W9-ABQ-380

PROFESSIONAL PRACTICE FOR

Interior Designers

PROFESSIONAL PRACTICE FOR

Interior Designers

Third Edition

Christine M. Piotrowski, ASID, IIDA

John Wiley & Sons, Inc.

Published by John Wiley & Sons, Inc.

Published simultaneously in Canada.

Library of Congress Cataloging-in-Publication Data:

Piotrowski, Christine M., 1947–
Professional practice for interior designers / Christine M. Piotrowski.—3rd ed.
p. cm.
Includes index.
ISBN 0-471-38401-1 (cloth : alk. paper)
1. Interior decoration—Practice—United States—Management. 2. Design services—United States—Marketing. I. Title.
NK2116.2.P57 2001
729'.068—dc21 2001022370

Printed in the United States of America.

10 9 8

For my parents, Martha and Casmer:
I am sorry you are not here to share this with me.

Contents

Preface

Interior design is a great way to make a living. An interior designer can be creative and see exciting commercial spaces or sophisticated residences become reality. An interior designer can utilize the most beautiful, sensuous, or elegant products to fill those spaces. The designer can help a business be more productive, be inviting to guests, or give comfort. All of these scenarios and many more allow the interior designer to utilize his or her creative side of the brain to solve problems for clients and to carve a path in the profession.

Interior design is, of course, a business. Whether the interior designer is a sole practitioner who is slowly developing a reputation in residential design or is a member of a team of designers that is creating a casino hotel—or anything in between—he or she must also care for the business side of the profession. In this very competitive profession, all interior designers, regardless of size of firm or design specialty, must understand and conduct themselves both as businesspeople and as creative interior designers.

Today, clients are more inclined to question fees and charges. Even though the economy has been very good to the interior design profession since the late 1990s, competition has increased while profits on projects have decreased. Clients want designers to be better project managers and to accept the legal responsibility involved in the design process. Technology scares some designers, while other designers embrace the advantages that technology has provided to speed work, to market to clients across the country or the world, and to help find needed products or other information easily.

The topics in this book are important, whether the reader is a student who is ready to embark on his or her first position as an interior designer, a professional who is planning to open a practice, or an already engaged professional who is looking for answers to practical questions about the practice itself. Understanding not only what is expected of a professional interior designer but also appropriate ways of managing and operating the practice must be embraced to keep the business from being one of the thousands of new businesses that fail each year.

Most students and practitioners have limited preparation or exposure to business practice. That is part of the reason that this book has always included information on a wide variety of topics in everyday business. It is not enough for a designer to learn about fee methods, where to buy products at a discount, or how to master the creative side of design. Interior design professional practice is also about managing and working with other designers, allied professionals, clients, and vendors. It is about calculating fees in sufficient amounts in order to make a profit. It is about knowing how to structure a contract and prevent legal problems, rather than deal with them when they occur. It is concerned with locating clients and presenting one's ideas in order to close the deal. For many, the practice of interior design eventually becomes the management of employees or team members, treating them with respect and mentoring them so that they can be contributing members of the firm and the profession. The professional practice of interior design is also about conducting oneself in an ethical manner and being professional, taking part in an association, and advocating for professional conduct and practice.

The business side of the profession of interior design has continued to evolve, and many changes in practice operations and technology have occurred since the previous edition of this book. This new edition has been developed to include those changes and challenges. In preparing the third edition, I have sought information from working professionals and industry associations. I have reviewed the literature on business topics concerning general business and interior design business, in particular. I have talked to educators, and I have received input from students.

Each chapter has been reviewed and updated to discuss the practice of interior design as it has evolved in the twentieth century and as it has been practiced at the beginning of the twenty-first century. Some sections have been relocated to improve the logical arrangement of topics. New material has been added to every chapter, whether through updated information, new examples, revised methods of practice, or topics that have evolved since the previous edition. Technology issues have been addressed within chapters.

The text remains easy to read and full of examples to help explain some of the more difficult topics, such as legal responsibilities. Most illustrations have been replaced to give the text a fresh look. Many of the illustrations are from design firms, so students and practitioners can see how other designers conduct business. Practitioners will find this book to be a thorough discussion of every aspect of planning and maintaining an interior design practice. Topics have been expanded or included to continue to create a comprehensive text on interior design business practices.

If you have used an earlier edition of this book, you will find much new material in this edition. Let me take this opportunity to explain some of the changes that have been made to this third edition. In Part I, Chapter 1 has been thoroughly updated and includes the latest requirements on the major professional associations, the NCIDQ examination, as well as on licensing. Chapter 2 is new and discusses the very important topic of professional ethics. It is hoped that this chapter will challenge both the student and the professional to consider the importance of ethical behavior. Chapter 3 has revised exercises on goals and material on creating a personal mission statement.

Part II provides important additional considerations concerning planning a new interior design practice. Discussion of the limited liability company and updates on legal filings have been added. A new chapter has been included that considers many issues involved in working alone—whether it is in a home office or not—and other topics related to start-up that have not been previously covered.

Parts III and IV have many changes. Part III brings together all the chapters on business organization, planning, personnel issues, and legal responsibilities. These chapters have been thoroughly updated and include new illustrations, examples, and sections of information. A new chapter in Part III consolidates previous sections on business planning methodologies and places an emphasis on strategic planning—a planning technique that has gained favor with interior designers in recent years. Part IV focuses on business finances, with chapters on financial accounting, fees, pricing, contracts, and the Uniform Commercial Code. New illustrations, new information on computer applications, and continued clarification of these topics have been provided.

Part V on marketing has been expanded considerably. There is an expanded discussion of target marketing. Several new items have been included that are related to promotional tools, calling for two chapters that make it easier to discuss these tactics. A discussion of using a web site for marketing has been added. The chapters on selling techniques and presentations have been expanded to include a different look at selling and presentation methods, as well as at the use of a formal proposal as a marketing tool and the presentation of the proposal. Chapter 26 is new and covers topics that assist students and professionals in improving their "personal power" through better nonverbal communication and business etiquette.

Topics on project management are included in Part VI. Sections have been included that update the discussion of current practice, with a more detailed discussion of the current philosophy behind the project phases. Sections about understanding working relationships, using the Internet for product information, and additional discussion on the paperwork that commonly is used during the contract document and contract administration phases are new to this edition.

The chapters on careers in Part VII have been revised and updated to cover alternate career options, using the Internet for job searches, preparing electronic resumes, and issues concerning the transition from student to professional. A discussion of career change issues for professionals concludes the text.

The Appendix includes an extensive list of organizations and businesses that might be a source of information or assistance to the student and professional. As much as possible, these contacts include web addresses to aid in informational searches. The Glossary has been expanded to include all the new terms that have been introduced in this edition of the text. And, of course, each chapter contains an extensive list of references that were used to research the material presented and to provide additional information for the instructor, student, or professional.

For the first time, an *Instructor's Manual* is available to assist educators in preparing discussion material and assignments. The *Instructor's Manual* includes a list of important terms for the chapter, discussion questions, and a test bank of true-false and multiple-choice questions with answers. In addition, a variety of exercises have been included that can be used for class discussions or out-of-class assignments.

I am honored that, since its first edition, this book has been embraced by educators who teach the business side of interior design and has been honored by professionals. But, as the business of interior design evolves, so must this book. So I invite feedback. Thoughtful criticism and suggestions from students, educators, and professionals alike have helped to improve this book over the years. I hope you will help make it what it will be in the future.

Acknowledgments

Suggestions for additions and improvements to this text have come from many sources. Foremost are the suggestions and comments from students whom I have taught over the years since this book was first published in 1989.

Educators also have provided many suggestions, and I would especially like to thank Tom Witt from Arizona State University and Susan Coleman from Orange Coast College for their great suggestions. I have also picked the brains of numerous professionals throughout the country in an attempt to be sure what is covered is relevant to the practice of interior design at the beginning of the twenty-first century.

The information in this text comes not only from practical experience and numerous discussions with professionals, but also from reviewing an extensive amount of literature on business practices, in general, and the interior design and related professions, in particular. I would like to thank the authors and publishers who graciously have granted permission to use their materials.

Previous editions acknowledged the many individuals and design firms or organizations that provided assistance or documents. There are a few people, however, whom I would like to acknowledge again, since they have had an especially important impact on the development and continued life of this book. I would like to acknowledge once again Fred Messner, IIDA, Jan Hancock, and Barbara Wallis for all their encouragement and assistance over the years.

A special thank you is due to those designers who graciously provided their thoughts about the interior design profession as it enters the twenty-first century. I am very grateful to Rosalyn Cama, FASID; Susan Coleman, FIIDA, FIDEC, CID; Marily Farrow, FIIDA; Charles D. Gandy, FAISD, FIIDA; Jain Malkin; Linda E. Smith, FASID; and Lisa M. Whited, IIDA, ASID for allowing me to include their thoughts as part of this textbook.

Many interior design practitioners and organizations have provided information and documents to help update and improve this book. Other individuals have provided reviews of chapters, suggestions on content, and new illustrative material. I am indebted to all the firms that have allowed me to reproduce their proprietary materials here: Fred Messner, IIDA, of Phoenix Design One, Phoenix, Arizona; Jain Malkin, of Jain Malkin, Inc., La Jolla, California; Jan Hancock and Christopher Babcock, of Walsh Brothers Office Environments, Phoenix, Arizona; John Schabow, of John Schabow, Ltd., Phoenix, Arizona; Suzanne Urban, ASID, IIDA, of Studio 4, Phoenix, Arizona; Betty Upton, Allied ASID, of Cunninghams Interiors, Flagstaff, Arizona; Michael Thomas, ASID, of Design Collective Group, Jupiter, Florida; Grei Hinsen, ASID, of G. S. Hinsen Co., Nashville, Tennessee; Sally Thompson, ASID, of Personal Interiors, Gainesville, Florida; James Tigges, ASID, IIDA, of Pinnacle Design, Inc., Phoenix, Arizona; Jeffrey Rausch, IIDA, of Exclaim Designs!, Scottsdale, Arizona; Dave Petroff, IIDA, of Office Designs, Phoenix, Arizona; Jeanne C. Crandall, ASID, of Crandall and Associates, Scottsdale, Arizona; Debra May Himes, ASID, IIDA, of Debra May Himes & Associates, Mesa, Arizona; Sandra Evans, ASID, of Knoell & Quidort Architects, Phoenix, Arizona; Donna Vining, ASID, of Donna Vining Associates, Inc., Houston, Texas; Wade Carter, of the Interior Surfaces Guild, Scottsdale, Arizona; Michael Schroder, AIA, of Langdon Wilson Architecture, Phoenix, Arizona; Gail Adams, FASID, of Gail Adams Interiors, Ltd., Phoenix, Arizona; Joan Gaulden, FASID, IIDA, of designonlineinc.com, Greenville, South Carolina; Merritt Menefee, IIDA, of Facilitec Interiors for Business, Phoenix, Arizona; Jeanine Hill, of Steelcase, Inc., Grand Rapids, Michigan; Jan Bast, ASID, of Bast/Wright Interiors, San Diego, California; Mary Brannon, ASID, of Brannon Design Associates, Inc., Del Mar, California; Niklas Moeller, of K. R. Moeller Associates, Ltd., Ontario, Canada; Sandy Friend, ASID, CID, Ashland, Oregon; Allyson Grenier, Allied ASID, Phoenix, Arizona; Charles Cooper, ASID of Scottsdale Community College, Scottsdale, Arizona; Gera King, ASID, of Scottsdale Community College, Scottsdale, Arizona; John Elmo, FASID, of Elmo Design Group, Ltd., Yonkers, New York; Denise Harmon, of Kahler Slater

Architects, Milwaukee, Wisconsin; Barbara Clapp, of US Business Interiors, Baltimore, Maryland; Perkins and Will, Chicago, Illinois; Miles Treaster and Associates, Sacramento, California; and Herman Miller, Inc., Knoll International, and Transcom Lines.

I would like to acknowledge the American Society of Interior Designers, the National Council for Interior Design Qualification, the International Interior Design Association, the Foundation for Interior Design Research, and the Interior Design Educators Council, the Interior Designers of Canada, the International Code Council, the Foundation for Design Integrity, the American Institute of Architects, the Construction Specifications Institute, and ARCOM Masterspec for allowing me to reproduce documents and other information.

A big thank you goes to Dawson Henderson, of Flagstaff, Arizona, for assisting in the production of many forms and digital images.

Finally, I would like to give a special thank you to Amanda Miller at John Wiley & Sons—my editor and friend—for being so patient, supportive, and understanding, and to the many others at John Wiley & Sons for their help in completing this edition of the text.

Lisa M. Whited, IIDA, ASID, was President of a commercial design firm in Portland, Maine for 14 years, and has served as president of the National Council for Interior Design Qualification (NCIDQ). She believes that collaboration between the architectural and interior design professions will strengthen the public perception of good design, and has taken a leadership role in bridging the respective professions. In her ongoing efforts to enhance the credibility and value of professional interior designers, Ms. Whited has created and presented seminars, written articles, and spoken to groups across the country.

Photographer—Abbie Sewall

NCIDQ—for some interior designers these letters spell "dread." For others, it is a challenge they cannot wait to tackle. I believe that the NCIDQ (National Council for Interior Design Qualification) must become an experience for designers to embrace rather than reject—it is here to make sure we have the knowledge and experience to call ourselves professional interior designers. The NCIDQ exam is simply the starting point to becoming a professional. The years spent after the exam—working with clients, contractors, architects, and engineers—will refine, shape, and sharpen an interior designer's skills. The NCIDQ acronym means "begin," not "dread!"

Photographer—Maine Audio Visual Services

Maine State House, Senate Chamber, Augusta, ME

Certified Interior Designer: Lisa Whited

Registered Architect: Weinrich & Burt

Contractor: Granger Northern

PART I

An Introduction to the Profession of Interior Design

1. The Profession
Defining a Profession *History of the Profession* *Divisions of the Profession*
Educational Preparation *Professional Associations* *NCIDQ Examination*
Licensing and Title Acts *Continuing Education*

2. Ethics
Ethics in the Business Environment *Professional Conduct* *For Discussion*

3. Personal Goal Setting
Goals *Risks in Goal Setting* *A Personal Mission Statement* *Setting Goals*

Chapter 1

The Profession

Look around you. The room in which you are reading this book was designed by someone. Maybe even you. Interiors are all around us—figuratively as well as literally. We probably spend 90 percent of our day in some sort of interior: where we live, work, shop, eat, seek professional services, and so on. Someone planned that space. And that individual or group of individuals made sure the interior space met building, fire, safety, and accessibility codes. He or she planned that space to meet functional needs of the client and visitors. The individual probably decided what colors, fabrics, materials, and textures would be needed to compliment the furniture items and to create a pleasing environment.

Hopefully, it was done by a professional interior designer. What does the title professional interior designer mean? "People who decorate interiors are interior decorators," believe much of the public. The most commonly quoted definition of an interior designer comes from the National Council for Interior Design Qualification (NCIDQ): "The Professional Interior Designer is qualified by education, experience, and examination to enhance the function and quality of interior spaces. For the purpose of improving the quality of life, increasing productivity, and protecting the health, safety, and welfare of the public."*

Of course, not everyone who has something to do with the planning and design of an interior has received formal education and training and has been certified by examination. That's because interior design as a profession is still evolving and gaining recognition as a profession both in the minds of the people who take up the business of interior design and in the minds of the public. This is, in part, due to the fact that it is a young profession. The use of the term *interior design* did not appear in general usage until after World War II.

The design of interiors plays a crucial part in all our lives. Designing interiors is not only a fun way to make a living but also an awesome responsibility. Part of that responsibility lies in being professional and businesslike about what we do as a professional. A position in interior design is not only an opportunity to be creative and, quite honestly, spend a lot of other peoples' money wisely but also a business. Design firms do not last long if they are not operated and managed in a businesslike manner and do not generate a profit somewhere along the line.

* Excerpted from the short definition of the National Council for Interior Design Qualification. The entire definition can be found in the Appendix.

After you have read this chapter, you will easily see why interior design today is a profession—different from other traditionally thought of professions but a profession nonetheless. Yet, it is still evolving. Chapter 1 begins by defining a profession according to sociologists. It continues with a short history of the profession. Educational standards, which have become increasingly stringent over the years, are important especially for those readers who are just now considering a career in interior design. A brief discussion of the major professional associations will help the reader appreciate the breadth of design specialties within the profession. The chapter also reviews the qualifying examination that has been established as the benchmark for licensing and for professional-level association membership, which provides evidence of competence. The chapter examines licensing and title registration issues, as well as continuing education. A discussion of ethics, which previously was included in this chapter, follows as its own chapter.

It must be noted that each of these topics in itself could constitute a book. However, the purpose here is to introduce these topics briefly as a reference about the growth and changes of the interior design profession itself.

Defining a Profession

This text discusses the issues associated with the operation and management of a professional interior design practice. To discuss the broad range of topics involved in the professional practice of interior design without discussing the profession itself would do it an injustice. So we begin this discussion by presenting information on how interior design meets the criteria of a profession based on the definition of "profession," as expressed by sociologists.

A profession is defined by sociologists as existing when a specific set of characteristics can be associated with it. According to Nicholas Abercrombie, they are as follows:

1. The use of skills based on theoretical knowledge
2. Education and training in these skills
3. The competence of professionals ensured by examinations
4. A code of conduct to ensure professional integrity
5. Performance of a service that is for the public good
6. A professional association that organizes members*

Gordon Marshall (1998, p. 527) writes: "A profession includes some central regulatory body to ensure the standard of performance of individual members; a code of conduct; careful management of knowledge in relation to the expertise which constitutes the basis of the profession's activities; and lastly, control of number, selection, and training of new entrants."

The profession of interior design, as we know it today, is guided by all of the points noted by both of these authors. But the profession itself, and the professionals associated with it, did not evolve overnight; and, of course, it is still evolving.

A professional does not emerge merely as a consequence of learning the technical principles needed in the profession. To become a professional also

* *The Penguin Dictionary of Sociology*, by Nicholas Abercrombie, Stephen Hill, and Bryan S. Turner (Penguin Books, 1994), copyright © Nicholas Abercrombie, Stephen Hill, and Bryan S. Turner, 1994, 335. Reproduced by permission of Penguin Books Ltd.

requires an attitude of dedicated commitment to the work one does and to the advancement of the profession. In addition, he or she must have some understanding of the history of the profession and the issues that are important to maintaining the vitality of the profession. Understanding what it takes to organize and maintain an interior design practice follows understanding the roots and contemporary concerns of the profession. Being a professional also involves keeping oneself informed about the latest advances in the design specialty in which one chooses to work. It also means learning to have a professional attitude in one's dealings with others in the industry and operating (or working in) a design firm as a knowledgeable business person.

History of the Profession

In some ways, it can be argued that the work of today's interior designer dates from the earliest times, although it was not called interior design until nearly the mid-twentieth century. The ancient Greeks were some of the first civilizations to put on theatrical performances in specialized spaces, referred to as theaters. Monasteries provided some of the earliest settings for healthcare facilities and were among the most important early school settings. Of course, religious facilities have always existed in one form or another. The hospitality industry dates back many, many centuries as well, beginning with taverns and inns that sheltered travelers. Perhaps you recall seeing the market stalls of the seventeenth century—the forerunners of today's malls—in recent, popular movies. During the Renaissance, the aristocracy began collecting antiquities and displaying them, creating, in effect, early museums. And, of course, homes have progressed from caves and dugouts to a variety of residential spaces, as can be seen throughout the world today. The "interior design" of all these different types of early architecture and consequent interiors came into being out of necessity at first. Interior design evolved as technology, and skills, and education improved.

Before the twentieth century, interior decoration was the responsibility of architects and artisans, such as the Michelangelo, the Adam brothers, Antonio Gaudi, and William Morris. No matter what their "profession" was in the arts, they clearly served as interior decorators. These architects, painters, sculptors, and other artisans were considered artists or craftsmen. Those who designed and produced the fabrics, carpets, and furniture items were considered shopkeepers. Called *ensembliers* or *ateliers* in Europe, the shopkeepers and shops did not deal with interior decoration as a profession but, rather, they were suppliers.

Elsie deWolfe (1865–1950) was among the first individuals who brought the concept of professionalism to interior decoration. It was approximately during her career that the term *interior decoration* began to be used in relation to the work of individuals such as herself. Born in New York City and a member of the upper class, deWolfe began her career as a professional interior decorator in 1904, when she was 39 years old. Her first commission, in 1905, was for the design of the Colony Club in New York City. Her use of white and pastels was a decided change from the dark colors that were popular in the Victorian period. Among deWolfe's clients were such notable figures as Henry C. Frick and Anne Pierpont Morgan. Because these early decorators often had wealthy clientele, the term *society decorator* was often associated with them. DeWolfe also wrote one of the earliest books about interior decoration, *The House in Good Taste* (1913), in which she related her philosophy of decoration for homes. She also is credited with being responsible for another milestone in the profession, when she received a fee for her design services rather than a commission on the sale of furniture (Cambell and Seebohm, 1992, p. 70).

DeWolfe's success inspired other women to enter the profession. It was, after all, one of the few acceptable professions for women at the turn of the century. Formal training, however, was difficult for them to obtain. It was not until 1904 that courses in interior decoration became available. The New York School of Applied and Fine Arts (now known as Parsons School of Design) in New York City was one of the first to offer such courses. Those who could not afford such courses or were unable to avail themselves of formal courses, would learn from magazines of the time, such as *House Beautiful* or *House and Garden*.

After World War I, postwar prosperity became more widespread, allowing an increased interest in, and employment of, the interior decoration professional. Department stores, with their displays of home furnishings, flourished as women had more time to shop. Furniture manufacturing centers grew in places such as Grand Rapids, Michigan, and High Point, North Carolina. At first, most of these manufacturers produced inexpensive imitations of period pieces that were popular in the United States at that time. By the 1920s, furniture manufacturers were producing finer-quality furniture. However, the society decorators were still traveling to Europe to purchase antiques.

In the 1920s, the Art Deco style had an important impact on the interior design of houses and offices. Department stores such as Macy's, Wanamaker's, and Marshall Fields constructed vignettes* to display the new style. These efforts did much to popularize the Art Deco style in the United States. Art Deco also revolutionized the interior and exterior design of office buildings and other commercial structures. At that time, most interior design in commercial structures was done by men. Dorothy Draper (1889–1969) is credited with being the first woman interior decorator who specialized in commercial interiors (Tate and Smith, 1986, p. 322). During that time, other educational programs of interior decoration were being established in New York and other cities in the United States.

By the late 1920s, many local Decorators' Clubs had been started in various parts of the country. Design education strengthened as an increasing number of formal college courses and programs in interior decoration became available. The profession was becoming more formalized and began to change its image from that of the untrained decorator to that of the trained professional.

Grand Rapids, Michigan, bears mention, as it was the site of one of the earliest and largest to-the-trade-only semiannual furniture markets. The Grand Rapids Furniture Exposition, as it was officially called, was first held in December 1878 (Carron, 1998, p. 72). The market was held in January and June for 87 years. Local manufacturers displayed their products, educational programs were held, and manufacturers from other locations rented storefronts to show their goods.

The economic depression of the 1930s was having a profound effect on the furniture industry—much of it centered in Grand Rapids at the time. The Great Depression had a disastrous effect on the ability of the middle class to purchase furniture produced in the United States and Europe. Many furniture manufacturing centers were on the brink of closing. The leading society decorators remained relatively unaffected by the depression, since their wealthy

* *Vignette,* as used in the interior design profession, means a display of furniture and furnishings that simulates an actual room.

clients could still purchase goods. However, most of these decorators were still purchasing goods from Europe rather than using American-made goods.

The leaders of the Grand Rapids manufacturing center conceived of an idea that would bring the decorators to Grand Rapids, they would hold a larger furniture market than they had ever held before. With William R. Moore of Chicago, they put together a conference to organize a national professional organization. The conference was held during July 1931, in Grand Rapids, and speakers such as Frank Lloyd Wright were scheduled to appear in order to entice decorators to the conference. The manufacturers provided the money—and furnishings—for the decorators so that they could design model rooms displays. And, of course, the decorators were invited to the various manufacturing plants and showrooms to see the furniture firsthand.

By the end of the conference, the American Institute of Interior Decorators (AIID) had been founded, with William R. Moore as its first national president. In 1936, the organization moved its headquarters from Chicago to New York City and changed its name to the American Institute of Decorators (AID). The early organization established membership requirements based on education and work experience. Over the years, these requirements changed and became more stringent. However, for many years, there was no formal testing for competency.

From the 1930s on, the modernism of the Bauhaus school had a great effect on the design of buildings and interiors in the United States. The industrialism of post-World War II also led to new manufacturing techniques that changed furniture and design styles. For example, molded plywood and molded fiberglass designs, such as those by Charles Eames, revolutionized seating design. After World War II, nonresidential design became an increasingly important aspect of the profession. Florence Knoll established the Knoll Planning Group in the 1940s. This design company's focus was on commercial interior design (Russell, 1992, p. 11). The evolution of giant corporations was one factor. Curtain wall construction, suspended ceilings, and changes in construction to allow for vast, open interior spaces in office buildings all impacted architecture and interior design and the role of the decorator/designer. In the 1940s and 1950s, more stringent educational opportunities meant that the decorators of the post-World War II era would have to rely on educational preparation rather than on just having "good taste" in order to obtain jobs and commissions.

The furniture and furnishings industry, inexorably tied to the interior design profession, forced further changes in the profession. Trade shows, first held at manufacturing centers like Grand Rapids and later, at metropolitan market centers like the Merchandise Mart in Chicago, became a popular way for manufacturers to present their new products to decorators, designers, and other tradespeople.

Changes in the philosophy of the workplace created new furniture concepts, such as that of the office landscape. Office landscape was first introduced in Germany in the early 1950s by the Quickborner Team für Planung und Organisation, often referred to as the Quickborner Team. Office landscape, as practiced in Germany, produced offices that were laid out without walls, utilizing plants, bookcases, and file cabinets as "screens" while creating wide-open floor plans. As companies embraced this planning philosophy, new specialists in space planning, lighting design, acoustics, and so forth, became part of the profession. These new design concepts and other issues created tension and arguments over admission and educational requirements for interior designers. A debate even ensued over the words *decorator* versus *designer*.

In 1957, a group belonging to the New York branch of AID broke off and formed the National Society for Interior Designers (NSID). For many years, deep-seated disagreements over qualifications, testing, and terminology continued between the two organizations. In 1961, the American Institute of Decorators became the American Institute of Interior Designers (AID). Finally, in 1975, the American Institute of Interior Designers and the National Society for Interior Designers overcame their differences and merged into one national organization, the American Society of Interior Designers (ASID). Today, there are over 30,000 members of ASID.

All through the 1960s, there existed discussions regarding educational training and testing procedures for qualification. NSID likewise favored licensing to restrict practicing to qualified professionals. According to Olga Gueft, the Southern California chapter of AID was fighting for licensing as early as 1951, whereas some chapters of NSID were lobbying for licensing in the 1960s. AID favored creation of a qualifying examination. An examination was devised, and in the 1960s and early 1970s, prospective members of AID had to pass the examination for membership. Because of philosophical differences, NSID designed and utilized its own qualifying exam. In 1974, the National Council for Interior Design Qualification (NCIDQ) was formed to develop an examination that both organizations could use.

As interest in the profession grew, the numbers of programs in colleges, universities, and professional schools increased, as did the number of faculty involved in education. Since most of these educators considered teaching as their full-time occupation, many limited their practice of interior design. Needing an organization to keep abreast of the profession as well as of advances in educational goals, they formed the Interior Design Educators Council (IDEC) in 1963 (IDEC web site, 2000). Today, IDEC publishes the only scholarly journal of the profession, the *Journal of Interior Design Education and Research*.

As concerns about educational programs evolved, AID, NSID, and IDEC worked together to encourage the creation of the Foundation for Interior Design Education Research (FIDER) in 1970 in order to deal with the accreditation of educational programs. Today, FIDER is the agency charged with evaluating interior design education programs and determining which ones meet the standards established for formal accreditation. This organization yearly publishes a list of the schools that provide accredited undergraduate interior design programs in the United States.

In the late 1960s, a new professional organization, the Institute of Business Designers (IBD) was incorporated to meet the needs of the commercial/contract designer. IBD was conceived in 1963 by members of the National Office Furnishings Association (NOFA), who were concerned about the importance of interior design service in office furnishings dealerships. Later, in 1963, NOFA-d (NOFA designers) was formed as a branch of NOFA. Membership was open to interior designers who were working for office furnishings dealers, although membership was basically limited to those designers who were working in Chicago and New York City. In 1967, NOFA was renamed NOPA (the National Office Products Association) after it merged with stationery and office supply dealers. Meetings began at this time concerning the status of NOPA-d. After discussions and a pledge of assistance from NOPA, NOPA-d became an independent organization in 1969 and was renamed the Institute of Business Designers (IBD). Charles Gelber was elected the first president in 1970. Along with the incorporation of IBD in 1969, that year saw the first Neocon (National Exposition of Contract Furnishings) market in Chicago. Today, Neocon Chicago is the largest contract furniture exposition in the country and is attended by thousands of interior designers, architects, planners, and end users.

Many special-interest professional associations, such as the International Society of Interior Designers (ISID) and the Institute of Store Planners (ISP), were established during the 1970s and 1980s. Those designers who work in specialized areas, such as for the federal government, store planning, or retail furniture and furnishings merchandising, facility planning, and lighting design, often have found it to be advantageous to join a specialized association. Several of these professional associations are discussed in a later section of this chapter.

A proliferation of new pressures and responsibilities began to be imposed on the interior design profession in the 1970s. After several tragic fires occurred in public buildings, stringent fire codes were passed to make commercial facilities safer. Today, interior designers must deal with many fire safety issues in the design of commercial interiors. The energy crisis and the increased cost of electricity have forced designers and suppliers to find new ways to provide satisfactory lighting at low cost. Rapid increases in the size of many businesses, as well as the energy crisis, have created a need for new, space-efficient furniture products and space-planning solutions. The mid- to late 1970s saw an explosion of products for open office design. These new products created many new design challenges and opportunities for interior designers. Although legislation for interior designers had been an issue for many decades, a renewed effort to formalize legislative efforts began around the mid-1970s. Efforts to license individuals working as interior designers finally became a reality in the 1980s. In 1982, Alabama passed the first legislation for title registration of interior design. The passage in 1992 of the Americans with Disabilities Act (ADA) provided yet another challenge to licensed professionals working in the United States. Canadian designers and designers around the world have had to learn to design with similar regulations. Designers and manufacturers, who increasingly have been concerned with interior environmental and health factors, began the "greening" of interiors. Environmentally safe or protected products were specified over products designed and manufactured from unhealthy or endangered natural materials.

Those designers who were members of IBD are now members of the International Interior Design Association (IIDA). IIDA was created in 1994 as a result of the discussions by the member organizations of the Unification Task Force. Representatives from ASID, IBD, ISID, ISP, Interior Designers of Canada (IDC), and IDEC formed the task force and began meeting in 1989 to discuss the creating of one umbrella organization that could address the needs of all aspects of the interior design profession. With NCIDQ, FIDER, and the Council for Federal Interior Designers (CFID), the Unification Task Force worked to develop a unified professional association. In early 1993, the president of the IDC reported that it would withdraw from the unified voice discussions. Although it strongly supported the unification concept and process, the IDC board felt that it would be in the best interests of IDC to withdraw from the talks. In addition, the ASID board voted to withdraw from the unification discussions in September 1993. According to a press release from ASID, the board voted against continuing discussions based on a membership response that was not in favor of unification (ASID, 1993). During the early part of 1994, members of the remaining organizations debated unification. In the end, members of IDEC and ISP decided to remain separate from the new group under discussion. Members of IBD, ISID, and CFID approved the merger, and formed the International Interior Design Association (IIDA).

The word *explosion* barely describes the emergence of the personal computer in the office and in most commercial interiors in recent decades. Personal computers on every desk in large- and small-sized businesses have created a new challenge for interior designers. While the computer has helped small and big business alike, it also has brought new problems for the designer—glare from overhead lighting, carpel tunnel syndrome from improperly placed equipment and incorrect seating specifications, and a recognition of health problems that are caused by poorly designed or specified seating.

Technology has also offered designers the opportunity to integrate computer-aided design and drafting (CAD) into their practices. Since the mid-1990s, the Internet has changed the way in which designers work, as rapid communication via E-mail has facilitated the transfer of information and graphics between designers and their clients on the World Wide Web.

And let us not forget that, while all these challenges were having a dramatic impact on commercial interior designers, those who chose to work in residential design were also seeing changes in their professional area. The changing makeup of the family has required renewed considerations about how the family and its members use their home environment. Issues of the "green" environment have become even more important in homes, as the various volatile odors and gases released by the increasing numbers of products that are being made from hydrocarbons have affected the lives of residential clients. Design styles, color trends, new product development, and bigger interior spaces also have challenged the residential designer.

At the turn of the twenty-first century, one of the biggest challenges to the residential interior designer will be to find appropriate ways to design and remodel homes for an aging population. With huge numbers of baby boomers (those born between 1945 and 1964) fast approaching their "senior years," homes and assisted-living facilities are needed to satisfy their changing lifestyles.

This section by no means attempts to be a definitive history of the interior design profession. The author leaves that task to other capable authors. Rather, this overview of the history of the profession and of the influences on its growth is meant to give readers an appreciation of the roots of the profession called *interior design*. Figure 1-1 summarizes its chronological development.

Interior design has seen many changes in its brief history and will continue to see changes as efforts such as licensing and certification increase and as outside influences continue to affect professional practice. In an earlier 1931 statement, AIID prepared the following definition of a decorator: "A decorator is one who, by training and experience, is qualified to plan, design, and execute interiors and their furnishings and to supervise the various arts and crafts essential to their completion" (Gueft, 1980, p. 8).* The reader is invited to compare this definition with the one quoted in the introduction to this chapter.

The major professional associations in the United States and Canada endorse the definition of a professional interior designer prepared by NCIDQ. That definition also has been endorsed by the International Federation of Interior Architects/Interior Designers (IFI), by FIDER, and by those states in the United States and provinces in Canada with licensing or certification statues. It has been reproduced in its entirety in the Appendix.

Today, the profession thrives during one of the greatest economic booms in decades. But it has been a long time in coming. Interior design professionals and students are faced with continuing changes in the profession. As members work on projects while being restricted by legal constraints, licensing issues, educational and qualification concerns, public opinion, and better business practice, the profession will continue to grow and evolve.

* Reprinted with permission, ASID. Copyright 1988, American Society of Interior Designers.

1878	First of its kind semiannual furniture market. Held in Grand Rapids, Michigan.
1904	First real use of term "interior decoration."
	First courses in interior decoration offered at the New York School of Applied and Fine Arts.
1905	Elsie deWolfe obtains her first commission as an interior decorator. She is credited as being first interior decorator.
1913	Elsie deWolfe publishes first true book on interior decoration, *The House in Good Taste.*
1920s	Greater effort by department stores to market home furnishings.
	Manufacturing centers of home furnishings begin to develop.
	Art Deco period creates greater interest in interior decoration of homes and offices.
	Dorothy Draper credited as being the first woman interior decorator to specialize in commercial interiors.
	Decorator clubs begin forming in larger cities.
	Design education strengthened in many parts of the country.
1931	Grand Rapids furniture show. Meeting to create a national professional organization.
	In July, American Institute of Interior Decorators (AIID) is founded.
	William R. Moore elected first national president of AIID.
1936	AIID's name changed to American Institute of Decorators (AID).
1940s	Post-World War II industrialism encourages new technologies in furniture manufacturing.
	Industrialism produces increased need for, and importance of, nonresidential interior design.
1950s	Development of open landscape planning concept in Germany by Quickborner Team.
1951	First time a state considers legislation to license interior design.
1957	National Society for Interior Designers (NSID) founded from a splinter group of the New York AID chapter.
1961	AID changes its name to American Institute of Interior Designers (AID).
1963	National Office Furnishings Association (NOFA) creates NOFA-d (NOFA-designers), a professional group for interior designers who work for office furnishings dealers.
	Interior Design Educators Council (IDEC) founded to advance the needs of educators of interior design.
1967	NOFA and NOFA-d change names to NOPA and NOPA-d, respectively, when NOFA merges with stationery and supplies dealers to form National Office Products Association.
1968	Introduction of "Action Office," designed by Robert Probst for Herman Miller, Inc. First true open-office furniture product.
1969	Institute of Business Designers (IBD) incorporated. NOPA-d is parent organization.
1970	Charles Gelber elected first national President of IBD.
	Foundation for Interior Design Education Research (FIDER) founded. Is responsible for reviewing and accrediting undergraduate and graduate interior design programs.
1974	National Council for Interior Design Qualification (NCIDQ) incorporated. Charged with the development and administration of a common qualification examination.
1975	American Society of Interior Designers (ASID) formed from the merger of AID and NSID. Norman De Haan is first national ASID president.
1982	Alabama becomes first state with title registration legislation for interior design.
1988	First major discussion of 1995 Hypotheses, the document that begins a discussion of unification of interior design professional associations.
1992	Passage of Americans with Disabilities Act (ADA), which provides accessibility standards for all public buildings.
1994	Unification of IBD, ISID, and CFID to form International Interior Design Association (IIDA).

FIGURE 1-1. Chronology

Divisions of the Profession

An in-depth discussion of the divisions of the profession and the many career choices within it is presented in Chapter 32. At this time, it would be beneficial to point out that many consider that there are two universally accepted divisions of the profession: residential interior design and commercial interior design.

Residential interior design is concerned with the planning and/or specifying of interior materials and products used in private residences. A private residence can be a freestanding home, a condominium, a townhouse, a mobile home, or an apartment.

Commercial interior design, sometimes called contract interior design because of the use of a contract for services, is concerned with the planning and specifying of interior materials and products used in public and private spaces, such as offices, stores, hotels, restaurants, schools, airports, hospitals, and so on.

Educational Preparation

The development of formal educational preparation in interior design began approximately in 1904 when what is now the Parsons School of Design began offering a specific program. Informal preparation in this career came from a few courses that were offered in art or home economics. Of course, architecture programs were in existence prior to the beginning of the twentieth century, but these offered few classes in interior decorating, as it was called then. Throughout the twentieth century, educational programs developed all across the country. Curriculums varied for many years, resulting in uneven preparation. As we read in the section on the history of the profession, the beginnings of some type of educational standards began as the numbers of decorators grew and the industry blossomed after World War II.

The traditional roots of interior design education are in the fine arts, home economics (referred to as human ecology today), and architecture. Current interior design programs at universities, colleges, community colleges, and professional schools generally assign interior design academic programs within one of these three areas, although they may be found in other departments or divisions as well. In addition, interior design programs are interdisciplinary, drawing from these three academic areas as well as from the supporting areas of business and the liberal arts. Depending on the location of the program, the professional and technical course work will have a slightly different focus.

Programs range from two years to as long as seven years. Two-year programs are primarily offered in community colleges and some professional schools. In many situations, students begin at one of these two-year programs and transfer into a four-year (or longer) program in order to obtain a bachelor's degree. Other students are satisfied with a two-year associate degree in interior design and move on to employment. Most of these graduates work in small interior design studios or retail stores. Graduates of four-year (or more) programs generally accept initial employment with larger-sized interior design firms or architectural firms.

Voluntary accreditation of interior design programs was not available until the creation of the Foundation for Interior Design Education Research (FIDER), which was established in 1970. FIDER, a nonprofit organization recognized by the Council on Higher Education Accreditation, is considered the reliable authority on the quality of postsecondary interior design education in North America.

The mission of FIDER is expressed by its mission statement: "FIDER leads the interior design profession to excellence by setting standards and accrediting academic programs" (FIDER web site, 2000). With the organization of FIDER, educational standards were developed to evaluate an interior design program prior to granting accreditation. These standards are reviewed from time to time; this was last undertaken in late 1999. An abbreviated statement of the standards is presented in Figure 1-2. The reader may wish to contact FIDER for a complete report.

Research studies in the 1980s revealed distinct differences in educational programs throughout the United States and Canada. The length of the programs varied from two years to as much as seven years. The number of credit hours of interior design classes varied considerably as well. With the research study information, FIDER, with assistance from NCIDQ and additional ongoing research, has defined a common body of knowledge and skills that are needed by competent professional interior designers. The common body of knowledge, according to FIDER, is shown in Figure 1-3.

1. **Curriculum Structure**
   The curriculum is structured to facilitate and advance student learning.
2. **Design Fundamentals**
   Students have a foundation in the fundamentals of art and design, theories of design and human behavior, and discipline-related history.
3. **Interior Design**
   Students understand and apply the knowledge, skills, processes, and theories of interior design.
4. **Communication**
   Students communicate effectively.
5. **Building Systems and Interior Materials**
   Students design within the context of building systems. Students use appropriate materials and products.
6. **Regulations**
   Students apply the laws, codes, regulations, standards, and practices that protect the health, safety, and welfare of the public.
7. **Business and Professional Practice**
   Students have a foundation in business and professional practice.
8. **Professional Values**
   The program leads students to develop the attitudes, traits, and values of professional responsibility, accountability, and effectiveness.
9. **Faculty**
   Faculty members and other instructional personnel are qualified and adequate in number to implement program objectives.
10. **Facilities**
    Program facilities and resources provide an environment to stimulate thought, motivate students, and promote the exchange of ideas.
11. **Administration**
    The administration of the program is clearly defined, provides appropriate program leadership, and supports the program. The program demonstrates accountability to the public through its published documents.
12. **Assessment**
    Systematic and comprehensive assessment methods contribute to the program's ongoing development and improvement.

FIGURE 1-2. FIDER Professional Standards 2000

Each interior designer may have unique qualities and possess highly specialized abilities in certain areas but will, in common, hold knowledge of:

- The basic elements of design and composition that form the foundation for creative design, and an awareness of the various media in the visual arts that assist in the understanding of the universality of these fundamentals;
- Theories of design, color, proxemics, behavior, visual perception, and spatial composition which lead to an understanding of the interrelationship between beings and the built environment;
- The design process, i.e., programming, conceptualization, problem solving, and evaluation, firmly grounded on a base of anthropometrics, ergonomics, and other human factors;
- Space planning, furniture planning and selection, developed in relationship to application to projects, including all types of habitation, whether for work or leisure, new or old; for a variety of populations, young and old, disabled, low or high income;
- Design attributes of materials, lighting, furniture, textiles, color, etc., viewed in conjunction with physical, sociological, and psychological factors to reflect concern for the aesthetic qualities of the various parts of the built environment;
- The technical aspects of structure and construction, building systems, i.e., HVAC, lighting, electrical, plumbing, and acoustics, sufficient to enable discourse and cooperation with related disciplines;
- Technical aspects of surface and structural materials, soft goods, textiles and detailing of furniture, cabinetry, and interiors;
- The application of laws, building codes, regulations, and standards that affect design solutions in order to protect the health, safety, and welfare of the public;
- Communication skills, oral, written, and visual for the presentation of design concepts, the production of working drawings, and the conduct of business;
- The history and organization of the profession; the methods and practices of the business of interior design; and an appreciation of a code of ethics;
- Styles of architecture, furniture, textiles, art, and accessories in relation to the economic, social, and religious influences on previous cultures;
- Methods necessary to conduct research and analyze the data in order to develop design concepts and solutions on a sound basis.

FIGURE 1-3. The FIDER common body of knowledge in interior design, developed collaboratively by professional associations (Reprinted with permission, Foundation for Interior Design Education Research)

Currently, FIDER accredits a single program of interior design education, the professional level. The program most commonly results in a bachelor's degree, although three-year programs also exist. The professional degree level of preparation must contain a minimum of 30 hours of liberal arts, sciences, and humanities courses. What is included in the total number of credit hours and their emphasis is up to the institution granting the degree. These programs provide curriculum preparation for professional-level interior designers and are also the common preparation for those seeking a master's degree in interior design. Effective during the fall of 2000, FIDER no longer accredits two-year programs, unless the program requires a minimum of 30 semester credit hours of liberal arts and science, in addition to the interior design curriculum (FIDER Professional Standards, 2000).

The master's degree level of preparation is for those designers who are seeking advanced studies or research work in interior design. Master's degree work commonly requires a minimum of 30 semester credit hours, with actual degree requirements being left up to the institution. A graduate student's work culminates in a graphic or written thesis, depending on his or her academic focus and the requirements of the institution. FIDER does not accredit master's degree or other postprofessional programs any longer.

Each interior design academic program has a different emphasis because of the mission of the institution and department, and the focus of the faculty. FIDER-accredited programs indicate to the student that the program meets the educational standards that are accepted and supported by the profession of interior design. Many other programs exist that are not FIDER accredited. It is up to the individual student and his or her family to investigate carefully the academic programs of all the institutions (accredited or not) in which the student has an interest. Prospective students should talk to academic advisors, alumni of the program, and any design businesses in the area that may have knowledge of the preparation given at a particular school. Students should understand the differences in focus of a program in fine arts versus one in architecture or human ecology. Professional, educational training in interior design must provide the student with the theory and skills of the profession as well as with the general education that is required in the twenty-first century. The focus of that training must also meet the interests, abilities, and career goals of the student.

Professional Associations

An important part of being a professional is to become an active member of a professional association. Interior design professional associations provide members with many tangible and intangible benefits. Some feel that the greatest tangible benefit of professional association membership is the privilege to place ASID, IIDA, IDC or other association appellations after a member's name. It is not the primary benefit; it is only one benefit. A list of other intangible benefits are:

- *Pride in accomplishment*. It is important to have a sense of pride in having achieved the educational, experience, and testing milestones that indicate that one has achieved the highest level in one's profession.
- *Recognition*. Consumers and allied professionals recognize the dedication and credentials of the interior designer who is affiliated with professional associations. To many others, peer recognition as a member of an association is gratifying.
- *Interaction with colleagues in design*. Interior design is both a large and a small profession. There are thousands of individuals who are affiliated with associations, and yet the profession is small enough so that many professionals meet and become friends with colleagues across the country—or across the globe.
- *Educational opportunities*. It is vital in this age of technology and regulations that designers continually update their skills and knowledge in their field. Professional associations help in many ways to provide opportunities for continual educational upgrading through chapter meetings, newsletters, seminars, workshops, national conferences, research studies, and lively discussions of issues and concerns.
- *Important friendships*. Professional colleagues are competitors at times, but many consider each other as friends as well. Through an association, designers get to know their competitors, not only as great designers or good business people, but also simply as people. Designers are proud of the professional and personal friendships that they have made through association activities.

These are just some of the intangible benefits of membership. The reader may think of others that are just as important.

Professional associations also provide tangible benefits for members. Some of these have already been mentioned—chapter meetings, educational updating, and national conference activities. There are many others, among which are the following:

- *Association leadership.* Membership offers an opportunity to be involved in the growth of the profession through positions as chapter and national officers.
- *Leadership training.* Association chapter and national board members and officers receive training to assist them in accomplishing their association responsibilities. Much of this training can be directly applied to an individual's work experience as well.
- *Mailings.* Associations provide mailings to members that keep them informed of the associations' activities as well as of external influences on the profession. Mailings might take the form of member magazines, supplemental newsletters and news bulletins, chapter newsletters, and conference reports.
- *Practice aids.* A number of associations provide sample contracts, business forms, marketing tools, reference books, and other useful aids for members to use in their practice in order to become better professionals.
- *Government affairs.* The associations maintain contact with federal, state, and/or provincial government agencies that may have an effect on the right to practice. Members are kept informed of any pending legislation that might affect design practice.
- *Group insurance.* It is possible for members to take advantage of low group insurance rates for a variety of personal and business insurance needs.
- *Business services.* Discounts and special pricing are available from some associations for car rentals, telephone service, express shipping, credit cards, and other similar business services.
- *Design competitions.* Professional prestige can be achieve through juried national competitions for projects, research, and writing.
- *Industry liaison.* Members receive technical information from industry suppliers.
- *World Wide Web.* Members may obtain information from association national offices, be informed of association business and issues affecting the members, and even carry on on-line chats with the national office or, with other members. Chapters may also offer marketing programs in which a member may link his or her web site to the chapter's web site.

Many other tangible benefits might be thought of by the reader.

There is no lack of reasons for becoming affiliated with an association that is appropriate to the interior designer's interests and needs. The remainder of this section briefly describes the major professional associations. The reader will want to contact the national or provincial offices (listed in the Appendix) for membership applications or for more specific details about the association.

American Society of Interior Designers (ASID)

The largest of the interior design professional associations, with over 30,000 members, is ASID. Its members are engaged in both residential and commercial interior design. An ongoing mission of ASID is to "satisfy the needs of the Society's customers through professional education, knowledge sharing and expansion of the interior design practice and market" (ASID, 1999). In the year 2000, "ASID's mission is to be the definitive resource for professional education and knowledge sharing, advocacy of interior designers' right-to-practice, and expansion of interior design markets" (ASID Membership information, 1999). ASID provides many membership benefits, including chapter meetings and activities at the local level, a national conference that offers numerous continuing education classes and seminars, on-line and World Wide Web interface, a membership magazine called *ASID ICON*, legislative support for states that are seeking licensing, and many other programs, documents, and activities for the support of the association, its members, and the profession. The members-only link to the association's web site provides specialized information for ASID members on a continually updated basis.

The five membership categories that ASID offers (as of January 2000) are (1) professional, (2) allied, (3) industry partner, (4) retail partner, and (5) student. The highest level of membership is *professional*. Members in this category have satisfied rigorous standards of education, work experience, and testing in order to qualify as professional-level members. The minimum requirements for professional-level membership are: (1) graduation from a recognized college, university, or design school with a major in interior design or a related field,* (2) successful completion of the NCIDQ examination, and (3) a minimum of two years of full-time employment in interior design. A combination of six years of interior design education and work experience is the minimum requirement for qualifing for the NCIDQ examination. Therefore, individuals who have completed at least two years of interior design postsecondary studies and have four years of work experience or another combination of specified education and work experience may also qualify. Individuals who have had no formal accredited educational preparation in interior design or a related field might not qualify for professional-level membership in ASID, since they will not have met NCIDQ's qualification standards. The educational program must include a minimum of 45 semester credit hours or 67 quarter hours in interior design related courses at a school that is accredited by a recognized accrediting agency. Only professional-level members may vote in association elections and may use the appellation *ASID* after their names and in advertising.

The second level of membership is *allied*. Allied Practitioner members are practicing interior designers. Educators who are teaching or working as full-time administrators in postsecondary programs of interior design may obtain Allied Membership (Education). Allied practitioner members must meet the same general membership requirements as for professional membership but have not as yet satisfactorily completed the NCIDQ exam. An allied practitioner member may have a four- or five-year interior design or architecture degree, a two- or three-year certificate in interior design, or a minimum of six years of full-time work in interior design. Allied practitioner members are able to use the appellation *Allied Member, ASID* after their names.

Students who are enrolled in interior design programs may become *student* members of an ASID chapter at their school, if the school has one, or *student corresponding* members, if their institution does not have an ASID student chapter. Students receive mailings from the national office and have the opportunity to participate in the local professional chapter. Students who are in good standing through graduation may apply for allied membership immediately upon graduation. Student members may use the membership appellation *Student Member, ASID*.

Industry Partner (IP) members are those who work for suppliers to the interior design industry. For the most part, these members are wholesalers and suppliers. Many representatives of the manufacturers and suppliers, trade

* NCIDQ requires a minimum of two years of educational preparation in order to take the examination. See the discussion on NCIDQ later in this chapter.

showrooms, and market centers become IP members in order to interact with the membership. Industry partner members also have generously provided financial backing to the profession through sponsorship of continuing education classes, chapter activities, and design competitions.

Retail Partner members are those retail businesses that supply goods and services to consumers. A key difference between the industry partner member and retail partner member is that the retail partner member sells directly to the end user and must have a least one ASID professional or allied practitioner member on his or her staff.

Affiliate Membership is a category for individuals who do not participate in interior design, and it is usually held by members of the press, government agencies, nondesign employees of design firms, and other nonpracticing design-related individuals.

International Interior Design Association (IIDA)

The IIDA represents interior designers who specialize in all areas of commercial and residential interior design. Many of its over 10,000 members were formally part of IBD, ISID, and CFID. The mission of the International Interior Design Association is as follows: "IIDA is a professional networking and educational association committed to enhancing the quality of life through excellence in interior design and advancing interior design through knowledge" (IIDA, 1999). IIDA provides many membership benefits, including local chapter meetings and activities, a national conference, a national news magazine called *perspective*, educational programs, industry liaison, design competitions, and many other programs and activities. It has a very strong commitment to the concept of the "virtual association." The IIDA web site provides a communication avenue to and from its national office to members around the world. The members-only section of the web site provides specialized information for IIDA members.

There are five membership categories in IIDA: (1) professional, (2) associate, (3) affiliate, (4) student, and (5) industry representatives. Professional and associate members may choose to designate a specialty forum as part of their membership. Specialty forums provide in-depth information related to specific interests in the interior design industry. There are eight forums: corporate, residential, healthcare, hospitality, retail, facility planning and design, government, and education and research.

Professional membership is the highest category of membership in IIDA. It is reserved for those members whose work experience, educational background, and successful completion of the NCIDQ examination permits them to apply for this membership category. To obtain professional membership level, the member must meet one of these standards: (1) the educational and experience requirements of the NCIDQ in order to take the examination or (2) proof of satisfactory completion of the NCIDQ examination or the National Council for Architectural Registration Board (NCARB) examination and six years of experience in interior design for architects. Only professional members who hold voting privileges may use the appellation *IIDA* after their names. IIDA also requires that professional members complete 1.0 continuing education units (CEUs), or ten hours, every two years. CEUs will be discussed in detail later in this chapter.

The second level of membership in IIDA is called *associate* membership. Associate members are actively engaged in the profession of interior design or design education, similarly to allied members of ASID. Associate members meet the same educational requirements of professional members but have not completed the NCIDQ examination. Associate members are also required to complete 1.0 CEUs every two years. These members may use the appellation *Associate IIDA* after their names for marketing purposes.

The third membership category is called *affiliate* membership. These members are individuals who are involving in an area related to interior design, such as graphic design, lighting design, or landscape architecture, but do not qualify for professional membership.

Student memberships at a national level are available to students who are enrolled in a recognized design school or college program. Student members of IIDA frequently become members of the local chapter in addition to the national student organization. Students who maintain their student membership in good standing through graduation may apply for allied membership immediately upon graduation.

Industry members are individuals who are interested and supportive of interior design but who are not practicing designers. These members include manufacturers, individual representatives, design centers, and schools.

Interior Design Educators Council (IDEC)

The IDEC is a professional association whose members are individuals who are actively engaged in teaching interior design. Many IDEC members are also professional or educator members of ASID, IIDA, and other associations. IDEC is "dedicated to the advancement of education and research in interior design. IDEC fosters exchange of information, improvement of educational standards, and development of the body of knowledge relative to the quality of life and human performance in the interior environment. IDEC concentrates on the establishment and strengthening of lines of communication among individual educators, practitioners, educational institutions, and organizations concerned with interior design education" (IDEC, 1999). IDEC provides many member benefits, including an annual conference and regional meetings, where speakers, seminars, and workshops are provided for the presentation of research and for the exchange of ideas; publication of the *Journal of Interior Design Education and Research*, a refereed journal, as well as the *IDEC RECORD*, a member newsletter; and many other programs, reference materials, and activities to assist members in improving the teaching of interior design. The IDEC web site contains information for the general public and has a members-only link that gives members access to a large body of interior design information specifically for use in teaching.

Full-time interior design educators who also have received appropriate interior design education and have professional work experience may become *professional* members, the highest membership level. Qualifications for professional member status are a diploma, a bachelor's degree or master's degree in interior design or a related field; two years of full-time teaching experience in interior design. If a professional member also practices professionally in interior design, he or she also must complete the NCIDQ examination or be a professional member of an association.

Members who teach interior design courses but do not qualify for professional membership may join as an *associate* member. Associate members may advance to professional membership when they meet the qualifications. Associate members who practice professionally in interior design also are required to pass the NCIDQ examination or to be a professional member of an association.

Affiliate membership is open to those who are not eligible for other membership but who are interested in interior design education.

Graduate student membership is available for those who are enrolled in postgraduate degree programs.

Interior Designers of Canada (IDC)

Interior Designers of Canada (IDC), founded in 1972, is the national professional association in Canada. IDC works in coordination with eight provincial associations:

- Interior Designers Institute of British Columbia
- Registered Interior Designers of Alberta
- Interior Designers Association of Saskatchewan
- Professional Interior Designers Institute of Manitoba
- Association of Registered Interior Designers of Ontario
- Société des designeurs d'Intérieur de Québec
- Association of Registered Interior Designers of New Brunswick
- Association of Interior Designers of Nova Scotia

The purpose of IDC is to "advance the interior design profession and to promote high quality in education and practice from coast to coast" (IDC Web site, 2000). Its members work in all specialties of interior design and design education throughout the provinces of Canada. Members of IDC must hold the highest level of membership in their provincial association and must pass the international NCIDQ qualification examination.

IDC offers its members conferences, a newsletter entitled *Communiqué*; education and learning opportunities through continuing education classes and programs; and forums related to government relations, the environment, and cross-disciplinary collaboration; and assistance to members who are working in the global market.

The eight provincial associations have individual membership categories and requirements. The reader should contact the appropriate provincial association for information. There is a direct link to those associations at the IDC web site. Their address can be found in the Appendix.

Other Professional Organizations

A few words should be said about other professional organizations with which the interior designer may wish to affiliate. First, interior designers who specialize in the design of retail stores and shopping centers may wish to affiliate with the Institute of Store Planners (ISP).

International Facility Management Association (IFMA) is a professional association for those who are actively engaged in corporate facility management and planning. IFMA has several membership categories, depending on the applicant's actual work experiences in corporate facility management and planning.

Some interior designers may be eligible for affiliated membership in the American Institute of Architects (AIA). The AIA is, of course, the professional organization for professional architects. Interior designers cannot become professional members of the AIA unless they meet the qualifications as an architect.

Designers who are interested in specializing in kitchen or bath design often affiliate with the National Kitchen and Bath Association (NKBA). There are several membership categories in NKBA, based on the type of work in which the candidate is engaged.

There are several other smaller or more specialized professional associations for interior designers or for those who are affiliated with the interior design profession. Complete information regarding the qualification and application procedures of these associations can be obtained from the national offices listed in the Appendix.

NCIDQ Examination

The NCIDQ is an independent corporation that was formed in 1974 and is concerned with maintaining standards of practice through the testing of members of the profession and the establishment of requirements for legal qualifications for licensing and title registration. The mission of NCIDQ is "to aid and assist the general public by establishing and administering an examination to determine which practitioners of interior design shall be certified as competent to practice in the field of interior design" (NCIDQ, 2000).

The NCIDQ examination is the recognized qualifying examination for professional membership in ASID, IIDA, IDC, and IDEC. The NCIDQ examination is also the primary examination in those U.S. states and Canadian provinces that have licensing, certification, or other registration statutes.

Ongoing research is conducted by NCIDQ to evaluate and analyze candidate performance, educational and professional practice skill and knowledge requirements, and methods to promote public protection by the interior design profession. The board of directors of NCIDQ conducted a major research study in 1998, in order to gather the most up-to-date information about the practice of interior design so as to revise the NCIDQ examination. Using the research study as its guide, the board of directors determined that the format of the examination needed to be revised.

The NCIDQ examination is given twice during the year—usually in April and October—at examination centers throughout the United States and Canada. When a designer has achieved a minimum combination of six years of education and work experience, the designer contacts the NCIDQ office for application materials. In some states, such as in Texas, candidates must apply to the state regulatory board in order to take the examination.

Eligibility requirements consist of a minimum of six years of combined educational and practical experience. A candidate may take the examination if he or she has (1) a four- or five-year degree in interior design, or equivalent educational credit, plus two years of professional experience; (2) a three-year certificate in interior design or equivalent credits plus three years of professional experience; or (3) a two-year certificate or equivalent credits, plus four years of professional experience. Educational requirements at the different levels have a minimum number of semester or quarter hours that the candidates must complete in interior design-related classes. All candidates must have a minimum of two years of academic training in interior design, in combination with four years of work experience, to equal a minimum of six years. All candidates must have a minimum of two years of full-time professional work experience. Recommendations and academic transcripts are also required of all candidates.

As of the fall of 2000, the examination is divided into three sections and is given over two consecutive days—usually Friday and Saturday. A candidate may take all three sections of the exam at one time or may elect to take individual sections or combinations of sections at different times. Only sections of the examination that are not passed must be taken again. Unless a professional association or a state statute has different requirements, there is no time limit within which a candidate must pass the examination.

The three sections of the examination are divided into two multiple-choice, computer-graded tests and one practicum section. The multiple-choice exams are based on six performance domains that are characterized within the work of interior design: (1) project organization, (2) programming, (3) schematics, (4) design development, (5) contract documents, and (6) contract administration. A discussion of the project activities that occurs within these domains is presented in Chapter 27 on project management. A brief description of the three exam sections follows.

Section I: *Principles and Practices of Interior Design.* This is a multiple-choice test consisting of 150 questions. It addresses the domains of project organization, programming, schematics, and design development.

Section II: *Contract Development and Administration*. This multiple-choice test addresses the domains of contract documents and contract administration.

Multiple-choice questions focus on practice situations, knowledge, and activities associated with the domains. Many questions incorporate drawings, pictures, symbols, and textual formats that are typical in the interior design profession, requiring candidates to recall, apply, and analyze information.

Section III: *Schematics and Design Development*. This is the practicum section of the exam. It requires that candidates produce a design solution. In this version of the examination, candidates are required to plan a multifunctional facility. All candidates are given the same problem. Besides being required to interpret a design program and to provide a design solution, all candidates are required to apply principles of accessible design to their solutions.

An examination guide is available from NCIDQ. This guide provides the candidate with an overview of the three sections of the examination, a bibliography of source information, sample multiple-choice questions, and a sample practicum exam. It provides valuable general information about the examination, the rules for the exam, the schedule, and other important information.

The STEP Program

ASID has devised special study programs to help candidates prepare for the NCIDQ. Though sponsored by ASID, any candidate for the NCIDQ exam may participate. This Self-Testing Exercises for Preprofessionals (STEP) program helps applicants learn the study and design skills that are needed to pass the examinations. STEP program leaders point out that the program is not a crash course in design; rather, it is a means to help preprofessionals learn to study.

The STEP workshop, conducted by educators and professionals who are specially trained by ASID, provides a review of applicable material and study skills for both the multiple-choice and practicum sections of the examination. Emphasis is generally placed on the practicum portion of the examination. Workshop activities take candidates through various exercises, which help them assess where they need additional work prior to taking the examination. Practice tests covering the multiple-choice sections of the examination are available as well.

The STEP workshop is commonly conducted over a two-day period. Workshops are generally sponsored by local ASID chapters. Registration fees are slightly higher for non-ASID members. Registration information can be obtained from either local ASID chapter offices or the ASID web site.

Licensing and Title Acts

Licensing, title acts, legal recognition, certification—all of these are topics that are important to the interior design professional and student. Licensing efforts have been a part of the profession's activities since 1951, when the Southern California chapter of AID attempted to get a bill passed in the state legislature. They failed. However, AID did prepare an examination at a later time. Today, the ASID and IIDA national organizations, as well as chapter organizations in numerous states, continue to fight for licensing. The professional associations seek licensing and/or title registration on a state-by-state basis.

Licensing and title acts are related, because both require legislation and state control. Title acts are, in fact, a type of licensing. *Title acts* are concerned with limiting the use of certain professional titles, such as *interior designer, registered interior designer,* or *certified interior designer* to individuals who meet agreed-upon qualifications and who have registered with a state board. Licensing, or *practice acts*, establish guidelines concerning what an individual can or cannot do in the practice of a profession in a particular state. Individuals who wish to engage in a profession guided by a licensing or practice act must also register with a state board.

To differing degrees, licensing and title acts, in some respects serve to limit who can practice a profession. A title act does very little to limit who can practice the activities of interior design, whereas practice acts do a great deal. The intent of legislation, however, is to indicate to the consumer which individuals have met the specific criteria that are related to education and work experience, indicating that they have acquired professional competence in the field. Licensing or title registration legislation also provides a definitive measure of experience and educational preparation for those who practice interior design. Licensing serves to protect the consumer from unregulated practice by those who do not have proper educational background, training, and experience in the profession of interior design.

Title acts only restrict the use of the title *interior designer* (or other designated title) to those who meet the qualifications of the state title act. Interior designers who meet these qualifications must also register with a state agency or board. An individual who does not meet the qualifications of the title act may not use the title of *interior designer* in any of his or her business dealings. With title registration, the title of *interior designer* connotes to the public that the individual has met the highest standards of the profession and can thereby provide the most competent service to the consumer. These standards are related to education, experience, abiding by a code of conduct, and passing a qualifying examination.

Practice acts are commonly legislated for those professions that deal with the health and safety of the public and that employing individuals in those professions. Lawyers, doctors, architects, and engineers have had to meet state practice act regulations for many years. Practice acts definitely limit who may practice a profession, since they usually require that individuals meet very stringent qualification criteria. When a person enters into a contractual relationship with an unlicensed professional, the contract may or may not be enforceable, depending on the statutes in the individual states.

Registered interior designers are allowed to stamp their drawings with a stamp or a seal and signature, showing that the drawings have been prepared by a registered professional. Work executed by a nonregistered designer would not have this stamp.

In the 1980s, some of the emphasis on licensing was the result of increasing pressure to limit the practice of interior design. Architects, building contractors, and taxing authorities in various states, sought to limit the practice of interior design by trying to legislate certain activities that are common to the interior designer to other more "traditional" professions (ASID, 1985). Unfortunately, this occurred again in 1999 when the International Code Council met to develop a revised model building code. As of this writing, the International Code Council upheld that the term "design professional," for the purpose of stamping drawings, is as follows: "The definition of 'design professional' be as defined by the statutory requirements of the professional registration laws of the state or jurisdiction in which the project is to be constructed" (International Code Council, 2000). This alone helps to protect an interior designer's right to practice, where some regulation of interior design already exists. However, in several states, there remain efforts aimed at limiting what the interior designer can do.

Those who have been actively engaged in bringing licensing legislation to their states would all agree that it has not been an easy task. Nor will it be in the future. Despite the frustration of many years of struggling with legislators and those who would rather that interior design not be licensed, many states have obtained some type of interior design legislation. In 1982, Alabama became the first state to pass a title registration act. As of January 2000, there are 21 jurisdictions that have passed licensing legislation: Alabama, Arkansas, California, Connecticut, Florida, Georgia, Illinois, Louisiana, Maine, Maryland, Minnesota, Missouri, New Mexico, Nevada, New York, Puerto Rico, Tennessee, Texas, Virginia, Washington, DC, and Wisconsin. Eight provinces in Canada have passed similar title registration acts. Florida, Washington, DC, Puerto Rico, Louisiana, and Nevada currently are the only jurisdictions with practice acts for interior design. Many other states are working on legislation for either title registration or practice acts.

Readers may wish to contact the Government and Public Affairs Department of ASID, the Legislative Issues Committee of IIDA, or the national offices of other professional associations for information on legislation within the reader's jurisdiction.

Whether one works toward licensing through title registration or practice acts, interior design professionals and students must be prepared to accept the legal and ethical responsibilities that such recognition brings. The next chapter discusses the codes of conduct of ASID and IIDA; later chapters cover the legal responsibilities that one must face.

Continuing Education

Like all other professionals, interior designers receive continuing education through seminars, workshops, lectures, and intensive professional studies in their field. Many designers seek postgraduate education in interior design, architecture, and business, to name just a few broad areas. Sometimes, designers obtain additional education in order to increase their technical skills and to allow themselves an opportunity to advance within the firm in which they work. Sometimes, they seek additional education in order to retrain for a new area of expertise, such as lighting design or CAD, or to move into management. Not all professionals have the time to seek college credit, however. And many professionals do not really desire the depth of study that is required when taking college courses.

Courses that provide continuing educational units (CEUs) furnish short-term course work in a variety of areas. Continuing education courses last anywhere from one hour to a few days; most common are all-day courses. The course length and level of difficulty are primary factors in determining the number of CEU credits available for the class. Most CEU classes are under 1.0 credits. One-tenth of an hour of credit (0.1) is given for each hour of the class. CEU classes provide a means for professional interior designers to remain current in the practice of interior design. Courses are available in almost every topic and area of the profession: theory and creativity; interior design; interior design education; design specialties; technical knowledge; codes and standards; communications systems; business and professional practice; and history and culture. The practitioner and student can find seminars on color and light, rendering techniques, designing with accessibility standards, kitchen design, improving personal and professional effectiveness, and areas of business practices, such as business planning and marketing. This provides only a very minuscule view of the breadth of available seminars and CEU classes.

Each association provides a number of CEU classes each year, most often sponsored at the local chapter level or as part of a national conference. In addition, numerous CEU classes of various credit amounts are offered at the professional association national and regional conferences. CEU classes are also offered at major market shows, such as Neocon.

It is important to note that reciprocity exists between many of the professional associations. It is possible for an ASID member, for example, to take a class sponsored by IIDA, IFMA, or another association. The member should check with his or her association to determine if a course offered by a different professional association will be applicable to his or her association. In some cases, the member may need to send a formal request to the association to determine if the course will be accepted.

Members also need to understand clearly that it is up to the individual member to keep track of his or her CEU credits. To receive CEU credit, members must be sure they complete the course credit application and provide a CEU fee that is generally in addition to the course fee. The individual member's CEU file is maintained by the NCIDQ. If the reader's association requires CEU credits to maintain membership, the member must request that transcripts be sent to the association's office. The NCIDQ does not automatically inform the professional association of a professional's CEU course work each year.

Continuing education is also very important because several states that have passed licensing or title registration acts require continuing education for maintaining registration. The exact requirements are the responsibility of the licensing board in each state. It is the individual's responsibility to inform state boards of any CEU activity.

Today's technological, litigious society makes it incumbent upon interior design professionals to keep current regarding the many technical, legal, and business skills and concepts of the profession. Changes in the ways in which design services are offered, changes in the products we specify, changes in the legal influences with which the designer must deal—all of these make continuing education an important part of being a professional interior designer.

Summary

This chapter is filled with a large amount of information. It tries to set the stage for the practical discussion of topics related to the professional practice of interior design from the business person's point of view. This background or, to use a design metaphor, foundation of information about history, professional associations, education, licensing, and more is important to the overall study of the profession and how it functions as a business.

Having an understanding of what the roots and issues of a profession are is an important part of being a member of that profession. Knowing what it is all about is crucial to making the time spent in the career a meaningful commitment of one's time and effort rather than an ordinary "job." Society tends to grant professionals higher status, money, and respect. Yet these do not come only with accomplishing the educational criteria of the profession. They come to the individual who has the attitude of service, commitment, and knowledge that is expected of the professional.

Being a professional means commitment to one's colleagues, clients, allied professionals, and students. Being a professional means being involved in an appropriate association, not just becoming a member. Being a professional means having sufficient pride in one's profession to fight for the profession throughout ethical performance and legislation. All these concepts and more demonstrate what a professional interior designer should be.

REFERENCES

Abercrombie, Nicholas, Stephen Hill, and Bryan S. Turner. 1994. *The Penguin Dictionary of Sociology.* New York: Allen Lane Publications (Penguin Books).

Abercrombie, Stanley. October 1987. "News: Leaders Meet." *Interior Design.*

Allwork, Ronald. 1961. *AID Interior Design and Decoration Manual of Professional Practice,* 2nd ed. New York: American Institute of Interior Designers.

American Society of Interior Designers. Web site information, 2000.

———. September 1993. "ASID Board Votes to Withdraw from Unification Talks: Pledges Cooperation with Unified Organization." (Press release).

———. September 1993. *Interior Design Registration Laws.* (Brochure).

———. 1992 and 1999. Membership Information.

———. 1992. *Professional Closeup.* (Brochure).

———. 1986. "First Interior Design Practice Act Passed in Nation." *Report.*

Anscombe, Isabelle. 1984. *A Woman's Touch.* New York: Elisabeth Sifton Books (Viking).

Ball, Victoria. 1982. *Opportunities in Interior Design.* Skokie, IL.: VGM Career Horizons.

Ballast, David K. 1992. *Interior Design Reference Manual.* Belmont, CA.: Professional Publications.

Borgatta, Edgar F., ed. 1992. *Encyclopedia of Sociology,* vol. 3. New York: Macmillan.

Campbell, Nina, and Caroline Seebohm. 1992. *Elsie de Wolfe: A Decorative Life.* New York: Clarkson N. Potter.

Carron, Christian G. 1998. *Grand Rapids Furniture.* Grand Rapids, MI: Public Museum of Grand Rapids.

Castlelman, Betty. June 1987. "How Will Licensing Affect Me?" *Designers West.*

Collier's Encyclopedia. 1984. "Interior Design and Decoration," vol. 13. New York: Macmillan.

"Design Revolution: 100 Years That Changed our World." *Interior Design.* December 1999.

deWolfe, Elsie. [1913] 1975. *The House in Good Taste* (reprint). New York: Arno.

Ebstein, Barbara. January–March 1985. "Licensing: The Design Concern for the Eighties." American Society of Interior Designers. *Report.*

Foundation for Interior Design Education Research. Web site information, 2000.

———. February 1993. *FIDER Fact Kit.* Grand Rapids, MI: FIDER.

Friedmann, Arnold, John F. Pile, and Forrest Wilson. 1982. *Interior Design—An Introduction to Architectural Interiors,* 3rd ed. New York: Elsevier Science Publishing.

Gueft, Olga. 1980. "The Past as Prologue: The First 50 Years. 1931–1981: An Overview." *American Society of Interior Designers Annual Report 1980.* New York: ASID.

Gura, Judith B. Fall. 1999. "Moderism at the Millennium." *Echoes.*

Hampton, Mark. 1992. *Legendary Decorators of the 20th Century.* New York: Doubleday.

Herman Miller. Inc. 1994. *A Brief History of Herman Miller.* Zeeland, MI: Herman Miller.

Hughes, Nina. June 1987. "Interiors Platform." *Interiors.*

Interior Design. December 1999. "Design Revolution: 100 Years That Changes Our World."

———. February 1992. "More Trouble on the Certification Front."

———."News: Leaders." October 1988.

Interior Design Educators Council, Web site information, 2000.

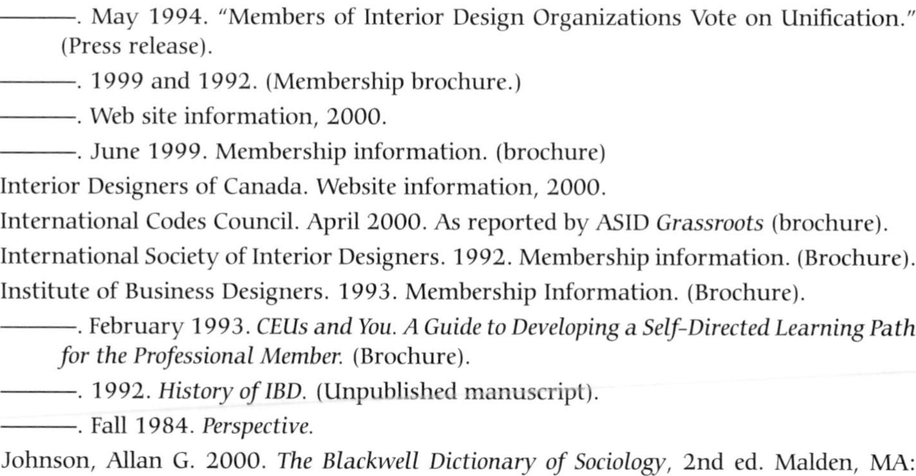

———. May 1994. "Members of Interior Design Organizations Vote on Unification." (Press release).

———. 1999 and 1992. (Membership brochure.)

———. Web site information, 2000.

———. June 1999. Membership information. (brochure)

Interior Designers of Canada. Website information, 2000.

International Codes Council. April 2000. As reported by ASID *Grassroots* (brochure).

International Society of Interior Designers. 1992. Membership information. (Brochure).

Institute of Business Designers. 1993. Membership Information. (Brochure).

———. February 1993. *CEUs and You. A Guide to Developing a Self-Directed Learning Path for the Professional Member.* (Brochure).

———. 1992. *History of IBD.* (Unpublished manuscript).

———. Fall 1984. *Perspective.*

Johnson, Allan G. 2000. *The Blackwell Dictionary of Sociology*, 2nd ed. Malden, MA: Blackwell Publishers.

Jones, Carol. September 1999. "Defining a Profession: Some Things Never Change." *Interiors and Sources Magazine.*

Kettler, Kerwin. "Is There More to Licensing Than a License?" *Designer Specifier.* May 1985.

Klein, Judy Graf. 1982. *The Office Book.* New York: Facts on File.

Kroelinger, Michael D. Spring. 1992. "Unified Voice Update." *Perspective.* Institute of Business Designers.

———. 1993. *Mission and Benefits of Unification.* (Unpublished material).

Marshall, Gordon. 1998. *A Dictionary of Sociology*, 2nd ed. New York: Oxford University Press.

Massey, Anne. 1980. *Interior Design of the 20th Century.* London, England: Thames and Hudson.

National Council for Interior Design Qualification. Web site information, 2000.

———. 1998. *Analysis of the Interior Design Profession.* Washington D.C.: NCIDQ.

Piotrowski, Christine M., and Elizabeth A. Rogers. 1999. *Designing Commercial Interiors.* New York: John Wiley.

Polites, Nicholas. "Arkansas Enacts Tiered Licensing System: Interior Designers Weigh Consequences." *Interior Design.* July 1993.

Rayle, Martha G. *Unified Voice Task Force (UVTF) Update.* (Newsletter published by American Society of Interior Designers). April 1992.

Russell, Beverly. 1992. *Women of Design.* New York: Rizzoli.

———. "Into the Ninth Decade: A Historic View of Interior Design Through the Contribution of Women." *IBD Perspective.* Fall 1992.

———. March 1985. "Interiors Business: New Moves Toward Interior Design Licensing." *Interiors.*

Staffelbach, Andre. "Does the Public Consider You a Professional?" *IBD perspective.* Summer 1992.

Steelcase, Inc. 1987. *Steelcase the First 75 Years.* Grand Rapids, MI: Steelcase.

Stein, Harry. 1982. *Ethics (and Other Liabilities).* New York: St. Martin's Press.

Sweet, Justin. 1985. *Legal Aspects of Architecture, Engineering, and the Construction Process*, 3rd ed. St. Paul, MN: West Publishing.

Tate, Allen, and C. Ray Smith. 1986. *Interior Design in the 20th Century.* New York: Harper and Row.

Thompson, Jo Anne Asher, ed. 1992. *ASID Professional Practice Manual.* New York: Watson-Guptill.

Unified Voice Task Force. April 1994. Newsletter sent to IBD members.

———. April 1994. Newsletter sent to IDEC members.

———. September 1993. *Interior Design Organizations Target July 1994 for Unification.* (press release).

Veitch, Ronald M., Dianne R. Jackman, and Mary K. Dixon. 1990. *Professional Practice.* Winnipeg, Canada: Peguis Publishers.

Voss, Judy. 1996. "White Paper on the Recent History of the Open Office." Holland, MI: Haworth.

Zeiger, Lisa. "House Fraus." *Interiors.* September 1999.

Note: There are dozens of additional articles, brochures, newsletters, and mailings on these topics. It is not possible to list all of these in this list.

Chapter 2

Ethics

The news headlines in the 1990s gave us all a lesson in ethical behavior—or, rather, the lack of it. Politicians, business leaders, corporations, sports figures, and medical practitioners in almost every walk of life tested how far ethical behavior could be stretched before someone would notice and take action. As a result, the teaching of ethics in all professional education programs has increased in importance, at least in part due to the headlines. Although the unethical behavior of an interior designer is very unlikely to garner headlines in one's local newspaper or to be discussed on MSNBC, ethical standards have become just as important in interior design as in any other profession.

On occasion, designers will come to on an ethics crossroad; down one path leads to behavior that is expected of a professional; down the other path leads to behavior that is contrary to one or more ethical standards. The decision has consequences for the individual, his or her company and client, and the profession as a whole.

As our world continues to become more complex and to make more demands on us, the expectations and demands for ethical professional behavior increase. If we expect other professionals who affect our lives to behave ethically, interior designers can demand no less of themselves. Thus, it is imperative that ethical behavior be treated as more than just a brief discussion in class while the class anticipates getting into subjects that are "more important."

This chapter has been added in order to present an overview of ethical concepts and issues as they relate to the professional practice of interior design. It is only a beginning, and the author hopes that the reader—whether a student or a professional—will seek additional information and guidance related to this important topic from an association chapter or an organization. Questions are raised through examples in order that the reader will think about and discuss ethical solutions to the examples. It is hoped that, in this way, the reader will begin to connect the code of ethics to situations that might occur in the profession.

Ethics in the Business Environment

Making ethical decisions in the general business environment often comes down to making choices that have something to do with such things as competition, conflict of interest, misuse of proprietary information, and employee theft (Ivancevich et al., 1994, p. 97). Of course, other problems can cause ethical dilemmas as well. However, only these four are discussed, since they represent major ethical issues in business and also can affect the interior designer as an individual or the individual's design business.

The free-market system creates rivalry between businesses—in other words, competition. When there are many businesses, the competition can be intense. When competition becomes intense, business owners, managers, and some employees may stretch ethical boundaries in order to win customers. Maybe a designer asks for a special discount (without passing it on to the client) from the manufacturer in order to specify one product over another and insure the winning of a project. On the other hand, what if the vendor offers a special discount (on the side) in order to have his or her product specified?

Related to this issue is the practice of accepting commissions. Some interior designers receive a commission from vendors when the client purchases products directly from the vendor. These commissions constitute additional revenue to the interior designer. However, these commissions raise ethical debates and ethical problems. Is the interior designer required to tell the client about these commissions? According to the codes of ethics from both ASID and IIDA, it is necessary to disclose all forms of compensation to the client. Some interior designers debate whether their colleagues should accept these commissions at all. Many interior designers feel that there really is no problem with competition in interior design. However, this is not really true. All design firms in any given market are in competition with each other, in one way or another. Architectural firms, retail stores, and vendors who sell directly to the client are also competitors of interior designers. In a practical sense, they are not likely to be pursuing the exact same clients, but some are. And when the economy is slow, even more designers are competing for the same clients. Regardless of the size of the interior design firm and how well the local economy is doing, plenty of competition exists between interior design firms.

A competitive, ethical crossroad can be met from another direction. Rather than designers bending competitive ethics, clients can put designers into such a position that they can test their ethics. Some clients shop around for a designer's ideas and prices, which in some ways is fine. Sometimes a client, however, who has a contract with designer A takes drawings prepared by designer A to designer B in order to get a lower price. What is designer B to do?

These examples also deal with conflict of interest. According to Bryan Garner, editor-in-chief of *Black's Law Dictionary*, *conflict of interest* is "a real or seemingly incompatibility between one's private interests and one's public or fiduciary duties."* *Fiduciary duties*, by the way, means that one person acts in a position of trust or confidence for someone else. When a supplier offers a *personal* advantage to a designer for specifying a certain product, the designer, if he or she accepts it, acts in a manner that is a conflict of interest. Putting personal gain above the good of the person or the organization that the designer is supposed to represent is an example of unethical behavior.

Another issue that has an impact on ethics in business is the misuse of propriety information. *Proprietary information* comprises a wide variety of data or information, graphics, or designs that belong to a particular person or business. Employers own all sorts of propriety information, such as financial data, client lists, discounting policies, and many others. Clients also can own

* Reprinted from page 295 in *Black's Law Dictionary*, 7th ed., by Bryan A. Garner, ed., 1999, with permission of the West Group.

proprietary information, such as trade secrets about a product or the business development of the company, or unique information about the operations of the business. In either case, the owner of the proprietary information would not want an interior designer or (anyone else) to divulge the information to competitors or to the public. For example, a designer leaves a company, taking and using proprietary information on that company's bidding strategies, and goes to work for a competitor. If the employee does share that information, he or she could be sued by the original employer. Firms try to combat this issue by having employees sign nondisclosure agreements, which means that the employee is not allowed to take proprietary information upon termination or voluntary separation.

Here is another situation. Gerald Smith is under contract to design the research and development offices for Netscape. Shortly after receiving the contract, his firm is contacted to provide design services for the same type of department at Microsoft. The Microsoft project is a much larger project and, therefore, more lucrative than the Netscape project. Would it be a conflict of interest for Gerald Smith's company to contract with Microsoft at the same time that he is working on the project for Netscape?

Employee theft is another common problem in the general business environment. Technically, taking home office supplies that are provided by the employer for personal use is employee theft. It is rare, indeed, for any employer to press charges against an employee for taking a few pens home. But employees have taken money, goods from the sales floor or warehouse, or even office equipment—all of which are of greater value to the company. Perhaps a designer "borrows" a lamp for his home, "forgetting" to sign it out on approval. Or, a designer makes an extra copy of Autocad for her home computer so that she can use it for personal business. Theft by employees, although, hopefully, it is not a great problem in interior design offices, does occur. What would you do if you knew that a colleague had "borrowed" a copy of some software to use while he was moonlighting in his spare time?

Why do some people behave unethically? According to Brown and Sukys (1997, p. 8), it is because people are (1) motivated by self-interest, (2) careless, and (3) they see no harm in the behavior. When someone places his or her own interests before others', he or she may be behaving unethically. Consider the case of a design student who shows work to an employer that has been done by someone else in her portfolio and represents it as her own. Since, in reality, she cannot do that quality of work, she has put self-interest first. The employer, at some point, will figure out that something is not right.

People become careless about ethical behavior when they get into a habit of being unethical. Perhaps a designer has gotten away with overbilling clients for services. Maybe a designer consistently overorders upholstery fabrics by a few yards and charges the extra yardage to the client, not to ensure that the amount will be enough for the project, but to warehouse the extra fabric in order to use it to make throw pillows for other clients.

"Everybody does it." This "I see no harm. . . ." excuse is another reason why people behave unethically. "Everybody uses down payments from one client to pay for orders for another client." This statement could be made by many designers. This practice is unethical and can be illegal if the state that designer works in requires that those down payments be held in escrow and used only for the client who made the down payment (see Chapter 19 for a further discussion of this). Just because "everybody does it" does not make it right. Harm is caused by this kind of thinking.

Professional Conduct

Ethical behavior has always been a concern of the professional associations. Adherence to the Code of Ethics and Professional Practice was expected of members of the AID in its earliest years (Allwork, 1961, p. 13). In fact, the AID Code of Ethics and Professional Practice was published in a professional practice manual at least as early as 1961 (Allwork, 1961, p. 13). As discussed in the first chapter, one of the characteristics of a true profession is that the profession and its members are guided by a set of *ethical standards*. These ethical standards define what is right and wrong in relation to the professional behavior of the members and even the practice of the profession.

While the teaching and discussion of ethics and an enforceable code of ethics that comes from professional associations provide definable and enforceable standards, a code of ethics cannot, by itself, produce ethical behavior. Ethical behavior must come from individual designers themselves in their daily dealings with clients, peers, the public, and allied professionals.

The codes of ethics of the professional associations deal with enforceable ethical standards of practice and provide philosophical comments concerning the professional conduct of its members. The ASID Code of Ethics and Professional Conduct (see Figure 2-1), reviewed annually, contains standards related to five areas of responsibility: (1) to the public, (2) to the client, (3) to other interior designers and colleagues, (4) to the profession, and (5) to the employer. The IIDA Code Code of Ethics (see Figure 2-2) is also reviewed annually. It consists of four sections: (1) the designer's responiblity to the public, (2) the designer's responsibility to the client, (3) the designer's responsibility to other designers and colleagues, (4) the designer's responsibility to the association and interior design profession. Of course, the other associations also have their own code of ethics or conduct. Readers interested in the code of ethics from other associations should contact them directly.*

These rules of conduct exist for members of the organizations, and members should use them when they deal with other designers, whether or not the other designers are members of one of the organizations. Just because someone who is practicing interior design or interior decoration is not a member of one of the associations does not mean that the individual can behave unethically. However, an ethical charge cannot be made against an unaffiliated designer. It is important for anyone in this profession to behave within ethical and moral standards. To not do so is not only harmful to that individual but also to the entire profession.

The examples that we have mentioned pose serious ethical problems. However, they do not discuss the most common ethical problems that have found their way into the national associations' ethics committees for disciplinary hearings, according to the interior design professional associations. Some broad examples of ethics complaints during 1999 that were filed with the ASID national office are shown in Figure 2-3.

Although the list does not contain all the issues reported to ASID, it does give the reader an overview of the most common ethics complaints that may occur in just one year. The largest number of complaints deal with financial or compensation questions and miscommunication.

* The code of ethics from ASID and IIDA have been used, since these two organizations represent the majority of professional association memberships in interior design.

1.0 PREAMBLE

Members of the American Society of Interior Designers are required to conduct their professional practice in a manner that will inspire the respect of clients, suppliers of goods and services to the profession and fellow professional designers as well as the general public. It is the individual responsibility of every member of the society to uphold this Code and Bylaws of the society.

2.0 RESPONSIBILITY TO THE PUBLIC

2.1 Members shall comply with all existing laws, regulations and codes governing business procedures and the practice of interior design as established by the state or other jurisdiction in which they practice.

2.2 Members shall not seal or sign drawings, specifications or other interior design documents except where the member or the member's firm has prepared, supervised or professionally reviewed and approved such documents, as allowed by relevant state law.

2.3 Members shall at all times consider the health, safety and welfare of the public in spaces they design. Members agree, whenever possible, to notify property managers, landlords, and/or public officials of conditions within a built environment that endanger the health, safety and/or welfare of occupants.

2.4 Members shall not engage in any form of false or misleading advertising or promotional activities and shall not imply through advertising or other means that staff members or employees of their firm are qualified interior designers unless such be the fact.

2.5 Members shall neither offer, nor make any payments or gifts to any public official, nor take any other action, with the intent of unduly influencing the official's judgment in connection with an existing or prospective project in which the members are interested.

2.6 Members shall not assist or abet improper or illegal conduct of anyone in connection with a project.

3.0 RESPONSIBILITY TO THE CLIENT

3.1 Members' contracts with a client shall clearly set forth the scope and nature of the project involved, the services to be performed and the method of compensation for those services.

3.2 Members may offer professional services to a client for any form of legal com pensation.

FIGURE 2-1. ASID Code of Ethics. (Reprinted with permission, American Society of Interior Designers, Government and Public Affairs, Washington, DC)

3.3 Members shall not undertake any professional responsibility unless they are, by training and experience, competent to adequately perform the work required.

3.4 Members shall fully disclose to a client all compensation which the member shall receive in connection with the project and shall not accept any form of undisclosed compensation from any person or firm with whom the member deals in connection with the project.

3.5 Members shall not divulge any confidential information about the client or the client's project, or utilize photo graphs or specifications of the project, without the express permission of the client, with an exception for those specifications or drawings over which the designer retains proprietary rights.

3.6 Members shall be candid and truthful in all their professional communications.

3.7 Members shall act with fiscal responsibility in the best interest of their clients and shall maintain sound business relationships with suppliers, industry and trades to insure the best service possible to the public.

4.0 RESPONSIBILITY TO OTHER INTERIOR DESIGNERS AND COLLEAGUES

4.1 Members shall not interfere with the performance of another interior designer's contractual or professional relationship with a client.

4.2 Members shall not initiate, or participate in, any discussion or activity which might result in an unjust injury to another interior designer's reputation or business relationships.

4.3 Members may, when requested and it does not present a conflict of interest, render a second opinion to a client, or serve as an expert witness in a judicial or arbitration proceeding.

4.4 Members shall not endorse the application for ASID membership and/or certification, registration or licensing of an individual known to be unqualified with respect to education, training, experience or character, nor shall a member knowingly misrepresent the experience, professional expertise or moral character of that individual.

4.5 Members shall only take credit for work that has actually been created by that member or the member's firm, and under the member's supervision.

4.6 Members should respect the confidentiality of sensitive information obtained in the course of their professional activities.

FIGURE 2-1. Continued

5.0 RESPONSIBILITY TO THE PROFESSION

5.1 Members agree to maintain standards of professional and personal conduct that will reflect in a responsible manner on the society and the profession.

5.2 Members shall seek to continually upgrade their professional knowledge and competency with respect to the interior design profession.

5.3 Members agree, whenever possible, to encourage and contribute to the sharing of knowledge and information between interior designers and other allied professional disciplines, industry and the public.

6.0 RESPONSIBILITY TO THE EMPLOYER

6.1 Members leaving an employer's service shall not take drawings, designs, data, reports, notes, client lists, or other materials relating to work performed in the employer's service except with permission of the employer.

6.2 A member shall not unreasonably withhold permission from departing employees to take copies of material relating to their work while an employee of the member's firm, which are not proprietary and confidential in nature.

6.3 Members shall not divulge any confidential information obtained during the course of their employment about the client or the client's project or utilize photographs or specifications of the project, without the express permission of both client and employer.

7.0 ENFORCEMENT

7.1 The society shall follow standard procedures for the enforcement of this Code as approved by the society's Board of Directors.

7.2 Members having a reasonable belief, based upon substantial information, that another member has acted in violation of this Code, shall report such information in accordance with accepted procedures.

7.3 Any deviation from this Code, or any action taken by a member which is detrimental to the society and the profession as a whole shall be deemed unprofessional conduct subject to discipline by the society's Board of Directors.

FIGURE 2-1. Continued

CODE OF ETHICS
TAKE RESPONSIBILITY

PREAMBLE

Professional and Associate Members of the International Interior Design Association shall conduct their interior design practice in a manner that will encourage the respect of clients, fellow interior designers, the interior design industry and the general public. It is the individual responsibility of every Professional and Associate Member of IIDA to abide by the Code of Professional Ethics and Conduct, Bylaws, Policies and Position Statements of the Association.

HOW ARE TERMS DEFINED?

The terms used in this Code shall be defined in the same manner in which they are defined in the Bylaws, Policies and Position Statements of the Association.

RESPONSIBILITY TO THE PUBLIC

In performing professional services, Professional and Associate Members shall exercise reasonable care and competence, and shall conform to existing laws, regulations and codes governing the profession of interior design as established by the state or other jurisdiction in which they conduct business.

In performing professional services, Professional and Associate Members shall at all times consider the health, safety, and welfare of the public.

In performing professional services, Professional and Associate Members shall not knowingly violate the law, or counsel or assist clients in conduct they know or reasonably should know is illegal.

Professional and Associate Members shall not permit their name or signature to be used in conjunction with a design or project for which interior design services are not to be, or were not, performed under their immediate direction and control.

Professional and Associate Members shall not engage in any form of false or misleading advertising or promotional activities and shall not imply, through advertising or other means, that staff members or employees of their firms are Professional or Associate Members unless such is the fact.

Professional and Associate Members shall not make misleading, deceptive or false statements or claims about their professional qualifications, experience, or performance.

Professional and Associate Members shall not, by affirmative act or failure to act, engage in any conduct involving fraud, deceit, misrepresentation or dishonesty in professional or business activity.

In performing professional services, Professional and Associate Members shall refuse to consent to any decision by their clients or employees which violates any applicable law or regulation, and which, in the Professional and Associate Members' judgment, will create a significant risk to public health and safety.

Professional and Associate Members shall not attempt to obtain a contract to provide interior design services through any unlawful means.

Professional and Associate Members shall not assist any person seeking to obtain a contract to provide interior design services through any unlawful means.

RESPONSIBILITY TO THE CLIENT

Professional and Associate Members shall undertake to perform professional services only when they, together with their consultants, are qualified by education, training or experience to perform the services required.

Before accepting an assignment, Professional and Associate Members shall reasonably inform the client of the scope and nature of the project involved, the interior design services to be performed, and the method of remuneration for those services. Professional and Associate Members shall not materially change the scope of a project without the client's consent.

Prior to an engagement, Professional and Associate Members shall disclose, in writing, to an employer or client any direct or indirect financial interest that they may have that could affect their impartiality in specifying project-related goods or services, and shall not knowingly assume or accept any position in which their personal interests conflict with their professional duty. If the employer or client objects to such financial or other interest, Professional and Associate Members shall either terminate such interest or withdraw from such engagement.

Professional and Associate Members shall not reveal any information about a client, a client's intention(s), or a client's production method(s) which they have been asked to maintain in confidence, or which they should reasonably recognize as likely, if disclosed, to affect the interests of their client adversely. Notwithstanding the above, however, Professional and Associate Members may reveal such information to the extent they reasonably believe is necessary (1) to stop any act which creates a significant risk to public health and safety and which the Professional or Associate Member is unable to prevent in any other manner; or (2) to prevent any violation of applicable law.

RESPONSIBILITY TO OTHER INTERIOR DESIGNERS AND COLLEAGUES

Professional and Associate Members shall pursue their professional activities with honesty, integrity and fairness, and with respect for other designers' or colleagues' contractual and professional relationships.

Professional and Associate Members shall not accept instruction from their clients which knowingly involves plagiarism, nor shall they consciously plagiarize another's work.

Professional and Associate Members shall not endorse the application for membership in the Association of an individual known to be unqualified with respect to education, training or experience; nor shall they knowingly misrepresent the experience, professional expertise, or moral character of that individual.

Professional and Associate Members shall only take credit for work that has actually been created by the Member or the Member's firm or under the Member's immediate direction and control.

RESPONSIBILITY TO THE ASSOCIATION AND INTERIOR DESIGN PROFESSION

Professional and Associate Members agree to maintain standards of professional and personal conduct that will reflect in a responsible manner on the profession.

Professional and Associate Members shall seek to continually upgrade their professional knowledge and competency with respect to the interior design profession.

Professional and Associate Members shall, wherever possible, encourage and contribute to the sharing of knowledge and information among interior designers, the interior design industry, and the general public.

Professional and Associate Members shall offer support, encouragement, and information to students of interior design.

Professional and Associate Members shall, when representing the interior design profession, act in a manner that is in the best interest of the profession.

Professional and Associate Members may only use the IIDA appellation in accordance with current Association policy.

Professional and Associate Members shall not knowingly make false statements or fail to disclose any material fact requested in connection with their applications for membership in the Association.

Check out the IIDA Web site at www.iida.org.

08.99

FIGURE 2-2. IIDA Code of Ethics. (Reprinted with permission, International Interior Design Association, Chicago, IL)

- Withholding merchandise that is already paid in full
- Undisclosed methods of compensation
- Overbilling, doublebilling
- Failure to disclose all business practices and compensation methods
- Purposely avoiding or not returning phone calls, faxes, letters, and other forms of communication
- Designer not qualified by professional history and experience to do the job
- Merchandise ordered is of a poor or unacceptable nature
- Failure to pay suppliers after deposits or full payment has already been made
- Failure to adhere to budget, unless discussed and approved by client first
- Unclear or nonspecific contract
- Contract alteration as the job progresses without prior client approval
- Not performing in best interest of client
- Unprofessional or improper business relationships

FIGURE 2-3. Some of the most typical complaints heard by ASID in 1999. (Provided by ASID, Washington, DC)

Both ASID and IIDA have judicial councils and ethics committees that review ethical charges brought against its members. Generally, when someone feels that it is necessary to file an ethics complaint, the process is this. The person against whom a complaint is made, of course, must be a member of one of the professional associations. The complainant must make the complaint in writing, explaining the details and facts of the situation. The letter is sent to the national office of the appropriate association. The national office sends a copy of the complaint to the designer, and the designer is given an opportunity to respond. If the member does not respond within the allotted time or if the complainant feels that the response is inadequate, the complainant can request that the ethics committee review the complaint. The complaint is reviewed by the association's legal counsel, who may feel that it is necessary to pass the complaint to the national association's ethics committee. When the appropriate committee or legal counsel determines that a violation may very well have occurred, the complaint is reviewed by another committee, which then determines if the complaint should go before the association's disciplinary committee. If that occurs, each party to the complaint is permitted to provide testimony and/or documentation before the disciplinary committee. The parties may also have legal counsel present. The disciplinary committee then determines if the facts provided by each party truly indicate that the designer charged by the complainant has violated the association's code of ethics or not. The committee may take several courses of action, from dismissing the case to terminating the designer's membership in the association.

Disciplinary hearings are not "courts of law" and have no legal bearing on either party. Thus, a disciplinary committee functions to investigate allegations of unethical behavior by members of the association. It has no authority over nonmembers who may behave unethically. The complainant is always free to peruse legal action in civil court if he or she chooses.

Actions taken to the disciplinary committee are no light matter. ASID publishes, in the *ICON*, the names of those members whose membership have been revoked by the disciplinary committee. Although this may be personally embarrassing to the member whose name appears in print, it also serves to advise all members that the Code of Ethics will be enforced by the association.

For Discussion

As this discussion of ethics in interior design draws to a close, let us look at just a few situations that "test" ethical standards. Do any of these situations represent unethical behavior? If so, if you were the designer in each case, what would you do to avoid ethical complaints? What would you do if you were a coworker? What would you do if you were a designer at another firm and heard about any of these situations?

- John has been running radio ads in his community, which give the impression that he and all his staff are professional-level members of one of the associations. John and half of his staff are not professional members of the associations.
- Samantha goes to the home of a new client. The client shows Samantha boards and plans that obviously were not prepared by the client. The designer would really like to do this project, because the client is quite a well-known celebrity.
- Marty's employer is seeking a design contract to redesign the interiors of a major hospital. Marty's wife, Jane Austin, is on the selection committee. Marty's employer knows this.
- George takes his client to a furniture trade showroom. A few days later, the client goes back alone and, while there, meets the representative of a furniture company, who tells the client details about the discount and commission program that the furniture company has offered to George.
- During her initial marketing presentation, Mary makes it clear to the client that she is experienced in handling a complex restaurant design. In fact, Mary has no experience in this area. Numerous errors have already been made in the floor plans.
- Roberta owns a design studio and specializes in the design of high-end residential projects. She recently has lost two projects to a competitor. One of those projects was for a former client, who is building a very large penthouse in Manhattan. Roberta plans to ask vendors about her former competitor.
- Anne has started her own design practice after having been fired from Miller/Jones Interior Architecture. A client is interviewing Anne and comments that he is also talking to Miller/Jones. Anne makes very disparaging comments about Miller/Jones, which seem to dissuade the client from considering that firm.
- Richard works at GBS Interiors and has been asked by a rival design firm to work for them. Richard has been hinting to some vendors that he is responsible for three or four major model home designs, but that his boss is taking all the credit. Richard feels that, since all the boss did was meet with the client to show ideas that Richard had developed, the projects are really his own.

The 1980 version of the IBD Code of Ethics remains a fitting conclusion to this brief discussion: "To be a professional involves the acceptance of responsibility to the public. . . . Ethical conduct is more than merely abiding by the letter of explicit prohibitions. Rather, it requires unswerving commitment to honorable behavior, even at the sacrifice of personal advantage."*

* "Code of Ethics." Reprinted with permission from the Institute of Business Designers, 1980, p. 3.

Summary

Some feel that it is not possible to teach ethics once an individual has become an adult. It is argued that we learn our values and morals as we grow up and that our ethics spring from those years of learning. Value systems and moral conduct start with what parents and other relatives teach us or show us, say philosophers. Ethics and values also come from others with whom we come in contact, such as clergy, teachers, coaches, and friends.

Whether it is possible to teach ethics or not is not the point of this chapter. Rather, the discussion of ethics in this chapter is offered so as to encourage further discussion of ethical behavior in the interior design field, whether or not one has chosen to belong to a professional association. If one chooses membership in an association, ethical behavior is expected in order to remain in good standing in that organization. If one does not choose to join an association, ethical behavior should still be practiced and is expected. Behaving unethically hurts oneself and the profession in which one chooses to practice.

REFERENCES

Allwork, Ronald. 1961. *AID Interior Design and Decoration Manual of Professional Practice.* New York: American Institute of Interior Designers.

American Society of Interior Designers. "Primary Basis of Complaints Being Filed." Information from ASID Ethics Office, August 2000.

———. "Procedures for Filing and Ethics Complaint." ASID web site, June 2000.

———. 1998. *ASID Code of Ethics and Professional Conduct.* Washington, DC: ASID.

Blanchard, Kenneth, and Norman Vincent Peale. 1988. *The Power of Ethical Management.* New York: William Morrow.

Brown, Gordon W., and Paul A. Sukys. 1997. *Business Law.* New York: Glencoe/McGraw-Hill.

Chewning, Richard C. 1984. *Business Ethics in a Changing Culture.* Reston, VA: Reston Publishing.

Cushman, Robert F., and James C. Dobbs. 1991. *Design Professional's Handbook of Business and Law.* New York: John Wiley.

Dale, P. Adrianne. "The Ethics Process: Inside Perspective." *ASID Report.* September 1995.

Garner, Bryan A., ed. 1999. *Black's Law Dictionary*, 7th ed. St. Paul, MN: West Group.

Garrett, Thomas M., and Richard J. Klonoski. 1986. *Business Ethics*, 2nd ed. Englewood Cliffs, NJ: Prentice-Hall.

Institute of Business Designers. 1989. *Code of Professional Conduct.* (Brochure).

———. 1980. "Code of Ethics."

International Interior Design Association. 1997. *IIDA Code of Ethics.* Chicago: IIDA.

Ivancevich, John M., Peter Lorenzi, and Steven J. Skinner (with Philip B. Crosby). 1994. *Management.* Burr Ridge, IL: Irwin.

Joiner, Colene. "Your Code of Ethics—how can it help you?" *ASID Professional Designer.* May/June 1998.

Kanungo, Rabindra N., and Manuel Mendonca. 1996. *Ethical Dimensions of Leadership.* Thousand Oaks, CA: Sage Publications.

Kaplinger, Eunice, and Susan Ray-Degges. "Can Ethics Be Taught or Is It Too Late?" *Journal of Interior Design*, vol. 24, no. 1, 1998.

Leider, Richard J. 1997. *The Power of Purpose.* San Francisco, CA: Berrett-Koehler.

Leone, Bruno. 1995. *Ethics.* San Diego, CA: Greenhaven Press.

Long, Deborah H. "Why We Need Ethical Decision-Making Skills." *ASID Professional Designer*. May/June 1998.

Newton, Lisa H., and Maureen M. Ford, eds. 1996. *Taking Sides*, 4th ed. Gilford, CT: Dushkin Group.

Siegel, Alan M. "ASID Code of Ethics and Professional Conduct: A Primer." *ASID Report*. September 1995.

Singer, Peter, ed. 1994. *Ethics.* Great Britain: Oxford University Press.

Stein, Harry. 1982. *Ethics (and Other Liabilities).* New York: St. Martin's Press.

Thompson, Jo Ann Asher, ed. 1992. *ASID Professional Practice Manual.* New York: Watson-Guptill.

Veitch, Ronald M., Dianne R. Jackman, and Mary K. Dixon. 1990. *Professional Practice.* Winnipeg, Canda: Peguis.

Chapter 3

Personal Goal Setting

Our world certainly has grown more complex, challenging, and stressful since the first edition of this text was published. It is also exciting, filled with almost unlimited opportunity for anyone who is willing to seek and achieve success in the interior design profession. New specialties have emerged. New ways of working have evolved. Markets have expanded for designers, even in small cities and towns. Options seem almost unlimited. But which specialty should you pursue? Which market do you want to conquer? What professional accomplishments do you seek to achieve?

Opening an interior design studio remains the dream for many who have entered the profession of interior design—and, if not in one's own studio, then perhaps as a design director in a major firm. Maybe one's dream is to have a project published or winning an award. For some, the dream might be to be a chapter or national officer in one of the professional associations. For others, the career dream might be to work for a major manufacturer. For still others, it might be, of course, to hold any number of other career and professional titles and achievements. Yet for many, these goals are never reached.

Goals are, of course, achieved through hard work, determination, and focusing on goals. However, goals are also achieved through planning. Sometimes family, friends, children—all of these and others—may enter the picture and delay or prevent an individual from reaching personal goals. But, in most cases, the inability to achieve a goal or a dream is not due to other individuals or job responsibilities; rather, it is usually due to a lack of planning and of setting goals—or maybe setting the wrong goals.

Although businesses spend a lot of time and energy on determining and setting goals for the coming year, individuals often ignore their own goals for the future. In this chapter, we will look at personal goal setting.

Goals

If You Don't Know Where Your Going, You'll Probably End Up Somewhere Else is the title of a wonderful book by David Campbell, PhD. (1974). Even though it was published in 1974 and dozens, if not hundreds, of other books have been written about setting goals, it still has value in the discussion of setting goals. To know where you are going can sometimes be very difficult. But, without some kind of direction, your personal and professional life can be very frustrating and unfulfilling.

Several years ago, I was visiting a friend in San Diego, California. Because she had not lived there for long, I admired her intuitive ability to find her way around a strange city. We never checked a map. Her intuition was uncanny. Many people approach all aspects of their lives in the same way. Flying by the seat of their pants, purely on intuition, they seek out educational preparation, make career decisions, move to other cities, or invest in stocks, experiencing life with little planning. For a few lucky people, this method works fine. Unfortunately, for the majority of us, living life purely on intuition leaves us like the book title mentioned above—somewhere other than where we want to be.

There is nothing wrong with using your intuition. There is also nothing wrong with just experiencing life—letting it happen. However, a far greater number of individuals who are viewed by their peers as successful people have achieved their success by planning and goal setting. The pyramids, St. Peter's Basilica, and your most recent design project were not accomplished without some kind of plan. Whatever your concept of success is, it will be far easier to achieve it if you have a plan.

Most people have dreams, but many have no goals. There is a difference. Dreams are imaginary hopes, whereas, to many, goals are concrete ideas that represent something that a person wants to achieve. Philosophically, goals are brief stops along the way of life that mark achievement in an individual's personal and professional life. Owning your own studio someday is not an end in itself, even though it may have been the goal. Now you must be ready to create new goals related to the success and growth of the studio. Goals are concrete ideas requiring effort and commitment for their achievement.

Whether an indivdual is a professional who has been actively practicing in interior design for several years or a student who is still negotiating his or her way through design classes, personal and professional goal setting is important. The professional who may feel unfulfilled or who is out of a job, even after several years of work, needs to take stock of what he or she has accomplished and the skills that he or she possesses. When tighter job markets limit choices, students must have a clearer idea of the type of job they are interested in pursuing while remaining open to any reasonable opportunity.

Even though you may have some general idea about what you want out of your personal and professional life, without some kind of concrete plan, you will find yourself reacting to what happens to you rather than having some control over events in your life. Taking control can and does make a big difference. The most successful people are those who create and develop a vision of what they want their career and personal life to be. They establish goals and strategies that help accomplish that vision. And they continually evaluate possibilities that are presented to them to determine how those possibilities positively or negatively will affect their career and personal life. Those who do not do this may find themselves saying, like the cartoon character Pogo: "We have met the enemy and he is us!"

Risks in Goal Setting

Many people have difficulty in setting goals or do not consciously bother to continue to do so, once they have achieved some immediate goal, like getting a job in the interior design field. To set a goal requires commitment of time, energy, and mental processes. Some people do not wish to really make a commitment of any kind beyond their immediate physiological needs. In setting goals, a person runs the risk of failure, that is, of not achieving the goal. But not achieving the goal does not automatically mean failure. The goal may be unattainable at the present time for one reason or another.

Because there are risks in setting goals, goals must be set with certain considerations in mind. First, set goals that satisfy you—not a spouse, a boyfriend or girlfriend, parents, or peers. If you are setting a goal to please someone else, then you will probably never achieve it. And, if, you do achieve it, it may never bring you satisfaction.

Second, some goals are unattainable without the proper experience. To become a design director at a major interior design or architectural firm does not happen overnight. It takes time to gain the experience to have such opportunities. Professionals and students alike must understand that certain goals take time to achieve. For a professional to set a goal of increasing his or her income by 50 percent in one year or for a student who is about to graduate from college to set a goal of being a design director in two years would invite disappointment. The attainment of such goals happens in only the most extraordinary situations.

Third, do not be afraid to change goals or change direction. Life is not perfect, and reality usually does not match fantasy. Be flexible in goal setting. Whatever first brought you into the interior design profession will probably change somewhat as your opportunities and experiences change. All of your career and life challenges will affect your potential ability to accomplish the goals that you set in college or after you have worked a few years in the interior design profession. This author remembers having a student who accomplished commercial projects far faster than anyone else in the class. When she was asked how she managed to do this, her response was, "I hate doing commercial design so much, I just want to get the projects finished." Her goal was to work in residential design, and she obtained that kind of a job right after graduation. About two years later, she was on campus again and she asked me, "Do you know of anyone hiring in commercial design? I hate what I am doing in residential design!" Unexpected circumstances and a lack of understanding of career requirements are just a few things that can affect reaching your goals.

There is one indisputable fact about life: life will change. For most, change means growth. So don't be afraid to grow. Being open to a change of plans may offer you an opportunity for personal and professional growth that you have not even considered. For example, Jim has a goal of becoming a design director at a major firm. One day, he was offered a two-year position as a designer in Hawaii. He did not look at the possibilities that the opportunity provided for the future and refused the position, and continued working in a medium-sized city in the Northwest. Several years later, he still was not in a position to be a design director, and he looked back longingly at that lost opportunity. Do not be afraid to consider or even embark upon different paths when they arise.

A Personal Mission Statement

Many readers have heard of Steven Covey and his very popular book, *The Seven Habits of Highly Effective People*. To Covey, a personal mission statement helps a person set a direction for what that person wants to do in his or her personal and professional life. Much like a business mission statement, "it focuses on what you want to be (character) and to do (contributions and achievements) and on the values or principles upon which being and doing are based" (Covey, 1989, p. 106).

Once you develop a personal mission statement, it will help you with many life decisions that are necessary as you travel through personal and professional relationships and activities. It will help you define your focus, which, in turn, will help you determine on what you most wish to spend your emotional, psychological, and financial resources. According to Covey, a personal mission statement will help you more effectively handle the changes that will constantly affect your life.

Creating a personal mission statement starts with allowing your innermost self to make you aware of what you most want in life—not just today, but in the future. It starts by determining the end you most desire: to own a successful design practice; to be the principal project designer at one of the top five design firms in the country; to have a highly respected international reputation in design; to have both a satisfying family and professional life; or anything else you can imagine.

Here is a brief example of a personal mission statement:

To believe in myself and allow myself to try, to experiment, to experience, thus to learn.
To strive each day to be willing to pay the price to achieve greater happiness, confidence, and spiritual growth.
To do some work that benefits others and that is enjoyable to me.
To treat others based on the principles that I hold as important.

Perhaps you would like to write a personal mission statement before you continue reading this chapter. Think of what you want to be known for at the end of your career, or even your life. Make notes about the roles that you now play within your family, in your career (or potential career), with friends, and in the community at large. Are you satisfied with those roles? Consider the principals that mean the most to you. Make notes about the things, words, places, and activities that inspire or excite you. Then take some time away from the hustle and bustle of your daily life to write down a personal mission statement. It doesn't have to be structured like the example. Any format or length will do.

Setting Goals

Whether you write a personal mission statement or not, the best way to set goals is to try to look at yourself in terms of the future. Steven Covey calls it, "beginning with the end in mind." In many ways, a similar approach is to write your own obituary *now*—a rather jarring thought at the age of 21 or at any age. This exercise in goal setting was required by an instructor whom I had in college. The idea was to focus on long-range goal setting. Occasionally, we all need to look at what we want to be remembered for—what we hope we will be able to accomplish by the time we pass away.

Understandably, writing your own obituary is difficult to do. It may be easier to start thinking about what you want to accomplish by the time you are 30, 40, 50, and at retirement age. And, if you find *that* too difficult to do, just try to figure out where you want to be in your professional and personal life during the next five years.

If you are unsure of what you want to accomplish, it might help if you use Figures 3-1 and 3-2 to get started. Find a quiet place where you can think undisturbed. Be brutally honest with yourself as you answer the questions.

The purpose of this exercise is to analyze your skills, interests, and abilities in relation to the kind of job opportunities you will be seeking in interior design. Completing this exercise will make you more aware of what you have to offer your present or future employers. It will also help you discover goals that you need to work on in the next year or so.

1. **What is your number one interest in interior design?**
2. **What or who influenced your interest in this profession? (family, teacher, mentor, the media, work experience, etc.)?**
3. **What kind of skills in interior design do you have right now?**
4. **What special skill(s) do you have to offer your present employer or another employer?**
5. **If you were going to a job interview tomorrow, what specific career goal would you share with the interviewer?**
6. **What could you do right now to improve the chances of getting the job you most want?**
7. **List three of your biggest successes.**
8. **List five goals you wish to accomplish during the next calendar year.**
9. **List three goals you hope to accomplish by the time you are 30 years old.**
10. **List three goals you hope to accomplish by the time you are 50 years old.**
11. **Assuming it were possible for you to achieve any goal in interior design, what would it be?**
12. **List ten mini-goals needed to support the goal stated in number 11.**

FIGURE 3-1. Personal goals exercise.

Once you have some idea of where you want to be, you can start looking at goals in terms of the concrete things that need to be accomplished in order to achieve them. For example, "I want to own my own studio by the time I am 35." What kinds of work experience will be needed to meet that goal? Where do you want that studio to be located? Where will you get the finances to open the doors? Do you want to work alone or with someone else? Being your own boss sounds good, but are you willing to sacrifice family and personal time to keep the studio in operation? These are some of the questions related to that goal. Some of the "mini" goals related to achieving this goal might be:

- Work with a residential firm for five years to gain experience in residential practice.
- Work with a commercial firm for five years to gain experience with general commercial clients.
- Become a senior designer or design manager with either a residential or a commercial firm to gain business and management experience.
- If necessary, take additional business classes at a community college or enter an MBA program to gain the business knowledge to own a studio.

These are all examples of concrete mini-goals that you would need to accomplish in order to bring about the larger goal of owning your own studio. Once the opportunity of opening a studio occurs, new goals must be decided upon, related to the business and the next "stop" on the road.

The process is the same for any goal. If the goal is the end, activities and accomplishments (called strategies and tactics in business planning) must be determined to reach the end—the goal.

The process, in some ways, is never ending. New opportunities occur all the time if they are recognized and acted upon. Unexpected problems and challenges might derail you momentarily or even forever. Ask any designer who is 10 or 20 years older than yourself how he or she got to where he or she is today, and you will probably find that the designer took many roads to get where he or she is. But isn't that part of the fun?

In these questions, you are asked to look at a variety of issues concerning your professional and personal life. Combined with the questions in Figure 2–1, these questions provided you an opportunity to look at some additional issues that can help clarify your professional and personal goals.

1. **List at least three things that drew you into a career in interior design. Write several comments about each of these items.**
2. **List any three people you most admire. Write down a few words or sentences that explain why you admire them.**
3. **List three or four companies (or types of firms) that provide the kinds of design work you wish to do.**
4. **Which of the following is most important to you in your career: money, recognition, self-satisfaction, or creative expression?**
5. **If you had the means to do so, what would you most like to do—personally and professionally? Remember, no restrictions.**
6. **What do you think you need to change to make yourself happier in your professional and personal life?**
7. **What frustrates you most about your professional and personal life?**
8. **What do you like most about work in interior design? What do you like least?**
9. **When are you at your best and most secure (professionally and personally)?**
10. **Do you prefer to work independently or with a group?**
11. **Write a paragraph that would sum up what you most want to be remembered for in your professional (and/or personal) life.**
12. **On a sheet of paper, make two columns. On the top of one column, write the word *problem,* and on the other, the word *solution.* Then write in the "problem" column those things that you feel are holding you back or are problems in your professional and/or personal life. In the "solution" column, write down potential solutions to each problem. In some cases, you may find that you are really writing down thoughts rather than true solutions, but those thoughts will help you find solutions to the problems.**

FIGURE 3-2. Professional goals questionnaire.

Summary

It is important for all of us to make goals in order to provide direction in our lives. Setting goals is risky and takes commitment, but, if the goals we set are goals that interest us, they likely will be fulfilled.

Achieving a goal may or may not be within our control. It must be remembered that some goals take a certain kind of expertise or maybe a credential like an M.B.A. Without the expertise or credential, accomplishing the goal may be unlikely. Goals take time to reach. Just as Rome was not built in a day, obtaining the credentials to teach in a university, to work for a major manufacturer, or to create designs that are purchased by custom furniture manufacturers does not come overnight. Always keep in mind that life changes either by actions that we take ourselves or by actions that have an effect upon us. Do not be afraid of those changes, and do not be afraid of making changes if new opportunities look interesting.

REFERENCES

Barnhart, Tod. 1995. *The Five Rituals of Wealth.* New York: HarperCollins.

Bliss, Edwin. 1983. *Doing It Now.* New York: Bantam Books.

Bolles, Richard Nelson. 2000. *What Color Is Your Parachute?* Berkeley, CA: Ten Speed Press.

Brothers, Dr. Joyce. 1978. *How To Get Whatever You Want Out of Life.* New York: Ballantine Books.

Buscagila, Dr. Leo. 1982. *Living, Loving, and Learning.* New York: Charles B. Slack.

Campbell, David. 1974. If *You Don't Know Where You're Going, You'll Probably End Up Somewhere Else.* Niles, IL: Argus Communications.

Covey, Stephen R. 1989. *The Seven Habits of Highly Effective People.* New York: Fireside Books.

Covey, Stephen R., A. Roger Merrill, and Rebecca R. Merrill. 1994. *First Things First.* New York: Simon and Schuster.

Freudenberger, Dr. Herbert J. 1980. *Burn Out.* Garden City, NY: Anchor Press (Doubleday and Co.).

Friedman, Martha. 1980. *Overcoming the Fear of Success.* New York: Warner.

Gray, John. 1999. *How To Get What You Want and Want What You Have.* New York: HarperCollins.

Griessman, B. Eugene. 1994. *Time Tactics of Very Successful People.* New York: McGraw-Hill.

Harragan, Betty Lehan. 1977. *Games Mother Never Taught You.* New York: Warner.

Helzel, Leo B. and friends. 1995. *A Goal Is a Dream with a Deadline.* New York: McGraw-Hill.

Hirsch, Arlene S. 1996. *Love Your Work and Success Will Follow.* New York: John Wiley.

Hyatt, Carole, and Linda Gottlieb. 1993. *When Smart People Fail,* rev. ed. New York: Penguin.

James, Muriel, and John James. 1991. *Passion for Life.* New York: Dutton Books.

Jones, Katie. 1998. *Time Management.* New York: American Management Association.

LeBoeuf, Michael. 1979. *Working Smart.* New York: Warner.

Lloyd, Joan. 1992. *The Career Decisions Planner.* New York: John Wiley.

MacKay, Harvey. 1997. *Dig Your Well Before You're Thirsty.* New York: Currency/Doubleday.

Mayer, Jeffrey J. 1999. *Success Is a Journey: 7 Steps to Achieving Success in the Business of Life.* New York: McGraw-Hill.

Ponder, Catherine. 1973. *The Prosperity Secret of the Ages,* rev. ed. Englewood Cliffs, NJ: Prentice-Hall.

Roger, John, and Peter McWilliams. 1991. *Life 101. Everything We Wish We Had Learned About Life in School—But Didn't.* Los Angeles, CA: Prelude Press (Bantam-Prelude).

Rubin, Harriet. 1999. *Soloing: Realizing Your Life's Ambition.* New York: HarperCollins.

Sheehy, Gail. 1995. *New Passages.* New York: Ballantine.

Sher, Barbara, with Annie Gottlieb. 1979. *Wishcraft—How To Get What You Really Want.* New York: Ballantine.

Sinetara, Marsha. 1987. *Do What You Love, the Money Will Follow.* New York: Dell.

Viscott, David, MD. 1985. *Taking Care of Business. A Psychiatrist's Guide for True Career Success.* New York: William Morrow.

Waitley, Denis. 1984. *The Psychology of Winning.* New York: Berkely Books.

———. 1983. *Seeds of Greatness. The Ten Best Kept Secrets of Total Success.* New York: Pocket Books (Simon and Schuster).

Webber, Alan M. "Are You a Star at Work?" *Fast Company.* June/July 1998.

Yohalem, Kathy C. 1997. *Thinking Out of the Box.* New York: John Wiley.

Rosalyn Cama, FASID is the President and Principal Interior Designer of the interior planning and design firm CAMA, Inc. in New Haven, Connecticut. CAMA, Inc. has completed design work for many institutional, corporate, professional, hospitality, and residential clients; however, its main areas of activity have been healthcare facilities, and academic settings for higher education. A former President of the American Society of Interior Designers, Cama has lectured at New York University and is often sought as a spokesperson/author for the professional in the area of healthcare interior design.

In a time when more evidence is needed to substantiate value, there is a transformation from the perception of interior design as a luxury to interior design as a necessity to improve behavior in the built environment. What this means is that as interior designers, we can no longer be complacent to just know design trends. We must be well versed in all aspects of our future, i.e., political, economic, environmental, sociological, and technological trends. With a more evidence-based approach to our problem solving, our clients will begin to value us as an important ally in the achievement of their strategic plans.

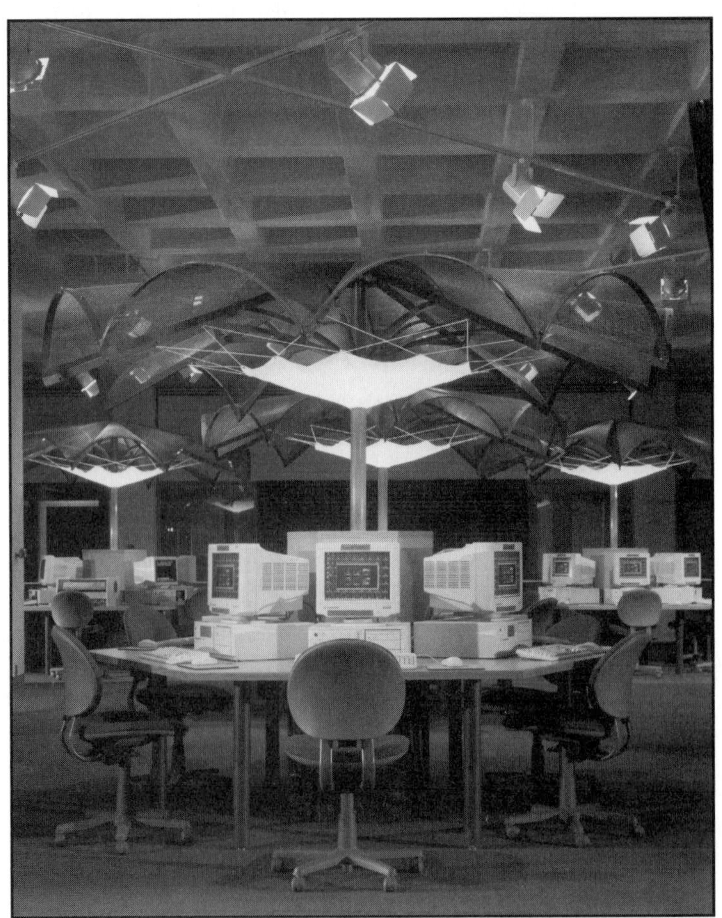

Part II

How to Establish an Interior Design Practice

Chapter 4

Planning a New Interior Design Practice

No one knows exactly how many new interior design practices are opened in any one year. To be sure, it is a large number, as many more designers seek the independence of working on their own or with a small number of partners or employees. Many of these ventures succeed and go on to flourish. Many others fail. According to the US Small Business Administration (SBA), approximately 1.5 million small businesses are launched each year. Statistically, a large number of thesese businesses fail within one year (SBA, 1991). Due in large part to the booming economy in the last few years, the number of business failures in 1997 was very low—less than 3 percent (SBA, 1998). Although there are numerous reasons for the failure of a business, many are related to not having a clearly defined plan before opening the doors. Businesses fail because the services that a business owner wishes to provide are unwanted, there are too few potential customers in the area, or the owner has insufficient funds to survive during the difficult first months. These factors and more are the kinds of things that the entrepreneur must investigate before "opening the doors" of the new enterprise.

Is it possible to start a design practice without a thorough business plan? Of course it is. However, a plan helps the budding business owner to clearly consider the business idea, establishing such things as which design services will be offered, how many customers might potentially be interested in those services, and the amount of financial resources that will be necessary until revenue starts coming in.

Anyone who might consider starting a design practice needs to do serious research, thinking, and planning. The potential business owner needs to research his or her own business skills and experience. In addition, the potential business owner must also evaluate his or her motivation for starting a design practice. Planning formalizes the decisions and ideas surrounding the creation of a new business. It helps the potential business owner see if the idea is feasible and what will be required to make it work. It provides an operational tool for the owner to handle potential problems with thought rather than by pure gut reaction.

The first sections of this chapter summarize information about the numerous decisions that must be made. The remainder of this chapter looks at suggestions on how to go about putting together a business plan. Chapters 5, 6, 7, and 8 address other issues that need to be reviewed and considered when a designer plans to start up a new interior design practice.

What Is an Entrepreneur?

An *entrepreneur* is someone who starts and manages his or her own business. An entrepreneur might work alone or might hire employees. Entrepreneurs generally try to do things differently. Often, the reason they have started a business is that they feel they have a better way to provide design services, to manage an office, or to sell products. Today, an entrepreneurial small business is the leading type of business being created. According to the SBA, virtually all of the new jobs in 1996 were created by small business firms, and 99 percent of the business tax returns filed in 1996 came from small businesses (SBA, 1998).

Numerous books and articles about entrepreneurs define the traits and characteristics of these individuals. However, do not become trapped into thinking that only those persons that "fit" these characteristics can be successful business owners. Charles Banfe, in his book *Entrepreneur,* feels that entrepreneurs come in all shapes, sizes, ages, experience levels, educational backgrounds and that there really is no typical entrepreneur. In fact, many small business owners of the late 1990s are totally different from the traditional picture of the entrepreneur.

The main characteristic that will help sustain a potential business owner through all the decisions and all the crises in starting and owning a business is *drive*. Willingness to work and to work hard. Owners of businesses do not punch in at 8 A.M. and punch out at 5 P.M. They commonly put in 12-hour days—often, even longer. They commonly take work home as well, if not in terms of actual paperwork or design work, then in terms of thinking about existing problems that must be resolved. Business owners seek out advice from books, consultants, friends—from any source that will help them do a better job of managing and sustaining their business. And, while many owners of design practices have said occasionally, "If someone would offer to buy my studio, I'd sell in a minute!" they have not and probably will not because, deep down, the challenge of ownership is too exciting to give up.

However, successful owners of design practices do have some common characteristics. They have technical design expertise gained through education and work experience. It is difficult to offer design services without knowing how to perform those services properly. Most have worked for someone else, either in a design firm or in some type of business situation. Working in a design firm provides an opportunity to experience and perhaps help manage a business. These people are highly self-motivated. Self-motivated individuals do not wait for the boss to assign them work. Designers who need to be prodded into working will find it difficult to put in the time and effort necessary to operate a business. Once again, they must have the drive to succeed.

Being the boss is fun. It is also risky and a lot of hard work. Those who may be considering owning their own business have already met the first prerequisite for ownership—they have the dream of ownership. Next, they must get the skills and background in design and business that will make it easier to achieve that dream. And they should not forget to get advice from specialists who are available to help the potential business owner.

Advantages and Disadvantages of Business Ownership

As with any risk, there are good things and bad things about owning a business. Designers see the boss leaving for long lunches, going home early, maybe driving an expensive car. Employees rarely consider the disadvantages, because employees do not always see the long hours, financial sacrifices, and continual stress that goes along with being the boss. Part of the decision-making process in owning your own business is to look at both the advantages and the disadvantages—especially the disadvantages—of ownership, to be sure that you are prepared to accept these constraints. Some of these appear below.

Advantages

- Not having to report to a boss. As the boss, the owner makes the decisions.
- Personal satisfaction in achieving success.
- Having the opportunity to perform the kind of design work the individual most enjoys.
- Making a potentially higher income, which includes potential gains from the profits of the company, as well as the income drawn from the business.
- Potential long-term job security. The job exists as long as the business succeeds and the owner wishes to remain in the business.
- The chance to develop a creative style, which is not often possible when one is working for someone else. Designers who are working for others often must design in the style of the design firm.
- Increased contact with clients, suppliers, and other industry members. The owner makes more client contacts, deals directly with suppliers, and has the opportunity to meet others in many aspects of the design industry.
- Greater responsibility in being in charge and making all the decisions. For some, of course, this becomes a disadvantage.

Disadvantages

- Large financial risk. Depending on the business formation, the business owner might also be risking personal assets.
- Greater legal liability. Owners are liable for their own actions, as well as for those of their employees.
- Longer hours. Typically, owners work 12-hour days, sometimes even seven days a week, with little time off for vacations or for a personal or social life. This is especially true in the first few years of the life of the business.
- Greater stress. The owner is concerned about bringing in enough business to meet all the bills and to prevent any kind of bad publicity or poor customer service. He or she also must worry that the employees are all doing their jobs properly and legally, and must worry about many other problems and constraints that affect the business.
- Minimal income in the early months and perhaps for the entire first year. Profits for a new business are traditionally low and are often plowed back into the business, either to pay expenses or to expand the business.
- Less design input. As the business grows, the design owner often finds that he or she is spending less time on design and more time on managing the business.
- Need to satisfy customers. Even though a business owner is the boss, he or she is now controlled by the wishes of the client.
- A great deal of management responsibility. Many designers who start

their own practice lack management skills. Thus, many new businesses, whether owned by one person or many people, stumble and even fail.

- Less flexibility. It is not easy to quit if the business owner finds that he or she does not enjoy ownership or otherwise no longer wishes to remain in business. A financial loss might result from closing down. It may be difficult to find someone to buy the business.
- Market changes. The changing needs of potential customers may drain away business.

It is not entirely by accident that the list of disadvantages of business ownership outnumber the advantages. Many business owners would agree with these lists. The intention here is not to discourage anyone from starting his or her own business; on the contrary. The intention is to be sure that the potential business owner realizes the risks involved and contemplates the business venture thoroughly before starting the new design practice.

Starting a New Design Practice

The decision to start a new design practice must involve careful evaluation of personal motivation; consideration of the financial, physiological, and legal risks; and a commitment to doing the research and to making the numerous decisions that will be required. Too many designers begin an interior design practice without carefully thinking through the business concept and its numerous decisions, let alone the risks involved.

If you are considering opening your own design practice, you must carefully look at your motivation. Since so many interior design businesses begin in a home office, it does seem attractive not to have to commute to work every day and to use that time with family or for oneself. Maybe your motivation comes from a desire to work only with clients who really want to buy your creative design ideas rather than the need to meet the demands of an employer. You may be motivated by the idea of making more money or working for yourself rather than for someone else. Or, you may be motivated by a feeling that you can somehow "do it better" than other designers in the marketplace.

These examples all have some validity for some of you. For others, these mean nothing. Whatever motivations you have for wanting to have your own design practice, the important point is to know and recognize what they are. Although the motivations noted above may appear to be positive, they can also result in negative issues. Working from home does save commuting time, but it also requires a great deal of discipline. The distractions of running a household and taking care of children may steal away time that is needed for running the business. Many designers start out picking and choosing clients but find that, in leaner economic times, they cannot do this. Besides, it will not take the new business owner long to realize that the client most often is not buying a designer's creative ideas as much as solutions to his or her problems. The motivation of making more money may be only a dream for many years, as the number of projects, low margins, and costs of operating the business reduce the profits of all small businesses.

Figure 4-1 provides numerous questions that will help the potential business owner evaluate his or her motivations and attitudes concerning starting a new design practice. This exercise is very important and should not be taken lightly.

Motivations and attitudes are only one part of the evaluation that any potential new business owner must make before starting a business plan.

The following provides sample questions that you should use to evaluate your motivations and attitudes toward starting your own business. If you are seriously thinking of starting your own business in the near future, use these questions only as a starting point to determine your interest and sincerity.

1. **Why do you want to own your own business?**
2. **Are you dissatisfied with your present job? Why?**
3. **Are you prepared for the sacrifices of your personal time and energy that you will have to make?**
4. **How do your present skills and abilities prepare you for business ownership?**
5. **Do you have finances available to commit to the business venture, or must you obtain outside start-up financing?**
6. **Are you willing to survive financially without a regular salary or paycheck?**
7. **Do you have sufficient experience in the interior design industry to operate and maintain a design practice?**
8. **Do you have clients who will switch to your business, should you leave your current employer?**
9. **Are you a self-starter, or do you need direction in your present work situation?**
10. **Are you good at performing many tasks at the same time, or are you better when you only have to do one thing at a time?**
11. **What skills and abilities do you have that you can offer your potential clients?**
12. **Have you done any evaluation of potential competitors?**
13. **Can you work without others around, or do you need others to help keep you motivated?**
14. **What kinds of business skills or experiences do you have to operate a business?**
15. **Are you a good organizer?**
16. **Do you have a lot of self-confidence?**
17. **Are family members prepared to accept your long hours and lack of attention as you start and operate your own business?**
18. **If your business is to be located at home, do you have sufficient space and privacy to perform your work activities?**

FIGURE 4-1. Personal motivations and attitudes about starting a new design practice.

A second important exercise is to evaluate the personal financial risk that is involved. Financial risk changes depending on many factors. It can take several thousands of dollars, if not tens of thousands of dollars, to start up a design practice and to survive during the first year. In addition, the entrepreneur must consider how he or she will pay personal expenses while waiting for revenues to be realized. Banks are reluctant to loan much, if any, money to many small businesses. Furthermore, banks will not loan money to a budding entrepreneur for living expenses, regardless of how great the business idea is.

An evaluation of the personal financial risk entailed in starting a new design practice begins by determining the amount of funds that are needed each month to pay living expenses. Figure 4-2 is a simple form that will help determine those expenses. It is generally suggested that the entrepreneur set aside at least one year's living expenses before starting a small business, since it may take that long for the business to be able to pay the entrepreneur a salary. Obviously, the next step is to determine where the funds will come from to cover those personal living expenses. For most entrepreneurs, it comes from savings and/or the funds available from the income of a family member. Some use the credit line on their personal credit cards. However, this is not advisable, since the interest rate on personal credit cards is commonly quite high.

The entire business concept has an impact on personal financial risk. The more ambitious the plans are for the business, the more risk is involved. Any

Personal Expenses

Item	Monthly Amount	Annual
Housing (Rent):		
Home Owners Association		
Insurance		
Property Taxes		
Utilities:		
Electricity/Gas		
Telephone		
TV (Cable)		
Internet		
Water/Sewer		
Food		
Automobile:		
Payment		
Insurance		
Gas and Maintenance		
Health Insurance		
Credit Cards		
Other Loans		
Clothing & Laundry		
Child Care		
Dues and Subscriptions*		
Savings/Investments		
Entertainment		
Gifts & Charities		
Miscellaneous		
TOTAL:		

*Those that are not business expenses.

FIGURE 4-2. A form for calculating personal expenses.

design practice with a high overhead will put more strain on the designer's ability to meet personal financial obligations. Willingness to live on less while the business gets on its feet may be an important consideration while funds to pay personal bills are limited. Careful evaluation, savings, and planning as to how the designer's personal financial responsibilities will be met is a very important part of planning a new design practice. Business start-up budgeting will be discussed later in this chapter.

Defining the Business

At this point, the potential business owner has evaluated his or her own motivations for starting a practice and has determined how to meet personal financial obligations during the tough start-up months of the business. Another important exercise to do, to prepare a business plan, is to define the business. "That's easy," one might say. "I'm going to have an interior design business." Okay, but what does that really mean? Students and professionals alike know that there are many different kinds of interior design businesses. That was briefly discussed in Chapter 1 and will be discussed more fully in Chapter 32.

The challenge is to clearly define what the purpose of the business will be and the services that will be offered in order to help create a positive start-up. In any given geographic area, there are dozens, maybe even hundreds, of other businesses that provide interior design services. In order to survive for many years, it is important to know what makes the new firm different from all the others. Answering the questions in Figure 4-3 will help the entrepreneur appraise the fundamental business idea. When this has been completed, it is a good idea to also create a draft of the business' mission statement.

The *mission statement* is a philosophical statement that provides a concise explanation of a firm's direction and purposes and why it exists. A mission statement generally contains the following information: a description of the business; a description of its customers; the services and products offered; and the geographic area served. It does not have to be long and commonly consists of only a few sentences. The following is a simple example:

> AllanBee Interior Design, Inc. is a full-service interior design company providing the highest level of professional skills and creative solutions for healthcare and assisted-living facilities clients throughout the southeastern United States.

Another example of a company mission statement is shown in Figure 4-4. Note that this example is very simple and straight forward. This illustrates the fact that mission statements can be and are different from company to company, expressing the individual firm's philosophy in a way that makes sense to that business.

Defining the business will help the prospective owner with marketing decisions, operational choices, hiring employees, financing, and many other management issues along the way. A clear definition will help the business owner realize what unique qualities the business brings to prospective clients. It will help the business owner know which projects to take and which ones to refuse, and what to look for when employees are needed. Financing choices becomes easier when a clear picture of the purpose and direction of the firm has been established. Defining the business makes it easier for the owner to determine what kinds of technology are needed. All of these decisions and many more are made easier for a firm that has a clear idea of what it is all about.

Carefully answer these questions in order to help you define your overall business idea. Remember to be as specific as possible in your responses. The information from this questionnaire can be used to develop your business plan.

Have you clarified your design and business skills? (If you will have partners, answer these questions for them as well.)

What experience do you have in interior design, architecture, and/or construction?
What experience do you have in sales and marketing?
What experience do you have in managing other individuals?
What business experience or knowledge do you have?

Define your business.

What services (exactly) will you offer initially?
Will you sell products?
Will products be from inventory or special order only?
How will you price your services (fee methods)?
How will you price the products you sell?
How will you receive and deliver goods to clients?
Have you considered what language will go into design contracts?

Do you know who your customers will be?

How many potential customers are in your business area?
How many of these customers do you think you can attract?
Will your customers perceive your prices as competitive?
Will your customers see a difference in your services from your competition?
What income group will your business appeal to?

What kind of finances will be required to start your business?

What business licenses will be required? Cost?
Are you going to start your business at home? Is this legally possible in your community?
If you are going to have your business in a commercial space, have you investigated rental costs?
What kind of equipment and furniture will be necessary to start your business? What is the estimated cost of purchase? What are the possibilities to lease these items?
What kind of income are you seeking for yourself for the first year? Use this (along with estimated expenses) to determine how much revenue you will need to generate monthly. Is this possible, considering your business idea, number of potential customers, and competition?

Have you researched the competition?

Who are your main competitors?
How many other firms like yours exist within 2 miles?
How many other firms like yours exist within your business area?
What can you do that your competition is not already doing?
Do you know how much your competition charges for its services/products?
Why would your customers buy from you rather than an existing competitor?

How will clients find out about your business?

Will you do mass mailings?
Will you use advertising? What kind and in what media?
Are you going to develop marketing tools, such as a brochure?
Have you considered the design of your letterhead and other business stationery?

FIGURE 4-3. A questionnaire to help the potential business owner define his or her business idea.

Mission Statement

We create architecture
sensitive to people and place.

Vision Statement

We are a team of professionals with
unique talents, enriched through rewarding
architecture, recognized for
excellence and innovation.

Knoell & Quidort Architects, Phoenix, Arizona

FIGURE 4-4. A sample mission statement. (Reproduced with permission, Knoell & Quidort Architects, Phoenix, Arizona)

The Business Plan

As was pointed out in the introduction to this chapter, preparing a business plan—even a very rudimentary one—provides the business owner a far greater chance of success than if he or she started a business without preparing a plan. Evaluating and planning the services to be offered, researching the customer base, determining operational procedures, and clarifying financing help the prospective business owner map a strategy for the business's start-up and growth.

"The business plan is a written document prepared by the entrepreneur that describes all the relevant external and internal elements involved in starting a new venture" (Hisrich and Peters, 1992, p. 12). For an interior design practice that will resell goods, the business plan may well be the key to obtaining the necessary funding from banks or venture capitalists to purchase needed inventory. However, an interior design practice that expects to obtain revenue from selling services requires less initial funding. In this case, the business plan is prepared to provide substantive thought as to what the business is all about and how it is going to operate.

There is no surefire way to prepare a business plan, as the numerous books on the topic testify. One should not look for a perfect "template" that requires the prospective owner to only fill in the blanks. Nor should one look to his or her attorney, accountant, or banker to provide all the answers. The business plan is a personal expression of what the owner feels the firm is all about and how he or she hopes it will grow. Although preparing a business plan will not guarantee success, the process of thinking the business through will help the prospective owner face the realities of starting a business. A plan, if it is thoroughly done, also provides an opportunity to anticipate problems and to avoid them, if possible—or at least to know how to cope with them as they arise.

The business plan is not something that can be done overnight. If an interior designer is anticipating opening a practice, then he or she should allow time to develop the business plan. It may take weeks or even months to prepare it, depending on how much time can be devoted to research and writing it. If outside financing is required from a bank, far more information will be needed, requiring more preparation time, than if the business is self-financed. At times, outside consultants may be required, especially if a formal plan is being prepared to obtain substantial financial backing.

If the owner prepares the plan after opening for business, an even greater amount of time may be required, since the owner must simultaneously keep the business going. In this case, an outside business consultant who is familiar with the interior design profession may be helpful.

The plan, once completed, helps the prospective owner in many ways to reach the goal of having his or her own practice. The plan helps the prospective owner see if the idea is realistic and feasible. Financial backing will be easier to obtain with a well-prepared plan. The business plan also sets initial goals and objectives of the firm, which can be measured by the firm's performance. Later, if performance does not meet these initial objectives, the plan and the ongoing analysis of the plan help the owner determine what to do to get back on track, assuming the plan was feasible in the first place.

Business Plan Research

An important ingredient of all business plans is research. A very thorough period of research should be undertaken before the business plan is written. Certain kinds of information always are expected to appear in the plan. It is necessary to complete research in areas of skills and abilities, the marketplace, and operational considerations, such as pricing, expected capital required, and projected financial planning. For all prospective interior design practices, the items in the following list must be thoroughly investigated and considered. The steps outline a suggested sequence in which the research should be conducted.

1. Analyze personal abilities and interests related to owning an interior design business.
2. Carefully consider the purpose and mission of the business, who prospective customers might be, and why the business is being started.
3. Develop a personal income plan that assures payment of all personal expenses during the first year of the life of the business.
4. If you have hired employees or anticipate hiring additional employees, analyze operational needs and their required skills.
5. Analyze the potential market for the firm's services. Do not forget to research existing competition.
6. Draft a marketing plan that includes the aspect of the market that the firm will address. Determine what services the firm will offer, target market, pricing policies, and considerations for advertising and/or promotional activities.
7. Determine which type of business formation will be used: a sole proprietorship, a partnership, a form of corporation, or possibly some other legal form.
8. Determine legal responsibilities and tax obligations. Consult with an attorney concerning contracts and liabilities, an accountant concerning record keeping, and an insurance representative regarding insurance obligations.
9. Estimate how much capital will be required to "open the doors." Estimate the first year's expenses. Determine sources of initial capital.
10. Develop a financial plan and income projections. Include projected balance sheets, income statements, and cash flow forecasts.
11. Develop a concept of the firm's image: appearance of letterhead, business cards, exteriors of delivery trucks, title blocks for drawing paper, and so on.

12. Prepare an organizational plan that includes projected personnel needs, job descriptions, employee benefits, and purchasing procedures.
13. If the firm will engage in retail selling of inventoried goods, develop an inventory plan of what will be purchased, when it will be purchased, and where it will be stored.
14. Produce the business plan.

The most important parts of the research for the business plan are Steps 1, 2, and 9. Understanding motivations and abilities is a very important part of the planning research. One must clearly determine if the services that the interior design business will provide are needed in the community and if one can obtain the capital to start and maintain the business. If the research results for either of these concerns shows that success is doubtful, the business venture should be reconsidered or possibly rejected. Figure 4-5 provides a list of questions that the prospective owner must ask about the proposed organizational structure of the new business, which will help in the research for the business plan. The remaining chapters in Part II give details about many of the points raised in figures 4-1, 4-3, and 4-5.

An important consideration for the prospective business owner when he or she is researching and developing the business plan is to analyze the financial needs and revenue expectations of the business. Earlier in this chapter, we addressed the evaluation of personal financial risk and the determination of how much financial resources would be needed to pay for personal living expenses during a business start-up. In this part of the chapter, we will look briefly at the issue of start-up expenses.

Regardless of the location of the business—whether at home or at a commercial office or retail location—an interior design business will have similar financial needs at its inception. One group of start-up expenses are those that are one-time expenses, including such things as purchase of equipment and furniture for the office, utility deposits, legal fees, start-up promotional items like advertising or mailings, and sellable inventory, if any. Other start-up expenses become ongoing expenses, such as stationery, office supplies, telephone and fax charges, insurance, and promotional activities. A third group of expenses are those that are ongoing yet are not necessarily needed at the initial start-up of the business. Figure 4-6 provides a list of the common expense items needed for an interior design practice. It can be applied to one that is based in the designer's home or in a commercial facility.

To prepare the financial part of the business plan, the business owner, perhaps with the help of an accountant, prepares pro forma income statements and other accounting reports. In business terms, *pro forma* means a projection. It can also mean in advance. So, a pro forma income statement is one that has been created with projected numbers instead of actual numbers or in advance of actual numbers.

The basis of a pro forma income statement (also called a profit and loss statement, or P & L) is any known numbers, such as expected overhead expenses like rent and utilities.* Assumptions and "best guesses" as to what might happen in the future are factored in to produce the numbers on the income statement. Generally, people more often will overestimate than underestimate the projected revenue for a business. The designer utilizing a pro forma statement must do some real homework on such things as the current and potential future economic situation, inflation, and changes in expenses. It is suggested that the reader review the opening sections of Chapter 15 if he or

* Other overhead expenses will be discussed in Chapter 15.

Select the name of the business.

Use your own name?
Use a fictitious name (Requires a legal filing; see Chapter 7)?

Where will the business be located (see Chapters 7 and 8)?

In a residence (will this violate zoning laws)?
In a commercial site?
Will customers easily be able to find the business location?
Can the business location (home or commercial site) easily be modified to meet your needs?
Will you rent or lease space?

Select a legal structure (see Chapter 6).

Sole proprietorship?
Partnership?
Corporation?
Other form?

Are any licenses required (see Chapter 7)?

Interior design registration?
Contractor's license?
Business licenses?
Transaction privilege tax license?

Will the business have employees other than the owner(s) (see Chapters 7, 11, and 12)?

Are any federal or state filings required?
What type of benefits will be provided to employees?
What kind of equipment will be provided for employees to do their jobs?
How will employees be recruited?

How will business records be maintained (see Chapters 15 and 16)?

What accounting bases will be used?
Who will do the daily bookkeeping?
Who will keep payroll and tax records?
Who will prepare any formal accounting records that are required?

How will the business be financed for the first year (see Chapter 4 and 5)?

Personal investment by owner(s)?
Investments by friends or relatives?
Loans?
Have an estimated cash flow statement and pro forma income statement been prepared for the first year?
Have personal living expenses for the first year been estimated?
Have start-up costs and expenses for the first year been estimated?

Have insurance requirements before investigated (see Chapter 5)?

What kinds of insurance are needed initially?

Will the business require inventory (see Chapter 8)?

What will the initial inventory consist of?
How will the purchase of initial inventory be financed?
Where will any back-up inventory be stored?
How will goods be delivered to clients?
Have your inventory ideas been compared with those of nearby competitors?

How will the business be promoted and clients obtained (see Chapters 21, 22, and 23)?

What marketing tools (such as a brochure) will be needed?
Do you have a marketing plan?
Will you utilize a web page?
Will you market to clients only close to your business location?

Have you thought about how fees will be set (see Chapter 17 and 19)?

Will services only be provided, or will merchandise also be sold?
On what basis will fees be set?
How will fees be set?
Are you comfortable in quoting more than one fee method?

Will design contracts or letters of agreement be used (see Chapter 17 and 18)?

What needs to be in a contract for it to be legally binding?
Have possible clauses been discussed with an attorney?
Will clients be billed for services covered in a design contract?
Will reimbursable expenses be billed?
Will compensation requirements be considered using more than one method?

FIGURE 4-5. Key questions to ask about the organizational structure of a business start-up.

Initial, essential one-time expenses:

Office furniture (desks, files, shelves, etc.)
Office equipment (computer, printer, copy machine, and other electronic equipment)
Remodeling of office/studio space
Initial inventory (if any)
Utility and lease deposits (for commercial location)
Licenses and permits
Catalogs, samples, and so forth
Miscellaneous office equipment (coffee maker, radio, small refrigerator, etc.)

Ongoing expenses needed at start-up:

Stationery
Utilities
Phone and fax
Internet provider
Drawing supplies
General office supplies
Insurance premiums—related to the practice of interior design
Marketing materials, such as brochures, direct mail items, and so forth
Possible consultant fees, such as accountant, attorney, insurance agent
Cleaning and janitorial fees
Transportation

Additional items or expenses that may be needed to initiate a design practice, as required

FIGURE 4-6. Common start-up expenses for a typical interior design firm.

she is unfamiliar with the parts of an income statement before proceeding with this section of the business plan.

By estimating the total amount of start-up and ongoing business expenses for one year, the prospective business owner will have an estimate of the minimum amount of revenue needed for the year. However, remember that, if the amount of revenue collected in a year just matches the amount of expenses estimated for the year, the firm has only reached a break-even point* and has experienced no profits.

Writing the Business Plan

After the research has been done, the actual writing of the business plan can begin. In most cases, an overview of the company should come first, with the financial material, second. The books listed in the References section at the end of this chapter provide several outlines of business plans. The following outline is but one suggestion.

I. Business summary
   A. Provide name of owner or board of directors
   B. Give location of business
   C. Identify type of business formation (legal structure)
   D. Describe business, including types of services to be performed
   E. Provide a summary of the owner's and/or manager's expertise in running the business

II. Market research
   A. Describe how the information concerning the business was obtained
   B. Describe the need for the firm's services in the community; include the number of potential clients
   C. Describe as much as possible the known competition
   D. Detail existing sales for this kind of firm in the community; might be available from the local chamber of commerce
   E. Describe any industry or local trends that might affect the success of the projected business

III. Marketing plan
   A. Detail what portions of the market the business will address
   B. Describe what services the business will offer; may be detailed enough to explain how sample boards will be done
   C. Determine how services and/or products will be priced
   D. If a warehouse/delivery service is used, determine how these charges will be passed on to clients
   E. Outline what kinds of advertising and promotional activities will support the business
   F. Describe any problems concerning expected seasonal business, if applicable

IV. Operational plan
   A. Provide the organizational structure of the business
   B. Analyze hiring of personnel and job descriptions
   C. Describe how records will be kept and controlled
   D. Analyze employee benefits
   E. Project dealings with suppliers, delivery people, and subcontractors

* The break-even point is the point at which revenues equal expenses. At this point, the firm is neither making nor losing money.

F. Frame customer relations
G. Project personnel needs

V. Financial information
A. Project initial capital and first-year estimates for keeping the business operating; detail how the money will be spent
B. Estimate additional revenue (monthly) beyond break-even points
C. Provide month-by-month, projected profit-and-loss statements
D. Decide on accounting practices that will be used, especially those related to depreciation, leasing, and inventories
E. Provide a beginning balance sheet
F. Explain how projections were made
G. Provide any additional information required of a corporation

Remember that starting a business should involve serious thought and time, or failure may result. If the prospective owner is not willing to devote the time and effort needed to producing a well-written business plan, he or she may not be ready to expend the energy to keep it going either.

Control and Evaluation

Planning an inter design business is very important. But it is equally important to evaluate the progress of the practice. Many portions of the business plan will establish some of the control mechanisms that can be used to evaluate financial and organizational success. For example, financial projections that have been prepared for the business plan can easily be compared to actual performance. Project pricing that has been developed for the marketing section of the business plan can be compared to actual performance. Additional control reports might well be suggested by the firm's accountant, attorney, or the experience of the owner/manager. These reports should address issues of asset management, productivity, and profitability. Many of these control and evaluation reports are discussed in Chapter 16 on financial management control.

Summary

Knowing that you want to open an interior design practice and having the required skills and experience in interior design are not enough. It is important also to establish goals and policies of the proposed practice as well as to analyze the abilities of all the individuals who may be involved in the business. Through research and analysis, the best possible decisions about the configuration, direction, and future of the practice can be made. If the prospective owner or the current owner/manager is not willing to put forth the effort needed to develop a well-thought-out business plan, he or she may not be ready to own or operate a practice. The business plan could very well be the most important piece of "design" work that the owner/manager does in his or her career.

In this chapter, we have provided an overview of business ownership. We have defined an entrepreneur and have looked at some of the advantages and disadvantages of business ownership. This chapter also has summarized the decisions that must be made before starting a new design practice and has discussed the need for and definition of, the business plan. The chapter also describes the steps that need to be taken in developing the research material required to prepare a business plan and provides a general outline for the business plan. The prospective owner or current owner/manager who is interested in preparing a business plan for an interior design practice should refer to one of the suggested books in the References. Other sources may be found at the public library, bookstores, or from the Small Business Administration.

REFERENCES

Alderman, Robert L. 1997. *How to Prosper as an Interior Designer*. New York: John Wiley.

Banfe, Charles. 1991. *Entrepreneur*. New York: Van Nostrand Reinhold.

Bangs, David H., Jr. 1995. The *Business Planning Guide*, 7th ed. Chicago, IL: Upstart Publishing.

Busse, Erwin. 1989. *The Business Plan. First Step to Success.* LaConner, WA: Haldon Marketing Services.

Cooke, Robert A. 1999. Small *Business Formation Handbook*. New York: John Wiley.

Dible, Donald M. 1974. *Up Your Own Organization!* 2nd ed. Reston, VA: Reston Publishing.

Edwards, Paul, and Sarah Edwards. 1999. *Working from Home*, 5th ed. New York: Tarcher/Putnam.

———. 1996. *Secrets of Self-Employment*, rev. ed. New York: Tarcher/Putnam.

Halloran, James W. 1991. *Why Entrepreneurs Fail*. New York: Liberty Hall Press.

Hansen, Jeffrey A. 1998. *Surviving Success*. Grants Pass, OR: Oasis Press.

Heinecke, William E. (with Jonathan Marsh). 2000. *The Entrepreneur.* Singapore: John Wiley.

Hisrich, Robert D., and Michael P. Peters. 1992. *Entrepreneurship*, 2nd ed. Homewood, IL: Richard D. Irwin.

Holtz, Herman. 1994. *The Business Plan Guide for Independent Consultants.* New York: John Wiley.

James, Muriel, and John James. 1991. *Passion for Life*. New York: Dutton.

Jenkins, Michael D. 1999. *Starting and Operating a Business in the U.S.* Milpitas, CA: Oasis. (This books comes with a CD for state-by-state information.)

Jenkins, Michael D., and Max Perlman. 1986. *Starting and Operating a Business in Arizona.* Milpitas, CA: Oasis.

J. K. Lasser Institute. 1994. *How To Run a Small Business*, 7th ed. New York: McGraw-Hill.

Jones, Katie. 1998. *Time Management*. New York: American Management Association.

Kaderlan, Norman. 1991. *Designing Your Practice.* New York: McGraw-Hill.

Loebelson, Andrew. 1983. *How To Profit in Contract Design* . New York: Interior Design Books.

Malburg, Christopher R. 1994. *The All-In-One Business Planning Guide.* Holbrook, MA: Bob Adams.

Mancuso, Joseph R. 1996. *Mancuso's Small Business Resource Guide.* Naperville, IL: Sourcebooks.

———. 1993. *How To Prepare and Present a Business Plan.* New York: Fireside Books.

———. 1985. *How To Write a Winning Business Plan.* Englewood Cliffs, NJ: Prentice-Hall.

McCarroll, Thomas. "Entrepreneurs: Starting Over." *Time Magazine*, 6 January 1992.

McCaslin, Barbara S., and Patricia P. McNamara. 1980. *Be Your Own Boss.* Englewood Cliffs, NJ: Prentice-Hall.

McKenzie, Ronald A., and Bruce H. Schoumacher. 1992. *Successful Business Plans for Architects.* New York: McGraw-Hill.

Morgan, Jim. 1998. *Management for the Small Design Firm.* New York: Watson-Guptill.

Piotrowski, Christine. 1992. *Interior Design Management. A Handbook for Owners and Managers.* New York: John Wiley.

Rice, Craig S. 1990. *Strategic Planning for the Small Business.* Holbrook, MA: Bob Adams.

Rogak, Lisa. 1997. *Smart Guide to Starting a Small Business*. New York: John Wiley.

Rouse, William B. 1994. *Best Laid Plans*. Englewood Cliffs, NJ: Prentice-Hall.

Rubeling, Albert W., Jr. 1994. *How To Start and Operate Your Own Design Firm*. New York: McGraw-Hill.

Silvester, James L. 1988. *How To Start, Finance and Operate Your Own Business*. Secaucus, NJ: Lyle Stuart.

Siropolis, Nicholas C. 1994. *Small Business Management. A Guide to Entrepreneurship*, 5th ed. Boston, MA: Houghton Mifflin.

Small Business Administration. 1998. *State of Small Business: A Report of the President*.

———. 1991. *State of Small Business: A Report of the President*.

Smart Start Your Arizona Business. 1997. Grants Pass, OR: Oasis Press. (Note that similar books are available for other states.)

Stasiowski, Frank A. 1991. *Staying Small Successfully*. New York: John Wiley.

Chapter 5

Advice and Counsel

Would you design an elaborate custom cabinet with inlays and special stone tops without obtaining advice from an experienced cabinet maker? Or would you suggest taking out a wall in a home or commercial building before checking on the existence of bearing walls? Of course not. Nor should you decide to open the doors of a new interior design practice without talking to an accountant, a lawyer, and other business advisors.

All business owners need certain professional advisers and counselors. Since very few people have expertise in all areas of business, the prospective business owner should find the best advisers possible to help establish and maintain an interior design practice.

In this chapter, we will discuss the most important advisers one should consider engaging when starting or operating an interior design practice. Those advisers are an attorney, who renders assistance in many legal areas; an accountant, who provides information concerning financial matters; a banker, who may help obtain the financing needed to operate the interior design practice; insurance advisers to help obtain proper insurance protection; and technical consultants, who are the many allied professionals who help the interior designer with specialized design problems.

Attorney

An attorney is a valuable adviser to the owner of a new and continuing interior design practice. Although generally it is not required that a prospective entrepreneur use an attorney to plan a new business, it is a good idea for him or her to obtain professional advice before signing any papers. Attorneys can assist the new owner in understanding the numerous legal questions in starting a business. Existing businesses will have other incidents and dealings that require the attention of an attorney throughout the life of the business.

Firms that are organized as corporations are required by many states to use an attorney to prepare the articles of incorporation. Attorneys also help the existing business deal with the many questions of liability, employee issues, contracts, and many other issues surrounding the continuation of a business.

The firm's attorney can:

- Provide specific reasons for different business formations, based on the prospective owner's goals, and advise the owner who is considering a change in legal formation
- Prepare legal filings required, depending on the formation of the business
- Provide counsel concerning required licenses and permits
- Review design contract formats and clauses
- Review legal clauses in leases, rental agreements, purchase agreements, purchase orders, and other business forms
- Resolve employee rights, safety, and compensation questions
- Assist with questions concerning estate planning
- Assist with collection problems
- Advise on many questions related to the growth and/or change of the design firm

With the escalating number of liability suits that are being filed today, the attorney can provide counsel on how to avoid a potential lawsuit. The professional designer must be aware of what kinds of actions can get him or her into legal trouble. Awareness should help the designer avoid legal consequences. An attorney, of course, will be needed to represent the design firm if any lawsuits are brought by other parties. The small design firm should work with an attorney who is familiar with small business practices. When contract issues are involved, it may be advisable to engage an attorney who specializes in contract law.

Accountant

Another very important source of advice and counsel is the firm's accountant. Only the larger design firms hire an accountant as an employee. Most new firms and sole practitioner practices will probably retain an accountant on an as-needed basis. A large, existing firm may have one or more bookkeepers or accountants on their staff and may retain an outside accounting firm to do special reports.

The accountant's job is to help the business owner decide what kinds of operational reports are going to be needed, to provide guidance on how to prepare those reports, to assist the owner in interpreting these reports, and to prepare the needed financial accounting reports, such as the profit and loss statement,* balance sheet, and cash flow statement. An accountant also prepares quarterly income tax statements and any annual financial audits that are required for a corporation. The accountant or accounting firm also may be needed for other important financial reporting activities, discussed below.

It is important, even for the sole practitioner, to utilize the expertise of an accountant to prepare income tax statements. Tax laws change every year, and interpretation of those laws can become quite involved. A professional tax preparer, or certified public accountant (CPA), will have the training and experience to interpret tax laws in relationship to the owner's actual business operations.

Day-to-day operational accounting, commonly called bookkeeping, may be done by the owner in a small firm or by an experienced bookkeeper. Larger

* A *profit-and-loss statement* is a clearing account that summarizes the net income or loss for the accounting period. In most cases, the profit and loss statement looks very much like a formal income statement, and the terms might be used interchangeably.

firms utilize full-time bookkeepers or accounting firms. Daily bookkeeping reports are the means for the owner to keep track of income and expenses. From daily operational bookkeeping records, formal financial reports, such as the balance sheet, can be prepared. These records, along with any other reports suggested by advisers or required by the owner, provide the quantitative financial and managerial picture of the operation of the firm. More specific concepts in accounting will be discussed in Chapters 15 and 16.

Accountants can do many things for a design firm besides prepare income tax returns and formal accounting reports. Depending on the size of the firm and the owner's specific needs, an accountant can:

- Recommend bookkeeping and accounting systems
- Help the small-business owner organize office management procedures
- Help analyze financial statements to discover potential problem areas
- Provide counsel concerning financial requirements for normal business operations and future plans of the design practice
- Help the owner to collect records that may be needed to obtain loans
- Provide investment counseling
- Recommend operational changes that can help the firm reduce income taxes
- Depending on the license of the accountant, serve as a representative of the design practice to the Internal Revenue Service concerning tax questions
- Suggest changes in business operations and procedures as the design practice grows

Another area in which the accountant can be of help is in advising the firm on the sales tax liabilities that it will have. A sales tax is imposed by governmental jurisdictions at many levels whenever tangible property is exchanged between a seller and a consumer. Even though the consumer is liable to pay the tax, the seller must actually collect and return this money to the appropriate tax agency. Each taxing authority has different regulations on what items or services must be taxed. The accountant should advise the interior designer on this important issue.

Although all accountants can provide the many services that the design practice will need, few accountants are really familiar with the intricacies of an interior design practice. If possible, the owner should seek out an accountant who has worked with other interior design firms or related professionals. Regardless of the accountant's experience with other interior design firms, it is important that the accountant be someone who will talk plainly and will answer questions about the design firm's financial situation. Many small-business owners become intimidated by their accountant and never understand the actual financial condition of their company. Don't let this happen to you.

Banker

Any new business owner needs to have a banker on his or her "team" of advisers and counselors. First, a banking facility that will handle the firm's account needs to be located. The business will need a commercial checking account, a savings account, and perhaps a payroll account. A commercial account, especially for a sole proprietorship, shows the business community that the firm is a serious business.

A banker can also advise the owner about methods and procedures for obtaining start-up capital or infusions of capital that may be needed by an existing firm. Unfortunately, banks are reluctant to finance a new business, especially a service-oriented business, if the owner has little or no collateral. As discussed in Chapter 4, an entrepreneur requires funds to plan and begin operations of the design firm. However, a banker, along with the firm's accountant, can advise the entrepreneur on the pros and cons of various alternative funding sources, based on the entrepreneur's personal situation.

In addition, the banker can help the interior design practice in many ways. The firm's banker can:

- Offer credit card services
- Provide the designer with help in checking credit references of clients
- Advise and be a source of funds when the business needs to borrow money
- Provide information on investors who may wish to invest in, or loan money to, the firm
- Provide investment services

The prospective business owner should look for a bank that is interested in working with a small business. Any bank that is comfortable working with the small business owner will be able to grow as the business grows. The prospective business owner should be sure that the loan officer and others with whom he or she is working always will be willing to explain how things work, will answer all the owner's questions about how the loan process is structured, will understand what the charges are for commercial checking accounts, and are experts in other banking issues of concern to the owner. If this does not happen, the business owner should ask to work with another person or go to another bank.

Financing the Firm

No matter how much of the initial assets come from personal sources, eventually every business needs outside financing. A growing business may need funds for purchasing additional inventory, new office equipment, or even its own office space. Business loans are a major funding source for design practices. In addition, many firms, especially those that resell products, work to establish credit with suppliers. However, as mentioned, banks generally shy away from making loans to small businesses until the business has shown for several years that it is successful. Still, it is important to discuss the basic terminology associated with business financing. This section explains important financial terminology related to outside financing and briefly describes some of the major credit-granting organizations associated with interior design practices.

Operating funds often initially come from personal assets that have been contributed by the proprietor or partners. Stock sales provide initial operating funds for corporation formations. Operating funds also are obtained from banks and other private lending organizations, from loans guaranteed through the U.S. Small Business Administration (SBA),* and investors such as friends and relatives.

Funds that come from creditors as loans are called *debt capital*. Funds that come from investors are called *equity capital*. Creditors expect the debt capital to be repaid with interest. Investors are gambling that they will receive some kind of return on their investment and know, if the business fails, that they may not even get their investment back. For example, if June receives a

* The SBA does not give loans. It guarantees loans provided by an SBA agent-lending institution.

$25,000 loan from a bank or her father to begin operating her business, she has received debt capital. The bank or June's father has asked for an interest rate to be paid monthly on the unpaid balance as well as repayment of the $25,000, called the principle. However, if June's father has invested $25,000 in June's business as a limited partner (discussed in the next chapter) and will patiently wait for a return on his investment, then she has received equity capital from her father.

Anyone who has tried to buy a car, a house, or even to obtain a credit card has dealt with establishing credit. For most proprietorships and partnerships, business credit starts with a personal credit history of the individuals involved. If the business owners have good personal credit, the business will have an easier time obtaining credit. New corporations, since they are legal entities themselves, must establish credit, just like an individual.

It has become much easier during the last several years for the small-business owner to obtain business or "corporate" credit cards from a variety of lenders. Business owners may use these credit cards for travel expenses, items that alternatively might be paid for with petty cash,* or any number of other expense items for the business. However, these cards should be used cautiously, as monthly payments and interest charges could become a problem for the small-business owner with a cash flow problem. In a similar vein, many entrepreneurs have used personal credit cards as a source of start-up capital for a new business. This convenient source of capital, however, is very expensive, with its high interest rates, making it far too easy for the new owner to go deeply into debt quickly, which possibly could pose problems concerning future personal credit needs. This source of capital should be used very cautiously.

The business plan discussed in Chapter 4 is a key document that is needed by any business to obtain credit. Business plans require careful thought in its description of the proposed business venture and financing of the venture. Careful planning will provide answers to key questions that all creditors want to know:

- Who are the owners?
- How much money do the prospective business owners want?
- What do the prospective business owners want the money for?
- How will the prospective business owners pay the money back?
- What happens if the prospective business owners cannot pay the money back?

Private lenders, such as commercial banks and finance companies, offer long-term and short-term loans. Long-term loans are for more than one year and are usually granted to purchase capital items, like office equipment and delivery trucks, or an office location. The items being purchased with long-term loans are usually the security for the loans. Long-term loans for simple, daily operating expenses, like stationery, are generally not available.

Short-term loans last for one year or less. Also called *lines of credit*, short-term loans help cover purchasing inventory and credit purchases from suppliers. These loans are used to satisfy a temporary need for cash rather than long-term needs. In many cases, these loans are also called *unsecured loans*, meaning that collateral is not required. If collateral is required as protection against nonpayment, the loan is considered a *secured loan*. Unsecured loans

* In accounting, petty cash is currency used to purchase small or minor items, such as office supplies, with cash on hand.

are made on the basis of a business owner's ability to repay it. In addition, unsecured loans generally carry a higher interest rate than secured loans. As a business performs positively, the owner will be able to obtain larger lines of credit. New businesses and businesses with poor credit histories have to function on a cash basis for many purchases.

When a supplier allows a designer to purchase on credit, the designer is working with the supplier's money, or what is called *trade credit*. This is especially useful to the small-business owner who often does not have the cash on hand to pay for orders "up front." Suppliers may extend some customers 30, 60, or even 90 days of credit without charging interest. Of course, a supplier usually does not extend this courtesy to new buyers. When a designer begins to order from a supplier, it is necessary for the designer to pay the full price for the goods in advance of the shipment. This requirement is referred to as pro forma credit, which means the supplier must be paid in advance. This is why designers ask for a down payment or deposit from customers. The down payment or deposit becomes the prepayment required by suppliers from whom the designer cannot order on credit.

The designer establishes credit with a supplier by first filling out a credit application provided by the supplier. This information is verified, along with further checks on the designer's general credit-rating through credit reporting organizations. The supplier then determines the credit limit and conditions for the designer so that he or she can order without making down payments.

When the designer pays bills promptly, his or her credit rating goes up with those suppliers. With small suppliers and tradespeople, this information is sometimes shared, so, for example, a good credit history with a wallpaper hanger may help get custom cabinets built on credit.

Credit listing agencies serve as clearinghouses on the credit soundness of a business. Other businesses, such as manufacturers, look for these credit listings before extending credit to an interior design firm. The design firm should strive for a credit listing with one of these agencies.

A very important agency is Dun and Bradstreet (D & B). The D & B is a national credit agency that gathers information on thousands of businesses, big and small. It obtains information on a business's operations, legal structure, financial condition, and payment history. It also reviews and makes available to a business owner who requests it information on a creditor's banking records, financial records such as income statement, the D & B credit rating, and whether legal proceedings against the business have occurred or are in process. The design firm should seek to have a good credit rating with D & B and can use the D & B reporting service to obtain information on the credit rating of potential business clients.

The Allied Board of Trade (ABT) is a credit agency specific to the interior design industry. Designers register with ABT in order to show to trade sources that they and/or the design firm are a member of the design community. To obtain a listing with the ABT, designers must show proof of academic training, of professional standards of practical experience, and of business. This procedure is usually done by reporting a sales tax number and previous trade relations with suppliers. The *Credit Green Book* references thousands of registered designers and is used both by interior designers to find trade sources and by suppliers to clarify credit information on designers.

Financing a design firm's operations is an ongoing activity. Few firms use profits to continually finance the daily operations of the company. Investors expect a return, and some portion of the profits is paid to investors. No matter how small or large the design firm is, obtaining funds and maintaining credit with suppliers is very important.

Insurance Advisers

Owning a business comes with inherent risk. Not only is the owner liable for his or her actions, but also the owner is liable for the actions of his or her employees. In today's litigious society, few design firms can afford the risk of operating without appropriate business insurance. Business insurance minimizes the financial risk of the firm in the course of the business day. Of course, it is best to operate so as to avoid risk rather than depend on insurance policies and an attorney to limit liability. However, as we have witnessed, natural disasters, riots, employee psychological distress, accidents, and other unforeseen events create the need for insurance so that a business and its employees will be protected.

The interior design practice, whether it provides only specifications and drawings or also goods to clients through the resale process, will have some insurance requirements. The firm with part-time or full-time employees also is required by law to have certain kinds of insurance for employee protection. Design studios and retail stores that display goods for sale and have inventory have many more insurance needs than the designer/specifier.

A qualified insurance agent who handles commercial businesses is another adviser that a business owner will need. The exact combination of insurance that a firm requires depends on the design practice itself. An insurance agent can assist the business owner in determining precise insurance needs. Professional associations or sometimes an association chapter sponsors certain types of insurance for its members. Of course, insurance can be obtained through private insurance companies. The following briefly describes basic types of insurance coverage.

Professional Liability Insurance. Called malpractice insurance by many, professional liability insurance protects the design professional in the event an action causes such things as incorrect spatial layouts, financial loss to the client because the project was not finished on time, or errors that resulted in plans failing to comply with building codes. This insurance also covers the interior designer should bodily injury or property damage occur as a result of the professional negligence of the designer. Interior designers also can be held responsible for errors or omissions for work performed or advice given to a client. This type of insurance is called *errors and omissions coverage* (E & O).

Errors and omissions coverage is very important for the interior designer to have. Should the interior designer or his or her employees make a mistake, such as improperly specifying materials to meet codes (an error) or forgetting to charge for the installation of wall covering, even though the paper itself was billed (an omission), the designer technically has committed an act that could result in legal proceedings being filed by the client. This insurance provides coverage for claims should judgments against the designer occur. The reader is directed to Chapter 13 for additional discussion on professional liability.

Property Damage, Liability, and Personal Injury Insurance. Available to many businesses as a package, property damage, liablity, and personal injury insurance is especially important for those who own a studio, store, or warehouse. Designers who rent space can obtain variations on this package to take care of their needs. Property damage insurance protects the building and its contents from loss due to fire, theft, and wind. Any business that has lost all its computer records when a bolt of lightning struck the building understands the importance of property damage insurance. Note there that may be exclusions for events like floods or earthquakes. Supplemental coverage can be obtained for businesses that are in areas that are prone to these events. Liability insurance protects the business should it be sued by a third party for injury or property damage due to negligence, product failure, or other claims of that kind. Note that the business can be sued for the acts of the owners, employees, agents, and suppliers. For example, if a carpet installer who has been hired by the designer breaks a lamp at the client's home, the designer is potentially as liable as the installer. Personal injury insurance is part of liability coverage and provides insurance in case of slander, libel, defamation, false arrest, and other personal injury torts. These personal injury torts are discussed in Chapter 13.

Automobile Coverage. Cars or other vehicles owned by the company require automobile insurance just as one needs personal automobile insurance. Policies should also cover employee use of their personal car on company business or the owner of the company must be sure that the employee has proper automobile insurance when using his or her car for business purposes. Design firms that hire trades people should be sure that the trades person has auto insurance so that the designer is not sued if the tradesperson has an accident while on a job for the designer.

Specialty Insurance. There are numerous types of specialty insurance coverage that may be necessary for a design firm. The insurance professional, perhaps along with the design firm's accountant, will advise the designer on whether it is necessary to have any of these types of special insurance coverage. Business income insurance pays for the loss of net profit and for operating expenses in case a fire or other specifically covered event prevents the business from operating. Accounts receivable insurance covers the loss of accounts receivable records due to fire or other specific events. Crime insurance protects the firm in case of theft of money by employees or individuals other than employees. Flood and earthquake insurance provides repayment on property losses due to floods or earthquakes.

When employees are added to the firm, additional insurance coverage may be either required or desirable. The government requires that the employer provide workers' compensation insurance in order to protect the employee in case of work-related injuries. The employer may also wish to provide health and possibly life insurance to employees as a benefit of working for the company.

Owners of sole proprietorships are commonly advised to obtain disability income insurance. This type of insurance provides continuing income if certain covered injuries or illnesses occur that prevent the business owner from working. The insurance provides benefits to help pay personal and business expenses.

It is important to mention that, for designers who are working from their home, most straight home owner's policies do not cover them for the loss of equipment (such as computers), if that equipment is used primarily for business purposes. There may also be other exclusions related to liability and injury on the residential property to clients or others doing business with the home-based design practitioner. This exclusion also can apply to the designer's personal automobile, if it is used for business.

Technical Consultants

Almost every interior design firm will require the advice and counsel of allied professionals from time to time. Architects, electrical engineers, lighting designers, other mechanical systems consultants, and contractors are some of the allied technical counselors whom an owner of an interior design business will call on to assist with parts of a project.

Technical consultants may be hired to obtain advice or to explain how part of a project will be accomplished. For example, a codes consultant may be retained to discuss code requirements for a particularly large, complex project and also to review drawings to check for codes compliance. Depending on the technical consultant's specialty, the laws within the jurisdiction, and the requirements of the project, a technical consultant might be called upon to perform such duties as

- Meet with the client to determine needs related to his or her specialty
- Prepare drawings to be used to obtain needed permits
- In some situations, prepare drawings that can become part of the interior designer's set of construction documents
- Provide on-site supervision during the construction and/or installation of the particular phases of work
- Provide guidance to the interior designer on appropriate courses of action on smaller projects
- Work as a directly paid subconsultant or subcontractor to the client
- Provide other help as might be related to the consultant's particular specialty

Most jurisdictions no longer allow a professional such as an architect to affix the architect's stamp to drawings that have been prepared by an interior designer who is not an employee of the firm and who thus is outside the supervision of the technical consultant. The interior designer must understand the laws within his or her state concerning this issue and properly plan this extra service and fee into design fees for the project.

The owner of a small interior design firm will establish a working relationship with technical professionals and will hire them on a per-job basis, just as a client would hire an interior designer. Larger firms often have one or more of these allied professionals on staff. The owner of an interior design firm should not be afraid to admit the need for these professionals. Interior designers who prepare documents without the proper license and expertise can easily be sued by the client. A listing of a few of these specialists and how they can help the interior designer follows.

Architects: They are needed to prepare and review plans that require an architect's stamp, usually for residences over 3000 square feet and commercial spaces that will have more than 20 employees.*

Electrical engineers: They assist the designer with planning questions on electrical components for projects. Electrical engineers also may be needed to prepare and stamp electrical plans in order for the owner to obtain a building permit.

Contractors: General and specialty contractors can provide advice on ways to build or specify interior design concepts. For example, a cabinetmaker can advise the designer on how to detail drawings for a tradi-

* Both these criteria vary with the local ordinances. Check with the building department.

tional, custom conference wall that might include storage, plumbing, and audiovisual equipment. General contractors will oversee all tradespersons needed for a project's build-out.*

Lighting designers: They can provide assistance or can provide the design and planning of specialized lighting concepts.

Commercial kitchen designers: They can provide planning and plans for commercial kitchens in restaurants, hotel foodservice areas, healthcare foodservice areas, and so forth.

Acoustical engineers: They are needed because large, open office spaces and other large, open areas often have critical acoustical problems that need to be solved. Acoustical engineers can advise on materials and finishes for furniture and architectural surfaces, and locations of acoustical treatments to solve noise problems.

Computer-aided drafting (CAD): Smaller design firms may not have chosen to implement in-house CAD services. These services often can be obtained from specialty companies and freelance professionals to provide all types of construction drawings as well as projected drawings.

Landscape architects, interior plantscapers, florists: Interior plants are excellent for an interior environment, but incorrect specification and placement can be expensive. These specialists can advise the designer on the proper selection and positioning of plants in the interior. They can also provide the designer with maintenance instructions.

Healthcare facility specialists: Individuals who have worked in healthcare may be hired by designers to consult with them on the design of healthcare professional offices. Designers often hire nursing professionals as consultants.

Miscellaneous consultants: There are many other consultants that the business owner may wish to retain from time to time. The small-business owner may have a hard time managing all the issues of the firm without occasional special help. In addition to the advisers and consultants already listed, the owner of an interior design firm may wish to talk to public relations agencies, advertising and marketing agencies, employment agencies, management consultants, computer consultants, web page designers, and communications consultants.

Sources of Information and Assistance

The small-business owner particularly needs information and help during the organization and planning stages of a new business and later as the design business continues operating. Even a design firm that is considered large also frequently needs assistance. There are many private organizations and government agencies that provide consultation or reference materials to the business owner. Although it is not possible to list all these sources in this book, the addresses of many helpful organizations are provided in the Appendix. The reader can also find innumerable sources of help by investigating web sites on the Internet.

* The term *build-out* is industry jargon for the construction process.

Private Organizations

Professional organizations such as the American Bar Association can provide assistance to business owners who are seeking an attorney. Other professional organizations can help the business owner select a consultant as well. Check the yellow pages for the phone number or address of a professional organization's local chapter. To find the name and address of a specific trade association, check the *Encyclopedia of Associations*. This book is available at libraries.

Local chapters of the chamber of commerce are business lobbying groups for businesses. They provide information to consumers on businesses in the local area and work for the benefit of all businesses in the community. Although the chamber of commerce does not necessarily provide direct assistance to businesses, members can network, learn about various topics of interest at meetings, and obtain useful information about the business community, which may be of use in the business owner's marketing efforts.

Universities and community colleges often have a small-business development center or small-business institutes in conjunction with the SBA. These groups provide seminars and one-on-one counseling to the small-business owner.

Government Agencies

The Small Business Administration (SBA) is a federal agency that provides many kinds of assistance to the small-business owner. Assistance may come in the form of informational pamphlets and books, seminars, clinics, and one-on-one counseling. In addition, the SBA may be able to provide financial assistance for qualified small businesses through its program of guaranteeing loans provided by member banks. The main address for the SBA is in the Appendix. Local offices may be found in the U.S. government section of the white pages in the local phone book.

The Internal Revenue Service (IRS) has business tax kits for different business operations. Publication Number 334, "Tax Guide for Small Business," is especially useful to the owner of a sole proprietorship. Addresses for local IRS offices are in the U.S. government section of the white pages.

Designers who are considering starting a new interior design practice can obtain information on local regulations by contacting their state's department of commerce and department of revenue. Many cities have small-business development centers or economic development offices. These offices can provide pamphlets, seminars, and one-on-one consulting services. They can be located through the government section of the telephone white pages or the local government web page. Many local governments also provide a small-business resource center at the local public library.

Summary

It is easy to see that there are many very important advisers with whom the owner of an interior design firm should consult. No one designer, or even group of design professionals, will have the educational or job experience to have all the answers. Business advisers such as attorneys, accountants, bankers, and insurance advisers can help with specialized business questions that may arise for any interior design practice. Allied professionals can offer advice on technical matters that the staff of the design firm may not be familiar with or legally qualified to handle. These advisers can be engaged to help the firm remain professionally competent, to stay out of legal problems, and most important, to remain a viable business.

In this chapter, we also looked at a few issues concerning operating a business that must be considered during the creation of a new venture or the maintaining of a design firm. Ways in which businesses can obtain funding and establish credit, different kinds of business insurance, and sources of information were also discussed.

REFERENCES

Anthony, Robert N., and James S. Reece. 1983. *Accounting Text and Cases*, 7th ed. Homewood, IL: Richard D. Irwin.

Berger, C. Jaye. 1994. *Interior Design Law and Business Practices*. New York: John Wiley.

Berk, Joseph, and Susan Berk. 1991. *Managing Effectively. A Handbook for First-Time Managers*. New York: Sterling Publishing.

Blum, Laurie. 1996. *Free Money from the Federal Government for Small Businesses and Entrepreneurs*. New York: John Wiley.

Caplan, Suzanne. 2000. *Finance and Accounting*. Holbrook, MA: Adams Media.

Dawson, George M. 1991. *Borrowing for Your Business*. Dover, NH: Upstart Publishing.

Dible, Donald M. 1974. *Up Your Own Organization!* 2nd ed. Reston, VA: Reston Publishing.

Dun & Bradstreet. 1999. *D & B Business Rankings*. Bethlehem, PA: Dun & Bradstreet.

Edwards, Paul, and Sara Edwards. 2000. *Working from Home*, 5th ed. New York: Tarcher/Putnam.

Entrepreneur Media, Inc. 1999. *The Entrepreneur Magazine Small Business Advisor*, 2nd ed. New York: John Wiley.

Eyler, David R. 1994. *The Home Business Bible*. New York: John Wiley.

Haviland, David, ed. 1994. *The Architect's Handbook of Professional Practice, Student Edition*. Washington, DC: AIA Press.

Heinecke, William E. (with Jonathan Marsh). 2000. *The Entrepreneur*. Singapore: John Wiley.

Hinkelman, Edward G. 1997. *Canada Business*. San Rafael, CA: World Trade Press.

Hisrich, Robert D., and Michael P. Peters. 1992. *Entrepreneurship*, 2nd ed. Homewood, IL: Richard D. Irwin.

J. K. Lasser Institute. 1994. *How To Run a Small Business*. New York: McGraw-Hill.

Jenkins, Michael D. 1999. *Starting and Operating a Business in the United States*. Palo Alto, CA: Running 'R' Media. (Includes a CD-ROM, which covers information for all 50 states).

Kaderlan, Norman. 1991. *Designing Your Practice*. New York: McGraw-Hill.

Loebelson, Andrew. 1983. *How To Profit in Contract Design*. New York: Interior Design Books.

Mancuso, Joseph R. 1996. *Mancuso's Small Business Resource Guide*. Naperville, IL: Sourcebooks.

Rubeling, Albert W., Jr. 1994. *How To Start and Operate Your Own Design Firm*. New York: McGraw-Hill.

Siegel, Harry, and Alan M. Siegel. 1982. *A Guide to Business Principles and Practices for Interior Designers*, rev. ed. New York: Watson-Guptill.

Stasiowski, Frank A. 1991. *Staying Small Successfully*. New York: John Wiley.

Stitt, Fred A., ed. 1986. *Design Office Management Handbook*. Santa Monica, CA: Arts and Architecture.

Whitmyer, Claude, Salli Rasberry, and Michael Phillips. 1989. *Running a One-Person Business*. Berkeley, CA: Ten Speed Press.

Chapter 6

Business Formations

A very important decision for the entrepreneur to make is to determine which legal formation the new business should take. There are several kinds of business formations for an interior design practice. All have their advantages and disadvantages. It is important for the entrepreneur to understand the differences between these formations as they relate to financial liability, taxes, personal liability, and other issues so that he or she may choose the business formation that is most suitable to the business plan. Eventually, the business owner may need to consider changing the type of business formation in order to better suit an increasingly complex interior design business. An appreciation of the various forms by the student is necessary for understanding the responsibilities of the owner.

This brief discussion will not provide all the answers concerning the selection of a business formation. It does, however, emphasize how important it is for the interior designer to consult with an attorney and an accountant to be sure he or she is making the right choice. In some cases, it is absolutely necessary to consult with an attorney to help set up the necessary legal papers. Changes in the tax laws occur every year. The prospective business owner should discuss the merits of the different business formations with his or her accountant as well.

We will discuss sole proprietorship, general and limited partnerships, the corporation, the limited liability company, and some specialized formations. These specialized formations are the S corporation, the professional corporation, and the joint venture. Figure 6-1 provides a summary of the key characteristics of each business formation. Chapter 7 discusses many of the various legal filings of each form of business. The designer who is contemplating starting an interior design business is urged to read Chapters 6 and 7 together.

Sole Proprietorship

The *sole proprietorship* is the simplest and least expensive form of business ownership. In this form of business ownership, the company and the owner are one and the same. Business is most commonly conducted under the owner's name (e.g., Mary Jane Smith Interior Design) but may also be conducted under a company trade name (e.g., Creative Interior Designs). Since the owner and the company are the same, the company has no existence if the owner quits

	Owners	Personal Liability of Owners	Who May Legally Obligate Business	Continuity	Organizational Paperwork	Business Profits Taxed
Sole Proprietorship	Sole proprietor	Unlimited personal liability	Sole proprietor	Ends when proprietor wishes; might be able to sell it	Minimal	Individual rates of proprietor
General Partnership	General partners	Unlimited personal liability	General partner	Ends with death of a partner; may be transferred with consent of all partners	Minimal; partnership agreement recommended	Supplement to Form 1040
Limited Partnership	General and limited partners	General partner has unlimited liability; limited partner up to limit of investment	General partner only	Same as general partnership; limited partners can sell their share	Start-up filing required; partnership agreement recommended	Individual tax of general and limited partners
Corporation	Stockholders	Stockholders have no personal liability; officers and directors have liability	Board of directors and officers	Continues unless corporation ends by decisions of board or reason of law; stock transferred without needed consent	Articles of incorporation; bylaws; annual meeting of stockholders	Corporation pays taxes on profits; stockholders, on personal taxes
S Corporation	Same as corporation	Same as corporation	Same as corporation	Same as corporation	Same as corporation	Taxed as partnership
Limited Liability Company	Members	No personal liability of members	Members or manager/ member	May have to dissolve, depending on state	Start-up filing; operations agreement recommended	Individual tax rates unless elects corporation tax status
Professional Corporation	"Partners"	Similar to corporation	"Partners"	Same as corporation	Same as corporation	Same as corporation

FIGURE 6-1. Chart showing the key characteristics of business formations.

operating the business, unless the business is sold to another owner. This is done by selling the assets of the business to another person.

Advantages

- It is the simplest to start. In most states, all that is necessary to start a sole proprietorship is to establish a location, obtain any local business licenses required, and begin operation. The sole proprietor will want to open a bank account in the firm's name, prepare the appropriate business stationery, and begin to establish credit with trade sources.
- There is great freedom in management. Since there is only one owner, that individual makes all the decisions as to how to organize and operate the business, unless a manager is hired as an employee.
- All profits (and losses) go to the proprietor. There are no other owners or investors with whom profits must be shared.
- There are minimal special fees and minimal formal actions to create the proprietorship. Generally, fees for business licenses, resale licenses, and registering the business name are minimal. These fees may be under $500, depending on the city where the sole proprietorship is located

(note that these are annual fees). A resale license is required only if the company plans to sell merchandise to clients. If the owner uses a name for the business other than his or her own name, a Fictitious Business Name Statement is required (see Chapter 7 for information on both these filings).

- There are no required filings with the federal government to begin the business, unless employees are hired.
- Depending upon the location of the business, it is not required that the owner pay unemployment tax for any income.
- Profits are taxed as income on the sole proprietor's regular income tax statement. Similarly, the deductions of the business also can affect the individual income tax due.

Disadvantages

- There is personal liability for all debts and taxes. Creditors may seek payment from the owner's personal savings or property if business assets are insufficient.
- There is personal liability for legal claims from lawsuits. If a lawsuit results in damages that must be paid by the sole proprietor, the plaintiff can collect from the firm's assets and, if necessary, from the owner's personal assets.
- Illness or death of the owner could result in failure of the business.
- It is difficult for a sole proprietor to take vacations, because when they are not available to operate the business, income generation is stopped or slowed.
- The owner could experience tax problems, since business and personal income are easily mixed. (This should not be done!) Here is an example. Joanne's Interiors was audited by the IRS. Discovered in the audit was the fact that the records of Joanne Smith (the owner) insufficiently showed a separation of business income from personal income and expenditures. She was fined for insufficient payment of taxes.
- It is difficult to obtain loans to finance the business or to establish credit with manufacturers and suppliers. It is difficult for a sole proprietor to obtain loans from banks, unless he or she has an excellent personal credit rating or substantial personal assets. For many banks, having substantial personal assets or an excellent personal credit rating does not, in itself, mean that the business will be successful. Many suppliers will only sell initially to a sole proprietorship that has made substantial down payments or payments in full prior to shipping.
- The owner must pay self-employment taxes (social security and Medicare contributions). These taxes, which will be discussed in Chapter 7, are paid by employers. The self-employed individual must make these payments. The rate is double what the individual would pay if he or she were an employee.
- A sole proprietorship that also operates in other states may need to obtain licenses or prepare other types of registrations in order to do business in those other states.
- The sole proprietor cannot collect unemployment benefits if the business closes its doors. It requires multiple management skills. Not many designers gain experience in marketing, employee management, accounting, and other management skills while working for other design firms.
- It may be difficult to sell the business. Interior design businesses often flourish because of the personal reputation of the owner. Clients may not stick with the business if it is sold to someone else. This reduces the potential value of the firm when the original owner tries to sell the firm.

- In states with community property laws, if a couple divorces, the sole proprietor may be forced to sell or close the business in order to divide the proceeds of the business.

Partnership

A *partnership* is created when two or more individuals agree to start a business. Although no formal written agreement is required by law, it is widely recommended that a partnership agreement be prepared. If a partnership agreement has not been written, most states refer to the Uniform Partnership Act (UPA) for the terms of the partnership. Partners are co-owners, unless some other agreement about the level of ownership has been made. Partners also act in each other's behalf and, depending on the type of partnership formed, are each able to bind the company to agreements. There are two types of partnerships that can be created: the general partnership and the limited partnership.

General Partnership

When two or more people join for the purpose of forming a business and these people alone share in the profits and risks of the business, a *general partnership* is formed. The name of the firm may be a trade name, like Creative Interior Designs, ID Associates, or it may consist of the partners' names, such as Brown and Williams Associates, or any other legal business name. Two or more interior designers often start a business as a general partnership (1) because it brings more design talent (perhaps some skill or experience that one partner lacks) to the company, (2) because of the assets and credit rating of the partners, and (3) because the responsibilities of the company are shared. A formal partnership agreement is not required to form a general partnership, though it is recommended that one be prepared. Figure 6-2 lists the most common items that partners need to discuss as they develop a partnership agreement.

Advantages

- It is relatively easy to form. It is very similar to a sole proprietorship. State law may require registration of the partnership with the secretary of state.

The following are among the most common questions that must be answered when two or more people are developing a partnership agreement. An attorney may suggest additional items, depending on the nature of the business.

What will be the name and address of the business location?
Where will the partnership be located?
What is the purpose of the partnership?
What are the names and addresses of the partners?
What are the responsibilities of each partner?
How much capital will each partner contribute?
How will business profits be distributed?
How will business holdings be divided in the event of the dissolution of the partnership?
How will each partner's drawings (salary) be distributed?
How will the partnership be dissolved in the event of a partner's disabling illness, death, retirement, or other reason?
How can ownership be transferred to another partner?
Which partners have fiduciary responsibility?
How will disputes be resolved?

FIGURE 6-2. Common items outlined during the development of a partnership agreement.

- There is the benefit of having two or more people involved in the affairs of the business.
- It is easier (than a sole proprietorship) to raise capital and to establish credit, because more than one person is involved in the business.
- The tax responsibility on profits is low—similar to a sole proprietorship. Individual taxes on partnership profits are reported on Schedule E of Form 1040. Other filings are required, however, for the partnership itself (see Chapter 7).
- Partners do not have to pay unemployment taxes on partners' income.

Disadvantages

- Although the general partnership is inexpensive to set up initially, it is more expensive to do so than for a sole proprietorship.
- There is unlimited financial liability for any losses or debts that the partnership incurs. Liability goes beyond the initial investment of the partners. If assets of the partnership are insufficient to satisfy debts, personal assets (up to the limitations established in each state) of the partners are vulnerable.
- Disagreement between partners as to how to manage the partnership may create difficulties.
- Profits are split, as determined by the partnership agreement (or equally, if no written agreement has been prepared).
- Partnerships are required to file many more forms with the federal and state tax authorities than for a sole proprietorship (see Chapter 7).
- A partnership doing business in other states may need to obtain licenses or file other registrations in order to do business in those other states.
- If one partner is unscrupulous, the others can lose their share of the partnership assets and possibly their personal assets as well. The firm and each partner of the firm is responsible for the actions of all the other partners. This means that any wrongdoing by one partner or any promises made by one partner are also the responsibility and obligation of the other partners. For example, if John Jones, one of the partners of Jones, Smith, and Brown, contracts with Knoll International for $50,000 of Bertoia chairs, the assets of Jones, Smith, and Brown and the personal assets of Mr. Jones, Ms. Smith, and Mr. Brown might be needed to pay for the order if the company's assets are insufficient.
- Any change in the relationship of the partnership can dissolve the partnership. If any of the partners wishes to withdraw from the partnership, the original partnership is usually dissolved. Depending on many factors, the remaining partners may vote in new partners, and the business can continue with adjustments to the partnership agreement. Should one of the partners die or become physically incapacitated so as not to be able to perform agreed-upon duties, the partnership is likewise dissolved.

Limited Partnership

A *limited partnership* is a variation on the general partnership. It is formed according to statutory requirements, and a limited partnership agreement must be filed with the state in which it was formed. Because of this requirement, it is more expensive to start up than a general partnership. If the limited partnership operates in other states, it may be necessary for the partners to file an agreement in those other states.

A limited partnership is formed with at least one general partner, and other partners can be designated as limited partners. The general partners have responsibility for the management of the firm. They also assume the same kind of personal financial and liability responsibility that is true for members of a regular partnership. The role of the limited partners is limited to that of investor.

The limited partners contribute assets toward the operation of the partnership and receive a portion of the profits. They cannot make any management decisions regarding the operation of the firm. The limited partners have financial responsibility for only the losses and debts of the partnership to the amount of each limited partner's investment in the firm. The general partners in a limited partnership have the same legal responsibilities as members of a general partnership. Should any one of the limited partners become involved in the management of the design firm, he or she is no longer a limited partner but is, rather, a general partner. When this happens, the former limited partner now shares in the liability of the firm, as do the general partners. If any of the partners (limited or general) withdraw from the business, the business may need to cease operations.

A limited partnership used to be a good option for designers who were looking for people to invest in their company. However, now that the limited liability company (LLC) formation is available, the limited partnership is a less attractive alternative.

Corporation

A *corporation* is an association of individuals created by statutory requirements and, as such, is a legal entity. The corporation, (sometimes referred to as a C corporation), exists independently of its originators or any other member. It can sue and be sued by others, it can enter into contracts, and it can commit crimes and be punished. A corporation also has powers and duties distinct from any of its members and survives even after the death of any or all of its stockholders. Simply stated, a corporation is like a person, legally and financially separate and distinct from any of its originating or ownership members (called stockholders or shareholders), yet legally and financially responsible, like any individual person. A stockholder's liability extends only to the ownership and value of his or her stock. Individual stockholders of a corporation cannot be sued, cannot enter into contracts, and so on.

How a Corporation Is Formed

The rules governing the right to form corporations is held by the individual states. The states establish regulations concerning chartering a corporation and its general organizational and operational limitations. If a firm engages in interstate commerce, it also will be regulated by the federal government. The term *incorporate* means to create a corporation. The term *incorporation* is the act or process of forming a corporation.

Corporations that might be formed for the interior design profession are called *private*, or *general*, *corporations*. They are the most common type of corporate structure. This type of corporation is formed for private, profit-making interests. *Public corporations* are those formed by some government agency for the benefit of the public. The U.S. Postal Service is an example of a public corporation.

When all the shares of stock of a corporation are privately held by a few individuals, and the stock is not traded on any of the public markets, the corporation is called a *close corporation*. Other names for a close corporation are family corporation or closely held corporation. If a corporation sells its stock on one of the formal stock exchanges, such as the New York Stock Exchange, the American Stock Exchange, or NASDAQ, it is commonly called a public corporation, although, by the definition given, the term is technically misleading.

In this case, the sale of the stock would be regulated by the Securities Exchange Commission.

Firms generally incorporate in the state in which they do business, if they engage only in intrastate commerce. A corporation formed in one state and doing business only in that state is called a *domestic corporation*. A domestic corporation is also a corporation that has been organized within the United States. When a firm engages in interstate commerce, it may be advantageous or required for that firm to incorporate in some other state as well. In this case, the corporation must obtain permission from the second state to operate in the second state. The business also may be required to register with the state of origination the fact that it is operating in a different state. A corporation formed in one state but doing business in another state is referred to by the other state as a *foreign corporation*. A foreign corporation does not have an automatic right to operate in the second state.

A corporation may be formed by one or more persons, depending on the state of origination. The organizers of the corporation must prepare a document called the "Articles of Incorporation." This document is most often prepared by an attorney and is submitted to the proper authority in the state. Figure 6-3 shows the general outline of articles of incorporation.

When the articles of incorporation are completed, they are usually sent to the appropriate authority in the state, generally the secretary of state, along with a filing fee. After approval, a certificate of incorporation is returned, along with the articles, by the state's secretary of state.

The first organizational meeting, the date of which is stated in the articles of incorporation, is then held. During this meeting, the board of directors is elected, the bylaws are prepared, discussions or actions concerning the sale of stock take place, and so on. When this agenda has been completed, the corporation may formally begin operation.

It should be noted that, when the organizers of a corporation are a husband and wife and they own all the stock, many of the described activities and documents are not necessarily required. In this instance, the reader must check the state's requirements to know if formal articles are required and to be sure that the proper filings are submitted to the appropriate governmental agency.

It is possible for anyone to start his or her own interior design business as a corporation. The many advantages of the corporate form influence interior designers to begin their business in this manner. However, there are also some disadvantages for the small-business owner or the designer who will be working alone while the business is getting established.

1. The name of the corporation
2. The purpose and nature of the business in which the corporation will engage
3. The initial capital structure
4. The number and classes of shares of stock
5. Shareholders' rights
6. The place where the corporation will do business
7. The names of the initial board of directors
8. The names of the original incorporators and statutory agents
9. Other information as might be required by the state for that type of business

FIGURE 6-3. A basic outline of items that comprise the "Articles of Incorporation," which is required for a new corporation.

Advantages

- There is limited financial liability for the originators and stockholders. Financial liability of the originators (or principals) and stockholders is limited to the amount of money each invests in the corporation. The personal assets of the principals and stockholders cannot be touched to pay any operational costs or to satisfy legal judgments resulting from the operations of the business or initiated by any individual employee of the business.
- Corporations generally have an easier time of deducting business expenses for such things as equipment, automobile usage, entertainment, and so on, than do partnerships and sole proprietorships. This changes as tax laws change.
- Corporations have continuity, even if the originators and stockholders change or cease to be involved with the corporation. The originators may sell their interest in the corporation to other stockholders or to outside parties at any time, and the corporation goes on. Stockholders also may sell their stock back to the principals or to outsiders, and the firm goes on without any major changes. If the principals or any of the stockholders die or otherwise withdraw from the operation of the business, the corporation still remains intact.
- It is relatively easy to raise capital through the sale of stock. The primary way in which a corporation raises capital is to sell stock. When the corporation is formed, the initial board of directors determines how many shares of stock will be issued and how much of this first issue will be sold. Later, the corporation may sell additional stock to raise more capital.
- A corporation can obtain debt financing (loans) more readily than individuals. It also can raise capital by going to lending institutions and pledging future assets as collateral in order to secure loans. Although this method is open to partnerships and sole proprietorships as well, it is much easier for a corporation to obtain loans than it is for these other forms of business. However, a purely service-oriented design firm that carries no inventory and has little other collateral will still have difficulty in obtaining a loan from a bank.
- Shareholders elect the board of directors. This gives shareholders a say in the management of the corporation.
- The corporation is a legal entity. This fact legally separates the business from the owners and managers.
- The nature of the corporation, even if it is only by legal appearance, may make it easier to attract employees.

Disadvantages

- A corporation is the most complicated and expensive of the business formations. Initial costs of incorporation include lawyer's fees and filing fees for the articles of incorporation (although some states allow businesses to incorporate without hiring an attorney).
- A great deal of paperwork is necessary to continue the corporation. City, state, and federal regulations involve the filing of numerous reports. These include unemployment insurance, taxes, funds for the employer's share of social security, and payment of city and/or state sales taxes on merchandise sold to clients. Of course, many of these forms also must be filed for other business formations, especially if the business has employees.
- The officers and directors of the corporation are liable for any criminal actions that they or their representatives perpetrate in the name of the corporation.

- Stockholders have little to say about how the corporation is managed other than with regard to the election of the board of directors and officers. Their only opportunity to influence management or have a say in how the firm is being managed is at the annual stockholders' meeting.
- Annual stockholders' meetings must be held. Corporate officers are required to inform the stockholders of the financial condition of the corporation and to conduct other such business as might be dictated by the board of directors or stockholders. An annual financial report must be prepared by an accounting firm and must be provided to the stockholders.
- There is double taxation. The corporation must pay taxes on its profits. In addition, stockholders pay taxes on dividend income. Corporation officers also pay employment taxes, social security and Medicare contributions, and unemployment taxes. The corporation must pay these same taxes for all employees of the corporation.
- Business activities are limited to those described in the Articles of Incorporation.
- Corporations are more heavily regulated by state and federal agencies than the other business formations.
- A corporation must qualify and register to do business in other states.

Limited Liability Company

A relatively new type of legal business formation is the *limited liability company* (LLC). Essentially, an LLC is a hybrid of the general partnership and the corporation. The name of the company must contain the words *limited liability company*, or the initials LLC or LC. It is set up much like a partnership but has the limited liability protection that is given to corporations.

Investors are called members, not partners, and those who manage the business are called managers. In most situations, at least two members are needed to form a LLC, although many states allow single-owner LLCs.* This type of business formation is organized under state law, and the requirements differ between states. Since this form of business is relatively new, legal and operational issues are not always clear. Before forming an interior design business as an limited liability company, be sure you understand the laws that govern such a formation in your state.

Advantages

- It is simpler to operate than a corporation.
- It is managed similarly to a general partnership. However, it is possible to have nonmembers as managers.
- There are few limitations on the number and nature of members.
- The liability is limited to a member's investment, thus personal assets are protected. A member has no personal liability.
- Although a multimember LLC is taxed as a partnership or a corporation, as the owners elect, tax regulations for LLCs are not as clearly defined as for other business formations. This could be problematic for the design firm. The firm's accountant should be consulted before this formation is elected.

Disadvantages

- In most cases, articles of organization must be filed with the state. In addition, the state will likely require that an operating agreement be developed, much like a partnership agreement or Articles of Incorporation.

* The first state to pass legislation allowing for LLC's was Florida (Cooke, 1999, p. 212).

- Annual reports or fees and filings will be necessary, as with any corporation.
- In many states, professionals such as lawyers and accountants are prohibited from registering the business as an LLC. This might affect interior designers who work in states that have licensing for interior design.
- The loss of a member might result in the dissolution of the LLC.
- Liability issues are still unclear, since liability challenges have not been significantly tested, as have those in a corporation or other forms of business.
- If the company does business in other states, it should register with those other states. If the LLC was formed with only one owner, it may have limited ability to conduct business in other states.

Interior design firms are finding this to be an advantageous business formation to begin an interior design practice. However, the prospective business owner should discuss the pros and cons of this business formation carefully with an attorney and an accountant.

S Corporation

The *S corporation* (formally called a subchapter S corporation) enjoys all of the advantages of the corporation. It is formed in a very similar manner and is expected to meet all the same requirements for Articles of Incorporation, stockholders' meetings, election of a board of directors, and so on as the corporation. The difference between the two relates to taxes. If a business elects to be an S corporation for tax status from the Internal Revenue Service, it then pays taxes as a partnership. Many interior designers use the S corporation form when they begin their practice in order to have the liability protection of the corporation. Designers also may wish to elect S corporation status in the early years of the business, when it is most likely to experience business losses. These losses are absorbed by the shareholders rather than by the business. It is necessary to change to the corporate form when the firm no longer meets the eligibility requirements of an S corporation.

The owner of a design business who chooses to qualify it as an S corporation must apply to the Internal Revenue Service. The eligibility requirements include the following: (1) the firm must be a domestic corporation (incorporated within the United States), (2) the shareholders can only be individuals, not other corporations, (3) there cannot be more than 75 shareholders, (4) all shareholders must be American citizens, (5) the corporation has only one class of stock, and (6) the S corporation obtains no more than 25 percent of its revenues from investments. Any changes in these will result in the termination of S status for the corporation. Because of these requirements, it is common for smaller, family, or closely held corporations to elect to be treated as S corporations.

The S corporation does not pay taxes on its income, though the corporation must file special tax reports with the government (see Chapter 7). Corporate earnings and losses for this business formation are paid or deducted by the shareholders on their personal federal and state income tax forms, in proportion to the share of stock they hold in the corporation. These payments are called distributions.

Since the advantages and disadvantages are very similar to those of a corporation, they will not be repeated here. Business owners who are considering the S corporation election should carefully discuss this issue with their accountant.

Professional Corporation

A *professional corporation* (referred to as a professional association in some states) is a corporation formed by persons in professions such as law, medicine, dentistry, accounting, or architecture. In many states, only professional services that are licensed or have other legal authorization by the state may register as professional corporations. Thus, an interior design practice cannot use the professional corporation form unless the state within which the practice operates requires that interior designers be licensed and the formation is allowed for interior designers in that state. The letters *P.C.* (professional corporation), *P.A.* (professional association), or *S.C.* (service corporation), following the name of the firm, identify it as a professional corporation.

The rules governing the right to form this kind of corporation are held by the individual states. All states and the District of Columbia allow professions to utilize this formation within the guidelines of state statute; some have very limiting restrictions related to the professional corporation. One important consideration about forming a professional corporation is that all shareholders must be licensed to practice the service being provided. This kind of business is formed in the same manner as an ordinary corporation. Tax benefits are the same as for any other corporation. And, in most instances, the professional corporation must act like a normal corporation in order to receive tax benefits.

Liability of the members is a little different from the normal corporation. All shareholders are liable to clients, even if only one member is negligent. However, personal assets are protected from business debts. As in corporations, any shareholder of a professional corporation who is guilty of a negligent act is personally liable for the injury and damages.

Strict laws enacted in the latter part of the twentieth century limited the formation of professional service corporations in many states. These laws were passed because many felt that professional service businesses were taking too many tax advantages with this business formation. The newer rules do not allow many of the tax loopholes that formerly were permitted. The restrictive requirements for the professional corporation does not make this business formation especially attractive to many in the design field. And, generally, only those corporations operating in states where licensing is required even have the option of professional corporation status.

Joint Venture

A *joint venture* is a temporary contractual association of two or more persons or firms that agree to share in the responsibilities, losses, and profits of a particular project or business venture. The key to the joint venture is its temporary status. It is treated much like a partnership, but it is for a limited time period or for a certain activity. Not being a legal entity, it cannot be sued, but the individual members of the joint venture can be sued. Each firm independently and the joint venture as a whole is liable to the client. Depending on the state in which the joint venture is formed, the profits and losses of the venture are usually taxed as they would be for a partnership or are passed along to the participating members of the joint venture.

A joint venture is not the same as "partnering," a term that has received a lot of attention in recent years. Partnering brings together the stakeholders of a project in order to manage a project. *Stakeholders* comprise all the parties to a project who have a vested interest in the completion of the project, such as the client, interior designer, architect, and vendors. Partnering is not a business formation. It is a way of managing a project.

The firms agreeing to enter into a joint venture should prepare a formal agreement that clearly explains the responsibilities of each party, the conditions of the arrangement, the manner in which the profits and losses will be divided, the method for paying employees, and so on. In essence, a general partnership agreement should be prepared. Because a joint venture is like beginning a brand-new business, a joint venture company often selects a new name for the temporary partnership for the duration of the project. When this happens, neither firm loses its original identity, and both generally go on with other projects that are separate from the joint venture project. When the project has been completed, the temporary partnership ends, and each firm goes back to working on a completely individual basis.

This kind of business relationship most often is entered into by architectural offices for very large projects, but it is something that can also be used by interior design firms. Architectural and interior design firms enter into joint ventures for several reasons. The most common reason is that a project is so large that no single firm—large or small—would have the time and support team to do it alone. Devoting the entire work force to one project, especially commercial projects that often take a substantial amount of time, would leave any design firm without a steady source of income. Depending on the income from that one project might leave the design firm in difficult financial straits until the project has been completed.

A design firm that is seeking to obtain a design project in another state may want to create a joint venture firm with a design firm in that other state. This would provide a base of local knowledge for codes, design, and construction variances. An out-of-state firm could benefit from the reputation and licensing of a local firm, should the interior designer come from a state that does not license interior designers.

A joint venture also gives a firm an opportunity to gain experience in the kind of project for which it has little or no experience. For example, one firm may have the staff to prepare the construction documents and other documentation that is needed for a hospital project but may have no experience with the interview and design development stages of hospital design. A second firm may not have enough designers or technicians to handle the increased workload but may have the interview and design development experience to plan the hospital. If these two firms create a joint venture, both will gain from the project.

The joint venture also provides a very strong design team for the client. Using the expertise of two firms can mean better design and follow-through for the client than if there is only one firm, which may not have the support staff or expertise to complete the project in a timely fashion.

Combining the staffs of two or more firms increases the speed inherent in a large staff. If one firm were to obtain the contract, it might be necessary to hire additional designers, to work either on the new project or on other existing projects. The cost of doing this could be a problem in completing any of the projects the firm has under contract and could be too high for the design firm even to undertake. The temporary partnership would bring the staffs of both firms together and might negate any need to hire additional employees on a short-term basis.

Through the joint venture, both firms continue under their own individual identities and with projects other than the joint venture project. If the firms did not create a joint venture but wished to join together, one firm would have to merge with the other. This, of course, would mean that one firm would no longer exist.

Finally, a joint venture gives the two firms an opportunity to learn from each other in areas other than design. The relationship between the two firms might bring about exchanges of information on how to make presentations, ideas on general business practices, marketing strategies, and so on. Although competing firms do not willingly give away their design and business secrets, some ideas and concepts can be shared while respecting the integrity of both firms.

Summary

Determining which business formation to use is one of the many important decisions that an interior designer who is planning his or her own business must make. It is important to understand the many differences in the formations so as to appreciate the obligations of the owner(s). The decision impacts the amount of funds required to initiate the business, legal liability, and personal responsibility, should legal actions be brought against the company, to name just a few considerations.

As the business changes and grows, the owner of the design firm also may wish to consider changing the business formation. The primary reasons for changing it would be for financial or tax reasons, as well as for liability protection.

This chapter briefly outlined the advantages and disadvantages of the many legal forms of business that can be used by the interior designer when starting a new interior design practice. We have covered the advantages and disadvantages of the sole proprietorship, partnership, corporation, S corporation, limited liability company, professional corporation, and joint venture. In our next chapter, we will discuss the legal filings that are necessary for the major business formations.

REFERENCES

Anthony, Robert, and James S. Reece. 1983. *Accounting Text and Cases*, 7th ed. Homewood, IL: Richard D. Irwin.

Bangs, David H., Jr. 1995. *The Business Planning Guide*. Chicago, IL: Upstart Publishing.

Barnes, A. James. 1981. *A Guide to Business Law.* Homewood, IL: Learning Systems.

Berger, C. Jaye. 1994. *Interior Design Law and Business Practices*. New York: John Wiley.

Brown, Gordon W., and Paul A. Sukys. 1997. *Business Law*, 9th ed. New York: Glencoe/McGraw-Hill.

Clarkson, Kenneth W., Roger LeRoy Miller, and Gaylord A. Jentz. 1983. *West's Business Law, Text and Cases*, 2nd ed. St. Paul, MN: West Publishing.

Clarkson, Kenneth W., Roger LeRoy Miller, Gaylord A. Jentz, and Frank B. Cross. 1989. *West's Business Law*, 4th ed. St. Paul, MN: West Publishing.

Conry, Edward J. 1993. *The Legal Environment of Business*, 3rd ed. Boston, MA: Allyn and Bacon.

Cooke, Robert A. 1999. *Small Business Formation Handbook*. New York: John Wiley.

Cushman, Roger F., and James C. Dobbs, ed. 1991. *Design Professional's Handbook of Business and Law.* New York: John Wiley.

Epstein, Lee. 1977. *Legal Forms for the Designer.* New York: N & E Hellman.

Haviland, David, ed. 1994. *The Architect's Handbook of Professional Practice, Student Edition.* Washington, DC: AIA Press.

Hisrich, Robert D., and Michael P. Peters. 1992. *Entrepreneurship*, 2nd ed. Homewood, IL: Richard D. Irwin.

Internal Revenue Service. 1999. *Tax Guide for Small Business.* Washington DC: Department of the Treasury.

Jentz, Gaylord A., Kenneth W. Clarkson, and Roger LeRoy Miller. 1987. *West's Business Law—Alternate UCC Comprehensive Edition*, 3rd ed. St. Paul, MN: West Publishing.

Kaderlan, Norman. 1991. *Designing Your Practice*. New York: McGraw-Hill.

Loebelson, Andrew. 1983. *How To Profit in Contract Design.* New York: Interior Design Books.

Mancuso, Anthony. 2000. *Nolo's Quick LLC*. Berkeley, CA: Nolo Press.

McKenzie, Ronald A., and Bruce H. Schoumacher. 1992. *Successful Business Plans for Architects.* New York: McGraw-Hill.

Oasis Press. 1997. *Smart Start Your Arizona Business*. Grants Pass, OR: Oasis Press. (Books of similar material are available for most other states.)

Piotrowski, Christine M. 1992. *Interior Design Management.* New York: Van Nostrand Reinhold.

Rubeling, Albert W., Jr. 1994. *How To Start and Operate Your Own Design Firm.* New York: McGraw-Hill.

Siegel, Harry, and Alan M. Siegel. 1982. *A Guide to Business Principles and Practices for Interior Designers*, rev. ed. New York: Watson-Guptill.

Siropolis, Nicholas C. 1990. *Small Business Management. A Guide to Entrepreneurship*, 4th ed. Boston, MA: Houghton Mifflin.

Sweet, Justin. 1985. *Legal Aspects of Architecture, Engineering, and the Construction Process*, 3rd ed. St. Paul, MN: West Publishing.

Veitch, Ronald M., Dianne R. Jackman, and Mary K. Dixon. 1990. *Professional Practice. A Handbook for Interior Designers.* Winnipeg, Canada: Peguis Publishers.

Chapter 7

Legal Filings

Depending on the exact nature of the interior design practice, some legal forms are required in order to begin most types of businesses. This chapter discusses some of the various legal papers or applications—other than partnership agreements, articles of incorporation, and articles of organization—that must be processed in order to start an interior design business. Some of the filings are only necessary once employees are hired. A few specialized filings that do not necessarily relate to starting a practice but that may be required or needed are also covered in this chapter. Such filings include interior design title registration and copyright protection.

A caution about legal filings. Changes are made annually to many of the requirements for business filings, especially those applied to tax laws. The documents discussed in this chapter are broad guidelines of what is required of each form of business. The business owner or prospective business owner must consult with his or her accountant and attorney to be sure the correct forms are filed each year. This chapter briefly describes the forms that are most common to any of the business formations that can be used by the interior designer.

Federal Forms

The forms required by the federal government vary based on the type of business formation and whether the business has employees. The most common federal form required of a business is the Application for Employer Identification Number (EIN). Additional forms are required of all businesses that have employees. Different income tax reporting forms are required, depending on the form of business. Since the tax laws change so frequently, this chapter does not discuss the specific income tax forms that are required by the different business formations.

Form SS-4, *Application for Employer Identification Number (EIN)*, which is issued by the Internal Revenue Service (IRS), identifies to the federal government that the interior design firm is a business. This form is required of all businesses that have employees. A sole proprietorship formation with no employees would not be required to apply for an EIN. In that case, the proprietor can use his or her own social security number. However, obtaining an EIN is recommended for the sole proprietorship form so that a change would not need to be reported should employees be hired. In addition, many banks will not provide a commercial checking account to a sole proprietor if the proprietor does not have an EIN.

Remember, when the interior design practice has been formed as a corporation, anyone working for the corporation is an employee. This means that, even if only one individual actually *generated income* for the corporation and was a member of the board of directors/stockholders of the corporation, that individual would be considered an employee.

Another form commonly used for almost all business sizes and formal formations is *Form 1099*. This income tax reporting form is commonly referred to as an information form. There are many different types of 1099 that are used to report specific information. In certain circumstances, the employer will have to file one or more copies of Form 1099. These forms report taxable income that does not fall under the normal wages category. Some special types of income include dividends on stock and nonemployee compensation, such as compensation paid to contract labor.* Other 1099s may have to be filed, depending on the exact nature of the business and the benefits program offered by the firm.

When the firm has employees, additional federal forms must be completed. The two with which the reader is most familiar are Forms W-4 and W-2. *Form W-4, the Employee's Withholding Allowance Certificate*, is filled out by each employee upon being hired. The employer is required to keep this form on file and must send a copy of the W-4 to the IRS if the employee claims ten or more exemptions or claims an exemption from withholding. This form indicates the number of deductions to which the employee is entitled, which determines how much income tax is withheld from wages. Employers and employees should consult with an accountant to be sure they are fulfilling their legal responsibilities related to Form W-4.

Form W-2, the Employer's Wage and Tax Statement, is prepared by the employer and is sent to the employee no later than January 31 of the calendar year. Form W-2 shows all wages paid; federal, state, and city taxes withheld; and social security taxes (shown as FICA)† withheld for the employee. Other information also may be reported on this form, depending on the firm's structure of benefits and wages.

Few design businesses with employees will be exempted from paying federal and state unemployment taxes and worker's compensation insurance. Generally speaking, *unemployment taxes* provide funds to eligible employees in the event that they are laid off from their job. *Worker's compensation insurance* is an insurance program that provides funds to the employee to cover the expenses of work-related injuries. Federal financial requirements for unemployment tax responsibility are set at a low threshold, and almost all businesses with employees, even if there is only one employee, pay unemployment tax. Sole proprietorships and partnerships do not have to pay unemployment taxes on the compensation to the owners. State laws generally require that most businesses, regardless of their size, provide worker's compensation insurance. Some states require that sole proprietors and partners also be covered by worker's compensation insurance.

Businesses are required to file other forms either annually or quarterly. A business owner is advised to check with the firm's accountant to clarify which forms must be filed and when for individual needs.

* Individuals working for the design firm who are not true employees. Independent contractor status is discussed fully in Chapter 12.

† FICA stands for Federal Insurance Contribution Act. Social security is the more common name for FICA.

SCHEDULE SE (Form 1040) (O) Department of the Treasury Internal Revenue Service	**Self-Employment Tax** ▶ See Instructions for Schedule SE (Form 1040). ▶ Attach to Form 1040.	OMB No. 1545-0074 **2000** Attachment Sequence No. **17**
Name of person with **self-employment** income (as shown on Form 1040)	Social security number of person with **self-employment** income ▶	

Who Must File Schedule SE

You must file Schedule SE if:

- You had net earnings from self-employment from **other than** church employee income (line 4 of Short Schedule SE or line 4c of Long Schedule SE) of $400 or more **or**
- You had church employee income of $108.28 or more. Income from services you performed as a minister or a member of a religious order **is not** church employee income. See page SE-1.

Note. Even if you had a loss or a small amount of income from self-employment, it may be to your benefit to file Schedule SE and use either "optional method" in Part II of Long Schedule SE. See page SE-3.

Exception. If your only self-employment income was from earnings as a minister, member of a religious order, or Christian Science practitioner **and** you filed Form 4361 and received IRS approval not to be taxed on those earnings, **do not** file Schedule SE. Instead, write "Exempt–Form 4361" on Form 1040, line 52.

May I Use Short Schedule SE or Must I Use Long Schedule SE?

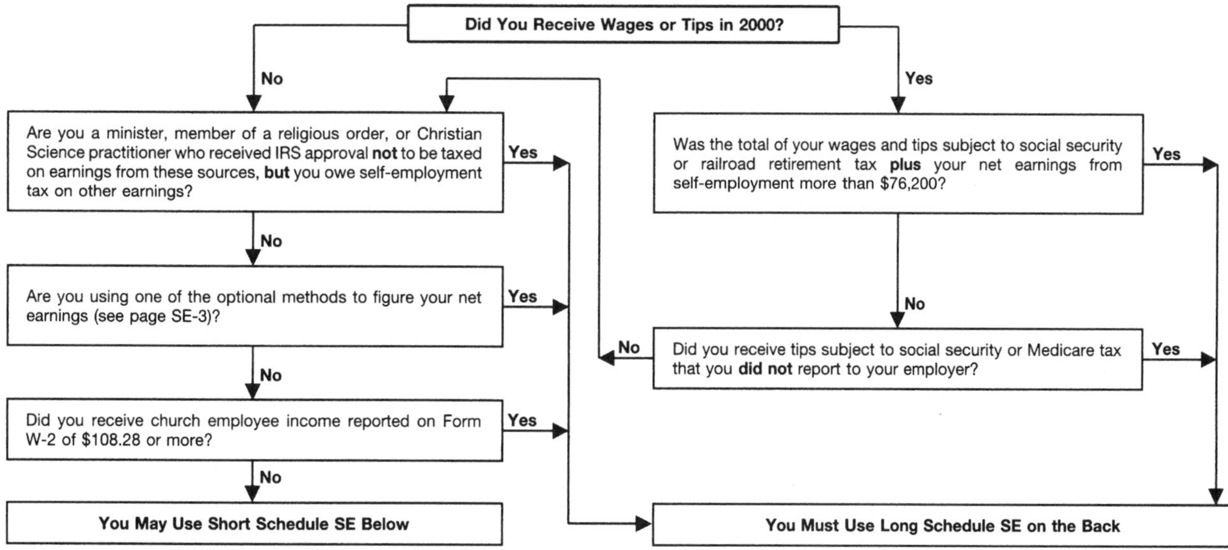

Section A—Short Schedule SE. Caution: *Read above to see if you can use Short Schedule SE.*

1	Net farm profit or (loss) from Schedule F, line 36, and farm partnerships, Schedule K-1 (Form 1065), line 15a	1	
2	Net profit or (loss) from Schedule C, line 31; Schedule C-EZ, line 3; Schedule K-1 (Form 1065), line 15a (other than farming); and Schedule K-1 (Form 1065-B), box 9. Ministers and members of religious orders, see page SE-1 for amounts to report on this line. See page SE-2 for other income to report	2	
3	Combine lines 1 and 2	3	
4	**Net earnings from self-employment.** Multiply line 3 by 92.35% (.9235). If less than $400, **do not** file this schedule; you do not owe self-employment tax ▶	4	
5	**Self-employment tax.** If the amount on line 4 is: • $76,200 or less, multiply line 4 by 15.3% (.153). Enter the result here and on **Form 1040, line 52.** • More than $76,200, multiply line 4 by 2.9% (.029). Then, add $9,448.80 to the result. Enter the total here and on **Form 1040, line 52.**	5	
6	**Deduction for one-half of self-employment tax.** Multiply line 5 by 50% (.5). Enter the result here and on **Form 1040, line 27** 6		

For Paperwork Reduction Act Notice, see Form 1040 instructions. Cat. No. 11358Z **Schedule SE (Form 1040) 2000**

FIGURE 7-1a. IRS Form Schedule SE (Form 1040), used to calculate the self-employment tax.

Name of person with **self-employment** income (as shown on Form 1040)	Social security number of person with **self-employment** income ▶	

Section B—Long Schedule SE

Part I Self-Employment Tax

Note. If your only income subject to self-employment tax is **church employee income,** skip lines 1 through 4b. Enter -0- on line 4c and go to line 5a. Income from services you performed as a minister or a member of a religious order **is not** church employee income. See page SE-1.

A If you are a minister, member of a religious order, or Christian Science practitioner **and** you filed Form 4361, but you had $400 or more of **other** net earnings from self-employment, check here and continue with Part I . . . . . . ▶ ☐

1	Net farm profit or (loss) from Schedule F, line 36, and farm partnerships, Schedule K-1 (Form 1065), line 15a. **Note.** Skip this line if you use the farm optional method. See page SE-3			1		
2	Net profit or (loss) from Schedule C, line 31; Schedule C-EZ, line 3; Schedule K-1 (Form 1065), line 15a (other than farming); and Schedule K-1 (Form 1065-B), box 9. Ministers and members of religious orders, see page SE-1 for amounts to report on this line. See page SE-2 for other income to report. **Note.** Skip this line if you use the nonfarm optional method. See page SE-3.			2		
3	Combine lines 1 and 2			3		
4a	If line 3 is more than zero, multiply line 3 by 92.35% (.9235). Otherwise, enter amount from line 3			4a		
b	If you elect one or both of the optional methods, enter the total of lines 15 and 17 here			4b		
c	Combine lines 4a and 4b. If less than $400, **do not** file this schedule; you do not owe self-employment tax. **Exception.** If less than $400 and you had **church employee income,** enter -0- and continue ▶			4c		
5a	Enter your **church employee income** from Form W-2. **Caution:** *See page SE-1 for definition of church employee income*	5a				
b	Multiply line 5a by 92.35% (.9235). If less than $100, enter -0-			5b		
6	**Net earnings from self-employment.** Add lines 4c and 5b			6		
7	Maximum amount of combined wages and self-employment earnings subject to social security tax or the 6.2% portion of the 7.65% railroad retirement (tier 1) tax for 2000			7	76,200	00
8a	Total social security wages and tips (total of boxes 3 and 7 on Form(s) W-2) and railroad retirement (tier 1) compensation	8a				
b	Unreported tips subject to social security tax (from Form 4137, line 9)	8b				
c	Add lines 8a and 8b			8c		
9	Subtract line 8c from line 7. If zero or less, enter -0- here and on line 10 and go to line 11 ▶			9		
10	Multiply the **smaller** of line 6 or line 9 by 12.4% (.124)			10		
11	Multiply line 6 by 2.9% (.029)			11		
12	**Self-employment tax.** Add lines 10 and 11. Enter here and on **Form 1040, line 52**			12		
13	**Deduction for one-half of self-employment tax.** Multiply line 12 by 50% (.5). Enter the result here and on **Form 1040, line 27**	13				

Part II Optional Methods To Figure Net Earnings (See page SE-3.)

Farm Optional Method. You may use this method **only** if:

- Your gross farm income[1] was not more than $2,400 **or**
- Your net farm profits[2] were less than $1,733.

14	Maximum income for optional methods	14	1,600	00
15	Enter the **smaller** of: two-thirds (⅔) of gross farm income[1] (not less than zero) **or** $1,600. Also include this amount on line 4b above	15		

Nonfarm Optional Method. You may use this method **only** if:

- Your net nonfarm profits[3] were less than $1,733 and also less than 72.189% of your gross nonfarm income[4] **and**
- You had net earnings from self-employment of at least $400 in 2 of the prior 3 years.

Caution: *You may use this method no more than five times.*

16	Subtract line 15 from line 14	16		
17	Enter the **smaller** of: two-thirds (⅔) of gross nonfarm income[4] (not less than zero) **or** the amount on line 16. Also include this amount on line 4b above	17		

[1]From Sch. F, line 11, and Sch. K-1 (Form 1065), line 15b.
[2]From Sch. F, line 36, and Sch. K-1 (Form 1065), line 15a.
[3]From Sch. C, line 31; Sch. C-EZ, line 3; Sch. K-1 (Form 1065), line 15a; and Sch. K-1 (Form 1065-B), box 9.
[4]From Sch. C, line 7; Sch. C-EZ, line 1; Sch. K-1 (Form 1065), line 15c; and Sch. K-1 (Form 1065-B), box 9.

FIGURE 7-1b.

Self-employment tax is required of designers who own a sole proprietorship or partnership. The self-employment tax is paid on the income that a sole proprietor and any partners receive on their share of the owner's income of the business. It is the equivalent of the social security and Medicare tax paid by employees and employers on an employee's income (see Figure 7-1). Since the income for those who have ownership in certain business formations is considered self-employment income and is not subject to normal withholding taxes, the self-employed individual must report and pay this tax at the time at which normal income taxes are due. The government acts as an agent to collect this tax for the Social Security Administration.

Estimated Taxes for the Self-Employed

Federal and state income tax is a "pay-as-you-go" tax. An employee who is working for a small business has a portion of his or her wages withheld from each paycheck to help offset the eventual total amounts of income tax due to the IRS or to his or her state's revenue department. Self-employed individuals do not have this done and must pay estimated taxes.

Self-employed individuals pay quarterly estimated taxes in lieu of withholding taxes. The amount due each quarter is based on the level of taxes that were paid the previous year. Of course, other types of business formations may also have to pay taxes on a quarterly basis. Penalties are imposed for underpayment of estimated taxes. Sole proprietors and other business owners should discuss the method of calculating and payment of estimated taxes with the firm's accountant.

State Forms

It is not possible in the space allotted in this book to discuss fully all the specific legal filings that are required by the various states. The following is a rather general discussion of the legal filings that would be common to all the states. Generally, a firm that is located in one state and that is doing business in another state must also file specific forms or obtain licenses to operate in that other state. This is especially true of corporations. The owner of an interior design practice must check with the proper counsel to be sure he or she is fulfilling the requirements of each state in which the firm will be located.

Many states require that the business obtain a *state employer identification number* in addition to the federal employer identification number. This number, issued by the state revenue service, identifies the business and helps to determine what rate of tax the business must pay. In the states where an employer identification number is required, usually it is required whether or not the business has employees.

The following is a brief discussion of the most common state permits and filings that are required of interior design practices. Some states may not require all those listed, and other filings may be required by a specific state. Advice as to proper filings can be obtained from the firm's accountant and attorney.

State Transaction Privilege (Sales) Tax License

Most states require that all businesses obtain the *Transaction Privilege (Sales) Tax License*, whether or not the business will be selling goods. This license is commonly referred to as a resale license. It is imperative for businesses that intend to resell goods to the end user. The sales tax license allows the interior designer to pass on the state sales tax to the client. It must be remembered that if the business fails to collect and pay this tax to the state and/or the city, the taxing authority will hold the business responsible for the tax monies. The amount collected must be reported and paid on a monthly basis, whether or not sales for the period have occurred. These monthly reports must be filed as long as the business remains in existence. Sales taxes are discussed further in Chapter 19. In some states, the state department of revenue collects sales taxes that are required by individual cities. However, since not all cities in any one state may be a part of a program such as this, the business owner must determine to which jurisdiction(s) he or she should send sales taxes.

Use Tax Registration Certificate

Use Tax is a companion to the sales tax. If the business will be purchasing goods from out of state for use or sale and these goods are taxable in the state in which the interior design firm is doing business, the business is required to obtain a Use Tax Certificate and to pay sales tax on those items. This insures that sales taxes or use taxes are collected either by the state that is selling the goods to the interior design firm or by the firm to the state if the goods are sold to end users.

Corporation Identification Numbers

Since the privilege of operating a corporation rests with the states, the states require that all businesses formed as corporations be registered with the state before operations begin. In most cases, corporation identification numbers are obtained from the state department of revenue. In many states, the corporation may also be regulated by either the state attorney general's office or some other state office.

Employee Withholding Reporting

For businesses with employees, the firm must file income tax withholding, unemployment, and workers' compensation reports with the state revenue department. In most states, this will require obtaining a withholding number and an unemployment number from the state. The manner in which these are collected, their amounts, and the reporting methods vary from state to state. The interior design firm must check with the proper agency to be sure it meets the legal obligations of the particular state.

Personal Property

Many states tax the personal property of the business. In most cases, the personal property taxes cover furniture and equipment that are used in the business. Sellable inventory is not taxed. Of course, if a business owns any real estate, that may also be subject to taxation by the state. In most cases, these filings are sent to the county attorney or county assessor of the county in which the business is located rather than to the state revenue department. Then the county tax assessor automatically bills the owner of record annually for personal property taxes that are due.

Income Taxes

All forms of business have to report income and losses of the business on a yearly basis in some way or another. Since most states model their income tax reporting on the federal laws, the reporting methods are similar. Forms and actual reporting methods are, of course, different for each state.

There are some additional similarities between federal and state income tax filing requirements. Most business formations have to pay estimated taxes based on profitability. The tax period for the state is the same as for federal taxes.

There are no special filings for sole proprietorships other than the fictitious business name statement. Partnerships must also file a fictitious business name statement (discussed below) if the name of the business does not reflect the ownership of the firm. Limited partnerships and corporations must file specialized forms (as discussed in the previous chapter) to start the business. Corporations must file their articles of incorporation with the state's secretary of state and may have to file these additionally in other states in which the business operates. Limited liability companies must file articles of organization with the state. As with federal regulations, businesses with employees are required to file and pay many similar employee taxes to state revenue agencies.

Fictitious Business Name Statement

If the business is operating under a name other than that of the owner(s), the state requires that the business file a fictitious business name statement. Many business people refer to this as a DBA statement. The acronym means, "doing business as." This filing is required of all forms of business, except corporations, and is usually filed with the county clerk. Its purpose is to identify to the state and to the general public the owner(s) responsible for any business formed within the state. In some states, it may also be necessary for the new business to publish a statement of ownership. It is relatively common for corporations to print a copy of the corporation papers in the business section of the local newspaper. When the business uses a fictitious name for its business, the owner must be sure that no other business in the state is already using that name.

Local Forms

Each city and county may also have particular licenses, property taxes, or tax requirements that the business must obtain and file. The interior design business owner should check with local city and county authorities to be sure that these requirements are satisfied.

City Transaction Privilege (Sales) Tax License

Many cities also require transaction privilege (sales) tax licenses. In some states, the owner can obtain this form at the same time that he or she applies for the state license; the taxes are then collected by the state and are forwarded to the appropriate cities. If this joint license is not available from the state, the city license can be obtained from the offices of the city in which the business is located. The city license serves the same function as the state license.

Zoning Restrictions

Cities have certain zoning restrictions as to where businesses may operate. Many interior design businesses begin their operations out of a private home. If the interior design firm is selling merchandise to clients, the business may very well be operating illegally, especially if delivery trucks arrive and depart from the home or the business has more than one employee in addition to the owner. Should neighbors complain to the city that the designer is operating a business in a residentially zoned area, the designer may be liable to pay a fine.

It is best that the owner check with the local zoning office before applying for a city business license. If the business does not have employees, does not have delivery trucks arriving at the residence, keeps visits of clients to a minimum, or conducts direct sales, it may be legal for the interior designer to operate a business out of his or her home, even if the area is residentially zoned. In some cases, it may be necessary to apply for a zoning variance. The *zoning variance* allows the business to operate legally in the residentially zoned area. A request for a zoning variance usually requires notification of neighbors and a hearing before the zoning commission.

In addition to zoning regulations, businesses operating out of a residence may be restricted by the home owner's association's restrictions and covenants. Refer to Chapter 4 for more information on this restriction.

Specialized Filings

There are many kinds of specialized filings that may apply to an interior design practice. Exactly what is required will vary from state to state. The business owner must check with the firm's accountant and attorney to ensure that the proper licenses and filings are taken care of, as required by the jurisdiction in which the business is located.

Interior Design Title Registration or Licensure

Interior designers who are working in states where title registration or licensing requirements have been passed must meet certain regulations so as to maintain their practice under the title of *interior designer* or some similar title. In some states, the interior designer is required to take an examination such as the NCIDQ examination in order to obtain the license to practice interior design. A few jurisdictions require supplemental tests, especially related to codes. Several states require that the license holder take a certain amount of approved continuing education classes each year.

Title registration and licensing regulations vary among each of the regulated states. Students and professionals must keep abreast of any new laws being formulated in their state and must be prepared to meet the specific requirements of the statutes. In general, the state board of technical registration (or other like agencies) set the standards for licensing and title registration in conjunction with approval by state legislatures. The state boards are also responsible for enforcement and termination of license privilege. Refer to Chapter 1 for a detailed discussion of interior design title registration or licensure.

Contractor's Licenses

The requirements related to the use of licensed contractors for construction work and installation of architectural interior finishes or attachments vary from state to state. Most states require that work done for private residences and commercial facilities be performed only by licensed contractors. If the designer hires unlicensed contractors to perform work that a licensed contractor must perform, the client may not have any legal obligation to pay the designer. It may also be a criminal offense for the interior designer to use the unlicensed contractor.

In many states, the supervision of construction work and the installation of architectural finishes that an interior designer might specify for a client need to be done by a licensed contractor as well. Such items as structural work, carpet laying, wall-covering installation, and other items that are attachments to the building often must be done only by a licensed contractor. Although it is rare for interior designers to be required to obtain a general contractor's license or one of the several specialized contractor's licenses for supervision of this work, some firms obtain these documents as a means to expand the potential of the practice. Some states require these licenses or a specialty contractor's license to sell, contract for, or supervise the installation or construction of these types of products. For example, if the design firm purchases and contracts an installer to install wall covering and if payment for both is made by the interior design firm, then the designer must have a specialty license (or other appropriate contractor's license). If the interior designer does not have the contractor's license, he or she can instruct the client to hire contractors who hold these licenses to do the supervision. Other designers focus on design rather than construction and installation, and provide consultation regarding these activities to the client. In this situation, the client then reports back to the tradesperson, construction project manager, or general contractor and asks that person to take care of the problems.

States have various provisions regarding the definition of a contractor, as it is discussed here. The owner of the interior design firm should be familiar with the statutes of the state in which the firm is located, and of *any* state in which it may be doing business. Questions should be directed to the state registrar of contractors or other appropriate authority.

Work Authorization Verification

With the passage of the Immigration Reform and Control Act of 1986, it is unlawful for individuals and businesses to hire aliens who do not have proper authorization to work. Since it is also unlawful for the company to discriminate in its hiring practices, companies are required to have all applicants hired after November 6, 1986, submit acceptable identification and work authorization information.

Not only must the applicant be asked to provide acceptable documents, but also the individual or business that is doing the hiring must keep a record of the request and verification on file. Several different kinds of documents can be used to verify identity and employment eligibility. The business owner should obtain Form I-9 from the Department of Justice, Immigration and Naturalization Service, to insure compliance with the law.

Copyrights, Trademarks, and Patents

The work of the interior designer usually results in a great deal of intangible design work, in the creation of floor plans, sketches, and sample boards. Often, it is hoped, these intangible items will result in a completed interior or, possibly, a custom-designed product. There will be instances in which the designer will wish to legally protect these design ideas so that they cannot be duplicated or copied without permission and fair compensation. In some cases, the client may also wish that these designs not be duplicated.

Creative work such as design drawings, fine art, photography, and writings are considered intellectual property because they are essentially intangible. The section of law that deals with the protection of these creative achievements is called *intellectual property law* and is governed primarily by federal statutes. The plans, specifications, and other documents created by the interior designer fall under the laws of intellectual property and are specifically protected by the use of copyrights, patents, and trademarks.

Copyright is the method by which written, artistic, and graphic designs, such as floor plans, sculptures, and this textbook, are legally protected. The legal protection of a custom-product design that results in a tangible object is a *patent*. When an individual or company receives a patent on a design, the patent gives the holder an exclusive right to make, sell, and use a product for a specific period of time—17 years for the product and 14 years for the design of a product. A *trademark* protects words and/or symbols specific to a person or a business that are very creative and out of the ordinary. Distinctive names, logos, packaging, and the like are commonly registered as trademarks. A design firm's logo could be considered a trademark if it were distinctive and not used by any other business. The designer who creates a logo that could be protected by a trademark would apply for protection of this design. However, the trademark is most often applied for, and granted to, the company for which the trademark was designed.

This section focuses on copyright protection, since most of what an interior designer creates can be copyrighted. Although a designer may wish to obtain a patent on a design or an actual custom-made product that he or she has designed for a client, the process of obtaining a patent is quite complex and any discussion of it is beyond the scope of this book. Readers who may want information on this process are urged to contact the U.S. Patent Office or to discuss the process with an intellectual property attorney.

In a very broad sense, the Federal Copyright Act of 1976 protects works of authorship and pictorial or graphic works. Design specifications fall within the authorship category, whereas drawings and plans fall within the latter category. The design idea itself is not copyrightable, it is the expression as a written, graphic, or artistic work that is protected. For example, floor plans for a prototype fast-food restaurant would be copyrightable, but the idea for that restaurant would not be. The idea for a custom-made dining room table is not eligible for a patent or copyright protection until the design of that table has been put down on paper. The object itself, if it is substantially different from any other cabinet design, must be patented to receive legal protection from unauthorized duplication.

The rights to a copyright last for a substantial period of time. Any written or graphic work that was created on or after January 1, 1978, is protected by copyright for the life of the author or designer, plus 70 years for an individual. If the work was created by an employee, the copyright, which belongs to the employer, lasts for 95 years from the date of publication or 120 years from the date of creation, whichever comes first. The difference between works created as an individual and as an employee are discussed later in this section.

The copyright begins at the moment at which the interior designer begins the act of completing the work. This means that the moment the interior designer begins drafting the working drawings, sketches, or specifications, then the right to legally protect the work begins. Thus, common law provides the creator of an artistic work automatic protection—to a limited degree. If the work is distributed without any copyright notice protection, then the work is considered to be in the public domain and can be used by anyone in any way without compensation to the creator. The work must bear a copyright notification prior to its being "published" and must be registered with the copyright office in order to receive full, legal statutory protection.

Many designers neglect to put a clause in their design contract concerning copyright and ownership of documents that they have prepared for a client. It has been upheld in court that work commissioned by a client from a designer belongs to the designer or company, even if there are no clauses in the design contract that gives ownership to the designer or company. Full statutory protection, however, is afforded only when the work contains the proper notification and meets registration and publication requirements.

So what exactly is "publication" and "notice?"

Publication occurs when the creator has somehow distributed the work to others for review without restriction of use by the creator. It does not mean that the work has been published by a publishing house. For example, if an interior designer gives a floor plan to a client for his or her review, the floor plan has been published. Providing to the client or to others copies of the work for the purpose of display constitutes publication.

Copyright notification must contain the following elements:

1. The word *copyright*, the abbreviation *copr*, or the copyright symbol ©
2. The year of publication
3. The name of the copyright claimant for the copyright

Notice of these three elements does not begin the copyright. Notice serves to protect what the claimant publishes. Copyright begins at the moment of creation.

The copyright notification itself, however, does not provide complete legal protection. The proposed copyrighted materials must be registered with the federal government in order for the interior designer to be able to file suit in a federal district court for copyright infringement. In order to register a copyrightable item, the creator must obtain the proper forms from the copyright office. The "VA" form is used for graphic works and the "TX" form is used for books, articles, and other general written works. The best way to obtain information and forms is to contact the copyright office at www.loc.gov/copyright. Forms can be downloaded from the Internet.

An original form, not a photocopy of the form, must be accompanied by one copy of the work, if the work is unpublished, and two copies of the work, if it has already been published. The copy of the work must be a "best edition" copy. Since originals cannot be readily submitted, properly prepared photocopies, photographs of the work, or plots of floor plans may suffice. What constitutes a best edition copy, however, is up to the copyright office. A fee to process the copyright is also required.

It is not necessary to send each project under a separate copyright form. A bulk of work, called a collection, may be submitted at one time. A collection can constitute any work that has been created within the same year, as long as all the work is of the same basic type and falls under the same form.

In order for full statutory and actual damages to be awarded, registration must occur either prior to the work's being published or under specific circumstances. If the work is registered within three months of first publication, the copyright holder is still able to claim statutory and actual damages. If the work is registered up to five years of first publication, there is a presumption of a valid copyright. After five years, the claimant has to prove that he or she is the original author. In these example cases, the copyright claimant may receive actual damages but not statutory damages or attorney's fees and costs.

Statutory damages refer to amounts determined by the court for each infringement. Actual damages relate to damages that the copyright holder suffers as a result of the infringement. Actual damages may mean payment of design fees, profits the designer may have lost, and profits the infringer may have made by the infringement.

Infringement refers to any unauthorized use of copyrighted materials. This can best be explained with a few examples. As discussed earlier a designer prepares the custom design of a table, and a cabinetmaker not only produces the table for the interior designer but also begins to produce the design for his or her own clients. Assume that the designs have been properly copyrighted. Since the plans were provided to the cabinetmaker for the exclusive use of producing one table, the cabinetmaker has infringed on the designer's copyright by producing additional copies of the cabinet. In a second example, a designer has prepared a set of working drawings for the interior of a prototype fast-food restaurant in a specific location. If the owner of the fast-food restaurant later duplicates the plans in another location, the restaurant owner has infringed on the designer's copyright.

On the other side of this issue, infringement also occurs if a designer uses the design created by someone else to create a "custom-made" piece of furniture. Even making very small changes, such as using a different finish, can be construed as infringement. Assuming the original designer copyrighted or even obtained a patent on the design, then the second interior designer has infringed on the original designer's copyright when he or she "knocks off" or imitates the original design. Of course, this is not legal and is not ethical. Numerous court cases have been heard over the last several years about just such an issue. An organization called the Foundation for Design Integrity (FDI) represents dozens of manufacturers and designers and aids them in the protection of their designs and litigation for design infringement by designers. The mission for the FDI is as follows:

"The Foundation for Design Integrity honors those who conceive, design, engineer and develop innovative new products for the Architectural and Interior Design Community and their clients. It seeks to educate and inform the industry, and the public, about the importance of original design. It seeks to foster integrity in the specification and procurement of interior and architectural products. And it seeks to set standards, protect original design and serve as the voice of the industry" (FDI, 1999). The address for this organization can be found in the Appendix.

Copyrights of any design work created by individuals who are employees of an interior design firm belong to the employer, not the employee. This is true as long as the work was done as part of the normal responsibilities of the employee. The copyright of work that an employee does falls under the concept of "work for hire." Any design that has been created by an employee as part of the normal responsibilities of the employee and for clients of the employer belongs to the employer, not the employee. An independent contractor (contract laborer) who performs interior design work for a firm might not own the copyright if the firm hiring the independent contractor specifically contracted for the ownership. The definition of an independent contractor is discussed in Chapter 12.

What if the employee creates an item that can be patented? The *shop right* doctrine says that employers hold a nonexclusive free license to any creation or invention of tangible products an employee designs that result as a part of employment (Garner, 1999, p. 1384). "The theory is that because such inventions are developed with the employer's funds or property, the employer should at least be able to use them" (Elias, 1999, p. 288). The employee is still the patent holder, however. An example might be a situation in which an interior designer creates a software program that provides a new way to handle the firm's data processing and the program is, for some reason, sold to a local software company. If the program is created on company time, the employer has an interest in using the program without paying royalties to the employee.

This distinction is important, because designers, being creative and thoughtful people, often dabble in works that stretch their job responsibilities in different ways. Generally, designs created on the employee's own time, using his or her own materials and facilities, belong to the employee, unless there is a statement to the contrary in an employment agreement.

Although it may not always be necessary for the interior designer to be concerned with the copyrighting of design documents, there may be instances in which certain projects or parts of projects would require this protection. Knowing how to prepare the documents for legal protection is very important. Including a clause in the design contract related to "design ownership" or "copyright permission" would also aid in legally protecting the designer.

Summary

An individual or group of designers may have the skill, experience, and finances to open a design practice. Once the business plan, partnership agreement, or articles of incorporation have been prepared, there are several other legal filings that are required by the federal, state, and local governments. This chapter briefly described some of those legal forms and documents.

Some states require specialized filings or documents. Those discussed were interior design title registration or licensure and contractor's licenses. One or more of these specialized filings affect almost all interior design practices in some way. This chapter also reviewed provisions of copyright law as they might apply to an interior design practice.

The reader, whether a professional who is considering opening his or her own practice or a student, should now be able to see that there is much work involved beyond design skill and ability in establishing a practice. The next chapter will look at some additional considerations in setting up an interior design practice.

REFERENCES

Bangs, David H., Jr. 1995. *The Business Planning Guide*, 7th ed. Chicago, IL: Upstart Publishing.

Berger, C. Jaye. 1994. *Interior Design Law and Business Practices.* New York: John Wiley.

Blue, Martha. 1990. *By the Book. Legal ABCs for the Printed Word*. Flagstaff, AZ: Northland Publishing.

Brown, Gordon W., and Paul A. Sukys. 1997. *Business Law*, 9th ed. New York: Glencoe/ McGraw-Hill.

Bunnin, Brad, and Peter Beren. 1998. *The Writer's Legal Companion*. Reading, MA: Perseus Books.

Conry, Edward J., Gerald R. Ferrera, and Karla H. Fox. 1993. *The Legal Environment of Business*, 3rd ed. Boston, MA: Allyn and Bacon.

Cooke, Robert A. 1999. *Small Business Formation Handbook*. New York: John Wiley.

Davidson, Marion, and Martha Blue. 1979. *Making It Legal.* New York: McGraw-Hill.

Elias, Stephen. 1999. *Patent, Copyright and Trademark*, 3rd ed. Berkeley, CA: Nolo Press.

Epstein, Lee. 1977. *Legal Forms for the Designer.* New York: N & E Hellman.

Fishman, Stephen. 1996. *The Copyright Handbook*, 3rd ed. Berkeley, CA: Nolo Press.

Foundation for Design Integrity. 1999. (Public relations materials).

Garner, Bryan A., ed. 1999. *Black's Law Dictionary*, 7th ed. St. Paul, MN: West Group.

Hisrich, Robert D., and Michael P. Peters. 1992. *Entrepreneurship*, 2nd ed. Homewood, IL: Richard D. Irwin.

Internal Revenue Service. 1999. *Starting a Business and Keeping Records*. Publication No. 583. Washington, DC: Department of the Treasury.

———. 1999. *Tax Guide for Small Business.* Publication No. 334. Washington, DC: Department of the Treasury.

———. 1999. *Employer's Supplemental Tax Guide.* Publication No. 15-A. Washington, DC: Department of the Treasury.

Jenkins, Michael D. (and the Entrepreneurial Services Group of Ernst and Young). 1992. *Starting and Operating a Business in Arizona.* Grants Pass, OR: Oasis. (Material is available for all 50 states and the District of Columbia).

Jentz, Gaylord A., Kenneth W. Clarkson, and Roger LeRoy Miller. 1987. *West's Business Law—Alternate UCC Comprehensive Edition*, 3rd ed. St. Paul, MN: West Publishing.

Mancuso, Anthony. 2000. *Form Your Own Limited Liability Company*, 2nd ed. Berkeley, CA. (The disk that is included with the book contains information for all 50 states.)

Oasis Press. 1997. *Smart Start Your Arizona Business*. Grants Pass, OR: Oasis Press. (Books are available for all 50 states.)

Patterson, L. Ray, and Stanley W. Lindberg. 1991. *The Nature of Copyright. A Law of User's Rights.* Athens, GA: University of Georgia Press.

Pressman, David. 1999. *Patent It Yourself,* 7th ed. Berkeley, CA: Nolo Press.

Steingold, Fred S., Barbara Kate Repa, ed. 1999. *The Employer's Legal Handbook,* 3rd ed. Berkeley, CA: Nolo Press.

Strong, William S. 1984. *The Copyright Book: A Practical Guide,* 2nd ed. Cambridge, MA: MIT Press.

Sweet, Justin. 1985. *Legal Aspects of Architecture Engineering and the Construction Process,* 3rd ed. St. Paul, MN: West Publishing.

Weiss, Donald H. 2000. *Fair, Square & Legal,* 3rd ed. New York: American Management Association.

Note: many other tax guides are available from the IRS. Local and state agencies have numerous publications available that can help the new business owner clarify requirements within each jurisdiction.

Chapter 8

On Your Own

So you still want to have your own interior design practice. Well, good for you! It is exciting to make that decision. It is also scary to tell your boss that you quit and plan to start your own business. Your friends will think you are crazy and will be jealous at the same time. Your family may also have the same reaction. Mine did. However, if you have thought it through, have calculated the possibilities and the problems, and have planned what you are going to do, then go for it!

The preceding chapters provided information to help the prospective entrepreneur and student understand and plan a new interior design practice. Whether the business is entered into alone or with several partners or co-owners, many critical decisions must be made. Other chapters in this text will provide information on specific operational activities and issues regarding the professional practice of interior design.

This chapter focuses on other general issues related to the start-up of an interior design practice. Although it is directed toward the sole practitioner, who essentially is working alone, readers also will find useful information in this chapter. The chapter begins with a discussion about the challenges of working alone. Additional topics include choosing a business location, equipping the design studio, and inventory issues.

Working Alone

Working alone. Free to work when you want and how you want. It has a lot of advantages. It can mean having the freedom to do interior design work in the way in which you really want to do it, without constraints being placed on you by a boss. It can also mean not having to dress according to a dress code, except when you are meeting with clients. It means that all the profits stay with the owner—you. However, "Free isn't easy. It means risks. It means responsibility. It means hard work" (Fisher, 1995, p. 14).

Working alone also has disadvantages and "traps" that can keep the entrepreneur from realizing the freedom that he or she imagined as well as from realizing the profits from the business that he or she expected. This section looks briefly at some of the challenges of working alone from a home office.

Working alone, and the isolation that comes with, can actually be quite hard on many people. For others, it can be very exhilarating. Designers who have a lot of energy when they are working with others may not have the same energy when they are working alone. Maintaining discipline to keep at whatever the task at hand happens to be is another problem that many people face when they work alone. When a designer starts a business and is working alone, there generally is no one to talk to about the ideas and problems that are generated by a project. Others find that they are procrastinators, putting unpleasant things, like record keeping, off. Then again, there is the possibility that the designer may become a workaholic, not taking time off to pursue personal interests.

Finding the time to get all the necessary tasks done in a timely manner can be another issue. It can be a struggle for the designer to find the time to meet with clients, prepare drawings and specifications, meet with vendors at the job site, supervise (to some degree or other) the installation, and also find the time to visit supplier showrooms in order to locate items for the project. Of course, working alone means that you also must take care of the bookkeeping, pay your taxes, and pay your bills. It is also up to you to find time to talk to prospective new clients, perhaps write an article every other month as a marketing aid, and deal with all the problems that occur as part of running a business. And attending to your family's needs also will require some of your time.

It is quite obvious that a sole practitioner must seriously consider what it means to work alone, perhaps surrounded by the distractions of the home office environment. Sometimes the realization of how alone "alone" can be, is pretty hard to take. It is a big issue in starting a solo interior design practice. It is not easy for many who enjoy the social interaction that comes with working in an office or a studio with other designers to make the transition to being the only one to answer the phone, do all the work, and maintain the discipline to work. For many, it is a big test of one's will.

The lack of companionship can become an issue for some. The silence of an empty home office can be unnerving and lonely. Going away for a few days and finding that no prospective client has called while you were gone can be very discouraging. Not getting the pats on the back that most individuals need can cause a sole practitioner to lose confidence.

For others, the privacy needed to function can be difficult to obtain. Working from home may mean that your children expect you to play with them more or that your pets want your attention. Suddenly you find yourself answering those telemarketing calls that you didn't receive when you were working for someone else. If the home office is not located in a quiet, private space, numerous other distractions can make it difficult to concentrate, to talk professionally on the phone with clients, or simply be a place where you want to work for several hours a day. And that refrigerator is so close for finding a nice snack. Being sure that there is a good place in your home to locate your design office is an important part of planning for your new venture.

Others start a business without understanding the risks involved. As a sole practitioner, it is up to you to find sufficient clients who will not only work with you but also pay you when jobs are completed. Those clients do not appear out of thin air. They must be prospected for, cultivated, and finally encouraged to sign contracts with you. Guess who gets to do all that? You—the sole practitioner. Granted, working alone and working from a home office means that the overhead expenses of operating the business will be low. However, you will still have expenses that are needed to operate the practice, taxes to pay on income earned, and bills to pay to suppliers who probably want 100 percent down on all orders. You are responsible for raising all that money. If you make a mistake that causes physical or business harm due to an error or omission in the executing of a project, you are responsible for the consequences and perhaps even legal judgments. All of this and more comes with starting a business and working alone.

Most of this section thus far paints a somewhat bleak picture of working alone. How can this be a positive experience? Here are some guidelines that you can follow that will help to make it a positive experience.

- Make sure you understand your abilities as an interior designer. It is not enough to be creative. To succeed as an independent designer, it is important that you have some understanding of managing a business and of your limitations regarding business skills.
- Determine that what you want to offer in the way of interior design services is readily needed by clients in your area. This may seem obvious, but far too many design businesses fail because they offer services to clients that they do not really want or need.
- Examine your ambition to be sure that you have the determination to keep going, even in the face of adversity. Understand how far you can go financially and emotionally by going it alone.
- Be clear that the probability of making a lot of money during the first year—even the first three years—is an illusion. Think about how much making money means success for you and whether money is the reason you have decided to go it alone.
- Keep yourself charged up. Become involved in your professional association chapter, network with clients at their associations, or start a network group of like-minded designers who could also use some camaraderie.
- Set goals that are challenging yet attainable. Do not undermine your confidence by setting goals that are impossible to meet.
- Do not berate yourself when your performance does not meet your expectations. Review why things have worked out as they have, try your best to change what you can, and move on. Negatives can be clues to things you need to do to increase positive results. Admitting that you are a procrastinator might finally get you to use good time management skills.
- Give yourself a break. Take that mini-vacation. Attend a trade show or a conference. Have lunch with old friends. Look out the window and remember to smell the roses!

Owning one's own business and being able to work alone is an exciting challenge as well as a scary proposition. It takes courage to start any new business. Carefully considering what you are trying to achieve and why, planning how to go about achieving those results, and then having the determination to do it will likely give you a great deal of pleasure and enjoyment!

Business Location

Behaving in a very businesslike way in dealings with clients is especially relevant for the sole practitioner who works from home. Not having a storefront or a formal office can be interpreted by clients as not being serious about being an interior designer. "It is often hard to be taken seriously when your office is at home, because clients think it's just a hobby rather than a business," says one Arizona sole practitioner.

Being taken seriously is very important to any practitioner, regardless of how large the design firm is or where it is located. This section focuses on the needs of the sole practitioner or the small design firm that has little or no retail sales space. Determining which location is the best—at home, in a commercial office building, or in a retail center of some sort—depends on many factors, including start-up expenses, the type of services that will be offered, and the firm's expected client base.

The Home Office/Studio

Interior design is one of those professions that many people think fits nicely into a home environment. In fact, a great number of designers begin their practice by working out of a spare bedroom or a converted garage. It is economical, since no additional rent needs to be paid. With the growth of home-based businesses and telecommuting in recent years, the federal government has been more lenient in allowing tax deductions for a home office. The "stigma" of working out of one's home disappeared in the 1990s as tens of thousands of small companies and employees in many corporations located their offices in their home. However, there can be problems with locating a business in the home.

One of the biggest problems relates to zoning restrictions. Local jurisdictions have zoning ordinances that spell how the land within its boundaries can be used. This is done to keep residential neighborhoods quiet and safe for families and to keep commercial and industrial facilities in restricted areas. Single-family dwellings are zoned R-1 in most communities, and it is expected that the primary use of the land will be for homes. A business, even a service business, may be restricted as to what it can do in an area that has been zoned R-1. Regardless of the huge increase in the number of home-based businesses and employees who are working at least part-time from home, cities remain earnest in their enforcement of zoning restrictions.

Before making the decision to operate the business from home, the designer must check with his or her local zoning board to make certain that a business can operate in the neighborhood. Many jurisdictions will allow small service businesses in a residential neighborhood, as long as the business does not appreciably increase traffic, parking problems, noise, pollution, or the aesthetics of the neighborhood. However, most jurisdictions prohibit a home-based business that has employees, other than the homeowner who operates the business.

If neighbors complain about traffic, parking, or even delivery trucks arriving around the home office, the owner may have to relocate or apply for a zoning variance (discussed in Chapter 7) in order to operate the business legally from the home. Do not forget that a home-based business must also obtain a city and/or county business license, sales and use tax licenses, and perhaps other licenses or permits that are necessary for practicing interior design. In some situations, these licenses may restrict the use of the home as a business location.

Related to zoning laws are home owner's associations restrictions. *Conditions, covenants, and restrictions* (CCRs) are specific regulations for condominiums, townhouses, and even single-family dwellings in planned communities. Even if the city allows a home-based business, CCRs may prohibit even a quiet business, such as an interior design practice, from working out of a home.

Another important issue to consider that is related to locating the interior design business within one's home is how to handle meetings with clients and suppliers. The designer may be a very talented, creative person, but oftentimes, the home office is a jumble of catalogs, samples, and files—not very attractive to a prospective client. Clients are often concerned about the location and the appearance of the office. After all, if the office does not appear businesslike and successful, the client may be reluctant to award the designer with a contract.

Two options regarding allowing customers into the designer's home are (if possible) (1) build an addition to the home or (2) create a studio with its own private entrance. In this way, the home environment is separated from the business. Another option is to rent space in an executive office complex, where the designer can use the conference room spaces and perhaps have mail delivered and have telephones answered when the designer is out of the home office. Of course, many designers who work out of a home office plan meetings with clients at the client's home or office, or possibly at a restaurant.

A home office location has other problems. For example, will the space selected have enough privacy when business telephone calls and faxes are received? Background noise of children, pets, or the TV over the phone are not conducive to giving the impression of being a professional business. It is not uncommon for many business faxes to be received after 5 P.M., some even after 10 P.M. or early in the morning, depending on one's time zone. Phones and fax machines that are ringing at all hours of the day and night can be very disturbing. The designer who has a studio at home must make it clear to the family that business hours are for business and must restrict, to the degree necessary for the designer, family and friends interrupting and disrupting business.

Another important consideration is that most home owner's insurance will not cover any furniture and equipment used in the home for business purposes without the addition of a special rider. The designer needs to confirm what will happen to office equipment that will be used in the home in the case of theft or fire, in order to ensure that the business will not suffer irreparable harm should something like this happen.

Commercial Location

A business office that is located in a commercially zoned part of town gives an impression of professionalism. The exact location of the business office will be determined, in part, by the nature of the business. If the practice is primarily commercial interior design and seeks an office suite and corporate client, a location in the downtown business district would be the most suitable. If the practice is specialized for a particular kind of business, such as hotels or restaurants, a location near the main hotel district or a downtown location, again, might be best. Residential design studios are often located near other suppliers, such as furniture, carpet, wallpaper, or lighting retail stores. This relationship could bring a client to the designer when he or she visits these other establishments. A residential practice that has a small showroom for retail sales may want to locate in a shopping area where the design firm's potential customers shop.

Design offices that do not sell displayed furniture or accessories can be located in many places. The first thought should be convenience for the client so that the design firm can be easily found by prospective clients. Depending on the exact services offered and design specialty, locations in high-rise office buildings, where other professionals such as architects are also located, are very common. Other interior designers locate in low-rise office complexes, where street entry and visibility are available. Some locate in mixed-use centers with other professionals, like accountants and small retail stores of various kinds. Locating near peer groups and related professionals should be a primary consideration when the designer is selecting a commercial location.

Of course, the interior designer must also consider the expense of the prospective commercial space. The amount of the rent, the terms of the lease, and how much of the utilities, insurance, and maintenance costs will be covered by the landlord are important factors to consider. All of these costs add to the total overhead of the business and require monthly payment, even if the firm does not generate any revenue in a particular month.

Interior design studio or office spaces must have a professional "look" that meets the expectations of its customers (see Figure 8-1). The commercial space must be of the highest quality to reflect the image that the firm is trying to achieve. Some owners and managers say that the studio, office, or store that has merchandise, samples, and documents spread out gives the office or studio the appearance of casualness. It is important for the owner of the studio or office to decide whether the kind of client that he or she wishes to attract will be turned off by the casual appearance of the studio or office.

The studio or office should give an expression of the general style of the design firm (contemporary, traditional, or a mixture), as this will play a part in attracting prospective clients. Clients who wish a traditional home or an advertising agency that is looking for a high-tech, high-energy office appearance will migrate toward a design firm that has shown it knows how to provide these. They will rarely go to a firm that has a reputation of or displays an opposing style to what they are seeking.

FIGURE 8-1. An interior design office in a commercial location. (A) selling area; (B) part of office work area. (Photos courtesy of Michael Thomas, The Design Collective Group, Jupiter, Florida)

In a commercial space, the tenant needs to negotiate with the landlord concerning improvements to the space to suit the firm's needs. The amount of allowance for interior partitions and improvements that will be covered by the landlord is important. Some locations do not provide for much more than very basic painting, floor covering, and drop-in ceiling fixtures. The designer must carefully review what is provided and must state very specifically in the *building standard workletter* from the developer or landlord what changes are desired for the space. This document outlines what quantity and quality of work will be undertaken by the developer in the construction of the tenant's office or studio space. If the allowances are minimal, the interior designer must decide to pay for *tenant improvements* (also called leasehold improvements) out of his or her own pocket. These are expenses that can be deducted in all likelihood, but they are not recovered upon vacating.

Last, but certainly not least, is the determination as to how much space will be required. It must be carefully calculated, because each square foot of office or retail space leased, whether it will be filled by furniture, equipment, and samples or used for circulation or as a visual impact that creates an aesthetic look, must be paid for each and every month. If there is too little space, the office/studio will become quickly cluttered and will look unprofessional. A successful practice in too small a space may also find that it must relocate to accommodate additional employees. Too big a space requires greater overhead expenses that must be met, possibly draining away revenues from new equipment purchases, marketing efforts for the business, or hiring additional employees.

Equipping the Office/Studio

Exactly what kinds of equipment are needed for the interior design office vary as much as do designers who work in the field. The type of interior design the company specializes in, as well as the services offered, compound the decisions that must be made. If the reader has been working in the interior design profession for several years, he or she will have some idea as to what kind of equipment will be needed for the studio or office. Those readers who are still students but who wish to have their own business someday are well advised to work for someone else for several years, not only to gain experience in the field, but also to see what kinds of equipment and supplies a studio or office needs.

In the same way in which the designer gathers information and makes decisions for a client, he or she must determine his or her own equipment needs. An evaluation of specific needs of the firm is logically the beginning of the decision-making process. Technology changes so quickly that a computer, for example, can be "out of date" before it arrives at the new office location. Therefore, it is important to consider future needs and the ability to upgrade the system or equipment before purchasing it.

File cabinets are required for storing numerous kinds of communication, documents, and records of the design firm's business activities. Paper was supposed to disappear with the use of the computer, but, in fact, we seem to use more paper than ever before, so storage of paper files remains a critical need for all sizes of interior design practices.

The need for client files and job books poses another storage issue. Some designers use plastic storage tubs of various sizes to hold samples and job files of active projects and even to retain them for archival use. Others find that file folders or three-ring binders are sufficient, while still other designers use magazine holder boxes or numerous other methods to store client records.

It is hard to imagine any size or specialty of a professional interior design office operating without a fax machine, a computer for word processing and record keeping, a copy machine, and, of course, a telephone. These basic pieces of office equipment are absolutely necessary for the sole practitioner and small studio. Even the smaller design firm looks for CAD packages to help with producing working drawings and construction documents. Color scanners and printers/plotters allow designers to scan photos from catalogs and magazines to help explain design concepts or to provide photos of products for presentations.

The telephone remains the most common way in which a client will make contact with an interior designer. Even in the home-based office, more than one phone line may be necessary. If a shared line is used for incoming calls, fax machines, and a hookup to the Internet, the design practitioner may lose important telephone contacts—even new business. It is important, then, to dedicate one line to incoming calls and reserve the second line for the fax and Internet. It would be wise for the designer to discuss options with a communications consultant at the telephone company in order to take care of those times when the designer will be away from the studio. The designer also needs to consider the greeting that he or she or any employees will be using when answering the phone. It should sound professional and businesslike. The design practitioner should rehearse the greeting and should have a few friends call in to make comments on the professional image that it might portray. It must be remembered that background noise of children playing, dogs barking, or the dishwasher running are not very businesslike.

Throughout this book, the text mentions how computers or other electronic office equipment can help in the management of the business practice. It is hard to imagine an interior design firm in the twenty-first century functioning without some type of computer system. Interior design firms, large and small, need to evaluate how computers can be used in the firm. Let us look very briefly now at how some of these devices help an interior design firm.

Everyone seems to know how basic computer software applications can help in the design office. Word-processing software is used to produce letters, marketing mailings, specifications—anything that is word-intensive. Spreadsheet software is used for accounting, numerical aspects of specifications, even "what if" analyses of pricing and specifications. Accounting software is used to record financial transactions and to produce many reports that can be given to the firm's accountant to prepare income tax records and formalized reports when needed. Database software keeps the office in touch with its clients by creating files of information on those clients (former and potential) that can be accessed easily for specific needs. Databases also can be used to organize a lot of information in product libraries. Software helps many designers organize their day and keep track of their marketing efforts.

More specialized kinds of software applications assist in other ways in the interior design office. Project-scheduling and time-recording software packages allow accurate record keeping and project scheduling. Many of these software packages also provide charting and integration of statistical information. Such software makes it easier to bill clients accurately for design time as well as to have good control of the status of design projects. Some design offices utilize sophisticated desktop publishing software to produce newsletters, case studies, brochures, and many other direct mail promotional items. And do not forget CAD and the Internet.

There are, of course, many other kinds of equipment that are needed to start up a design practice. Storage shelves or cabinets for material samples, catalogs, and cut sheets can take up a considerable amount of space and come in a wide variety of forms. Gone are the days when vendors willingly gave catalog binders to every interior designer who asked for one. However, it is still easy for large numbers of catalogs, tear sheets, and sample books to accumulate quickly. It is necessary to decide not only how to store these items but also which ones to have on hand. Each sample and catalog on hand should be included in the firm's library because it expects to need it at some point in the near future. Just like clothing that has been hanging in the closet for years but has not been worn, catalogs and samples that have been in the library for some time—a year or two perhaps—but have not been used should be re-evaluated and discarded. Not doing so can mean that the designer might inadvertently price goods at prices that are far out of touch with present-day reality.

One item that, in a way, seems to multiply on its own is memo samples and large textile cuttings. These are fabric swatches that the designer needs in order to clarify pattern and appearance to the client. However, many are never used for the project and somehow never seem to be returned to the vendor. These large cuttings must be paid for if they are not returned. Some design firms that do a substantial amount of custom fabric treatments can add thousands of dollars to their overhead by retaining memo samples. The design firm owner and employees should be clear on pricing policies from the textile vendors and consider sending back unused and unimportant samples.

Fortunately, in the last few years, information about resources have become more available on the Internet. Practitioners need only to locate the web address of vendors and suppliers to obtain detailed product information, pictures that can be downloaded, and, by special arrangement, pricing. In some situations, direct orders also can be placed with the supplier over the Internet. This use of the Internet is discussed in more detail in Chapter 28.

The Internet can be a valuable research tool in many ways. The interior design firm owner can obtain information concerning the professional associations with which he or she has chosen to affiliate. Up-to-date information from other organizations also can be easily obtained over the information highway. Designers also have access to educational opportunities as colleges, universities, and associations offer classes over the Internet. The opportunities for searching for information that can be of help to the interior designer are unlimited. And, of course, the interior designer may determine that a web address for his or her interior design practice is a useful marketing tool.*

All the kinds of office equipment that we have been discussing—and more—make it possible to conduct business in the interior design field wherever the office or studio is located. Although the foregoing list is not all-inclusive, it does provide the student or professional who is considering starting his or her own design practice with an idea of what needs to be planned for and budgeted.

Inventory Issues

Even though this chapter is directed toward the small interior design practice that does not involve retail display, every design firm accumulates inventory. Goods purchased and held by the business for resale to clients are considered inventory. For the most part, inventory can be items that have been rejected

* Web pages for marketing purposes are discussed in Chapter 23.

by clients that cannot be returned to the vendor. Some inventory can also be accumulated as a designer shops for items for one client and finds some unique item that might be used for some future client.

When the owner of a design firm decides to handle inventory for the studio, regardless of how that inventory is obtained, the owner must be clear as to the purpose of retaining or accumulating inventory items. Rejections are going to happen, no matter how careful the design firm is in specification of products, approval by the client, and delivery methods. And this is an important point. The design firm must have good procedures and policies in place to prevent as many returns and rejections by clients as possible. Some of these will be discussed in later chapters. Purchasing just one more of that "really neat" basket for some future client might seem like a good idea at the time—if it then gets sold in a reasonable length of time. These inventory items represent dollars that cannot be used by the firm for anything else until the items are sold. All those baskets, drawer pulls, and returns stored somewhere in a garage, in a warehouse, or a public storage unit also create storage costs and insurance liability, which result in additional drains on financial resources that many small firms cannot afford.

If the designer has to purchase an item "just in case," he or she should try to purchase an item that can be sold in a reasonable length of time—perhaps within a few months or weeks. The designer should make sure that these items are not so specialized that none of the firm's other clients might be interested in buying them. For example, the designer should not stock up on American Indian baskets because one client wanted that accessory if most of the firm's work is in eighteenth-century Georgian-style historical restoration.

The design firm should keep good records on these items as to how long they have been in inventory and even where they are located. The records will be needed for tax purposes. The author has heard many designers comment on the fact that they had lost track of some items because they had been in storage so long. If inventoried items become damaged or stolen, the records will help the firm recover insurance claims. Good records also help the design firm's owner know how to get rid of items—possibly at a designer's "ding-and-dent" sale through an association or even by making a donation to a charitable organization.

Summary

Most of the chapters in Parts I and II of this book have discussed the many issues and concerns of starting an interior design practice. For the most part, these chapters were written for the prospective entrepreneur, regardless of the type of design practice or size of business desired. This chapter has focused on many topics that are relevant to the practitioner who is more inclined to work alone than with a partner or with employees. Of course, some of the topics covered in this chapter, such as location and equipment procurement, are necessary considerations for any size interior design business.

The chapter concludes with a discussion of topics related to the overall planning and organization of an interior design practice. The chapters in Parts III, IV, V, and VI discuss specific details relevant to the management and operation of any interior design practice. Part III covers topics on business organization, personnel management, and legal issues that affect the interior design practice. Part IV provides discussions on managing the financial areas of the business and includes an overview of financial accounting methods, methods of charging fees, preparing design contracts, and pricing products. Part V gives information and ideas on how to market the interior design practice, while Part VI discusses many topics in the area of project management, contract administration, and project completion.

REFERENCES

Bond, William J. 1997. *Going Solo*. New York: McGraw-Hill.

Collin, Simon. 1997. *Doing Business on the Internet.* London, England: Kogan, Page.

Edwards, Paul, and Sarah Edwards. 1999. *Working from Home*, 5th ed. New York: Jeremy P. Tarcher/Putnam.

———. 1996. *Secrets of Self-Employment*, rev. ed. New York: Jeremy P. Tarcher/Putnam.

Emery, Vince. 1996. *How To Grow Your Business on the Internet*. Scottsdale, AZ: Aoriolis Group.

Entrepreneur Magazine. 1999. *Starting a Home-Based Business*, 2nd ed. New York: John Wiley.

Eyler, David R. 1994. *The Home Business Bible.* New York: John Wiley.

Fisher, Lionel L. 1995. *On Your Own*. Englewood Cliffs, NJ: Prentice-Hall.

Gerber, Michael E. 1995. *The E Myth Revisited.* New York: Harper Business.

Holtz, Herman. 1993. *How To Succeed as an Independent Consultant*, 3rd ed. New York: John Wiley.

LeBoeuf, Michael. 1996. *The Perfect Business.* New York: Fireside.

Lewin, Marsha D. 1995. *The Overnight Consultant.* New York: John Wiley.

Pack, Thomas. 1997. *10 Minute Guide to Business Research on the Net.* New York: Que/Macmillan.

Rappoport, James E., Robert F. Cushman, and Karen Daroff. 1992. *Office Planning and Design Desk Reference*. New York: John Wiley.

Warshaw, Michael. "Get a Life." *Fast Company.* June/July 1998.

Whitmyer, Claude, Salli Rasberry, and Michael Phillips. 1989. *Running a One-Person Business.* Berkeley, CA: Ten Speed Press.

Linda Elliott Smith, FASID is President of Smith and Associates, Inc., an award-winning interior design firm specializing in contract, hospitality, and residential interior design in Nashville, TN. She served three years as President of the National Council for Interior Design Qualification and has held numerous positions within the NCIDQ organization. In addition to her design practice, Smith holds a principal position in education-works, inc., a professional development seminar group in Dallas, TX.

The future of interior design in the twenty-first century is dependent upon two major factors: 1) the recognition of the true value of ideas—ideas that are valuable solutions to problems, and 2) the efficient and effective use of technology to maximize time efficiency.

Interior design professionals must fully realize the value of design solutions, and the overall impact these solutions have on the quality of life within the built environment. They must realize the true value of their creative abilities. The focus must be on ideas, not products.

Part III

The Business of Interior Design

9.Business Organization and Management

Organization of the Interior Design Practice   The Stages of a Business Organizational Structure within the Office   Types of Business Organizations   Management   Functions of Management

10. The Planning Function

Importance of Planning   Kinds of Plans   Budgeting Measuring Performance

11. Personnel Management

Job Classifications   Job Descriptions   The Performance Evaluation The Employee Handbook   Compensation and Fringe Benefits

12. Legal Issues of Employment

Federal Laws Regulating Employment   The Agency Relationship Employment at Will   Employment Contracts Independent Contractors   Sexual Harassment

13. Legal Responsibilities

Criminal versus Tort Law   Negligence   Intentional Torts Against a Person   Intentional Torts Against Property   Codes Compliance Plan Review Boards

14. Warranties and Product Liability

Warranties   Products Liability

Chapter 9

Business Organization and Management

The business organization of a small interior design practice is not very complicated, nor should it be. However, once the practice begins to grow in terms of profits, number of clients, and employees, an organizational structure becomes necessary. The purpose of this organizational structure is to aid all employees in understanding the various activities of the firm and to show who is responsible for those activities. The larger the firm is, the more complex the organizational structure will become. As long as the firm continues to plan for changes in the organization rather than reacting to them, the firm will continue to grow and prosper.

Obviously, the design firm's organization does not come out of the sky. Rather, it comes through thoughtful consideration and decision making by the owners and managers. These activities of planning and decision making are two additional functions or responsibilities of managers and management. The more the firm grows, the more important these responsibilities become. For, as the firm grows, the "pact" between owner and employees grows. This pact is that the owner and/or managers vow to keep the interior design firm viable and income producing so as to meet all of its financial and legal obligations. And, frankly, regardless of the design talent of the owner, this pact cannot be met without some concern for planning, organization, decision making, and controlling the business of the interior design firm.

Starting an interior design practice, no matter how talented the designer or how well intentioned the owner/manager is, cannot be taken lightly. Whereas at first the responsibility of making the firm viable might only affect one or two people (a proprietor or set of partners), eventually, it also affects employees. Thus, management responsibility grows and becomes more time-consuming.

This chapter briefly describes the most typical ways in which an interior design firm comes into existence and grows. It also provides a short discussion about the role of management and the functions of a manager.

Organization of the Interior Design Practice

An interior design practice often begins as a sole proprietorship, with one owner and no employees. In some cases, two or more designers form a partnership or create a company with multiple owners and a number of support employees. A new design practice also might start out as a small retail studio, offering design services to supplement sales of merchandise. Maybe the new design practice is a joint venture that has done so well that the two companies merge to form a new, large design firm.

Although there are no statistics available, a very large number of design practices began as one-person studios, located in the owner's home. In this smallest of interior design practices, the owner is the president, business manager, marketing director, designer, salesperson, draftsperson, order entry clerk, expediter, complaint department, bookkeeper, secretary, librarian, installer, and any other person required to get the job done.

Eventually, the practice becomes prosperous enough to add one or two support people. The first employee added to the sole practitioner's interior design practice is often a part-time bookkeeper or a full- or part-time design assistant. Designers commonly maintain day-to-day financial records themselves as the business gets off the ground. They commonly hire a part-time bookkeeper once the workload has increased to the point where the practitioner cannot keep up with the records himself or herself. A design assistant is also a valuable addition to the design firm as the number and complexity of projects increase. As might be expected, the design assistant is commonly an upper-level student or recent graduate from a nearby college or university's design program.

Of course, many interior design businesses also start as partnerships or some other business formation that is appropriate to multiple ownership. Now decisions must be made as to which of the two partners (for simplicity) will be responsible for which business functions: marketing, financial management, operational management, and employee supervision, as well as to who will be responsible for the creative design work of the company. The partners need to sit down and honestly evaluate their strengths and weaknesses in order to determine who will do what. For example, it must be decided if employees will be hired and given responsibility for certain activities, such as office management or bookkeeping, or if one of the partners will take on these responsibilities. Egos must be put aside to ensure that each owner brings appropriate skills and resources to the venture.

Depending on the success and desires of the owner(s), the design practice may grow in size as well as revenues generated for the year. What happens to a business as it grows, in terms of its overall needs?

The Stages of a Business

A business will go through several different stages, from start-up until, for some reason or another, it no longer exists. These stages reflect the energy put into the business by the owner and employees, as well as the general viability of the business. In marketing textbooks, authors describe product life cycles. When a new product hits the market, the sales of the product are generally low, as consumers have not really found the product or seen the need for the product. This first stage is called market introduction. The next phase, called market growth, happens when sales of the product increase substantially, providing increased profits to the company—at least for a while. When a product becomes successful, competitors come into the market and sales of the original product decrease or the profit margin decreases. In the third phase, called market maturity, sales for the originating company fall off as competitors enter the market and siphon off sales. Unless something dramatic is done, the product enters the fourth and final phase—market decline—as sales of the product diminish for the original company as well as for most of the competition (see Figure 9-1).

What has this to do with the business stages of an interior design firm? It is not difficult to use this same cycle when looking at the life of many interior design firms (see Figure 9-2). In the earliest stage of any new practice, the emphasis is on introducing the company to the marketplace, obtaining clients, and earning sustainable revenues. A client base must be established and a good design reputation and excellent customer service must be developed. Owners of small businesses frequently have difficulty in placing the proper emphasis on management issues, since few have many, if any, employees or any management experience. The main concern is survival, and the focus of all tasks is on producing the work that will result in revenue. This is comparable to the market introduction stage of a product's life cycle.

As the reputation of the firm grows and employees are added, the focus changes somewhat. More structure is needed to handle the added employees and any project/operations management issues. The business expands, demanding more of each employee. Increasing the client base continues to be important at the same time that the owner must consider whether he or she will spend his or her time on design projects, marketing, or managing the firm. This stage is akin to the market growth stage in a product's life cycle. The small, personal, "family" business of the early days begins to disappear in many cases, because the owner has to be in too many places at the same time to micromanage all the issues of the business. Owners quickly find that

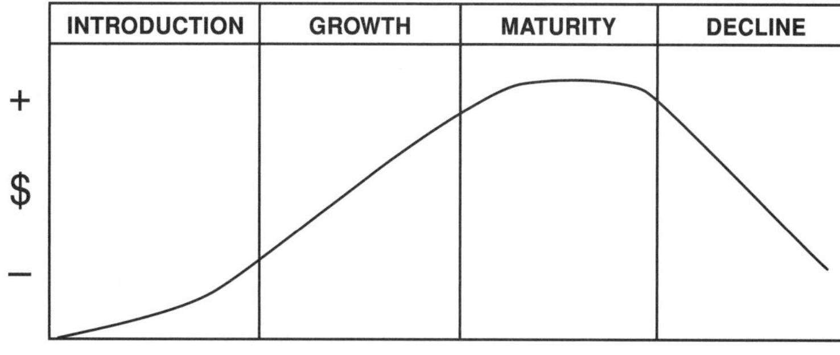

FIGURE 9-1. The standard product life cycle.

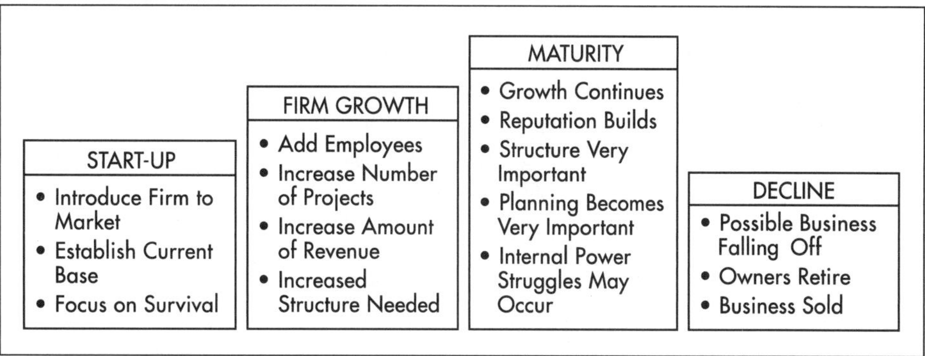

FIGURE 9-2. The growth cycle of a typical interior design firm.

management and organizational issues become very important as the business grows, perhaps overwhelming any opportunity to do creative project work. Inappropriate office organization and project or process management can quickly create chaos if the growing firm continues to operate in the same way that it did when it was a very small organization. This is often the time when the owner seeks out individuals with specialized management or other business skills so that the owner can continue to generate designs.

If the owners are looking to continually expand the breath and scope of the practice, then they will continue to add employees. However, additional pressure exists to increase revenues in order to pay for the added overhead of new employees. The firm also finds itself competing with many other interior design firms and architectural offices, which are providing services to similar clients. This situation can be compared, in some ways, to the market maturity stage of a product's life cycle. Structure definitely becomes an issue at this stage, since it is necessary to define how things are done with so many projects and employees. Structure becomes more important at the same time that many owners and staff desire responsibility to handle projects and problems on their own. In addition, planning for the future becomes even more important.

Continued growth and expansion finds the firm in a mature stage that, hopefully, will never duplicate the last stage of a product's life cycle, market decline. The design firm now has a confirmed reputation, perhaps even an award-winning staff, and is in a position in which perhaps it can even pick and choose clients. It may have grown to the point that strong departmentalized units have been formed. If it has, then department heads have been given the responsibility to organize and manage their departments in such a way that the overall goals of the company have been met. The chain of command becomes increasingly important the larger the firm grows. *Chain of command* refers to the formal reporting links that exist between one level of employee and another. Good yearly planning is now necessary to guarantee the future of the design firm. The regular evaluation of the company's mission and goals are necessary for it to retain the freshness and drive that will keep it from losing customers and seeing revenues decline.

Of course, any interior design firm can enter the decline phase of the life cycle. A firm's business can decline because the design style of the firm has become dated. Or a major contributing member of the firm has moved on to start his or her own practice. Or the owners may have reached a point at which doing design and managing the office are no longer fun or a challenge. Some owners reach retirement age and desire to retire. And, of course, some firms simply decline due to poor management, poor marketing, and mediocre financial management.

It is important to note that these stages or cycles of the design firm are going to occur, regardless of the size of the firm. A sole practitioner is going to be as busy handling the business and management issues described as the owner and managers of a firm that adds employees. These issues become critical and complex as the owner decides to allow the company to grow. Planning for growth, regardless of what form that growth takes, is important to the success of the company.

Organizational Structure Within the Office

To some degree, organizational planning is obvious and necessary. Everyone knows that designers are one group of workers, that secretaries and clerks constitute another group, and that bookkeepers and warehouse and delivery people constitute still another. Authority must be delegated within these work groups in order that each group is managed properly. When the group is large enough, the staff will require titles that differentiate seniority and responsibility. Decisions as to who will manage each work group need to be established as the number of employees increases. The owners will need to evaluate each of the existing employees to see if any of them can take on the management responsibility. If the owners do not find any employees who can take on management responsibility, then they will need to determine what to do until individuals can be interviewed and hired.

Job descriptions need to be worked out for each different job or job level in the work groups. An employee handbook, describing specific personnel policies, also needs to be prepared. In addition, policies regarding work activities for each group needs to be established. And, assuming that this was not done in the past, a procedure for developing yearly marketing plans, financial plans, budgets, and strategic planning for future growth has to be established—overwhelming tasks for many business owners. Yet, these are things that must be done to assist the practice in continuing to achieve healthy, profitable growth.

How projects are managed administratively is an important part of the firm's organizational structure. When the sole practitioner obtained a client, it was very obvious who was responsible for all the design activities. When a partner joined the firm, each partner most likely was responsible for his or her own design project work. As design employees were added as assistants, some project responsibilities were delegated to the less experienced individuals. But what starts to happen when the company grows to include about six or eight designers/salespeople plus the owners? Who brings in new work? What happens to it once the client signs the contract? Who is responsible for all the design work? Who writes the specifications?

The answers to these questions and many more concerning the operations and procedures of the growing design firm need to be addressed. Like it or not, the bigger the design firms, the more structure will be required to keep the CAD plotters humming and design revenues coming in the door. Planning for the growth of the design practice is discussed in the next chapter. Job descriptions, the employee handbook, and other personnel issues are discussed in Chapters 11 and 12. Operational and project management matters are covered throughout the later chapters in this text.

Types of Business Organizations

The following discussion covers the primary business organizations that are found in the interior design profession. The purpose is to describe the different ways in which a practice can be organized. Of course, these brief descriptions are very general and should not be considered as the only ways in which an interior design business can be organized. They do not represent all the types of business organizations in which an interior designer may practice.

Residential Retail Stores

Retail stores that are involved in furniture sales and services often have a group of individuals who are strictly floor salespeople. These individuals work in the store and sell merchandise to clients who do not really need an interior designer's services. These clients are often just looking for one or two items to supplement or replace something in their homes or offices. If the retail store is large enough, these in-house salespeople may specialize in areas such as furniture, wall coverings, and floor treatments. In-house salespeople may or may not be trained as interior designers.

A second group in the retail store is comprised of interior designers. When clients require the services of an interior designer, they are referred to one of the people in this group. The interior designer is responsible for finding out what the client needs in the way of products and services, for discussing contracts (if the company charges a fee for design service), and for all the design work that needs to be done. In some situations, the designer may have an assistant (an entry-level interior designer) who will help him or her gather information, find appropriate products, and prepare necessary documents. However, the experienced interior designer is the primary person who deals with the client.

Office Furnishings Dealers

Office furnishings dealers, which generally are retail establishments, will have outside salespeople and a group of designers working for them. The salespeople are responsible for selling products, but their efforts often also bring in a major portion of the interior design work done by the company. When they find a client who also needs interior design services, they will alert the appropriate department.

In smaller firms, interior designers work out of an interiors department. In this situation, it is common for any one of the designers with the time and experience to handle a client to meet with the client and be responsible for the project. In larger firms, there might be an interiors department or even a separate, affiliated interior design company. In either of these cases, the interiors department is likely headed by a design director, and the salesperson contacts him or her concerning the project. The design director either visits with the client face-to-face or assigns one of the senior designers to the task. Whoever then meets with the client must get the complete picture of the project, determine if and what amount of fees will be charged, and determine who will be responsible for preparing all the design work.

In addition, some office furnishings dealers are organized based on a team concept. Designers are assigned to work with specific sales personnel or for a specific project manager most of the time. These team members work and coordinate their efforts to program, plan, and ultimately sell the project to the client.

In a small firm, a contract is prepared by the designer, who visits with the client. In larger firms, the contract is likely to be prepared by the design director or, with approval of the design director, by the project designer who has interviewed the client.

Independent Interior Design Firms

Independent interior design practices may or may not sell furnishings or have a retail showroom. Client contact, contract development, design, and project management in a small firm are all part of what each designer in the firm is expected to do. Most likely, the owner is also doing a lot of project work in addition to managing.

The larger firms will have various management and staff levels. Client contact is usually the responsibility of the owner, the senior designers, or possibly a design marketing manager. Senior designers are primarily responsible for managing projects and they often supervise a team of designers and support personnel during the completion of the project. In some firms, there are also individuals who have many specialized job functions, such as specification writers and renderers, who can free the project designers from such activities.

Architectural Firms

Over the years, many large architectural firms have added interior design services to their list of services. In many ways, the organization of an architectural firm is similar to the independent interior design firm. In this context, it commonly has one or more interior designers working on the projects obtained by the firm. In larger firms, interiors projects that are worked on independent of the architectural staff are sought. Interior designers in smaller firms may be responsible to an architectural services project manager or a senior architect. In larger firms, there may be a sufficient number of designers so that a design director or an interiors managing partner is required to supervise the interiors staff.

For the most part, these firms do not sell merchandise to clients. Although some firms find that this is a way to generate additional revenues for the firm, most focus on design and specification activities instead. Further discussion of the job classifications mentioned in this section can be found in Chapter 11.

Management

Management is the business function of a manager, who works to plan for and coordinate the myriad activities of a design office. More precisely, management means the effective direction of staff members and financial resources under a manager's control toward the goals and objectives that the owners of the firm have established.

Most interior designers do not receive much formal management training. Few schools require that interior design majors take a basic management course, despite the fact that many interior design students proclaim a desire to own their own business one day. The lack of understanding of the functions of management is unfortunate, since, even if the designer has no desire to own a practice, understanding the manager's job will help him or her be a better employee.

It does not really matter if the firm is a sole practitioner in which the owner is responsible for managing the operations of the company as well as for producing all the creative work for clients, or a large multidiscipline design firm with layers of employees. Managing the practice is a necessary activity for achieving success.

Managers (and, of course, the owner) must be able to see the big picture as well as be concerned about the details. What is meant by seeing the big picture? The manager must understand the workings of the entire company—all of its parts and responsibility centers. The big picture involves future plans for the company as well as its day-to-day operational issues. Future plans involve decisions that must be made as to whether the company will stay small or will grow, and will add employees, space, or open branch locations. As for the day-to-day operations, looking at the big picture means that the owner and manager are responsible not only for creating excellent design work but also for estimating fees properly to ensure that there will be sufficient revenues to pay salaries and expenses; marketing to bring in a continuing stream of clients; and motivating and, when necessary, reprimanding employees, regardless of their experience level. It also means encouraging employees to understand and assist with the big picture. Seeing the big picture means dealing as a professional with the firm's accountant, attorney, and all the other professionals that the firm needs from time to time, as well as making numerous decisions that affect the ongoing life of the design firm.

A big part of managing involves directing and motivating employees. People do this differently, based on their experience and style. There are two extremes of management style—autocratic (or authoritative) and democratic (or facilitative). If a manager uses an autocratic style, planning and decision making comes down from the manager to the staff. Very little staff input is requested or even tolerated. This autocratic style of management is often apparent in small firms, where the owner performs all the management functions. A sole proprietor is naturally very connected to making decisions as to how things will be done. After all, it is his or her business. However, it can also exist in larger firms that often require more structure and organization. Accepting a position with a company that has an autocratic manager does not mean that the manager is going to be a difficult person to work for. It probably will mean that the employees are expected to do the design work and project management the way in which the owner/manager dictates it, with little room for individual decision making and initiative.

In a company that is managed in a democratic or faciltative style, staff input is desired and responsibility is often given to staff members to accomplish certain managerial tasks. Employees are often empowered by the owner/manager to take responsibility for getting many kinds of tasks done in a reasonable way. *Empowerment* can be defined as "giving employees [who are] responsible for hands-on production or service activities the authority to make decisions or take action without prior approval" (Ivancevich, Lorenzi, and Skinner, 1994, p. 261). When employees are empowered, they make things happen themselves, without having to check with the boss. This responsibility is very satisfying for most interior designers, who want to "do it right" for the client and the job.

Sometimes a democratic style of management can be a problem for the design firm. If employees start making promises, for example, that cannot be kept by the firm, the reputation of the design firm diminishes. Or maybe the promises can be kept but only through the extraordinary efforts of some or all of the staff. It can be argued that extraordinary efforts can sometimes be justified for the goodwill that it can create with the client. However, if a firm begins to make extraordinary efforts frequently, then clients may begin to expect them. Now the extraordinary becomes practically impossible without adding employees or stretching workloads into overtime, adding to the overhead costs of the firm, which might be more than the efforts might actually bring in in terms of revenue or added projects.

A democratic type of manager can exist in any size firm, just as the autocratic type of manager can show up in any size firm. There is no way to predict which management style will exist in a particular interior design firm. Design employees prefer the democratic style of management, since most creative people like the freedom that this style of management provides. Knowing which style of management under which you work best can help you make a decision as to what firm you will accept an offer of employment. Knowing one's own style of management will also help when you are hiring employees.

Functions of Management

Managers perform four broad, generally accepted functions:

1. Planning
2. Organizing and directing
3. Decision making
4. Controlling

In *planning*, managers help chart the future direction of the firm. This involves research of staff capabilities and resources of the firm in its various segments. With this knowledge, managers prepare goals, objectives, and strategies. These goals, objectives, and strategies involve every aspect of the firm: its operations, including personnel and production; marketing; and financial planning. The preparation of the strategic plan is an example of this function. Since this function of management is so important to the ongoing success of an interior design practice, it will be discussed in depth in the next chapter.

The *organizing and directing* function occurs as the manager determines how best to use the resources at his or her disposal in order to perform the work activities of the firm. For example, if the firm is large enough so that a division of labor for completing projects is desired, the manager determines who will perform which tasks and how these tasks will interrelate.

Decision making is the act of making reasonable choices between the alternatives available. It is a part of all the other management functions and seems to occur almost all the time in the manager's day. For example, in firms where new projects are generated through a manager, salesperson, or marketing individual, the manager must decide which designer will be responsible for completing which project.

In the *control* function the manager monitors the activities of the interior design department and takes any necessary steps to ensure that the plans, policies, and decisions of the manager and the firm are being carried out. This is done, in part, when a manager reviews the kinds of reports that will be discussed in Chapter 16. It also occurs when the manager makes adjustments or develops new evaluative mechanisms to help the firm achieve its goals and objectives.

Although each of these functions are discussed separately, they are continually intermixed. Managers find themselves engaged in all these functions every day. This reality is part of the stress and excitement of the management role.

This section only briefly discusses the role that management plays in the practice of interior design. There are many fine books on management in libraries and bookstores. The reader may wish to review one or more of these books or even take a course in management to gain a more complete understanding of the management function.

Summary

All design firms go through stages of development and growth, from its inception until the owner passes the leadership on to someone else or the company dissolves. Growth, in whatever form it takes, puts different pressures on the owner and employees at each stage of the firm's development and as it moves from one stage to another. As an interior design firm grows, it becomes increasingly important for the owner(s) to review and define the organizational structure. Job responsibilities become more specialized and roles must be defined. Free-wheeling procedures of the early years do not provide an adequate framework for controlling project management and internal operations. Owners find it necessary to spend more time in managing the firm and its employees rather than in primarily creating design work for clients.

Unless one is content with a sole practitioner arrangement, in which a few projects per year bring in a limited amount of revenue, the design firm will grow. With that growth comes the need for management activities and skills, whether they are provided by the owner or employees. This chapter briefly described management responsibilities and functions as they relate to an interior design practice. Developing the design practice takes the business beyond the entrepreneurial beginnings discussed in Chapter 4. In some way, the interior design practice must be organized and managed as it moves into its next and subsequent stages. The chapters in the remainder of Part III, as well as those in Parts IV, V, and VI discuss many of these issues.

REFERENCES

Aaker, David A. 1995. *Developing Business Strategies*, 4th ed. New York: John Wiley.

Alderman, Robert L. 1997. *How To Prosper as an Interior Designer.* New York: John Wiley.

Applegate, Jane. 1995. *Strategies for Small Business Success.* New York: Plume.

Bennis, Warren. 1994. *On Becoming a Leader*. Reading, MA: Perseus.

Bennis, Warren, and Burt Nanus. 1985. *Leaders.* New York: Perennial Library.

Berk, Joseph, and Susan Berk. 1991. *Managing Effectively. A Handbook for First-Time Managers*. New York: Sterling Publishing.

Blanchard, Ken (with John P. Carlos and Alan Randolph). 1996. *Empowerment Takes More Than a Minute*. New York: MJF Books.

Covey, Stephen R. 1991. *Principle-Centered Leadership.* New York: Simon and Schuster.

Coxe, Weld. 1980. *Managing Architectural and Engineering Practice.* New York: John Wiley.

Cramer, James P. 1994. *Design Plus Enterprise.* Washington, DC: AIA Press.

DePree, Max. 1992. *Leadership Jazz.* New York: Currency/Doubleday.

———. 1989. *Leadership Is an Art.* New York: Currency/Doubleday.

Drucker, Peter F. 1995. *Managing in a Time of Great Change*. New York: Truman Talley.

Gerber, Michael E. 1995. *The E Myth Revisited.* New York: Harper Business.

Haviland, David, ed. 1994. *The Architect's Handbook of Professional Practice, Student ed.* Washington, DC: AIA Press.

Head, George O., Jr., and Jan Doster Head. 1988. *Managing, Marketing, and Budgeting for the A/E Office.* New York: Van Nostrand Reinhold.

Hisrich, Robert D., and Michael P. Peters. 1992. *Entrepreneurship*, 2nd ed. Homewood, IL: Richard D. Irwin.

Ivancevich, John M., Peter Lorenzi, Steven J. Skinner (with Philip B. Crosby). 1994. *Management: Quality and Competitiveness.* Burr Ridge, IL: Richard D. Irwin.

Johnson, Spencer, MD. 1998. *Who Moved My Cheese?* New York: G. P. Putnam.

Kotter, John P. 1996. *Leading Change.* Cambridge, MA: Harvard Business School Press.

Laurie, Donald L. 2000. *The Real Work of Leaders.* Cambridge, MA: Perseus Publishing.

Maister, David H. 1993. *Managing the Professional Service Firm*. New York: Free Press.

Maslow, Abraham H. (edited by Deborah C. Stephens). 2000. *The Maslow Business Reader*. New York: John Wiley.

———. 1998. *Maslow on Management.* New York: John Wiley.

Maxwell, John C., and Jim Dornan. 1997. *Becoming a Person of Influence*. Nashville, TN: Thomas Nelson.

Morgan, Jim. 1998. *Management for the Small Design Firm*. New York: Watson-Guptill.

Pressman, Andy. 1997. *Professional Practice 101: A Compendium of Business and Management Strategies in Architecture.* New York: John Wiley.

Siropolis, Nicholas C. 1990. *Small Business Management*, 4th ed. Boston, MA: Houghton Mifflin.

Stasiowski, Frank A. 1991. *Staying Small Successfully.* New York: John Wiley.

Wheatley, Margaret J. 1994. *Leadership and the New Science*. San Francisco, CA: Berrett-Koehler.

Chapter 10

The Planning Function

Regardless of the size of the interior design firms, some planning is essential for the ongoing life and success of the company. Planning is an everyday occurrence for designers as they work through the process of completing a design project. Too few design firm owners, however, formally plan for the continuation of their business.

Chapter 4 discussed the importance of creating a business plan for a new venture. A business plan helps the entrepreneur understand what kind of business he or she intends to create. It helps the entrepreneur think through what services to offer, how design services will be performed, where clients will come from, and make many other decisions to keep the company prosperous and healthy.

Completion of the business plan, however, is not the end of business planning.

Owners and managers of an interior design firm should plan for many aspects of the business. When new markets for the firm are desired, a marketing plan will be needed. As the company grows, a time may come when the firm must either move to larger quarters or purchase a building for the offices or store. A financial plan will be necessary at that juncture. And design firms, regardless of size, must plan for the future. A strategic plan that tries to determine that future is necessary.

This chapter will provide many good reasons for planning, even for the one-person design firm. It will discuss some of the typical, specialized plans used by businesses, with emphasis on strategic planning. It will also discuss budgeting as part of the planning process and concludes with information about the importance of measuring performance of the planning process.

Importance of Planning

Ongoing planning of a business is a necessity for any owner who wants the company to grow. In fact, planning is necessary even for the owner who wants the firm to stay small and not become a huge management headache. Many forces continually affect a business, especially the small business, and planning is an important way for the owner to keep control and be responsive and competitive in the marketplace. According to Ivancevich, Lorenzi, and Skinner (1994, p. 166), "Planning enables a firm to respond quickly to changing business demands, market conditions, and customer expectations."

There are several common reasons for planning for the future of a business. Figure 10-1 outlines those reasons, and a discussion of each follows below.

First, planning helps the owner clarify and define his or her mission or vision of the firm. This was discussed in Chapter 4; however, the definition of the interior design firm's mission bears repeating here. The mission statement is a philosophical statement that explains the direction and purpose of the design practice, its values, why it exists, and who it serves. Each year the owner and employees of a firm must revisit the mission statement to see if it is still valid with regard to the current direction of the design firm and how it relates to the future of the firm. How is this done?

The owner needs to do some thinking about what he or she perceives the firm is all about. He or she should also talk to former clients to get positive and negative feedback about the firm's performance and about their satisfaction with the firm. Employees should be encouraged to openly provide their comments about what the firm is all about to them. From this discussion and examination, a philosophy of the firm will emerge. Recall the sample mission statement provided in Figure 4-4.

Planning helps a firm set priorities. There are many demands placed upon a firm's time and resources—both human and financial. Only good planning will help a firm determine most effectively how to use its resources to the best advantage. Maybe the firm wants to produce a brochure to assist with marketing. Perhaps the company needs a new office space for its growing number of employees. Staying abreast of technology updates is a constant need for many design firms. Through the use of planning, the owner and staff determine which wants and needs are most important. Just like planning one's day based on the most important activities required, planning helps set the priorities to determine the items of greatest need.

Another good reason for planning is that it helps a firm with financial resource allocation. For example, there are tremendous pressures on design firms to utilize many kinds of computer software and technological aids. The need to use CAD, fax machines, pagers, cell phones, the Internet, specialized software for presentations, good project management, and accounting are just a small part of the technological demands placed on design businesses in the twenty-first century. Many firms, however, cannot afford all these aids at once. Planning provides a formalized mechanism for the owner to determine what is needed and when so that resources can be budgeted to obtain or achieve desired results.

Planning provides a yardstick to measure and evaluate success. A written plan makes it much easier to evaluate what was "planned" versus what "actually" happened. Taking the time to create a plan, put it on paper, and implement it takes a great deal of time. A year later, the owner and employees

- To clarify and define the company's mission or vision
- To help set priorities
- To help with financial resource allocation
- To provide a yardstick to measure and evaluate success
- To integrate management and employee thinking for a common purpose
- To avoid failure

FIGURE 10-1. Typical reasons to plan for the future of a business.

can then carefully look at what was done and what was not accomplished as they prepare to plan for the next year. Formal evaluation does not have to wait for a year, however. Accountants suggest that their clients look at quarterly or even monthly variance reports. *Variance analysis* shows budgeted and actual financial performance in many ways as well as the variance, or the deviation, from the budgeted amounts. The variances can be immediately evaluated so that negatives can be dealt with quickly before they become financial problems. The same concept can be applied to the business plan, with periodic reviews scheduled to determine success (or not) against plans. Certain activities, such as marketing efforts, might need to be evaluated quarterly, while other items can be put off for a year. Variance analysis and reports are discussed further in Chapter 16.

Planning helps to integrate management and employee thinking so that they both have a common purpose. It has been proven time and time again that small businesses are more likely to be successful when the employees really feel that they are a part of the business. This means that they are taken seriously by the owner, their input is respected, and they are made to feel that they have a stake in the firm beyond their expected work responsibilities. Involving employees in the planning process helps create this common purpose and feeling that they are important to the overall success of the design firm. When the employees are involved in planning, it is also much more likely that they will work to achieve the goals of the company. If the owner hands down the goals without having requested any employee input, employees may be resentful and may assume that their ideas are not wanted, with the probable result that the plans will not be achieved or the employees will leave the company.

The primary reason it is important for any size business to use planning on a periodic basis is that businesses that fail to plan are more likely to fail. Managing by the "seat of the pants" often leads to difficulty in handling problems that occur. Not knowing where the company is headed can lead to disjointed efforts, with confused priorities. Planning helps the design firm determine a destination and forces the owner and staff to create a road map of how to get to that destination in a logical manner.

Kinds of Plans

A plan can be developed for many specific areas of the business. Large companies have a human resources or personnel plan in place. They might also have a capital spending plan, which will help them budget funds to purchase their own office building rather than leasing space. Many firms develop a marketing plan, perhaps to enter a new market with the company's design services.

An annual plan is developed by many companies to establish goals and objectives for the coming year. This plan is replaced, for the most part, by the strategic plan. A strategic plan primarily focuses on the long term—three to five years into the future. However, many businesses create a "rolling strategic plan" that takes into consideration the current (or short-term) as well as the long-term goals of the company. This section focuses on the strategic planning process. Marketing plans are discussed briefly in this chapter but are presented in more depth in Chapter 21.

Strategic Planning

Strategic planning is a process for creating a specific written vision for the design firm and its future. It is comprehensive and future oriented, requiring the business owner and employees to predict what they would like to see for the business concerning the many operational and organizational areas of the design firm in the future. Goals and objectives are set for a minimum of one full year into the future, with an emphasis on two to three years ahead. Figure 10-2 represents a partial strategic plan.

A common component of the strategic plan is the mission statement. When the strategic planning process is begun, one of the early tasks is to revisit and possibly revise the company's mission statement to accurately reflect the current situation and purpose of the design firm. Many texts on how to go about making a strategic plan suggest writing it before completing the rest of the work of the plan. Others put it off until the end. The author feels that drafting a mission statement at the beginning of the process is useful but that a finalized statement at the beginning is difficult to achieve. The in-depth analysis that a firm should do as part of the strategic planning process often leads design firms in slightly different directions than might even be expected. If a company's mission statement exists, the planning process should begin by reviewing this statement and getting a feeling for what, if any, of it remains valid. Then the planning team should wait to finalize the mission statement until the rest of the planning process is complete.

The first important step is arguably the most important—analysis of the firm's current condition. It is very difficult to determine what the possibilities for the firm are until the owner and employees know what they can do right now. By carefully looking at all the forces that affect the design firm, the planning team can make better judgments for the future. The most commonly used method of analysis is called *SWOT analysis*. SWOT stands for strengths, weaknesses, opportunities, and threats.

SWOT analysis, when taken seriously and constructively, can result in much useful planning information. It is important to consider carefully a firm's strengths, for, as Peter Drucker points out, strength analysis "shows where there is need to improve or upgrade existing strengths and where new strengths have to be acquired" (Drucker, 1995, p. 43). Unfortunately, it is common for firms to spend too much time on lauding their strengths and seeing how "great" they already are rather than spending enough time on their weaknesses. It is even more important to know what can't be done or what is being done in an inferior manner. In addition, SWOT is sometimes criticized because responses

Goal 2: Increase marketing and promotional efforts in order to create potential client awareness of Johnson/Clark Designs.

- **Strategy 1:** Review existing promotional materials.
  - Tactic 1: Collect copies of promotional materials used in last three years.
  - Tactic 2: Categorize materials into types of promotional tools.
- **Strategy 2**: Identify potential venues for speaking programs.
  - Tactic 1: Develop database of local target client professional associations.
  - Tactic 2: Develop database of target client professional associations in the three adjoining states.
  - Tactic 3: Develop database of any other possible clubs or groups that might host a program.
- **Strategy 3**: Brainstorm with staff for at least six possible topics for programs.
- **Strategy 4:** Identify potential venues for informational and educational articles to show our company's expertise.
  - Tactic 1: Obtain copies of all local magazines and other print media in our local market.
  - Tactic 2: Obtain copies of local magazines in major cities of the three adjoining states.

FIGURE 10-2. A portion of a strategic plan for a small interior design practice.

can be either too harsh or too meaningless to have validity. However, if taken seriously, it does help firms carefully look at what it can do and how it operates in order to create the basis for future goals and objectives.

SWOT analysis is done by preparing statements that analyze the internal and external forces and activities of the design firm. Internal forces are those within the firm that the firm can control. They would include such things as the services the firm offers, financial resources, project management, and the way in which the firm markets itself. External forces are those forces outside the design firm that are essentially out of the design firm's control, such as government regulations, competition, technology, economic forecasts, and the firm's customers.

The internal factors are those that are related to the strengths and weaknesses of the firm (in SWOT analysis), while the external factors are the opportunities for, and threats to, the firm (in SWOT analysis). Examples of these are shown in Figure 10-3. Opportunities and threats are often harder to determine, because they are factors that are "outside" the business. Firms that are busy keeping up with its current day-to-day practice often miss seeing potential opportunities for, or threats to, the practice. An opportunity might be a contact with the real estate brokerage company that is helping a corporation locate housing for its headquarters' personnel's move into the design firm's city. A definite threat would be new legislation limiting aspects of traditional interior design practice, such as requiring contractors' licenses for supervision of materials installation.

This kind of formal analysis helps the design firm to understand what it can do, what it wants to do, and what it must work on to improve present services so that the firm will be in a position to offer additional services. It also helps define outside influences on the firm that can affect its mix of services and its ability to offer services to specific groups of clients.

Strengths

Our firm is well known.
Our firm has a strong financial position.
Our firm has a focused client target market.

Weaknesses

Our firm receives too many customer service complaints.
Some support staff members have a bad attitude.
None of our designers are NCIDQ qualified.

Opportunities

Angel Carpeting is offering co-op advertising.
The studio will be relocating to an uptown location in order to increase our potential for high-end clients.
A major competitor has overextended itself financially.

Threats

Three strong competitors have moved into our market area.
A former employee has taken away two former repeat clients in the last six months.
State licensing will be required for supervision of installations.

FIGURE 10-3. Examples of items that might be included in a SWOT anlaysis.

SWOT analysis can be started by reviewing the skills and interests of the owner and all the staff. A firm cannot seek hospitality projects, for example, if no one has experience in that kind of field. Of course, the analysis must look at how the firm operates as well and must evaluate the strengths and weaknesses of the operations and processes of the company. If customer service has been notoriously bad, this factor will not help the company when it seeks to obtain a new market, like hospitality design. At the same time, a firm that wants to enter the hospitality market needs to know if that market exists for the company, based on economic forecasts, the competition, and a possible customer base for that kind of design service. These are important issues that can only be resolved through external analysis and research.

External analysis often involves the use of primary and secondary sources of information. The easiest sources of information to obtain are from secondary sources. *Secondary sources* are generally those sources of information that are already in existence or are produced by others. These include such things as government, trade association, and general business publications such as the *Wall Street Journal*. Local business reports in newspapers, chamber of commerce publications, and reporting services such as the "McGraw Hill Dodge Reports" are other secondary sources of information. Any information that the firm gets from some source other than its own work is considered a secondary source.

These publications give the design firm various forms of information, such as general economic trends and the announcement of new firms opening in the local area. Local, glossy consumer magazines and chamber of commerce reports present economic outlooks and forecasts, show increases or losses in population, and provide business and demographic information. All this gives valuable hints as to potential clients for the residential and commercial interior designer.

Primary sources are sources of information that provide specifics from people who may have direct knowledge about the information being sought. Some scientific research methods used to gather primary data are surveys or questionnaires, observation, and interviews. The most common method of gathering primary data used by design firms is a casual interview, or, more precisely, casual conversation.

Some means of obtaining information through the use of casual conversation include "picking the brain" of past clients, meeting with design professionals at conferences and seminars, and talking with professionals such as architects, contractors, and developers. In addition, contacts with government agency employees, manufacturers' representatives, vendors and subcontractors, and even employees of the firm will provide information that can be used in developing a marketing plan.

Another relatively easy form of primary research—observation—can be done whenever anyone who is working for the firm is driving around town. Everyone should keep his or her eyes open for new construction, remodeling, or work in progress related to the interior design firm's practice. This kind of observation might not bring an immediate lead but could result in a contract at a later time.

An expensive form of primary marketing analysis is the formal questionnaire or survey. Surveys may be conducted by mail, by telephone, or in person. The decision as to which survey to use involves the size of the audience, the length of the survey, and the immediacy of response. Although surveys can be helpful to the design firm for some specific kinds of research information, the cost and time involved usually limit its use to large practices.

When all the analysis and research have been completed, it is time for the design firm to begin developing the actual strategic plan. Goals and objectives are developed for as many operational areas of the company as are practical. In the best case, considerations are made for such areas as marketing, project management, operational management, finances, and personnel. If this is done, all areas of the practice are planned for the future.

Establishing goals and objectives is an important aspect of financial and overall management control. An organizations' *goals* are broad statements of what the firm wishes to achieve, without regard to any time limit. One of the goals for an interior design firm might be "to become the premier residential design firm in the city." *Strategies* are specific statements that describe how the firm plans to achieve a goal. They can be combined with time limits. Strategies for our sample goal might be, "During the next year, we will refine our resource library to obtain materials on the highest quality merchandise." Also, "The owner will begin submitting articles on interior design to a local shelter magazine to gain publicity."*

To further ensure successful accomplishment of these goals and objectives, more specific tactics must be established. These *tactics* are highly specific actions that are needed to accomplish the strategies. To continue with our example, a tactic might be, "During the next three months, the owner will schedule meetings with the editors of three local magazines concerning a column on design." All the goals, strategies, and tactics of the strategic plan must relate back to the firm's mission statement.

Marketing Plan

The marketing plan is one of the very specific plans that most firms develop to one extent or another. Whether the firm is large or small, having a detailed and specific marketing plan helps that firm understand what it is about and what its market is. This is because marketing plans commonly involve thinking through the marketing efforts of the firm, whether it is a large or small firm, by analyzing what is commonly referred to as the four "Ps" of marketing: product, price, place, and promotion. Briefly, for an interior designer, the product refers to the services being offered as well as the mix of actual furnishings, fixtures, and equipment specified and/or sold to the client. Price, of course, investigates and establishes how and how much the firm will charge for its "products." Place refers to where the clients are for the specific services the design firm wishes to offer. And promotion refers to the ways in which the firm plans to make itself known to potential clients. The marketing plan is discussed in more depth in Chapter 21.

Budgeting

Budgeting, which is a part of the management planning function, involves creating annual managerial goals that can be expressed in specific, quantitative monetary terms. Budget is defined as "a predetermined amount of resources linked to an activity" (Ivancevich, Lorenzi, and Skinner, 1994, p. 183). Budgeting encourages the owner and manager to plan for the financial needs of the company in a thoughtful and organized way. It helps them control the budget in a way that is proactive rather than reactive. When there is no plan or budget, owners must "react" to what happens to them. This is thought of as "stamping-out-the-fires" management. Using a budget provides just one more opportunity for success. Formal budgeting also permits the discovery of

* Shelter magazines are generally considered to be those sold to the general public on newstands or by subscription such as *Better Homes and Gardens*.

potential problem areas and provides the opportunity to determine a course of action prior to their occurrence. Finally, budgeting focuses the efforts of the whole organization toward the firm's annual goals by coordinating all the various individuals' and groups' efforts.

Budgeting that is related to the planning process can be done as plans are developed. However, it is more common for budgeting to be done when the goals, strategies, and tactics are determined and prioritized. This timing makes it easier for the owner and manager to estimate the financial and even human resources necessary to accomplish important, agreed-upon goals and, if necessary, make adjustments to them.

It is generally agreed that strategies and tactics are the items that receive budget consideration, whereas goals are budgeted based on the total cost of the strategies and tactics that are needed to achieve the goals. Each strategy and tactic should be reviewed, and preliminary cost estimates for each item should be established. Revenue production strategies and tactics also should be budgeted. It is just as important for the firm to create revenue budgets as it is for the firm to determine what level of revenue is needed and is possible to accomplish for all the items that require "costs."

By reviewing figures of prior years, owners and managers can begin to forecast what will likely happen in the coming year (see Figure 10-4). With

Design Department Proposed Budget 200x

Revenue		
From Fees	420,000	500,000
Cost of Sales		
Direct Labor	271,875	290,000
Supplies	8,500	7,000
Reproduction Expense	9,350	7,500
Telephone (long distance)	3,700	4,800
Total Cost of Sales	293,425	309,300
Gross Margin	126,575	190,700
Total Cost of Sales	293,425	309,300
Gross Margin	126,575	190,700
Operating Expenses For Design Dept.		
Salaries	61,990	84,000
Payroll Taxes	16,000	24,000
Group Insurance	1,750	1,700
Promotion	2,750	2,000
Travel Reimbursements	6,800	7,000
Supplies and Postage	6,300	6,000
Professional Dues	3,000	2,500
Printing and Reproduction	8,400	10,000
Technical Consultants	12,900	5,000
Total Operating Expenses	119,890	142,200
Net Income	6,685	48,500
Profit to Sales	2%	10%

FIGURE 10-4. A simple budget report.

further analysis, budgeting for what the company will actually attempt to accomplish becomes more realistic. However, budgeting should not be done by merely adding a modest percentage of increase for the coming year. Although this might work for some expenses that do not increase or decrease from month to month and year to year, it does not provide an accurate budget for expanded activities, like marketing in a new geographic market, or for new activities, such as hosting an educational seminar for potential clients. It is better to develop more accurate cost estimates when the firm creates the budget.

The simplest and most common method of budgeting in many firms is to look at figures of the prior year and then, by applying various percentages of increase or decrease, come up with a new budget. This can work fairly well in normal circumstances but could be disastrous in a slow economy or during a period in which the economy goes down or becomes volatile for some reason. The past is always a good starting point, but it should be used in conjunction with good research and planning.

When totally new tactics are called for as part of the plan, the firm, naturally, will have to do some research through appropriate consultants to determine budget figures. For example, if the plan includes developing a web site, it will be necessary to check with web site designers to establish a budget for the design of the web site as well as the ongoing costs of a web master and provider fees.

Some firms use the zero-based budgeting method as their starting point. This budgeting method received a lot of attention during the presidential administration of Jimmy Carter. Zero-based budgeting assumes that each year the managers of the firm start with a zero budget level and must justify all costs, as if the department or activity were starting new. This means that no costs are considered as ongoing from year to year. It also means that the firm must accurately forecast revenues to cover and, of course, to exceed the amount of the expenses.

Measuring Performance

Inherent in all types of business plans are the means of measuring performance. Having goals and objectives with no way of determining success results in a meaningless expenditure of energy in the planning and writing process.

Performance evaluation not only is part of the individual employees' productivity results but also relates to all other planning. Such things as whether the job descriptions were actually written and were adhered to during hiring, whether the newly purchased truck was cost-effective, and whether projects were obtained from the hospital market are all part of the performance evaluation portion of the planning process.

One measure of performance is variance analysis, which was mentioned earlier in this chapter. Another measure of performance can be accomplished by doing postproject reviews at the conclusion of all significant projects. This can be very formalized, and a standard report form can be created by the design owner in order to obtain such information as revenue dollars and reports on expenses, or it can be informal. The numerical/financial data can also be supplemented with a short narrative review of the project. This postproject review is discussed further in Chapter 31.

It does not matter if one is monitoring a marketing plan, a personnel plan, a strategic plan, or any other type of plan. Stopping to review progress is essential to good business practice. A large firm may not do a review until a full year has gone by if there are plenty of staff members who are keeping track of what is happening in the company. A small design firm needs to look at the big picture painted by the plan a little more often—at least twice a year. Scheduling a half-day to review progress or the lack thereof is just as important as developing the plan in the first place.

Summary

Planning is not only an important management function but also a necessary function of management which helps an interior design firm owner and possibly managers achieve success. Owners generally know where they want to go with their business, though, of course, some do not! But far fewer think about how they are going to achieve their business goals. Planning can create a road map to help the firm achieve its goals, whether those goals are lofty or not.

Plans can be developed for very specialized purposes, such as marketing the design firm into a new type of design service or a new geographic area. They can be far-reaching, such as looking into the future via a strategic plan.

This chapter reviewed the several different types of plans that commonly are used by an interior design practice and discussed the planning process, with a focus on the strategic plan. It also discussed the importance of putting budget figures to the plans and monitoring the progress of the plan. A plan will not guarantee overwhelming success for the firm, but it will provide an important basis for proper decision making in the present and the future.

REFERENCES

Aaker, David A. 1995. *Developing Business Strategies*, 4th ed. New York: John Wiley.

Aaker, David A, V. Kumar, and George S. Day. 1998. *Marketing Research*, 6th ed. New York: John Wiley.

American Society of Interior Designers. "Strategic Planning for the Small Design Practice." *ASID Professional Designer.* March/April 1998.

Anthony, Robert N., John Dearden, and Norton M. Redford. 1984. *Management Control Systems*, 5th ed. Homewood, IL: Richard D. Irwin.

Bangs, David H., Jr. 1998. *The Market Planning Guide*, 5th ed. Chicago, IL: Upstart Publishing.

———. 1995. *The Business Planning Guide*, 7th ed. Chicago, IL: Upstart Publishing.

Berk, Joseph, and Susan. 1991. *Managing Effectively. A Handbook for First-Time Managers*. New York: Sterling Publishing.

Collins, James C., and Jerry I. Porras. "Building Your Company's Vision." *Harvard Business Review*. September/October 1996, 65–77.

Cook, Kenneth J. 1994. *AMA Complete Guide to Strategic Planning for Small Business.* Chicago, IL: American Marketing Association.

Cowley, Michael, and Ellen Domb. 1997. *Beyond Strategic Vision*. Boston, MA: Butterworth-Heinemann.

Czinkota, Michael R., Masaaki Kotabe, and David Mercer. 1997. *Marketing Management: Text and Cases*. Cambridge, MA: Blackwell Business.

DePree, Max. 1989. *Leadership Is an Art.* New York: Doubleday.

Drucker, Peter F. 1995. *Managing in a Time of Great Change.* New York: Truman Talley/Dutton.

———. 1992. *Managing for the Future: The 1990s and Beyond.* New York: Truman Talley Books.

Frey, Fred L., and Charles R. Stoner. 1995. *Strategic Planning for the New and Small Business*. Chicago, IL: Upstart Publishing.

Graham, John W., and Wendy C. Havlick. 1994. *Mission Statements*. New York: Garland.

Ivancevich, John M., Peter Lorenzi, and Steven J. Skinner (with Philip B. Crosby). 1994. *Management. Quality and Competitiveness.* Burr Ridge, IL: Richard D. Irwin.

Johnson, Spencer, MD. 1998. *Who Moved My Cheese?* New York: Putnam.

Kotter, John P. 1996. *Leading Change.* Boston, MA: Harvard Business School Press.

Maister, David H. 1993. *Managing the Professional Service Firm.* New York: Free Press.

McCarthy, E. Jerome, and William D. Perreault, Jr. 1993. *Basic Marketing,* 11th ed. Homewood, IL: Richard D. Irwin.

McKenzie, Ronald A. 1992. *Successful Business Plans for Architects.* New York: McGraw-Hill.

Mintzberg, Henry. 1994. *The Rise and Fall of Strategic Planning.* New York: Free Press.

Morrisey, George L. 1996. *Morrisey on Planning: A Guide to Long-Range Planning.* San Francisco, CA: Jossey-Bass.

Piotrowski, Christine M. "Strategic Planning for the Small Design Practice." *ASID Professional Designer.* March/April 1998, 18–21.

Rice, Craig S. 1990. *Strategic Planning for the Small Business.* Holbrook, MA: Bob Adams.

Stasiowski, Frank A. 1991. *Staying Small Successfully.* New York: John Wiley.

U.S. Small Business Administration. *Developing a Strategic Business Plan,* No. MP21.

Zikmund, William G. 1994. *Business Research Methods,* 4th ed. Fort Worth, TX: Dryden Press.

Chapter 11

Personnel Management

The creative professional can be a challenge to manage. Interior designers, generally are self-motivated and do not need or like someone to stand over their shoulders to be sure they are working. For many, the creative process is personal and individual. Yet, the interior designer must often work as part of a team. Job satisfaction comes from making a client happy with the design created by the designer.

Personnel issues are important to any business organization. Individuals enter design professions for many reasons, which are different than for other professions. Yet designers wish to be treated fairly, receive adequate compensation, and be given greater responsibility, as would any professional in the twenty-first century. Thus, it has become increasingly important for employers to be concerned with employer/employee relationships and personnel policies. Although there is no documentation concerning the number of law suits filed that involve personnel issues within the interior design industry, it is certainly time for employers to be more formalized and careful in their dealings with employees.

For the owner and/or manager, processes that formalize personnel management can assist in the hiring, development, and retention of effective employees. Formalized processes also protect the employer should employees feel they have been treated unfairly. At the same time, formal personnel processes help employees understand what is expected of them and that the design firm intends to treat its employees fairly.

The areas of personnel management discussed in this chapter are job classifications, job descriptions, the performance evaluation, the employee handbook, compensation, and fringe benefits. Other legal considerations of personnel management, including the concepts of employment at will and employment contracts, will be discussed in Chapter 12.

Job Classifications

As was seen in Chapter 9, as an interior design firm grows, the need for structure and organization increases. Organization of office procedures and defining project responsibility becomes more critical when the design department has several interior designers who have varying amounts of experience and expertise. This structuring of job responsibilities leads to defining job classifications or job titles within the various responsibility centers of the firm. In a large firm, the need for layers of responsibility becomes obvious.

The chain of command or, more formally, the organizational structure, helps everyone in the organization understand what are the formal communication patterns. The *organizational chart* is a graphic representation of the chain of command. A formalized chain of command within an organizational chart rarely exists in smaller design firms. An informal structure representing the same concepts, however, does.

Even though it is commonly found that the "real chain of command" does not exactly reflect the organizational chart, larger organizations find it useful to create such a chart in order to show the formal flows of official communication. Figure 11-1 shows an organizational chart that includes the various job classifications. The descending order of responsibility reflects no specific organization and merely describes the most common levels. Staff positions such as bookkeeper, secretary, delivery person, and office manager are not included in this discussion.

Principal

A principal is a job classification or a title often used by the owner of the interior design firm. Some owners use the title president. Of course, there can be more than one owner. In some firms, the principal can be joined in upper-level management by a partner. A partner can be an owner or an upper-level employee who may or may not have some financial vested interest in the company.

Principals and partners are the most direct link to clients, since they are responsible for the vast majority of initial client contacts. They are often involved in presentations to clients to obtain design work for the office. Naturally, they also provide the vision and direction of the company. The amount of time they actually spend on designing a project, however, varies, based on the actual organization of the design practice. Principals in large design firms find that their design input is reduced, because they are faced with a large number of administrative and marketing responsibilities. Others find it important to

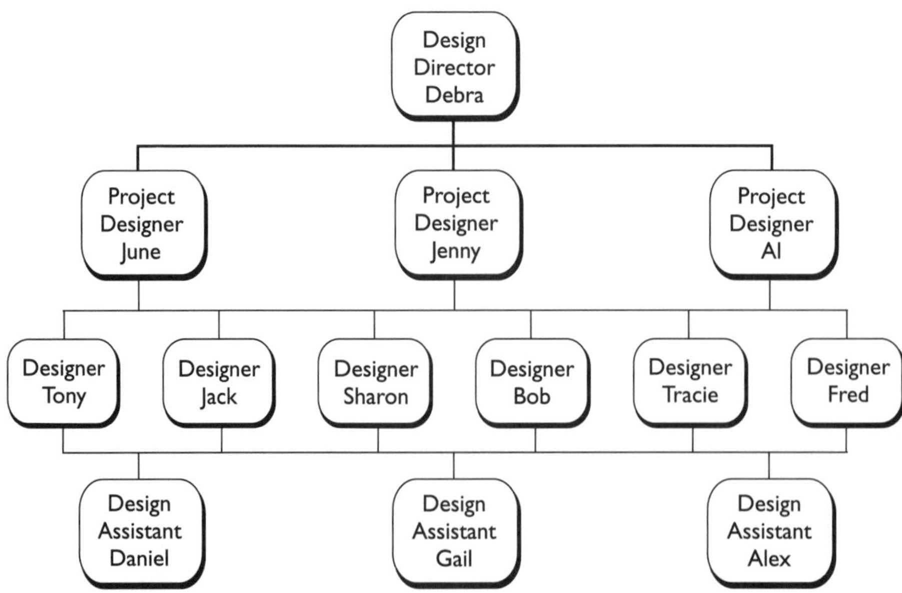

FIGURE 11-1. A sample organizational chart for an interior design firm.

retain design input in projects and hire others to take on many day-to-day management or administrative responsibilities.

Should a principal or partner be involved in a design project, his or her time would be billed at the highest rate quoted by the firm. The principal as a designer would be supervising project managers and other design staff in the execution of the needed design work.

Design Director

Below the principal on the organizational chart for an interior design department is the title of the first level of managers. The job title might be design director, vice president of design, design manager, or perhaps some other title indicating this person's leadership role in the design firm. This person can have many different job responsibilities, depending on the actual size of the firm, but usually the job responsibilities include (1) administration, (2) marketing, and (3) design.

Administrative duties include all the management functions. Planning, hiring and firing, assigning work, and preparing contracts are some of these. In addition, the design director is responsible for preparing various management control reports, establishing policies, and attending management meetings. The training and development of the design staff is an important part of the design director's responsibilities.

Depending on the roles of the principal, the most important marketing duties of the design director are establishing client contacts and making subsequent presentations to prospective clients. The design director is often involved in the development of marketing tools, such as brochures. In many firms, the design director is also the company's liaison with the public. And, of course, he or she is involved in planning and participating in the development of marketing plans.

The design responsibility of the design director may be minimal in large, very active design firms, or it may be an important part of the manager's responsibility in a small firm. By design responsibility, we mean that the design director is in charge of design projects when he or she plays the role of the project designer. In this situation, the design director makes client contacts, prepares design documents (or supervises others in their preparation), prepares and reviews purchase orders, and makes himself or herself available for supervision during the installation phase of a project.

In addition, the design director, with guidance from the principal, sets the minimum standards for all design work that leaves the office by reviewing projects during their progress and before they are presented to clients. In this second role, the design director remains involved with project activities without actually doing them.

In very large design firms, the leadership role might be broken down into two or more areas. The design administration and marketing group might be responsible for all administrative functions, such as hiring, and all marketing activities of the interior design department. The design production group might be responsible for ensuring the quality of project execution. It would be common for these two groups to be headed by different individuals, who would report to a design department head, such as a vice president.

Project Manager

The second level of management responsibility in larger firms comes under such titles as project manager, senior designer, and senior project designer. Project manager is the title that is commonly used today for interior designers who have primary responsibility for a design project. In large firms, where the design director is primarily involved in administration, this position becomes the key design and client contact level. Project managers commonly have five or more years of professional experience and have substantially developed the technical design skills needed by the hiring firm. They are also required to have good communication skills when dealing with clients and other designers.

The project manager is the lead designer and may supervise other designers. As the lead designer, he or she meets with clients to determine their needs, prepares or directs others in the completion of design documents, and is responsible for order entry supervision and installation supervision. Depending on the size of the firm, the project manager may not be very involved in developing design concepts. Rather, many project managers find themselves primarily involved in administrative management of the project, giving minimal input into the actual design. In some firms, the project manager is required to market the firm's design services in order to obtain new projects and may even be required to negotiate the design contract.

Designer

At the next level of the organizational chart, professional employees are given such titles as designer or staff designer. Designers commonly are required to have two or more years of professional experience and well-developed technical design skills. On large projects, these individuals work under the supervision of the project manager. They may be involved in client interviewing and any information gathering conducted by the project manager; they may be asked to prepare preliminary drafting and other documentation and preliminary product specification, in addition to other tasks assigned by the project manager. On smaller projects, they may be responsible for all phases of the project, from obtaining needed information from the client to being responsible for installation supervision. Administrative responsibility is limited.

Design Assistant

The entry-level position for most firms is commonly called design assistant,* or junior designer. Entry level means that these individuals have little professional experience other than as interns. They work under the direction of a more experienced designer for one or more years. The kinds of work performed most commonly are drafting, preparation of sample boards, preparation of specifications lists for furniture and furnishings, perhaps some installation supervision, maintenance of the library, and other tasks assigned by the design director. After working for several months in a smaller firm, the design assistant usually is given full responsibility for small-sized projects. As in the case of the designer, administrative responsibility include only time and record keeping for his or her own efforts.

Other Job Classifications

Depending on the actual interior design practice and size of the firm, there may be some additional, specialized job classifications. In many large interior design offices, the CAD operator is a common job classification. As most readers know by now, a CAD operator has experience in the use of computer-aided design equipment and software. Depending on how a CAD operator is used in the firm, the person may be a trained interior designer or a computer operator. The person may serve in a separate capacity in the firm or may be a part of the interiors department.

In large office furnishings dealers, commercial interior design firms, and architectural firms, a job classification called space planner might exist. A space planner is responsible for planning the overall use of space for a client or for tenant improvement work, but not for the specification of furniture and

* Note that FIDER defines a design assistant differently from the way in which it is used here.

furnishings. The documents that he or she prepares are working drawings and needed specifications for construction. In some firms, the space planner may have a job title of TI specialist (TI stands for tenant improvement).

Another specialized job classification is specification writer or estimator. As the title implies, this individual is responsible only for the preparation of finished specification documents. This job classification is most commonly found in very large interior design or architectural firms.

A job classification that can be a specialization or an expected responsibility of any designer is a renderer or a graphics designer. A renderer or graphics designer has, as a major responsibility, the production of perspectives and colored renderings of the interiors designed by the interior design staff. A graphics designer is also responsible for the design of graphics for such things as business cards and brochures, presentations, and presentation graphics for clients, as well as for similar graphics for the interior design firm. Only larger firms have specialized renderers and graphics designers.

In large design firms, one nondesign staff position that is fairly common is business development specialist. Some firms refer to this as marketing director. An individual with this title may or may not be a trained interior designer but generally has an educational background or extensive success in business development. The business development specialist exclusively works to identify and qualify potential clients, as well as assists the principal and project designers in developing presentations to obtain contracts. An additional responsibility of the business development specialist often includes being the liaison between the design firm and public relations and/or advertising specialists hired by the design firm.

Job Descriptions

The *job description* communicates the qualifications, skills, and responsibilities of each job classification within the firm. Many design firms with five or fewer employees rarely have job descriptions. In fact, many large design firms, especially those that have experienced rapid growth, often do not have job descriptions either. However, as the firm grows, job descriptions can help to organize and control growth, as well as help to organize the work in the office and keep work on track. Job descriptions should be provided to individuals when they are seriously being considered for a position or upon being hired. Job descriptions also should be available to existing employees so that they can see what qualifications and skills are required of higher-level positions.

Job descriptions do not need to be elaborate. The small firm may find a simple structure, such as the one shown in Figure 11-2, satisfactory. Larger firms may find that detailed job descriptions are of greater value (see Figure 11-3). Job descriptions are usually prepared in outline form. They should contain statements that are specific enough to differentiate among individuals, yet broad enough to allow the manager some flexibility in hiring. The content of the job descriptions must be kept current and complete. They also must accurately reflect the desired skills required to perform the responsibilities of the positions. As much as possible, the descriptions should be stated in measurable terms to aid in performance evaluation.

Job descriptions should contain statements related to qualifications, skills required, and responsibilities, and they may contain statements related to the job. The qualifications section outlines the minimal educational requirements. This section also specifies the minimum amount of work experience in years

Interior Design Consultant
Creative Design Consultants, Inc.

This job classification requires that the employee assist the owner with projects. The employee is also expected to bring his or her own clients to the company.

Responsibilities:

Assist clients.
Evaluate and specify products to meet client needs.
Prepare layouts, plans, and other documents as required.
Prepare color boards.
Obtain signed sales orders.
Prepare cost estimates for all work required on a project.
Complete all required purchase orders.
Coordinate installation and delivery.
Share in housekeeping chores in the office/studio/warehouse.

Qualifications:

Bachelors Degree in interior design. Associate degree in interior design with work experience in interior design would substitute for a college degree.

Work Experience:

Minimum of two years actual sales and interior design experience required.

Skills:

Portfolio should show training in color coordination, product coordination, drafting, and the ability to space plan.
Knowledge of residential products and how to specify those products.
Knowledge and familiarity with AutoCAD 2000.
Proven sales record.

FIGURE 11-2. An example of a basic job description. This example might be most useful to a small, residential interior design firm.

that is required. Statements such as "graduation from at least a four-year college or university, with a major in interior design" sets one of the minimum criteria for an interior design position.

In the section concerning skills required, statements related to any specific technical abilities, along with any skills or abilities of a general nature, are outlined. Although this section often comes second in a job description, it is often easier to finish writing this section after the responsibilities section has been completed. In any case, it is important for the skills required to correlate with the responsibilities expected and the qualifications demanded. These skills and general abilities should be listed in the order of their importance in the job. For a firm that is involved in commercial interior design, drafting skill may be of primary importance for an entry-level design assistant, and therefore it should be listed first. For a firm that is involved in residential interior design, color coordination may be of primary importance for an entry-level design assistant.

The responsibilities section must be detailed enough so that the individual in the position knows what is expected of him or her. Large corporations, which have a great deal of experience in the preparation of job descriptions, often have very detailed outlines of responsibilities. Interior design firms, which have

Job Description

Job Title: Senior Designer
Reports To: Design Director
Pay Rate: Salary

Responsibilities:
The following describes the essential responsibilities of this job classification. Other duties may be assigned from time to time by the Design Director or Owner.

- Determine scope of services required for projects.
- Assist Design Director with development of design contracts and project scheduling.
- Responsible for all phases and activities of design projects assigned, including but not limited to programming and data gathering, space planning, furniture layouts, development of contract drawings, product specification, budgeting, presentations to the client, and job site supervision.
- Maintain client confidence and good client relations.
- Supervise design team members to complete projects. Team members will be assigned by Design Director.
- Maintain client files for projects assigned, including all correspondence, drawings, and other materials, as described in our standard client file processes booklet.
- Keep Design Director informed of project status on all projects and other duties assigned.
- Attend all in-house meetings and programs.
- Be available to meet with manufacturer's representatives as assigned by the Design Director.
- Maintain design proficiency by attending seminars and workshops.
- Provide accurate time records to the Design Director each week.
- Provide marketing assistance by participating in marketing presentations as requested and by informing Design Director of possible projects that might become known to the designer.

Supervisory Responsibilities:
This job has no direct supervisory responsibilities; however, some direction of team members will be expected from time to time. This position does not participate in performance evaluations of team members.

Qualifications:

- Education: Bachelors degree from a four-year college or university with preferably a major in interior design, interior architecture; or an Associate Degree and a minimum of three years of experience in lieu of a four-year degree.
- Previous work experience: A minimum of four years full-time work experience.
- Portfolio and resume should show ability and competence to perform the required tasks of a senior designer with full competence and skill.
- NCIDQ qualification desired.
- Competence with AutoCAD, 2000 minimum. Competence with other computer applications is expected, or training will be required.

FIGURE 11-3. An example of a job description for a senior designer in a design firm that has many employees.

limited experience in this area, often have vague, unclear descriptions (if they have them at all).

A reference as to whom the person reports, either in a separate section or within the responsibilities section, should be noted. This helps clarify the chain of command and also aids new employees in learning who will be their supervisor. Since people do leave positions, reference is best made to job title rather than to an individual's name.

The Performance Evaluation

"I don't understand why I didn't get a raise!" complained one designer to her friend in the office. "I know I am working just as hard as everyone else around here—even more so." How do owners and managers make decisions about who will get a raise and how much that raise will be? Maybe such a decision is about who will get a promotion or extra training. The decision might even involve who is to be laid off or replaced. All these management decisions are ones that owners and managers must deal with throughout the year. One technique that they can use to help make these decisions is a performance evaluation.

A *performance evaluation* is a systematic evaluation of the positive and negative work efforts of an employee. They should be thought of as a positive management activity rather than as dreaded chore by both the employee and the owner/manager. For almost every owner or manager of a design firm, the preparation of performance evaluations of employees is an unpleasant task. In part, the performance evaluation is difficult for design managers because few have any training in, or experience with, the performance evaluation process. In far too many design practices, the performance evaluation consists of an informal mental review of each employee's work contribution. This informal review is almost always based on the manager's subjective opinions rather than on any objective evaluation of the employee's performance based on the responsibilities of the job. In addition, far too often, performance evaluations are used solely to determine compensation increases rather than to assist in the development and training of employees, which creates added stress. Considering the increase in employee lawsuits with regard to discrimination, harassment, and unfair termination during the last several years, laxity in performance evaluations should not be tolerated.

Managers also dislike performance evaluations because preparing them can take so much time. Even in an informal review process, it is not uncommon for a manager to spend many hours during the year considering each employee's past performance and discussing these impressions with the employee. To many managers, a formal process means that even more time must be spent on this activity.

Employees also find that the review process is an anxiety-producing, negative time period. Far too many employers use performance evaluations as a time for negative criticism rather than as an opportunity to help direct an employee's progress and development. It is no wonder that employees dislike the evaluation process.

Keep in mind that the primary goal of the performance evaluation should be the development of the employee, not the punishment of the employee for past performance (see Figures 11-4 and 11-5). These evaluations must be based on the responsibilities that the employee understands to be within his or her control during the period of the evaluation. Evaluations must be made objectively and must be based, as much as possible, on measurable criteria related to the employee's responsibilities.

Written evaluations also help protect the employer if an employee files a formal grievance. Written notes and evaluations placed in each employee's personnel file provide the owner of the design firm a credible document that can be used if any employee claims that some type of discriminatory practice exists or unfair termination has occurred.

A performance evaluation should be designed to do the following:

1. *Encourage the development of employees.* Encouraging the development of an employee so that he or she will be effective in the design firm

WALSH BROS. EMPLOYEE PERFORMANCE REVIEW

SECTION A	EMPLOYEE INFORMATION
Employee________________________	Department________________
Job Title________________________	
Supervisor________________________	Date Review Due____________
______________________ has missed _________ days of work due to _________________	
The past months from to	

Rating Scale

Outstanding (5) Performance and results achieved ***always*** exceed standards and expectations for the position requirements, standards, & objectives.

Exceeds Standards (4) Performance and results achieved ***consistently*** exceed the standards and expectations for the position requirements, standards, & objectives.

Meets Standards (3) Performance and results achieved ***generally*** meet the standards and expectations for the position requirements, standards, & objectives.

Below Standards (2) Performance and results achieved ***generally do not*** meet the standards and expectations for the position requirements, standards, & objectives.

Unsatisfactory (1) Performance and results achieved ***consistently do not*** meet the standards and expectations for the position requirements, standards, & objectives.

Section B	**5**	**4**	**3**	**2**	**1**	**Comments**
Punctuality: Overall adherence to work schedules, meetings, assignments, appointments and office hours.						
Attendance: Is faithful in coming to work daily and follows call-in and approval procedures for time off (Excused/Unexcused absences).						
Interpersonal Skills: Relates in a positive and professional manner with co-workers throughout the company.						
Positive Orientation: Is enthusiastic about his/her role in the organization. Demonstrates commitment, dedication, & positive attitude with changes in job/duties.						
Use of Time: Effectiveness in utilizing available time in performance of job duties and responsibilities. Meets required deadlines.						
Quality of Work: Completes work assignments thoroughly and completely in an accurate, prompt, neat manner (including all appropriate paperwork).						
Empowerment: Is an active problem solver who helps plan how to get things done and then does them.						
Sense of Urgency: Acts promptly and is proactive in accordance with their job.						
Participates in Quality Alliance: Works together on improving performance continually, achieving higher levels of productivity.						
Attract Customers: Demonstrates knowledge of product/services. Responds positively and proactively to internal & external customer needs.						
Serve Customers: Follows through on satisfying internal & external customer needs with effective communication. Provides high quality service.						
Keep Customers: Exceeds customer expectations. Goes beyond minimum standards to deliver product/services to both internal & external customers.						
Think Solutions: Seeks solutions to resolve unexpected problems that arise on the job.						

FIGURE 11-4. One page of a sample employee performance evaluation review form. (Reproduced with permission, Walsh Bros. Office Environments, Phoenix, AZ)

WALSH BROS.
SIXTY-DAY REVIEW

Employee ______________________ Hire Date__________________

Dept. ______________________ Position __________________

Rating Scale

Outstanding (5)	Performance and results achieved ***always*** exceed standards and expectations for the position requirements, standards, & objectives.
Exceeds Standards (4)	Performance and results achieved ***consistently*** exceed the standards and expectations for the position requirements, standards, & objectives.
Meets Standards (3)	Performance and results achieved ***generally*** meet the standards and expectations for the position requirements, standards, & objectives.
Below Standards (2)	Performance and results achieved ***generally do not*** meet the standards and expectations for the position requirements, standards, & objectives.
Unsatisfactory (1)	Performance and results achieved ***consistently do not*** meet the standards and expectations for the position requirements, standards, & objectives.

	5	4	3	2	1	Comments
Punctuality: Overall adherence to work schedules, meetings, assignments, appointments and office hours.						
Attendance: Is faithful in coming to work daily and follows call-in and approval procedures for time off (Excused/Unexcused absences).						
Problem Solving: Recognizes problems and acts to resolve unexpected problems. Develops alternative courses of action that are based on logical assumptions.						
Follows Instructions: The quality of assuming and fulfilling job assignments in accordance with directions given.						
Use of Time: Effectiveness in utilizing available time in performance of job duties and responsibilities. Meets required deadlines.						
Quality of Work: Completes work assignments thoroughly and completely in an accurate, prompt, neat manner (including all appropriate paperwork).						
Teamwork: Ability to function in a joint cooperative manner while supporting the Company and departmental plans, programs, policies, procedures and other employees						
Responds Cooperatively to Supervision: Willingness to perform as a team member including understanding of goals and accepting direction where appropriate.						
Overall Job Performance: Demonstrates knowledge of job skills, requirements, and techniques required by the job.						

PLEASE EXPLAIN ANY "BELOW STANDARDS" OR "UNSATISFACTORY" RATINGS IN THE SPACE BELOW.

____

____

____

____

____

______________________ ______________________
Employee Signature Date

______________________ ______________________
Supervisor Signature Date

____
Dept. Manager Agree Disagree

FIGURE 11-5. A form used for a 60-day performance review. (Reproduced with permission, Walsh Bros. Office Environments, Phoenix, AZ)

is a costly proposition. It can cost a company up to two year's of an employee's salary for that employee to reach a level of competence that results in positive work effectiveness. Companies that continually hire designers, train them, and then see them take a job with more responsibility at another company costs the firm more in the long run.

2. *Aid the employer-employee relationship.* Individuals in management positions in interior design offices should have aspects of their job with regard to the supervision and training of design staff employees clearly defined. Even though the design director is often expected to wear many hats in the office, his or her management of design personnel should not be the design director's least important responsibility. Managers must take the time to observe the design staff in terms of how they do the work assigned. When necessary, they must be ready to train employees in aspects of the firm's design processes. And they must be ready to recognize when employees are in need of training from outside sources.
3. *Determine compensation increases, promotions, and dismissals.* Too many firms and employees view the performance evaluation as a means to getting a salary increase or a promotion. When this is the primary goal, individuals who do not get the expected increase or promotion often become frustrated and leave the firm. This occurs most often when the reason for not receiving the increase or promotion is not clarified or when the employee suddenly finds out that he or she had not been doing what was expected in order to receive the increase or promotion. However, a well-thought-out performance evaluation process can be used as a way to determine those adjustments as well as to help motivate employees to achieve agreed upon goals related to responsibilities and job performance.
4. *Aid human resource planning.* The performance evaluation process helps a manager determine which areas of expertise existing employees have and which areas of expertise they lack. The manager then can choose either to provide those employees with further training or hire new employees. For instance, if the design firm decides to pursue contracts in healthcare facilities planning, performance evaluations will help the manager decide whether or not someone within the firm can do the work. Understanding this, the manager then can recruit someone who is experienced in healthcare facilities planning or someone to take over the current staff member's ongoing responsibility as he or she shifts into the new area of responsibility.
5. *Protect the employer from false claims by employees.* Written records of performance, reprimands, and the like provide evidentiary documents that can help fend off claims by former employees who have been fired for legitimate reasons.

The performance evaluation should tell each employee how he or she is doing. It should also tell the employee where he or she can likely progress in the future and how to advance there. For new employees, this means that the manager must indicate clearly what the responsibilities of the position are and what kind of performance level is expected. A well-written job description defines responsibilities. If, however, the individual's actual job responsibilities deviate from the job description in some way, this should be written down and clearly understood by both parties. Performance levels also need to be discussed and agreed upon. Interim evaluations should focus on the achievement of goals, and, where satisfactory progress does not exist, constructive criticism should be given to help the employee succeed.

For the employee who has previously had a performance evaluation, the evaluation must be based on responsibilities and performance levels agreed upon at the last evaluation. Since the performance evaluation is for development of the individual, pointing out deficiencies must be done in terms of correction and future achievement, not punishment. There also should occur a discussion regarding new goals and how current and future responsibilities and performance levels fit into these goals. This becomes the performance criteria for the next evaluation.

The Performance Evaluation Process

In this section, we will discuss the performance evaluation process. Suggestions will be made that can help make the process more useful to the employee and the employer, and perhaps less difficult for them both.

Although informal performance evaluations may occur at any time for any level of employee, most companies find that a formal evaluation should take place on a yearly basis. It is a very good idea, however, for new employees to be evaluated more frequently during the first year. The first evaluation takes place commonly at the end of the probationary period, which is usually 90 days. Many firms find it advantageous to have reviews at 30-, 60-, and possibly 75-day intervals for new employees during the 90-day probationary period. Subsequent evaluations occur after the first six months and then after one year. The one-year date can be either on the anniversary date of hiring or on a day set for all evaluations.

The performance evaluation is most commonly performed by the employee's immediate supervisor. In design firms, where people often work in teams to complete projects, individuals who are not truly an employee's supervisor may be asked to evaluate an employee's performance. If this occurs, the employee should be made aware of who is making the evaluations and why he or she is involved, if that person is not, in fact, the employee's supervisor.

Often individual evaluations are supplemented by self- or peer evaluations. Self-evaluations can be helpful, but it is not uncommon for employees to be either harder or easier on themselves than their superior. Peer evaluations, in which employees rate their coworkers, only seem to work when employees trust each other, when they are truly in a position to be very familiar with each other's work, and when they are not competing with each other for raises or promotions. Experience has shown that peers will be either too easy on each other (so as not to get their coworker angry) or too hard on those individuals whom they do not like.

It is best to use a formalized performance evaluation form such as the one shown in Figure 11-4. The criteria on this form should deal only with those factors that are relevant to an individual's performance. For example, a design assistant may be told that drafting is a primary responsibility of the position. If the quantity of work produced is not relevant but the quality of work (i.e., no mistakes) is, then only the quality of work should be evaluated.

The evaluation form and its application to personnel matters must be written as objectively as possible. Dealing with specific skills and skill levels as they relate to job responsibilities is one way to maintain objectivity. Being sure the evaluation form does not contain a lot of questions that focus on either the personality, attitude, or appearance of the employee also helps to maintain objectivity. The evaluation form also should not evaluate the employee based solely on the employer's personal opinion, especially if that personal opinion has not been satisfactorily communicated to the employees. The correct kind of evaluation form will help maintain objectivity in the evaluation, which is necessary to make it fair for all employees.

A performance evaluation interview should be scheduled sufficiently in advance so that both the manager and the employee can adequately prepare themselves to discuss the employee's past performance with respect to previously agreed-upon goals. The evaluation interview should be private, and only the employee and the manager should be present. Sufficient time must be scheduled so that it can progress without being interrupted by telephone calls, clients, or anything else. A minimum of one hour is generally required, if the evaluation interview does not include a discussion of the next year's goals, but two or more hours may be needed in order to discuss both issues fully.

The manager should start the performance evaluation interview by making a positive statement. This helps put the employee at ease and also from being put immediately on the defensive. The employer should seek to be as descriptive as possible in positive and negative comments, and these comments should be based on performance criteria, not personal feelings. This attitude will help the employee understand more precisely what he or she is doing right or wrong. During the performance evaluation interview, the employee should be asked to evaluate his or her own progress. It is necessary for the employee to comment about his or her own performance so that the employer can understand how the employee views his or her own role.

The last portion of the evaluation interview should focus on the future, with discussions concerning what the employee can do to resolve any performance deficiencies. Discussion and negotiation must occur so that the course of action becomes an agreed-upon plan, not one dictated by the employer. Success comes from focusing on two or three of the more important negative areas. This is a more satisfactory approach, since it is difficult for people to try to improve on many things in which they have been deficient and, at the same time, maintain a positive attitude. A realistic timetable for improvement should also be agreed upon as an aid in future evaluations.

The evaluation interview should be concluded with a summary of the satisfactory and unsatisfactory areas of the employee's performance, as well as an action plan for the resolution of agreed-upon unsatisfactory areas. The evaluation interview should end on a positive note, with the employee understanding clearly how his or her performance is viewed by the employer and what the future will bring for that employee.

After the evaluation, the employer should prepare some notes related to what occurred during the evaluation interview and place the performance evaluation form and notes in the employee's personnel file. It is also a good idea for the employee to keep notes as well. The goals and timetable should be prepared as soon as possible. It should then be reviewed individually and any discrepancies should be discussed and agreed upon immediately.

The employer should follow up the performance evaluation by monitoring of the employee's progress. Some areas may need special monitoring, and the manager must be ready to spend the time either training or working with the employee. Remember that performance evaluations fail when the employer thinks that only evaluation and development are the important issues in a formal performance evaluation process.

The Employee Handbook

The purpose of an *employee handbook* is to provide owners, managers, and employees with a concise reference regarding the company's policies. In some design firms, the employee handbook might include general operating policies, such as policies related to special ordering merchandise for clients, as well as

FOREWORD

The purpose of the Smith and Hardy Interiors Employee Handbook is to provide employees with a complete source of the policies and procedures of the firm. Our experience has shown that providing each employee with a handbook of this information helps to promote consistency in the operations of Smith and Hardy Interiors. This consistency results in a more efficient, productive, and, therefore, more profitable association for the employees and the firm.

As you flip through the pages, you will see that the handbook is broken down into four parts; **Introduction, Personnel Policies, Operating Policies,** and **Department Policies and Procedures**. The Introduction provides you with the philosophy and Mission Statement of Smith and Hardy Interiors, a brief history of the firm, and a presentation on the organizational structure of the firm. In the section on Personnel Policies, there is an explanation of hiring, performance evaluation, termination policies, and employee benefits. The section on Operating Policies explains general business policies, such as the business hours, holidays, sick leave, overtime, and so forth. The final section contains specific policies and procedures of your department. The material in this section may be supplemented by additional information provided to you by your supervisor. These, of course, should be inserted in this section.

The policies and procedures of this firm have evolved over many years. As the firm changes, so may some of its policies. As policies and procedures change, these will be completely presented and discussed with employees.

We are happy to have you as an employee at Smith and Hardy Interiors and look foreword to working with you for many years. The management wishes you great success as you grow with us.

Randolph Hardy, Managing Partner
Smith and Hardy Interiors, Inc.

FIGURE 11-6. An example of an opening statement for an employee handbook.

personnel policies. In other design firms, it is possible for there to be one handbook that describes personnel issues and one or more additional handbooks that explain operational policies for each department. As with job descriptions, many design firms—especially smaller firms with five or fewer employees—do not have an employee handbook.

A well-designed employee handbook, however, helps to clarify policies so that complaints, grievances, and morale problems can be prevented before they occur. The handbook can help the company prevent lawsuits related to equal employment opportunity laws from being filed against it. Well-defined policies assist managers and owners in the decision-making and control process by providing consistent treatment of defined issues. These are some of the key reasons why any interior design firm with employees should develop an employee handbook.

In recent years, some legal issues have surfaced concerning employee handbooks. Numerous state courts have applied the rule of implied contracts to employee handbooks, especially concerning employee termination. An *implied contract* is one in which "a contract (is) implied by the direct or indirect acts of the parties" (Brown and Sukys, 1997, p. 98). Courts have determined more frequently that implied contracts exist as represented by statements and promises in employee handbooks. This legal issue is discussed in Chapter 12. Due to changes in interpretations of the law, the small-business owner should not shy away from preparing an employee handbook. On the contrary, it is a useful management tool for any size interior design business.

To be sure all policies remain current, the owner should review the handbook once a year. The state department of labor can advise the owner on current labor policies. Of course, the firm's attorney can also advise on specific legal issues that might arise regarding the contents of the handbook.

How to Prepare a Handbook

In relatively small firms, the owner most likely prepares the employee handbook, although it is a good idea for the owner to solicit input from employees. In departmentalized firms, managers may be asked to submit policies related to their areas. Then either through committee meetings or through the efforts of one manager, a composite handbook can be produced.

Many policies may already exist in writing, or employees may already know what they are, even if they are not written down. These become the starting point for an employee handbook. Some information may have to be obtained from company records. For example, paid holidays may have varied over the years. Company records will show which holidays were considered paid ones each year. Records regarding vacation and sick time allowance may also only be obtained from company records.

Many companies have unwritten rules that have sprung up over the years but that have dubious authority. These unwritten rules should be discovered, and decisions should be made as to their current validity. An example of an unwritten rule might be that "no employee may make client appointments outside the office from 8 to 9 A.M." This unwritten rule may have addressed an earlier need to ensure that someone would be in the studio to answer the phone until the bookkeeper arrived at 9:00. Now that there is a secretary who comes in at 8:00, the unwritten rule probably has no validity.

The organization and contents of the handbook should be logical, clear, and concise. For example, the firm may wish to use a format that mirrors the logical sequence of events of an organization. In this case, issues related to hiring would be placed first, perhaps followed by hours of work and the issue of absenteeism, with employee benefits placed in the middle, and the policy with regard to termination placed at the end.

As much as possible, clear and concise wording is important. Terminology that everyone understands or is in common usage should be adopted. For example, the sentence "Scheduled work hours for all departments are Monday to Friday, 8:30 A.M. to 5:30 P.M." should be used instead of "The studio, workrooms, warehouse, and bookkeeping areas will be open and maintained by appropriate personnel on a daily basis, Monday through Friday, from 8:30 A.M. to 5:30 P.M."

Remember that the employee handbook and the included policy statements are meant to inform employees, not impress them with flowery prose. Also remember that some employees are not interior designers and may not be familiar with some of the jargon of the interior design profession. For a small company with just a few employees, the handbook can be kept short and simple. As the company grows, the foundation for the handbook will already exist and can be expanded upon to meet the needs of the growing company.

The new handbook, when completed, should not just be handed to employees, especially if the firm has never had a handbook. It is important for the owner and/or managers to meet with employees to explain why the handbook was prepared, to define the purpose of the handbook, and to go over its contents with employees. Even if employees have not been a part of the process of creating the handbook at least they will feel less threatened by a new set of rules if the rules are explained to them before the rules are put into effect.

What to Include

Precisely how much information should go into an employee handbook should be up to the interior design firm. The complexity of written policies should match the management style and philosophy of the owners and/or managers

A. **Overview**
B. ***Introduction*: Provides an overview of the company.**
C. ***Organization*: Provides a description of the responsibility areas and organizational structure.**
D. ***Employment and hiring policies*: Details hiring procedures, if performance evaluations are performed, and promotion policies.**
E. ***Compensation*: Details compensation policies for all levels of employees. This section commonly defines pay periods, bonuses, and fringe benefits (if any).**
F. ***Time off*: Details company paid holidays (if any), vacation policies, sick leave, and other paid or nonpaid days off.**
G. ***Training*: Provides information about any company training or reimbursement for training for educational purposes.**
H. ***General rules and policies*: Details work week, overtime, tardiness, and such things as use of company phone and mail for personal business, dress code, and other general work conditions.**
I. ***Leaving the company*: Includes information on termination policies, expected notice, severance pay (if any), and policies on references.**

FIGURE 11-7. The common parts of an employee handbook.

while, at the same time, should provide the policies needed to aid managers in control and decision making. Many people begin a career in interior design because they seek freedom of expression and a certain freedom of time. In a studio that is composed primarily of self-motivated, self-directed individuals, those individuals will rebel or even quit if a great number of strictly enforced rules are suddenly thrust upon them. Figure 11-7 summarizes the common parts of employee handbooks.

A new employee handbook should begin with a statement related to the purpose of the handbook and the reason for its development and implementation. Figure 11-6 gives an example of such an introductory statement. All the policy statements for each category within the handbook should follow. Figure 11-8 provides an example of policies related to hours of work.

After the handbook has been prepared, the owner must remember that it is never really finished. The owner and manager should periodically review the contents to keep it as up to date as possible. As the business continues to change, policies need to be reviewed and possibly modified.

Whatever the size of the firm or the type of interior design practice, written policies related to operational and personnel issues aid the owners and managers of the firm in running the practice in a professional manner. Written policies also help clarify how things are done and where employees stand in their relationship to the firm. Policies that are clear and can be easily followed will be adhered to by all employees. Those that run counter to what is happening in the firm or that seem to be constantly ignored by some employees in the firm cannot be enforced and also will tend to undermine the manager's role.

5. Hours of Work

A. Business Hours

Monday through Thursday, 7:00 A.M. to 5:00 P.M.

Friday, 7:00 A.M. to 12 Noon

Both hourly and salaried employees are expected to be at work during normal business hours.

B. The Work Week

The normal work week for hourly and salaried employees is forty (40) hours.

C. Lunch Hours

Hourly employees are entitled to one hour for lunch. It must be taken between 11:30 A.M. and 2:00 P.M. Salaried employees are expected to take one hour for lunch. It should be taken between 11:30 A.M. and 2:00 P.M.

D. Breaks

Hourly employees are entitled to two 15 minute breaks. One should be taken in the morning and one in the afternoon.

E. Overtime

Hourly employees must have the approval of their supervisor to work overtime. Overtime pay begins after a minimum of forty (40) hours of work in a normal work week. The pay rate for overtime is 1–1/2 times the normal hourly rate. Hourly employees may take compensatory time in place of overtime pay. One hour of compensatory time may be taken in place of the overtime pay rate. Approval and arrangements must be made with the employee's supervisor.

Salaried employees are not entitled to overtime pay. Compensatory time can be arranged for extended overtime work. Approval must be made with the employee's supervisor.

F. Absences

You must keep your supervisor informed of absences that you know of in advance.

If you must be unexpectedly absent for illness or some other reason, you must telephone your supervisor as soon as possible. If you must be absent for more than one day, telephone your supervisor daily.

G. Lateness

You should contact your supervisor if you find that you will be unavoidably late.

FIGURE 11-8. A page of policies related to working hours from an employee handbook

Compensation and Fringe Benefits

The salary for any employee who is working in an interior design firm is a very important consideration for both the employee and the employer. There is more than one way for employees to be compensated. *Compensation* is any kind of payment made to an employee for work performed. It most commonly is provided in the form of a weekly or biweekly paycheck. *Fringe benefits* are other kinds of payments given to the employee that are optional or that may not even be provided by an employer. Fringe benefits, such as paid vacations and health insurance, also make a significant contribution to the total compensation package. The most common methods of compensation will be briefly discussed in this section.

Compensation

The most common methods of compensating employees are straight salary, commission, and hourly wage. Bonus plans, technically called incentive compensation, are sometimes tied to any of these.

The *straight salary* provides a fixed amount of salary to the employee no matter how many hours in the week he or she works. Of course, the firm still requires that the employee on a straight salary work a normal work week of 35–40 hours. The employee's weekly salary is determined by dividing the yearly salary by 52 weeks. This is the most common method of compensating interior design and other design professional staff, especially when product sales are not part of the compensation arrangement.

An employee who is compensated on a straight-salary method is generally not eligible for any overtime pay. When the employee works overtime, he or she usually is expected to, at some convenient time, utilize compensatory time. *Compensatory time* is time off during the normal work week that makes up for the overtime hours that an employee has worked. In all cases, the utilization of compensatory time must be approved by the manager so that the absence of the employee will not be detrimental to the regular office work. Firms generally have an additional policy that compensatory time cannot be "saved up" for an extended period nor added at the beginning or end of a vacation period.

Interior designers whose work responsibilities are more involved with the selling of products or services rather than in design work may be paid a *commission*. When commission is used as the compensation method, the employee is paid some percentage of the gross, net sale, or gross margin of the merchandise sold, or the amount of the contract.

Commission on the gross sale means that the commission percentage is paid on the amount for which the client has been billed. For example, if the designer is paid 10 percent of the gross sale and the client has been billed $5000, the commission that must be paid is $500.

When commission is based on the net sale, the percentage is calculated after certain items have been deducted. Deductions could include discounts, freight charges, delivery charges, returns—even interior design services of in-house designers. For example, assume a gross sale of $5000 has a commission on the net sale of 10 percent and a $250 deduction for delivery and freight charges. The commission that should be paid to the designer would be $475.

In the gross margin method of paying a commission, the commission percentage is paid based on the gross margin of the sale. *Gross margin* (also called *gross profit*) is the difference between the selling price and the cost price of the goods or services being sold. Designers are motivated to sell merchandise and services for the highest gross margin possible in order to receive the most commission possible. In the preceding example of a $5000 gross sale, with a 10 percent commission, assume that the cost price of the sale is $2500. The amount of commission that should be paid in this case would be $250.

Some firms utilizing the gross margin commission method also often incorporate a sliding scale of commission. In this situation, different percentages are paid depending on the amount of the gross margin percentage. For instance, if the gross margin is 90 percent (nearly retail price), the commission percentage might be 50 percent. If the gross margin is only 5 percent (nearly cost price) the commission percentage might only be 2 percent.

In the *hourly wage*, the employee is paid some rate for every hour that he or she works. Because of the nature of interior design work, the hourly wage is used less often as a method of compensation, except when the monitoring of the employee's productivity and work responsibilities is relatively easy. It is more commonly used to compensate entry-level employees and "production" employees, such as secretaries, bookkeepers, and delivery people. Regular full-time interior designers are rarely paid based on a true hourly rate.

Although most readers are familiar with how the hourly rate of compensation is calculated because of their own part-time work experience, it is briefly discussed here as a point of overall reference on compensation methods. The weekly salary is computed by figuring the average workday (e.g., 8 hours) and the average work week (e.g., 40 hours). If an employee is paid $9.00 an hour, his or her weekly gross salary would be $360 per week for a 40-hour work week. Some firms, however, have slightly shorter work weeks. It is possible for a company's work week to be 35 or 37 hours. It is up to the individual company to determine the length of its normal work week. Since the federal wage and hour laws apply to interior design firms, the firm has to pay hourly wage employees overtime for any hours worked beyond the normal work week. This amounts to time-and-a-half for weekday overtime work and double time for work done on Sundays and holidays.

Gross salary, as anyone who has held some kind of a job realizes, is the amount of employee compensation before any deductions. The employer must withhold (deduct) amounts for federal income tax, social security* and Medicare contributions, possibly state income taxes, and possibly voluntary contributions for such things as health insurance. The amount of compensation left after these deductions is called net pay, or take-home pay. It is common for the basic withholding deductions for taxes and social security to amount to 20–35 percent of gross pay.

Incentive compensation is payment over and above regular compensation. The two common types of incentive compensation are merit pay and bonus plans. *Merit pay* is an amount added to an individuals' basic annual compensation amount, often as a reward for quality work done in the past. It is commonly referred to as a raise or salary increase. Another kind of compensation that is added to the basic annual compensation is a cost-of-living adjustment. *A cost-of-living adjustment* (also referred to as COLA) is generally given across the board, meaning that all employees may receive a cost-of-living adjustment to help off set increases in inflation. Merit pay is an increase that can go to all employees but usually is given to those individuals whose high level of performance during the past year warrants it. Incentive compensation is primarily awarded to hourly and salaried employees. Those on commission rarely receive incentive compensation.

A *bonus plan* is a method of paying extra compensation to employees based on their producing more than a specific personal quota. Bonuses most commonly are paid to design employees who sell merchandise. If they meet or exceed their sales quotas, the employees are paid some kind of bonus. Since designers who are responsible for creative design work cannot easily establish a quota of design work, bonuses are less often paid to these individuals. However, some interior design firms do have a bonus plan that rewards creative staff. Bonuses are usually based on the employee meeting or exceeding the amount of contracts budgeted or on exceeding a budgeted amount of specifications on a certain kind of furniture or furnishings.

Fringe Benefits

Compensation only represents part of the payments that employers make to employees. Approximately 20–60 percent of payments to employees is for fringe benefits. Depending on the size of the firm and allowances for fringe benefits, these items can represent from 25 to 35 percent of the overall payroll.

Fringe benefits take many forms and are not offered consistently from one interior design firm to another (see Figure 11-9). This is due, in part, to the fact that benefits vary based on the size of the company. The larger the firm is, the more benefits will be provided. Federal and even state labor laws are an important factor in the benefits packages offered. Of course, competition during a tight labor market (as has been experienced at the turn of the twenty-first century) also have an impact on benefits paid to employees.

* Social security contributions show up on the paycheck stub as FICA. FICA stands for Federal Insurance Contributions Act. Social security is the common name for FICA.

Health insurance
Life insurance
Supplemental insurance such as dental, disability, and vision care
Retirement plan, such as profit sharing
Paid holidays, vacations, and sick leave
Employee purchase discounts
Payments for employee professional association dues
Payments for NCIDQ or other testing and licensing fees
Reimbursements for employee use of personal automobile
Payments for employee educational enhancements

FIGURE 11-9. The most common voluntary fringe benefits provided by businesses.

The most common fringe benefits given or paid directly to employees are paid vacations, paid holidays, group health insurance, and employee discounts on purchases. Other benefits offered to employees might include group life insurance, supplemental health insurance such as dental programs, paid sick leave, profit-sharing plans, and professional-growth benefits. Professional-growth benefits include such things as paid educational benefits, partial or full payment of professional association dues, and partial or full payment of NCIDQ testing fees.

Other benefits that would not be paid directly to the employee but must be paid by the employer include social security tax contributions, worker's compensation taxes, and unemployment insurance taxes. These are benefits that the employee may or may not draw from for some time. Social security is not payable until the employee retires (or is physically disabled and can no longer work). Worker's compensation covers on-the-job injuries, and unemployment insurance is only paid, under certain circumstances, if the employee has been laid off from the design firm.

When an individual is applying for a job, is considering a promotion, or is weighing the merits of staying with the present employer, he or she must look carefully at the complete benefits package. A position with one firm with a slightly lower salary but a good employer-paid health insurance program may be better than another position where the salary is a bit higher but there is no health insurance program available to employees.

Summary

As an interior design firm grows, it becomes increasingly important for the owners and managers to review and define the organizational structure. Job responsibilities become more specialized and roles must be defined. The development and utilization of job classifications and job descriptions assist owners of growing design firms in managing employees.

To keep good employees, research has shown that more must be done for employees than give them occasional raises. Performance evaluations that are keyed to job descriptions help employees understand how they are doing. They also show employees how they can advance in the firm. In addition, performance evaluations help protect employers when disputes concerning termination occur. Employee handbooks clarify work rules and operational procedures.

Fair compensation and fringe benefits vary widely in the interior design industry. Employers do not want to pay more than they have to, and, at the same time, employees want to feel they are being treated fairly. Compensation and fringe benefits are particularly important issues during a tight job market when a few extra benefits can make the difference between an employee accepting a position or not. Of course, these issues are also important in a good job market, when design firms, frankly, become less concerned about keeping employees. Fair methods are needed to attract and retain qualified and appropriate employees.

All these issues are of critical importance to the owner and managers of an interior design practice. A firm is really made up of individuals who must be managed and motivated to achieve the business goals of the firm. Without effective office organization and employee management, the smooth operation of the firm becomes difficult, if not impossible. In the next chapter, we will cover legal issues of employment, such as the employer-employee relationship and employment contracts.

REFERENCES

Beam, Burton T., Jr., and John J. McFadden. 1998. *Employee Benefits*, 5th ed. Homewood, IL: Dearborn Financial Publishing.

Berk, Joseph, and Susan Berk. 1991. *Managing Effectively. A Handbook for First-Time Managers.* New York: Sterling Publishing.

Block, Judy R. 1981. *Performance Appraisal on the Job.* New York: Executive Enterprises Publications.

Brown, Gordon W., and Paul A. Sukys. 1997. *Business Law*, 9th ed. New York: Glencoe/McGraw-Hill.

Charnov, Bruce H. 1985. *Appraising Employee Performance.* Westbury, NY: Caddylak Publishing.

Coxe, Weld. 1980. *Managing Architectural and Engineering Practice.* New York: John Wiley.

Finter, Andrea. "Senior Designers' Average Pay: $37,300." *Contract.* June 1985.

———. "Designer Salary Poll Links Job Tenure and Compensation." *Contract.* July 1984.

Getz, Lowell. 1986. *Business Management in the Smaller Design Firm.* Newton, MA: Practice Management Associates.

Gibson, Woody. "Design Wages Depend on Function," *Contract.* October 1980.

Hood, Jack B., Benjamin A. Harady, Jr., Harold S. Lewis, Jr. 1999. *Worker's Compensation and Employee Protection Laws.* St. Paul, MN: West Publishing.

Imperato, Gina. "How To Give Good Feedback." *Fast Company.* September 1998.

Joel, Lewin G., III. 1996. *Every Employee's Guide to the Law.* New York: Pantheon Press.

Johnson, Spencer. 1998. *Who Moved My Cheese?* New York: Putnam.

Kotter, John P. 1996. *Leading Change.* Cambridge, MA: Harvard Business School Press.

Lawson, J. W., II. 1970. *How to Develop a Company Personnel Policy Manual*, 5th ed. Chicago: Dartnell Corp.

Maister, David H. 1993. *Managing the Professional Service Firm.* New York: Free Press.

National Institute of Business Management. 1998. *Fire at Will: Terminating Your Employees Legally.* Special Bulletin No. 239A. McLean, VA: National Institute of Business Management.

Shapero, Albert. 1985. *Managing Professional People.* New York: Free Press.

Slavin, Maeve. "Jobs Are Not What They Used To Be." *Interiors.* September 1983.

Steingold, Fred S. (edited by Barbara Kate Repa). 1999. *The Employer's Legal Handbook*, 3rd ed. Berkeley, CA: Nolo Press.

Stern, Natalie. "Top Contract Furniture Sales People Can Boost Earnings 33% with Timed Move." *Contract.* November 1982.

Stitt, Fred A., ed. 1986. *Design Office Management Handbook.* Santa Monica, CA: Arts and Architecture Press.

Tobias, Sheila, and Alma Lantz. "Performance Appraisal." *Working Woman.* November 1985.

Wagner, Michael. "Interiors Business. Salaries and Bonuses Are Up for Designers." *Interiors.* September 1985.

Weiss, Donald H. 2000. *Fair, Square & Legal*, 3rd ed. New York: American Management Association.

Whitmyer, Claude, Salli Rasberry, and Michael Phillips. 1989. *Running a One-Person Business.* Berkeley, CA: Ten Speed Press.

Woodward, Cynthia A. 1990. *Human Resources Management for Design Professionals.* Washington, DC: AIA Press.

Chapter 12

Legal Issues of Employment

Employers are responsible for abiding by many federal and state laws regarding the hiring and firing of employees. Although some statutes have an impact only on large design firms, many affect the small interior design firm as well. Meeting the spirit of employment laws is, at the very least, the ethical thing to do in any size or type of interior design firm. Added to this ethical consideration is the fact that the number of employees suing employers over some issue or another has increased. Although there are no actual figures for the interior design industry, it is likely that interior design firms are being affected by employee lawsuits.

Interpretations of older laws and the enactment of new laws to protect employees have made it difficult for employers to hire or fire individuals when they do not perform as expected. Firms that never before found it necessary to have job descriptions and performance evaluations are busy developing them in order to clarify the responsibilities of their employees. Strategies that were seldom used by design firms in the past are now being used to protect the employer. Employment contracts and more formalized record keeping of disciplinary actions and performance evaluations have become necessary in the interior design industry. Even small design studios with just a few employees are looking to develop formalized personnel management systems in order to protect themselves from the possibility of employee complaints and lawsuits.

More and more employees are utilizing the courts to satisfy their grievances. In the interior design profession, lawsuits occur as a result of misunderstandings about work requirements, company policies, or layoffs, for which there is seemingly little reason. As women claim their right to be treated fairly and equally in the workplace, sexual harassment and discrimination complaints are increasing. Far too many interior design employees find out about their legal rights and obligations only after some unpleasant experience.

In this chapter, we will look at many issues related to legal regulation of employment. We will briefly discuss federal laws regulating employment, the agency relationship, the concept of employment at will, implied contracts, and employment contracts. This chapter will define the difference between employees and independent contractors and will discuss sexual harassment. Legal issues concerning interviewing for a position are detailed in Chapter 33.

Federal Laws Regulating Employment

There are many laws at the federal and state levels that were written during the twentieth century to protect employees. These laws were created to stop the brutal working conditions that were prevalent in factories and in some ways even the office environment during the early part of the twentieth century. Many of the laws written to protect employees have more of an impact on firms that are unionized. Since it is almost unheard of for an interior design firm to be unionized, there will be no attempt in this text to discuss those laws. However, several federal laws do affect employment in the nonunion professional interior design office.

Employment Discrimination

Whether it occurs in a large or a small firm, employment discrimination is a key concern for employers. Several laws exist to protect employees from job discrimination. Title VII of the Civil Rights Act of 1964, along with the Equal Employment Opportunity Act of 1972 and the Civil Rights Act of 1991, prohibit an employer from discriminating on the basis of sex, race, color, religion, or national origin. The Age Discrimination in Employment Act of 1967, which was amended in 1990, prohibits employer discrimination based on the age of the employee. A most familiar law to the reader is the American Disabilities Act. This act concerns accommodation in public buildings and will be discussed in Chapter 13. However, it also affects the workplace.

These laws and their subsequent amendments reinforce various employment prohibitions, as well as prohibitions related to educational opportunity and other public issues of discrimination. Although these laws generally apply to firms with 15 or more employees, all interior design firms should abide by their intent. Complaints are most commonly reviewed by the Equal Employment Opportunity Commission (EEOC). Should the EEOC determine there is sufficient cause, it will file a civil lawsuit against the employer in the name of the employee.

Equal opportunity employment laws make it illegal for employers to ask verbally or on a job application for such things as the employee's (1) age, (2) date of birth, (3) maiden name, (4) marital status, or (5) gender, or for any other information related to age, gender, religion, national origin, race, or marital status. Discrimination laws do not stop at the hiring process. They apply throughout all the stages of employment. For example, Jane has repeatedly asked for flexibility in her work hours to take a class at the community college. Without being given a reason, her request is refused each time. Harvey has been granted the same request the first time that he has asked. On the face of it, it appears that Jane has grounds for filing a discrimination complaint with the EEOC.

It is possible for the employer to obtain information in less direct ways, if the information has significance as to whether the interviewee is capable of performing the job responsibilities. For example, it is legal for an employer to ask something like, "Are you between the ages of 23 and 50?" or "Are you a citizen of this country?" The key, of course, is whether the questions and the way in which they are asked are being used to discriminate against potential employees. Additional sample questions that are illegal in the hiring situation are given in Chapter 33.

Title I of the Americans with Disabilities Act (ADA) affects the hiring and promoting of employees. This portion of the ADA restrains employers from discriminating against any handicapped person who is otherwise qualified for a job. Employers with 25 or more employees were required to comply with the law beginning in July 1992. Employers with 15 or more employees were required to comply with the law by July 1994. Furthermore, the employer is required to make "reasonable accommodation" in the structuring of the job and/or modification of the work as necessary for the employee to do the job. For example, a paraplegic designer who has the qualifications and skills required for a design position must be given equal consideration with a nonhandicapped person. If the handicapped person is hired, the employer must attempt to make reasonable changes in the work areas. The drafting station, for instance, could be reconfigured using modular furniture that is more flexible and accommodating to a person's specific needs.

Interior design practices that are involved in work with the federal government would need to comply with some additional federal laws. Executive Order 11246 requires that firms that do more than $10,000 of business with the federal government have nondiscrimination clauses in their contracts. If an interior design firm does more than $2500 of work for the federal government, the Rehabilitation Act of 1973 and 1974 requires that the design firm accommodate handicapped employees. Other requirements may be enforceable, depending on the exact nature of the design firm's work with the federal government.

Other Issues

The Equal Pay Act of 1963 requires that employers pay all employees who have the same basic work responsibilities and work experience the same amount of salary or wages. In this case, if two employees with the same job title and job responsibilities are hired at the same time and start with approximately the same work experience, each must be paid the same starting wage. If future proven performance or responsibility issues become different for the two individuals, then each can be paid a different amount. Another federal law dealing with pay and wages is the Fair Labor Standards Act, commonly called the wage-hour law. First passed in 1938, it primarily governs wages for employees who are working in companies that are involved in interstate commerce and hourly wage employees.

The Occupational Safety and Health Act (OSHA) of 1970 requires that all employees be given a safe place to work. OSHA inspectors, although primarily found in production facilities, do make inspections in the office environment. In the interior design studio, an OSHA inspector may look for properly located and functioning fire extinguishers, first-aid kits, and a proper reporting procedure for employee injuries. In 1999, OSHA proposed dramatic requirements related to ergonomic workstations for office workers. Additional proposals by OSHA would also affect home office workers. At the time of the writing of this third edition, these changes have not become law.

The National Labor Relations Act, also called the Wagner Act, protects employees from many kinds of activities by employers that could cause unfair labor practices. Most of these laws protect union employees and will not be discussed here. One issue that might affect an interior design practice is related to an employee being fired or otherwise discriminated against as a result of the employee's filing any kind of charges or giving testimony against the employer. An example might be that an employee is fired after he or she files a complaint related to wage discrimination with the Federal Wage and Hour Board. Depending, of course, on the exact nature of the complaint and the manner in which the firing took place, the employer would be liable for illegally firing the employee.

Additional laws affecting the employer-employee relationship include the Family and Medical Leave Act of 1993. In companies with 50 employees or more, the Family and Medical Leave Law Act, requires that an employer give employees up to 12 weeks of leave for child, spousal, or parental care without jeopardizing the employee's job. This leave is not automatic and does not accrue until the employee has worked at the company for at least one year on a full-time basis.

When an employer provides some sort of health insurance as a benefit, the employee is entitled to continue that health benefit even after he or she has been fired or quits. An exception is if the employee is fired for gross misconduct. The Consolidated Omnibus Budget Reconciliation Act of 1986 (COBRA) requires that the employer continue health benefits for the employee and the employee's spouse and dependents. The time period of the benefits is generally 18 months. Of course, the employee must pay the insurance premiums. Employees of companies with 20 or more employees are covered under the federal law. Note that states have variations on the law and requirements regarding the length of time that the insurance must be made available.

State legislatures have also passed many laws that affect legal issues related to employment. Employers are urged to speak to an attorney to be sure that their business is in compliance with employment laws. Prevention is cheaper than having to deal with employees through the court system. Employees should speak to an attorney or contact the EEOC if the employee feels that he or she may have experienced any kind of employment discrimination.

Of course, this section does not discuss all the federal statutes that in one way or another affect employment. The reader may wish to review one or more of the books listed in the References at the end of this chapter or check on-line for additional information on employee rights and/or employer responsibilities.

The Agency Relationship

In common law, an *agency relationship* occurs when one person or entity agrees to represent or do business for another person or entity. In the most common use of the agency relationship, an agent is empowered to represent another party, called the principal. Many readers are familiar with the fact that agents represent professional athletes during negotiations for contracts with sports teams. The agency relationship also gives the principal the right to control the conduct of the agent in the matters entrusted to the agent. In our example, the agent cannot make a deal with the sports team if it is not agreed to by the principal—the sports figure.

The agency relationship is also applied to employment. The employer-employee relationship is a type of agency relationship. The principal of the interior design firm is the owner (or controlling board member), whereas the agents are all the employees, whether they are in management positions or staff positions.

An employee is defined as "a person who works in the service of another person (the employer) under an express or implied contract of hire, under which the employer has the right to control the details of work performance."* In many ways, employees are also agents, since they also represent the owner. However, an employee is a legal agent of the firm only if he or she has the authority to act in place of the owner. For example, Roger, Phyllis, and Kelley work for Marjorie. All four designers are expected to call on clients, obtain the information to prepare a design contract, and prepare the required design

* Reprinted from p. 543 in *Black's Law Dictionary*, 7th ed., by Bryan A. Garner, ed., 1999, with permission of the West Group.

activities to complete the project. Only Marjorie, who is the owner, is allowed to sign the design contracts. If Roger, Phyllis, or Kelley signed a design contract, the contract would not be binding on the firm.

The agency relationship, in some manner, specifically spells out the extent of the relationship between the employer and the employee. Unlike most contractual relationships, the conditions of the agency relationship do not have to be in writing. There does have to be an agreement to the effect that the employee is willing to be an agent for the employer. Accepting a position and knowing what the responsibilities of the position cover imply agreement. Since all positions in the firm have different responsibilities and different levels of trust within the employer-employee relationship, it is important for employees to fully understand their responsibilities. For example, not all employees have the right to sign purchase orders or to buy supplies for the office. Carefully prepared job descriptions, as discussed in Chapter 11, explain most of these responsibilities.

Because of the agency relationship, each party is obligated to perform certain duties with respect to the other party. Each party has a primary duty to the other to act in good faith toward the other party. There are specific legal duties of each party in an agency relationship. Let us look first at the duties that the employer has to the employee.

Employer to Employee

The employer is obligated to provide the employee with a reasonable amount or kind of compensation for the completion of the agreed-upon services. What this reasonable amount is is not defined by law, except that the law states that it must conform to what would be customary compensation for the services performed. The employer is also required to provide reimbursement to an employee for reasonable expenses while the employee is working for and under the direction of the employer. It is common for the employer to reimburse employees if the employee uses his or her own automobile when traveling on company business.

The employer also has a duty to assist and/or cooperate with the employee so that he or she is able to perform the agreed-upon services. It could be construed as a violation of the employer-employee agreement if the employer prevents or inhibits the employee from performing his or her duties. For example, if it is understood that the employer will provide all the necessary tools and materials for the employee to do drafting work and later requires that the employee pay for those tools, the employer is inhibiting the employee from performing his or her duties.

Common law, as well as federal and state regulations, requires that the employer provide safe working conditions for employees. Should an employee feel that his or her working environment is unsafe, the employer cannot dismiss the employee for reporting unsafe conditions.

The preceding examples relate to general duties of the employer to the employee. Other duties may also be required of the employer, depending on the exact nature of the agreement between the employer and employee.

Employee to Employer

The employee has several basic duties to the employer and may have additional ones, as outlined by any formal agreement or written contract. The employee has an obligation to perform his or her duties with reasonable diligence and skill. At what level the diligence and skill must be performed is related to what would be considered common for the services required and experience level expected. For example, if an employee is hired on the basis of his or her skill in, and knowledge of, architectural CAD software, the employer has a right to expect that the work performed be representative of someone who fully understands the software.

A second duty of the employee is to be loyal to the employer. An employee is expected to act in the interests of the employer, not for the benefit of any outside party or even of the employee. This means, for example, that a designer who prepares the design work for a major company cannot be hired by that company to design an additional area in the company "on the side." If the designer engaged in moonlighting* in this way, the employer would have the right to terminate the employee for breach of the agency relationship because of a conflict of interest.

A third duty of the employee to the employer is to keep the employer informed of anything related to the relationship. "What the agent actually tells the principal is not relevant; what the agent *should have told* the principal is crucial"† (Jentz et al., 1987, p. 479). The following provides an example. One day Tom mentions to his boss that a client appears to be ready to order 100 chairs from a certain manufacturer. The boss, thinking that this would be a good opportunity to order an additional number of the same chair for inventory, orders another 100. After the order has been placed, Tom learns, but neglects to tell his boss, that the client has changed his mind and will not order the chair after all. The boss, who now is responsible for paying for all the chairs, could consider Tom in breach of the agency relationship.

A fourth duty of the employee is to be obedient to the employer. By this is meant that the employee is required to follow all legal and clearly stated instructions or policies of the employer. For example, if the company has a policy that warehouse workers may not use the company vehicle for personal business, it would be a violation of this duty if one of the drivers used a company truck on the weekend without getting permission from the proper supervisor. Only certain emergency situations would allow the employee to deviate from these obligations.

Employees are hired because of the skills they possess, which match the tasks and responsibilities required by the employer. The employer expects that those tasks and responsibilities will be performed by the employee, not a third party. It is unlikely that an employee will hire someone else to perform the work required by that employee without telling the employer; however, this duty is part of the relationship and personal service that are required by the agency relationship.

Finally, for the employee who has access to company funds or property, the employee has a duty to keep a proper accounting of the inflows and outflows of funds or use of property. A designer who has authorization to sign purchase orders for supplies would be breaching this duty if he or she used one of the purchase orders to obtain supplies for his or her own needs. In this case, the breach is also a criminal act, and the employer could press charges.

Employment at Will

The concept of *employment at will* relates to the doctrine that an employee, who is not bound by a written contract and who has no written terms of his or her employment spelled out, can be fired by the employer at any time without any explanation. Traditionally, the courts have ruled that, since the employee may

* Moonlighting is when an individual holds or engages in work outside his or her main job.

† Copyright West Publishing Company.

quit at any time without giving a reason, the employer has the right to fire the employee at any time without giving a reason, as long as the firing does not violate any federal or state employment laws.

The vast majority of employees in the interior design profession are subject to the employment-at-will doctrine. Most design employees are put to work and continue in specified duties without ever signing an employment contract. Since there is no contract, the employer is not bound by law to give the employee any reason for termination. Likewise, the employee has the right to give notice and leave the firm at any time without giving any reason.

There are some restrictions on the employer's right to terminate an employee under the employment-at-will doctrine. An employee cannot be fired merely because of his or her sex, race, religion, age, or handicapping condition. An employer cannot fire an employee out of malice, in retaliation, or because of bad faith. Unless there is a contract between the employer and the employee, the employer can fire the employee without giving any reason. Of course, an employer can have many reasons to terminate an employee that are perfectly legal. A few examples of these include insubordination, violating company rules, excessive absence or lateness, low productivity, misappropriating company property, or a downturn in business.

Unfortunately, some employers take advantage of the employment-at-will doctrine and terminate employees unfairly. If an employee believes that he or she has been fired unfairly or not in accordance with his or her written or implied contract, the employee may have grounds for a wrongful discharge suit.

Wrongful discharge basically means that the employee has been fired without good cause. Wrongful discharge litigation, also called unjust dismissal, stems from rulings by judges who feel that the employment legislation passed by federal and state governments have not always gone far enough to protect employees. Common-law wrongful discharge is based on legal precedent rather than on statutes. Under the concept of wrongful discharge, workers cannot be fired for performing "public obligations," such as jury duty or voting. Employees also cannot be fired for reporting company violations of health or safety laws (called whistle-blowing). These are examples of a public policy tort and are grounds for an employee lawsuit.

Another aspect of wrongful discharge involves implied contracts. Many courts have ruled that verbal agreements about working conditions constitutes an implied contract between employer and employee. A written or oral assurance made to an employee by the employer can restrict the employer's right to fire the employee for anything other than cause.

According to Lewin Joel (1996, p. 55), to see if an implied contract exists, the courts will look at such things as how long the employee has worked for the firm; if records show a lack of criticism of the employee; whether promises or assurances have been given to the employee; and the firm's overall employment practices.

Recent judgments have also determined in some states that statements in an employee handbook can constitute an implied contract related to the firing and possibly other conditions of employment. In the case of terminations without reason, if the handbook describes the procedure for dismissal, an employee cannot be terminated unless the firm has followed that procedure. For example, if a company named Business Office Furniture has the statement, "No employee will be dismissed without good cause" in its handbook, an employee cannot be fired unless the employee has been told what that "good cause" reason is. To avoid this problem, it is necessary to add a statement in an employee handbook such as that the employee has no contract for employment unless the contract is in writing and has been signed by the employer and/or that the company reserves the right to fire the employee for reasons that may have been stated in the handbook (such as insubordination) or for no reason at all. These kinds of statements help protect the employer.

If an employee has been fired illegally, the employee must be able to prove in court that the firing was due to discrimination or wrongful discharge. This can be very difficult for the employee to prove. The employee can protect himself or herself by requesting written information regarding expectations and performance evaluations on a regular basis. It is also important for the employee to document any events that might relate to the firing. The employee should also maintain copies of performance evaluations that have been signed by the supervisor, as well as notes about any meetings concerning job performance.

Large firms have attempted to protect themselves from potential charges by changing management practices. Regular performance evaluations of all employees hired "at will" is one way to prove that a terminated employee has been fired because of inadequate job performance. Documented meetings, during which the manager talks to and warns an employee that he or she is not meeting expectations, is another method the employer can use to protect his or her right to fire noncontract employees. Adding disclaimer statements to employee handbooks also affords the employer protection against lawsuits.

Although it is harder for an employer to fire an employee for little or no reason, the courts still support the idea that the employer must retain the right to fire employees who are incompetent, unqualified, unwilling to work, and so on. As more and more court cases related to improper termination occur, it is important that both employers and employees take the hiring, evaluation, and termination process more seriously.

Both employers and employees should be aware of each other's rights with regard to employment and termination. Employers no longer can terminate an employee capriciously if the employee is fulfilling his or her duties in accordance with satisfactory levels of performance. And employees have the right to retain employment without fear of retaliation, sexual harassment, and discrimination.

Employment Contracts

Some design firms use employment contracts or agreements to spell out conditions of employment or special perks and benefits. The use of employment contracts has always been more prevalent for various sales and management positions, while professional staff positions in interior design are more often considered to be employment at will. However, a tight job market has brought an increase in employment contract lawsuits for all types of professional staff in the interior design industry.

An employment contract does not have to be in writing. An oral employment contract would be formed technically when the employer and employee have agreed about things with respect to responsibilities, compensation, and terms of employment. Written contracts are prepared to clarify more complex issues that may be of interest to the employer or the employee. An interior designer who is responsible for sale of goods or is otherwise eligible for a commission or a bonus may want a written contract to spell out what will be paid and how the commission or bonus will be paid. Many employers seek written contracts to limit the employee from taking clients to competing firms if the employee quits. Figure 12-1 shows a sample employment contract.

Corporate Interiors Group, Inc.
7000 N. Lincoln Avenue
Anywhere, Pennsylvania

August 200x

Mr. Tony Smith
8142 E. Dempster St.
Anywhere, Pennsylvania

Dear Tony:

Let me welcome you to the Corporate Interiors Group, Inc. family! We are very pleased you have decided to join our company.

The following constitutes the employment contract between Corporate Interiors Group, Inc. employer, and Tony Smith, employee.

Employment

You shall devote your full time and best efforts to interior design activities and perform these activities to the best of your ability. You are not allowed to work for clients or other design firms outside the employ of Corporate Interiors Group, Inc.

The starting job classification for your employment is **Project Manager.** The duties and responsibilities of a Project Manager include: marketing presentations, project design and specification, production of contract documents, working with designers and design assistants, job site supervision or coordination, and other duties and responsibilities as called out on the attached job description.

Compensation

Project Managers are compensated on a salary basis. Your starting salary will be ________ annually. This salary will be paid on the basis of 26 equal pay periods.

You are eligible for the bonus program after you have worked full-time for a period of three (3) consecutive months. Bonuses are determined based on a percentage of income. The details of the bonus calculations are outlined in the attachment, "Corporate Interiors Group, Inc. Bonus Policies." This attachment is considered part of this employment contract.

Project Managers are entitled to a ____ percent commission on all accessory specifications. Payment is made only after receipt of payment from the client.

Merit and cost-of-living increases are only awarded at the beginning of the calendar year. Merit raises are determined on the basis of performance reviews. Any salary increase thus earned will begin at the next regular pay period after the completion of performance reviews. Performance reviews are conducted for all employees during November and December. Cost-of-living increases are at the discretion of the owners, not the design department manager.

Benefits

All benefits are described in detail in the company handbook. There is a company retirement plan. Eligibility and details are available from the Personnel Manager.

Termination

Your employment may be terminated by either party upon written notice. This notice must specify the date of termination and be hand-delivered or delivered by certified mail.

A. Within thirty (30) days of termination, you will be paid outstanding commission on sales of accessories made prior to your termination where all the merchandise has been delivered and accepted to the customer.
B. Commissions due on sales begun prior to your termination but not delivered prior to your termination will be paid within 30 days of receipt of payment by the customer.
C. Bonus payments will be prorated on the number of calendar days you worked between the last date of the previous bonus payment and the date of termination notice.

Noncompetition Provision

The employee may not go to work for a competitor of Corporate Interiors Group, Inc. for a period of 15 days from the date of termination of employment with Corporate Interiors Group, Inc.

The employee will not make available to a subsequent employer any confidential information concerning the operations and clients of Corporate Interiors Group.

Return of Company Property

Upon termination of employment, the employee will surrender all handbooks, files, equipment, price lists, catalogs, customer information, and other company records or property. The use of photographs for a personal portfolio of projects which the employee was primarily responsible when an employee of Corporate Interiors Group can be used only if Corporate Interiors Group is cited as the employer.

Modifications to the Contract

No changes, modifications, additions, or deletions shall be made to this contract unless those changes, modifications, additions, or deletions are in writing, and are signed by both parties.

The above constitutes the total legal agreement between the parties named. Signatures below signify agreement to the terms of the employment contract. One copy shall be placed in your employment file. The second copy should be retained by the employee.

______________________________ ______________________

Tony Smith, Employee **Date**

______________________________ ______________________

Jordan Jones, President **Date**
Corporate Interiors Group, Inc.

Attachments:
Job description, Project Manager
Corporate Interiors Group, Inc. Bonus Policies

FIGURE 12-1. An example of an employment contract for an interior design position.

In general, the written employment contract covers the following:

1. *Compensation*. Will the employee be paid hourly, on a salary, or by commission? If by commission, the method of payment should be spelled out.
2. *Employment responsibilities*. This clause should indicate, in sufficient detail, what the employee has been hired to do. Many companies refer to and attach a copy of the appropriate job description.
3. *Termination*. Statements about procedures and policies concerning termination notice and the manner in which either party must give notice should be in the contract. For the protection of the employee, statements should also outline how any outstanding commission (if commission is part of the compensation method) is to be paid.
4. *Termination for cause*. This clause protects the employee from being terminated for some capricious reason. Reasons for termination for cause include negligence, incompetence, dishonesty, disloyalty, and nonadherence to company policies.
5. *Territory rights*. Sales personnel especially are limited to working with clients only in certain territories. This territory might be certain cities or states, or even certain clients. If the employee is limited to a territory, this fact should be stated in the contract.

There may be other clauses in the contract to protect either party. A clause regarding return of company property may be in the contract. Although most employment contracts in the interior design profession would not have an ending date, the employer or the employee might wish to have a duration clause that specifies a fixed date when the contract would expire. It is understood that the contract remains in force as long both parties agree to the employee's continuing employment.

Some employers put a *restrictive covenant* (also called a noncompete agreement) in an employment contract. A restrictive covenant "limits a worker's employment options after leaving her or his present job. The objective . . . is to protect the present employer from an employee who might take trade secrets, customer lists, or other confidential material to a competitor" (Brown and Sukys, 1997, p. 157). The restrictive covenant can effectively prevent the employee from working for a competitor of the employer or from starting his or her own business, and can limit the territory in which the employee seeks new employment. A restrictive covenant is enforceable by the court as long as it does not last for an unreasonable length of time or unfairly restricts the individual from making a living in the same location as the former employer. What the length of time is and what the area is that are considered reasonable is up to the court in the area.

Employment contracts can protect both the employee and the employer. If the employer requests that a written contract be signed, the prospective employee should be certain that he or she understands all the terms of the contract. If an oral agreement is made, the same advice is suggested. In fact, many authors on employee rights suggest that the employee prepare a letter that summarizes the oral agreements and then send this letter to the employer. It is far more pleasant for both the employer and the employee to be in agreement concerning the terms of employment, compensation, and other conditions of the employment relationship rather than at odds about those conditions later on in court.

Independent Contractors

The use of independent contractors is not a new concept in business or in the practice of interior design. A designer who hires a wallpaper hanger is hiring an independent contractor. The delivery crew that has been hired on an as-need basis to deliver furniture for a design firm is considered an independent contractor, as far as the interior design firm is concerned, although the crew probably are employees of the delivery service company.

During the sluggish economy of the early 1990s, design firms began to hire design personnel as independent contractors. This was done so that a company intermittently could supplement its staff with design personnel when necessary. In some cases, designers who had been laid off by an employer were asked back on an as-needed basis. Some designers started their own businesses and freelanced their design services to design firms. Employers categorize these temporary workers as independent contractors, since the designation means that they are not required to pay many kinds of benefits to them. However, this designation is not always used legally.

According to the IRS, the general rule is that an individual is an *independent contractor* if the employer has the right to control or direct only the result of the work and not the means and methods of accomplishing the result (IRS, 2000). The independent contractor usually has a specific, short-term working relationship with the firm, and the work often is defined by a written contract. The worker is paid upon completion of the work.

Designers and others who work freelance* are generally independent contractors. Wallpaper hangers, floor-covering installers, contractors, and subcontractors are all examples of independent contractors, as long as the work that they do and the equipment that they use to do the work are *not* controlled and provided by the designer who has hired them. Designers who hire architects to review drawings that have been produced by the designer are hiring an independent contractor. Design firms that hire consultants are hiring independent contractors.

However, as John L. Vollmer has reported, design firms have taken advantage of the independent contractor designation when they hire workers (2000, p. 56). Whether this occurs by mistake or is intentional, this practice can have serious consequences for both the employer and the workers.

Independent contractors are not employees of the design firm and have no rights to the benefits that employees have. Employers are not required to withhold deductions for income tax and generally are not required to pay or withhold social security or Medicare contributions, or worker's compensation insurance for an independent contractor. Also, employers are not liable for the negligent acts of independent contractors while they are performing their contractual work responsibilities.

As far as the independent contractor is concerned, he or she cannot file for unemployment insurance when the work has been completed. He or she also is not entitled to worker's compensation insurance if he or she is injured while working for the contracting business. The independent contractor must pay self-employment tax on this supplemental income. If the worker does not report the supplemental income and pay self-employment taxes in accordance to IRS regulations, the worker can be subject to penalties by the IRS.

The primary issues that define a worker as an independent contractor or employee focus on the degree of control that the employer has over the worker.

* *Freelance* is generally accepted as meaning a self-employed worker.

The greater the control, the more likely it is that the worker is an employee. Along with this is the degree to which the worker controls his or her own work schedule, whether the worker is working solely for one employer or is working for more than one at a time, and where the contracted work is being performed. Again, all these issues related back to control held by the employer. There are strict guidelines for defining independent contractors. Figure 12-2 summarizes these guidelines. If the reader is considering hiring someone as an independent contractor or is working as an independent contractor, he or she is urged to obtain IRS Publication 15-A for clarification of this type of employment status.

Part-time workers are not considered independent contractors by the IRS. It may be that the part-time employee receives little, if any, company benefits, such as health insurance; nevertheless, the employer is required to withhold social security, worker's compensation, and other mandated contributions for all part-time workers.

Sexual Harassment

Sexual harassment is a type of discrimination, covered under federal statute Title VII of the Civil Rights Act of 1964. It has become an increasing issue in the last decade for women and men. Unfortunately, *sexual harassment* can be

According to the Internal Revenue Service, the following factors will be considered when determining whether an individual is to be considered an independent contractor or an employee. Individual state departments of revenue and worker's compensation insurance providers also may be called to audit whether an individual is an employee or an independent contractor.

- The person hiring the independent contractor has no control over *how, when,* or *where* the contractor does the work for which he or she has been hired. This is a very key issue in determining the status of an independent contractor.
- An independent contractor uses his or her own methods and receives no training from the person who buys the services.
- An independent contractor hires his or her own assistants when necessary to complete the assignment.
- An independent contractor works when and for whom he or she chooses. He or she also sets the hours of work, though this may be negotiated by the requirements of the assignment.
- The independent contractor provides his or her own equipment and supplies to perform the job duties required.
- The independent contractor is usually hired for a short time, with no expectation of permanent employment. Often the independent contractor is hired "for the job," which means only for a specifically defined task.
- Payment for services is commonly at the end of the job or by means of one or more partial payments (depending on the length of the job).
- The expenses of working are born by the independent contractor, though some expenses may be billed to the buyer, based on the assignment.
- An independent contractor can work for more than one company or individual at a time.
- The independent contractor must engage in professional work that is distinctly different from that of the person hiring the contractor. Interior designers hired by interior design firms to do interior design work might not be considered independent contractors, especially if the other conditions mentioned in the preceding are not met.
- An employee can be fired or quit at any time. An independent contractor agrees to work until the assignment has been completed and cannot be fired as long as he or she produces a result that meets the specifications of the assignment.

FIGURE 12-2. Guidelines for defining an independent contractor, from IRS Publication No. 15-A. (US Department of the Treasury, Internal Revenue Service)

a problem in the interior design office. Women and men in large and small interior design firms have been exposed to, or have been recipients of, sexual harassment at one time or another. "Sexual harassment is generally defined as sexual advances, requests for sexual favors, and other verbal or physical conduct of a sexual nature when submission to such conduct is made either explicitly or implicitly a term or condition of employment or some related activity" (Jones and Philcox, 2000, p. 92).

Sexual harassment is commonly thought of as the unwelcome sexual advances that a supervisor or business owner makes toward an employee who is a subordinate of that supervisor or business owner. Yet, there are two types of sexual harassment. The most common is called *quid pro quo*, which is Latin for "something for something" and is associated with the most commonly understood type of sexual harassment. For example, an employee is told he or she will receive a promotion if he or she gives sexual favors to a superior. The other type of sexual harassment is the creation of a hostile work environment. This second type is more subjective, and it is generally not tied to a promotion, raise, or the like. Examples are explicit cartoons, jokes, or gestures that become commonplace in the work environment. Obviously, this issue is very important, since many cases have come before the EEOC and the courts in recent years.

Most cases of sexual harassment occur between employers and employees, but some peer harassment is also considered illegal sexual harassment.* In some cases, the employer might be liable for sexual harassment of an employee by a customer, especially if the employer has been informed of the situation and does nothing about it. Of course, the customer might also be liable.

As seen by widely publicized cases in the media, sexual harassment is not easy to prove. The first thing that someone who feels that he or she has been sexually harassed should do is to inform the person exhibiting the unwanted behavior to stop. If a designer feels that he or she is being harassed by a supervisor, he or she should, as soon as possible, document for his or her files any details about the episode. These notes would be needed to prove that harassment rather than, say, work deficiencies was the reason for termination, should that occur. The individual should file a written complaint with the proper supervisor or person in authority. If the individual is working in a small firm and the harassment is coming from the owner, the designer should submit the letter to the owner. In larger firms, the individual should check with other employees to determine if the harassment is widespread. Of course, if nothing positive results from the written complaint, the designer would want to speak to an attorney or the EEOC. Delays in contacting the proper authority might be interpreted as acceptance of the behavior and could result in jeopardizing a claim, if one is filed later.

Sexual harassment is unwanted sexual advances or sexual connotations. If the individual accepts the behavior, he or she cannot later claim that the actions constitute harassment. Do not tolerate this kind of behavior from coworkers, bosses, even clients. Learn more about sexual harassment by reading one of the books in the references or any of the other numerous books and articles that have appeared recently.

Summary

There are many laws that regulate the hiring, retaining, and firing of employees that apply to the interior design firm, especially one with more than

* Peer harassment, however, is not illegal under Title VII.

15 employees (depending on the law and the jurisdiction). Employers and employees should be familiar with these laws to avoid government intervention or lawsuits. The employer-employee relationship itself also involves specific legal obligations on the part of both parties.

Employees have rights in the design office, and they should become informed about those rights. Discrimination in all phases of the work situation and sexual harassment are among the most widely occurring problems in employee-employer relationships. Employees—even those who work part-time—are entitled to certain benefits that are paid in part or entirely by the employer. It is important for the employer and the worker to understand when the worker is classified as an employee and is entitled to certain benefits and when a worker is truly an independent contractor.

All these legal issues are not meant to handcuff the employer or employee. Rather, both sides must realize that hiring employees or accepting a position with a company must be done in good faith and within legal restraints. It is too expensive for companies to hire, train, and fire, or watch employees leave design firms. It is too emotionally draining for the employee to have to sue or even threaten to sue over employment misunderstandings or mistreatment. As the profession continues to grow and change, employers must accept the responsibilities related to employees just as it accepts responsibilities related to the client.

REFERENCES

Beam, Burton T., Jr., and John J. McFadden. 1998. *Employee Benefits*, 5th ed. Dearborn Financial Publishing.

Bennett-Alexander, Dawn D., and Laura P. Hartman. 2001. *Employment Law for Business*, 3rd ed. Boston, MA: Irwin/McGraw-Hill.

Berger, C. Jaye. 1994. *Interior Design Law and Business Practices.* New York: John Wiley.

Bernardo, Stephanie. "Fire Me . . . and I'll Sue!" *Success!* July/August 1985.

Brown, Gordon W., and Paul A. Sukys. 1997. *Business Law*, 9th ed. New York: Glencoe/McGraw-Hill.

Clarkson, Kenneth W., Roger LeRoy Miller, and Gaylord A. Jentz. 1983. *West's Business Law*, 2nd ed. St. Paul, MN: West Publishing.

Clarkson, Kenneth W., Roger LeRoy Miller, Gaylord A. Jentz, and Frank B. Cross. 1989. *West's Business Law*, 4th ed. St. Paul, MN: West Publishing.

Conry, Edward J., Gerald R. Ferrera, and Karla H. Fox. 1993. *The Legal Environment of Business*, 3rd ed. Boston: Allyn and Bacon.

Epstein, Lee. 1977. *Legal Forms for the Designer.* New York: N & E Hellman.

Eskenazi, Martin, and David Gallen. 1992. *Sexual Harassment. Know Your Rights!* New York: Carroll & Graf.

Garner, Bryan A., ed. 1999. *Black's Law Dictionary*, 7th ed. St. Paul, MN: West Group.

Goodale, James G. 1992. *One to One: Interviewing, Selecting, Appraising, and Counseling Employees.* Englewood Cliffs, NJ: Prentice-Hall.

Harragan, Betty Lehan. "Career Advice." *Working Woman.* September 1986.

Hauser, Barbara R., ed. 1996. *Woman's Legal Guide.* Golden, CO: Fulcrum.

Haviland, David. 1994. *The Architect's Handbook of Professional Practice, Student Edition.* Washington, DC: AIA Press.

Hood, Jack B., Benjamin A. Hardy, Jr., Harold S. Lewis, Jr. 1999. *Worker's Compensation and Employee Protection Laws.* St. Paul, MN: West Publishing.

Internal Revenue Service. January 2000. *Publication No. 15-A. Employer's Supplemental Tax Guide.* Department of the Treasury.

Jentz, Gaylord, Kenneth W. Clarkson, and Roger LeRoy Miller. 1987. *West's Business Law—Alternate UCC Comprehensive Edition*, 3rd ed. St. Paul, MN: West Publishing.

Joel, Lewin G., III. 1996. *Every Employee's Guide to the Law.* New York: Pantheon Press.

Jones, Nancy L., with Phil Philcox. 2000. *The Woman's Guide to Legal Issues*. Los Angeles, CA: Renaissance Books.

Lawson, Joseph W. R., II. 1998. *How To Develop an Employee Handbook*, 2nd ed. New York: American Management Association.

Liddle, Jeffrey L. 1981. "Malicious Terminations and Abusive Discharges: The Beginning of the End of Employment at Will." *Employee Termination Handbook*. Englewood Cliffs, NJ: Executive Enterprises Publications.

Maister, David H. 1993. *Managing the Professional Service Firm*. New York: Free Press.

McWhirter, Darien. 1989. *Your Rights at Work*. New York: John Wiley.

O'Shea, Tracy, and Jane LaLonde. 1998. *Sexual Harassment*. New York: St. Martin's Griffin.

Petrocelli, William, and Barbara Kate Repa. 1999. *Sexual Harassment on the Job*, 4th ed. Berkeley, CA: Nolo Press.

Phillips, Patricia, and George Mair. 1997. *Know Your Rights: A Legal Handbook for Women Only*. New York: Macmillan.

Sack, Steven Mitchell. 1998. *The Working Woman's Legal Survival Guide*. Paramus, NJ: Prentice-Hall.

———. 1990. *Employee Rights Handbook*. New York: Facts on File.

———. 1981. *The Salesperson's Legal Guide*. Englewood Cliffs, NJ: Prentice-Hall.

Schulhofer, Stephen J. 1998. *Unwanted Sex. The Culture of Intimidation and Failure of Law*. Cambridge, MA: Harvard University Press.

Shilling, Dana. 1998. *The Complete Guide to Human Resources and the Law*. Paramus, NJ: Prentice-Hall.

Steingold, Fred S., and Barbara Kate Repa, ed. 1999. *The Employer's Legal Handbook*, 3rd ed. Berkeley, CA: Nolo Press.

Sweet, Justin. 1985. *Legal Aspects of Architecture, Engineering and the Construction Process*, 3rd ed. St. Paul, MN: West Publishing.

Vollmer, John L., Ph.D. "Sole Practitioner: Self-Employed or Contingent Worker? Investigating Worker Misclassification and Its Implications to Commercial Interior Design." *Journal of Interior Design*. vol. 26, no. 1, pp. 56–61. 2000.

Weiss, Donald H. 2000. *Fair Square and Legal*, 3rd ed. New York: American Management Association.

Woodward, Cynthia A. 1990. *Human Resources Management for Design Professionals*. Washington DC: AIA Press.

Chapter 13

Legal Responsibilities

In almost every major interior design firm, it is now common to hear of a few interior designers who act as expert witnesses in legal disputes. These interior designers are asked to provide testimony regarding reasonable professional practice, either for an interior designer or for a client who is suing an interior designer. Legal responsibility is not a matter of choice in the twenty-first century; it is a fact of professional life.

Interior designers are legally liable for the work they or members of their staff do and, as such, can be sued. This exposure includes the planning, specification, and execution of the design and design documents. Even the smallest design project involves activities and responsibilities that can lead to potential legal actions against the designer.

As the professional stature of interior design continues to grow and as the fight for licensing of the profession continues, the recognition and acceptance of legal responsibilities must increase as well. Interior designers must be aware of how lawsuits can negatively affect their practice because of such activities as malpractice and negligence, even as they can also protect them. It is the responsibility of the professional designer to be aware of the legal responsibilities that affect his or her practice. It is not necessary to become a lawyer, but it is necessary to understand all the ramifications of engaging in a professional practice so as to avoid legal problems.

Legal responsibility and issues of the professional practice of interior design are woven into almost every aspect of the business. Many of these issues are discussed throughout this text. This chapter will briefly introduce the differences between criminal and tort law and will discuss issues of tort law that are important to the designer. Legal issues related to employment are explained in Chapter 12. The next chapter will cover warranties and product liability. Legal responsibilities concerning preparing design contracts for services is covered in Chapter 18. Chapter 20 covers legal responsibilities related to the selling practices of designers, as defined by the Uniform Commercial Code (UCC).

The examples given in this chapter are simple illustrations that help clarify the legal concepts discussed in the chapter. In reality, a great many factors are involved in the determination of the actual guilt or innocence of persons in situations that are similar to the examples given in this chapter. These chapters do not constitute legal advice. The information provided should not substitute for any discussion with an attorney.

Criminal versus Tort Law

When a person (or a business, in the case of a corporation) commits an offense that is regulated by statute, the offense is a criminal offense and referred to as a *crime*[*]. Statutes are created to protect the public at large, thus crimes are wrongs against all of society. The punishment for the criminal act is imprisonment and/or a fine.

Although most people think of a crime as an offense against another person, there are some crimes that affect businesses. Embezzlement, or the fraudulent taking of another person's property or money by the one entrusted with it, is a well-known crime affecting businesses. Falsifying public records or altering legal documents are forms of forgery. These are but a few of the areas in which crimes are committed against businesses or even by businesses. If a corporation is involved, the corporation officers can be held responsible for their acts or for the neglectful acts of employees acting on behalf of the corporation.

Most legal problems that interior designers experience do not involve criminal acts, but, rather, they involve torts. A *tort* is "a private wrong that injures another person's physical well-being, property, or reputation" (Brown and Sukys, 1997, p. 72). When one person causes injury to another person or his or her property, the injured person may seek various remedies for the damages caused. Since the act is against one person by another, a tort is a civil action, in which the person harmed sues, in a civil court, the person who has done the harm. Some torts, such as assault and battery, are also criminal acts if there are statutes that define them as such.

By far, the most common kinds of tort cases that involve interior designers are related to negligence and breach of contract. Negligence liability, often referred to as professional negligence, legally means that the designer has failed to use due care in carrying out his or her design responsibilities. Breach-of-contract liability refers to the failure of the designer to complete the requirements of a contract. Breach of contract is discussed in Chapter 18. Other torts that can affect the interior practice, although these are less likely to occur, are torts for false imprisonment, defamation, and misrepresentation. Strict liability, a tort related to product liability, is another tort that can entangle the design practice. Strict liability is discussed in the next chapter.

Negligence

One kind of tort that commonly involves interior design practices is *negligence*. "Negligence is the failure to use due care to avoid foreseeable injury which might be caused to another person or property as a result of the failure to exercise due care" (Barnes, 1981, p. 11). The person accused of negligence creates a risk. This risk is such that a reasonable person can anticipate it and prevent it. If there is no creation of risk, there cannot be negligence. Because of this factor, it is a way of committing a tort rather than a kind of tort.

Negligence is also considered an unintentional tort. Negligence in unintentional because the designer did not think that any wrongful consequences of an act would occur and did not want them to occur. Nevertheless, the conduct created a risk, and that risk created the environment for the tort of negligence.

* Statutes are created to protect the public at large, thus crimes are wrongs against all of society.

To prove negligence, the harmed party must prove several things: first, that the defendant owed a duty—most commonly, "reasonable care"—to the plaintiff; second, that there was a breach of that duty either intentionally or unintentionally; third, that the act was the proximate cause* of the harm; and fourth, that there were damages or harm to persons or property. For example, inadvertently switching numbers on a purchase order, which results in the wrong wallpaper being hung in the client's home, is negligence. Selling and installing a carpet that the designer knows does not meet fire codes is negligence. An improper specification of textiles that has been proven to contribute to a fire is negligence.

Professional negligence indicates that the designer in some way was negligent in his or her conduct while executing a project. All the elements of negligence apply to professional negligence. Some examples of professional negligence, pointed out in Justin Sweet's *Legal Aspects of Architecture, Engineering, and the Construction Process* are worth repeating here.

Specifying material that did not comply with building codes

Failing to inform client of potential risks of using certain materials

Drafting ambiguous sketches, causing extra work

Designing closets not large enough for the clothing to be contained in them

Designing a project that greatly exceeded the client's budget

Failing to engage and check with a consultant (Sweet, 1985, pp. 329–330)

As can be seen by these examples, there are a large number of relatively unintentional acts related to everyday responsibility that can be considered professional negligence. Let us look specifically at the factors that must be proven in order to show negligence and how they relate to an interior design practice.

Duty of Care

Interior designers owe a duty of care to their clients in many ways. This duty relates to the care in selection of materials and products that are proper and adequate to meet the functional and legal (if codes are binding) needs of the project. Specifying residential grade carpet in most commercial interiors would give inadequate performance and would be negligent. The correct preparation of working drawings is another professional duty owed by the designer. Making a mistake in labeling dimensions for a custom cabinet is a mistake; but it is also negligence if it results in the wrong size cabinet being constructed. A designer owes a duty to the client to not allow defective work to be done on the job site. For example, if a designer who is visiting a job site sees that the carpet installer is using a non-quick-release glue to affix carpet tiles when a quick-release glue was specified, the designer has a duty to the client to stop the work and have it corrected.† The designer also has a duty not to expose others to risks created by defective designs. The designer must be sure that the structure of a building will support any wall-hung units that are specified. The designer owes a duty to write specifications that are within the budget stated by the client. Designing and writing specifications for a project that are in excess of the budget also constitutes negligence.

* This is formally referred to as causation.

† Although the duty may "always" exist, the actual legal ability to remedy the situation will vary, depending on local laws regarding supervision of construction and/or installation work. Refer to Chapter 6 for more on this issue.

Breach of Duty A breach of duty results when a designer fails to act in a way that is considered reasonable for the professional designer. The breach may be an act, such as knowingly specifying the wrong carpet for the client (intentional), or an omission, such as not stopping the work when the designer sees that the carpet being installed is incorrect (carelessness). The benchmark of "reasonable" is sometimes hard to define, so expert witnesses are often used to help the court determine what is reasonable for an interior designer concerning the case in question.

Proximate Cause A person may have a duty to another, and he or she may in some way breach that duty, but the act (the breach of duty) must cause some injury or harm for a tort to have been committed. In legal terminology, this is called proximate cause. *Proximate cause* "is the connection between the unreasonable conduct and the resulting harm" (Brown and Sukys, 1997, p. 80). If the injury occurs exclusively because of the designer's act, then there is proximate cause. An example will help to explain this. A designer knows that a certain manufacturer requires 5/8-inch drywall to support its wall strips and knows that the client already has installed 1/2-inch drywall. If the designer has the wall strips hung anyway, there is causation in fact. Often the "but for" test is used to determine causation in fact. "But for the wrongful act, the injury would not have occurred."

"The question is whether the connection between an act and an injury is strong enough to justify imposing liability" (Clarkson et al., 1983, p. 53).* If the consequences of the act that does harm are unforeseeable, there is no proximate cause. For example, if the wall strips pull out from the wall and, as a result, the falling books hit a lamp, which shatters and starts a fire that then burns down the house, there would probably be proximate cause if it were shown that the lamp would have created a fire if it had broken in such a manner. How foreseeable one act is over another is determined by the courts and is not easy to establish. For the designer to be held liable, actual cause between the act and the harm created must be present.

Injury or Harm A tort of negligence does not occur unless there is some legally recognizable loss, harm, wrong, or invasion to a plaintiff. Injury must occur in order for the plaintiff to recover compensation. There does not have to be an injury to a person for this element to exist. The delay in delivery of sufficient furniture for a business to operate can be considered an injury if the delay is the fault of the designer. Remember, plaintiffs in tort cases seek compensation for damages from the defendant; they usually do not seek to imprison the defendant. Courts more often find in favor of the plaintiff when personal injury, rather than property or economic damage, occurs.

Principal Defenses for Negligence The principal defenses for negligence are assumption of risk and contributory negligence. In assumption of risk, the plaintiff who knowingly and willingly enters into a risky situation cannot recover damages if injury occurs. If a client agrees to purchase a residential grade carpet, knowing it will not provide the wear required in his or her commercial installation, the designer is absolved of negligence.

In using contributory negligence as a defense, it must be shown that both sides have been negligent and that injury has resulted. This comes from the idea that everyone should look out for his or her own interests and safety.

Where contributory negligence is successfully used as a defense, the plaintiff is not able to recover damages no matter how great the injury or how slight the contributory negligence.

Many states have also added a defense of comparative negligence to soften the effects of contributory negligence. In this situation, the courts determine the degree of fault by both sides and grants damages related to it.

Intentional Torts Against a Person

Intentional torts against a person must show intent; that is, the person must have consciously performed the act and must have known or have been substantially certain that the act would harm another person. Assault, battery, false imprisonment, defamation, invasion of privacy, and fraud are some of the torts included in this area.

Assault occurs when a person intentionally performs an act so that another person has a feeling of apprehension or fear of harm or physical injury. Actual contact or physical harm is not necessary for an assault to occur; causing another to be apprehensive is enough. Battery occurs when there is intentional touching or other physical contact by one person upon another without the person's consent or without any justification.

False imprisonment (or false arrest) is the intentional confinement of a person for an appreciable duration of time. This is of particular importance to designers who are engaged in retail selling. A business owner must be reasonably certain that a customer has shoplifted in order to detain that customer or the customer can sue for false imprisonment. In many jurisdictions, shoplifting has not occurred until the person has walked out the door of the business with goods that have not been properly paid for.

Defamation is the wrongful harming of a person's good reputation. If the defamation is in writing, it is called *libel*; if it is oral, it is *slander*. To be defamatory, statements must be made to, or read or heard by, a third party. It is not necessary for the defamed party to hear or read the defamation. Again, some harm must result from the statements made in order for them to be considered to be defamation by a court. It is for this reason that interior designers must be careful about what they say or write concerning their competitors or competitors' products. For example, telling a client that Jones Interiors "did a lousy job" on their last three residential commissions would be defamation by slander if Jones Interiors lost work because of the comments. Jones Interiors could sue the offending designer.

Invasion of privacy is a tort against a person's right to freedom from others' prying eyes. For this reason, it is important to obtain written permission to photograph an installation. This is especially important if the photograph becomes part of an advertisement or a printed promotional tool of any kind. Permission should be obtained, even if the designer does not intend to cite the location in the promotional piece or display. In addition, a release must also be signed by any people who are seen in the photograph, even if permission has been given to photograph the interior by the employer. Care must also be taken when obtaining information concerning a person's or a business's affairs, for example, about credit information, without permission. This type of information must be kept confidential by the designer and must not be distributed intentionally or unintentionally.

Fraud (also thought of as misrepresentation) is another intentional tort against a person. When a designer intentionally misrepresents facts to deceive a client in order to receive personal gain, fraud has been committed. Informing a client that a certain product will meet specific needs of the client if the designer or salesperson knows that it will not, is fraud. The common test in this situation is misrepresenting facts. A misstatement of facts, not opinions, unless the person expressing the opinion is considered an expert in the subject matter, is what is considered to be fraud. These "untrue facts" must be made with the intent that the client will rely on them. The deceived party must have justifiably relied upon the information, and the reliance must have caused damages to occur.

It is not unusual for designers or salespersons to use language that might exaggerate a service or a product. If a designer's or salesperson's statements are not misrepresenting facts, then those statements are likely to be considered seller's talk or "puffing." The use of puffing, or offering personal opinions about intangible qualifiers of a product or a service, is not usually considered fraud unless the seller represents as fact something that he or she knows is not true. To say that your design firm is the "best interior design office in town" is not fraud, since the word *best* is subjective, not objective. To say that your design firm is the only firm in town that can do the work when it is clearly not true is misrepresentation if, in fact, your firm is not the only firm in town that can do the work. Factual deception in order to obtain personal gain is a form of misrepresentation.

Intentional Torts Against Property

The three torts against property are trespass to land and personal property, conversion, and nuisance. Although each may be a problem to the interior designer, the torts of trespass to personal property and conversion are potentially the most damaging.

Trespass to land occurs when a person enters land that does not belong to him or her. Trespass to personal property occurs when a person either injures the personal property of another or interferes with the owner's right to exclusive possession or use of the personal property. The most common form of trespass of personal property is conversion. *Conversion* occurs when the rightful property of one person is taken by another. In criminal law, this is commonly called stealing or theft. For example, if an employee takes merchandise or supplies that belong to the employer and uses them for his or her own use rather than for company-related use, conversion has occurred. Although most employers do not prosecute or sue (remember, both are valid here) when employees take home pens and paper paid for by the employer, they have a legal right to do so. Here is another example of conversion. Bean Interiors refuses to deliver merchandise previously paid for by the client to the client's home, because the client will not control a dog on the premises. Withholding the goods that rightfully belong to the client can be considered a tort of conversion against Bean Interiors.

A suit for nuisance can also be brought against an interior designer. "A nuisance is an improper activity that interferes with another's enjoyment or use of his or her property" (Jentz et al., 1987, p. 55).* For the designer, this could mean that the designer and the client can be sued by a neighbor if the noise and dust from a remodeling project has interfered with the neighbor's enjoyment of his or her home.

* Copyright West Publishing Co.

Codes Compliance

An area of professional responsibility that is very important to all interior designers but that generally has more effect on the commercial interior designer is compliance with various codes. *Codes* are systematic bodies of law created by federal, state, and local jurisdictions to ensure safety. Codes are written by many different independent agencies and adopted and modified by federal, state, and local jurisdictions. During the course of a project, the interior designer's work may need to be judged against building codes, life safety, or fire codes, and barrier-free (handicapped access) codes. Other codes that the project may have to be in compliance with include electrical codes, health department codes, and zoning laws. Codes affect the work of the commercial designer generally more than the residential designer, since far more code requirements are directed toward public buildings than toward private residences.

Interior designers must be sure they understand which codes apply in the locations where they are designing. The code that applies to a specific project is the code that is in effect within the community where the project is being built or remodeled, not the location of the interior design firm. For example, an interior design firm located in Phoenix, Arizona, is preparing design drawings for a hospitality project in Tempe, Arizona (adjoining Phoenix), and Santa Barbara, California. The designer must meet the code requirements within Tempe and Santa Barbara, not those in Phoenix.

Code compliance is not an option; it is a legal necessity. Information can be obtained from local fire marshals, planning and building departments, and state and federal agencies responsible for specific types of structures. It is usually possible to purchase the necessary code books from the local planning and building department. Noncompliance with codes can result in work being stopped, torn out, and/or redone, generally at the expense of the interior designer.

Building Codes

Building codes primarily regulate structural and mechanical features of buildings. They define minimum standards for the design, construction, and quality of materials, based on the use, type, and occupancy of the building.

A new set of model building codes was approved in late 1999 by a joint commission. It was hoped that, within a reasonable length of time, all jurisdictions would adopt these codes so that there would be only one building code. Called the International Building Codes (IBC), these codes replace the several model building codes discussed in previous editions of this text. Basic concepts discussed here apply to the IBC codes, though, at the time of publication, it was unknown which jurisdictions had adopted the new codes. With this in mind, a brief discussion of existing codes is retained in this text.

New codes will go into effect only when a jurisdiction adopts them. The three existing model codes used in the United States until the International Building Codes are adopted are:

1. *Uniform Building Code* (UBC). Written by the International Conference of Building Officials (ICOB), the UBC has been adopted by most states west of the Mississippi River.
2. *Basic/National Building Code* (NBC). Written by the Building Officials Code Administrators International (BOAC), the NBC is used primarily by states east of the Mississippi River.
3. *Standard Building Code* (SBC). Written by the Southern Building Code Congress International (SBCI), the SBC is also used by states east of the Mississippi River.

The model building codes are revised every two to three years. Although it is a good idea to obtain each new addition of the applicable building code, the designer should be aware that not all jurisdictions change to the new code each time it is revised. In addition, local building conditions may require additional code requirements. Designers who work in metropolitan areas or who design work in several different cities also need to be sure that they are using the right version of the building code for each jurisdiction. Two cities next to each other in an urban area may have slightly different requirements. The local planning or building department can advise the designer on the applicable code.

Fire Safety Codes

Fire safety, or *life safety*, codes and regulations exist to provide a reasonable measure of safety in a building from fire, explosions, or other comparable emergencies. The model code used by most jurisdictions is the Life Safety Code written by the National Fire Protection Association. Covering many of the same concerns with design, construction, and materials as in the building codes, the Life Safety Code attempts to lessen the danger to life from fire, smoke, and hazardous fumes and gases. The intent of these codes is to prevent a fire whenever possible. However, since all fires cannot be prevented, the codes also focus on fire control. Fire prevention is facilitated by the regulation of hazards and such things as controls on the kinds of materials—both construction and furnishings—that can be used in buildings. Fire safety control is facilitated by the requirement of fire sprinklers, fire doors, and the like.

Fire codes focus on such matters as egress (corridors, halls, doors, etc.), interior architectural finishes, and fire protection equipment such as sprinklers and smoke detectors. Fire regulations related to furniture construction and fabrics or finishes are more a matter of federal, state, and local regulations. Codes developed by the New York Port Authority, the Boston Fire Department, and the California State Fire Marshall's Office (to name a few) have been adopted by many of the states in order to regulate furniture construction and the fabrics or finishes of furniture. The most far-reaching fire code related to furnishings is California TB 133. This code requires that the whole of the upholstered seating piece be tested and meet standards related to smoldering and ignition. In other words, the frame, stuffing, and padding, as well as the upholstery itself, must meet the standards. This is a very stringent standard for furniture and applies to only certain types of commercial installations. Note that not all jurisdictions have adopted this model code. The designer is again cautioned to check with local or appropriate fire marshals or building departments to clarify which fire safety standards are applicable in the firm's working area.

Barrier-Free Regulations

Building codes have worked to make public buildings more accessible to the handicapped and thus are *barrier-free*. In January of 1992, the Americans with Disabilities Act (ADA) opened the door, literally and figuratively, to making all buildings—public and private—accessible to those who are handicapped in the United States. The ADA itself is civil rights legislation, not a building code. Until a state or a local jurisdiction creates statutes of enforcement or incorporates the ADA regulations into its building code, a complainant would have to file a civil rights action in federal court. ADA regulations do not apply in the Canadian provinces.

The ADA legislation deals with four distinct areas: employment, public service and transportation, public accommodations, and telecommunications. This means that the legislation is a comprehensive package of requirements that denies discrimination against disabled individuals in many areas of their life. Applicable to our discussion in this section are a few items concerning Title III, Public Accommodations.

The intent of Title III is to provide access for a disabled person that is equal to that of the general public. New construction must be designed and built to meet the new design criteria called for in Title III. Existing buildings may have to make what are called "readily achievable" accommodations and changes to meet the criteria. If an existing building is going to be remodeled, it has to include all reasonable design changes. If an existing building is not undergoing any remodeling, the owners have to make the readily achievable changes if it is economically feasible to do so. Of course, if an individual files a civil rights lawsuit against the building owner, the end result of that lawsuit may be a requirement to make changes even in an old building. For example, for a new restaurant, seating must be provided that is as accessible to the disabled as it is to the general public. Public restrooms must also be designed to meet the new standards. In an existing restaurant, the owners may be required to make seating as accessible to the disabled as it is to the general public, since that is readily achievable. Modifying undersized restrooms might not be required because of cost or unless an individual wins a civil rights lawsuit against the restaurant.

The ADA affects every public and private building and type of business, with few exceptions. Private residences are excluded, as are commercial facilities. Commercial facilities are defined in the ADA as nonresidential buildings used by a private entity and that only employees of the entity are given access to.* A designer's warehouse and the offices of a private corporation (as long as the general public is denied access) are examples of a commercial facility. The designer's studio or office is considered a commercial facility as far as the ADA is concerned, assuming that the designer's clients are given access to the studio or office. There are special application requirements for restaurants and cafeterias, medical care facilities, business and mercantile buildings, libraries, transient lodging, and transportation facilities.

This author, having had a disabled parent for nearly 30 years, understands and appreciates the importance of this landmark legislation. It is hoped that designers will not view the ADA—or any code or regulation, for that matter—as infringement upon design creativity but, rather, as part of making all interior environments enjoyable to all individuals. Unfortunately, it is beyond the scope of this book to discuss in depth all the design criteria and regulations of the ADA. Numerous reference guides have been published recently to assist the designer in complying with the law. A few are listed in the references. An excellent reference for the interior designer on the various codes is *The Code Guidebook for Interiors* by Sharon Koomen Harmon.

Plan Review Boards

All jurisdictions have *plan review boards* (PRB) or design review boards (DRB), whose responsibility it is to review construction drawings prior to issuance of building permits. Depending on the contract responsibility, the owner, architect, or interior designer submits copies of plans and specifications to the plan review board. The plans are first reviewed by a member of the building department. This individual looks for any omission or discrepancy in design as regulated by building, mechanical, fire, and accessibility codes and regulations, as well as compliance with all other local building and construction standards.

* Commercial facilities may have to make reasonable, readily achievable accommodations for employees, based on Title I of the ADA.

Plans get *red lined* or are marked in red to show where problems exist. If too many red marks occur, the plans are rejected and must be redrawn, and perhaps, if necessary, redesigned. If only a few red marks appear on the plans, these are usually worked out among the owner, architect, designer, contractor, and the building department prior to or during construction. Many projects also are reviewed by the fire department, engineering department, planning and zoning department, state health department, or other groups that are looking specifically for compliance with regulations and codes within their jurisdictions.

Since meetings of the plan review board are subject to open meeting laws, anyone can sit in on the meeting. Designers who have never been "under the fire" of a PRB meeting should sit in on one sometime. If nothing else, it will make the designer more careful about the production of plans and specifications for all future projects!

Summary

As interior designers seek professional recognition, they must also accept professional responsibilities and liabilities. Students beginning their pursuit of a career, as well as those who already are actively engaged in the profession, must realize that their design efforts—whether in residential or commercial design, or in the specification of products or the drafting of floor plans—place them in a position of responsibility to their clients that goes beyond designing an aesthetic environment.

This chapter briefly discusses the differences between criminal and tort law. It also discusses many of the common tort classifications that can result in a civil lawsuit being brought against an interior designer. Chief among these are negligence and the concept of professional negligence.

The designer is responsible for being familiar, if not thoroughly cognizant of, the many regulations and legislation that affect the interior design and related professions. Building codes, earthquake protection, fire safety codes, barrier-free regulations, performance testing for flammability, and quality standards are just a few of these regulations.

Designers must gain awareness of their legal responsibilities in designing interiors as well as in their everyday professional practice. Today's interior designer is held accountable for his or her activities in design. The information in this chapter is provided to help the designer gain some understanding of that accountability so as to avoid legal problems. The reader may also wish to review items in the references, obtain copies of the applicable regulations, or take CEU classes for familiarization.

REFERENCES

Barnes, A. James. 1981. *A Guide to Business Law.* Homewood, Ill.: Learning Systems.

Berger, C. Jaye. 1994. *Interior Design Law and Business Practices.* New York: John Wiley.

Brown, Gordon W., and Paul A. Sukys. 1997. *Business Law*, 9th ed. New York: Glencoe/McGraw-Hill.

Building Owners and Managers Association. 1991. *ADA Compliance Guidebook. A Checklist for Your Building*. Washington, DC: BOMA.

Clarkson, Kenneth W., Roger LeRoy Miller, and Gaylord A. Jentz. 1983. *West's Business Law, Text and Cases*, 2nd ed. St. Paul, MN: West Publishing.

Conry, Edward J., Gerald R. Ferrera, and Karla H. Fox. 1993. *The Legal Environment of Business*, 3rd ed. Boston, MA: Allyn and Bacon.

Cushman, Robert F., and James C. Dobbs, eds. 1991. *Design Professional's Handbook of Business Law*. New York: John Wiley.

Federal Register. *Nondiscrimination on the Basis of Disability by Public Accommodations and in Commercial Facilities; Final Rule*, vol. 56, no. 144. 1991. Washington, DC: Department of Justice.

Garner, Bryan A., ed. 1999. *Black's Law Dictionary*, 7th ed. St. Paul, MN: West Publishing.

Harmon, Sharon Koomen. 2000. *The Codes Guidebook for Interiors*, 2nd ed. New York: John Wiley.

Hopf, Peter S., and John A. Raeber. 1984. *Access for the Handicapped*. New York: Van Nostrand Reinhold.

Jentz, Gaylord A., Kenneth W. Clarkson, and Roger LeRoy Miller. 1987. *West's Business Law—Alternate UCC Comprehensive Edition*, 3rd ed. St. Paul, MN: West Publishing.

Schweich, Thomas A. 1998. Protect Yourself from Business Lawsuits. New York: Scribner.

Steingold, Fred S. 1999. *The Employer's Legal Handbook*, 3rd ed. Berkeley, CA: Nolo Press.

Sweet, Justin. 1985. *Legal Aspects of Architecture, Engineering, and the Construction Process*, 3rd ed. St. Paul, MN: West Publishing.

Chapter 14

Warranties and Product Liability

Let us say that your firm has specified tables and chairs for the dining room of an assisted-living facility. From the catalog literature, the project manager is convinced that the chairs would be appropriate for the ambulatory residents who sit in the assisted living area of the facility. After all, the manufacturer is one of the many that specialized in furnishings for healthcare facilities. Would it be fair for your firm to be held responsible if any of the chairs, within a reasonable time frame—broke, causing harm to one of the residents? This is the type of question that this chapter will address.

Today's litigious society means that interior designers must fully understand the implications of warranties and product liability. Specifying and selling furniture and other goods to clients creates a legal responsibility. Whether the designer sells furniture, fixtures, and equipment for a small residential studio or specifies large quantities of products for a commercial project, the client expects to receive properly specified goods.

Designers are liable for the performance of the products that are specified in any project. Products must meet the expectations of reasonable use and fitness for the situation in which they will be used. The designer is also responsible for making sure that the products are specified and installed in such a way as not to cause injury to the people who will use the products or to the space in which the products will be installed. These requirements are expected of all individuals who are licensed or who call themselves interior designers.

This chapter will review basic concepts of warranties on products and legal concepts of product liability. This information goes hand in hand with the discussion on negligence in the previous chapter.

Warranties

The days when the phrase "buyer beware" was standard for consumers has long since past. Consumers are protected by a large number of regulations and laws that place much of the burden on the marketplace to provide safe products rather than on the buyer to be wary. Other regulations and laws help to satisfy the customer so that what he or she purchases meets correct standards of design, manufacturing, and use. Warranties are one way that the buyer is protected.

Warranties place a burden on the seller that the goods he or she sells meet certain standards. Four important kinds of warranties are governed by the Uniform Commercial Code (UCC):*

1. Warranty of title (Section 2-312)
2. Express warranty (Section 2-313)
3. Implied warranty of merchantability (Section 2-314)
4. Implied warranty of fitness for a particular purpose (Section 2-315)

When a designer or a design firm offers a warranty on a product, failure to honor that warranty is a breach of contract duty and gives the client the right to sue. The seller's breach also allows the customer to cancel the order.

Warranty of Title

The first aspect of warranty of title is that the seller has title to the goods and can legally sell them to others. *Title* signifies legal ownership of the goods. Basically, this means that the seller,† knowingly or not, is not selling stolen goods or goods that he or she does not have authorization to sell. For example, if an interior design firm does not have authority to buy and sell Steelcase systems from Steelcase because it does not have an agreement with a Steelcase dealer, the firm would not be able to tell the client that it could purchase the goods from Steelcase and sell the products to the client. Since the design firm cannot take title to the goods from Steelcase, it cannot pass the title on to the client.

A second aspect of warranty of title is that the buyer is protected from loss if he or she unknowingly buys goods with a lien attached. A *lien* means that someone other than the person who has ownership or possession of the goods has a security interest in the goods. If the buyer buys the goods knowing that there is a lien, he or she will not be able to collect from the seller.

A third aspect of warranty of title concerns infringement. This means that the goods do not have any patent, copyright, or trademark claimed by anyone. For example, a designer creates a logo for a client of the design firm in which he works, and the copyright is registered by the design firm. However, the client was not shown the design at that time. Six months later, the designer starts a design practice and contacts the former client about possible work. The client hires the designer to produce a logo and is shown the logo that the designer has designed for his previous employer. The client has bought that design and has incorporated it into all of the client's letterhead. The original design firm can sue both the client and the designer for infringement.

Express Warranty

Promises, claims, descriptions, or affirmations made about a product's performance, quality, or condition that form the "basis of the bargain" is an *express warranty*. In effect, the *basis of the bargain* means that the information provided is what primarily influences the decision of the buyer. Interior designers and salespeople, in the course of their discussions with clients about a product's viability, often make statements about what the product can or cannot do. When are these statements covered under express warranty and when are they not? It depends on the words used or circumstances surrounding the sales interaction.

* The UCC is a body of law that regulates commercial transactions. Section 2 of the UCC sets out laws related to the sale of goods, warranties, and product liability. The law that regulates contracts for the sale of goods is discussed in Chapter 20.

† A seller is anyone who sells something. A merchant is someone who is in the business of selling a certain type of goods. Anyone can be a seller; people selling as a business are merchants.

The seller does not need to use words such as *warranty* or *guarantee* in the sales presentation, nor does he or she even need to intend to make such a warranty. How precise these statements have to be and how strongly they must be worded is not clear in the UCC, so care must be taken to say exactly what is meant to avoid misunderstandings.

When statements made by the seller are only the seller's opinion or relate only to the worth of the product generally, no express warranty is made. For example, Jim Jones says to a client, "This is the best open office system on the market." It is an expression of opinion, not based on statements of fact. This kind of salesmanship is called *puffing*.* On the other hand, such a statement from Jim Jones as, "This wood flooring is care-free," is a promise that can be interpreted by the customer as meaning that he or she will not have to wax the floor. In this situation, an express warranty very likely is being made by Jones. It is very likely an express warranty because, like so much in the law, different judges can interpret the words and intention behind the words in many ways. Therefore, care should always be taken when using words that express quality.

If the salesperson is believed to be an expert concerning the goods being sold, the statements of opinion are more likely to constitute express warranties. Although opinions expressed by an interior designer who specifies but does not sell products about a manufacturer's product would probably be considered puffing, the statements made by a manufacturer's representative who has worked for that company for many years could be considered express warranties. Since the UCC does not make it clear what puffing is and what an expression of warranty is, it is important to be careful when making statements about quality and performance of a product. If the statement is reasonable and a reasonable person believes the statement, a warranty may be created.

Implied Warranty of Merchantability

Implied warranties exist as operations of law. The implied warranty of merchantability affects sales made by merchants. In its simplest form, the UCC says that the goods must be "fit for the ordinary purposes for which such goods are used" (Quinn, 1991, p. 2). As long as the merchant is a merchant of the kind of goods in consideration, he or she is held liable.

Under this section of the UCC, goods sold must be of fair to average quality and must be comparable in quality to other similar goods. They must be fit for the normal purpose of the good. They must be packaged and labeled adequately, and must conform to the statements made on the packaging or labels. For example, strippable wallpaper must be strippable; fire retardant fabric must not ignite or burn within the limits stated on the binder; a solid brass headboard must be made of solid brass.

This section of the UCC makes an implied warranty of merchantability applicable to every sale by a merchant. Liability does not disappear even if the merchant is unaware of any defect in the product. The interior designer most likely will be liable, along with the manufacturer, when a product fails or causes some injury to a person or property.

Implied Warranty of Fitness for a Particular Purpose

Implied warranty of fitness for a particular purpose affects the goods that any seller—merchant or not—sells to another. When the seller knows the intended purpose for the goods and the buyer must rely on the seller's knowledge to select or recommend goods for the purpose, an implied warranty of fitness for a particular purpose exists.

* Puffing was also discussed in Chapter 13.

The seller does not need to know the exact purpose of the purchase. However, if he or she has a general idea of the purpose and if the buyer has relied on the seller's knowledge or skill in selecting the goods, an implied warranty of fitness also has been created. For example, Mrs. Damon hires John Simmons to redecorate her home. As part of the services offered, Simmons sells to Damon the wall coverings for the kitchen and the bathrooms. Damon makes it clear to Simmons that the wallpaper in the bathroom must be able to withstand a lot of steam and dampness, since her husband takes long, hot showers. A few weeks after installation, the wallpaper begins to peel away. Since Simmons knew the purpose of the goods and Damon relied on the professional knowledge of Simmons, a breach of an implied warranty of fitness exists. Of course, the paperhanger, if he or she also knew the purpose of the purchase, is also liable for breach.

Magnuson-Moss Warranty Act

The Federal Trade Commission (FTC) enforces the Magnuson-Moss Warranty Act. This legislation was enacted to make it easier for the consumer to understand what is being warrantied in any product sold to end users. Warranties between merchants are regulated by the UCC rules.

The act does not require that sellers provide a written warranty for goods sold to consumers, "but if a seller chooses to make an express written warranty, and the cost of the consumer goods is more than $10, the warranty must be labeled as 'full' or 'limited.'" (Jentz et al. 1987, p. 314.) In addition, if the goods have a value of over $15, the Magnuson-Moss Warranty Act requires that a written warranty be provided to the potential consumer. In this case, who warrants the goods, what is covered, any limitations, the legal rights of the consumer, and how enforcement is made must all be spelled out.

Full warranties require repair or replacement at no charge to the buyer, should goods be defective. There cannot be a time limit for the replacement. If there is, it is not a full warranty but, rather, a limited warranty. When repairs cannot be made in a reasonable time, the product must be replaced or a refund must be given the consumer. Limited warranties must be clearly stated as to what is warrantied and the time limit of the warranty.

Disclaimers of Warranty

An express warranty can be disclaimed if the manufacturer or seller does not make any express promises or statements of fact relating to or describing the goods. This is true whether the statements are written or verbal. Saying, "We guarantee that this fabric will not show wear for five years," constitutes an express warranty. A disclaimer to that statement might be, "We provide no warranty beyond that of the manufacturer, and their tests under normal use in a home indicate the fabric will show no significant wear for five years."

An implied warranty of merchantability can be verbal, but it must be specific as to disclaiming merchantability. For example, Michael Cobb of Cobb Designs sells Mr. Smith a budget-priced guest chair to be used as a desk chair based on the needs described by Smith. Cobb verbally informs Smith that he does not warrant merchantability of the chair, since it is not fit for use as a desk chair. Cobb also attaches a note, making the same disclaimer to the sales agreement. The chair does not hold up, and Smith wants Cobb to replace it. Since it was disclaimed as to merchantability, Cobb is not liable to replace the chair on those grounds.

An implied warranty-of-fitness disclaimer must be in writing. For example, a designer sells a client a kitchen stool with a cane seat, which will be used at a kitchen counter. The confirmation says something like, "ABS Designs provides no warranty of fitness beyond that of the manufacturer's for normal, reasonable use." A few weeks after purchase, the client uses the stool to stand on and the cane breaks, resulting in injury to the client. The designer is not liable, since the client was using the stool in a manner that was not normal and reasonable for the product; the manufacturer did not design the chair to be used as a ladder.

Disclaimers of fitness are also written with such words as *as is*. It is common to see retailers label used furniture "as is" to protect themselves against claims on used or damaged goods. According to the UCC, however, even new merchandise is sold "as is" to imply that no warranty other than what the manufacturer has provided exists.

If a client refuses to inspect goods before signing a delivery ticket, there is no implied warranty concerning defects. This is because the client has refused, for whatever reason, to inspect the goods prior to acceptance. If the seller does not ask the buyer to inspect the goods and the goods are damaged or defective, the seller is liable.

Products Liability

Anyone who purchases products, whether the person is a designer purchasing goods from a manufacturer for a client or a client purchasing goods from a designer, expects the products to be safe and not cause harm or damage to the purchaser. There is an expectation that the products will meet certain minimal standards of materials, workmanship, and design for its intended use. If the products fail, certain express or implied warranties may have been breached. Manufacturers and sellers of products may be liable to end users, bystanders, and other merchants if individuals are physically harmed or if property damage occurs. This is called products liability. Products liability includes the areas of tort law related to negligence and strict liability and contract law related to warranty.

Products Liability and Negligence

In Chapter 13, we defined negligence as a failure to use the care that is expected of a reasonable person, and this failure to use care results in injury to another person or his or her property. Manufacturers of products must use this same care in the design, materials selection, production, and testing of their products so that they will be safe when they are used as intended.

The plaintiff must show that the manufacturer did not use due care and that the defective product caused an injury. The plaintiff must also show that he or she used the product as designed and knew the risk of using the product incorrectly. For example, Mr. and Mrs. Franklin purchased a dining room suite, including eight chairs for their new home, from interior designer May Jefferson. Jefferson knew that the manufacturer was a reputable company and had used the company's products numerous times. The Franklins liked the style of chair and relied upon Jefferson's expertise in design when they approved the chairs. The Franklins gave a dinner party a short time after the chairs had been delivered. One of the guests leaned back on the chair, causing the chair to tilt up and rock on its back legs. One leg cracked, causing the chair to collapse, and, consequently, the arm of the guest was broken. The guest attempted to sue the manufacturer and the designer. His products liability lawsuit would only succeed if he could prove that the chair had been manufactured improperly, that the chair had been sold in a defective condition, and that the guest had been using the chair for its intended purpose. Although the designer did not specify the chairs for "rocking," Jefferson would be involved in the lawsuit, because she had specified the chair. The example tries to show that, regardless of what the intended purpose of a product, clients might use their purchases in ways that could cause them harm and could leave the designer open to legal problems.

Designers must take the time to be sure that they specify products that are suitable for a client's use and that the client has been warned if the designer feels the client is demanding a product that is unsuitable for the client's use. Written disclaimers, indicating that warnings have been given and that the designer accepts no responsibility for misuse, should be given to the client, and a copy should be kept on file. This procedure may not eliminate all liability, but it would show the court that a conscientious effort to warn the client has been made.

Strict Liability

Strict liability means that "a seller is liable for any and all defective or hazardous products which unduly threaten a consumer's personal safety" (Black, 1990, p. 1422). This is true, regardless of the seller's intentions or care. Strict liability, as it applies to product liability, must be a concern of interior designers. The interior designer specifies a product, and, if the product fails, causing injury, the designer is almost always named in the lawsuit along with the manufacturer. It should be remembered that product liability usually is concerned only with reasonable, normal use of a product. If the client uses a product in a way in which it was not designed for use, the interior designer is not held liable.

Strict liability is sometimes called liability without fault. Generally considered a negligence tort, liability without fault involves some act that has departed from the use of reasonable care. For the designer, this may result from putting incorrect information in drawings, documents, and/or specifications that causes injury. For example, if the designer incorrectly labels a material in a construction drawing and the structure later fails, causing injury, the designer is responsible, based on this premise.

It is also important to note that, under strict liability, people are responsible for their acts, regardless of their intent or use of reasonable care. For example, a painter who has been hired to paint the exterior of a home uses reasonable care when he is using spray-painting equipment. However, the next-door neighbor goes out to inspect her house and finds overspray of the blue paint on the side of her white house. The painter is liable under strict liability.

The strict liability doctrine can be applied to manufactured products when the purchaser can show that "(1) the product was defective, (2) that the defect made the product unreasonably dangerous and (3) that the defect was the proximate cause of the injury" (Clarkson et al., 1983, p. 393).

For strict liability to be applied to a products liability case, the injured party (plaintiff) must prove several things:

1. The goods were defective when purchased.
2. The seller or manufacturer was in the business of selling the product.
3. The defective goods would be unreasonably dangerous to any user.
4. Physical injury occurred to the plaintiff or to his or her property.
5. At the time of the injury, the goods were substantially in the same condition as when they had been purchased.

For example, Mr. Shasta of Shasta Commercial Interiors orders fabric from a textile company that is described as fire retardant for use on restaurant booths. A few months after it has been installed, a dropped cigarette smolders and ignites the fabric, causing extensive damage to the restaurant. A strict liability case is brought against the textile company and (probably) the designer, if it can be shown that the goods were defective at the time of purchase. Further, it has to be shown that injury was caused to the premises, that the untreated fabric was dangerous in its use, and that the fabric was in a basically unchanged condition since purchase. Although most of the liability in this case rests on the manufacturer of the fabric, there is nothing in tort law or in the UCC to prevent the unknowing designer from also being held liable.

Liability Without Fault for Design Defects

Interior designers create many design elements and custom products. Designers also specify and sell products that primarily have been designed and manufactured by someone else. In both cases, the designer may be liable if the design of the specified product causes injury due to defective design. For example, Mary Nixon designed and produced the drawings for a custom table desk. The table desk was manufactured according to the specifications and drawings provided by Nixon. Three months after delivery, the client was propped on the front edge of the table desk (but he was not actually sitting on the desk). The desk leg nearest where the client was propped split at the joint, causing the client to fall on his left side and break his left arm. It would appear that there was a design defect in the way the joint between the top of the table leg and the table desk top was designed. The specifications and drawings provided by Nixon appear to have been inadequate for safely using the desk for its intended purpose. It could be argued that the design was adequate as a desk. Had the client been actually sitting on the desk, Nixon would less likely have been held liable, since a desk is generally not designed to be sat on.

Interior designers must be careful that the custom treatments and products that they design are properly designed and meet performance standards relating to the structural integrity of the design. Those who are unfamiliar with product design should either refrain from creating custom designs themselves or retain the services of product designers, craftspeople, or other appropriate experts to help in the design of custom goods. Designers also need to be constantly vigilant that the goods that are specified from manufacturers are designed safely and have no history of liability from design defects.

Warranty Law and Products Liability

Warranty law and products liability is the only portion of products liability related to the UCC. Warranty responsibility and product liability are based on the areas of warranties that have been discussed in the previous sections. They are mentioned here in relation to an injury to a third party.

In contract law, the only parties that have regress for injuries are the parties to the contract. However, much of what is governed by the UCC easily affects third parties who are not a part of the original contract. The UCC provides regulations that make the manufacturers and/or sellers liable to injuries to parties who are not a part of the original contract. For example, Mrs. Johnson hires an interior design company to redecorate her home. Through this company, she has some wall-hung shelves installed in the living room. One day, a bracket pulls out of the wall so that a shelf strikes a guest of Johnson. The guest sustains a head injury. If it were not for UCC Section 2-318, the guest would not be able to sue the installer for an implied warranty of merchantability—only Johnson could.

However, the UCC is not clear as to how responsible sellers and manufacturers are. It was written with three alternatives, which give different levels of responsibility. Alternative A is limited to household members and their guests who use or are injured by the goods. Alternative B is broader, not limiting injury to family members or guests, and alternative C is the broadest, protecting anyone who is injured by the defective product. Thus, should someone who is using a product sustain some injury if the product fails, though he or she did not purchase the product, the person has grounds for filing a lawsuit.

Summary

This chapter looked at many of the legal responsibilities expected of the professional interior designer when he or she sells and specifies goods to the consumer. The public and the profession expect that anyone who is engaged in the practice of interior design will accept the legal responsibility of his or her practice activities. In a legal sense, it matters very little whether an interior designer primarily does residential spaces or commercial spaces. As it becomes increasingly common for many not to accept responsibility and blame others for their problems or misfortunes, it becomes even more necessary for the interior designer to understand and accept his or her legal responsibilities.

The legal responsibilities that were described in this chapter and in the previous chapter should be of concern to any size or type of design practice. Of course, the size and complexity of many commercial projects makes the commercial interior designer more exposed to liability, especially as concerns warranties and products liability.

Specifying and selling goods and materials to consumers as part of one's interior design business comes with legal responsibilities and sometimes consequences. Constant care is very important. The designer should not get involved in design projects that may be out of his or her area of expertise. The designer must understand the needs of the client so that he or she can create proper specifications that go beyond aesthetic decisions. The designer must take care to specify products that he or she is familiar with or has researched and must maintain accurate records to limit his or her liability.

This concludes the portion of the book that specifically is devoted to the organization and legal responsibilities of the design firm and owner. Part IV provides several chapters that deal with the financial and revenue-producing activities of an interior design practice.

REFERENCES

Berger, C. Jaye. 1994. *Interior Design Law and Business Practices*. New York: John Wiley.

Black, Henry Campbell, (with Joseph R. Nolan and Jacqueline M. Nolan-Haley). 1990. *Black's Law Dictionary*, 6th ed. St. Paul, MN: West Publishing.

Brown, Gordon W., and Paul A. Sukys. 1997. *Business Law with UCC Applications*, 9th ed. New York: Glencoe/McGraw-Hill.

Clarkson, Kenneth W., Roger LeRoy Miller, and Gaylord A. Jentz. 1983. *West's Business Law, Text and Cases*, 2nd ed. St. Paul, MN: West Publishing.

Clarkson, Kenneth W., Roger LeRoy Miller, Gaylord A. Jentz, and Frank B. Cross. 1989. *West's Business Law, Text and Cases*, 4th ed. St. Paul, MN: West Publishing.

Conry, Edward J., Gerald R. Ferrera, and Karla H. Fox. 1993. *The Legal Environment of Business*, 3rd ed. Boston, MA: Allyn and Bacon.

Cushman, Robert F., and James C. Dobbs, eds. 1991. *Design Professional's Handbook of Business and Law*. New York: John Wiley.

Jentz, Gaylord A., Kenneth W. Clarkson, and Roger LeRoy Miller. 1987. *West's Business Law—Alternate UCC Comprehensive Edition*, 3rd. ed. St. Paul, MN: West Publishing.

Quinn, Thomas M. 1998. *Uniform Commercial Code Commentary and Law Digest*. Cumulative Supplement. Boston, MA: Warren, Gorham and Lamont.

———. 1991. *Quinn's Uniform Commercial Code Commentary and Law Digest*, 2nd. ed., vol. 1. Boston, MA: Warren, Gorham and Lamont.

———. 1991. *Uniform Commercial Code Commentary and Law Digest*. Boston, MA: Warren, Gorham and Lamont.

Reznikoff, S. C. 1989. *Specifications for Commercial Interiors*, rev. ed. New York: Watson-Guptill.

Sweet, Justin. 1985. *Legal Aspects of Architecture, Engineering and the Construction Process*, 3rd ed. St. Paul, MN: West Publishing.

West Publishing. 1998. *West's Encyclopedia of American Law*, vol. 8. St. Paul, MN: West Publishing.

A commercial interior designer by background, Marilyn Farrow, FIIDA has served the Institute of Business Designers as National President and the International Design Association as International President. Farrow's writings, speeches, television appearances, and consulting on the professional practice of interior design, client needs, and workplace trends have been featured internationally. She is currently self-employed, providing consulting services to corporate and design firm clients nationwide.

The twenty-first century has opened with low unemployment driving heightened competition for employees, expansion of global employment, and segregation of economies respondent to available workforces. Taken together, these tumultuous times have brought forward "quality of life" as a driving force in homes and workplaces across America—and that bodes well for design industries.

Part IV

Managing the Business's Finances

Chapter 15

Financial Accounting

Financial accounting is concerned with the day-to-day and periodic measurement and reporting of a firm's monetary resources. This measurement and reporting is of interest to individuals outside the firm, such as bankers, government agencies, stockholders, and auditors. Of course, the owner and managers of a design practice also use the basic financial reports to analyze and understand the financial position of the design firm. All the various accounts, journals, and ledgers that are kept by the firm and that are used to prepare balance sheets, income statements, and statements of cash flow are part of financial accounting. Financial accounting reports can be prepared by the firm's accredited business accountant, a public accountant, or a CPA,* and, until recently, that has been the most common situation. It is important to hire an accounting consultant who is familiar with the interior design business. Many general accountants, who are unfamiliar with the seeming peculiarities of this industry, have problems in properly advising interior designers.

Today, reliable and inexpensive accounting software programs make the preparation of reports easy for even the sole practitioner. Of course, formal audits and reports for tax purposes generally are still prepared by trained accounting personnel. Software programs, however, give the sole practitioner and the owner of an interior design firm many useful reports in order to keep up with the financial position of the firm at any given moment. It is especially important for a firm's owners and management to be able to read, interpret, and analyze the primary reports discussed in this chapter.

In this chapter, we will introduce the reader to several essential components of financial management. First, there will be a discussion of the different accounting methods used to record information, followed by a review of the elements of the balance sheet, the income statement, and the statement of cash flow (formally, the funds flow statement). Other accounting documents, such as the journal and ledgers, are the daily bookkeeping records that must be maintained. This chapter will not cover how to actually do daily bookkeeping but will introduce the reader to basic concepts. Finally, the last sections of the chapter will explain cash management, a very important factor in the financial health of a business, and the use of the computerized accounting systems for financial record keeping.

* CPA is the abbreviation for certified public accountant.

Accounting Methods: Accrual versus Cash Accounting

Before we discuss financial accounting reports, it is important for us to look at the accounting methods used by businesses. The two most common accounting methods (or bases) are the accrual method and the cash accounting method. Central to the difference between the two methods is the time when revenue and expenses are recognized (recorded). *Revenue* is the amount of inflows from the sale of goods or the rendering of services during an accounting period. *Expenses* is the amount of outflows of resources as a consequence of the efforts made by the firm to earn revenues. Rent, monthly utility bills, salaries, and advertising costs are examples of expenses.

In *accrual accounting*, revenue and expenses are recognized at the time they are earned (in the case of revenue) or incurred (in the case of expenses), whether the revenue has actually been collected or the expenses have actually been paid. This means that the income and expenses for the year are recognized in the year in which they have incurred. For example, Jane Doe Interiors has revenues of $5250 for January. Of that, $3250 is from cash sales and $2000 is from invoices to clients that have not yet been received. In the same month, expenses of $4000 have been incurred for the period—$3500 has already been paid, and $500 is still due. Using the accrual method, there is a $1250 gross profit for the month. In this case, the profit is a "paper profit," since $2000 has not been collected yet (see Figure 15-1). This accounting method requires double-entry accounting, which will be discussed later in the chapter.

In *cash accounting*, revenue and expenses are recognized in the period in which the firm actually receives the cash or actually pays the bills. In the preceding example, only $3250 of revenue and $3500 of expenses are recognized for the month, since this is what actually has been received or paid out. Using the cash accounting method, Jane Doe Interiors shows a $250 loss for the month. Cash accounting is commonly used by small design practices for daily bookkeeping purposes. It is simpler to use than the accrual accounting method and allows for use of single-entry accounting.

A firm generally can use whichever accounting method it chooses, though the regular corporation form of business cannot use the cash method. The cash method also cannot generally be used to calculate income (loss) for tax purposes by any form of business, if that business maintains an inventory or if the business uses inventory as the means of arriving at the business's income. However, as this issue is currently in flux with the Internal Revenue Service, advice from the firm's tax accountant is critical for compliance with the law. In some cases, the Internal Revenue Service expects businesses to pay income taxes based on the accrual method (Pinson and Jinnett, 1998, p. 11). Businesses that sell products or maintain sellable inventory must also pay income taxes based on the accrual method, in certain circumstances. The cash method can

	Accrual Method	Cash Method
Revenue	$ 5,250	$ 3,250
Expenses	−4,000	−3,500
Gross Income	$ 1,250	$ −250

FIGURE 15-1. A comparison of accrual and cash accounting methods for the realization of revenue.

be used for daily or nontax accounting needs. Since tax laws change annually and accounting standards also change on a regular basis, it is important for the business owner to discuss appropriate accounting methods with the company's accountant.

It is commonly recommended that all firms use the accrual method for an additional reason. Even though the accrual method may require extra accounting time, it provides a more comprehensive picture of profit and loss for the firm at any given period. Having a more accurate financial picture of the firm at all times helps the owner/manager make more intelligent management decisions. Moreover, with cash accounting, it is too easy for unpaid invoices to accumulate, thus allowing debt not to be obvious, which would put the firm in a serious situation.

This chapter discusses accounting principles based on the accrual method.

The Balance Sheet

A *balance sheet*, sometimes called a statement of financial position, shows the financial position of a firm at a particular moment in time and provides a statement of its assets (resources) and liabilities (claims against total resources) at that moment. The balance sheet is composed of two parts that must equal each other. These two parts are called assets and liabilities.* A design firm's assets are typically shown on the left side or top of the page, and the liabilities are shown on the right side or bottom of the page.

There are two important formulas you should keep in mind when reviewing a balance sheet.

Total assets = Liabilities + Owner's equity
Total assets − Liabilities = Owner's equity

The first reflects the final outcome of all balance sheets. The total amount of asset accounts must always equal the total amount of liability accounts. The second formula shows the breakdown of the two sections that make up the liabilities side of the balance sheet. Liabilities are moneys that the firm owes to creditors. Owner's equity represents moneys invested in the firm by the owners or stockholders. Liabilities accounts always have first claim on the assets of a firm.

Remember these formulas as we discuss the balance sheet. The reader may wish to refer also to the balance sheet in Figure 15-2 during this discussion.

Assets

Assets are any kind of resource—tangible or intangible—that the firm owns or controls and that can be measured in monetary terms. Assets are of three kinds: (1) *current assets*, which are resources that the firm would normally convert to cash in less than one year; (2) *fixed assets*, also called property, plant, and equipment, which are the long-lived items used by the firm; and (3) *other assets*, which are such assets as patents, copyrights, and investment securities of another firm.

Current assets typically include the following accounts: cash, accounts receivable, inventory, prepaid expenses, supplies, and marketable securities. *Cash* is the cash on hand in the firm's bank account, checking account, cash register, or petty cash box. *Accounts receivable* is the account that shows what

* Earlier editions of this text referred to assets and equities. Common practice today uses the term liabilities rather than equities.

Balance Sheet
Bently and Jordan Interior Designs
As of January 31, 200x

Assets		
Current Assets:		
Cash	$ 8,625	
Accounts Receivable	31,750	
Inventory	11,900	
Supplies	1,250	
Prepaid Expenses	2,250	
Total Current Assets		$ 55,775
Fixed Assets:		
Plant and Equipment:		
Office Furniture at Cost	$ 25,500	
Less: Accumulated depreciation	−2,400	
Office Equipment at Cost	11,500	
Less: Accumulated depreciation	−1,800	
Automobile at Cost	19,500	
Less: Accumulated depreciation	−5,600	
Net Plant and Equipment		46,700
Total Assets		$ 102,475
Liabilities		
Current Liabilities:		
Accounts Payable	$ 8,725	
Notes Payable	4,000	
Accrued Expenses	7,000	
Deferred Revenues	6,750	
Total Current Liabilities		$ 26,475
Other Liabilities:		
Long-Term Debt		29,500
Total Liabilities		$ 55,975
Owner's Equity		
Common Stock	$ 35,000	
Retained Earnings	11,500	
Total Owner's Equities		46,500
Total Equities		$102,475

FIGURE 15-2. A typical balance sheet for the corporation form of business.

others owe to the firm as a result of sales or billings for services. *Inventory* shows those items purchased by the firm for resale to the firm's customers. For an interior designer, a chair that the designer has purchased for sale to a client is inventory; a chair that the designer has purchased that is used by the bookkeeper in the office is equipment, the value of which is recorded in the fixed assets account. A *prepaid expense* is early payment of expenses, such as insurance policies paid on the equipment that the firm owns or rent that may have to be paid in advance. Supplies represents the value of normal office supplies. Marketable securities are investments that are expected to be sold within the year for cash.

The fixed assets, or property, plant, and equipment, account includes the following categories: building and equipment, which is represented by the building, if owned by the firm, and any capital equipment—furniture used by the office staff and computers, plotters, copying machines, delivery trucks, and so on. The accumulated depreciation on these items is also shown on the balance sheet. Property or land is shown as a separate entry, since it is not depreciated—land does not "wear out." Note that in Figure 15-2, the company does not own its building, so it is not listed as an asset.

Depreciation results from the concept that capital equipment has a limited useful life. It is intended to express the usage of a fixed asset in the firm's pursuit of revenue. Although many think of deprecation as a way to express the wearing out of an object, it more accurately relates to the usage of the object, not its wear and tear. Accountants predict what will be the useful life of the equipment and determine the depreciated value of the equipment for each year the firm owns the item. Depreciation is set for a fixed period of time and varies based on the item and current tax laws.

The category for other assets includes investments that the firm has made in other firms. If the investments are to be held for more than one year, they are listed here. If they are expected to be sold within a year, they are listed under current assets. The value of copyrights, trademarks, patents, licenses, and similar intangible assets that the firm might have are also listed under other assets. Of special interest to the design firm is the value placed on copyrighted designs or patents on any furnishings the firm may have obtained. These copyrighted designs or patents solely belong to the design firm and cannot be used by others without the permission of the firm. Patents and copyrights are *amortized*, which is the practice by which the value of the patent or copyright is reduced over time to record its usage in the firm's earning activities. Amortization is essentially the same as depreciation, except that it applies to intangible assets.

Liabilities

Liabilities are claims by outsiders and/or owners against the total assets of the firm. The liabilities side of the balance sheet is made up of two sections—liabilities, which can be current and concurrent (or long-term), and owner's equities. Liabilities are amounts that the firm owes to others as a result of past transactions or events. Liabilities always have first claim on the firm's assets. Should a business cease operation for any reason, all outstanding liabilities must be paid before owners or stockholders receive any funds. The two categories of liabilities are current and noncurrent.

Current liabilities are obligations that are due within one year or less. The following accounts are considered current liabilities: *Accounts payable*—claims from suppliers for goods or services ordered (and possibly delivered) but not yet paid for; notes payable (short-term loans); and *accrued expenses*—expenses owed for the period but not yet paid. Examples of accrued expenses are salaries due, rent, utility bills not yet paid, and so on. *Deferred revenues* are revenues received for services or the future sale of goods, but the services or goods have not been delivered yet. The most common source of deferred revenues for a design firm is retainers or down payments that the client has paid to the designer.

Two other current liabilities accounts are taxes payable (sometimes called estimated taxes), which represent the amount of income tax or other taxes owed to government agencies but not yet paid, and current portion of long-term debt, which show how much of the long-term debt, perhaps resulting from the purchase of a delivery truck by the firm, is to be paid during the next one-year period.

Other liabilities or noncurrent liabilities are amounts owed that will not be paid during the coming one-year period. The main item listed would be the balance of principal owed on a long-term loan.

The *owner's equity* section on the balance sheet shows the amount the owners have invested in the firm. How this section is shown on a balance sheet will vary, based on the legal business formation. For a sole proprietorship, owner's equity would be shown as "Michael Smith, Capital" and the amount Michael Smith invested to start the firm, plus any additions he made to the capital of the firm. For a partnership, it is customary to indicate the amount invested by each partner as a separate line, in much the same way as for a sole proprietorship. A partnership and a sole proprietorship also show a beginning and ending balance to show any withdrawals (or drawings) made by the owners against the assets. *Drawings* are fixed amounts withdrawn by proprietors or partners as salaries. Drawings are not truly salaries, however, and are not treated as salaries in the bookkeeping process. A separate drawing account is set up for each partner. Figures 15-3 and 15-4 show owner's equity in these forms of business. It is not uncommon for the balance sheet for a sole proprietorship not to show an owner's equity section.

A design firm that is a corporation would show stockholders' equity, since the corporation is owned by stockholders. The amount of money obtained to run the corporation is listed as capital stock and paid-in capital stock. Par value of issued and outstanding stock is reported to represent the legal minimum claim on assets associated with the stock itself. Paid-in capital stock is the excess of par value representing the claims on assets arising purely from the value of stock at the time of its issuance.

Owner's Equity	
Michael Smith, capital as of January 1, 200x	$25,000
Deduct: 1999 drawings	−5,000
Michael Smith, capital as of December 31, 200x	$20,000

FIGURE 15-3. Reporting format of owner's equity for a sole proprietorship on a balance sheet.

Owner's Equity	
Helen Sampson, capital	$ 15,000
Margaret Wallace, capital	10,000
Burt Anderson, capital	10,000
Total Partnership Equity	$35,000

FIGURE 15-4. Reporting format of owner's equity for a partnership on a balance sheet.

Another item shown under stockholders' equity is *retained earnings*. This represents the claim on assets arising from the cumulative undistributed earnings of the corporation after dividends are paid to stockholders for use in the business. Retained earnings does not refer to cash in and of itself. It may be in some other form, such as a vehicle, equipment, or marketable securities. There is no retained earnings section on the balance sheet of a sole proprietorship or a partnership. Earnings are treated as noted above for these forms of business.

Each general category is added to obtain total assets and total equities. Total assets must always equal total equities.

The Income Statement

The *income statement* (also commonly called a *profit-and-loss*, or *P & L, statement)* formally reports all the revenues and expenses of the firm for a stated period of time. The period of time may be a month, a quarter, or a year. The result shows the net income (or loss) for the firm during the period. The brief format of the essential information reported on an income statement is show in Figure 15-5. Revenues are the inflows of moneys to a company from the sale of goods and services. For an interior design firm, revenues may result from the fees it charges clients or from the amounts received from the sale of goods. For the sale of goods to yield revenue for the firm, the goods must be goods that *pass through* the design firm. What this means is that items that are specified by the designer but are sold to an end user by someone else are not revenue producing for the design firm. For example, Meghan O'Connor specified tables and chairs for a new restaurant, but the restaurant owner purchased the goods directly from the manufacturer. Since the sale did not pass through O'Connor's books, she cannot recognize those funds as revenue. The design fee to specify those goods, however, would be revenue for O'Connor, since those funds were billed through O'Connor's office. This distinction is very important concerning sales tax funds and income taxes for the firm.

Expenses are the outflows of assets used to generate revenue. Since assets must always equal liabilities, expenses are also decreased in owner's equity. Net income (or profit) is the eventual difference between revenues and expenses. A loss occurs when expenses are greater than revenues.

The income statement used in the following discussion is formatted with the consideration that the firm uses the accrual basis and has instituted a cost accounting system to measure and evaluate costs of doing business against the revenues that the firm has generated (see Figure 15-6). In a cost accounting system, certain, if not all, costs directly related to the generation of revenue are costed or charged to the particular revenue-producing activity. For a design

Net Revenue
− Cost of Sales
Gross Margin (or Gross Profit)
− Operating Expenses
Profit (Loss) Before Taxes

FIGURE 15-5. The brief format used for an income statement, showing the main items reported to determine profit or loss.

Income Statement
Grand Designs
For Year Ending December 31, 200X

Income		
Gross Revenue		
From Fees	185,350	
From Reimbursable Expenses	11,540	
From Sale of Goods		
Product	227,820	
Freight-in	24,680	
Delivery	14,100	
Installation	8,610	
Total Gross Revenue		$ 472,100
Other Revenue		
Interest	3,575	
Net Revenue		$ 475,675
Cost of Sales		
From Fees:		
Direct labor	35,800	
Supplies	2,350	
Reproduction expense	3,760	
Telephone / Fax (long distance)	1,290	
CAD—contract labor	6,750	
Reimbursable expenses	9,540	
From Products:		
Cost of Goods	177,699	
Freight-in	19,750	
Delivery	10,200	
Installation	7,650	
Total Cost of Sales		$ 274,789
Gross Margin		$ 200,886
Expense		
Operating Expenses		
Salaries	30,940	
Payroll taxes	15,200	
Group insurance	6,000	
Rent	28,800	
Heat, power, and light	9,800	
Telephone	7,500	
Advertising and promotion	10,000	
Travel reimbursements	12,600	
Supplies	4,800	
Postage and express	1,300	
Depreciation expense (furniture and equip.)	5,600	
Depreciation expense (auto)	2,500	
Insurance	5,700	
Dues and subscriptions	2,750	
Professional development	1,800	
Professional consultants	3,000	
Printing and reproduction	2,200	
Interest expense	4,800	
Bank charges	1,750	
Web/Internet provider and serv.	2,400	
Misc. expenses	2,575	
Total Operating Expenses		$ 162,015
Net Income Before Taxes		$ 38,871

FIGURE 15-6. An income statement showing the separation of direct expenses from overhead expenses.

firm, this means that all costs related to a particular job are recorded for that job. These costs show up on the income statement under the category of cost of sales as either direct labor or direct expenses. The author believes that it is important for a design firm to use this method in order to have an accurate view of the activities of the firm. This point will be discussed further.

The easiest way to understand the parts of an income statement is to start at the top entry and work down to the various parts. The income statement in Figure 15-6 shows income generated from fees and goods sold. First note the heading. The date indicates the status of the firm prior to the date shown in the heading.

Gross Revenue to Net Revenue

Gross revenue consists of all the revenue generated by the firm for the period of time noted. For our purposes, we will break this down into revenue from fees, which are the design fees for interior design services, and revenue from sale of goods, which are revenues related to the sale of products to clients. We further break down the revenue from sale of goods to show (1) product, or the amount the client paid the design firm for the goods; (2) freight-in, the freight charges the client paid for goods; and (3) delivery, the delivery and/or installation charges that the design firm has billed to the client.

Total gross revenue is the total amount of revenue generated from all means by the firm for the period of time noted. Adjustments are made for such things as returns and allowances, damages, or any extra discounts that the designer has offered to clients for prompt payment. These are subtracted from the total gross revenue to obtain net revenue.

Cost of Sales to Gross Margin

Cost of sales refers to the costs paid in the direct generation of revenues. In retail sales businesses, such as a clothing store, this is called cost of goods sold and relates to changes in inventory. In our example, cost of sales is broken down into two parts, as was revenue—from fees and from products. Under the section cost of sales from products, there are three lines corresponding to those in revenues. The first is cost of goods, which shows the change in inventory and any special orders delivered during the period. The second, freight-in, shows the actual charges the firm has been billed for goods that have been delivered to the firm. The third is delivery and installation, which shows the cost of delivery and/or installation of products to the company (this includes salaries paid and cost of trucks, equipment, and so on that are needed to deliver products to the customer).

Under cost of sales from fees, there are four items. The first, direct labor, should be the easiest to determine. *Direct labor* is the time the designers spent directly involved in the generation of the designs under contract for which fees for services are charged. The amount of direct labor can easily be determined from the time sheets kept by the design staff. This amount can be calculated against the salary paid to the various designers. Direct labor also can include the time that secretarial and management staff spend working on the projects under contract. Since this is often harder to keep an accurate account of, the time spent on projects by management and support staff are more commonly figured as overhead.

In Figure 15-6, other line items shown are for supplies, reproduction, and long-distance telephone charges. These are legitimate costs against projects done under contract. They are presented to give a more accurate view of the profitability of the firm's activities. Many firms do not show these charges at all, putting them into appropriate categories of overhead expenses.

All these adjustments (costs) are totaled and subtracted from net revenue. The result is gross margin, which is sometimes called gross profit but which does not represent profit. "Gross margin is the difference between the revenues generated from selling products (goods or services) and the related product costs."* Gross margin shows the amount of revenue that is available to cover overhead expenses in order to keep the firm in business.

Overhead Expenses

Overhead expenses, also called selling and administrative expenses, are those expenses that are incurred whether the firm produces any revenues or not. They are often thought of as those expenses needed to keep the doors open. They are reported in as much detail as is needed by the firm for anyone who would be looking at the income statement. Expenses listed in Figure 15-6 represent the many expense items that are common to an interior design firm.

A few comments about some of these items should be made here. The item salaries represents the amount of expense paid out for non-revenue-generating labor activities (or activities that cannot be easily costed to projects). This usually includes salaries for secretaries, accounting personnel, and management personnel. However, if the firm is using a true cost-accounting methodology, it also would include that portion of the design staff's salaries that cannot be considered direct labor. Telephone represents those normal telephone charges and other telephone charges that the firm cannot or chooses not to cost back to specific revenue-generating activities. Advertising and promotion can be actual promotional expenses such as magazine advertising or the cost of placing the firm's ad in the yellow pages, but it can also represent the expense of a business lunch.

As can be seen from the example, a firm can go into quite a bit of detail in order to have an accurate picture of its financial standing. If an interior design firm has invested in a good computer system, the detailed record keeping and data entry that are required is made easier. Many management reports that would be helpful in the control of the design firm can then be generated. More detail on this topic will be covered in Chapter 16.

All these expenses are totaled and subtracted from gross margin to obtain net income. *Net Income* (or loss) represents the amount of income (or loss) that results when all remaining expenses (deductions) are subtracted from gross revenues. If the result is positive, net income represents the dollar amount of profit that the firm has made for the period reported. If expenses are greater than revenues, then a loss (a negative result) is reported for the period. If the design firm is a corporation, this result would be called net income before taxes, since it is necessary for a corporation to show its estimated income taxes on the income statement. Unless the firm has some extraordinary expenses, such as a loss from fire, the next line should show a Provision for Income Tax, which is the estimated tax for the period. This amount is subtracted to determine Net Income. If the firm receives income from sources other than from those brought in as a result of the normal operation of the firm, such as interest earned on checking or savings accounts, it is added before the net income before taxes result is determined.

This is not true for sole proprietorships or partnerships, since the income of these types of businesses is personal income and is reported along with any other income made on individual or family tax statements. These forms would not necessarily show a provision for income tax. The next line, in these cases, would be net income.

* Anthony, Robert N., and James S. Reece, *Accounting Texts and Cases*, 7th ed., Richard Irwin, 1983, p. 908.

The Statement of Cash Flow

In the *statement of cash flow*, "information regarding a company's cash inflows and outflows (from) operations, investing, and financial activities" (Chasteen et al., 1995, p. 265) are reported. This information is useful to potential investors and creditors, as well as to management when they are making various decisions concerning the firm. The information used to prepare the statement of cash flow comes from the balance sheet, the income statement, and, for corporations, from the retained earnings portion of the income statement. Although the report can be useful for those who need to review the financial condition of any business formation, it is primarily prepared for the corporation form of business ownership. Many lending institutions require a cash flow statement from all types of businesses when they seek loans.

Prior to 1987, this type of financial information was reported as part of the statement of changes in financial position (sometimes called the funds flow statement). This statement reported the sources and uses of funds during a given period. Because of an increased emphasis on reporting this information on a cash basis format, the Financial Accounting Standards Board recommended that cash flow information be recorded in the statement of cash flows format. This practice was begun in 1987 (Imdieke and Smith, 1987, p. 646) and is still recognized today. The most widely used format for this information is the indirect method, shown in Figure 15-7.

Tanner Interior Design, LLC
Statement of Cash Flows
For the Year Ended December 31, 200x

Net Cash Flow from Operating Activities:	
Net Income	$ 120,400
Adjustments to Convert Net Income to Net Cash Flow from Operating Expenses:	
Depreciation Expense	10,600
Increase in Accounts Receivable	−25,650
Decrease in Inventory	22,300
Increase in Prepaid Expenses	−12,300
Decrease in Accounts Payable	−22,360
Increase in Accrued Expenses	−8,700
Net Cash flow from Operating Activities	101,690
Cash Flows from Investing Activities:	
Purchasing of Equipment	−$ 22,500
Net Cash Used by Investing Activities	−22,500
Cash Flows from Financing Activities:	
Proceeds from Customer Retainers	18,900
Proceeds from Customer Deposits	33,000
Proceeds of Long-term Debt	27,000
Payments on Long-term Debt	−7,750
Cash Dividends Paid	−1,250
Net Cash Provided by Financing Activities	69,900
Net Increase in Cash	$ 149,090

FIGURE 15-7. A statement of cash flows (direct method).

Although the statement of cash flow provides information about cash receipts (inflows) and cash payments (outflows) from all areas of the firm, its primary purpose is to report inflows and outflows for a given time period. Cash, for accounting purposes, is money, checks, or items such as money orders that are accepted by banks. The statement of cash flow also reports the inflows and outflows of cash equivalents. Cash equivalents are very liquid, short-term investments, such as money market funds, that can be converted to cash quickly. However, if these kinds of investments are made only for the temporary investment of excess cash, they are not to be considered a part of the data that make up the statement.

The inflows and outflows come from three areas: operations, investments, and financing. Operations activities are those that are involved in the normal revenue-generating activities of the firm. Operations flows come primarily from the payments and receivables from clients, and the payments that the firm makes to others in the generation of revenues. Depending on the nature of the firm, operations flows also can come from interest earned, if the firm has loaned money to someone, or from dividends from certain kinds of investments. Investments inflows and outflows result from lending money and receiving payments on those loans; purchasing or selling certain kinds of securities; and purchasing or selling assets such as property, buildings, or equipment that the firm owns. Financing inflows and outflows comes from the finances that the owners have invested in the company and subsequent payments to those owners for the investment, as well as payments received and returned to creditors, such as banks, for mortgages.

The methods for actually constructing these forms are quite complicated and are generally done by the firm's accountant. They will not be discussed here. Interested readers may want to review appropriate material that can be found in one of the references or, as a necessary part of business management, may want to discuss the statement of cash flow with the firm's accountant.

Accounting Records and Systems

The balance sheet, income statement, and statement of cash flow are summary reports. They are generated from the information that the firm has maintained in its accounting records. These accounting records are commonly referred to as the daily bookkeeping records.

In accounting terminology, events that affect the financial aspects of a firm, either as revenue generating or expense generating, are called *transactions*. These transactions must be recorded in an organized manner so that the firm can report or review its financial condition.

Design businesses may use either single-entry or double-entry bookkeeping systems. A single-entry system is very simple. It is set up based on the income statement and includes business income and expense accounts. Because of its simplicity, it is used by many small businesses. However, many accountants feel that it is not an adequate way of properly accounting for transactions. Most accountants today recommend using the double-entry bookkeeping system because of its built-in checks and balances. The double-entry bookkeeping system uses journals and ledgers (discussed below), and the accounts are based on the entries found in both the income statement and the balance sheet. In the double-entry system, transactions are first entered in the journal and then summary information is transferred to the appropriate ledger. The next section provides additional information about the double-entry system.

Accounts

Financial organization is established in accounts. *Accounts*, with different names for clarification, show additions (increases) to the account and subtraction's (decreases) to the account. In its simplest form, the account record looks like the letter T, hence the name T-account (Figure 15-8).

The left-hand side of the T-account is called the *debit* side, whereas the right-hand side is called the *credit* side. In these accounts, debit and credit have no meaning in accounting other than "left" and "right," respectively. They are not substitutes for the words *increase* or *decrease*, since, for some accounts, the increase side of the T-account will be on the right and the decrease on the left. Figure 15-9 shows this accounting situation.

Journal, Ledger, and Chart of Accounts

Following a business transaction, entries are made in a journal. A *journal* is a chronological record of all accounting transactions for the firm (see Figure 15-10). Today, it is usual for record keeping to be done using some sort of computer software. However, some small sole proprietorships retain a manual system. Whether the record keeping is done manually or on the computer, the concepts are the same. Journal entries show the date of occurrence, the name of the account to be debited or credited, the amount of the debit or

T-Accounts

Assets

(Increases on left, decreases on right)

Cash

DEBIT	CREDIT
300	900
1,700	450
1,000	

Accounts Receivable

DEBIT	CREDIT
8,700	9,100
7,500	
1,700	

Equities

(Decreases on left, increases on right)

Accounts Payable

DEBIT	CREDIT
900	
450	

Fees Revenue

DEBIT	CREDIT
	8,700
	7,500
	12,000

Note: These Accounts are not represented to balance.

FIGURE 15-8. A sample format of typical T-accounts.

Assets		=	Liabilities		+	Owner's Equity	
increase	decrease	=	increase	decrease	+	increase	decrease
(+) debit	(-) credit		(-) debit	(+) credit		(-) debit	(+) credit

FIGURE 15-9. Some accounts show increases as a debit, while other accounts show decreases as a debit.

200X		Accounts	Ledger	Debit	Credit
Oct	6	Cash	1	1,250	
		Sales	26		1,250
	6	Accounts Receivable	2	3,400	
		Design Fees	3		3,400
	6	Inventory	5	17,700	
		Cash	1		7,000
		Accounts Payable	21		10,700

FIGURE 15-10. Simple journal entries.

credit, and a reference to the ledger account to which the entry has been posted. Entries are posted to different ledger accounts from the journal. *Posting*, therefore, is the transferring of a journal entry to the correct ledger account.

The *ledger*, often called a general ledger, is a group of accounts. Some readers may be familiar with the general ledger book, a bound book for recording all entries. But a ledger does not need to be a bound book, and in most cases today, it is not. Such a book may work for a small firm, but larger firms use computerized accounting programs. The general ledger is often supplemented by various subsidiary ledgers. These provide detailed information to support the general ledger. For an interior design firm, an important subsidiary ledger is the accounts receivable ledger (see Figure 15-11). This ledger has separate accounts for each client who purchases on credit from the designer. A few other ledgers are:

Cash receipts ledger: Shows all the moneys received by the firm
Cash disbursements ledger: Records moneys paid out to cover expenses

Sydney Orlando — Client #: R842
1526 E. Seaport Drive

Date		Explanation	Debit		Credits		Balance	
May		Balance					150	00
	9	Sales Check # 6801	325	00			775	00
	14	Received on Account			500	00	225	00
	29	Sales Check # 7002	120	00			345	00
June	8	Received on Account			300	00	45	00

FIGURE 15-11. A sample page from an accounts receivable ledger.

Accounts payable ledger: Records amounts that the design firm owes to others

Purchase order ledger: Shows outstanding orders for goods and/or services for clients or the firm

Payroll ledger: Records payments to employees

A *chart of accounts* is a list of all the accounts that a firm is using. Typically, the chart of accounts is set up to have account names that mirror the items shown on the balance sheet and income statement and is based on management's and the accounting consultant's desires about what needs to be accounted. Figure 15-12 is a portion of a chart of accounts. A useful starting place is the accounts that relate to the information needed to prepare the balance sheet and income statement. Accounts are set up for cash, accounts receivable, fixed assets, accounts payable, payroll, telephone, rent, sales revenue from fees, and so on. The chart of accounts is a statement about how the firm categorizes the events that it seeks to control. The list is numbered in some

Sample Chart of Accounts

Account #	Description	Account #	Description
Assets		**Revenue**	
1000	Cash	6000	Sales of goods/products
1010	Cash: checking	6100	Freight in
1020	Cash: savings	6110	Delivery fees
1030	Petty cash	6200	Professional fees
1099	Total cash	6300	Reimbursable expenses
1100	Accounts receivable	6400	Cash discounts
1190	Allowance for bad debts		
1199	Total accounts receivable	**Expenses**	
1200	Inventory	7000	Cost of sales
1299	Total inventory	7100	Cost of goods sold
1300	Fixed assets	7125	Freight in
1310	Office furniture & fixtures	7200	Direct labor
1320	Office equipment	7300	Telephone
		7325	Supplies
Liabilities		8150	Payroll tax
2000	Accounts payable: cost of sales	8200	Rent
2050	Accounts payable: general	8300	Telephone
2100	Accrued payroll	8320	Utilities
2110	Federal withholding	8400	Group insurance
2120	Unemployment compensation	8450	Insurance
2125	Social security	8500	Professional consultants: attorney
2200	Note payable	8550	Professional consultants: accountant
2300	Interest payable	8600	Supplies
2400	Sales tax payable	8625	Catalogs/samples
3000	Long-term liabilities	8650	Postage
3010	Note payable long term	8675	Promotion
4000	Capital	8900	Depreciation expense
4100	Owner's capital	8925	Bank charges
4300	Owner's drawings	9000	Federal income tax
		9999	Net Income

FIGURE 15-12. A partial chart of accounts. (Excerpt from Christine M. Piotrowski, *Interior Design Management*, 1992, John Wiley & Sons)

logical order. These code numbers are the ones used to cross-reference journal entries to posting entries. The chart of accounts should be set up so that it can increase in complexity as the firm grows, with appropriate accounts added as needed.

Trial Balance

Remember that assets must equal liabilities and debits must equal credits. This does not mean that debits and credits will be equal within each account but that when all accounts are considered, they will be equal. A test to see if accounts are balanced and if all the account balances with the debit and credit side are totaled separately is called a trial balance.

There are two purposes of a trial balance. One is to check the accuracy of the posted entries to see if total debits equal total credits. The other is to establish summary balances in all accounts in order to prepare the balance sheet, income statement, and changes in financial condition. A trial balance can be done whenever the accounts are up to date.

Cash Management

For interior design firms to stay in business, a constant inflow of cash that equals or exceeds the outflows is needed to pay the expenses for a given period. The statement of cash flow, discussed earlier, reports to those outside the firm the sources and uses of funds for a given period. In this section, we will briefly discuss a simple cash flow statement that can easily be prepared by a manager and can be used in cash management. They are generally considered to be two different reports, although they contain similar information. The statement of cash flows is used to report information to outsiders. The cash flow statement is an internal tool used by owners and managers to forecast revenue and expense needs and to pinpoint cash needs for a specific period.

Cash management is really cash forecasting. The firm estimates how much revenue will be realized each month (or quarter) and how much expenses will be for the month (or quarter). Because it is a forecast, the estimate for cash receipts (revenue) can never be 100 percent accurate. All kinds of things may happen to upset forecasts for obtaining revenues. Projects fall through, clients do not pay on time, projects are delayed due to construction problems, just to name a few potential problems. For this reason, it is also a good idea to project a small, though realistic, percentage above expected and needed cash receipts for the period. If this is done, then it is easier to meet actual needs if (and when) forecasts are lower than actual receipts. It should also be remembered that not all income turns into cash immediately. Accounts receivables may take 30, 60, even 90 or more days to be received. So although the cash could be recorded for several months, it should not be forecasted as in hand until the the income has been actually received.

Cash disbursements for expenses is much easier to forecast. These outflows are usually known for any given period and are more easily controlled. The expected purchase of supplies or a piece of capital equipment can be put off when cash receipts do not materialize as forecasted.

The important thing is to keep reviewing cash flow. An existing business would probably want to do a cash flow report monthly. Computer programs allow this to be done fairly easily.

Figure 15-13 shows a simple cash flow statement. A cash flow statement begins with the current, known cash balance. If the entire cash flow statement is for projected cash flow, then the beginning cash balance for each month can

Cash Flow Statement: December to March 200x

Description	Actual December	Projected January	Projected February	Projected March
Beginning Cash Balance	$ 8,000	$ 6,500	$ 19,100	$ 21,200
Projected Revenue	95,000	92,000	100,000	105,000
Other income		1,100	1,100	1,100
Projected Gross Revenue	103,000	99,600	120,200	127,300
Operating Expenses	77,000	78,000	79,000	81,000
Purchase computer	17,000			3,400
Purchase office furniture			17,500	
Line-of-credit debt	2,500	2,500	2,500	2,500
Ending Cash Balance	6,500	19,100	21,200	40,400

FIGURE 15-13. A simple cash flow statement. Notice how it repeats the format of an income statement.

be estimated. In order to show how the cash flow statement works, however, the beginning cash balance is the actual balance (as determined by revenue minus expenses). The next line shows the known and projected revenues for the months being reviewed. Projected revenues combine the known work-in-process* amounts for each period with forecasts of additional work in each month. Adding the beginning cash balance to the projected revenue provides the projected gross revenue.

Operating expenses are the projected combined expenses for each month. These include salaries, fringe benefits, rent, utilities, and other costs of doing business. On another line is shown each month's responsibility for a bank line of credit that has been obtained in a previous month. This amount is the amount of principal and interest due each month. Note that in March, the firm expects a one-time expense of $3400 for a computer. The last line shows the ending cash balance for each month. This balance is carried up to the beginning cash balance line in the forecast months. The reader may wish to fill in April's figures to obtain the ending balance for the month (and to see how well the firm is doing)!

A cash flow budget allows the owner to compare actual results of the business against forecasted goals. When the revenues are lower than forecasted, the owner will want to renew marketing efforts or possibly find new revenue sources. The owner can also look at how he or she has been extending credit to customers or may want to change payment requirements. If expenses exceed forecasts, the owner can look quickly at what has happened and determine ways in which he or she can hold down expenses.

Many small design firms operate in markets in which they must survive on seasonal design business, especially those with a large number of second homes. Understanding on paper what the cash flow situation will be in the slow months can help the owner determine how to generate alternative revenue sources for those slow months. For example, perhaps the owner can work with real estate agents, providing brief consultations for sellers. Alternately, the owner may need to generate larger pools of revenue or hold down costs during busy periods.

* *Work in process* means work under way for a client that has not yet been billed.

New firms and those in the first year also have a built-in cash flow problem. If the firm also sells merchandise, it may be extending credit to clients several months into the future. Revenue is often delayed as the firm waits for full payment on delivery. On top of this problem is the requirement for many new businesses to pay up front for merchandise that they have purchased for clients. Recall from Chapter 7 that this is often referred to as pro forma credit. Obviously, the cash could easily be going out faster than it is coming in, unless the firm has a well thought out retainer and deposit policy. Even if the firm has no debt expense for a line of credit from a bank (operating on an all-cash basis), the design firm can quickly get into financial problems.

For design firms that do not sell merchandise, the cash flow cycle is relatively short. Firms that sell merchandise often have a constant cash flow problem because they have not received enough cash from some source to pay for the merchandise that is on order. Whatever the case, there must always be enough cash available to pay current bills. Employees expect to be paid within 7 to 14 days of completing their work. Suppliers generally have a 30-day grace period before they start charging penalties. The faster the firm can collect on its receivables, the more efficient its cash flow cycle will be. However, it is not uncommon for a firm to have a significant percentage of its receivables over 120 days outstanding.

Cash flow falls back on the cash accounting method rather than on the accrual accounting method. Good cash flow records of cash receipts (deposits of cash) and outflows (when a check to a supplier or other liability account clears the bank) are necessary. To accurately record cash receipts, the owner must keep track of new orders or contracts for services; when deposits or retainers are to be received; when partial payments are expected; when delivery of goods are expected; and so on.

Cash management has a relationship to other business operations. When the owner sees cash needs months in advance, that information encourages the owner to market beyond what is needed to pay today's bills. Small firms frequently have an uncanny habit of looking at the work that they are doing right now, neglecting marketing until the current project is done. When this happens, a business may be without any revenue for weeks or even months as the owner finally gets around to seeking new business. Cash management actually forces the owner to recognize marketing efforts as an ongoing part of his or her ownership responsibilities.

Good, basic business practices aid in keeping cash flow operating efficiently. Here are a few examples of them.

- Constant monitoring of outstanding orders and receivables aids the firm in protecting narrow margins of profit.
- The firm must have good pricing policies for both fees and products.
- Credit reports on clients with whom the firm is unfamiliar should be obtained before the firm orders merchandise.
- Inventory, returns, and exchanges must be carefully monitored so that cash is not tied up in inventory. This cash cannot be used to pay other expenses.
- The firm must prepare design contracts to help protect from possible stoppages or losses of revenue.
- The firm should require substantial retainers and deposits before work is begun or products are ordered.
- Careful time keeping, scheduling, and project management are also helpful in cash flow forecasting.
- A thorough monitoring of budgeted versus actual time estimates and fee estimates can eliminate project shortfalls.

- Constant monitoring of outstanding orders and receivables aids the firm in protecting narrow margins of profit.

Positive cash management can be helped by establishing policies that require substantial retainers and deposits as well as tracking and collecting receivables. When the firm needs cash the owners may be able to obtain short-term loans from the firm's banker. Keeping the banker informed of the financial situation of the design firm helps the firm in the loan approval process, as does a good history of prompt repayment of those loans. But going to the bank every time that the firm needs cash to pay bills is not the best solution. Good management of the firm and the firm's cash flow is the answer.

Finally, cash flow and profit are not the same thing. Even a company with good cash flow can be losing money. If bills are not paid or are deferred, even if there is a positive cash inflow, those unpaid bills will have to be paid one day. And Murphy's Law says that those will always be due when the cash reserves are low. Design firm owners and managers must not let this happen but should constantly review the cash flow statements against the P & L to help them make management decisions that will keep them out of financial trouble with creditors.

Computer Applications

As mentioned earlier, most design firms, whether they are a sole practitioner or a large firm with dozens of employees, use some type of computerized accounting system for financial record keeping. Of course, for a sole practitioner, it remains relatively easy to maintain regular bookkeeping records using a manual system that has been suggested by the firm's accountant. However, more and more sole practitioners are utilizing one of the simplified, computerized accounting software programs to assist in this important management activity.

Computer programs have many other advantages that help organize basic record keeping. They may also accommodate check writing to pay bills, payroll and payroll tax reports, quick creation of managerial reports beyond the balance sheet and income statement that can help the owner manage the company's finances, and many other regular accounting and financial record-keeping documents.

Many software programs exist for both Windows® and Macintosh® computer systems that can be adopted by interior designers. Software for Windows is more universally accepted by businesses, especially for business functions, than Macintosh software. There are also specialized programs available that have been created specifically for interior designers. The author does not recommend any one particular software program, but three common ones used by interior design firms are Quickbooks Pro, Peachtree Accounting, and MYOB. Computer programs should not be used with the idea of eliminating any involvement of a qualified accountant. Selection of appropriate software should be made after the owner discusses all pertinent issues with the firm's accountant. The firm's accountant generally is familiar with different software programs for accounting needs and can help the design firm owner with this decision.

Summary

This chapter by no means fully explains financial accounting. Interior designers rightly utilize the services of accountants to prepare the formal accounting statements that are needed periodically. Many leave the day-to-day bookkeeping chores to bookkeepers, accountants, or others who better understand these financial matters. However, the owner should still have knowledge of the firm's financial condition, since he or she is ultimately responsible for the company's finances.

It is important to understand the financial aspects of the interior design business and to be conversant with the terminology and concepts of financial accounting. No matter who does the daily bookkeeping in the long run, the owner of a design firm is responsible for accurate recording of financial transactions.

In this chapter, we have looked at the basic concepts, definitions, and parts of the balance sheet, income statement, and statement of changes in financial condition. We also have looked briefly at the concepts related to accounting records and systems, and cash management.

In the next chapter, we will discuss managerial accounting and some brief concepts concerning management control systems. These concepts relate to reporting methods generated from the financial statements, which have been created to help owners and/or managers plan, organize, and control the finances of the design firm.

REFERENCES

Anthony, Robert N. 1983. *Essentials of Accounting*, 3rd ed. Reading, MA: Addison-Wesley.

Anthony, Robert N., and James S. Reece. 1983. *Accounting Texts and Cases*, 7th ed. Homewood, IL: Richard D. Irwin.

Caplan, Suzanne. 2000. *Finance and Accounting*. Holbrook, MA: Adams Media.

Carmichael, D. R., Steven B. Lilien, and Martin Mellman. 1999. *Accountant's Handbook*, 9th ed. New York: John Wiley.

Chasteen, Lanny G., Richard E. Flaherty, and Melvin C. O'Connor. 1995. *Intermediate Accounting*, 9th ed. New York: McGraw-Hill.

Donnahoe, Alan S. 1989. *What Every Manager Should Know About Financial Analysis*. New York: Simon and Schuster.

Finkler, Steven A. 1992. *Finance and Accounting for Nonfinancial Managers*. Paramus, NJ: Prentice-Hall.

Getz, Lowell. 1997. *An Architect's Guide to Financial Management*. Washington, DC: AIA Press.

———. 1986. *Business Management in the Smaller Design Firm*. Newton, MA: Practice Management Associates.

Getz, Lowell, and Frank Stasiowski. 1984. *Financial Management for the Design Professional*. New York: Watson-Guptill.

Haviland, David, ed. 1994. *The Architect's Handbook of Professional Practice, Student Edition*. Washington, DC: AIA Press.

Head, George O., Jr., and Jan Doster Head. 1988. *Managing, Marketing, and Budgeting for the A/E Office*. New York: Van Nostrand Reinhold.

Horngren, Charles T. 1981. *Introduction to Financial Accounting*. Englewood Cliffs, NJ: Prentice-Hall.

Horngren, Charles T., George Foster, and Srikant M. Datar. 2000. *Cost Accounting*, 10th ed. Upper Saddle River, NJ: Prentice-Hall.

Imdieke, Leroy F., and Ralph E. Smith. 1987. *Financial Accounting*. New York: John Wiley.

Ittelson, Thomas. 1998. *Financial Statements*. Franklin Lakes, NJ: Career Press.

Loebelson, Andrew. 1983. *How To Profit in Contract Design*. New York: Interior Design Books.

Meigs, Robert F., Mary A. Meigs, Mark Battner, and Ray Whittington. 1996. *Accounting: The Basis for Business Decisions*, 10th ed. New York: McGraw-Hill.

Mose, Arlene K., John Jackson, and Gary Downs. 1997. *Day-to-Day Business Accounting*. Paramus, NJ: Prentice-Hall.

Pinson, Linda, and Jerry Jinnett. 1998. *Keeping the Books*, 4th ed. Lincolnwood, IL: Upstart Publishing.

Piotrowski, Christine M. 1992. *Interior Design Management*. New York: John Wiley.

Plewa, Franklin J., Jr., and George T. Friedlob. 1995. *Understanding Cash Flow*. New York: John Wiley.

Ragan, Robert C. 1992. *Step-by-Step Bookkeeping*, rev. ed. New York: Sterling Publishing.

Siegel, Joel G., and Jae K. Shim. 1995. *Accounting Handbook*, 2nd ed. Hauppauge, NY: Barron's.

Siropolis, Nicholas C. 1990. *Small Business Management*, 4th ed. Boston, MA: Houghton Mifflin.

Stasiowski, Frank A. 1993. *Cash Management for the Design Firm*. New York: John Wiley.

Williams, Jan R. 2000. *Miller G. A. P. Guide*. San Diego, CA: Harcourt Professional Publications.

Chapter 16

Financial Management

All interior design businesses have limited financial resources. The smaller the design practice is, the fewer financial resources the firm has. However, design firms, regardless of their size, have similar requirements for those financial resources. Funds must be available to pay employee salaries as well as the rent and other overhead expenses in order to keep the firm in operation. Many interior design firms also must have funds to cover the expenses related to selling goods to the client and installing them. From time to time, the design firm will need to purchase equipment of various kinds, such as a new computer or computer software, furniture for new employees, or perhaps a delivery truck.

Depending on the type of design firm and its actual ownership, some firms need to pay out dividends to stockholders or at least some sort of return on financial investment. At the very least, the sole proprietor wants to be paid a salary or possibly to draw against the profits. It can easily be seen that managing these limited financial resources is as important as generating the revenue in the first place.

The development of the summary reports discussed in the previous chapter is the primary type of information that an owner uses to manage the financial resources of the firm. However, for many firms, the balance sheet, income statement, and cash flow reports do not provide enough information to assist the owner in making important financial decisions. Owners and their accountants turn to other financial management techniques for assistance.

There are many managerial reports that can be developed from data that are available to the firm. These reports provide additional information that the owner or manager can use to assist them in decision making. As the interior design firm grows, this function becomes more important. In this chapter, we will review several useful financial ratios and percentages, as well as various kinds of reports that the owner can use to make financial decisions. The chapter concludes with a brief discussion concerning controlling overhead. This discussion has been added to this chapter because it is a continual problem for owners and managers.

What Is Financial Management?

Financial management, or managerial accounting, is concerned with the analysis and reporting of all the financial aspects of the firm. The reports that are prepared are used to help individuals within the firm to manage and control the performance of the firm.

Financial management goes beyond financial accounting. By means of financial management, owners and managers generate reports that will help them analyze any kind of financial or numerical information that is of interest to them. These accounting reports can show many things. One simple example is a report that summarizes how much of all possible work time for each designer is billable to clients as opposed to house or nonbillable time. This is commonly called a utilization report. A second type of important report is called an aged receivables report. It provides information about how many dollars are owed to the firm by clients and for what period of time that money is owed.

Financial management is the responsibility of the owners and possibly the business manager and design director—those in the firm who are entrusted with the responsibility of planning, organizing, and controlling the organization. In small firms, financial management is always the responsibility of the owner, who receives assistance from the firm's accountant in developing reports. In medium- and large-sized firms, the reports are usually generated and analyzed by the managers.

There are numerous ratios that can be applied to the data that are summarized in the balance sheet and income statement. These ratios help the owner by giving him or her evidence of performance (or the lack of performance) of such things as the amount of profit actually realized from the revenues generated, the amount of working capital that actually results from comparing current assets to current liabilities, and even the relationship of direct labor to nonbillable labor.

Managerial reports can be narrative reports. Perhaps, for example, a design firm is considering locating a branch office in another state. The owner may direct an appropriate party to analyze the business potential of this new location. The report can be in narrative form or a combination of narration and numerical data. This report will help the owner/manager make a decision about the potential viability of the branch office.

Analyzing appropriate data helps the owner make sense of the efforts of staff and the business as a whole. Financial management reporting assists the owner in determining ways in which he or she can keep the firm viable. It is not necessary for the small-business owner to become an accountant in order to do this. It is incumbent upon the owner to seek appropriate help until he or she becomes familiar with reading and interpreting results. Accredited public accountants and certified public accountants generally offer assistance in the development of these reports or in assisting the owner in determining which reports are helpful for a firm's particular situation.

Financial Ratios and Percentages

One way to analyze and report on the financial performance of a business is through the use of financial ratios and percentages. As any accountant would say, understanding financial reports is only part of really understanding whether a business is financially successful or not. Looking at ratios and percentages provides many important clues to the success of, or possible problems in, the financial performance of a design firm. There are several ratios and percentages that are used to evaluate the numerical information contained in the balance sheet and income statement. These ratios and percentages give an even clearer message as to the overall financial success (or lack of it) of a business.

By using ratios and percentages, a designer can evaluate almost anything that can be measured in numerical terms. Ratios are quite common and are used every day by almost everyone in one way or another. In our everyday experiences, we might use ratios to determine the amount of fat in a portion of food, the miles per gallon our car gets, or how much estimated time has been completed on a project. Ratios, as we remember from math class, is one number over another—the relationship between two or more things. With ratios, we are comparing two numbers. A ratio can become a percentage when we divide one number into another. Of course, for a ratio to become a percentage, the large number (the denominator, in this case) must be divided into the small number (the numerator). For example, if we divide 75 by 100 (75/100), we will get a percentage of 75. When using ratios, remember that when we compare a part to the whole, the whole is always the denominator.

There are many ratios that accountants and financial analysts use to evaluate a business. In this brief discussion, we will discuss only a few of the key ratios. Figure 16-1 shows several financial ratios.

One important group of ratios is profit ratios. A business can only remain viable if it sustains a profit. As a rule, profitability (or income) is affected by increases in volume and changes in price, or both. One way for a design firm to increase its profitability is to increase its fee base. Another is to bill more hours at its design fee. And a third can be to find ways to reduce expenses. The profit margin on sales ratio tells the business how much profit has been obtained from every dollar of sales. Using the information in Figure 16-2, you can see that the firm's profit margin on sales (fees only) is 17 percent. Find the data in the income statement that you can use in the formula in Figure 16-1 to calculate this percentage. How can the firm increase this ratio?

A second important profitability ratio is the ratio that tells the return on (total) assets, often expressed as ROA. This ratio measures the amount of profit generated by the use of the assets of the company. The ROA for Wallis Design Group is five percent. Is this firm using its assets effectively to achieve a reasonable profit?

Numerous efficiency ratios can be developed to review how well the business is operating. One very important efficiency ratio is the average collection

1. **Profit margin on sales = net income/total sales**
2. **Return on total assets (ROA) = net income/total assets**
3. **Return on equity (ROE) = net income/owner's equity**
4. **Current ratio = current assets/current liabilities**
5. **Quick ratio (or acid test) = current assets – inventory/current liabilities**
6. **Debt ratio = total debt/total assets**
7. **Working capital = current assets – current liabilities**
8. **Net profit = earnings before interest and taxes (EBIT)/net sales**
9. **Return on investment = EBIT/total assets – total liabilities**
10. **Average collection period = accounts receivables × 360/total sales**
11. **Inventory turnover ratio = cost of goods sold/average inventory**
12. **Gross margin percentage = gross margin dollars/net revenue**

FIGURE 16-1. Financial ratios that are useful to business owners when they are determining the financial performance of the business.

Income Statement
Wallis Design Group
Period Ending December 31, 200X

Gross Revenue	
From fees	$18,400
From sale of goods	
Product	$37,500
Freight-in	2,625
Delivery	3,250
	43,375
Total Gross Revenue	$61,775
Net Revenue	$61,775
Cost of Sales	
From products:	
Cost of goods	$25,000
Freight-in	2,500
Delivery	3,000
From fees:	
Direct labor	12,750
Materials supplies	185
Reproduction expense	95
Telephone (long-distance)	105
Total Cost of Sales	43,635
Gross Margin	$18,140
Operating Expenses	
Salaries	10,500
Payroll taxes	1,900
Rent	850
Heat, power, & light	250
Telephone	265
Promotion	225
Supplies & postage	225
Insurance	200
Dues & subscriptions	57
Printing & reproduction	50
Interest expense	200
Total Operating Expenses	$14,722
Other Revenue	
Interest	350
Net Income Before Taxes	$3,418
Less: Provision for income taxes	−627
Net Income	$3,141

FIGURE 16-2. The income statement of a design firm.

period ratio. This ratio tells the business how many days, on average, it takes to collect accounts receivable. If this ratio is low, it means that the business is receiving payments from clients quickly. If it is high, it means that clients are taking a long time to pay, and this can seriously affect cash flow for the business. The data for the average collection period ratio comes from the balance sheet and income statement. Note that the 360 in the denominator of the formula represents the number of days in the year.* Should this firm try to improve its collection policies?

For design firms that have inventory, it is important for the owner and manager to know how long the merchandise has been in stock. The longer the inventory is held in the office or warehouse, the longer dollars are tied up that can be better used in some other way. Design firms, like any business that sells from its inventory, needs to turn over that merchandise and keep what it sells fresh. The information for this ratio comes from the balance sheet and the income statement. It appears that the firm is turning over its inventory quite quickly. Is it possible that this might not actually be true?

Two other groups of ratios that are of particular importance to investors are the liquidity ratios and the debt ratios. Liquidity ratios show the design firm's ability to pay its debts. Of particular importance is the firm's ability to pay its current liabilities with available current assets. A second liquidity ratio is the working capital ratio. It measures the amount of cash that is available to operate the business on a daily basis. If a firm's working capital is less than its operating expenses, it may not be able to pay all of its current bills. Debt ratios indicate how much of the firm's financing has come from debts—loans and lines of credit—rather than direct investment by the owners and/or stockholders. Potential new investors will be concerned about high debt ratios, since they mean that the loans must be paid off before any return is made on investments in the firm.

Ratios help determine the financial health of the firm and locate some of the potential financial or operational problems of the firm. Ratios are more important to the owner or manager of the firm than to employees. However, employees should understand that there is a lot of number crunching that goes on behind the scenes in the operations of a design practice. Awareness brings about concern, and concern brings about the realization that every employee in the design firm affects the financial health of the company.

Reporting Performance

Two important types of reports that are used by management to determine if the firm's plans are being accomplished are information reports and performance reports. Information reports are generally not made up of financial or other numerical data. They are prepared in a narrative form and are used to provide management with information that is needed in the operation of the organization. A summary of an article related to general economic forecasts for the geographic area of the design firm, which also discusses how these forecasts may affect the design firm, is an example of an informational report.

The second type of report, which is more important to our discussion here, is the performance report. The performance report consists primarily of financial or other numerical information. By sifting through financial and other numerical information, such as time records, many detailed performance reports are possible.

Using today's computer accounting programs and database management programs, a design firm owner can generate dozens of reports with relative ease. However, not all reports that can be created are necessary. In fact, too many reports can confuse rather than help the owner. It is therefore necessary

* Accountants generally use 360 rather than 365 days to determine the number of days in a year in this type of ratio.

for the owner and the firm's accountant to determine which reports will be reliable and timely. What this means is that any report must be based on accurate data or information. In the old days of creating computer programs, there was a saying, "garbage in, garbage out." If the information inserted into a reporting format is inaccurate or in any way comes from improper data, then the usefulness of the generated reports will be questionable. Let us look at a simple example. If an owner is concerned about the revenue productivity of the firm's senior designers, he or she will want to analyze accurate time records for those individuals. If in some way the designers have "fudged" their time records, the resulting analysis will be of little use to the owner. Of course, providing inaccurate time records is very serious, if the design firm is billing the client for that design time.

Reports must also be timely. Owners or managers who are trying to make decisions regarding assigning new projects to the staff, for example, need to know the current status of all projects on at least a weekly basis. Accepting new design projects when the staff is completely booked and overworked, as it might well be in some companies, might look like a good idea, but when the work cannot be accomplished, the staff's enthusiasm will backfire. Some firms may want daily time sheets; others can live with weekly or even monthly reports. An aged receivables report is needed monthly at the very least, but it might be needed on a weekly basis if a firm has a serious cash flow problem.

Many kinds of performance reports are most effective when they are reviewed in terms of variance analysis. In variance analysis the owner or manager looks at financial and numerical data in relation to the differences between planned (or budgeted amounts) and actual amounts (see Figure 16-3). In variance analysis, accountants use the terms favorable and unfavorable. An unfavorable variance generally means that the actual amount is more than

Expense Report($)
April 200X

Expense	Actual	Budget	Variance over Budget
Salaries	$75,000	$78,500	$−3,500
Payroll taxes	4,575	5,000	−425
Group insurance	750	750	0
Rent	1,500	1,500	0
Heat, power, & light	650	500	150
Telephone	375	300	75
Promotion	450	525	−75
Travel reimbursements	790	600	190
Supplies and postage	450	500	−50
Depreciation expense	900	900	0
Insurance	750	750	0
Dues & subscriptions	250	150	100
Professional consultants	2,300	1,000	1,300
Printing and reproduction	570	450	120
Interest expense	875	875	0
Total Expenses	90,185	92,300	−2,115

FIGURE 16-3. Performance report—variance analysis for the expense report.

Creative Interior Design
Projected Revenue by Client Type
200X, 200X (Est.), 200X (Est.)

	200X	**200X**	**200X**
Open Office Planning:			
Under 15,000 sq. ft.	$23,500	$65,000	$75,000
15,000–30,000 sq. ft.	12,000	36,000	40,000
Over 30,000 sq. ft.	20,800	27,000	35,000
Subtotal	$56,300	$128,000	$150,000
Medical Facilities:			
Physician's suites	32,500	48,000	55,000
Hospitals	35,000	40,000	25,000
Subtotal	$67,500	$88,000	$80,000
Banking Facilities:			
Branch offices	10,000	20,500	28,000
Corporate offices	15,500	20,000	30,000
Subtotal	$25,500	$40,500	$58,000
Professional Offices:			
Attorneys	28,700	42,000	55,000
Accountants	13,600	25,000	30,000
Corporate	45,900	55,000	60,000
Real estate	5,000	7,500	10,000
Others	10,000	20,000	25,000
Subtotal	$103,200	$149,500	$180,000
Hospitality:			
Restaurant	65,500	80,500	90,000
Lodging	38,500	49,000	72,000
Subtotal	$104,000	$129,500	$162,000
Grand Total	$356,500	$535,500	$630,000

FIGURE 16-4. Performance report—projected revenue by client type.

the budgeted amount. A favorable variance generally means that the actual amount is less than the budgeted amount. For example, if the budgeted amount of direct labor for a project is 300 hours and the actual amount of hours worked is 365 hours, there is an unfavorable variance. Assuming there is the same number of budget hours, if the actual hours were 280, there would be a favorable variance.

However, a manager must not only look at the quantitative differences. For the data to be truly meaningful, he or she must also ask questions as to why the variances occur. This analysis quite often begins with informal meetings with the individuals involved. The manager uses his or her judgment, then, to make decisions related to the variances.

It is important for firms to look at certain blocks of information to determine if goals and objectives are being met. Reports related to revenue generation (see Figure 16-4), expenses, and profits are the most important. To have the most use, summary reports should be prepared on a monthly basis.

Some examples of specific reports that can be useful, depending on the size and complexity of the interior design firm, are as follows. Figures 16-5 and 16-6 are examples of some of these reports.

1. Revenues from sources—fees and sales of goods
2. Work in process and aged receivables
3. Deferred income
4. Employee utilization and productivity
5. Comparisons of fees earned with budgeted estimates
6. Revenues by client type (or size of project)
7. Month-by-month profit-and-loss statements (with variances)

How often should reports be prepared? This would largely be determined by the firm's ability to produce the required reports. As mentioned above, computer applications allow for fast turnaround of many reports. In some

Excellent Interiors, Inc.
Work in Process/Age Analysis
As of July 200X

				Accounts Receivables			
Client	**Total**	**Work in Process**	**Current**	**30 Days**	**60 Days**	**90 Days**	**120 days and Over**
Nelson's Real Estate	$8,900	$2,250		$900			
Smith, Jones Corp.	15,000	5,000	$5,000				
Astro Business Park	12,500	3,000	2,500	1,000	$2,000*		
University Computing Center	29,500	9,750	7,750				
Phoenix Corporation	25,500			5,500	2,000*		
Financial Trust Bank	8,500	5,000	3,000	500			
Oceanview Development Co.	70,500					$21,000*	
Carter Residence	5,000	1,500					1,550*
Robbins Residence	6,500	2,000	1,500	1,500			
Totals	$181,900	$28,500	$19,750	$9,400	$4,000	$21,000	$1,550

*Sent letter: work stopped until account is current.

FIGURE 16-5. Performance report—work-in-process/age analysis.

Manpower Utilization Report
Excellent Interior Design, LLC
Week Ending April 1, 200X

Week ending	No. of employees	Total hours	Billable	% Billed	House	Meetings Admin.	Misc.
3/3	8	335	280	84%	55	42	13
3/11	8	365	274	75%	91	73	18
3/18	8	385	375	97%	28	13	15
3/24	8	330	300	91%	30	21	9
3/31	8	342	320	94%	22	15	7
4/01	9	355	337	95%	18	12	6

FIGURE 16-6. Performance report—employee productivity.

cases, assuming data are available, a report can be generated on the computer by the end of a business day. If the report is done manually, as is the case for many small design firms, getting it done on a monthly basis can be considered fast, since some reports are prepared only every three to six months—if at all. Ideally, most reports should be prepared on a monthly basis when the previous month's data is available within the first ten days of the month.

Even small design firms or sole proprietors can take advantage of performance reporting by using accounting and database management. Computer systems can link accounting and other numerical data to generate tabled reports relatively easily. Software that also can automatically prepare charts and graphs from the numerical data provides additional aid for the manager.

Controlling Overhead

Controlling overhead is very definitely a financial management issue. Keeping overhead expenses under control is an important task in producing a profit for any size design business. Even the sole practitioner who works out of a home office needs to control overhead, or profit margins will be nonexistent.

As you will recall from the previous chapter, overhead consists of those expenses that are necessary to keep the doors of the design firm "open." For almost all businesses, overhead expenses exist even if no revenue is produced during a business day. In Chapter 15, we briefly discussed common overhead expenses. In this section, we will look at the concept of controlling overhead expenses as part of financial management.

A monthly review of overhead expenses is the starting point for controlling overhead. Reviews need to be made so that the owner and/or manager can see if any areas of the business have increasing overhead costs. For example, if utility rates are rising, the owner needs to determine if this is solely due to an increase in utility rates by the supplier or if a sudden amount of overtime is the culprit. Working longer hours means an increase in the use of utilities. Although it might not be possible to eliminate this increase—the workload is the workload—it can be taken into consideration when the owner is determining billing rates and fee methods for future projects.

Indirect labor is an important factor in the overhead expense totals for a firm. You will recall that indirect labor is any work performed that cannot be directly charged to a particular revenue-producing account or project. Informational meetings with manufacturers' representatives and with vendors who drop by the office or call on the phone is an example of indirect labor that can sometimes get out of hand. Deciding not to have the secretary keep track of time spent typing and preparing specifications for projects is another example of indirect labor that can create big overhead expense problems. While the drop-in visit by a vendor cannot be billed to a client, the secretary's time for typing can be billed or at least costed to the project.

Other ways in which overhead expenses can sometimes be reduced to help improve profit margins include the following:

- Purchasing equipment rather than renting or leasing.
- Subletting office or studio space from another design firm (for the sole practitioner).
- Rotating designers who are sent to major market shows.
- Arranging for in-house training seminars rather than sending designers out of state. A firm could sponsor a CEU and invite nonfirm designers to participate.

The most important way to control costs is to know what the costs are. Many smaller interior design practices keep minimal records on direct or indirect expenses of operating the practice. "It takes too much time to record all my time," and "It's too much trouble to keep track of how many copies I make for a client," are common excuses for minimal expense recording. Carefully recording time and other expenses should not be considered an intrusion. This type of record keeping is good business practice. Working from knowledge allows the owner to make better estimates of fees and to come closer to meeting expected profit forecasts, both of which make it easier to expand the business and obtain needed equipment or hire experienced personnel.

Creating methods and procedures to control overhead can become overly obsessive and can actually be an intrusion into the orderly completion of work in the firm. Determining which overhead activities will be controlled and studied should be carefully limited to ensure positive assistance to the owner while not creating extra work for the staff. For example, while it is useful to know how many sheets of plot paper are wasted in the development of a project, this bit of information can actually be considered "micromanaging" and may not even be kept accurately. Discussions with the firm's accountant to determine which areas of overhead need to be controlled, along with meetings to carefully explain to the staff the importance of these procedures, are vital when the owner is instituting methods to control overhead.

Summary

Managerial financial reports provide important information to the owner and manager of an interior design firm. These reports help the owner and manager make decisions related to many financial, personnel, and operational issues of the interior design practice.

Interior design firms that utilize computers for accounting and data management can quickly produce many useful financial managerial reports. However, the variety and complexity of these reports must aid the managerial function, not burden it with the preparation and analysis of useless documents.

Managerial reports are prepared to assist in the management of the firm, not to become a burden or overriding issue. Companies or managers who become slaves to the numbers may miss the opportunity to involve the company in new design areas, to hire designers who have a chance to grow with the firm and become loyal employees, or to explore other issues related to the overall mission and goals of the design firm.

The next four chapters discuss how design firms produce revenue. Chapter 17 will discuss fees for services. Chapter 18 then covers what constitutes a legal contract and what should go into an interior design contract. Chapters 19 and 20 review product pricing and the law as it relates to the sale of goods.

REFERENCES

Anthony, Robert N., John Dearden, and Norton M. Bedford. 1984. *Management Control Systems*, 5th ed. Homewood, IL: Richard D. Irwin.

Anthony, Robert N., and James S. Reece. 1983. *Accounting Texts and Cases*, 7th ed. Homewood, IL: Richard D. Irwin.

Berk, Joseph, and Susan Berk. 1991. *Managing Effectively. A Handbook for First-Time Managers.* New York: Sterling Publishing.

Caplan, Suzanne. 2000. *Finance and Accounting*. Holbrook, MA: Adams Media.

Carmichael, D. R., Steven B. Lilien, and Martin Mellman. 1999. *Accountant's Handbook*, 9th ed. New York: John Wiley.

Chasteen, Lanny G., Richard E. Flaherty, and Melvin C. O'Connor. 1995. *Intermediate Accounting*, 5th ed. New York: McGraw-Hill.

Finkler, Steven A. 1992. *Finance and Accounting for Nonfinancial Managers.* Paramus, NJ: Prentice-Hall.

Fridson, Martin S. 1995. *Financial Statement Analysis.* New York: John Wiley.

Garrison, Ray H. 1985. *Managerial Accounting*, 4th ed. Plano, TX: Business Publications.

Getz, Lowell. 1997. *An Architect's Guide to Financial Management*. Washington, DC: AIA Press.

———. 1986. *Business Management in the Smaller Design Firm.* Newton, MA: Practice Management Associates.

Getz, Lowell, and Frank Stasiowski. 1984. *Financial Management for the Design Professional.* New York: Watson-Guptill.

Horngren, Charles T., George Foster, and Srikant M. Datar. 2000. *Cost Accounting*, 10th ed. Upper Saddle River, NJ: Prentice-Hall.

Ittelson, Thomas. 1998. *Financial Statements.* Franklin Lakes, NJ: Career Press.

Meigs, Robert F, Mary A. Meigs, Mark Bettner, and Ray Whittington. 1996. *Accounting: The Basics for Business Decisions*, 10th ed. New York: McGraw-Hill.

Mose, Arlene K., John Jackson, and Gary Downs. 1997. *Day-to-Day Business Accounting.* Paramus, NJ: Prentice-Hall.

Pinson, Linda, and Jerry Jinnett. 1998. *Keeping the Books*, 4th ed. Lincolnwood, IL: Upstart Publishing.

Shapero, Albert. 1985. *Managing Professional People.* New York: Free Press.

Siegel, Joel G., and Jae K. Shim. 1995. *Accounting Handbook.* Hauppauge, NY: Barron's.

Stasiowski, Frank A. 1993. *Cash Management for the Design Firm.* New York: John Wiley.

Stitt, Fred A., ed. 1986. *Design Office Management Handbook.* Santa Monica, CA: Arts and Architecture Press.

Walsh, Ciaran. 1996. *Key Management Ratios*. London, England: F.T. Pitman.

Williams, Jan R. 2000. *Miller G. A. P. Guide*. San Diego, CA: Harcourt Professional Publications.

Chapter 17

Determining Design Fees

For many interior design firms, the only source of income for the firm is from fees charged to the client for services. These fees must cover the cost of the designer's time or salary expense and overhead expenses, such as electricity, cost of drafting paper, and telephone calls, and must provide a margin of profit as well. Other interior design firms generate revenues from the sale of merchandise. Still others generate the revenues from both merchandise fees and service fees.

There is no one way to satisfy all situations and all types of interior design practice. Each firm must decide which fee method and revenue method is appropriate for its purposes. Many factors will impact this decision. The methods used by local competition may force the design firm into using certain fee methods, since clients may be used to specific practices. The type of design in which the designer chooses to specialize may mean that the firm must use one fee method over others. The designer's own experience and knowledge may direct the designer to use a particular fee method.

The variety of fee methods allows the design professional to choose a method with which he or she is a comfortable in order to "sell" it to the client more easily. Various fee methods allow the professional to customize how he or she charges clients to suit the clients needs and the specific project. However, the different fee methods can create confusion. Inconsistency can be a problem if the designer is working with clients who talk to each other a lot, such is often the case in residential interior design practice.

This chapter emphasizes fee methods related to compensation for interior design service as might be used by a designer or a firm. However, fee methods used alone or in combination with service fees are also discussed. Pricing methods for the sale of goods is discussed in Chapter 19.

The Billing Rate

In almost all cases, the method of charging a fee to the client is related to the billing rate of the firm. The *billing rate* is a dollar amount charged for each design professional, staff member, or, in some cases, the type of service provided. Most typically, the billing rate is expressed as an hourly rate. Some situations might call for a day rate, in which case, the billing rate is for a full day's work rather than determined on an hourly basis.

The billing rate is based on the salary rate of the employee. Since the salary rate alone does not cover expenses and provide a profit, the rate is actually calculated based on the firm's *multiple* (also called a multiplier). A multiple is calculated to include these other factors. For some fee methods, especially the fixed fee and square footage method, the billing rate is primary to the determination of the total fee. In other methods, such as cost plus or percentage off retail, it has an indirect bearing on the fee itself. The multiple is multiplied by the salary rate, and the individual's billing rate is then established.

Traditionally, the most commonly used multiple is 3.0. No one seems to know where this factor came from. It might be interpreted as meaning that one part is equal to the salary rate, one part covers overhead burden, and one part allows for profit. However, this is not necessarily accurate, since some firms have a multiple that is below 3.0 and some firms have one that is slightly above 3.0, depending on the size of the firm, which will affect overhead and salary expenses. A method commonly used in interior design and architectural offices is to determine the multiple of *direct personnel expense* (DPE). The direct personnel expense is a number that includes the salary of the employee and costs of employee benefits such as unemployment taxes, medical insurance, and paid holidays. The calculation of the DPE is an accurate determinant of a firm's multiple.

Many firms make the mistake of determining the billing rate only on the salary rate per hour of the employees, not taking into consideration direct and overhead expenses. If this is done, the firm is actually reducing the amount it will have to provide for direct and overhead expense coverage and for profit. On average, the cost of employee fringe benefits can add up to 60 percent to the cost of the employee. Many new owners of an interior design firm are very surprised to find a net profit of only 2–4 percent—if they find any net profit at all. Net profit rates of around 10–15 percent are more common, especially in firms that carefully control costs and accurately estimate profit plans into billing rates.

A multiplier based on the DPE is a factor that is based on the direct labor expense plus the cost of employee benefits. You will recall, from the discussion in Chapter 15, that direct labor and expenses are those that are incurred when employees are actually working on revenue-producing work. This discussion follows the numbers shown in Figure 17-1. All of this information could be obtained easily from the financial records of the design firm. First, the total annual salaries of all employees is determined. Then the total of employee fringe benefits expenses are found, such as unemployment taxes, worker's compensation, medical and/or life insurance, FICA, sick leave, pension plans, and paid holidays. (Figure 17-2 provides some examples of employee benefits.) Next, the owner needs to determine the total of overhead expenses for the year. Adding these three items together gives the total annual expenses for the firm. At this point, the owner should add on a factor for a profit goal. In Figure 17–1, we have added a percentage that would give a reasonable profit goal of 20%.

The total net revenue shown in the example is revenue that does not include any sale of furniture. It is purely related to the offering of design services. In this situation, the revenues are realized when designers work on design projects, thus, it is necessary to determine a factor for direct labor. Since it is very difficult for all professional staff to work at 100 percent billable time and little of the support staff's time is billable, it is necessary to create a multiplier based on direct personnel expense (DPE) to be accurate.

This is done by the calculations shown in the remainder of Figure 17-1. Assuming that only 70 percent of possible work time is billable (referred to as a utilization rate), then $70,000 would be direct labor. The remaining salary

Direct Personnel Expense and Fee Multiple

Total annual salaries	$100,000	
Total fringe benefits	20,000	
Total overhead expenses	32,000	
Total Expenses	$152,000	
Total profit goal (20% of revenue)	38,000	
Total Net Revenue (income goal for year)	$190,000	
Direct labor $100,000 × 0.70	$70,000	
Indirect Expenses:		
Indirect labor $100,00 × 0.30	30,000	
Payroll taxes and benefits	20,000	
Overhead expenses	32,000	
Total of indirect salary and expenses	82,000	
Total of Direct Salaries and Indirect Expenses	$152,000	
The DPE multiplier would be:		
Direct salary divided by direct salary: $70,000 divided by $70,000		1.00
Total indirect expenses divided by direct salary: $82,000 divided by $70,000		1.17
Adding profit: $38,000 divided by $70,000		0.54
Total DPE multiplier		2.71

FIGURE 17-1. Calculations of the direct personnel expense (DPE) and fee multiple.

expense is indirect labor—that salary expense that cannot be billed to clients. The amount of payroll taxes, fringe benefits, and overhead expenses is restated in the lower portion of the figure for clarification. Employees whose time is billable are the professional design staff. Secretaries, office assistants, and bookkeepers generally are not employees whose time can be billed.*

The net multiplier is then calculated against the salary rates to get the billing rates. For example, if the senior designer is paid $23.50 per hour, his billing rate would be $63.70, or probably rounded to $65.00 per hour. An entry-level design assistant who is paid $17.00 per hour could be billed at $46.07, or $50.00 per hour.

When determining the expense portion of the billing rate multiple, there is another concept that the owner should consider. As the business expands, the cost of direct expenses will expand as more revenue is generated. What is sometimes forgotten is that, as business expands, so might overhead expenses. It may be necessary for the owner, manager, and employees to stay after normal business hours in order to complete projects, adding to overall utility bills. This extra work could also mean additional work for support personnel. As

* That portion of time that a secretary spends working on such things as specifications and written documentation for a project *can* be billed, as it directly relates to the completion of a project. However, it is not very common for design firms to charge for this time.

Paid holidays
Paid vacations
Paid sick leave
Health insurance
Life insurance
Dental insurance
Retirement or profit-sharing programs
Employee discounts
Educational expense allowances
Professional dues reimbursements
Unemployment taxes
Social Security insurance
Worker's compensation insurance

FIGURE 17-2. Typical personnel benefits.

business expands, simple overhead expenses, like supplies, telephone services, and many other costs of doing business and those related to generating income, also increase. Calculating these extra overhead expenses into the multiplier may not be an easy thing to do, but recognition of their impact should be taken into consideration. Not to consider the effect that overtime work will have on the costs and fee estimates of projects will, at the very least, lead to a reduction in planned profit margins.

Billing rates also can be used to determine if the fixed fee and the percentage rate methods are sufficient. The fee divided by the billing rate multiple will give the amount of salary dollars that the owner can use for that project at the profit margin that is normally maintained. This method helps the owner determine if the amount of salary dollars available is sufficient to cover the expenses and desired profit for the project. If it is determined that the project cannot be done for that amount, then the owner can either reject the project or try a different fee method or a combination of methods in order to ensure that there will be proper compensation.

Which, When, Why?

As has already been mentioned, the interior designer has many different ways in which he or she can charge the client for design services. For the most part, no one method is better than any other. A lot of ingredients go into deciding which fee method should be used on any particular project. Of course, designers tend toward one or two methods most of the time. This may be because it is one they are used to or has worked before or better fits the way in which they do business with a majority of clients. It would be good for the student and the design professional who is just starting a practice to look at some of the elements that can affect the determination of a fee method.

- *The client's experience with an interior designer.* Clients—residential or commercial—who have had no previous experience working with an interior designer require more of the designer's time and patience, and more educating. These clients ask more questions, want more choices, and deliberate more before they make decisions. They also change their mind more often and generally challenge the interior designer more frequently. The client who has worked with a designer before, for the most part, will be just the opposite—though no "cinch" to work with either! And if the designer has never worked with the client before, the client will also require more of the designer's patience and time, even if the client has worked previously with other interior designers. Projects generally will take longer to complete for the client who has not previously worked with a designer.

- *The scope of services required to execute the project.* When the project requires the full range of design services—programming, schematic design, design development, contract documents, and contract administration—the fee methods used are quite different from those that are used when the project requires more decorative services and few if any, drawings. Interior designers who tend more toward the decorative side of design and who work little in the overall planning and limited architectural services often charge no fee for their services and earn revenue from the markup of furniture that they sell to their clients. Of course, more can go wrong with a complex project that requires a large number of services. Contingency planning in the selection of fee methods and amounts is necessary in a large, complex project.
- *The size of the project.* The larger and more complex the project is, the more time the designer will have to spend on the project, and the chance for something to go wrong exists. While there is no argument that the designer can make a very serious mistake when designing and specifying a custom window treatment or spectacular mahogany and granite cabinets for a residence, much more can go wrong in numerous places and ways in the design of corporate headquarters. Then there are some large projects that are large in terms of square footage but that do not require a lot of unique designs. Hotels may have hundreds of rooms, but most of the rooms have the same floor plan, and use perhaps a few different color schemes in the same pattern. Creating the prototype guest room is where the intense design effort occurs; less time is spent on the "copies."
- *The designer's experience with the type of project.* The less experienced the interior designer is with a particular type of project, the longer (logically) it will take him or her to execute the project. There is a learning curve with every project because the designer does not know a particular client or a project in depth. Perhaps new programming methods and tools must be found and used to elicit the needed information. In a commercial project, the designer may lack background information about the client's business and may find that research is in order. Maybe the client and project call for product specifications that are unfamiliar to the designer or are so unique that extra time is required to find the products. All of these examples and many others affect the amount of time that the designer needs to complete the project, thus requiring that he or she be compensated for that time without making the client pay for all the "learning" that the designer needs in order to complete the project.
- *Residential versus Commercial.* Residential interior designers tend to charge fees or earn revenue based on the sale of goods. Sometimes, charges for their design services are commonly "buried" in the price of the goods and are not charged directly. These designers frequently charge retail or at cost plus a markup percentage for the goods. Other residential interior designers charge a small fee for their services and

then sell merchandise at some sort of markup from cost or discount from retail in order to cover the remainder of the revenue that is required to cover the expenses of performing design services, paying overhead, and earning a profit. Naturally, some residential designers do not sell furniture and other furnishings at all and charge clients based on fees for services.

Commercial designers, on the other hand, predominately charge for the services they perform and less frequently sell merchandise. These designers use a variety of fee methods but commonly use the hourly or fixed fee methods. Others use the square footage method or perhaps some other method. The hourly fee is the most remunerative way of charging for design services, because the client pays for every hour (or potentially every minute) of design work. Clients, however, may be concerned that the designer may take too long to finish the project if the work is based on an hourly rate. This is why many commercial designers use other methods.

- *How much research is needed for special items.* Many high-end residential projects require extra time for researching products that are "just right" and that are appropriate for the client's project. Many times these items are not easily found in catalogs, in sample books at the studio, or in the design firm's inventory. Someone must travel to trade showrooms or request textile (or other) representatives to come to the studio and show many pieces of fabrics in a search for the right items. Some commercial projects require the same type of research. Accessories for restaurants and some hotels are very special and generally are not found in catalogs. I recall spending many days browsing antique shops for accessories that would finish a resort's guest rooms. Other commercial projects have simplified product specifications, and the items are available from manufacturers' catalogs. Interior designers who work for an office furnishings dealer may have very simplified specifications, since they must use what is in inventory in order to meet the client's demand to move into a modular office systems layout immediately.

Which method to use depends on all the factors just discussed, as well as many others that are particular to the design firm. Competition, the desire to do a particular project, the cash flow situation of the design firm, and many other things are thought of by the owner every time the client wants to know "How much will this cost?" Now let us look specifically at the typical fee methods that are used in the professional practice of interior design.

Methods for Setting Design Fees

There are a great number of factors that the owner of a design firm must take into consideration when determining which fee method he or she will use for each design project. No one method works for all projects for any one design firm, and there is no one fee method that can be guaranteed to work best all the time for a particular type of project. Before we discuss the different fee methods themselves, let us look at some differences between residential and commercial projects that can affect the choice of fee method and the amount of the fee.

Commercial projects are often large, commonly starting at about 3000–5000 square feet. Some can be very large—hundreds of thousands of square feet in a hotel, hospital, major office project, or department store. Commercial projects are complex because of their size, the dollars involved for the build-out and interiors, and short time frames. A considerable amount of coordination is necessary and to be expected between the designer and the architect, contractors, engineers, and, of course, the client. Although many of these projects can be finished in three to six months (more or less), others can take years. In addition, commercial projects can also go through many changes, even during the design stages. Clients may add employees or functional requirements, codes may change, construction and product costs may increase, and many other factors can have an impact on the project, which can affect the fee estimate. All these factors also point out the necessity for greater time management, time keeping, scheduling, and project management, all of which are time-consuming activities.

Commercial clients generally make decisions quickly when presented with interior design concepts by designers. Whatever their actual business, they do not take the time to discuss and make decisions leisurely on the interior of the project. They often will agree to the products presented at the earliest schematic and design development meetings. This is not to say that they accept everything at the first presentation—this would be any interior designer's dream—but, generally speaking, they do not expect the designer to resubmit items time after time. Fewer items are custom made and are primarily specified from items that are easily available in manufacturers' catalogs. For many projects, only a few manufacturers are used, which provides pricing advantages because of the economy of single-source purchasing. Finally, if these clients want the designer to continue to make changes, look for new alternatives, or add services or areas to the project, the commercial interior designer charges these clients for the changes and additions, in addition to whatever the original fee is.

In residential design, a professional interior designer prefers working on single-family residences, which are approximately 3000–5000 square feet. A rather large residential project can be 10,000–15,000 square feet. Some are larger, of course. A residential project can be quite complicated due to such things as multiple architectural finishes, custom cabinets, perhaps custom furniture, and numerous other details. An average home can be built in about six to nine months (barring weather or construction delays), though it can take longer for larger, more complex residential construction projects. These are just some of the differences between residential and commercial project execution.

In residential projects, it is common for the client to take longer to make up his or her mind concerning the decisions that must be made. Because of this, the designer often reworks plans and must do more research or "shopping" for the products that will go into the project. Since many custom-manufactured items are specified in residences, the delivery and completion time of the project can be delayed beyond the client's original expectation. In many cases, residential projects require more servicing, which has been described by professionals as "hand holding." Once a relationship with a client has begun, residential designers often find themselves providing telephone, in-studio, or in-home advice or consultation on what sometimes seems minor issues. For example, rather long discussions about a particular accessory that the client may have seen at a retail store can occur at any time during the project. Thus, the designer must sometimes be ready to go back to the client long after he or she has finished with the project mentally or on paper.

No matter what type of interior design practice the designer has, the client's reluctance to pay a fee for service as well as for furniture remains a problem. When the firm is one that produces designs and specifications, the client pays the firm only for interior design services. Designers who work from a retail store or a showroom are less likely to charge a fee for design services in addition to the markup on the furniture. However, when the firm both charges for the interior design service and then attempts to sell the merchandise to the client, the firm often runs into difficult negotiations with the client, because the client often thinks that he or she is being charged twice. In recent years, many designers have distanced themselves from this problem by reducing or eliminating the selling of merchandise along with their services or by selling products at greatly reduced prices. There is no doubt that this issue will continue to evolve in our profession as designers seek to be compensated for the design services and knowledge they have to offer.

As the reader can see, there are many factors that contribute to the designer's difficulty in selecting an appropriate fee method and amount of fee. Let us look at the specific fee methods that commonly are used in interior design.

Hourly Fee Method

The *hourly fee* is commonly charged based on the firm's DPE, as discussed earlier in this chapter. It is a very satisfactory way of ensuring that the firm will be compensated for all the work it does for a client. The hourly fee is a customary method of charging that firms use if they do not intend to sell merchandise to the client. And it can be used by those in residential or commercial practice.

Many clients, however, are reluctant to agree to an hourly fee, since the meter, metaphorically speaking, is always running. The longer the designer works on the project, the greater the charges will be. The client is often afraid to allow the designer this much freedom in setting the time schedule. Clients are often afraid that the designer will take extra time so that he or she can increase the fee. Many firms get around this objection by setting a "not to exceed" limit on the contract. What this means is that the designer must estimate the actual amount of time that he or she will spend on the project and must quote a maximum fee that will cover all the expected work. The client cannot be charged more than this maximum. The designer must be careful in estimating the time it will take to complete a project. He or she should also be sure that a clause is included in the contract to allow additional charges if the cause for delays or extra work is due to the client.

The hourly fee is often used

1. For the initial or specific consultations on small-scale projects
2. To cover travel time to the job site, to markets, or for other travel time
3. When the project involves a great deal of consultation time with architects, contractors, and subcontractors
4. When it is necessary to prepare working drawings and specification documents
5. When the designer perceives that the client will have difficulty in making up his or her mind
6. Whenever it is difficult to estimate the total amount of time needed to complete a job, for example, a law office in which each partner wishes to have his or her office designed in a very individual manner

The DPE is used by the owner to set a billing rate based on the salary level of the employee. Many firms set billing rates in this way to distinguish the professional levels of employees. Thus, work performed by less experienced designers is charged at a lower rate than work executed by senior designers and principals. The principal is billed at a very high rate, compared to the design assistant. For example, a principal might bill for his or her time at $75–200 per hour; a senior or project designer might be billed at $50–175 per hour; the charge for midlevel designers might be $40–125 per hour; and design assistants and draftspeople might be billed at $25–75 per hour. Additional dollar amounts might be added, based on the reputation of the designer and the value of his or her service. Of course, local competition may prohibit a firm from adding dollars above the DPE multiple.

Other firms find that averaging all the rates of the various levels of designers involved and charging one rate no matter who is doing the work is a satisfactory solution. The danger here is that, if the principal or senior designer is largely involved in the project, his or her time will not be generating adequate income. When entry-level designers are involved in the project, they often take longer than experienced designers. The averaging method can result in undercharging or overcharging the client.

Another way of charging the hourly fee is to charge by the kind of service rather than the personnel. In this case, the firm's owner determines that three or more levels of service are needed and sets a fee amount to charge for each level of service. Three levels might be design (or creative) service (the highest level of service); documentation and drafting (those activities involved in the preparation of final drafting of floor plans and other drawings, preparation of texture boards or documents, and bid documents); and at the lowest level, for supervision and/or miscellaneous time (that would involve such things as travel time within the city, meetings with architects and contractors, meetings with the client, site visits, and so on). Some firms break down the project based on the standard five phases of a project. This method has the same problems as the averaging method.

The hourly fee method provides a way of charging the client for all (or almost all) the time put into the client's project. However, clients often object to the open-ended nature of the hourly fee method. This method can be used successfully by many designers without including the "not to exceed" clause if the client trusts the designer's ability to manage the project.

Fixed Fee Method

The *fixed fee method*, also called the flat fee method or lump sum (or stipulated sum) method,* is similar to the hourly method, because it includes a not-to-exceed clause. With the fixed fee method (for simplicity), however, the estimated fee is usually charged to the client whether the amount of time estimated is correct or not. This means that, if the firm's owner has estimated badly and the time involved in completing a project exceeds the estimated fee, the firm cannot be compensated for the extra time. If the firm has estimated too high and the project does not require the full amount of estimated time, the firm is not obligated to refund any of the fee to the client. Of course, it is improper to overinflate the fixed fee as a way of seeking to obtain a huge profit at the client's expense. The fixed fee includes charges for all services and expenses other than those that the firm charges as reimbursable expenses. This fee method appeals to those clients who clearly are interested in the bottom line. Designers who wish to use this fee method should have a database of previous projects that will help them determine the approximate average times and expenses that are needed to execute various kinds of projects.

In order to use this method, it is important for the owner or project manager to consider the salary and overhead costs for the design firm and to have a thorough understanding of the services that must be performed. He or she must also have a feeling for the decision-making ability of the client so as to predict if the client will be difficult or easy to work with and if the client understands the time element so that all phases of the project can be

* The term lump sum or stipulated sum is commonly used by architectural firms.

satisfactorily accomplished. It is also important for the owner or manager to have a record of job histories for similar projects, which can aid in estimating and can be used as a guide in making decisions on new projects. And, of course, the owner or manager should have a very good idea of the client's budget.

The owner or manager must be very comfortable in his or her ability to estimate the time that will be necessary to complete various kinds of projects if the fixed fee method is used. The firm that has built up a history of time records and expense records from various kinds of projects is in the best position to use the fixed fee method. The fixed fee method, which can be used for both residential and commercial projects, is a satisfactory method of charging fees when

1. The client is not purchasing goods from the designer. This allows the designer to utilize goods that he or she might not normally use, since the designer is not selling the goods. For the client, this may mean that the goods specified are at a lower cost than those the designer might be trying to sell.
2. The amount of goods to be purchased is so small that it would result in an insignificant amount when compared to the time involved. The design firm will put the time into the project, knowing that the firm will be fully compensated for that time rather than depending on profits from selling a small amount of goods.
3. Whenever a large amount of the same items are to be purchased. This is often the case for projects such as restaurants and office complexes, in which standardized products are specified; little additional time is required for such projects after the final product selections are made.
4. When it is easy to determine the time and requirements of the project.
5. When the scope of the project is easy to define.

Square Foot Method

In this method, the fee is determined by some rate per square foot times the amount of square footage of the project being designed. Commonly used in commercial design and by some designers in residential practice, the *square foot method* can be a profitable way of determining the design fee. Whenever firms have sufficient experience in specific kinds of jobs, such that they can be comfortable with a fee rate, the square foot method is an excellent method to use.

With the square foot method, the owner must determine what factor will be used for charging for the various phases of the project. As mentioned in the discussion of the hourly fee method, the project can be broken down into phases. If the firm normally charges a different rate for each of these phases, then the firm must determine what fee rate correlates with a portion of the square footage fee.

An owner who has never used the square foot method for determining fees can gather data on several completed projects, for example, similar size doctors' suites or real estate offices. The actual design fee charged for these projects is divided by the square footage of the project, which provides a historical view of the square foot cost of the design work.

Recently, widely published data on setting fees based on a square foot factor appeared in an article in the 1996 issue of *Interior Design* magazine. If we used that data, the median fee in dollars per rentable square foot (RSF) for offices would be approximately $2.50. The fee for hotel spaces would be $3.75; restaurants, $7.00; and medical offices, $3.00.* It is easy to see from these

* Reproduced with permission from *Interior Design*, January 1996, Cahners Business Information.

variations in fees that the type of space and complexity of the project affects the amount that can be charged. In addition, regional factors, the design firm's experience, and local competition may drive fees up or down. The owner of each firm must look at the fee per square foot in relation to the national average, and the owner must determine if his or her fees are in line with the national average and with what is appropriate in that firm's geographic location. Charging a higher fee than what the local traffic will bear will bring frustration and a loss of work.

Percentage of Merchandise and Product Services Method

Akin to the architect's percentage of construction cost method, the design firm can determine and negotiate a percentage of the cost of the goods and installation that will be involved in the project. The percentage is then multiplied by the budgeted or final costs of the project. This might include the furniture, wall coverings, floor coverings, ceiling and window treatments, lighting fixtures, accessories, built-in cabinets, and even general construction costs. The *percentage of merchandise and product services method* is used frequently by commercial designers.

This method is very similar in concept to the cost plus percentage method, and it is often utilized by interior design firms that generally do not sell any merchandise to the client. It is used if clients suspect the designer of "double dipping," that is, of earning revenue from the specification and also from selling the merchandise. The percentage rate varies with the size or complexity of the project. The larger the project is, the smaller the fee will be. The more complex the project is, the greater the fee will be. For example, a large project like a hotel, with a large dollar volume but a potentially smaller number of design decisions, would require a smaller fee than a group of individually designed executive offices.

Since the project fee is based on cost, the client may actually save money if any extra discounts are provided on merchandise that the client purchases. The designer, however, must carefully negotiate the percentage of that discount, because the firm could lose a considerable amount of money if projects are bid and won by trying to "buy" a project at a very low price. Budgets must be carefully considered to ensure that the project is done as required and that the designer is compensated fairly. This method should be used cautiously and only in combination with another method that will ensure fair compensation for design time and services.

Value-Oriented Method

The dramatic increase in competition in many markets has led designers to consider a fee method, called the *value-oriented*, or value-based, method. This fee method uses the concept that the design firm prices services based on the value or quality of the services rather than on the cost of doing those services. It will only work for a design firm whose services have, for some reason, additional value in the marketplace. The value judgment is made by the client and is based on his or her perception of the value of the interior design firm.

Traditionally, most fee methods are based on time or cost rather than on value. With the value-oriented fee method, the designer must show the client how his or her services are superior to those of competing designers. The perception of most clients is that all designers do the same thing and provide the same services. The designer must show how he or she differs from the competition and is thus worth the fees requested. If the client perceives that what one design firm offers has greater value than what other design firms offer, the more valued firm will win the contract. In many cases, this perceived value also means that the design firm can charge a premium for its services. Firms with a lot of experience are expected to do a better job than a new firm or than designers who are trying to get into a different segment of the market. For example, a design firm that has specialized in restaurants for ten years has a far greater expertise in that type of facility than a firm that has done primarily offices for the same ten years. The first firm will try to show the client that experience has value and that value should be compensated fairly.

Clients who are unfamiliar with or do not appreciate the time and subtleties involved in completing a project react favorably to the value-oriented method. The fee is based on the designer's ability and experience to do the work and to meet the expectation of the client rather than on the time that it will take to complete the project. When the designer can clearly differentiate his or her experiences and ability, this fee method should be considered.

The remaining fee methods are those that are used most often by interior designers who depend upon the sale of merchandise as their primary source of revenue. Although these following methods are most commonly used by residential designers, commercial firms may also use one or more of these methods to generate revenue.

Cost Plus Percentage Markup Method

The *cost plus percentage markup* method allows the design firm to add a specific percentage to the net cost of the merchandise being purchased by the client. The percentage determined must be sufficient to cover the design firm's costs and allow for the desired profit margin, if it is the only compensation method used. Cost plus percentage markup is more commonly used in residential design but can be effective in commercial design as well. It can be the least remunerative method, if a very small markup is added to the net price. This method can be used as the exclusive fee method, if the amount of goods to be purchased from the firm is sufficient to compensate for the time the designer must put into the project.

The key in using this fee method is to charge an adequate percentage. Residential designers might charge from 10 percent to over 30 percent. There is no average markup, as each firm decides what percentage to use based on business needs, competition, and what the client is willing to pay. When commercial interior designers use this method, the percentage is generally quite low. That is primarily due to the competition for the sale of goods in the commercial area of interior design. It works well for firms as long as

1. The budget is not cut at the last moment
2. The client does not use a lot of existing furniture in the new project
3. The client does not decide to hold off purchasing any of the merchandise at a later time, thereby reducing the amount of fees the firm may collect

Of course, these three points also affect the profitability on almost all the fee methods that have been discussed in this chapter.

Another segment of the interior design industry that uses the cost plus percentage markup method consists of those design firms that are just getting started. Many new design firms offer this method of compensation as a way of competing with larger, more established firms that can operate at the retail method. If a firm decides to use this method of obtaining fees, it must be sure it is covering the costs of its design practice. Without a careful calculation of costs, the designer may not be fully compensated for his or her design talents. Any firm that is considering the use of this method should use it in conjunction with some other fee method to be sure the firm receives a reasonable gross margin to cover costs and obtain a profit.

Retail Method

The *retail method* has always been a very common method of obtaining fees if a design firm actually sells merchandise to the client. In the retail method, the design firm charges the client the retail price suggested by the manufacturer or supplier. If the manufacturer does not provide a suggested retail price, then the design firm marks up the merchandise from the net or cost price to achieve the retail price. Since both the suggested retail price and the common markup percentage used is 100 percent, the retail method provides a high gross profit margin for the firm.

The retail method is more commonly used by residential design firms than by firms that are primarily involved in commercial design. And it is commonly used by firms that perceive that the amount of time needed on any given project or client is small in relation to the budget for merchandise. If it is estimated that a great deal of planning, custom design, drafting, specification writing, or supervision work is required, the retail method is not a suitable fee method for the firm to use. Even though the markup provides a reasonable margin to cover the expense of these tasks, there is no guarantee that the client will purchase merchandise from the designer, which means that the designer will not be fully compensated for time spent working on the project. Should these kinds of activities be the major part of the project, then another fee method should be used, or the retail method in conjunction with another method might be used.

Because designers have become more willing to quote a design fee for services, the retail method is used less often today. Clients are becoming accustomed to the concept of paying for the professional services that an interior designer can offer and thus are willing to pay the separate design fees. In addition, clients are far more willing to shop around for a good price today. This has led many designers to use a different method for generating revenue.

Discounting or Percentage off Retail Method

Another common fee method that is directly related to the purchase of goods is *percentage off retail* method. In order to gain a competitive edge, some firms offer merchandise at a percentage off retail and expect that the volume of merchandise purchased by the client will offset the design services costs. It is a method that office furnishings dealers frequently use. This method is also used by those residential designers who sell large quantities of merchandise.

In this method, the design firm reduces the selling price of the merchandise by some percentage off the suggested retail price. Care must be taken when the design firm determines what that discount will be, since the resulting difference between the selling price and the net price is the gross margin, which is needed to allow for a profit and to cover overhead costs. As long as the discount allows for the needed gross margin, covers overhead expenses, and provides a profit margin, this fee method works. However, the larger the discount is, the smaller the gross profit margin will be and the less there exists the potential to pay off expenses and maintain profits.

Office furnishings dealers have found that this method does not always cover the cost of design services. This has become true because of the rash of deep discounting on systems projects and the highly competitive market in office furnishings. Because of these deep discounts (which will be discussed in Chapter 19), dealers have been forced to charge design fees, such as an hourly fee, to make sure the designer's time is covered.

Consultation Fee

In some situations, a client may feel that he or she wants some ideas from a designer but does not need complete design services. The interior designer would then charge the client a small fee for the consultation. The designer would provide ideas but generally would not execute plans or other documents. The consultation is generally limited to a maximum of a few hours, though any arrangement that the designer wishes to develop is possible.

Goods are generally not sold in this arrangement. Of course, the client may later decide that he or she does need the full services and/or purchasing ability of the interior designer. Generally, the interior designer applies this consultation fee later to the project.

Combination Method

In many cases, using only one of the described fee methods will not provide sufficient compensation to cover all the expenses and desired profit margin for the firm. It is often necessary for almost all commercial firms and many residential firms that are not primarily retail showrooms to use more than one method for obtaining design fees.

Since projects involve a variety of activities, it is defensible for the firm to charge the client a variety of fees. For example, let us consider a project that involves a lot of the designer's time in meetings with the client, contractors, and the architect for specifying interior finish materials but not a large dollar amount for the actual materials to be purchased. The designer might find that an hourly charge for meetings, travel, and on-site supervision in combination with either a cost plus percentage or percentage discount from retail for the merchandise sold would adequately compensate the designer in this situation.

In another case, a project might require that the designer spend a large amount of time in the preparation of contract documents and specifications for rooms that are basically the same. In this situation, it is common that the goods would be purchased from a vendor not the designer. This might occur for a hotel project or a major office complex. In this situation, the designer might charge an hourly fee for the drafting and a fixed fee or a percentage of the selling price for the design and preparation of specifications for the areas that are basically the same. If properly considered, a combination of design fee methods can provide excellent compensation to the designer at a fair price to the client.

The two most common combination methods are the cost plus percentage markup with a fixed fee and cost plus percentage markup with an hourly fee. The cost plus percentage markup with a fixed fee is very commonly used by interior designers. In this case, the designer charges a fixed fee for services and then sells the merchandise on a cost-plus basis. Both residential and commercial interior designers might use this method. It has become especially attractive to those residential designers who have moved away from the retail method.

The fixed fee can be sufficient to cover direct labor and overhead, and provide some profit for the project. When this is the case, the markup on the merchandise should be rather small, or the client might accuse the designer of "double-dipping." Generally, however, the fixed fee is calculated to provide only a portion of the revenues needed to cover labor, expenses, and profit. The remaining revenue to make the project profitable for the designer is generated by merchandise sales.

The cost plus markup with an hourly rate is very similar to the above, except the designer charges for all design and consultation time, as described in the contract, based on an hourly rate. It is necessary for the designer to determine which services will be charged at the hourly rate and which will be included in the markup of the merchandise. This method is used by both residential and commercial interior designers. However, designers who work in office furnishings dealerships use a slight variation on this method—they charge an hourly rate in conjunction with a discount from retail rather than a markup from cost. As with the combination of markup and fixed fee methods, some clients may feel that the designer is double-dipping for revenues.

Designers who use a combination of cost plus percentage markup and an hourly rate feel that they are more likely to cover all or most of the time that they actually work on the project. This does not always happen with a combination of the fixed fee and cost plus percentage markup methods.

The danger in using either of these combinations is that the designer may rely on the client's purchasing goods to generate some of the revenue. However, if the client purchases from some other source, delays purchasing, or buys goods at a lower price, the designer will receive less income than estimated. Depending on the size of the fixed fee and/or the services to be included in the hourly rate charges, these fees may not be sufficient to cover the time spent on the project. Safeguards can be incorporated in the event that some of these problems occur. They will be discussed in the next chapter.

Estimating Design Fees

Regardless of which fee method the designer uses, the key to profitability in providing design services is properly estimating the design fees. And the keys to effectively estimating the design fee are (1) understanding the scope of services to be provided and (2) carefully calculating costs to ensure that the fee method satisfactorily covers costs and provides a profit margin.

Design projects can be complex endeavors and can involve several people and many months, or they can involve one designer for only a few days. The first step must be a detailed analysis of what must be done, how much time each design activity will take, and how much time the project will take. Firms use estimating sheets, such as the one in Figure 17-3, to assist them in calculating what has to be done and how long it will take. The experience of the designer in doing similar projects helps the designer create an estimate of how much time the project will take once the designer determines what has to be done.

Interior design projects include costs beyond the time involved. Supplies of various kinds are needed, from stationery to plotter paper and CDs to files for storing information. A telephone, cell phone, and fax machine are necessary for researching information for the project and coordinating the execution of the work. Support personnel are needed to assist the interior designer with many phases of the project. And utility bills must be paid to keep the lights on and the heat or air conditioner working as the studio remains open to work on the project. Naturally, these are just a few expenses associated with completion of an interior design project. Of course, some of these expenses are straight overhead expenses, such as utilities. Others can be considered direct expenses, such as telephone calls. Regardless of how the owner determines to categorize expenses, they all play a part in the cost of operating the business and generating revenue. Somehow, they must be included in the estimate for design work.

With this information in hand, the designer or manager can apply one or more fee methods to the project to determine which method provides the greatest profit for the particular project. As previously discussed, projects requiring a lot of meetings, drafting, and specification writing are best charged at an hourly fee. Projects that have a lot of similar design decisions (multiple spaces like hotels and hospitals) might work out better if the desinger uses a fixed fee or a percentage of cost. Computer simulations can be set up that will compare costs and revenue generation based on the fee method that a firm generally uses. These simulations help the designer determine which fee method will generate the greatest profit for a particular job.

PROJECT SCOPE OF SERVICES

Project:

Address:

Size:

Budget:

Scope:

Project Goal:

Items Specifically Excluded:

Proposed Project Team:

Schedule:

PROJECT DELIVERABLES

Included	Not Included	Quantity	Project Deliverables
			DESIGN PHASE
			Interior Design
			Field Verification/CAD Setup
			Space Plan
			Design Details
			Furniture Selection
			Finish Selection
			Presentation Boards
			Illustration/Computer Rendering
			Programming
			Schedule
			Tenant Leasebook
			Furniture/Equipment Inventory
			Construction Budget Estimate
			Graphic Design
			Identity Development (logo, stationary, menus)
			Signage Development
			Design Sketches and Concepts
			City Code /ADA Research
			DESIGN PHASE MEETINGS
			Client
			Subconsultant
			Contractor
			Site Visit
			City Code Review

Page 2 of 12

FIGURE 17-3. A sample form that can be used to estimate design fees (partial). (Reproduced with permission, Jeffrey Rausch, Exclaim Design, Scottsdale, AZ)

Included	Not Included	Quantity	Project Deliverables
			DOCUMENT PHASE
			Interior Design
			Construction Specifications
			Demolition Floor Plan
			Demolition Reflected Ceiling Plan
			Construction Floor Plan
			Reflected Ceiling Plan
			Millwork/Finish Plan
			Construction Elevations and Details
			Millwork Elevations and Details
			Floor and Wall Finishes Plan
			Phasing Plan
			Site Plan
			Furniture/Equipment Plan
			Furniture, Fixtures, Equipment Specifications
			Furniture, Fixture, Equipment Bid Documents
			Construction Bid Documents
			ADA Compliance Survey
			Graphic Design
			Camera-ready Artwork (digital documentation)
			Design Intent Drawings
			Final Design Drawing
			DOCUMENT PHASE MEETINGS
			Client
			Subconsultant
			Contractor
			Bidding
			Site Visit
			City Document Submittal
			City Code Variance
			City Design Review
			Health Department Review
			PROJECT ADMINISTRATION
			General Project Management/Administration
			Punchlist
			CONSULTANT SERVICES
			Mechanical Engineer
			Plumbing Engineer
			Electrical Engineer
			Structural Engineer
			Signage Consultant
			Civil Engineer
			Fire Protection Consultant
			Landscape Consultant
			Audio/Visual Consultant
			Telecommunications Consultant
			Security Consultant

Page 3 of 12 

FIGURE 17-3. Continued

Included	Not Included	Quantity	Project Deliverables
			Food Service Consultant
			Lighting Consultant
			Artwork Consultant
			Asbestos/Toxic Substance Consultant
			REIMBURSABLE EXPENSES
		Actual Cost + 15%	Document Reproduction/Plotting and Blueprinting
		Actual Cost + 15%	Camera Ready Artwork/PMT's
		Actual Cost + 15%	Messenger/Delivery Service
		Actual Cost + 15%	Long Distance Telephone Charges
		Actual Cost + 15%	Travel and Expenditure
		Actual Cost + 15%	Presentation Materials
		Actual Cost + 15%	Film/Photography
		Actual Cost + 15%	Digital Services (diskettes, zips)
		Actual Cost + 15%	Color Prints (color printer-high end color outputs)
		Actual Cost + 15%	Additional Insurance required by Client's Insurance Coverage
		Actual Cost + 15%	Government Fees/Permits

PROJECT SCOPE

In describing these design services, reference is made to various people:

The Designer: the professional firm or individual that will provide the design services described here.

The Client: the user for whom the space is being designed, landlord of the premises or the tenant of the building.

The Contractor: The individual or firm providing the construction or fabrication of the project design of the Designer.

Note that only those items identified on the attached basic service list are included.

DESIGN PHASE

FIELD VERIFICATION/CAD SETUP

The Designer will verify the accuracy of documents provided by the landlord, confirm "as-built" conditions, measure existing suites in order to correct discrepancies and calculate square footage. Existing building conditions may create difficulties in obtaining complete as-built measurements. Some measurements may require verification after demolition and during construction. The Designer will prepare as-built drawings on AutoCad from field verification mark-ups showing the following: walls, doors, windows, cabinetry, electrical and voice/data outlets.

SPACE PLAN

The Designer will prepare, and present for approval, a preliminary space plan that illustrates a planning concept and design direction. Calculation of useable square footage is done using Building Owners and Managers Association (BOMA) area calculations methods. This floor plan will include:

Preliminary: Preliminary plan is schematic only and does not include notes and specifications for budgeting purposes

- Walls, doors, windows
- Furniture, for reference (reception, conference, open staff areas only. Private offices are excluded.)
- Room names, sizes
- Cabinet, sink, plumbing locations

Detailed: Detailed plan may be prepared for use in preliminary budgeting including:

- Walls, doors, windows
- Furniture, for reference
- Electrical and Telecommunication locations
- Room names, sizes
- Cabinet, sink, plumbing locations
- Specifications in CSI format

FIGURE 17-3. Continued

The owner of each design firm must make his or her own decision as to what method will be used for charge for design services and produce an appropriate level of revenue. Planning for a profitable business begins with understanding the financial side of the business. If a designer is clear about his or her expenses in operating the particular practice, then the designer has taken the first step toward maintaining a profitable and successful design practice. Understanding the scope of services required is a very important factor that will impact the profitability of a project. The designer must consider the kinds of clients with whom he or she will be working, the types of design spaces, and the local competition. The firm must be ready to modify its fee methods when necessary to remain competitive.

Indirect Job Cost Factors

In this chapter, we have looked at several common methods used for determining fees for the generation of income for an interior design firm. No matter how carefully the designer considers these methods, it is possible for the firm to lose a certain amount of profit because of unexpected events. Although some of these indirect cost factors can be calculated into the design fee, they occur more commonly once the project has begun.

One of the most common indirect cost factors for firms that are doing strict cost accounting is overtime. No matter how carefully a project has been estimated, if the design firm must pay overtime salary to any of its staff, the gross margin of the project and potential profitability will decrease. A career in interior design is rarely a 9 to 5 job. However, careful supervision of projects by the design director or project designers will help to hold down the amount of overtime needed for projects. Some firms control overtime costs by paying designers, not on an hourly basis, but rather on a salary basis, as discussed in Chapter 11. This does help with direct salary expense but not with overhead expenses, which are still incurred when the office is working past normal business hours. In addition, it is common practice (as pointed out in Chapter 11) for the firm to provide compensatory time for overtime worked by salaried employees. This time does not generate revenue.

A second indirect cost factor that occurs rather often is the indecisive client. This type of client just can't seem to make up his or her mind about any number of things—colors, furniture styles, patterns, the furniture or space arrangement, and so on. Experienced interior designers learn to recognize the indecisive client during the initial interviews. But often even the most experienced designer gets a client who just can't seem to make up his or her mind. If the fee method used is the hourly method, this would have little bearing on the final outcome of the project, since the designer continues to charge for all the changes and extra meetings. But when a fee method has been established that limits the amount of fee that can be charged, the designer must diplomatically find ways to urge the client to make up his or her mind and move on with the project.

Designers who depend on the sale of merchandise face another indirect cost factor. They are often frustrated by a client who goes along with design concepts but then purchases merchandise through some source other than the designer or perhaps purchases nothing at all. Interior designers in this situation must protect themselves from the client who uses them for ideas but buys from some other source. If no fee for service has been negotiated at the start of the project, the designer has worked essentially for free. This is no way to build a successful and profitable professional practice. Techniques that designers can use to help with the client who does this will be discussed in the next chapter.

Many times, the profit on a project is affected by changes and/or additions to the project, caused by the client. For example, the client may change his or her mind about some portion of the project, which necessitates extra planning or drafting work or perhaps respecification of products. Or perhaps the client may ask the designer questions and may request design work for other parts of the residence or commercial space that originally was not part of the project. If the designer continues to make changes or design extra spaces, any planned profit for the job can disappear. The best way to avoid this problem is to have in the design contract a very clear description of the project area to be designed and a detailed scope of services to be provided, and to specify charges for changes and additions to the project. This will also be discussed in the next chapter.

An added cost that occurs whenever a designer has ventured into a project that he or she has never done before is for unexpected technical or professional consultation. Oftentimes designers are asked to do projects that require the preparation of construction documents. Most cities have strict regulations as to who may prepare construction documents. Designers may suddenly discover that they must have an architect prepare those documents or that they must obtain an architect's or other professional consultant's stamp on drawings prepared by the interior designer. This unexpected fee reduces the expected profit margin.

Unusual job site and delivery costs can also add to the cost of a project. In projects related to open-office systems, for example, it is common for thermostats, light switches, air-conditioning vents, and the like to end up right where the interior designer has planned to hang a wall strip or to attach a divider panel. In residential design, it is common for a client to make some kind of change at the site without telling the interior designer. Sometimes a designer may specify a very large piece of furniture, which may be very difficult to deliver. For example, a designer specifies a very large conference table that cannot fit inside an elevator but must be placed on top of the elevator cab or must be hoisted up on cranes from the exterior of the building.

Unless there is careful project management, furniture may be ready for delivery to the job site, but the job site may not be ready to receive the merchandise. In situations where the design firm does not have a warehouse to hold merchandise until it is ready to be delivered, extra cost is involved in storing and later delivering it to the job site. In many cases, this extra cost is borne by the design firm, even though the design firm has not caused the delay, since management of the project is considered to be part of the normal and expected services of the firm.

All of these examples lead to extra design time that may not have been calculated for or otherwise considered in the fee and contract. The extra costs of some of these examples may be passed on to the client, if the proper clauses are in the design contract, which we will discuss in the next chapter. Unfortunately, the extra costs discussed in this section are often the responsibility of the design firm.

Summary

All interior design firms are in business to make a reasonable profit, while providing quality services to clients. The goals and operations of the design firm, as well as the clients whom the firm wishes to attract, all play a part in how the owner determines which fee methods to use and which revenue-generating strategies to use so that the firm will stay in operation.

The income that the firm generates, whether from fees for services only, from the sale of goods, or from a combination of both, must be sufficient to cover costs and to provide a net profit in order to sustain the firm. In this chapter, we have looked at the different ways in which a design firm can generate this income by means of several fee methods. No fee method is perfect for all circumstances for all firms. Each firm must determine for its own type of business which situations warrant a particular fee method.

Once the fee method for a particular project has been determined, the next step for the owner to take is to prepare a design contract or proposal. In the next chapter, we will look at the preparation of such a contract.

REFERENCES

Alderman, Robert L. 1997. *How To Prosper as an Interior Designer.* New York: John Wiley.

American Society of Interior Designers. "Design Fees and Profits." *ASID Professional Designer.* September/October 1998.

Birnberg, Howard. 1992. *New Directions in Architectural and Engineering Practice.* New York: McGraw-Hill.

Connor, Dick. 1989. *Increasing Revenue from Your Clients.* New York: John Wiley.

Cooper, David G. 1993. *Finding and Signing Profitable Contracts.* New York: John Wiley.

Foote, Rosslyn F. 1978. *Running an Office for Fun and Profit.* New York: McGraw-Hill.

Getz, Lowell. 1997. *An Architect's Guide to Financial Management.* Washington, DC: AIA Press.

———. 1986. *Business Management in the Smaller Design Firm.* Newton, MA: Practice Management Associates.

Getz, Lowell, and Frank Stasiowski. 1984. *Financial Management for the Design Professional.* New York: Watson-Guptill.

Haviland, David, ed. 1994. *The Architect's Handbook of Professional Practice, Student Edition.* Washington, DC: AIA Press.

Kubany, Elizabeth Harrison, and Charles D. Linn. "Why Architects Don't Charge Enough." *Architectural Record.* October 1999.

———. "How To Increase Your Fees in a Tough Market." *Architectural Record.* November 1999.

Loebelson, Andrew. "Interior Design Giants." *Interior Design.* January, 1996.

———. 1983. *How To Profit in Contract Design.* New York: Interior Design Books.

Morgan, Jim. 1998. *Management of the Small Design Firm.* New York: Watson-Guptill.

Piotrowski, Christine M. 1992. *Interior Design Management.* New York: John Wiley.

Shenson, Howard L. 1990. *The Contract and Fee-Setting Guide for Consultants and Professionals.* New York: John Wiley.

Siegel, Harry (with Alan M. Siegel). 1982. *A Guide to Business Principles and Practices for Interior Designers,* rev. ed. New York: Watson-Guptill.

Stasiowski, Frank. 1993. *Cash Management for the Design Firm.* New York: John Wiley.

———. 1993. *Value Pricing for the Design Firm.* New York: John Wiley.

———. 1985. *Negotiating Higher Design Fees.* New York: Watson-Guptill.

Stitt, Fred A., ed. 1986. *Design Office Management Handbook.* Santa Monica, CA: Arts and Architecture Press.

Thompson, Jo Ann Asher, ed. 1992. *ASID Professional Practice Manual.* New York: Watson-Guptill.

Chapter 18

Preparing Design Contracts

Interior designers enter into contracts of one sort or another every day. The most common of these occur when a designer offers to provide some service or product to a client and the client agrees to purchase that service or product. In these contractual relationships, it is the interior designer's responsibility to fulfill the contract. In many cases, designers and clients enter into contracts, but they do not know that they have done so. Or they should have entered into a contract but did not.

Designers and clients also may breach or break those contracts. Sometimes this is done knowingly and willingly (while hoping the other party does not sue), sometimes this is done by accident, and sometimes this is done by mutual consent (which is not really a breach at all). Interior designers also are sometimes faced with such threats as "I'm going to sue for breach of contract" or "I'm going to sue because we had a contract."

In this chapter, we will review the basic ingredients of a contract and contract law as they relate to a contract for services or a combination of services and goods. In the next chapter, we will discuss the specific differences concerning contracts for the sale of goods. The counsel of an attorney is strongly recommended for obtaining a complete explanation of the legal considerations of contracts. The information in this chapter is general in nature and should not be construed as legal advice.

Definition and Basic Elements of a Contract

Basically, a *contract* is a promise or agreement that is made between two or more parties to perform or not perform some act. The performance or lack of performance of this act can be enforced by the courts.

A legally enforceable contract must have certain elements in it, or it may not be enforceable. Currently, the basic requirements of a contract are as follows:

1. *Offer.* One party proposes to do something or not to do something for another party.
2. *Acceptance.* The party to whom the proposal has been made agrees to accept the offer and is bound exactly by the terms set up in the offer.
3. *Contractual capacity.* The legal ability to enter into contracts. This must exist for both parties involved in the contract.

4. *Consideration*. Something of value that is exchanged as it relates to the contract. It must be legally sufficient enough for a court to take it seriously.
5. *Mutual assent*. The giving of the offer and acceptance of the offer must be done willingly.
6. *Legality*. The contract must exist only to support the performance of some legal act.

Offer

An *offer* in a contract is made by the party who makes the offer—the *offeror* (for our purposes, the interior designer). In legal terminology, the client is referred to as the *offeree*. What a designer offers to do must be done with serious consideration and intent. If a designer makes statements in a contract that promise to do certain things and the designer is unable to achieve them or neglects to have someone else achieve them, this is very serious and can have legal consequences. Forgetting to put something into a contract can also have serious consequences. For example, if a designer has a contract with a client to design the client's home for a fee of $15,000, but in the terms of the contract, the designer does not ask for a retainer, the designer cannot later ask the client to pay a retainer, since that was not part of the original offer.

For an offer to be binding, there must be a serious intention by the offeror (the party who makes the offer to the other party, who is called the offeree). Merely expressing an opinion is not a form of valid intention. For example, if John Doe says to his client that "the project can probably be completed in five days," his client cannot sue if it actually takes ten days, since the "five days" is an opinion, not a promise.

An offer also must be given in terms that are definite enough for a court to determine whether the contract has been fulfilled or not. If an interior designer puts in the contract the statement, "select all finishes," this can leave the firm responsible for selecting interior and exterior finishes when the firm only considered selecting interior finishes.

The third element of a legal offer is that the offer must be communicated to the offeree so that the offeree knows of the existence of the offer. For example, unless the client knows that out-of-town travel expenses are over and above the design fees, the client is not expected to pay these expenses.

The last element in a legal offer concerns the ability of the offeror to terminate the offer or the acceptance of the offer. If the designer's proposal states that the price for the services is good for ten days but the client responds on the fifteenth day, the designer is not obligated to provide the services at the stated price. It should be noted that the time period of the offer begins when the offeree receives the offer, not when it is prepared or mailed by the offeror. If there is no time limit stated in the offer, the time limit terminates at the end of a reasonable period of time, based on consideration of the circumstances of the offer.

An offer can also be terminated if the offeror withdraws the offer before the offeree accepts it. It is, of course, important that the offer be withdrawn prior to its being accepted. For example, if an interior designer discovers that he or she has miscalculated his or her bid to the city of Chicago but has already turned in the bid, he or she must revoke his or her offer prior to the closing date and time of acceptance of all bids. If all bids are due by Friday at 5:00 P.M. and the designer discovers the error on Friday at 5:30 P.M., it is too late to revoke the bid.

Another way to terminate the offer is for the offeree to reject the offer. Should this happen, there is no obligation on either side to fulfill the contract.

Should the client later wish to accept the offer, the designer can refuse, accept, or modify the original offer. This is because the client's refusal of the offer has terminated the original offer. But if the client says something like, "Is this the best price you can give me on the sofa?" this does not constitute rejection of the offer.

The last method of terminating an offer is for the client to make a counteroffer. A *counteroffer* is an agreement to the offer in which the terms of the offer have been changed. For example, if Susan Jones says, "Your design fee is out of the question. I am prepared to pay only $5000 for these services," the offer of $5000 is now a counteroffer. The designer is now in a position to either accept or reject this counteroffer.

Interior designers are often invited to bid on design projects or sales of goods. An invitation to bid or to negotiate is not an offer but merely shows a willingness on the part of the client to enter into discussions with the designer about a potential contract.

Acceptance

If the offeree (the client) agrees to the terms of the offer, then acceptance has been given. "In order to exercise the power of acceptance effectively, the offeree must accept unequivocally. If the acceptance is subject to new conditions, or if the terms of the acceptance change the original offer, the acceptance may be considered a counteroffer that implicitly rejects the original offer" (Clarkson et al., 1983, p. 129). Unequivocal acceptance is referred to as the *mirror image rule* of acceptance in law textbooks. When someone accepts a contract proposal and does not make changes, he or she has "mirrored" the offer.

Generally, acceptance cannot be construed if there is "silence," or no response, from the client. However, if by silence the client has received a benefit from the services that the designer has provided, then the courts will rule that the client has accepted the contract. For example, if a designer decides to proceed with the space planning of an office for a client, even though the client has not yet accepted the terms of the contract, the client is not obligated to pay the design fee for the services provided, unless the client has taken ownership (a benefit) of the space somehow. Merely beginning work on the space planning does not generally translate into receiving a "benefit."

Finally, acceptance must be made within the time limit set in the terms of the offer. If no definite terms are stated, acceptance must be made within a reasonable time frame, considering the conditions of the offer and the subject of the offer.

Contractual Capacity

Both parties in a contract must have the legal capacity to enter into a contract. *Contractual capacity* relates to the full legal competency of the parties. It is very important for the designer to be sure that the person agreeing to and signing a contract has the legal capacity to enter into the contract. In residential design, the interior designer normally deals with a legally competent adult who is head of a household or a spouse. In commercial interior design, the designer often deals with people other than the actual owner of the business or the chairperson of the board of the corporation. Rarely does a minor (under the age of 18) have contractual capacity.

In a commercial project, the interior designer must be sure that the person who signs the contract has the authority to bind the corporation or business to that contract. Not all employees, even those with fancy job titles, have that authority.

Consideration

Consideration is the "price" that the offeree "pays" to the offeror for the offeror's fulfilling the promise made in the contract. Generally, in an interior design contract, the consideration is the design fees that the client must pay to the designer for providing the services agreed to by the client. The consideration must be adequate enough to be fair.

Consideration can be money, property, services, or anything else that is legal. For example, a designer might barter or agree to provide interior design services to his or her accountant in exchange for accounting services. An interior designer might also accept a piece of property, such as a painting from a gallery, for interior design services provided to the gallery. Of course, money is the primary type of consideration.

A promise to give consideration for something that has already occurred or that the designer is already obligated to do is not binding. If the client says, "Because you did such a great job on finishing the office installation on time, I will give you a $500 bonus," the client is not legally obligated to pay the bonus, since it is consideration for something that has happened in the past. Considerations are negotiated for actions that take place in the future or in the present, not in the past. Similarly, if the design contract says, for example, that the designer will provide a watercolor rendering of the client's living room and later the designer tells the client that he or she must pay the designer an additional $500 for that rendering, the client is not obligated to pay, since the firm is already legally obligated to supply that rendering for the consideration outlined in the contract.

Mutual Assent

The parties to a contract must be willing and free to enter into the contractual offer and acceptance. This is referred to as *mutual assent*. Sometimes a contract that is made by two parties who have the full legal competency to make a valid contract may not be able to be enforced because the reality of assent of one or another of the parties is being called into question. This might occur because of (1) a mistake (this must relate to a mistake by one or another of the parties with regard to the facts of the terms of the contract, not an error of judgment or quality); (2) fraudulent misrepresentation (the terms of the agreement have been intentionally presented with information that is incorrect in an attempt to deceive the other party); (3) undue influence, (one party exerts so much influence on the other party that that other party virtually is unable to exercise his or her own free will); and (4) duress (this negates a contract if the offeree is forced under certain kinds of threats to agree to the contract). If any one of these occurrences is proven to exist for either party, then the contract is not valid.

Legality

Contracts must describe legal acts for the courts to have the authority to enforce them. An illegal contract is any contract that, if performed, would constitute an act against legal statute, would break tort law, or in any way would be opposed to the public good. The main way in which the concept of legality might affect a contract into which an interior designer entered would be if it related to restraint of trade.

Contracts in restraint of trade are made intentionally to be detrimental to the public good and generally have an effect on the potential for fair competition in a given market. For example, if two or more interior design firms in a market area in which they were the only source for furniture got together and agreed to sell merchandise at the same markup, they would be guilty of collusion, and their agreement would be in restraint of trade. If one subsequently lowered prices and the other sued, saying they had an agreement, the lawsuit would be thrown out, and both firms would likely be charged with a crime.

Some contracts in restraint of trade are actually legal, however. Certain clauses in employment contracts that restrain the activities of former employees can be legal, if the restrictions relating to noncompetition are reasonable. This was discussed in Chapter 12.

These elements are primary to the formation of a contract for such services as might be offered by an interior designer. The interpretation of these elements and the enforcement of these contracts is governed by common law. When a designer sells goods to a client, these sales contracts are governed by the Uniform Commercial Code. These contracts will be discussed in Chapter 20.

Letter of Agreement or Contract?

Many interior designers prefer to use the terminology letter of agreement rather than contract when discussing a written agreement for services with clients. These designers feel that the word contract scares many clients. A *letter of agreement* is a contract, but it is generally less formal in content and terminology and looks more like a letter. A letter of agreement is more commonly used for residential projects, while a contract or the term contract is more commonly used for commercial projects. However, this is not a universal situation.

It should be clearly understood that a letter of agreement is a contract and affords the designer the same legal consideration for enforcement as a contract, that is, if it meets the criteria discussed in this chapter, as for any other contract. In fact, although a letter of agreement is thought to be less formal, it is often quite detailed and may contain many of the same types of clauses as a contract. It is up to the designer to decide whether the term contract or letter of agreement is more appropriate to his or her interior design practice. Format examples of both a letter of agreement and a contract are shown later in this chapter.

Form of the Contract

Steve Smith, an interior designer, says to his client, John Burton, of Burton's Travel Agency, "I will charge you $5000 to prepare a feasibility study of your new offices." Burton replies, "That will be fine. When can you start?" Have Smith and Burton entered into a contract for services? On the face of what we know, yes, because an oral agreement has been made by Smith and Burton for services. But is this good professional practice by Smith?

Although an oral agreement might seem to be the best way to work with a client for some designers, it is not a good idea and is also not very good business practice in today's world. But is an oral contract a legal contract? Yes, it can be legal, except in some specific instances that require a written contract. However, interior designers should not start any design work for clients without obtaining some sort of written agreement, whether it is required by statute or not.

A written contract is the strongest evidence that a designer has to show that a contract for services exists between the client and the designer. Designers whose major source of income comes from performing services rather than from selling goods should never begin any design work until a written contract has been executed and signed by the client, even though it might be legal to do so. Any designer who sells products as the major source of revenue should also make it a policy to only order merchandise for a client after the client has signed a purchase agreement. Designers should be concerned about conducting themselves in a professional and businesslike manner and should therefore insist on a written agreement prior to beginning design work and/or ordering merchandise. Although it is true that an occasional client's feelings may be bruised by the contractual situation, it is better to lose an occasional client than to lose revenue.

As the old saying goes, "an oral contract is as good as the paper it is written on." Some designers have worked for many years "on a handshake" and never have had any problems. Some designers work with certain clients without a contract and use a written agreement with other clients. In general, considering how litigious our society has become today, it is not particularly good professional practice to offer design services and/or to sell goods to clients without having a written agreement.

A written contract or agreement is actual evidence of what the circumstances to the agreement actually are. Written evidence is always preferred over someone's word by the courts when they are determining the facts. If a designer has a dispute with a client over whether certain work has been performed or not, the written agreement should provide the evidence to help clarify what is to be done. A written contract helps protect the designer.

Laws dealing with preventing fraud and perjury in relation to oral contracts have existed for many years. These statutes prescribe when a contract must be in writing and the form of that contract. Each state has its own statute of frauds, and a statement of statute of frauds is contained in the Uniform Commercial Code. Of the six types of contracts that must be in writing, three relate to the interior designer: (1) contracts for the sale of goods that amount to more than $500, (2) contracts that cannot be completed within one year of their origination, and (3) contracts for the sale of real estate. There are other situations in which the contract must be in writing, but these do not apply to the work of an interior designer.

Contracts Whose Performance Will Take More Than One Year

Interior designers often are involved in contracts that will take more than one year to complete. If the terms of the contract are such that the project or requirements of the contract cannot be completed in one year, the statute of frauds requires that the contract be in writing for the contract to be binding. If the terms of the contract indicate that the project will be completed within one year, it is not necessary for the contract for services to be in writing. The time limit begins one day after the contract is agreed to by both parties.

Contract for Sale of Goods

Interior designers often take orders for furniture and furnishings without obtaining any written agreement from the client: "I wouldn't think of asking Susan Smith for a contract to order a sofa." Yet many of these same designers sometimes find themselves owning furniture and furnishings that their clients have refused to accept.

The statute of frauds requires that a written contract be in existence for the sale of any goods of an amount over $500. This contract need not be any kind of formal contract but merely a written document that states quantity, description, and terms of the agreement; it must be signed by the party or parties involved. This aspect of a contract for the sale of goods will be discussed in detail in the next chapter. The written contract provides more authority for the designer to obligate the client to pay for the goods.

Contract for the Sale of Real Estate

A contract for the sale of real estate, which is any land and buildings, plants, trees, or anything else affixed to the land, must always be in writing. Any oral contract for this kind of transaction is not binding on either party. This situation is mentioned because many interior designers purchase real property for their business location.

Content Formalities

When a contract must be in writing, what does *writing* mean? "The writing should be intelligible. It may be embodied in letters, memos, telegrams, invoices, and purchase orders sent between the parties" (Brown and Sukys, 1997, p. 167). It can be written on any material that allows the writing to be readable. Of course, it is recommended by this author that the contract or purchase orders be prepared on the design firm's stationery and other business forms. The agreement should also provide enough information to signify that an agreement has been made between the parties, which can suffice as a contract. Sufficient information that describes what has been promised, which has been scribbled on a napkin from a restaurant and which has been signed by the party to be charged can serve as a legal contract, although this is not advisable.

To be more specific, however, to be fully enforceable, the contract must include the following information:

- Gives the date
- Identifies the parties involved
- Details what services are to be provided
- States how fees are to be charged and the terms of payment
- Is signed by the parties and especially the party being charged—the client

Such items as time limit of the agreement and other terms that seem appropriate are left up to the discretion of the designer. What must be covered in a contract for the sale of goods will be covered in the next chapter.

Just as there is no such thing as an ideal way to charge, there is no ideal way to write a design contract. To protect the design firm from the potential loss of income, an variety of contracts should be developed with the assistance of the firm's attorney. These different contracts should focus on the various kinds of business in which the design firm is engaged. Both ASID and IIDA, as well as the AIA, have standardized contracts that have been carefully developed based on input from interior designers and attorneys who specialize in contract law. Members of these professional organizations can obtain copies of these standardized contracts through the appropriate national office.

Developing the Design Contract

There are many things that the designer needs to know in order to properly prepare a design contract. Gathering the information needed to prepare a design contract that will protect the interior designer from future disagreements is very important. The ethics committees of the major professional associations report that disputes related to contracts are among the major source of ethics complaints filed by clients against interior designers. Therefore, this task should not be taken lightly and should not be trusted to one's memory. Designers regularly use questionnaires or other forms to help them obtain the necessary information (see Figure 18-1). Much of this information is obtained directly from the client. Additional information may have to be obtained from other individuals who are involved in the project, such as the architect.

Eagerness to become involved in a particular project sometimes leads designers to not really find out anything about the potential client. It is, of course, not possible to know each client well before beginning a project, but some investigation is possible. As the interior designer talks to a prospective client, he or she will begin to understand if the client is knowledgeable about

Project Information

Date of Contact: ______________________ Project # ______________________

Appointment Date: ______________________

☐ Existing Clients ☐ New Client

Move-in Date: ______________________

Client	Project Location
Address	Address
Phone	Phone
Fax	Fax
E-mail	Contact E-mail

Project Areas Involved:

Budget

Site Conditions:

☐ New Construction

☐ Renovation–Some Demolition

☐ Renovation–Finishes Only

☐ Movable FF&E Only

Architect ______________________

Scope of Services: (See Fee Estimate Form)	Additional Comments:

FIGURE 18-1. A type of form that designers can use to obtain detailed information about the design project in order to prepare the design contract.

Expected Deliverables:

- ☐ Design Concept Statement
- ☐ Programming Report
- ☐ Presentation Documents
  Specify
- ☐ Purchase Proposals
- ☐ Others ______
- ☐ Full Construction Documents
- ☐ Partial Construction Documents
  Specify
- ☐ Bid Documents

Expected Staffing

- ☐ Principal
- ☐ Senior Designer
- ☐ Project Manager
- ☐ Design Assistant
- ☐ Consultant:
- ☐ Consultant:
- ☐ Clerical
- ☐ Warehouse Service
- ☐ Other

Reimbursables:

- ☐ Travel: Airfare, Hotel, Per Diem
- ☐ Ground Transport
- ☐ Misc. Travel
- ☐ Printing / Copying Documents
- ☐ Other

Notes

FIGURE 18-1. Continued

the design process. Clients who have never worked with an interior designer before will need to be informed in more detail of the process and will probably have more questions and pose more problems during the course of the project. Interviewing will also help the interior designer understand if the client has unrealistic expectations concerning budgets, time lines, and overall responsibility of the interior designer. Budget expectations are particularly problematic, as clients who have not budgeted sufficiently for the project may be afraid to say that they do not have the funds to cover the design suggestions. Later, they may accuse the designer of not meeting the budget that they had in mind or might otherwise create problems related to their unrealistic budget.

The designer can check on clients before proceeding in several ways. One is by obtaining credit reports. This is a natural safeguard if the designer is intending to sell the client merchandise and to request design service fees. The firm's attorney might be able to do a check of court records in order to determine if the client has a propensity for suing. The Better Business Bureau can tell the designer if other businesses have had problems with a particular client. And, of course, there is always the gut feeling that some experienced designers have that warn them to stay away from a particular client.

Along with an understanding of who the client is, one of the most critical parts of the design contract is the scope of services that will be offered. The designer needs to be very clear about what the scope of the project will be and all the potential services that will be needed to complete the project. Each design activity takes time. Some require expense items (like the materials to build a model). For many projects, specific activities may require that more than one designer be involved (interviewing and documentation). Missing out on understanding the full scope of the project could mean that the designer might provide some services at no charge. Not including a complete scope of services could mean that, if part of the project is done improperly, there would be legal liability. Understanding the full scope of the project cannot be taken lightly by the designer. Figure 18-2 provides some of the questions that must be answered prior to the writing of a design contract.

Taking on a design project is a serious responsibility. The designer should not enter into a design contract for a project if the designer is not competent and capable of performing the work described. Designers are sometimes tempted to work with a client on a project when their capabilities to do the project are marginal. This is always a mistake. The errors that can be made can be costly in terms of both finances and reputation. The designer should not be tempted to take the project in such a case. However, if the project is something the designer wants to do in order to gain experience, then the designer might consider setting up a joint venture with an experienced designer. Otherwise, the designer should steer clear of working on any project in which his or her skills are marginal.

Interior Design Contracts: Content and Form

What the final form of a design contract will be is determined from information obtained in meetings with the client, the designer's knowledge and experience with similar projects, and a thorough knowledge of the abilities of the design staff of the firm. All three play an important part in determining which clauses should go into the contract and whether or not a contract should be prepared for the client.

Earlier we discussed the minimal requirements for a contract to be enforceable. Whether the contract is for a residential project or a commercial project, there are certain specific items that should be in the contract to protect both the designer and the client. Different forms and terms are appropriate for the different kinds of projects in which the designer might become involved. Which form or outline to use depends on the scope of the project, the experience of the designer, the experience of the client in working with interior designers, and the compensation method.

What the designer chooses to call the written agreement—a contract or a letter of agreement outlining design services—does not matter. A letter of agreement is a legal contract, as long as it spells out information concerning the offer in sufficient detail so that the courts (if necessary) can determine the nature and facts of the offer and agreement. In fact, a simple statement such as "ABC Designs agrees to prepare the plans and specifications for the remodeling of the family room for Mr. James Madison. The charge for these services will be $75 per hour," constitutes a legal contract, if it is dated and signed by the client

Who are the owners?
What is the exact location of project?
What spaces will be involved in the project?
Is the project new construction or a remodeling project?
What is the square footage of the project?
Does the owner occupy or lease the building?
Will designer/client CAD networking be required?
What is the budget?
What is the targeted completion date?
Are architectural floor plans available, or will the space need to be site-measured?
Have you worked with this client before?
Has the client worked with a designer before?
Will presentation graphics, such as perspectives, be required? What media is appropriate?
Does the current design staff have the time and experience to do this project?
Will consultants or additional staff be required in order to do this project?
If it is a remodeling project, what code requirements must be researched and met?
If it is new construction, who is the architect?
Who and how will the contractors be selected?
What kind of presentation will be required at preliminary and final meetings?
Will sample and image presentation boards be required?
If it is new construction, what code requirements must be researched and met?
Who will obtain permits?
How much demolition is expected?
How much supervision must be done on site?
Will the project go out to bid, or has a purchasing agreement already been established?
Will the project be completed all at once or be done in stages?
What portion of the construction or interiors project will be handled by the client?
Does the client require moving services, or will the client take care of this himself or herself?
How much existing furniture will be used?
Who is responsible for production of construction documents?
What styles of new furniture are preferred?
Are new architectural finishes to be selected?
Are custom cabinets, custom furniture items, or treatments expected?
Are office systems furniture (or other furniture) evaluations required prior to specifications?
Will art, graphics, accessories, interior plantscaping be required?

Note: This list, of course, is not all-inclusive.

FIGURE 18-2. Typical questions that the designer should ask prior to preparing a design contract for services.

and the designer. (The author strongly cautions, however, that such simplistic contract language not be used.)

Contracts in residential design projects used to be relatively short—perhaps a few pages. To safeguard the designer in today's litigious climate, longer contracts or agreements are recommended. They may still be written less formally than a commercial contract using simpler language and may look more like a letter than a contract. However, they still must contain the parts discussed earlier in this chapter. Commercial contracts are almost always relatively long and detailed, running about 4 pages at least. Some sample formal contracts used in commercial projects and architecture can even be as long as 12 pages, because detailed clauses are needed to protect the interior designer by clearly spelling out all the services, duties, and responsibilities of the designer, the client, and any other parties to the contract.

Both residential and commercial contracts have the same basic parts. Figure 18-3 shows a list of the common items found in a contract for interior design services. Some projects do not require the entire list of terms. A very complex project may actually include terms not shown in the figure or discussed in this chapter. We will discuss each item in the list as they relate to residential and commercial projects, noting any differences between the two. These items are discussed in the typical order in which they would appear in a contract. Refer to Figures 18-4 through 18-7 for sample contracts.

1. *Date.* Contracts must be dated with the day, month, and year.
2. *Client's name and address.* It is very important for the name of the client obligated to the contract to be clearly stated at the beginning of the contract. In residential design, it is important for the husband's and wife's names to be on the contract and for both to sign the contract. This obligates each in the event of divorce, separation, or death of either of the spouses.

   In commercial design, the name of the person having the authority to contract for the business should be listed, and the contract should be signed by that person. The address of the home office is usually listed when the business has several locations.
3. *Detailed description of project areas involved.* To avoid confusion and arguments over extra charges or threats of breach, it is important for the project areas involved to be detailed at the beginning of the contract. In a residential project, this may mean including a clause as broad as "your residence at 1234 Hummingbird Lane," which means the designer is responsible for the scope of services to be defined in the contract for the entire house. If the services relate only to the living room, the contract should say this.

1. Date
2. Client's name and address
3. Detailed description of project areas involved
4. Detailed scope of services to be provided
5. Detailed purchasing arrangements
6. Price guarantees
7. Method and payment of compensation
8. Reimbursements for out-of-pocket expenses
9. Charges for extra services
10. Designer responsibility disclaimer
11. Charges and responsibilities of third parties
12. Photographic and publishing rights
13. Termination of contract
14. Responsibilities of the client
15. Assignment and delegation
16. Ownership of documents
17. Time frame of the contract
18. Matters of arbitration
19. Mutual understanding and legality
20. Conditions and amount of retainer
21. Signatures

FIGURE 18-3. A checklist of typical types of clauses found in design contracts.

August 31, 200x

Mr. and Mrs. Michael Hamilton
1479 E. Stanford Drive
Hazelton, Rhode Island

Dear Mr. and Mrs. Hamilton:

This letter will confirm our agreement concerning the professional services we will provide for your residence at 1479 E. Stanford Drive, Hazelton, Rhode Island. It is understood that the project specifically involves the living room, dining room, family room, and kitchen.

We will provide the following services:

A. Design Concept Services
   1. Measure the existing spaces and prepare sketches or take photos of the existing interior.
   2. Discuss your specific needs and preferences.
   3. Prepare conceptual furniture floor plans.
   4. Make preliminary selections and color schemes for new furniture items to be purchased, as well as selections for walls, floors, and window treatments.
   5. Prepare a preliminary budget for the project.
   6. Review all of the above with you.

B. Purchasing Services
   1. Upon approval of the preliminary selections mentioned above, we will prepare finalized specifications and pricing proposals.
   2. It is understood that all items specified by the interior designer will be purchased only through the interior designer, should you wish to purchase them.
   3. All items to be purchased will be detailed as a specifiction and will require your signed authorization, as well as 75% of the total price for each item prior to placing the order. The balance, including applicable taxes, shipping, and handling fees, are due upon delivery.
   4. The price for each item shall be the regular or normal wholesale or cost price to the interior designer plus ______% purchase fee plus shipping and handling fees at actual cost. The fee is in addition to Design Concept and supervision fees, to be described below.
   5. As might be necessary, the designer will provide counsel and guidance in the selection of necessary contractors to perform the required work. Client will enter into any contract for these services directly with the contractor.
   6. Periodic visits to the residence will be made to observe that the work is being done in accordance with standard acceptable practice. Constant on-site observations are not part of the designer's responsibilities.

C. Compensation

   The fee for the concept and supervision services described will be ___________. Additional services requrested by you that are beyond the scope of services outlined in this agreement will be billed separately at ______ per hour.

   Billing for services shall be in the following manner:
   20% upon signing the contract (retainer)
   40% at the end of the preliminary review meeting
   30% when construction and furniture orders are placed
   10% upon completion of the project

   All payments are due ten days after receipt of invoice.

   The above fee does not include client-approved expenses for long-distance telephone calls, out-of-town travel to shop for resources, and special renderings. These charges, if required, will be billed separately at our actual cost plus 10%.

D. Other Matters
   1. The drawings and specifications are intended for design concept only and cannot be used for construction or architectural purposes.
   2. The designer does not include any responsibility for the design of structural, electrical, plumbing, heating, or other mechanical systems that exist or might be needed for the project.

3. The drawings and documents prepared by the interior designer remain the property of the design firm and cannot be used by you for any purpose other than the completion of the project by the interior designer.
4. We will perform the services described in good faith but cannot be responsible for the performance, quality, or timely completion of work by others. Further, we shall not be responsible for any changes to the project that the client or contractor(s) make without informing the designer.
5. You are expected to grant reasonable access to the premises for the designer and the designer's agents, as well as to contractors required to perform the agreed-upon work. By signing this proposal, you understand that the peace and privacy of your home may be disrupted for the time required to perform the work.
6. This proposal may be terminated for any reason by either the client or the designer, provided ten days' written notice has been given. In the event of termination by the client, the client will pay the designer for all work done and expenses due up to the date of termination.
7. Upon completion of the project, the designer may require permission to photograph the project for the firm's records. The interior designer shall not use the photographs for promotional purposes without the permission of the client.
8. This agreement is the complete statement of understanding between the interior designer and the client. No other agreements have been made other than those stated in this agreement. This agreement can only be modified in writing, signed by both parties.

It will be our pleasure to begin your project as soon as we have received a copy of this proposal signed by both of you and a check for the retainer. We appreciate your selection of our firm for your interiors project and look forward to working with you.

Sincerely yours,

EastCoast Interiors, Inc.

________________________ ________________________

(Owner) Mr. Michael Hamilton

____

Mrs. Betty Hamilton

FIGURE 18-4. A sample design contract for a residential project.

January 30, 200x

John Smith, Chief Executive Officer
Smith Serve, Inc.
1776 N. Adams
Boston, MA

Dear Mr. Smith:

We are pleased to submit the following proposal of professional interior design services for the space planning and interior design of your new office in Amherst, Massachusetts at ____________________.

SCOPE OF SERVICE

A. **Programming and Schematic Design**
1. Meet with you and/or selected members of your staff to determine all requirements that will affect the space planning and interior design of your project.
2. Obtain floor plans from the architect.
3. Inventory existing equipment that might be used in the new space plan.
4. Conduct interviews with staff to determine equipment needs and adjacency requirements.

5. Determine project objectives as well as budget considerations.
6. Review all programming findings with your project committee.
7. Prepare preliminary schematic layouts.
8. Develop preliminary furniture, color, and materials selections.
9. Review schematic layouts, selections, and sketches with your project committee.

B. **Design Development**

1. Finalize space plans showing locations of walls, furniture, and built-in equipment.
2. Finalize selections of all materials, finishes, and treatment for furniture, walls, flooring, windows, and ceilings.
3. Provide 3-dimensional drawings of typical workstations.
4. Provide 3-dimensional sketches of lobby and employee "think tank" space.
5. Finalize lighting specifications with lighting consultant.
6. Prepare a budget of all interior furnishings.
7. Present plans and product specifications for your approval.

C. **Contract Documents Phase**

1. After final approval of all space plans, furniture layouts, and product selections, prepare appropriate working drawings and documents for the construction of the space and installation of the interiors. This will include dimensioned floor plans, furniture plans, electrical location plans, reflected ceiling plans, and cabinet shop drawings as needed.
2. Prepare bid specifications for furniture and other moveable equipment.
3. Consult with you on developing the qualified bidder's list.
4. Provide information for the preparation of bid specifications for floors, walls, windows, ceilings, and lighting fixture materials or products (bid specification to be written by your facilities department).
5. Coordinate with your facilities department to develop complete set of bid documents.

D. **Contract Administration Phase**

1. Assist you in obtaining competitive bids for furnishings and equipment.
2. Assist you in coordinating the schedule for delivery and installation of the work.
3. Make periodic visits to the job site to ensure that the work is progressing according to the specifications in the bid documents.
4. Supervise installation of furniture and movable equipment covered in the bid documents.
5. Upon completion of the installation, the designer shall prepare a punch list of items needing attention by the designer or vendors. This will be reviewed with you prior to transmittal to appropriate parties.

TERMS OF COMPENSATION

For the interior design and consultation services outlined above, you will be billed a fee of $57,500 payable according to the following:

You will be invoiced monthly for actual hours worked. Payment is due within ten (10) days of receipt of invoice. A late payment charge of 1-½% per month (18% per annum) will be added to invoices thirty days past due. Note that a retainer is required to begin work. The amount is detailed later in this proposal.

The total fee is based on a maximum of two revisions after each client review. Work required or requested beyond the two revisions will be charged at the described hourly fees, but will be in addition to the maximum estimate.

Additional services not outlined in this proposal but requested by you or required after client approval results in changes in the project will be billed separately at an hourly rate of ___________.

Fees include provision of six sets of contract documents for the client's use. It is understood that your company is responsible for reproduction of all sets of contract documents required for the bidding process.

REIMBURSABLE EXPENSES

Reimbursable expenses are in addition to the charges detailed above. Such expenses as out-of-town travel and living expenses, long-distance telephone charges, special renderings, mock-ups, and reproduction costs other than those detailed shall be billed at actual cost to the designer.

Out-of-town travel in the interest of the project shall only be made with proper notification and approval of the client. At this time, it is estimated that a minimum of four site visits will be necessary during the progress of the project.

GENERAL CONDITIONS

1. The designer shall not be responsible for the quality, workmanship, or appearance of products should you purchase products other than those specified.
2. The designer is not responsible if you, architect, or contractor(s) make changes to the project without notification to the designer.
3. The designer or representatives of the designer reserves the right to photograph the project upon completion in order to provide a record of the project. The design firm shall have the right to use these photographs for business purposes.
4. This contract does not include provision for fees by third party consultants required to complete the project. Contracts for these services will be negotiated separately and their contract negotiations must be completed within 20 days of the execution of this contract.
5. You shall make provision for the design firm and/or its agents access to the project site as needed for the completion of the project in a timely fashion.
6. This proposal may be terminated by either party upon seven (7) days written notice. In the event of termination by you, you shall pay the designer for all services performed and reimbursable expenses due up to the date of termination.
7. Drawings, specifications, and sample boards, as instruments of service, are the property of the designer. The designer reserves the exclusive copyright to these items and provides them to you for your use on this project only. Any reproduction or reuse of the drawings, specifications, and sample boards without the prior written consent of the designer is not permitted.
8. The timely completion of this project and the fees quoted is based on this signed return of this proposal to the designer within ten (10) calendar days.
9. Any controversy or claims arising out of or relating to this project or breach thereof shall be subject to review and settled by arbitration in Massachusetts. Arbitration shall be in accordance with the rules of the American Arbitration Association. The decisions of the arbitrator shall be final and binding on both parties.
10. This contract represents the complete understanding between the designer and the client. Changes and modifications must be made in writing and signed by both parties.

Approval of this proposal is signified by your signature in the space below. Work will begin on your project when the designer receives a signed copy of this proposal along with a check for a retainer of ______________.

We would like to thank you for the opportunity to submit this proposal for professional interior design services. We look forward to a set of challenges which we pledge to meet with our best professional efforts and attention.

Sincerely,

Authorized:

Columbia Interior Design, Inc.

____
(Company)

____
(Design Director)

____
(By)

____
(Date)

____
(Title)

____
(Date)

FIGURE 18-5. An example of a design contract for a commercial office project with an extensive scope of services.

ASID Document ID124

RESIDENTIAL INTERIOR DESIGN SERVICES AGREEMENT

This **AGREEMENT** is

made this ______________day of____________________ in the year of Nineteen Hundred and ____________

BETWEEN the **CLIENT**:
(name and address)

and the **DESIGNER**:
(name and address)

The **CLIENT** and the **DESIGNER** agree as follows:

The Project pertains to the following areas within Client's residence located at

____:

(List areas below:)

FIGURE 18-6. ASID Document ID124: Residential Interior Design Services Agreement (flat fee). (Reprinted with permission, ASID, Washington, DC)

INTERIOR DESIGN SERVICES

1. Design Concept Services

1.1 In this phase of the Project, Designer shall, as and where appropriate, perform the following:

A. Determine Client's design preferences and requirements.

B. Conduct an initial design study.

C. Prepare drawings and other materials to generally illustrate Designer's suggested interior design concepts, to include color schemes, interior finishes, wall coverings, floor coverings, ceiling treatments, lighting treatments and window treatments.

D. Prepare layout showing location of movable furniture and furnishings.

E. Prepare schematic plans for recommended cabinet work, interior built-ins and other interior decorative details ("Interior Installations").

1.2 Prior to commencing Design Concept Services, Designer shall receive an Initial Design Fee of ______________________ dollars ($____________). This non-refundable Design Fee is payable upon signing this Agreement and is in addition to all other compensation payable to Designer under this Agreement. Not more than__________ (____) revisions to the Design Concept will be prepared by Designer without additional charges. Additional revisions will be billed to Client as Additional Services.

2. Interior Specifications and Purchasing Services

2.1 Upon Client's approval of the Design Concepts, Designer will, as and where appropriate:

A. Select and/or specially design required Interior Installations and all required items of movable furniture, furnishings, light fixtures, hardware, fixtures, accessories and the like ("Merchandise").

B. Prepare and submit for Client's approval Proposals for completion of Interior Installations and purchase of Merchandise.

2.2 Merchandise and Interior Installations specified by Designer shall, if Client wishes to purchase them, be purchased solely through Designer. Designer may, at times, request Client to engage others to provide Interior Installations, pursuant to the arrangements set forth in the Project Review services described in paragraph 3 of this Agreement.

FIGURE 18-6. Continued

2.3 Merchandise and Interior Installations to be purchased through Designer will be specified in a written "Proposal" prepared by Designer and submitted in each instance for Client's written approval. Each Proposal will describe the item and its price to Client (F.O.B. point of origin). The price of each item to Client ("Client Price") shall be the amount charged to Designer by the supplier of such item ("Supplier Price"), plus Designer's fee equal to ___________ percent (____%) of the Supplier Price (exclusive of any freight, delivery or like charges or applicable tax).

2.4 No item can be ordered by Designer until the Proposal has been approved by Client, in writing, and returned to Designer with Designer's required initial payment equal to ___________ percent (____%) of the Client Price. The balance of the Client Price, together with delivery, shipping, handling charges and applicable taxes, is payable when the item is ready for delivery to and/or installation at Client's residence, or to a subsequent supplier for further work upon rendition of Designer's invoice. Proposals for fabrics, wall coverings, accessories, antiques, and items purchased at auction or at retail stores require full payment at time of signed Proposal.

3. <u>Project Review</u>

3.1 If the nature of the Project requires engagement by Client of any contractors to perform work based upon Designer's concepts, drawings or interior design specifications not otherwise provided for in the Interior Specifications and Purchasing Services, Client will enter into contracts directly with the concerned contractor.

3.2 Designer will make periodic visits to the Project site as Designer may consider appropriate to observe the work of these contractors to determine whether the contractors' work is proceeding in general conformity with Designer's concepts. Constant observation of work at the Project site is not a part of Designer's duties. Designer is not responsible for the performance, quality, timely completion or delivery of any work, materials or equipment furnished by contractors pursuant to direct contracts with Client.

3.3 Time expended by Designer for all Project Review services will be charged to Client on an hourly basis at the rates set forth in paragraph 4.1 of the Agreement.

4. MISCELLANEOUS

4.1 Should Designer agree to perform any design service not described above, such "Additional Service" will be invoiced to Client at the following hourly rates:

Design Principal	$________
Project Designer	$________
Staff Designer	$________
Draftsman	$________
Other employees	$________

Hourly charges will be invoiced to Client ____________ and are payable upon receipt of invoice.

FIGURE 18-6. Continued

4.2 Disbursements incurred by Designer in the interest of the Project shall be reimbursed by Client to Designer upon receipt of Designer's invoices, which are rendered __________. Reimbursements shall include, among other things, costs of local and long distance travel, long distance telephone calls, duplication of plans, drawings and specifications, messenger services and the like.

4.3 Designer's drawings and specifications are conceptual in nature and intended to set forth design intent only. They are not to be used for architectural or engineering purposes. Designer does not provide architectural or engineering services.

4.4 Designer's services shall not include undertaking any responsibility for the design or modification of the design of any structural, heating, air-conditioning, plumbing, electrical, ventilation or other mechanical systems installed or to be installed at the Project.

4.5 Should the nature of Designer's design concepts require the services of any other design professional, such professional shall be engaged directly by Client pursuant to separate agreement as may be mutually acceptable to Client and such other design professional.

4.6 As Designer requires a record of Designer's design projects, Client will permit Designer or Designer's representatives to photograph the Project upon completion of the Project. Designer will be entitled to use photographs for Designer's business purposes but shall not disclose Project location or Client's name without Client's prior written consent.

4.7 All concepts, drawings and specifications prepared by Designer's firm ("Project Documents") and all copyrights and other proprietary rights applicable thereto remain at all times Designer's property. Project Documents may not be used by Client for any purpose other than completion of Project by Designer.

4.8 Designer cannot guarantee that actual prices for Merchandise and/or Interior Installations or other costs or services as presented to Client will not vary either by item or in the aggregate from any Client proposed budget.

4.9 This Agreement may be terminated by either party upon the other party's default in performance, provided that termination may not be effected unless written notice specifying nature and extent of default is given to the concerned party and such party fails to cure such default in performance within _________ (____) days from date of receipt of such notice. Termination shall be without prejudice to any and all other rights and remedies of Designer, and Client shall remain liable for all outstanding obligations owed by Client to Designer and for all items of Merchandise, Interior Installations and other services on order as of the termination date.

4.10 In addition to all other legal rights, Designer shall be entitled to withhold delivery of any item of Merchandise or the further performance of Interior Installations or any other services, should Client fail to timely make any payments due Designer.

FIGURE 18-6. Continued

4.11 Any controversy or claim arising out of or relating to this Agreement, or the breach thereof, shall be decided by arbitration only in the ______________________ in accordance with the Commercial Arbitration Rules of the American Arbitration Association then in effect, and judgment upon the award rendered by the arbitrator(s) may be entered in any court having jurisdiction thereof.

4.12 Client will provide Designer with access to the Project and all information Designer may need to complete the Project. It is Client's responsibility to obtain all approvals required by any governmental agency or otherwise in connection with this Project.

4.13 Any sales tax applicable to Design Fees, and/or Merchandise purchased from Designer, and/or Interior Installations completed by Designer shall be the responsibility of Client.

4.14 Neither Client nor Designer may assign their respective interests in this Agreement without the written consent of the other.

4.15 The laws of the State of ________________ shall govern this Agreement.

4.16 Any provision of this Agreement held to be void or unenforceable under any law shall be deemed stricken, and all remaining provisions shall continue to be valid and binding upon both Designer and Client.

4.17 This Agreement is a complete statement of Designer's and Client's understanding. No representations or agreements have been made other than those contained in this Agreement. This Agreement can be modified only by a writing signed by both Designer and Client.

FIGURE 18-6. Continued

5. ADDITIONAL TERMS

CLIENT:

____

____

DESIGNER:

____

____

FIGURE 18-6. Continued

STANDARD TERMS AND CONDITIONS [COMMERCIAL]

1999 EDITION
FORM IIDA01L

Consultation with legal counsel is recommended regarding the completion or modification of this document.

ARTICLE I – SCOPE OF SERVICES DEFINITION

A. Unless otherwise agreed upon in writing by the Client and Interior Designer, the Interior Designer shall provide the services specified in the Agreement in accordance with the following Terms and Conditions.

ARTICLE II – SCOPE OF SERVICES: CHANGES OR MODIFICATIONS

A. If the scope of the Project, Client's Representative, Interior Designer's services, or Project Schedule are changed, the Interior Designer's compensation shall be modified accordingly.

B. Any modifications to the Interior Designer's scope of services shall be authorized in writing by the Client.

ARTICLE III – CLIENT'S RESPONSIBILITIES

A. The Client shall designate a Representative authorized to act on the Client's behalf to provide decisions, approve drawings, reports, presentations, and other documents and data. The Client's written decisions, authorizations, and approvals for the Interior Designer's services shall be provided promptly in order to meet the Project Schedule. Services on a Phase shall commence only after receipt of the Client's approval of the previous Phase and authorization to proceed.

B. The Client shall grant the Interior Designer access to the Project site at all reasonable hours, and the Interior Designer shall be permitted to photograph the Project during construction and upon completion for its records and marketing purposes.

ARTICLE IV – SERVICES BY OTHERS

A. The Interior Designer shall not have control over or charge of, and shall not be responsible for, construction means, methods, techniques, construction schedules, sequences, or procedures; fabrication, procurement, shipment, delivery, receipt, inspection, or installation; or safety programs in connection with the General Contractor's work. The Interior Designer shall not be responsible for acts or omissions or failure to carry out the work in accordance with the Contract Documents by the General Contractor, Subcontractors, or any other persons or entities or their agents or employees performing or supplying the work.

B. The Interior Designer shall have no responsibility for the acts or omissions of the building Architect or Client's Consultant(s), supplier(s), vendor(s), fabricator(s), or anyone otherwise performing work directly for the Client.

ARTICLE V – USE OF DOCUMENTS

A. Instruments of Service include all drawings, plans, specifications, and other documents, including those in electronic format, prepared for this Project by the Interior Designer or the Interior Designer's Consultants. The Interior Designer and the Interior Designer's Consultants retain all rights of ownership and property interest therein, including copyrights.

B. Upon the payment of all monies due the Interior Designer, the Interior Designer shall furnish the Client with reproducible copies of the Interior Designer's Instruments of Service for the use and maintenance of this Project only. The Instruments of Service shall not be used on other Projects, extensions to this Project, or completion of this Project by others, except by written agreement and with appropriate compensation to the Interior Designer.

C. Upon the Client's request and for the Client's convenience, the Interior Designer shall provide Instruments of Service in electronic format to the Client or to vendors providing other necessary services for the Project for the use and maintenance of this Project only. Documents provided in electronic format are furnished without guarantee of compatibility with other software or hardware, and the Interior Designer's sole liability shall be limited to replacement of defective files within 30 days after delivery to the Client. In the event of a conflict in their content, printed hard copies shall take precedence over documents in electronic format.

D. Because of the potential for alteration of the data stored in electronic format and for misuse of the Instruments of Service, the Client agrees to indemnify, defend, and hold harmless the Interior Designer, the Interior Designer's Consultants, and the officers

continued

FIGURE 18-7. IIDA Form IIDA01L: Standard Terms and Conditions (commercial project). (Reprinted with permission, IIDA, Chicago, IL)

STANDARD TERMS AND CONDITIONS [COMMERCIAL]

and employees of any of them from and against any and all claims, liabilities, damages, losses, and costs, including but not limited to reasonable attorneys' fees and all legal expenses and fees incurred on appeal, and all interest thereon, accruing or resulting to any and all persons, firms, or any other legal entity, on account of any damage or loss to property or persons, including death, arising out of the alteration or modification to the data in electronic format in the Client's possession or released to others by the Client and arising out of uses specifically prohibited herein.

ARTICLE VI – DISPUTE RESOLUTION

A. In the event of any dispute, controversy, or claim arising out of this Agreement or any alleged breach thereof ("Dispute"), the Client and the Interior Designer shall participate in a mediation conducted under the auspices of a recognized neutral third-party professional mediation service, in a good faith effort to negotiate a resolution of the Dispute, prior to undertaking any legal action. A demand for mediation shall be made in writing to the other party within a reasonable time after the Dispute has arisen. In no event shall the demand for mediation be made after the date when institution of legal or equitable proceedings based on such Dispute would be barred by the applicable statutes of limitations. The selection of the mediation service shall be acceptable to the parties, and the cost of the mediation service shall be borne equally by the parties unless otherwise ordered by the mediator.

B. Should such mediation fail to resolve said Dispute, said Dispute shall be submitted to mandatory, binding arbitration under the auspices of a recognized neutral third party arbitration organization, or as otherwise agreed by the parties. The award rendered by the arbitrator or arbitrators shall be final, and judgment may be entered upon it in accordance with applicable law in any court having jurisdiction thereof. All costs, fees, and expenses incurred pursuant to any such arbitration shall be paid by the nonprevailing party.

C. The arbitrator shall award reasonable attorneys' fees and costs to the prevailing party in the arbitration. Any attorneys' fees and cost award inconsistent with this paragraph are subject to judicial review and enforcement. For purposes of this provision, "prevailing party" shall include a party that dismisses an action for recovery hereunder in exchange for payment of the sum allegedly due, performance of covenants allegedly breached, or consideration substantially equal to the relief sought in the action or proceeding.

D. The arbitrator must issue a written decision setting forth the legal basis of the decision, making findings of all relevant facts, and stating how the law was applied to the found facts, and the decision must be consistent with and apply to the law of the state where the Interior Designer's principal place of business is located. Any award inconsistent with said law is appealable within 30 days of the date of the parties' receipt of the decision, to a court of competent jurisdiction.

ARTICLE VII – TERMINATION, SUSPENSION, OR ABANDONMENT

A. This Agreement may be terminated by either party upon 30 days written notice. In such an event, the Client shall compensate the Interior Designer for services and Reimbursable Expenses incurred prior to the termination date, in accordance with the terms of this Agreement.

B. If the Client fails to make payment when due the Interior Designer for services and Reimbursable Expenses, the Interior Designer may, upon seven days written notice to the Client, withhold documents and suspend performance of services under this Agreement. The Interior Designer shall not be held liable for any claims or losses that may result therefrom.

C. If the Project is abandoned or suspended by the Client for more than ________ days, the Client shall compensate the Interior Designer for services and Reimbursable Expenses incurred prior to the date of written notice by the Client of such abandonment or suspension. In the event the Project is resumed, the Interior Designer shall be entitled to the reasonable costs associated with the resumption of services.

ARTICLE VIII – COMPENSATION PROVISIONS

A. Payment for fees and Reimbursable Expenses, billed monthly or as mutually agreed upon in writing by the Client and Interior Designer, shall be due upon receipt of the Interior Designer's invoice. Disputes or questions regarding an invoice shall be brought to the Interior Designer's attention within 10 days following receipt of the invoice, and shall not be cause for withholding payment for any undisputed portion of the invoice. A service charge of ________

FIGURE 18-7. Continued

STANDARD TERMS AND CONDITIONS [COMMERCIAL]

percent per month, in addition to reasonable collection expenses, shall be added to balances unpaid 30 days after the invoice date.

B. Reimbursable Expenses include air fare, delivery, electronic media, facsimile, ground transportation, hotel, meals, messenger service, mileage, models and renderings, out-of-town living expenses, parking and tolls, photography, plots, postage and shipping, printing, reproducibles, reproduction, sales tax and other transactional taxes, shipping, supplies, telecommunications, and any expenses incurred in connection with the Project or approved by the Client. The Interior Designer shall be entitled to a markup on Reimbursable Expenses.

C. All fees and conditions of this Agreement shall be subject to renegotiation if the Interior Design services are not completed within one year of the date of this Agreement through no fault of the Interior Designer.

ARTICLE IX – MISCELLANEOUS PROVISIONS

A. In providing any opinions of the preliminary or updated budget or the estimated cost of construction, the Client understands that the Interior Designer has no control over costs of the price of labor, equipment, or materials, or over the Contractor's method of pricing, and that any such opinions provided by the Interior Designer are made on the basis of the Interior Designer's qualifications and experience. The Interior Designer makes no warranty, expressed or implied, as to the accuracy of such opinions as compared to bid or actual costs.

B. Neither the Interior Designer nor any of the Interior Designer's Consultants shall have any responsibility for the discovery, removal, or disposal of hazardous materials of any type at the Project site.

C. The Client and the Interior Designer each binds itself, its partners, successors, and assigns to this Agreement. Neither party shall assign or transfer its interests in this Agreement without the express written consent of the other party.

D. This Agreement shall be governed by the laws of the state where the Interior Designer's principal place of business is located.

E. This Agreement may be amended by written instrument only and shall supersede all prior representations, negotiations, or oral or written agreements.

F. If any provision of this Agreement shall be determined to be invalid or unenforceable, all remaining provisions shall remain valid and in full force and effect.

Consultation with legal counsel is recommended regarding the use, completion, or modification of this document.

(The Client) ______________________ *has read and reviewed the Standard Terms and Conditions*

made as of the ______________ *day of* ______________ *in the year of* ______________
[*in words, indicate day, month and year*]

Approved as a duly authorized signatory and representative of (Client) ______________

NAME ______________ TITLE ______________

SIGNATURE ______________ DATE ______________

IIDA CAUTION: You should sign an original IIDA document which has this caution in red. An original assures that changes will not be obscured as may occur when documents are reproduced.

3

FIGURE 18-7. Continued

A contract for a commercial project needs to be even more specific. If the address of the project is different from the main office, it should be listed. It may be necessary to list the specific area by department or room and even the amount of square footage. "The main dining room, foyer, and meeting rooms, but excluding the kitchen of your restaurant at the Harbor Hotel, San Diego" is a clear definition of what rooms in what building will be involved in this contract. To say, "your restaurant at the Harbor Hotel," leaves the designer open to a lot of unplanned additional design. Should the client want additional areas to be included or added, a secondary contract or addendum to the contract might be prepared to cover these areas and the services they require.

4. *Detailed scope of services to be provided*. As mentioned, this is a very important part of the design contract. Services required for a project vary greatly from project to project. So that there is little room for disagreements about doing or not doing something, it is important for the scope of services to be considered thoroughly and spelled out in specific detail. It is best for these services to be outlined in the general order in which they will take place and, whenever possible (based on the type of project and in consideration of the fee method), according to the phases in which they will take place. Figure 18-8 shows a wide range of services that might be required of either a residential or commercial project, offered in the sequence suggested by the project process that will be discussed in Chapter 27. Only those services that the designer understands are to be performed should be listed in the contract.

   One service that should be mentioned before we proceed with our discussion is on-site supervision requirements. This service causes considerable misunderstandings between designer and client. To the designer, on-site supervision generally means making occasional trips to the job site to be sure that all furniture and furnishings are being installed properly and that all construction is going along as designed. Certain phases of the project require that the designer be on the job site for substantial periods of time. Other phases require only a short visit once a day or every few days. The client, however, often feels that on-site supervision means that the designer will be on the site all day, every day, seeing to every detail of the construction and installation. For most projects, this is, of course, impossible and impractical. How much supervision and what kind of supervision—even who in the office or representing the office is to supervise—should be clearly spelled out in the scope of services.

   Designers must also be careful when using words such as *supervise* or *manage* in relation to the installation of interior finishing materials or any actual construction. All states require that construction supervision be performed by licensed contractors, and many states require that the supervision of installation of interior finishing materials also be done only by licensed contractors.

5. *Detailed purchasing arrangements*. This clause should inform the client of the conditions under which the design firm will be selling any products to the client. If the design service is provided by designers on staff of a retail store, the purchasing arrangements will be outlined by store policy.* The minimal information that should be covered in this clause is how the

* A signed authorization should be part of this policy so that nothing is ordered or given to the client without his or her signature. Confirmation proposals are discussed in detail in Chapter 30.

Scope of Services

Programming Phase

Interview client to determine user needs and goals.
Evaluate existing job site or review any drawings for new construction.
Inventory existing furniture that might be used in the project.
Obtain scaled floor plans of the project space from the client (the architect or landlord).
Measure job site to obtain necessary dimensions of site.
Determine style, color, etc. preferences.
Meet with landlord concerning building standards and regulations.
Ascertain potential building code, life safety code, and barrier-free regulations as might affect the project.
Develop project schedule.
Develop project budget.
Coordinate (if needed) with appropriate consultants.
Determine feasibility of meeting the client's requirements; determine and inform the client of any restraints that will affect the feasibility of the project.
Prepare final design program.

Schematic Design

Develop spatial and communication adjacencies.
Develop preliminary space utilization plans.
Prepare preliminary furniture plans.
Preliminary selections of interior architectural finishes.
Preliminary furniture, furnishings, and equipment selections.
Review applicable building, life safety, and accessibility codes, and apply as required.
Make preliminary color selections.
Refine budgets.
Prepare design drawings, such as perspectives, elevations, etc., as needed.
Meet with consultants, such as architect, contractors, or others as required.

Design Development

Finalize relationship diagrams or charts.
Complete space plans and layouts.
Complete furniture, furnishings, and equipment plans.
Complete working drawings concerning custom furniture, cabinets, or architectural treatments.
Determine specifications of architectural finishes.
Prepare specifications of furniture, furnishings, and equipment.
Prepare other drawings, such as lighting plans, elevations, and sections, etc., as required.
Prepare presentation boards.
Prepare presentation graphics, such as renderings of perspectives, isometrics, or axonometric drawings.
Prepare a budget of expected costs for all construction and furnishings, as specified.

Contract Documents

Prepare working drawings and schedules for the construction and/or installation of the space. Prepare written specifications to accompany working drawings, schedules, and furniture, furnishings, and equipment.
Prepare furniture and equipment installation drawings.
Obtain approvals and permits from jurisdictional agencies.
Provide or assist client with the preparation of bid documents.
Qualify vendors, suppliers, and subcontractors.
Assist client in obtaining competitive bids for all phases of the project.
Provide guidance in the selection of necessary contractors.
Assist client with owner-contractor contracts.

Contract Administration

Assist with securing of bids.
Provide project management supervision of the job site during construction/installation.
Procure furniture and furnishings by submitting purchase orders to suppliers and installers.
Assist in the procurement of furniture and furnishings through bid administration.
Make periodic visits to the job site to ensure the work is being done in accordance with the contract documents and specifications.
Supervise installation of furniture, furnishings, and equipment.
Maintain project management and schedule records.
Assist in determination of substantial completion, payments to vendors, and securing releases.
Prepare and administer postoccupancy evaluations.

This list suggests a wide range of services and is not meant to be all-inclusive.

FIGURE 18-8. A detailed list of common services in a complete interior design "Scope of Services."

client will be charged for furniture and furnishings; the terms of payment; penalties for cancellation of orders; the design firm's responsibilities toward warranties of goods sold; charges for installation, freight, sales tax, delivery costs; and whether or not there is a late payment penalty on the sale of goods.

The clause also should have specific language regarding what would happen if the client purchased the goods specified from someone other than the designer. In some cases, the only way in which the designer is receiving compensation for services is through the sale of goods. If goods are purchased from someone else, the designer would not receive compensation, unless this was covered in the contract.

It is also common for all these considerations to be spelled out in the contract for the sale of goods and for only a reference to these conditions to be made in the contract for services. Since many commercial designers and some residential designers specify products only and do not sell the goods to the client, this clause may not even be in the contract.

It is quite common for outside sources or contractors to be necessary for the completion of the project. In some cases, the interior designer will want the client to hire these outside contractors rather than have to contract himself or herself with subcontractors. This section of the contract should inform the client as to expectations and requirements in this case.

6. *Price guarantees.* An important clause that ASID recommends including deals with price guarantees. It is quite possible for the prices for products and services to increase as the project moves from conceptualization through design development and final approvals by the client. Although the designer is responsible for maintaining a tight control on the budget and is responsible for keeping the client informed of any price increases, this clause helps to provide some protection for the designer if the actual bid prices of construction and goods increase over time.

7. *Method and payment of compensation.* This section details how the designer will be paid for his or her services. It should begin by describing how the design fees will be charged. Remember, there are many different ways of charging fees. The compensation section is the most common changeable part in standardized contracts that are available from the professional associations. Figure 18-9 provides examples of wording for three common compensation methods.

Hourly Fee

1. For the design services as described, you will be charged on an hourly fee basis of _____ per hour. You will be invoiced monthly for all hours actually worked.
2. Compensation for the design services described will be billed:
   _____ per hour for Principals
   _____ per hour for Senior Designers
   _____ per hour for Project Managers
   _____ per hour for Designers
   _____ per hour for Design Assistants
   _____ per hour for Draftspersons/CAD

Fixed Fee Method

1. The design fixed fee for this project will be _____. You will be billed as follows:
   20 percent upon signing of contract as a retainer
   20 percent at the end of the preliminary review meeting
   40 percent at the completion of the preparation of drawings and specifications
   10 percent when construction begins and purchase orders are placed
   10 percent upon completion of the project
2. The design fee for basic services will be _____ . You will be billed as follows:
   _____ Percent upon signing of contract as a retainer
   _____ Percent upon completion of Programming
   _____ Percent upon completion of Schematic Design
   _____ Percent upon completion of Design Development
   _____ Percent upon completion of Construction Documents
   _____ Percent upon completion of the project

Cost Plus Percentage Mark-up

1. Design Consultation
   The designer will be compensated for consultation services as described under the scope of services on an hourly basis at the rate of _____ per hour. Client will be invoiced on a monthly basis. Upon signing this agreement, the client shall provide _____ as a non-refundable retainer for design consultation services.
   (Note that a flat fee could be substituted for an hourly rate).
2. Purchasing Services
   The designer will be compensated at a cost plus percentage of mark-up on a basis of a _____ mark-up percentage of cost of furniture, furnishings, and equipment specified. Cost will be defined as the Designer's cost as stated by the manufacturer or supplier's invoice. The client will be required to pay an initial payment of _____ of the expected invoice cost prior to orders actually being placed with the supplier. The balance will be due upon delivery.
   Products specified shall be purchased only through the interior designer.
   (There are many other ways of stating the purchasing services section of a contract.)

Note that these examples may not include all the phrases or clauses you may wish to include in your agreements/contracts. Actual wording should be reviewed with your attorney.

FIGURE 18-9. Sample compensation clauses for three different ways of charging design fees.

This section should also detail how the client will be billed and whether or not there will be any penalties for late payment. Whatever compensation method is used, the payment terms must be clearly stated within the contract so that the designer is assured of being paid. The designer cannot charge a late payment penalty if the client is late paying invoices if this clause is not included in the contract. Such clauses as, "payments are due upon receipt," "payment is due upon receipt of invoice," or possibly "payments are due within ten days" are needed to clarify how quickly the designer expects the client to send payment. Moreover, the section should continue with a statement about late penalties. The amount of the late payment penalty is commonly 1–1/2 percent per month on the unpaid balance, which is charged for any invoices that are overdue. The monthly percentage varies and should be determined with the advice of the design firm's accountant.

8. *Reimbursements for out-of-pocket expenses. Reimbursable expenses* are those expenses that are not part of the design contract but that are made in the interest of completing the project. Some designers refer to these charges as disbursements. The most costly reimbursable expenses that might be incurred are for out-of-town travel and living expenses or per diem expenses incurred in connection with the project. *Per diem* refers to a dollar amount that is allowed to cover hotel, meals, and transportation costs. These expenses are something that the client should pay for, but they should not be part of the design fee. Other typical reimbursable expenses are long-distance telephone calls, postage, blueprinting, computer time, and overtime. Some firms include the cost of renderings, models, and mock-ups in reimbursable expenses.

   Most firms charge reimbursable expenses at actual cost. Some, however, add a service charge to the expense. If a service charge is added, this should be clearly stated in the contract.

   Many firms only put a clause concerning reimbursable expenses in the contract if they anticipate out-of-town travel, the need for renderings or models, or an inordinate amount of other kinds of expenses. Expenses such as blueprinting, telephone calls, and data processing are often considered costs of doing business and are not charged to the client.

9. *Charges for extra services.* A clause concerning charges for extra services is provided to deal with a situation in which the client requests more areas to be done or more kinds of services to be performed than were outlined in the initial list of scope of services. This clause protects the designer so that he or she will not be required to perform design services for free. It also informs the client as to how additional work can be added to the contract or done at the same time, and how the client will be charged. Many designers charge extra services as an hourly fee at a higher rate than stated in the contract.

   This section also spells out what happens if the client makes changes to the project after certain phases of work have been completed. If the designer has already received approval for certain phases of the project and changes are then made by the client, the designer should be compensated for the additional work. For instance, after the space planning was approved by the client and the designer began final drawings, the client decided to add three more offices that had not been originally planned. The designer should be compensated at some reasonable amount for the time it will take him or her to redo the space planning and the final drawings. This section allows for the designer to be compensated in such a situation.

10. *Designer responsibility disclaimer.* This section specifically describes any portions of the project for which the designer cannot claim responsibility. For example, if the designer is not required to plan the lighting for an interior, he or she should state that the firm claims no responsibility for the lighting in the finished interior. There are also some kinds

of activities that can only be done by licensed professionals. If the law requires that construction documents be drawn by a licensed architect, the interior designer should disclaim any responsibility for errors in those drawings.

The contract should also contain a disclaimer of responsibility concerning whether the designer is able to provide a variety of services. Most interior designers, depending on licensing regulations in their state, cannot prepare drawings related to structural load-bearing design and mechanical features. Thus, it is advisable that the contract clarify that the drawings are conceptual and are not for construction.

Another item that might be in this section would be a disclaimer if the client purchased products other than those specified. This would protect the designer from potential negligence or product liability suits, if the products the client purchased were not the same as those specified.

Another situation that might be covered in this section involves the designer's not being responsible for changes made by the owner, architect, or contractor without the designer's consent. Should the client or the contractor change the length of an alcove that is to receive a custom-made piece of furniture, the designer would not be held responsible if the furniture did not fit in the alcove, if he or she had not been informed of the change.

11. *Charges and responsibilities of third parties*. This clause is a "companion" to the preceding. After meeting with the client, the designer should have an idea of whether the project will require the consultation of any third parties, such as architects, specialized consultants such as lighting designers and commercial kitchen designers, contractors, or landlords. Although it is possible to calculate and add these charges to the design contract if they will involve short meetings, it is usually safer to make this a separate charge. If a project requires extensive architectural services, the services of a third-party may be better dealt with as a separate contract between the client and the third party. However, the designer should still charge for the time that he or she will have to spend with the third-party.

12. *Photographic and publishing rights*. It is unlikely that the designer will wish to photograph or use every project in one of the firm's publications. It should be standard practice, however, to include a clause that allows the designer to obtain permissions for all projects. Clients should know up front how the designer intends to use the photographs of the project for publication. Some clients may object to allowing this kind of intrusion. In some commercial installations, it may be against company policy because of security reasons. Often, when clients object to photographing their living or working quarters, the designer may be able to get permission if he or she does not publish the name of the client. Remember that releases must also be obtained from any recognizable people in the photographs, even if the owner of the space has given permission to photograph the interior.

13. *Termination of contract*. As a means of protection for the designer, a termination clause should be included. This clause is to ensure compensation for services rendered in the event that the project ends for some reason *other than* by the designer's wishes. If the client runs out of money, cannot take the space, and must end the project, it is important for the designer to be paid for design work that has been prepared. Without this kind of clause, it is more difficult for the designer to collect any fees. Something like the

following wording can be used; "In the event the project is terminated through no fault of the designer, the designer will be compensated for all work actually performed." Or something more clearly defined, depending on the kind of fee arrangements or exact nature of the project, may be necessary.

14. *Responsibilities of the client*. In many projects, there are certain tasks that the client should perform for the project to proceed successfully or to be completed with few headaches. Responsibilities of the client might include making it the client's responsibility to obtain needed permits and approvals (although this is commonly a responsibility of the designer); providing reasonable access to the job site; providing a place to receive, unpack, and store products prior to installation on the job site; and providing approvals expeditiously. For a commercial project, it is also necessary for the owner of the building or site to designate an employee as a liaison between the designer and the owner.

15. *Assignment and delegation*. Sometimes an event may occur that is unforeseen that prevents the designer (or even the client) from fulfilling the contract. If the rights in a contract are transferred to another party, it is called *assignment*; if they are given to someone else, it is called *delegation* (Conry et al., 1993, p. 227). For example, the designer/owner of a sole proprietorship might become ill or the lead designer in a larger firm might quit in the middle of a project to take a position with another firm. It might happen that the real estate office with which the designer is contracted to design is sold to another owner in the middle of the project. A clause that requires that the assignment or delegation of responsibility of either party to another cannot be done without written notice to and consent by the other party is recommended.

16. *Ownership of documents*. Many interior designers and other design professionals wish to protect their design ideas from being copied or imitated without their receiving fair compensation. It is necessary to put a provision in the contract that warns the client that he or she may not reuse the design ideas without compensating the designer. The designer must copyright his or her design documents as an added protection. Copyright is the legal means of protecting the drawings or plans and specifications that interior designers produce. A sample clause might be, "Documents and specifications are provided for the fair use by the client in completing the project as listed within this contract. Documents and specifications remain the property of the designer and cannot be used or reused without permission of the designer." This will clarify the issue. If the designer needs or wishes to use this clause, he or she should become familiar with copyright law so that he or she can answer the questions of the client. Refer back to Chapter 7 for more information on copyright.

17. *Time frame of the contract*. As we saw in the beginning of our discussion of contracts, the time frame or time limit of a contract is an important part of the offer. Interior design projects, whether they are residential or commercial, must work around some date, such as the move-in date.

    A second important issue concerning time has to do with the time limit that the designer can wait before he or she receives the signed contract in order to complete the project by the move-in date. A sample clause is, "In order to complete the project as specified in the scope of services, the signed contract must be received by the designer no later than June 20,

20xx." This should help the client in making up his or her mind quickly as to whether or not he or she will engage the designer.

Another clause that appears in many commercial contracts relates to renegotiation of the contract if the work is expected to be done over a long period of time. This could include a project that extends for more than one year, although this should be taken into consideration when the contract is drawn up. It concerns those relationships between the designer and the client when the designer is on a retainer for an extended period of time. In this relationship, design work may be scattered over time, and it may be necessary for the design firm to renegotiate a fair increase in its fees every so often.

18. *Matters of arbitration.* In any project in which disagreement might occur, a clause concerning *arbitration* should be included. This clause spells out what would happen in the event there was a disagreement between the parties that could not be resolved. Rather than going to court, an arbitrator (a disinterested third party) would be called in to listen to the arguments of both sides and then to render an opinion of what must be done. Both client and designer must agree beforehand to abide by the decision of the arbitrator.

19. *Mutual understanding and legality.* Designers sometimes add a clause that clarifies that the contract, as written, is the full and complete mutual understanding of the terms and conditions of the agreement. This is done in case there are claims by the client that some verbal comment has been made that creates an addition to the contract or supersedes the original intent of the contract. If this clause is included and a later claim is made, the later claim is unlikely to be upheld by a jury. Any changes to the project that the client requests or that the designer finds are needed should be made in writing as an addendum to the original contract.

A contract should note that the laws of a specific state or province govern the agreement and interpretation. The specific state or province generally is the one in which the design firm is located, since that is the legal location of the business.

20. *Conditions and amount of retainer.* A *retainer* is an amount of money that is paid by the client to the designer for professional services that will be done in the future. The retainer is applied by the designer to the total fee of the project as work progresses. In some ways, the retainer acts as "earnest money" from the client, showing his or her good faith in proceeding with the project. The retainer provides operating funds to the designer to purchase the needed production materials and services in order to begin the design services portion of the project. If a retainer is expected, the amount and when it is due must be spelled out in the contract. It is a good idea also for the designer to explain briefly how it will be applied to the total fee. Typically, the retainer clause appears at the end of the contract.

A deposit (or down payment) is similar to a retainer, but it is usually applied toward the purchase of furniture and furnishings. Refer to Chapter 19 for additional information on down payments and deposits.

21. *Signatures.* Space should be provided in the contract for both parties to sign. To enforce the contract, the client only must sign. The client, on the other hand, will want the designer to sign as a token of the designer's good faith.

Each contract, whether it is for a residential or a commercial project, must be developed to suit the individual project. A form or standard contract can be developed to cover almost all contingencies, and then parts can be "cut and pasted" to make the final contract. A word processor makes this task very easy.

As mentioned above, standardized contracts can be obtained from ASID, IIDA, and AIA. These organizations have standard contracts that meet the conditions of many normal projects. Space is provided to type in standard information, such as the designer's name and address, and some can be imprinted with the design firm's name. Whatever the final form of the contract is, it should be periodically reviewed by the firm's attorney to be sure that the contract meets the conditions of the firm's individual practice.

Now let us look at what constitutes legal performance and termination of a contract.

Performance

A contract terminates when both parties perform the acts or activities promised in the terms of the contract. Sometimes there is disagreement as to whether or not the terms have been fulfilled. This is especially true when the contract insufficiently specifies the required services. In contract law, there are three types of *performance*: (1) complete, (2) substantial, and (3) inferior, or performance far below what is considered reasonable.

For complete performance to occur, the terms expressed in the contract must be fully accomplished in the manner in which they are specified in the contract. If a design contract for a restaurant has as one of its terms the provision that "the designer provide two computer-generated color renderings of the dining room," the contract is not complete if these renderings have not been provided to the client. This is true even if all other terms in the contract have been fulfilled. In this case, the client has grounds to sue for breach of contract, if he or she so chooses.

Since it is sometimes impossible to satisfy a party's idea of complete performance, the courts hold that performance is complete if it is done so as to be substantially complete. *Substantial completion* means that the performance cannot vary greatly from what has been spelled out in the contract. If, in the preceding example, the designer provides two black-and-white computer-generated renderings of the dining room, the court might rule that the terms have been performed substantially and that the client must pay the designer for the services performed. Note that a substitution of a different medium, such as markers, technically constitutes a breach of contract.

Inferior performance is work that varies quite considerably from what is required. Inferior performance causes a material (or major) breach of contract and excuses the nonbreaching party from fulfilling his or her obligations in relation to the contract. In our example, should the designer provide only pencil or ink sketches of the areas, rather than the computer-generated color renderings, it could be argued that what was provided was inferior. A material breach would have occurred. The nonbreaching party would not have to pay agreed-upon fees and would likely be entitled to damages.

The phrase *breach of contract* has been used several times in this section. A breach of contract occurs when one of the parties of the contract does not perform his or her duties as spelled out in the terms of the contract. If the breach is minor (as when the designer does a black-and-white rendering rather than a color one), the client would not be excused from his or her obligation to the designer, but the client would not have to pay until the designer has provided the renderings in watercolor or until some other agreement has been worked out. If the breach is material (as when the designer only provides pencil sketches rather than color renderings), the client is excused from the contract and may also be entitled to damages. A decision of a material breach terminates the agreement when major or material ones occur.

A breach of contract could also occur if the designer was negligent or had performed tasks in what could be considered an unskillful manner. Interior design services must be performed to standards considered reasonable for a professional in this profession. If, for example, drawings are submitted that do not meet code, or the furniture as drawn does not fit into the actual rooms, the client can claim that the designer has breached the contract (among other things)."Wrongful performance or nonperformance discharges the other party from further obligation and permits that party to bring suit to rescind (the) contract" (Brown and Sukys, 1997, p. 197) or recover monetary damages as compensation.

If one party has breached a contract, the court may determine that the harmed party is not only due the performance of the contract but also damages. The term *damages* refers to money awarded to the party that has been harmed as a result of the breach. Actual, or compensatory damages, represent a sum of money that is equal to the financial loss that the harmed party has suffered. They are compensatory because they are meant to compensate for the loss. Another type of damages is incidental, which are meant to cover expenses that have been paid out by the harmed party. Consequential damages might be given in order to cover losses that could have been foreseen by the party who has breached the contract. Nominal damages may be awarded as a token to indicate that the breaching party has done something wrong but that the harm is not very great. The most serious kind of damages are *punitive* damages. In this case, the damages are given in order to punish the guilty party, because the harm is grievous in his or her breach of the contract. It is more common for punitive damages to be awarded in tort cases than for breach of contract. The reader should note that there are additional kinds of damage awards and may wish to review these in a business law textbook. While they may apply to an interior design breach-of-contract case, they are less of a factor in our discussion.

A type of remedy that is related to breach of contract is specific performance. *Specific performance* is an equitable remedy when the court requires that the breaching party perform what it is required to perform according to the contract. As it relates to breach of contract, the party that has breached the contract is ordered to perform whatever is required in the contract that he or she so far has not done. The nonbreaching party generally is satisfied with specific performance, since it requires that what has been bargained for actually is done. It is usually applied only if the monetary damages are insufficient to satisfy the party who has been breached. However, courts are reluctant to apply specific performance to service contracts, since such application requires that the courts force someone to perform a specific service (Jentz et al., 1987, p. 227).

A breach of a contract can occur easily, especially if the designer has not been careful in the preparation of the terms of the agreement. And, in fact, it is generally easier for the interior designer to breach the contract than it is for the client to do so. It is extremely important for the designer to understand the scope of the project and what the terms of the agreement are so that the designer does not leave himself or herself open to a breach.

Termination by Agreement

Contracts can be terminated by agreement. We saw in a preceding section, in which we discussed the termination of contract, how the designer seeks to protect himself or herself if something occurs that is not the designer's fault. It is not necessary for there to be such a clause in the contract for the contract to be terminated by agreement.

It is possible at any time for the contract to be terminated if both parties agree to the termination. If a clause does not exist in the original contract, it is necessary for a second contract dealing with the terms of the termination to be written as a protection for both parties. An oral agreement to terminate the contract is not advisable. All terminations by agreement, regardless of who initiates the termination, should be spelled out in writing.

Summary

The major portion of what the interior designer does for clients can be covered by contracts of one sort or another. Too often, designers have suffered a loss of fees as a result of their failure to understand what constitutes a contract, to prepare one properly, or to even have one. The professional designer must realize that, in order to protect himself or herself, he or she must insist on the preparation of contracts. The designer must also get the contract signed by the client before beginning design work. Regardless of the designer's enthusiasm to do a project, today the professional designer should not undertake a design project or order goods for clients until the appropriately prepared contract has been signed by the client.

This chapter described in a general sense what legally constitutes a contract and a contractual relationship. It then covered the kinds of clauses that are commonly found in an interior design contract. The chapter may not answer all the questions or special needs; therefore, the designer should discuss the matter and form of contracts with an attorney. Although most attorneys understand contract law, few understand the interior design, architecture, and construction professions. Ideally, the designer should work with an attorney who is familiar with the design industry. More information on contracts and contract law can be found in the references. A course in business law that emphasizes contracts also can provide additional material for study.

REFERENCES

Alderman, Robert L. 1997. *How To Prosper as an Interior Designer*. New York: John Wiley.

———. 1982. *How To Make More Money at Interior Design*. New York: Whitney Communications Corporation.

Barnes, A. James. 1981. *A Guide to Business Law*. Homewood, IL: Learning Systems.

Berger, C. Jaye. 1994. *Interior Design Law and Business Practices*. New York: John Wiley.

Brown, Gordon W., and Paul A. Sukys. 1997. *Business Law*, 9th ed. New York: Glencoe/McGraw-Hill.

Clarkson, Kenneth W., Roger LeRoy Miller, and Gaylord A. Jentz. 1989. *West's Business Law, Text and Cases*, 4th ed. St. Paul, MN: West Publishing.

———. 1983. *West's Business Law, Text and Cases*, 2nd ed. St. Paul, MN: West Publishing.

Conry, Edward J., Gerald R. Ferrera, and Karla H. Fox. 1993. *The Legal Environment of Business*, 3rd ed. Boston, MA: Allyn and Bacon.

Cooper, David G. 1993. *Finding and Signing Profitable Contracts*. New York: John Wiley.

Cushman, Robert F., and James C. Dobbs, eds. 1991. *Design Professional's Handbook of Business and Law.* New York: John Wiley.

Davidson, Marion, and Martha Blue. 1979. *Making It Legal.* New York: McGraw-Hill.

Getz, Lowell V. 1997. *An Architect's Guide to Financial Management.* Washington, DC: AIA Press.

Haviland, David. 1994. *The Architect's Handbook of Professional Practice, Student Edition.* Washington, DC: AIA Press.

Holtz, Herman. 2000. *Getting Started in Sales Consulting.* New York: John Wiley.

———. 1998. *Proven Proposal Strategies To Win More Business.* Chicago, IL: Upstart Publishing.

Jentz, Gaylord A., Kenneth W. Clarkson, and Roger LeRoy Miller. 1987. *West's Business Law—Alternate UCC Comprehensive Edition,* 3rd ed. St. Paul, MN: West Publishing.

Loebelson, Andrew. 1983. *How To Profit in Contract Design.* New York: Interior Design Books.

Morgan, Jim. 1998. *Management for the Small Design Firm.* New York: Watson-Guptill.

Neubert, Christopher, and Jack Withiam, Jr. 1980. *How To Handle Your Own Contracts,* rev. ed. New York: Greenwich House.

Shenson, Howard L. 1990. The *Contract and Fee-Setting Guide for Consultants and Professionals.* New York: John Wiley.

Siegel, Harry, and Alan M. Siegel. 1982. *A Guide to Business Principles and Practices for Interior Designers,* rev. ed. New York: Watson-Guptill.

Stasiowski, Frank. 1985. *Negotiating Higher Design Fees.* New York: Watson-Guptill.

Sweet, Justin. 1985. *Legal Aspects of Architecture, Engineering, and the Construction Process,* 3rd ed. St. Paul, MN: West Publishing.

Thompson, Jo Ann Asher, ed. 1992. *ASID Professional Practice Manual.* New York: Watson-Guptill.

Chapter 19

Product Pricing Considerations

The vast majority of small interior design practices that have five or fewer employees generate the largest part of their income from the sale of merchandise. In the last ten years or so, these same firms have begun to augment that income with fees for services. Yet selling products remains a way in which the sole practitioner—and even larger practices—can generate revenues. It seems that residential designers, in particular, depend upon the sale of goods for the largest part of their revenues, though many also charge fees for their services. Commercial interior designers tend to sell merchandise less frequently, though many also find that selling products is a good way to generate revenue.

Establishing the price for goods or product-related services is critical to whether or not the design firm will make a profit. The *price* is, of course, what something sells for. There are many factors involved in determining the price of a product or a service. And, unfortunately for the individual who is new to the interior design profession, there are many different prices with which the interior designer has to deal.

Designers who sell merchandise to clients must be acutely aware of the selling prices they quote to clients. In many cases, these sales may be the only revenue generated by the design firm. Making a mistake in calculating and quoting products' selling prices is always costly to the design firm and almost always comes out of the designer's commission.

Several product pricing concepts will be discussed in this chapter. To begin, in order to understand how prices are established, it is best to explain the different kinds of "prices." The terminology and methodology of creating prices for the tangible goods sold to the client as part of the interior design service will be explained. Designers frequently charge clients for the shipping of goods from the manufacturer to the designer. And, of course, there are additional expenses for the delivery and installation of goods at the client's home or commercial job site. Terminology related to shipping, delivery, and installation will be defined in this chapter.

It is also critical for designers to understand when sales and use taxes are required on the sale of goods. Forgetting to charge the customer sales tax does not remove the obligation of the payment of that tax. Designers can be fined quite heavily for failure to collect and pay sales taxes. We will look at some of the requirements of sales tax collection.

Many designers do not sell merchandise but do have the responsibility of pricing and budgeting the goods specified in the project. This chapter will briefly discuss the role of the designer/specifier in the pricing of merchandise.

Understanding product pricing terminology and the pricing practices used in interior design are critical for anyone involved in the profession. Clients are rarely nice enough to pay additional sums to the designer because he or she has made a mistake. Care in pricing and in budgeting merchandise is as important as determining how much to charge for a design fee.

Pricing Terms

In the interior design field, there are many terms related to pricing. The price is what is charged for the goods that the designer is selling. Some prices are quoted to the client by the designer, and some prices are quoted by a supplier to the designer. To add to the possible confusion, some of these pricing terms often mean the same thing. Other terms can also be interpreted as a "price," for example, fee is the term commonly used to represent the price of services; rent is the price for an office space. Students are familiar with the term tuition, which is the price for classes; and interest is the price one pays for a loan.

These differences must be learned quickly and completely, since calculating and quoting the wrong price more often means losing money rather than making it. Knowing what price has been quoted by a vendor or in a catalog is also very important. Not knowing the prices quoted in a catalog or carelessness in determining pricing can easily mean that prices quoted to clients are below the designer's price from the vendor. This is no way to make a profit! So, let's start this chapter by defining the many different terms that are related to buying and selling merchandise, as they apply to the interior design industry.

Pricing from the Supplier to the Interior Designer

There are three different terms that are used to represent the price that the designer must pay to the supplier for goods: (1) net price, (2) wholesale price, and (3) cost price. *Net price* and wholesale price generally mean the same thing and represent a 50 percent reduction (or discount) from the suggested retail price (or list price). The *suggested retail price* is a price suggested by the supplier. *Wholesale price* can also be defined as a special price given to a designer by a supplier, which is lower than what it would cost the consumer.

Cost price is the price that the designer must pay for the goods; it is not always the same as the net or wholesale price. Not all designers have the privilege of purchasing goods at a 50 percent discount from all suppliers. For example, if an interior designer occasionally buys one or two items from a certain supplier, he or she might only be given a 30 percent discount from the retail price. A designer who frequently purchases from the same vendor would be given the full 50 percent discount. A major reason why designers are not permitted the 50 percent discount from retail is because they do not have a quantity purchasing agreement. It should be noted that pricing from the supplier to the designer is governed by federal law. This point will be discussed at the end of this chapter.

Pricing from the Interior Designer to the Client

There are four different price terms that designers use to quote prices to clients. These are (1) suggested retail price, (2) list price, (3) selling price, and (4) retail price. The first two generally mean the same thing. Suggested retail price is the price suggested by the manufacturer for use by the seller. Sometimes the price might be shown by the acronym MSRP, which stands for manufacturer's suggested retail price. The price term *list price* is generally accepted as being the same as suggested retail price. Generally, they are the price to the ultimate consumer of the goods, called the *end user.* When you purchase an electronic product like a DVD player at a store, you are most likely paying the suggested retail price.

Selling price is a term many designers use to refer to the actual price at which they sell goods to the client. Since some designers sell goods at a discount (a price lower than suggested retail) and others may occasionally sell goods at a price that is higher than suggested retail, selling price is not always the same thing as suggested retail price and list price. The selling price to the end user may be different from the list or suggested retail price, because designers may sell merchandise to the end user at any price they wish. They are not obligated to sell goods at the suggested retail price. In fact, federal laws prohibit manufacturers from requiring merchants to sell goods to the end user at a set price.

Retail price is a term that is commonly used in retailing. Retailing involves businesses that sells goods to the consumer, or end user, such as department stores and specialty stores. In retailing, retail price generally is not a price suggested by the manufacturer but, rather, a price determined by the retailer. So, in fact, although the price term for the selling of the DVD player mentioned earlier could be the suggested retail price, it might actually be a retail price.

Who knows where all this confusion has come from. It is part of the long history of sales transactions over the centuries. Perhaps it is due in part to sellers' desires to keep the price they pay secret from the buyers or manufacturers who are trying to control who can sell their products.

In our discussions in this chapter, we will use the term selling price to mean the price quoted to the client and cost price to mean the price the designer must pay for the goods. However, the other terms are also used in the discussion but are carefully differentiated to prevent confusion.

Catalog Pricing

When a designer requests a catalog from a supplier, the catalog often comes with a price list. Many manufacturers send a price list for suggested retail or list prices. When this occurs, the designer must then negotiate with the manufacturer's representative for the discount percentage that the design firm may expect to receive. This may be as small as 10 percent or as much as 50 percent.* The manufacturer may offer variable discounts to different design firms, as long as these decisions are soundly based. Such things as purchasing an amount of goods over some specific time period or whether or not the designer will inventory goods are two possible factors that affect discount percentages. The cost price to the designer results from determining the price after the discount percentage has been subtracted from the suggested retail or list price.

Some manufacturers send net price lists with their catalogs. A net price list means that the designer can purchase the goods at the price listed in the catalog. This net price list, of course, is the designer's cost price.

It is common for suppliers to send price lists in terms of list price rather than net price, since many suppliers offer varying discounts based on the volume of purchases. However, enough firms utilize the net price list, so the designer must be very careful in understanding what price list he or she is reading. Most often, furniture price lists are retail or list price values, whereas

* For very large dollar-volume purchases, manufacturers may give the designer a larger than 50 percent discount.

price lists for textiles, wall coverings, and carpeting are net price values. A selling price determined by quoting or discounting a net price list means that the designer has sold the goods to the client for the same price that the designer has purchased the goods from the supplier. If the designer receives a price list that is not clearly marked "suggested retail," "list," "retail," "net," or "wholesale," the designer should contact the representative or the factory to determine what the price list represents.

Discounts

A *discount* is a reduction, usually stated as a percentage, from the suggested retail price. A designer receives a discount from a supplier for ordering goods. Some designers give clients discounts when the clients purchase goods. The full discount price given by most manufacturers is 50 percent from the suggested retail. Remember that this is also called net price.

Some manufacturers use a code word, such as *keystone,* to mean a 50 percent discount. Another price code used by some manufacturers is something like, "your discount is *5/10.*" This code might mean that the designer should take $5.00 off the dollar portion of the quoted price and $.10 off the cent portion of the quoted price. For example, if the retail price of the goods are $23.50, the designer's price would be $18.40. These price codes are used to protect designers, should clients try to contact suppliers directly in order to determine profit margins of the designer.

Recall that not all designers receive the full discount of 50 percent. A manufacturer may determine that a 50 percent discount will be given only to those companies that are stocking dealers or that purchase a certain minimal quantity of goods in a given time period. A *stocking dealer* is a vendor that stocks a certain inventory level of goods at all times. A designer who does not consistently buy from a certain retail store but has purchased a similar quantity of goods consistently, may be given the same discount as a stocking dealer.

It is simple to determine the cost amount by taking the discount percentage off the suggested retail price. For example, if a design firm received a 50 percent discount for purchases made from Martin's Wallcoverings, then wallpaper that has a suggested retail price of $35 per yard would cost the designer $17.50 per yard.

The following formulas might help:

$$\begin{aligned}\text{Discount in dollars} &= \text{Suggested retail price} \times \text{Discount percentage}\\ &= \$35 \times 0.50 = \$17.50\\ \text{Cost} &= \text{Suggested retail} - \text{Discount}\\ &= \$35 - \$17.50\\ &= \$17.50\end{aligned}$$

These same formulas are used whenever a designer is calculating discounts to determine cost.

A Quantity Discount

A *quantity discount* is a discount greater than the normal 50 percent discount because a large quantity of merchandise has been purchased at one time. For example, if a designer purchased one chair, the discount would probably be 50 percent, if that is the firm's normal discount. If the designer ordered 500 chairs, the manufacturer would most likely give a larger discount—perhaps

55 percent. Remember that quantity discounts given by manufacturers to designers are regulated by federal law to prevent price discrimination.

In some cases, the quantity discount might be cumulative. This means that the special discount due to quantity purchases over a given period of time is applied to purchases. The discount might increase as the quantity purchases increase. For example, perhaps a designer has more than one project in progress, which include the specification of plumbing fixtures. The plumbing fixture supplier may give a cumulative discount as an incentive or as an acknowledgment of loyalty to that plumbing fixture supplier. Of course, this type of discount could create cause for ethical concern on the part of the designer.

Multiple Discounts

Multiple discounts are a series of discounts from the suggested retail price. Multiple discounts are usually only given by manufacturers to designers for very large orders. They are not the same thing as a cumulative discount. Occasionally, the design firm may offer a multiple discount to the client—again, because of a very large order. The written notation for such a discount is given as 50/5 or 50/5/2. This does not mean that the designer takes 55 percent off the retail price in the first example or 57 percent off in the second. Rather, each discount is taken separately. For example, if the manufacturer offers a 50/5/2 discount on a large purchase of $500,000 of chairs, the cost to the designer would be figured as

Total retail price	=	$ 500,000
Less 50 percent	=	−250,000
		$ 250,000
Less 5 percent	=	−12,500
		$ 237,500
Less 2 percent	=	−4,750
Cost	=	$ 232,750

Trade Discounts

Trade discounts are discounts given as a courtesy by some vendors to designers and others in the trade. These are usually a small percentage off retail, though they can be as much as 50 percent. Many retail stores that sell specialized residential or commercial furnishings products offer trade discounts to the local design community. For example, if Interior Visions, a retail accessory store, offers designers a 20 percent discount for accessory items purchased from its store for resale, it is offering a trade discount. To calculate what the cost price to the designer would be, use the previous formula. Let us look at an example.

$$\begin{aligned}\text{Discount in dollars} &= \$150 \times 0.20\\ &= \$30.00\\ \text{Cost} &= \text{Suggested retail} - \text{Discount in dollars}\\ &= \$150 - \$30.00\\ &= \$120.00\end{aligned}$$

The interior designer can then add an additional amount to the cost price of $120.00 in order to cover costs and to make a small profit on the sale of the accessories to his or her client.

Cash Discounts

Another discount term that is familiar to design firms that sell merchandise is cash discount. More commonly used in accounting, *cash discounts* are given by manufacturers and suppliers to those customers who pay their bills promptly. A notation like 2/10 Net 30 must appear on the invoice if a cash discount is allowed. The notation translates into an additional 2 percent deduction from the cost price if the invoice is paid within 10 days of receipt of the invoice. If it is not paid within 10 days, then the cost price is as stated and is due within 30 days. The notation automatically establishes an interest-free credit of 30 days.

The cash discount is taken after all other discounts have been taken. For example, the cost to a firm for an order of goods is $5000. The invoice offers a cash discount of 2/10 Net 30. If the firm pays the invoice within 10 days, it only has to pay $4900.

$$\begin{aligned}\text{Cash discount} &= \text{Cost} \times \text{Percentage}\\ &= \$5000 \times 0.02\\ &= \$100\\ \text{Amount due} &= \$5000 - \$100\\ \text{Cash discount} &= \$4900\end{aligned}$$

Seasonal Discounts

A *seasonal discount* is given to encourage early purchasing of certain goods. This type of discount is to encourage retailers* to purchase certain items that are sold earlier than normal more frequently during certain seasons of the year. It is not something that particularly affects the interior designer, unless he or she has a location that is frequented by walk-in consumer traffic. It most often will be given by a supplier to a designer, though a designer might give a special seasonal discount to sell items such as Christmas decorations during the late summer.

Advertising Allowances

Some suppliers and manufacturers offer an interior designer a special *advertising allowance* if the designer uses their products in promotions and advertising. A small design firm in a midwestern city might use a carpet company's name in the design firm's advertising, perhaps as a special promotion before the holidays. The carpet company would then give the advertising allowance to the designer to pay for the advertising costs. It is not an extra discount on the purchase of the goods for clients.

Deep Discounting

A pricing strategy that is embraced by many manufacturers of commercial furniture, *deep discounting* represents an extremely large discount from the suggested retail price for very large orders. For example, a manufacturer might offer a deep discount of 75 percent off retail for a $5 million order of systems furniture for a large corporate installation. In many cases, these discounts are offered directly to the end user. The designer or dealer may be totally bypassed in the transaction or might receive a small percentage for servicing the job at the local level.

Many designers argue that deep discounting practices (sometimes called *buying the job*) have had a major negative impact on the design industry. They feel that these deep discounts, once enjoyed by a customer, will be expected for all purchases. They argue that deep discounts erode profit margins, hurting many firms that sell commercial goods. Other designers state that this pricing policy affects even those designers who sell goods but who rarely do larger jobs. These designers report that they often feel like "order takers" rather than designers.

Manufacturers counter by saying that deep discounts have become a part of the competitive nature of the industry. They state that commercial furniture

* Any interior design business that has a commercial store location is technically called a retailer, even if it does not actually sell merchandise at retail.

dealers have forgotten that commercial furnishings products are commodities and that deep discounting is a way of selling that commodity. The big profit margins and treatment of very large projects, especially systems projects, of the past are gone, say manufacturer's representatives. Many of these representatives feel that deep discounting is a pricing strategy that designers and sellers must understand and learn to accept.

Regardless of a designer's specialty or whether or not he or she sells goods, discounting techniques are an important part of the professional responsibility of interior designers.

Selling Prices

Most design firms operating retail showrooms sell merchandise to clients at the suggested retail price. However, since the designer can sell the merchandise at whatever price he or she determines, some firms mark up or add a dollar amount to their cost so that the resulting price is higher (or even lower) than the suggested retail price. This is a practice one finds in residential and commercial retail sales. In commercial design, it is more acceptable to use a selling price rather than the retail price, since the client commonly purchases at a price lower than retail for all the company's other needs.

The two methods of determining a selling price, other than using the retail price, are discounting from retail and marking up from cost. Both of these methods are used in commercial design. Residential designers who own their own interior design practice but who do not inventory furniture also may use one of these two methods.

Discounting from Retail

The designer can offer to the client any discount that he or she wishes. The selling price based on a discount from retail is calculated in the same way that the discount is calculated to find cost. For example, a designer has prepared a specification of products with a total retail price of \$6500. The designer has decided to offer the goods to the client at a 25 percent discount. The selling price, then, would be \$4875. This figure is determined in this way:

$$
\begin{aligned}
\text{Discount in dollars} &= \text{Retail price} \times \text{Discount percentage} \\
&= \$6500 \times 0.25 \\
&= \$1625 \\
\text{Selling price} &= \text{Retail price} - \text{Discount in dollars} \\
&= \$6500 - \$1625 \\
&= \$4875
\end{aligned}
$$

Markup from Cost

Although many in the design community use discounting from retail as a method for finding the selling price, many others use an approach that utilizes a markup from cost to arrive at the selling price. A *markup* is a percentage amount that is added to the cost of goods to get the selling price. Suggested retail is usually a 100 percent markup from the net price. The selling price, however, can be any markup percentage or dollar amount that the designer adds to the cost price.

When the designer knows the cost of the goods, it is necessary for him or her to multiply the cost by the percentage of markup. For example, an end table costs the designer \$250. With a 100 percent markup, the selling price would be \$500.

Markup in dollars = Cost price × Markup percentage
= 250 × 1.0
= $250
Selling price = Cost + Markup in dollars
= $250 + $250
= $500

If the same table were to be sold at only a 50 percent markup, the selling price would be $375.

Markup in dollars = 250 × .50
Markup in dollars = $125
Selling price = $250 + $125
= $375

There are two ways to find the markup percentage. In one you would find the markup percentage based on the retail price of the product. In the other, you would find the markup percentage based on the cost price of the product. For example, the retail price of a table lamp is $350, the cost price is $175, and the markup in dollars is $175. To find the markup percentage based on the retail price, use the following formula:

Markup percentage based on retail price = Markup in dollars ÷ Retail price
= $175 ÷ $350
= 50%

The formula for the markup percentage based on the cost price is as follows:

Markup percentage based on cost price = Markup in dollars ÷ Cost price
= $175 ÷ $175
= 100%

In practice, most retailers use the markup percentage based on the retail price as a method of determining the markup percentage, whereas most interior designers use the markup percentage based on the cost price for determining the markup percentage.

Prestige Pricing

Some goods, because of their quality, their reputation, the manufacturer, or other factors, have obtained a special place in the minds of some consumers. Thus, these goods can be priced at substantially higher prices than goods of a similar nature. "Prestige pricing involves setting a high price so that status-conscious consumers will be attracted to the product and buy it" (Berkowitz et al., 1994, p. 379). Products like a Ferrari, diamonds, and certain antiques are examples of items that are prestige priced.

Some interior designers or design firms charge higher rates for their services based on this same concept. This is discussed in Chapter 17 in the section, "Value-Oriented Method."

Gross Margin

As you will recall from Chapter 15, "Financial Accounting," the gross margin is the difference between revenue and cost. In relation to pricing, gross margin is the difference between selling price and cost. Many design firms use the gross margin or gross margin percentage to determine commission on sales. Since gross margin is also the amount of revenue left that will pay all overhead expenses, the gross margin is important for design firms that do not charge separately for design services. Among other things, the gross margin must cover the expense of design services. For example, the gross margin is $875 if we assume a net price for the designer's cost of \$2500 and a selling price of \$3375. The gross margin percentage would be 26 percent. To calculate the gross margin dollars for the example,

$$\begin{aligned}\text{Gross margin dollars} &= \text{Selling price} - \text{Cost price}\\ &= \$3375 - \$2500\\ &= \$875\end{aligned}$$

To calculate the gross margin percentage,

$$\begin{aligned}\text{Gross margin percentage} &= \text{Gross margin in dollars} \div \text{Selling price}\\ &= \$875 \div \$3375\\ &= 26 \text{ percent}\end{aligned}$$

Markdown from Retail

A term that is used in retail when discounts are taken for promotional sales of one kind or another is *markdown*. A markdown is calculated in the same way as a regular discount. Interior designers do not usually refer to the discount from suggested retail price to get their cost or the discount they will give to their clients as a markdown. They may, however, refer to a discount as a markdown if they mark down inventory during a clearance sale.

Pricing Review

The cost price to the interior designer could be retail, retail less a trade discount, or retail less a full discount that equals the net price or the wholesale price. It could also be retail minus a less than full discount given by the supplier, a cash discount after the cost amount was determined, or an amount after quantity discounts were taken from the retail price. The selling price to the client could be retail, suggested retail, list price, retail less a discount, or cost plus a markup. Specialty discounts that apply primarily to the designer from the supplier would include seasonal, advertising allowance, and deep discounts.

Deposits, Down Payments, and Retainers

These three terms are used by many designers interchangeably, although this should not be the case. They all have different legal definitions, even though they have similar meanings. This section will explain those differences.

Interior designers who sell merchandise to clients commonly are required by manufacturers and other suppliers to pay part or all of the price for goods and services up front, at the time the order is placed. This is also called pro forma credit (see Chapter 5). Of course, interior designers also establish credit with manufacturers and suppliers so that they do not have to pay anything at the time of the order.

Interior designers who have not established credit with suppliers require some prepayment from their clients. This money is then passed along to the suppliers. Prepayments from clients also are an important way for the interior designer to determine if the client is really serious about continuing with the project. Someone who is not really interested in the designer's ideas and concepts will be reluctant to pay a down payment or deposit for goods.

The term deposit has several legal definitions. For our purposes, *deposit* means money that is part of the purchase price, prepaid by the buyer as security in contracts for the sale of goods. It is common for designers to request that clients provide a deposit at the time the order is prepared in order to process orders. This is especially true if designers must special order goods for the client. The deposit is credited toward the full purchase price as the contract is fulfilled and is returned in accordance with the contract, if the contract is not fulfilled. Deposits generally do not have to be deposited in escrow accounts and do not have to be used solely for the client who has given the deposit. The term deposit must be used in contracts and agreements, and the designer should check with his or her accountant to be sure that this is true in his or her state.

A *down payment* is a portion of the total selling price paid at the time goods are ordered. Like the deposit, designers often use the down payment money as the prepayment that is required by the supplier. The designer may have to return all or part of the down payment if the client cancels the order.

The term down payment does create a problem for designers in several states. Some states require that money that is collected as a down payment be deposited in a separate escrow account and be used exclusively for the client from whom it has been collected. In other words, if your state requires this separation of funds, you are not able to use the down payment from Mr. Smith to order something for ABC Electronics. Check with your tax accountant or attorney to see if your state regulates the use of down payments.

A retainer is a payment to a professional to cover future services or advice by that professional. Retainers are not prepayments to be applied to the sale of goods but, rather, are for the contracting or retaining of design services or other professional services. It is common for people to "retain" his or her attorney or to put an attorney "on retainer." Interior designers and other design professionals in allied areas usually require that clients pay a retainer to show good faith. Designers can also create an open-ended design contract in which the designer is "on retainer" with a client. This means that the designer is more or less on call to the client whenever the client requires design services. The fee for those services already has been negotiated. Additional discussion about retainers for design services contracts can be found in Chapter 18.

Freight and FOB

Freight, also called shipping, is the cost and process involved in the delivery of goods from the manufacturer to the interior designer. Most frequently, freight is handled by trucking companies that are working as a transportation source for the manufacturer. Many manufacturers have their own trucks to handle the freighting of products from the factory to the interior designer's warehouse, but many use independent companies, especially for small orders. Goods are sometimes shipped by train, but this is generally done only for very large loads or when the manufacturer sends one of its trucks "piggyback."* Small items, like accessories, fabrics, and many wallcoverings, are shipped via a parcel delivery service, such as United Parcel.

The notation FOB is often found in the price list. *FOB*, according to the Uniform Commercial Code (UCC), means "free on board." There is usually a second notation, such as "factory" or "destination," following it. It also is referred to as "freight on board." Both interpretations mean the same thing. For our purposes, we will use "free on board," since that is the definition used by the UCC.

Free on board means that the manufacturer is responsible for the cost of loading the goods onto the truck or train. The cost of transporting the

* Piggyback means that the truck's trailer is loaded on a train flatcar and is shipped by train to the general destination. Then the trailer is removed from the train and is driven to the warehouse or the client's final destination.

goods to the destination are covered in the second part of the notation. This second notation indicates which party is responsible for the freight charges and when ownership of the goods changes hands. If, for example, a manufacturer's catalog says *FOB, Factory*, this means that the buyer assumes ownership or title of the goods when they are loaded on the truck at the factory. In this case, the interior designer pays all transportation costs and assumes all risks during transit. If the catalog has the notation *FOB, Destination*, then the manufacturer retains ownership of the goods and assumes all risks until they reach the destination. The cost of transportation is also paid by the manufacturer in this case.

Some manufacturers, as a means of reducing their own liability and as a convenience to their customers, may want to pass ownership of the goods to the buyer as they leave the factory loading dock but will pay the freight charges. In this case, the notation in the catalog reads something like *FOB, Factory—Freight Prepaid*. What this means is that the interior designer has ownership and responsibility for damages during transit, but the manufacturer pays the transportation charges to the destination.

A term found in some catalogs concerning shipping charges is *zone pricing*. In zone pricing, a manufacturer determines two or more shipping zones based on geographic distances from the factory. Anyone within each zone pays the same amount for shipping, each zone having a different rate. Shipping charges for locations within each zone are averaged. For example, perhaps a desk company that is located in California uses a zone price for shipping. Let us assume the zones have been divided similarly to the way time zones are divided. The cheapest shipping charges will be in the zone that includes California—the point of origin. As the zones progress toward the East, the shipping charges will be higher. With zone pricing for shipping, the seller pays the actual freight and bills the buyer for the zone average charge.

It is very important for the design firm to understand what the shipping policies are for the different manufacturers and suppliers it uses. Shipping charges can be quite costly for the interior designer, if the firm is located a great distance from the manufacturer's factory.

These charges are also legitimate charges that the client should pay if the goods are not sent prepaid by the supplier. Most interior designers charge clients "actual freight," which means that the designer will bill the client whatever the interior design firm is billed for the transportation of the goods to the designer's warehouse. Some firms add a small service charge to the actual freight charges to cover handling the payment and the necessity of dealing with the freight companies if there are any damages in transit.

Occasionally, firms will determine a "freight factor." This factor is obtained by finding the average and usual freight charges for all the kinds of goods and quantities of goods received FOB, Destination. This factor is added to the selling price or the cost price (as determined by the policies of the firm) of any goods ordered for the client that are shipped to the designer's warehouse. There are a few other terms related to the freight process, but these will be discussed in Chapters 30 and 31.

Delivery and Installation Charges

A project or sale is not complete until the merchandise has been delivered or installed at the client's job site. Chapter 31 includes a detailed discussion on the delivery and installation processes. Here, in this section, we will briefly cover basic information about charging for delivery and installation. For our purposes, *delivery* means taking tangible goods to the job site and placing them in their correct location. *Installation* means that some additional services are involved in the delivery process, such as assembly or construction of the products. For example, carpet must be installed to complete a job. An area rug, however, is delivered to the site. It is placed where the client wishes it to be placed.

Many retail stores do not charge for delivery, if the client's location is within a limited geographic area of the store's location or warehouse. Installation charges are added to the price of the actual goods, regardless of the job site location. Beyond this limited geographic area, most firms charge clients for the cost of delivering the merchandise. Delivery charges can be either a flat rate, determined by how far away the client is from the warehouse, like the zone shipping pricing discussed earlier, or an hourly charge. Hourly charges are often quoted as door-to-door. *Door-to-door* means that the client is charged from the time the delivery truck leaves the designer's warehouse loading dock to the time it leaves the client's location.

Delivery services include many activities that require the expense of adequately trained personnel as well as the cost of transporting the merchandise to the client from the designer's warehouse. Delivery services involve transportation of the merchandise to the client's location, uncartoning, simple assembly, and placing the merchandise in the desired location. Delivery services also include removal of any cartoning or packaging materials, and dusting or slight cleaning of the merchandise. As will be discussed further in Chapter 31, the delivery personnel or the designer should also explain to the client how to care for the merchandise.

Some items require installation. Wallpaper, carpet, drapery, and other architectural finishes need to be installed. A roll of carpet is not finished goods. Until the carpet has been installed, that item is not complete. The tradespeople-and craftspeople who do this work charge for their time and materials to complete the installation. As for architectural finishes, all these installation charges are the liability of the client, and the design firm must remember to pass them on in the pricing of the finishes. The charges to install architectural finishes might be higher for remodeling projects than for new construction projects. Designers must charge, not only for the installation of the new goods, but also for the removal of the old materials and for the preparation of the surfaces for the new goods.

Some furniture items also require installation or specialized assembly. A wall-hung bookcase unit in a home needs to be assembled and properly hung on the wall. Open-office systems furniture needs to be assembled by a trained installer.

Exactly what constitutes installation services depends on the products being installed. In general, the goods must be delivered to the job site, and some type of preparation of the surfaces or area is required prior to installation. In addition, specialized supplies are often required, such as tack strips for carpet, adhesives for wall coverings, and wall anchors for wall-hung furniture items. When the items are installed, some also require initial cleaning or dusting, and, as with the delivery of simpler items, maintenance and care instruction should be provided by the installer or the designer.

These installation charges are required to make a finished product and should be absorbed by the client and not the design firm. The designer must be familiar with the job site so that he or she can explain to the installer what services will be required. Neglecting to tell the carpet installer that the existing carpet is a glue-down installation (which will require removal of the carpet and preparation of the floor) will result in an improperly quoted price on the installation of the new carpet. In many design firms, this error in pricing comes out of the designer's commission. When the designer neglects to add these charges to the estimate and final pricing of the job, the client is under no legal obligation to pay for the work. However, the work must be completed and generally will be absorbed by the design firm or vendor. Thus, care in specification of all architectural finishes, custom cabinets, and goods requiring installation is very serious.

Sales and Use Taxes

It is very important for the interior designer and the design firm to fully understand the laws relating to the charging of sales tax on the goods and services they provide. Sales taxes that are not collected from the client will be collected by the state or city from the interior design firm.

In order to sell merchandise to clients, the design firm must obtain a resale license from the state sales tax agency (see Chapter 7). If cities, counties, or other similar entities also require the collection of sales tax, the business must also obtain similar permits from them. Permits also must be obtained if the business is located in other cities or states.* The resale tax certificate exempts the designer from paying the sales tax at the time that he or she orders the merchandise for the client. It is then the designer's responsibility to collect the sales tax from the client.

In many states, the design firm is required to pay a *use tax* on goods purchased by the design business. If the designer uses, stores, or consumes tangible goods for which tax has not been collected by the seller, the design firm must pay a use tax. Goods that the design firm purchased from out-of-state suppliers for use in the design firm's business would be subject to a use tax if those goods would normally have a sales tax charged against them if they were sold in the state in which the design firm was located. The liability to pay the use tax is on the buyer, not the seller. For example, ABC Interiors has purchased a computer from an out-of-state store for use in its accounting office. Since ABC Interiors is a business, it does not have to pay sales tax on the computer, but it does have to pay use tax. ABC Interiors must report and pay that use tax to the state tax agency. The use tax insures that the state will receive some tax moneys on the sale of goods used by the business.

There is much differentiation in the tax laws from state to state regarding when sales and use taxes must be collected. It is therefore very important for the firm to understand all the laws of the state in which they are doing business. What might be taxable for a design firm working out of an office in New York City and selling to a client in New York City might not be taxable in New Jersey.

The remainder of this section focuses on the sales tax—not use tax—that must be charged on purchases made by the designer firm's customers. Generally, the following guidelines are applicable anywhere, but in no way are they to be construed as absolutely true for all design practice areas.

As a rule, all items that are considered tangible personal property are taxable. *Tangible personal property* is any property that is movable, can be touched, or has physical existence. Some examples of personal property are sofas, desks, chairs, and draperies. Some processes such as labor, installation, delivery, and freight have various kinds of interpretations as to when sales tax must be collected and when they are exempt. A case in point is draperies. In many states, the labor to make the drapery and hang the finished product in the home is taxable, since it is considered a vital part of completing the

* The means for obtaining this license were discussed in Chapter 7.

item. However, the charges a drapery store might ask to rehang drapery after it has been cleaned are not taxable, since the labor of hanging the drapery is considered a service.

Items such as wall-to-wall carpeting, wall coverings, and installed mirrors, although they are, in essence, personal property (they are moved from the factory to the job site), are legally considered fixtures or sometimes capital improvements. A *fixture* is legally defined as "a thing which was once personal property, but has become attached to real property in such a way that it takes on the characteristics of real property and becomes a part of that real property" (Clarkson, 1983, p. 1203).* Sales tax must be charged if the installation of the product becomes part of the building or becomes permanently affixed to the structure in such a way as to make it difficult or impossible to remove it without damaging the structure. Depending on the answer to this analysis and the state laws that prevail, tax may or may not have to be charged. In many instances, sales tax is charged on the material and supplies needed to manufacture the finished goods, but not the labor. In some states, as in the drapery example, if the labor to manufacture and install the capital goods is necessary to make the "finished goods," then sales tax must also be charged on the labor.

Certain circumstances (for example, if the freight and delivery charge can be considered part of making the finished goods) require that sales tax be charged on freight and delivery. However, in most cases, these charges are either considered a service and generally are not taxable or are considered part of doing business and are calculated into the price of the goods. When freight and delivery charges are calculated into the price of the goods, sales tax technically can be calculated and must be paid to the state or city revenue office. It is important, as with all sales tax collection policies, for the design firm to obtain information from the firm's accountant or the state and city revenue departments regarding the requirements for charging sales tax in such situations.

In general, design fees, such as hourly fees that do not relate to specific purchases of goods, are exempt from sales tax. If, however, the design fee is added to the selling price of some goods, then the total price is taxable. For example, if the designer added a 25 percent charge for design services to the selling price of $5000 for office furniture, the taxable amount would be $6250—$5000 for the tangible goods and $1250 for the design fee. If the design fee was a separate line item, then sales tax would only be charged on the tangible goods.

The design firm is responsible for recording sales and use taxes and paying the appropriate amounts to the state tax agency. The firm must also keep complete records of items that are exempt from taxes. The burden of knowing which items are taxable and which items are not wherever the design firm does business is on the design firm. State tax auditors have the authority to seize the moneys and/or property of the business if they discover that the business has not submitted the proper amount of sales and use taxes.

The Role of the Designer/Specifier

The preceding discussion focused on how a designer who sells goods to the client prices those goods. Many designers do not sell goods to the client. These designers, often called designers/specifiers, prepare the plans and specifications for

* Copyright West Publishing Co.

residential and/or commercial projects but do not wish to involve themselves in actually selling merchandise. Interior designers who work in architectural offices are another group of designers who infrequently involve themselves in the direct selling of merchandise to clients. Designer/specifiers, however, are responsible for many of the same activities that those who do sell products are responsible for.

There are many responsibilities related to specifying a project, whether the designer will be directly selling the merchandise or not. Of these activities, three are of special concern to the designer who does not sell merchandise to clients: (1) estimating a project budget, (2) preparing the purchasing specifications, and (3) assisting the client in evaluating and selecting suppliers.

Estimating a Project Budget

Even though the designer/specifier is not selling merchandise to the client, the client naturally needs to have some idea of what the project will cost. However, the actual cost of the project cannot be known until the client either begins purchasing from suppliers or the bid process has been completed. Designer/specifiers who work with residential clients most often budget or price a project based on the retail prices of the specified goods. Since it is possible for the client to obtain some of the specified goods "on sale" or at a discount from a seller, the budgeted price will almost always be slightly higher than what the client actually pays for the completed project. Of course, if the client delays purchasing any of the items, the prices may be higher than the budgeted amounts.

When a designer/specifier works with a commercial client, the project will probably go out for competitive bidding. *Competitive bidding* is a process whereby several, perhaps dozens of, vendors, provide prices for the project to the client. The final cost of the project to the client is not known until the bidding process is over. This results in a more difficult budgeting situation for the designer/specifier and the client. The designer cannot guarantee a firm price, since he or she is not selling the merchandise. All that can be provided is a "best guess" based on methods such as: (1) a retail basis with estimates as to potential discounts, (2) a cost price plus percentage markup, or (3) a cost price plus a predetermined high-low negotiated markup. The first two are self-explanatory. The third budgeting option needs a bit of explanation. Occasionally, a bid is set up so that the sellers who are providing prices must agree to only a specified markup on their cost. This condition is clearly indicated in the bid documents that the sellers obtain at the onset of the bid. Sellers must carefully consider if this negotiated or set markup is sufficient to justify providing a bid on the project. The budget is then closer to the actual purchase price, since the costs of the products are fairly well known by the designer.

Preparing Purchasing Specifications

Purchasing specifications can be as simple as what many designers call an equipment list or as complex as formal competitive bidding documents. A comprehensive equipment list provides quantities, descriptions, manufacturers' names, and a budgeted unit price (see Figure 19-1). This equipment list is then used by the client when he or she is shopping in order to purchase the necessary goods. Along with the equipment list, the designer often also provides the names and addresses of recommended sellers, installers, and craftspeople who can meet the demands of the designer and the client in completing the project.

When a formal bid is used to purchase goods and services, the designer is responsible for preparing the specifications for all of the furniture, furnishings, and equipment (FF&E). Along with these specifications, additional documentation is included that clarifies the responsibilities of the sellers, installers, and

Specification list for:
Ralph Smithson
Job Number 20547

Quantity	Manufacturer	Prod. No.	Description	Unit price	Extend price
2	B&B Italia	D277B	Diesis Sofa Fabric: COM Maharam 451801090 Mohair Color: 090 Magenta	$6500	$13,000
2	Cartwright	20/123	Club chair Fabric: Black Leather Finish: Ebony	3165	6330
2	Bernhardt	2BB 36/914	End table Finish: Frame—Black Top: Maple	2009	4018
1	Excel Custom		Custom Coffee Table 60" x 60" × 18" Per drawings Finish: Marble	4500	4500
2	Atherton	L9968	Table Lamp Finish: Coffee	1295	2590
1	Amazing Custom Cabinets		Custom Entertainment Unit Built to drawings (see attached) Finish: Maple and Ebony per drawings	27,300	27,300
		Total for Product			$57,738
		Freight and Delivery			4,619
		Sales Tax			3,975
		Total			$66,332

FIGURE 19-1. A comprehensive equipment list that is used to prepare a project specification.

tradespeople who are awarded the bids, along with information about many other aspects concerning the completion of the project by the winning bidders. An explanation of the bid process and the documentation that must be included in a formal bid are discussed in Chapter 29.

Assisting the Client with the Evaluation and Selection of Sellers

As mentioned in the preceding section, even when the designer prepares a simple equipment list, he or she commonly makes recommendations as to potential sellers and suppliers of the merchandise and/or installation of products. One might argue that the responsibility of assisting the client with evaluating and selecting sellers is more critical if formal bid documents are necessary. The bidding process allows any seller who feels that he or she is capable of supplying the specified merchandise to provide a bid to the client. But not all sellers are really able to fulfill the coordination and requirements of bids, especially for major projects. For example, although J. D. Furniture Store, which is a small retailer, may wish to bid on a project like a major hotel installation, the designer and client must determine whether or not J. D. Furniture Store really is capable of ordering, delivering, and installing the merchandise called for in the bid.

In some bids, the exact specification of merchandise is left a little vague, so the client and the designer must evaluate alternative merchandise. Frequently, multiple sellers of office systems furniture are involved in providing bids. The designer must assist the client in determining if the products from several different manufacturers are sufficiently the same as the product named in the bid specification. Although the example is for office systems, the designer may have to provide this same type of assistance for every single product specified.

One of the major concerns of the designer who does not sell merchandise to clients is that clients may purchase different merchandise from what has been specified. The designer is concerned about proper quality and suitability for the intended purpose when the client purchases on his or her own. To limit liability, the designer must include clauses in the design contract and the purchase specification regarding this issue. This was discussed more fully in Chapter 18.

Federal Laws and Pricing Practices

The Federal Trade Commission was established by the federal government to prevent unfair or deceptive competition or practices between businesses. One of the most important pieces of legislation that the commission enforces is the Robinson-Patman Act. This legislation makes it illegal for a merchant to charge various merchants different prices for the same goods. "If goods of similar grade and quality were sold at different prices, and these differences could not be justified by differences in production and distribution costs, the practice would violate the Robinson-Patman Act" (Jentz et al., 1987, p. 778).* For example, if a manufacturer were selling the same quantity of product to two different design firms, it would have to offer the goods at the same price to both. However, if one firm had a record of purchasing a larger quantity of goods or stocking a quantity of goods, then the manufacturer could sell the goods at different prices to each designer. However, price discrimination only affects sales between merchants. A merchant has the legal right to sell to the consumer at any price that he or she determines. If Wendy Jones Interiors decided to sell a Knoll chair to Mrs. Smith for $1000 and the same chair to Mr. Peters for $750, the designer would not be in violation of any laws, as long as Smith and Peters were the end users.

Another important responsibility of the Federal Trade Commission relates to those practices by businesses that limit competition. The Sherman Act prohibits practices by which businesses make agreements in restraint of trade or engage in price-fixing. An example of restraint of trade is when two or more businesses have agreed not to sell in each other's territory or to each other's customers. This agreement limits the consumer's options. Price-fixing occurs when two or more businesses agree to sell the same goods to the consumer at the same price. This relates directly back to the concept of suggested retail. At one time, certain consumer goods were sold at the same price, no matter where someone went to purchase them. These prices were dictated by the manufacturers. Some people even referred to these goods as "fair trade goods." However, enforcement of the Sherman Act negated these "fair trade" pricing polices. Today, all goods sold to the consumer are sold at whatever price any merchant that carries the goods determines to sell them. This means that a suggested retail price by the manufacturer is just that—suggested. The designer can sell the goods at any price that he or she determines—higher or lower than the suggested retail price. If the manufacturer insists that the designer sell the goods to the consumer at a particular price, then the manufacturer is in violation of the Sherman Act.

There are several other pieces of legislation affecting businesses that prevent unlawful business practices; these are related to such things as monopolies, mergers, and labor relations. The ones already discussed, however, have the most relevance to an interior design practice.

Summary

The competition of the marketplace and the demands of the consumer—whether residential or commercial—have forced designers to review critically their pricing policies and strategies. The days of selling every item at more than 100 percent markup are gone for all but a small number of designers. Deep discounting practices have certainly cut into personal commissions and business revenues, forcing many designers and design firms out of the industry.

It is very important for interior designers to understand the many ways in which they can price the goods and services that they sell to their clients. The pricing terminology discussed in this chapter covers the more commonly used terms for the sale and cost price of the goods that the designer might sell. The chapter also covered the terminology related to down payments and deposits, and the shipping, delivery, and installation charges for getting goods to the client. In addition, a brief discussion of the applicability of sales and use taxes was provided.

The last chapter in this part will discuss the Uniform Commercial Code (UCC). The UCC deals with laws pertaining to the sale of goods, real estate, and regulations of the banking industry. The chapter will only provide a background into sales law as it pertains to the interior design industry.

REFERENCES

Alderman, Robert L. 1997. *How To Prosper as an Interior Designer*. New York: John Wiley.

American Society of Interior Designers. "Design Fees and Profits." *ASID Professional Designer.* September/October 1998.

Berkowitz, Eric N., Roger A. Kerin, Steven W. Hartley, and William Rudelius. 1994. *Marketing*, 4th ed. Burr Ridge, IL: Richard D. Irwin.

Black, Henry Campbell. (with Joseph R. Nolan and Jacqueline M. Nolan-Haley). 1990. *Black's Law Dictionary*, 6th ed. St. Paul, MN: West Publishing.

Brown, Gordon W., and Paul A. Sukys. 1997. *Business Law*, 9th ed. New York: Glencoe.

Caplan, Suzanne. 2000. *Finance and Accounting.* Holbrook, MA: Adams Media.

Clarkson, Kenneth W., Roger LeRoy Miller, and Gaylord A. Jentz. 1983. *West's Business Law, Text and Cases*, 2d ed. St. Paul, MN: West Publishing.

Czinkota, Michael R., Masaaki Kotabe, and David Mercer. 1997. *Marketing Management: Texts and Cases.* Cambridge, MA: Blackwell Publishers.

Haviland, David, editor. 1994. *The Architect's Handbook of Professional Practice, Student Edition*. Washington, DC: AIA Press.

Jentz, Gaylord A., Kenneth W. Clarkson, and Roger LeRoy Miller. 1987. *West's Business Law—Alternate UCC Comprehensive Edition*, 3d ed. St. Paul, MN: West Publishing.

McCarthy, E. Jerome. 1981. *Basic Marketing*, 7th ed. Homewood, Ill.: Richard D. Irwin.

McCarthy, E. Jerome, and William D. Perreault, Jr. 1993. *Basic Marketing*, 11th ed. Homewood, IL: Richard D. Irwin.

Morgan, Jim. 1998. *Management for the Small Firm.* New York: Watson-Guptill.

Quinn, Thomas M. 1999. *Quinn's Uniform Commercial Code Commentary and Law Digest*, 2nd ed. St. Paul, MN: West Group.

———. 1991. *Quinn's Uniform Commercial Code Commentary and Law Digest.* Boston, MA: Warren, Gorham and Lamont.

Siegel, Harry (with Alan M. Siegel). 1982. *A Guide to Business Principles and Practices for Interior Designers*, rev. ed. New York: Watson-Guptill.

Siropolis, Nicholas C. 1990. *Small Business Management*, 4th ed. Boston, MA: Houghton Mifflin.

Terry, John V. 1990. *Dictionary for Business and Finance*, 2nd ed. Fayetteville, AK: University of Arkansas Press.

Thompson, Jo Anne Asher, ed. 1992. *ASID Professional Practice Manual.* New York: Watson-Guptill.

Chapter 20

The Sale of Goods and the Uniform Commercial Code

When you buy goods from a store, do you know what your rights are as a purchaser of those goods, should you have a problem with one of them? What if you bought an item at a yard sale? As an interior designer, are you aware of the laws that affect your purchases from suppliers and manufacturers? Do you have any idea of what the law states about the ability of your client to refuse delivery of goods or to cancel an order? These questions and hundreds of others are regulated by common law, along with a uniform set of regulations concerning the law of sales called the Uniform Commercial Code (UCC).

In the UCC, the sale of goods involves the transfer of title for goods from one party to another. The offer to sell goods and the acceptance to buy those goods creates a contract. The nature of a sales contract has many differences from a contract for services and from many other contracts. The UCC is the primary authority that governs the transfer of title when goods are sold. This transfer of title is covered within the law of sales. The law of sales, as represented by Article 2 of the UCC, governs the sale of goods (not services), real property (real estate), or intangible property (such as stocks). These laws affect sales between merchants, between merchants and consumers, and between consumers and consumers—in other words, all sales transactions involving goods.

For the majority of the members of the interior design profession, selling and ordering goods for clients is an everyday occurrence, yet few have ever heard of the Uniform Commercial Code. It seems that most designers learn about the intricacies of selling and buying goods from experience. This may be fine if the reader is purchasing a loaf of bread from the grocery store. However, designers who own an interior design practice and make the sale of merchandise their major source of income need more knowledge about the rights and responsibilities involved in ordering and selling goods.

This chapter is not meant to be an in-depth discussion of the UCC. The section of the UCC that deals with sales is quite extensive. We will, however, attempt to provide some basic understanding regarding how the UCC affects the daily work of the interior designer who engages in the sale of goods.

History

Most laws related to commercial business activity, including interior design, come from the individual states. During the early years of this country, this fact often resulted in the passage of confusing and conflicting laws. As the nation's commercial business activity became more complex, the problems became more acute.

In the late 1800s, the National Conference of Commissioners on Uniform State Laws was established to create uniform statutes related to business activities. These statutes, revised over the next 55 years, helped to illuminate many of the problems of commercial business. Yet there remained instances in which these uniform statutes overlapped. Work was begun in 1945 to revise all the statutes into one uniform document. In 1957, after much work, the Uniform Commercial Code was completed (Stone, 1975, p. 2).

The purpose of the code is to help "state legal relationships of the parties in modern commercial transactions. The Code is designed to help determine the intentions of the parties to a commercial contract and to give force and effect to their agreement" (Clarkson et al., 1983, p. 9).

The code consists of nine articles:

1. General provisions
2. Sales
3. Commercial paper
4. Bank deposits and collections
5. Letters of credit
6. Bulk transfers
7. Documents of title
8. Investment securities
9. Secured transactions

This chapter will be limited to a discussion of sections of Article 2.

The UCC has been adopted by all states except Louisiana. This state has only adopted certain sections of the code and has state laws to cover other issues. However, according to legal texts, for practical purposes, the reader may assume that all states have adopted these laws. Since 1958, certain sections of the code have been revised to meet current needs and to refine the statutes. The following discussion is based on the 1989 revision, as amended up to 1994.

Definitions

The interpretation of the statutes stated in Article 2 vary, depending on whether the buyer of goods is an end user (consumer) or a merchant. It is therefore necessary to define some common terms as they relate to the code. Although there are many definitions in the code, the main ones that we wish to look at here are those for goods, sale, seller, merchant, buyer, and price.

Goods (Section 2-105) are any items that are tangible, that is, have physical existence and can be moved. Furniture and accessories are tangible goods. The sale of tangible goods is covered by the UCC. Items such as carpet, wall coverings, and window treatments are goods, because they have physical existence. When these items are permanently attached to a home or a building, they are generally considered real property. Or are they? The sale of the merchandise itself from the supplier to the designer and the designer to the client would be covered by the UCC, since the goods do not become real property until they are "permanently" attached to the home or office. If the client later wants to remove these goods from his or her home or office and sell them, or even sell the building with the merchandise intact, the sale would be governed by real estate law.

A *sale* (Section 2-106) occurs when the seller transfers title or ownership of the goods to a buyer and the buyer has provided some consideration to the seller. Whenever the designer agrees in good faith to sell a piece of furniture to a client for some amount of money and the client takes delivery of the furniture and sends the designer a check for the agreed-upon price, a sale has occurred. There are, however, some special considerations with regard to when "ownership" actually occurs. This will be discussed later in the chapter.

A *seller* (Section 2-103) is anyone who sells goods or contracts to sell goods. The interior designer, who sells goods to clients, is considered a seller. A manufacturer who sells goods to an interior designer also is considered a seller. However, both the interior designer and the manufacturer are also considered "merchants."

A *merchant* (Section 2-104) is anyone who is involved with the buying and/or selling of the kinds of goods with which he or she is dealing. In other words, "a person is a merchant when that person, acting in a mercantile capacity, possesses or uses an expertise specifically related to the goods being sold" (Jentz et al., 1987, p. 244). Thus, although the interior designer who sells a personally owned stereo to a friend is a seller, if he or she sells a chair to that same friend and that sale occurs through the business, the designer is now considered a merchant.

Many interior designers who sell goods never have a showroom, warehouse, or installation crew who are employees of the firm. Any interior designer, however, who purchases goods, whether or not through a firm's inventory account, and resells them to a client so that the purchase and the resale "pass through" the design firm's books, is a merchant.

A person becomes a *buyer* (Section 2-103) when he or she contracts to purchase or purchases some good. A buyer also is someone who buys from someone who is in the business of selling goods. A client who is purchasing a sofa from an interior designer is a buyer. Is the interior designer a buyer when he or she purchases the sofa for the client? Yes, and the designer is protected by the same rights as the end user, as long as the purchase is from a seller whose business it is to sell the sofa.

Finally, *price* (Section 2-304) can be any kind of payment from a buyer to a seller, including money, goods, services, or real property. Therefore it is possible, for example, for a client to offer to trade his or her own professional services as the price of a sofa.

The Sales Contract

For the most part, the statutes related to the sale of goods as covered by the UCC generally follow the principles of contract law. This means that an offer to sell something must be made, an acceptance to buy the goods must occur, and proper consideration must be exchanged from buyer to seller. However, there are some differences. This section will look at how "offer," "acceptance," and "consideration" occur in sales law.

As discussed in Chapter 18, the Statute of Frauds contains a provision that the sale of goods of over $500 must be in writing to be enforceable. This provision is contained within Section 2-201(1). Although a written contract for the sale of goods does not mean that the designer will force the client to take the goods, it does give the designer the legal right to sue for payment, if he or she so chooses.

As far as the form of the contract is concerned, Section 2-204 states, "A contract for the sale of goods may be made in any manner sufficient to show agreement, including conduct by both parties which recognizes the existence of such a contract" (Quinn, 1991, p.2/112). The contract might be made in writing through the mails, by fax, or even by E-mail or phone if the acceptance to the order is approved in a reasonable manner. The date, description of what is being sold, price, and signature by the person being charged—items discussed in Chapter 18 on contracts for services—are handled somewhat differently from a contract for the sale of goods. Those differences are discussed throughout this chapter.

Offer (Sections 2-204, 2-205, 2-206, 2-305, 2-308, and 2-311)

Normally, a contract exists when an offer is followed by an acceptance. In sales law, however, the nature of offers and acceptances renders the point at which a contract exists more inexact. Because offers and acceptances in sales contracts are exchanged verbally, through the mail, electronically by e-mail and faxes, and by the behavior of the buyer and seller, it is more difficult to determine exactly when a contract exists. To assist with this problem, the UCC in Section 2-204 states that a contract exists when there is sufficient agreement to an offer so that a contract has been formed. This agreement may be verbal, written, or by the actions of the parties. For example, the price for a sofa in a catalog is an offer. When the designer sends a purchase order for this sofa, a contract is formed.

In contract law, the terms of the offer and the acceptance must be clearly stated before the contract can be effective. Because of the unusual circumstances that surround offers and acceptances in sales law, the UCC allows for the offer to be valid even if one or more terms of the agreement are not stated, provided that the parties intend to go through with the contract and the courts can agree that a contract is intended and can determine a remedy for breach of contract.

Open-Terms Provisions—An Introduction

If the designer forgets to put all pertinent information on the purchase order that will be sent to a supplier, is the contract effective? There are provisions that allow the contract to be valid even when some of the terms of the contract are indefinite. Terms include quantity, description, part number, delivery location, payment, and price. In general, if the terms are incomplete, it is likely that the contract will be valid, as long as it can be shown that both parties intend to fulfill the contract. However, the more terms there are that are left incomplete, the more difficult it will be for the courts to determine if the contract is valid. For example, should a designer order some tables and all the terms needed in the purchase order are present except the finish of the wood, the order would still be valid. However, if the quantity is missing, the order is usually considered invalid, since the courts cannot determine the full value of the contract in order to establish a remedy. If the parties intend for a contract to exist, then one does exist, even if some of the information is missing.

Open-Price Term

If the price is missing, the other party can cancel the offer or determine a reasonable price. The question here is whether the two parties intend to conclude an agreement in "good faith." For example, should ABC Design Company agree to furnish drapery tiebacks for a client but forget to provide a price for those tiebacks, the client can either set a reasonable price for the items or cancel the order for the tiebacks. It is, obviously, not a good idea to leave the price off a purchase order to a supplier or to the client.

The reasonable price concept most often is only reasonable to the person who is setting the price. The interior designer should always be the person who sets the price to the client and who knows what the price will be from the supplier before placing an actual order. Any form or manner in which the interior designer gets a quotation from a supplier should clearly indicate it is just that—a request for quotation and not an order. In this way, the designer is prevented from inadvertently ordering goods at a price that is higher than what the client is willing to pay before the client agrees to even purchase the goods.

Open-Payment Term

A third open term that is related to offers is an open-payment term. If a payment due date for the goods has not been specified, the UCC stipulates that payment is due upon delivery to the buyer or at the time of "receipt of goods." The buyer receives the goods when he or she takes physical possession of the goods. Additionally, if payment terms have not been specified, the payment must be in cash, check, or agreed-upon credit. When the designer (or supplier) has included a phrase such as, "Payment due within 10 days of receipt of invoice," the designer has effectively given the buyer ten days of credit at no cost.

For the client, receipt of goods takes place when the goods are delivered to his or her home or office or when the client leaves the designer's place of business with the goods. According to subsections 2-310 (b and c), receipt of goods shipped from a manufacturer to the designer occurs when the goods are placed in the hands of the carrier. This is the reason that invoices often arrive prior to the goods. However, this means that payment is due before the goods can be inspected. All buyers have the right to inspect the goods before they make payment. These same subsections provide for that right of inspection, but the inspection must be done promptly. If the goods are not as ordered, the seller must be notified immediately if the buyer does not want to be bound to pay.

Open-Delivery Term

If the location for the delivery has been omitted, it is customary that delivery be made at the seller's business location. This could be quite costly to the designer in the supplier/designer relationship, since it would be the designer's responsibility to pick up the goods from the seller. It is unlikely that major manufacturers of goods would not call to check with the designer as to a delivery location. However, the manufacturer is not obligated to do so if the delivery location has been omitted from the order.

Section 2-307 states that delivery and payment are due at one time for all the items being sold, unless provisions in the agreement or "circumstances" allow for delivery and payment in lots.* The designer should have a term on the purchase order that informs the supplier as to whether shipment of less than the full order is acceptable.

The designer needs to protect himself or herself concerning partial deliveries to the client as well. For large-sized projects involving multiple items, it is not unusual for the client to want the goods delivered as soon as they arrive. The designer usually prefers to deliver the goods to the client promptly in order to

* *In lots* means partial shipments.

keep cash flow operating smoothly. However, in order to receive payments for goods delivered in lots rather than as a whole, a term in the sales contract must be provided that would notify the buyer of this fact. When several deliveries are made to the client to complete one order, without a written term in the contract, payment is not required until the entire order has been delivered.

The Firm Offer

Normally, in contract law, an offer to sell or buy goods has a time limit. That time limit can be set by the offeror (seller). If the offer is not in writing or is not accompanied with payment by the offeree (buyer), the offer can be revoked by the seller at any time before the buyer can accept. However, in sales law, special provisions are made when the seller is a merchant, and they apply whether the buyer is a merchant or an end user. If the merchant makes an offer in writing, whether or not consideration has been given by the buyer, or a time limit to the offer has been set, the merchant cannot revoke the offer either during the time limit or for a reasonable length of time. In such a situation, a *firm offer* has been made. For example, Mary Smith signs a written contract to sell $30,000 of furniture to Susan Rose, but Rose does not sign the agreement and does not provide any down payment. Ten days later, Smith realizes that she made an error in her calculations. If Rose accepts the contract within a reasonable length of time, Smith will lose $2000, since she used a net price list to discount some of the goods. Legally, Smith cannot revoke the offer, since it was a "firm offer" in writing and was signed by her.

The points in this discussion are important to the interior design practice. They show the value of good preparation of paperwork of the specification list, the contract for the client, and purchase orders. Designer omissions can cost time and money. They can even result in lawsuits against the designer.

Acceptance: Sections 2-206 and 2-207

In most situations, the seller establishes the way in which an acceptance can be made. If acceptance is not made in the manner specified, the acceptance can be rejected or considered a counteroffer. However, the law generally allows the acceptance to be valid if it is received within the time limit set, even if it is by a different method of acceptance. Usually the seller wants an oral acceptance, followed by a signed acceptance of the sales proposal. When the supplier sends or otherwise indicates an acceptance to the merchant to buy (receipt of the designer's purchase order), a sales contract has been formed. In general, the acceptance should mirror the offer; that is, if the offer was made via a purchase order sent through the mail, the acceptance should be mailed. If the order was placed via fax, than the acceptance should be faxed, and so on. Many designers still insist on telephone orders, although this is not advisable. For example, Ralph Brown telephoned in an order for mini blinds and did not follow up with a written confirmation. When the blinds were ready for installation, Brown found that they were the wrong size. The size of the length had been made the size of the width, and vice versa. Brown claimed that the blinds company had made the mistake. The blinds company played a tape recording of the telephone order. It was clear that Brown had given the dimensions incorrectly. He had to pay for the blinds and reorder them, using the correct sizes.

In the designer/end user relationship, there are usually few problems or questions related to the existence of the contract. This is because, in everyday practice, the designer prepares a confirmation proposal that states who is being charged; lists the quantities, descriptions, and prices of the items being sold; lists the terms of sale, such as when payment is due; and requires the signature of the client on the confirmation. Assuming price is not an issue, rarely does the client make acceptance in any way other than by signing the confirmation.

A key to the agreement between designer and client is the time limit of the offer and whether or not the client has signed the agreement. If the designer's proposal states that the offer is good only for ten days (or some other time limit), the client must respond within that ten-day period; if he or she does not, the designer does not legally have to honor the original offer. If there is no time limit stated, the client has a "reasonable length of time" to respond. For example, a month after receiving the proposal, the client signs and returns the confirmation. However, the price of the goods to the designer has increased during that time. The designer may very well be expected to sell the goods at the quoted price, thus lowering his or her profit margin. Thus, it is important that all offers to sell goods to clients have stated on the confirmation a time limit for acceptance.

In contract law, a contract exists only if all the terms of the offer are exactly matched by the acceptance. Any differences constitute a counteroffer. In sales law, it is not uncommon among merchants for the terms on the purchase order and the terms of the acknowledgment to contain some differences. In interior design practices, the quantity, description, and price commonly match. Terms such as ship date and general terms of the sale often vary. The UCC allows for a contract to be formed when the conditions of the purchase order and the acknowledgment are different, as long as the offeree's response indicates a definite acceptance of the original terms of the offer and there are no conditional terms in the offer or acceptance. For example, designer A sends a purchase order to manufacturer B for some custom-made bedspreads. The purchase order is prepared following the instructions in the catalog. The acknowledgment comes back from B with the statement, "On condition that a 50 percent deposit be submitted within ten days of receipt of acknowledgment. No work will be started until deposit is received." If this term is not stated in the catalog, no contract exists, unless the buyer agrees, because the seller has added a condition to the terms of the offer.

When the differences in terms are minor and neither party objects to the differences, a contract has been formed. If the offer and acceptance are made over the phone, the printed confirmation and acknowledgments are proposals to the oral contract, and, again, a contract has been formed, as long as no objections are made and the differences are minor.

What all this means to the designer is that he or she not only must carefully prepare the terms of sale on his or her purchase order but also must be familiar with the terms and conditions of sale from all the suppliers. What is ordered is usually not the problem in interior design orders. The price, ship dates, warranties, and payment terms are more often the issue. Chapter 30 contains an example of the terms and conditions on the back of a firm's sales order (see Figure 30-3).

Should the acknowledgment contain discrepancies with regard to quantities, descriptions, and so on, it is important for the designer to make prompt written notification of the errors to the supplier. There are literally only a few days to generally a maximum of ten days to catch and correct any changes in an order. Failure to do so means acceptance of the acknowledgment, hence a contract, and the designer then "owns" the merchandise, even if the error has been made by the supplier.

If there are material differences between the designer's purchase order terms and a supplier's acknowledgment terms, the designer may be protected by the UCC constraints against material differences. Material differences means that there are substantial or essential changes to the original. However, to be protected, the designer is encouraged to object in writing to any terms that are different from his or her own.

Facsimile (Fax) Agreements

As far as the UCC is concerned, an issuance of a faxed (facsimile) order from the interior designer and a mirrored faxed acknowledgment from the supplier create a contract for the order of the goods. There are two cautions when faxes are used for ordering. The first is that the designer should set his or her fax machine to print a report that shows that the fax was received by the vendor. This is a "machine talking to a machine" report (see Figure 27-3). A report of this kind is especially important when time is of the essence for an order. For the small design firm, this report helps the owner know that the supplier has received the fax and that it has not gone to a wrong party or is in cyberspace somewhere.

For a fax, the normal terms and conditions of sale, which are generally on the back of the sales order to a client or perhaps on the back of the acknowledgment from the supplier, are generally not faxed. A statement to the effect, "The product is sold subject to the terms and conditions of sale of goods by 'the design firm' which are available for review upon request," (Quinn, 1999, p.2/201), is necessary to protect the designer and suppliers who use faxes for acknowledgment of orders. It is the seller's responsibility to make sure that the buyer knows the terms and conditions of the sale, whether these terms are printed in a price list, on the sales agreement, or acknowledgment, or are covered by a clause such as the above for a fax.

Consideration: Section 2-304

In general, the UCC does not differ with the general contract law precept that consideration must be part of the acceptance. Between designer and client, the consideration is primarily a deposit that is paid when the agreement, which states that the client will pay full value at a later time, is signed. Between designer and supplier, consideration is generally the good faith credit that the supplier affords to the designer, knowing that the designer will pay the supplier after the goods have been shipped.

There are strict rules governing consideration when the buyer or seller attempts to modify the contract. For example, after the designer sends the purchase order to the supplier and the supplier acknowledges the order to the designer but merchandise has not been shipped yet, the supplier informs the designer that the price will go up 10 percent as a result of an increase in materials price. The designer subsequently notifies the supplier that he or she accepts the increase. Later, the designer changes his or her mind and says that he or she will only pay the original price. Whether or not the designer accepts the increase orally or in writing, he or she is bound by the new price. This is true as long as it can be shown by the supplier that the change in price is due to a reason such as a change in availability of materials to manufacture the finished goods, causing an increase in price for the finished goods. If the supplier makes a mistake in his or her pricing, the modification of the contract is invalid.

Once the terms and conditions are agreed to by the designer and the supplier, later modifications agreed to are binding, if they are reasonable as a result of something that is beyond the control of the party who is asking for the modifications. If the supplier later tells the designer that the price will be higher and the designer does not agree, the contract is revoked. If the original or modified contract must meet the statute of frauds or has a condition that changes must be in writing, these changes must be in writing to be valid.

Statute of Frauds

Although the Statute of Frauds (Section 2-201) is very specific that a contract for the sale of goods over $500 must be in writing to be valid, there are certain very specific exceptions.*

First, between merchants, an oral agreement is valid if one party sends the other party a signed confirmation outlining the details of the agreement. The receiving merchant has ten days to respond in writing to any conditions or content of the offer to which he or she does not agree. Failure to respond within the ten days forms a valid contract.

Second, an oral contract for the special manufacture of goods that are not suitable for anyone else and whose manufacture has substantially been started, forms a contract. For example, Mary Jones Designs places a telephone order to Smith's Drapery Company for the manufacture of ten different-sized arched mini blinds at a price of over $1800. A month later, after production has been started but not finished, the client cancels the order and Jones calls to cancel the order. If it is unlikely that the blinds can be sold to another client of Smith's Drapery Company, Mary Jones Designs is liable. It is for this reason that designers include in the terms of their confirmations a statement that a restocking charge, say at least 25–50 percent, is charged for any order the client cancels.

Third, if one party to the contract admits in court or in legal proceedings that a contract does exist, then an oral contract is binding for what was admitted. For example, Robert Class places a telephone order for 50 yards of Wilton weave carpet from an English mill. The value of the carpet is $6000. The mill ships 500 yards. Class refuses the shipment, and the mill sues. Class admits in court that he ordered 50 yards of carpet. Since Class admits that an oral contract did exist, he would be liable to pay for the 50 yards of carpet but not the extra yardage.

Finally, an oral agreement is enforceable up to the amount of payment made and accepted or the amount of goods delivered and accepted. For example, if a designer makes a verbal contract to order mini blinds for a client and the client provides the designer with a deposit, the client is liable to pay for and accept the quantity of blinds that the deposit covers. If the designer delivers a portion of the order for the blinds, the client is also liable for the value of the blinds that are delivered.

Far too many designers agree to sell goods to clients and/or order goods for clients without a written contract. The designer who places orders for clients without having the client sign a confirmation may not have legal recourse if the client later refuses delivery. If the designer fails to send a confirming order to the manufacturer, the manufacturer may not be bound to a sale. And, the designer who fails to read an acknowledgment for an oral agreement is obliged to accept whatever was orally agreed to.

Title

When goods are bought and sold, ownership of those goods changes hands from the seller to the buyer. In legal terms, that ownership is called *title*. For a sale to take place, goods must exist and must be identified in the contract. Section 2–401 of the UCC clarifies the law related to the title of goods.

* Additional information on the Statute of Frauds can be found in Chapter 18.

Title passes in several ways. The most common way is at the time and place that the physical delivery of the goods is made by the seller to the buyer. The designer should use a sales confirmation describing what has been sold. If the goods are delivered to the client's home or job site, a delivery ticket or other evidence of what has been delivered and accepted should be used. The delivery ticket also should be dated and signed by the client. This provides clear evidence of what has been delivered and that the title has passed to the buyer. The description of the goods on the delivery ticket should mirror what has been written on the sales confirmation, signed by the client prior to ordering (or turning over) the goods.

When the designer buys from a manufacturer, title often passes by use of a shipment or a destination contract. Recall that FOB, Factory* (or a *shipping contract*) means that the title to the goods passes to the buyer when the manufacturer (seller) places the merchandise into the hands of the shipper. When the seller uses the FOB, Destination (or a *destination contract*), the manufacturer retains title of the goods until they arrive at the buyer's delivery address. In this case, title passes to the buyer at the time the seller turns over the goods to some shipper.

The reader may be familiar with another term of shipment, called COD (cash on delivery). Shipments sent COD require that the buyer pay cash (or other approved payment) at the time the merchandise is delivered to the buyer's location.

Some buyers do not require shipping or delivery and take the merchandise right from the studio or showroom. When no delivery is required, the title passes to the buyer when the contract is made. If the buyer refuses delivery or wants to otherwise return the goods, title reverts to the seller.

Risk

Since title can change at differing times, the UCC must address who is liable for the risk of loss during the shipping of the goods. Shipping of goods is governed by the UCC in Sections 2-319 through 2–323.

Free On Board (FOB) also indicates who assumes the risk of loss, should the goods be damaged in transit. In a shipping contract, the risk for loss is transferred to the buyer when goods are passed to the carrier. If the goods have been damaged before they arrive at the buyer's location, it is the buyer's responsibility to recover damages from the carrier. For example, Darby and Smith Designs was waiting for a large shipment of furniture for a radio station in Chicago. The truck was in an accident on the freeway, damaging all the furniture. Darby and Smith Designs will have to deal with the shipping company concerning claims for damages. In destination contracts, the risk for loss is transferred to the buyer at the buyer's destination. If the goods have been damaged in transit, it is the seller's responsibility to recover the damages from the carrier. In the example, the manufacturer, not Darby and Smith Designs, must deal with the shipping company concerning claims for the damaged furniture, since the manufacturer retains title in this case.

When there is no delivery required, risk passes in different ways, depending on whether or not the seller is a merchant. If the seller is a merchant, then risk passes when the buyer receives the goods. If the seller is not a merchant,

* The price list does not have to say "factory." A shipment contract means from the place the goods are originally shipped.

than risk passes when the seller gives the merchandise to the buyer. This very subtle difference is there only to show that a merchant selling goods has more responsibility concerning the damage of undelivered goods than a nonmerchant seller. Additional discussions concerning FOB can be found in Chapters 19 and 30.

Sales on Approval

A common special sale situation in the interior design profession is the sale on approval. In this situation the client is not sure about a product and takes it to his or her home or business location in order to see if it is appropriate. If the client subsequently keeps the product, he or she pays for it; otherwise, he or she is obligated to return the product.

There is a normal condition to the sale on approval regulated by the UCC that is explained by the following example. Jane Miller finds a sofa on a showroom floor but is not sure that it will go with her decor. She asks if she can try it "on approval." The store allows her five days to decide. If she calls and says that she will keep the sofa before the five days are up or fails to call before the five days and makes no attempt to return the sofa, the store considers the sofa as sold and sends her a bill. If Miller damages the sofa before the five days are up and before she approves of the sale, the loss is Miller's. If it is damaged in transit or in some way but through no fault of Miller, the loss is the seller's (Sections 2-326 and 2-327).

The Seller's Rights and Obligations

Sellers are always concerned that the buyer will cancel the order or want to change the order after it has been placed. Designers as sellers should protect themselves from these problems by including clauses in the sales agreement that stipulate under what conditions an order can be canceled or changed. Many designers indicate that restocking charges will be assessed if the client cancels an order. This *restocking charge* is a fee to cover the paperwork costs that have already been accumulated as well as a small penalty for taking back merchandise that the client does not want.

The seller has other rights when the buyer refuses to accept the goods or in some other way breaches the sales contract. In general, when the buyer breaches the sales contract, the seller is allowed to withhold delivery of the goods.

One situation involves partial deliveries to clients. For example, Sarah Randolph ordered new dining room and living room furniture from Smyth's Interiors. Smyth's delivered the living room furniture, but the dining room items were not in yet. Since the goods had been delivered, Smyth's billed Randolph for the partial delivery. Randolph refused to pay the bill. If the terms and conditions on the sales contract from Smyth's Interiors stated that partial deliveries would be billed separately, then Randolph would be in breach of contract. Smyth's could withhold delivery of the other furniture items until Randolph paid for the previous delivery.

Another frequent problem for designers occurs when a client claims that the items delivered are not those specified in the sales agreement. Most frequently, this concerns a color of fabric. Let us say that New Age Foods ordered 50 forest green upholstered chairs. When the chairs were delivered, New Age

Foods claimed that the chairs were not the right color green and refused to accept and pay for the goods. If the designer can show that the fabric was substantially the correct color (barring anything greater than a dye lot variation), the buyer would be in breach of contract to refuse acceptance of the order. The designer, on written notification, would have a right to cancel the order and could sue the client for the breach of contract. However, if the designer was not justified in canceling the order, the buyer could sue the designer for breach of contract.

If a client becomes insolvent while he or she has taken delivery but has not yet paid for the goods, the designer has the right to demand the return of the goods. This must be done quickly, however. The written demand for the return of the goods usually must be done within ten days of delivery of the goods.

The seller has an obligation to deliver the goods described in the sales agreement to the client within a specified time period. In most situations, any discrepancy in what was delivered versus what was ordered is the responsibility of the seller. Designers must protect themselves from the potentiality of a buyer trying to cancel an order, refuse an order, or refuse to pay for goods. This can be done by being very careful in writing up the descriptions of the goods on the sales order, getting the buyer's signature on the sales order, carefully preparing the purchase order, and checking on the progress of orders.

To mitigate the problem of a client saying that the fabric (or other finish) color is not correct, designers order a cutting or sample from current stock that is sufficient to fulfill the order. The designer does not actually place the order for the goods until the sample has been received and approved by the designer and client. If the delivered goods are as described, the buyer knows what will be ordered, and the buyer knows the terms and conditions of the sale, the buyer has no choice but to pay for the goods. Figure 20-1 lists some hints on how to avoid problems in selling goods.

The Buyer's Rights and Obligations

If the seller has delivered the goods that are described in the sales contract, the buyer has an obligation to pay for those goods. Because of this obligation, it is important for the designer to describe what is to be ordered on the sales agreement in sufficient detail so that the client clearly understands what he or she is purchasing. If the sales agreement states, "one 30 × 60 desk," there is a lot of room for argument on both sides as to whether the right desk actually has been delivered. However, if the sales order states, "one Stowe-Davis, Number 3060DP, 30 × 60, double-pedestal desk; finish, walnut; trim, polished chrome," there is very little disagreement as to what is to be ordered. Any modification in what has been delivered versus what is described gives the buyer the right to refuse the delivery. If the delivered goods are as described in the sales agreement, they are referred to as *conforming goods*. If the goods are somehow different, they are nonconforming goods. *Nonconforming goods* are simply any goods that are not as described in an order.

The buyer is also obligated to make payment for the delivered conforming goods in accordance with the terms in the sales agreement. If the terms are cash payment upon delivery, the designer expects the client to pay in cash or with a check. If the terms are a credit purchase, the buyer is expected to make payment within the time frame indicated in the sales agreement. COD shipments are valid only if COD shipment has been agreed to in the sales contract (Section 2-601).

- Fully describe on the sales agreement the goods to be ordered and sold. Include dimensions, finish selection, and/or fabric name and color number for furniture items. Include similar information for other products.
- Do not process any purchase orders until the client has signed the sales agreement and has provided the required prepayment.
- Be sure to go over the terms and conditions on your sales agreement with each new client and whenever a client orders goods from the firm.
- Obtain credit reports on all new clients.
- Request textile cuttings of current stock to ensure color matches are correct before finalizing the purchase with the supplier.
- If you use faxes or E-mails to order goods, make sure that you receive a report copy of the fax that the supplier has received the purchase order and/or that you print a hard copy of all E-mails that you send or receive concerning purchases, acknowledgments, and quotes.
- Obtain client signatures or initials, approving all goods that might be questioned, such as upholstered furniture items.
- Make sure that your terms and conditions concerning the client's right to cancel an order are clear and protect the design firm. Be certain that you also explain the client's legal rights to cancel an order.
- Work only with manufacturers and suppliers who provide reputable service and goods. Understand the terms and conditions of sale from every supplier with whom the firm does business.
- Keep the client informed of the progress of all special orders.
- Inspect all merchandise at the time of delivery to the firm's warehouse. Make sure this is done prior to paying the supplier in full.
- Insist that the client signs off on all delivered goods. Take care of any discrepancies immediately so that the client has little room to argue for nonpayment.

FIGURE 20-1. Tips that may help the designer avoid problems when selling goods.

The buyer also has a right to inspect the goods prior to paying for them. When the designer sells goods to the client, the client has the right to inspect the items to be sure that the delivered goods are those specified in the sales agreement. The buyer may refuse the goods if in any respect they do not conform to what is described in the sales agreement. He or she may also accept any part of the order or reject the nonconforming goods, or even accept the goods even if they are nonconforming.

If they are nonconforming goods, the buyer (designer or client) has the right to refuse the goods (or any part of the order that is nonconforming) and to not pay for the nonconforming goods. Designers purchasing goods for the client also have the right to inspect the goods prior to paying the supplier. Even though it is common for the manufacturer to send a bill for goods prior to the designer receiving the goods, the designer has a right to inspect and verify that the order is correct prior to being obligated to pay for the goods. According to the UCC, this right is absolute for all buyers, except for COD orders (Section 2(606a)). This is just one reason that it is very important for the designer to check all deliveries from manufacturers and suppliers.

If the buyer rejects the goods as nonconforming, the buyer must promptly notify the seller of the same. A telephone call is notice, but the written notice is more binding, since it is tangible evidence. Written notification with a full description of what the problems are is the best way to provide notification. If the buyer does not provide notice and retains the goods, the seller expects the buyer to pay for those goods.

The longer the goods are in the hands of the buyer, the more likely it is that the buyer will be obligated to pay for the goods, even if they are nonconforming: "Inaction results in acceptance" (Quinn, 1999, p.2/171). The buyer's failure to inspect and reject the goods within a stated or reasonable time period constitutes acceptance. If the buyer rejects some or all of the goods as nonconforming but uses the goods without prior agreement from the seller, the buyer is taking ownership of the goods and the seller by law expects the buyer to pay for the goods. State laws generally allow buyers a 72-hour *right of refusal.* In some states, this is called a three-day right of cancellation. This means that, even if the goods are as ordered, the buyer has 72 hours in which to return the goods and receive full repayment. In many states, this right of refusal only applies to contracts signed in the buyer's residence. The right of refusal allowance for contracts signed in a residence was developed to protect buyers from feeling pressured into purchasing from a seller who has come to the residence. The exact conditions of the right of refusal vary by state.

Although many companies have the philosophy that "the customer is always right," according to sales law, this is not necessarily true. Designers who buy and sell goods need to understand not only their rights as a seller but also the rights of buyers.

Summary

Selling goods to clients is often a profitable way of producing revenues for the interior design practice. But the buying and selling of goods also has many legal considerations and constraints. Although it is easy for a designer to write a purchase order for goods, there are many regulations that govern legally how that order can be placed, how ownership of the goods can change hands, and what responsibility the seller has to the buyer concerning defects or injury that might be caused by the goods.

In this chapter, we have tried to explain the basic concepts of the law of sales, as regulated by the Uniform Commercial Code (UCC). We have defined basic terms related to sales and selling, discussed how a sales contract is made, and noted how a sales contract is different from a normal contract. We have also briefly discussed the Statute of Frauds, explained when title and risk passes from the seller to the buyer, and noted the responsibility of the seller and buyer in selling goods.

Although the UCC standardizes most of the laws related to the sale of goods, the designer must still check with the firm's attorney to know which part of the code is valid in his or her state and if there are any state or city regulations that supersede the UCC.

REFERENCES

Brown, Gordon W., and Paul A. Sukys. 1997. *Business Law*, 9th ed. New York: Glencoe.

Clarkson, Kenneth W., Roger LeRoy Miller, and Gaylord A. Jentz. 1983. *West's Business Law: Text and Cases*, 2nd ed. St. Paul, MN: West Publishing.

Conry, Edward J., Gerald R. Ferrera, and Karla H. Fox. 1993. *The Legal Environment of Business*, 3rd ed. Boston, MA: Allyn and Bacon.

Cushman, Robert F., and James C. Dobbs, eds. 1991. *Design Professional's Handbook of Business and Law*. New York: John Wiley.

Jentz, Gaylord A., Kenneth W. Clarkson, and Roger LeRoy Miller. 1987. *West's Business Law—Alternate UCC Comprehensive Edition*, 3rd ed. St. Paul, MN: West Publishing.

Quinn, Thomas M. 1999. *Quinn's Uniform Commercial Code Commentary and Law Digest*, vol. 1991-1: Cumulative Supplement. St. Paul, MN: West Group.

———. 1991. *Quinn's Uniform Commercial Code Commentary and Law Digest*, 2nd. ed., vol. 1. Boston, MA: Warren, Gorham and Lamont.

Stone, Bradford. 1975. *Uniform Commercial Code in a Nutshell*. St. Paul, MN: West Publishing.

Sweet, Justin. 1985. *Legal Aspects of Architecture, Engineering, and the Construction Process*, 3rd ed. St. Paul, MN: West Publishing.

As a healthcare designer, I look forward to greater understanding about the effect of the built environment on healing and to healthcare providers having an appreciation of the factors that play a role in the physical, emotional, and spiritual well-being of patients, their families, and staff. At the new millennium, interior designers have much to celebrate in the level of professionalism that has been achieved in a relatively brief period and in the number of projects of outstanding merit.

Jain Malkin is President and founder of a San Diego, California interior architecture firm that specializes in healthcare facilities. Her pioneering efforts to create life-enhancing hospital interiors have won her international acclaim and several first-place design awards. Malkin has lectured widely and written numerous articles on the psychological effects of healthcare environments. Through her publications she has been recognized for her research-based approach to the design of healing environments. She is the author of *Hospital Interior Architecture* and *Medical and Dental Space Planning: A Comprehensive Guide.*

Courtesy Jain Malkin Inc.
www. JainMalkin.com
Photographer: Steve McClelland

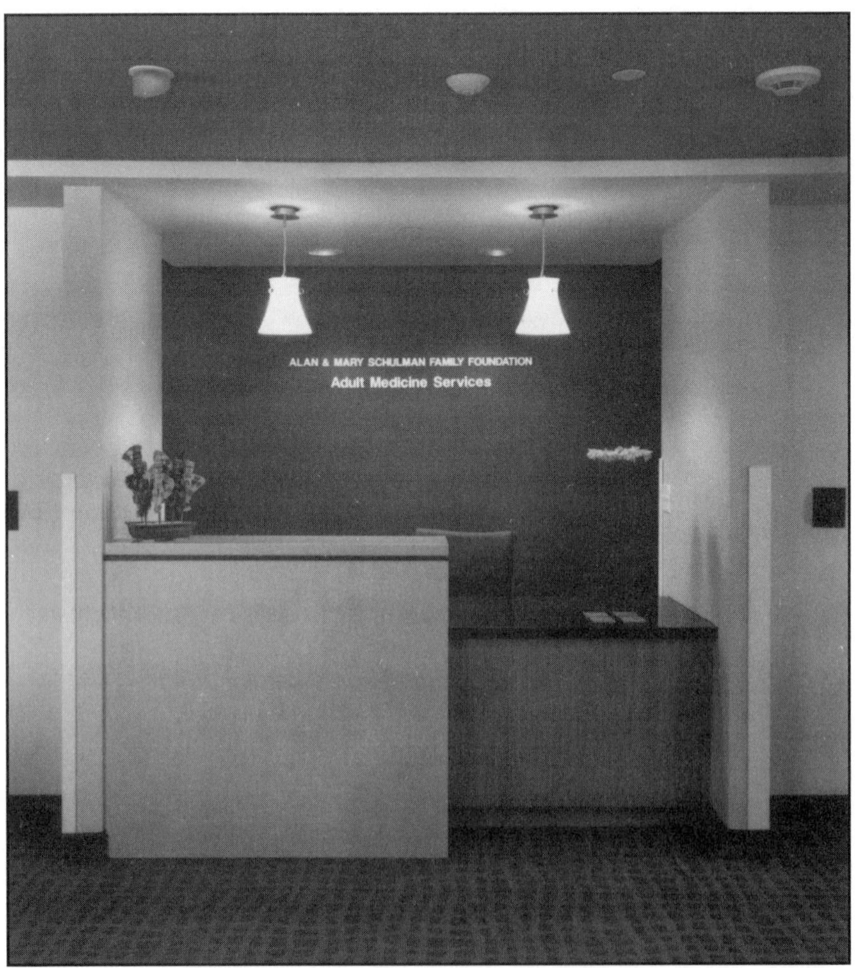

Photographer: Gary McGuire

Part V

Marketing and Business Development

21. Marketing Interior Design Services

Definitions   Target Marketing   Establishing a Niche   The Four Ps of Marketing   Marketing Analysis   The Marketing Plan

22. Promoting the Interior Design Practice

Public Relations   Publicity   Basic Promotional Tools   Referrals   Networking   Competitions

23. Advanced Promotional Tools

Publication   Direct Mail   Speaking at Seminars and Meetings   Premiums   Multimedia Presentations   Internet Marketing   Proposals   Advertising

24. Selling Your Services

What is Selling?   Selling Services versus Products   Building Client Relationships   The Selling Process   Selling Techniques

25. Design Presentations

Marketing Presentations   Proposal Presentations   Project Presentations   Overcoming Objections   Closing Techniques   Follow-up   Negotiating   Other Guidelines for Making Presentations

26. Personal Power

Image—Nonverbal Cues   Well Suited   Body Language   Business Etiquette

Chapter 21

Marketing Interior Design Services

Although many interior design firms are fortunate enough to obtain prospects or commissions from referrals and previous clients, it is also important for design firms to actively market their design services through other means. Design professionals who are committed to the expansion of their business must always be thinking past the current project and look for ways to attract a constant flow of new projects. This is especially the case in commercial design, since contacts may be promoted, change companies, transfer to other cities, retire, or lose responsibility related to the interior designer's interests. Residential designers must also look beyond today's client in order to keep their firms active, growing, and profitable.

Expanding competition is another reason that designers should actively market their firms. It is easy for an interior design firm to get lost in the crowd of new design firms. Many interior designers were "forced" to go out on their own in the 1990s due to the poor economy in the early part of the decade. Once the economy became very active in the late 1990s, many other new forms of business were created to compete with existing design firms. Major home centers offer interior design services. Many manufacturers open their catalogs to the end user. Architectural offices and residential developers continue to offer design services to clients. And the Internet allows firms in one part of the country—or world—to make contact with potential clients anywhere. In the twenty-first century, firms must look beyond traditional methods of obtaining commissions.

This chapter introduces the reader to some of the basic underlying concepts of marketing. These concepts serve as the basis for the use of specific marketing techniques to execute a design firm's marketing plan. We will begin with some definitions of marketing and will follow with a brief discussion of the strategy of target marketing. The chapter continues with a discussion of marketing analysis and the development of the marketing plan. Chapters 22 and 23 explore many of the promotional activities and tools used by interior designers. Personal selling techniques are reviewed in Chapter 24, and Chapter 25 discusses some techniques used to make presentations.

Definitions

Many designers do not like to think about marketing, because they are too busy with other work. Others think that marketing means selling and refuse to consider themselves as salespeople. Every time a designer makes a presentation, the designer is engaging in selling. And selling is a part of marketing. However, selling is not marketing, and marketing is not selling. A few definitions might help.

There are many definitions of *marketing*. Most include the concept of moving goods and services from producers to consumers. One definition says "marketing is a societal process by which individuals and groups obtain what they need and want through creating, offering, and freely exchanging products and services of value with others" (Kotler, 2000, p. 8). For comparison, the American Marketing Association defines marketing as "the process of planning and executing the conception, pricing, promotion, and distribution of ideas, goods, and services to create exchanges that satisfy individual and organizational goals" (Bennett, 1995, p. 166). The well-known management consultant, Peter Drucker, has written, "The aim of marketing is to know and understand the customer so well that the product or service sells itself" (Drucker, 1973, p. 64). Obviously, there can be many definitions to marketing.

Selling, on the other hand, "is the personal, oral presentation of products or services to prospective customers for the purpose of making sales. . . . The salesman ideally does more than make the customer desire the product; he tries to win the customer's regard for the company which sells the product (and) tries to extend the confidence and regard of the customer to himself" (*Collier's Encyclopedia*, p. 422). In selling, the designer must explain his or her services or perhaps his or her solution to the design project in a personal way in order to instruct and bring the client to accept the company or design idea. Many marketing texts therefore insist that selling involves "an inward-looking function in which you persuade the customer to take what you have. . . . Marketing, on the other hand, is an outward-looking function in which you try to match the real requirement of the customer" (Czinkota et al., 1997, p. 19). Interior designers, it can be argued, must do both. It takes personal selling to explain design concepts to clients, yet it also takes marketing to find out what the client really needs from the designer in order for the interior designer to secure new clients. Chapter 24 will discuss personal selling techniques used by the designer to obtain a commission or to finalize a project presentation as part of the marketing process.

Target Marketing

When a sole practitioner or group of designers decides to organize a design practice, they must determine the type of clients they seek to attract to the business. In the most rudimentary sense, this decision is whether to seek clients who wish residential or commercial interior design services. This decision can be considered the beginning of a business strategy, called target marketing.

More precisely, *target marketing* is a marketing method that helps a firm identify one or more groups of potential customers who are most likely to utilize the services of the firm. When a firm uses target marketing, it develops identifiable groups within the firm's total market, called market segments. A *market segment* is a group of customers that has some common characteristic.

For example, everyone living within the city of Beverly Hills can be a market segment for a residential designer located in Beverly Hills, California. All doctors practicing in Boise, Idaho, can be a market segment for a commercial designer in Idaho.

However, those examples are rather broad. Firms have greater success in target marketing when they are as specific as possible, because they cannot get every customer who may want some type of design services in these broad segments. By specifically defining segments within a broad segment, firms will have greater success in attracting clients and thus will utilize marketing resources to the best advantage.

Knowing what the design firm can do and wants to provide is only part of the challenge in reaching the right clients. The interior designer who is intent on expanding his or her market to high-quality clients must also find out what the client wants from an interior designer. If the designer provides what he or she thinks is needed, rather than what clients actually need, the designer will have little to do. Target marketing provides a way to help designers solve both these problems.

Target marketing begins with an understanding of what services the firm can offer. A thorough analysis of what each employee can do and the kind of projects the firm has done in the past helps the firm determine what it can do in the future. This analysis also may help a firm determine if it can offer new services. Any new services may open up a new market segment and produce additional revenue for the firm.

Internal analysis of strengths, weaknesses, and previous general market interest should be followed by in-depth research in order for the design firm to more clearly identify the market segments that most likely want and need the firm's services. The following characteristics are frequently used to further differentiate market segments.

1. *Demographics.* These are characteristics such as age, gender, occupation, level of income, stage in family life cycle, religion, and race.
2. *Psychographics.* These concepts define a person's lifestyle interests and attitudes, such as hobbies, sports interests, personality traits, and abilities (or lack of abilities).
3. *Geographics.* These define a location: for example, is the design firm willing to work only within the confines of the city in which the business is located, or is the firm willing to go out of state for work?
4. *Industry type.* This can be explained by differentiating the exact type of specialty within interior design. A commercial designer has many areas in which he or she can specialize, such as healthcare, retail, lodging, and so on. Residential designers can specialize as well, if they wish to limit their practice to designing apartments and condominiums rather than single-family dwellings.
5. *Benefits.* What is the client looking for? Benefits are related to why the customer buys; for example, the client may be looking for a more productive office staff and therefore may be seeking a design solution that will help accommodate that need.
6. *Product usage.* This defines how often the product or service is purchased or used. Although this factor relates more to product sales marketing than to design services marketing, it can be used to target services. Knowing how often a certain type of client will use design services will help the firm understand the type of marketing methods that it must use to attract repeat and new business.

Information to develop target market segments comes from many sources. A firm's historic data on completed projects is where many firms start their target market research. Additional data can be obtained from reports and publications at the library, the local chamber of commerce, city building departments, and small business development centers located at many community colleges, to name just a few other sources. Occasionally, large firms may fund a questionnaire or interviews. This is done to obtain very specific information that the design firm needs. Information gathered from the library or other sources by someone other than the design firm is called secondary research. When research such as a questionnaire is undertaken to answer specific questions, it is called primary research. Primary research, obviously, is more expensive than secondary research.

Creating a clear focus of the firm's target market is very important in the firm's overall marketing efforts. All firms have a limited amount of resources to put into marketing. Focusing marketing resources on clients who are most likely to be interested in the firm's services uses scarce marketing dollars and time to fullest advantage. In addition, when a firm determines its target market, it is then easier to establish what marketing methods will work most effectively to attract target clients.

Establishing a Niche

Some design firms have found that it is advantageous to establish a particular specialty in interior design. Specializing creates a targeted focus of the firm on some area of the industry that the owner finds particularly interesting and rewarding. It is easy to see how this would help a commercial designer. And yet residential designers can also specialize. When the specialty has some very refined focus or is somehow unique, the firm has targeted a *niche*. According to Martin and Knoohuizen (1995, p. 6), a niche "is a design specialty that focuses its services to meet the needs of a specific group—or segment—of the total market."

Some marketing books do not even mention the term niche; they simply refer to this concept as market segmentation. The idea is to choose a specific segment or part of the total market in which the designer has an interest or expertise and to work only with clients in that segment. Of course, some designers choose to specialize in two closely related segments. By becoming an expert in one or two segments of the interior design market, the designer can provide specialized services and a focused use of the firm's resources. For example, rather than market to all residential clients, perhaps the designer creates a niche in condominiums and townhouses. In a community of empty nesters, perhaps the niche helps clients downsize their homes by providing evaluation, restoration, and even disposal through resale of furnishings. A commercial designer with experience in the design of medical offices might further specialize by establishing the offices of dermatologists as a niche.

By having a niche, the designer can spend his or her time more productively researching and learning the peculiar functional problems of that niche. This allows him or her to be of special value to potential clients as a designer. When a designer is very knowledgeable about a particular niche, the client will not feel like the designer is learning on the job about his or her particular needs. In addition, the designer is also able to find unique specialty products and materials that are needed in, and appropriate to, that niche. Designers who do not specialize do not always know about specialty products for unique purposes.

It may seem that targeting a specialized segment can mean that the designer does not have enough clients to keep working. Of course, this can be true and is very important if the designer is trying to determine a possible niche to pursue. If a designer decides to specialize in a particular niche, he or she must be sure that sufficient work exists to support the goals of the design firm in terms of meeting business expenses and generating a profit. Even a sole practitioner who is working in a small town may find that not enough work exists in the area to support his or her business if the niche is too unique. This is why most niche designers market outside their immediate geographic area into different cities, states, and even outside the country.

If a designer has gained some expertise in a particular area of interior design, then the designer may be on the way to establishing a niche. Someone who has worked for many years in office systems may find tenant improvement work an attractive niche. Perhaps a designer has some medical experience and some residential experience. The designer may wish to choose assisted-living apartments as a niche. The hospitality market has been a boom area of design in recent years, and this is generally expected to continue. A designer who is located in a resort or vacation area may want to develop a niche designing bed-and-breakfast facilities. The possibilities are almost endless.

The niche should be something that the designer also has a passion for. If the designer does not like doing residential design very much, taking up a niche in assisted-living facilities is not a good idea. When the niche is related to a special interest or passion, then, as with most other things, the designer will do a better job.

Good market research is needed to establish a business niche. Everything discussed in this chapter becomes vital. Coming up with an idea for a niche that has few potential clients or is past its prime is a disaster waiting to happen, like the companies who continued to make buggy whips when the automobile took over as a mode of transportation in the early part of the twentieth century. The numbers of clients, the competition, the potential growth of the specialized area of design, the experience level of the designer, the ease in which the designer can enter the niche all play a part in the designer's determining whether a niche is a possibility.

The Four Ps of Marketing

Another factor in the development of a marketing plan relates to what is called the marketing mix. The *marketing mix* consists of operational elements that the design firm can control in the process of marketing and selling goods and services. Traditionally, the marketing mix consists of what is called the four Ps of marketing.

The *four Ps of marketing* are four basic variables—product, place, promotion, and price—that create a firm's marketing mix. An interior designer's product is generally considered to be professional design services rather than tangible goods. But, in marketing, a product can be either a service or goods. Designers who sell goods must also establish which goods they will sell. The product that the designer offers to its target market must be something that satisfies potential customers' needs. Offering computer rendering services to allied professionals in a market that does not demand computer rendering services is a futile venture. The firm must utilize its internal analysis and its preferred market area to determine which products are needed by potential clients.

The second variable is place. This means that the firm must find ways of getting its product to the places where potential customers exist. The designer offering computer rendering may not be able to get much business in a very small community. However, the designer probably would have greater success if he or she offered these services in large cities. Business owners must recognize that the client drives the need for products and that the products must be offered or made available where potential clients exist. The need is not based on the designer's desire to offer products that only the designer perceives as necessary or that exist only in a location where the designer wishes to reside.

The potential client finds out about the availability of a product through the third variable, promotion. Promotional activities inform potential clients of the existence of the design firm and the services that the firm offers, whether or not the designer is located in the same geographic area as the client. Promotional activities, which will be discussed in detail in Chapters 22 and 23, include public relations, the use of brochures, referrals, advertising, and other promotional techniques.

The last of the four variables of marketing is price. Establishing the right price for the interior design firm's "product," which was discussed in Chapters 17 and 19, is a difficult management activity. If the firm sets a price for services, for example, that is too high in relation to competition, the firm will not secure work with many clients. If the price for fees is set too low, clients will suspect the firm's ability to do the work and may not seriously consider using the design firm.

There is one other variable to be factored into the determination of a marketing mix—perception. Although perception is not in the accepted list of variables of the marketing mix, it is an important factor for the designer to take into consideration. Perception is an intuitive process of gathering information about people, places, events, and so forth, with which we come into contact. Clients perceive the designer in terms of such things as image, business professionalism, and, of course, design ability. If a designer's image does not meet the client's perception of the image of a designer, the client is less likely to hire the designer. Clients develop a negative opinion of interior designers who are, to some degree or other, not business professionals. Being consistently late for meetings, neglecting to return phone calls, making mistakes in estimates, not following through on promises are all factors that sour the perceptions of clients. Perception also impacts on the client's willingness to pay the price the designer is asking. If the designer's creative reputation, quality of service, and methods of doing business have a high value to the client, the client is more willing to hire that designer and even conceivably to pay a higher price for the design services. If the client does not perceive the high value of a designer's services, the client will not be willing to pay the price, even if the designer is a truly creative professional.

All these variables are important factors that a firm must investigate and consider when it is developing a marketing plan. One variable is not really more important than another. Each is important by itself as well as in relation to the others. Ignoring one variable could upset the marketing mix and make it difficult, if not impossible, for the design firm to successfully market its services.

Marketing Analysis

Another important step in developing a marketing plan is to conduct research and analysis of the firm's market. *Marketing analysis* involves gathering and analyzing data about such things as the abilities and interests of the staff, potential clients, the economy, and the competition. This research and analysis allows the firm to make better plans and decisions about the direction of the firm's business efforts. The goal of marketing analysis is to find out what the client wants and then to provide it.

In part, marketing analysis involves similar research to what is done for target marketing. In addition, marketing analysis provides information for preparing strategic plans and annual plans. This process was discussed in detail in Chapter 10. This section will review some key issues in this analysis process as they are related to the firm's specific marketing program and plan.

Marketing research and analysis is done by consulting firms that specialize in this kind of work. Sometimes advertising agencies do marketing analysis. Small firms and designers who are just beginning their practices often try to do their own marketing analysis. Although they can meet with success, it is a time-consuming and detailed process. Firms that are determined to do this work internally must be prepared for the fact that the designer who is responsible for the marketing analysis will generate less revenues for the firm.

An important first step in market analysis is answering the question, "What business are we in?" Although it seems like an easy question to answer, it really is not. If the firm believes that it is in the business of providing interior design services, it has done little to really answer the question in a way that will help the firm market itself to new clients. In many ways, almost every interior design and architectural firm, retail store, and many others in the built environment industry could say the same thing, thus not differentiating the firm at all from its competition.

In order for the design firm to answer the question about what business the firm is in, it must answer other questions. These key questions (see Figure 21-1) help the firm understand what business it is in (or wants to be in) and helps the firm realize the direction it wishes to take.

These questions relate to key issues, especially for new or relatively new firms, or firms that are seeking to move into some sort of new market. In a large city, there may be thousands of companies that can provide similar services. However, if a firm is really interested in attracting new clients, it needs to understand what business it is in so that it discovers ways in which it can to make itself appear different, even unique, from its competition.

A second step in marketing analysis is to conduct an in-depth review of the internal and external forces that can and do affect the firm. SWOT analysis, described in Chapter 10, is a common method that can be used to accomplish this. If the reader has not reviewed that chapter, it is suggested that he or she do so now.

1. **What design services do we offer?**
2. **What products do we intend to specify and sell?**
3. **Are there sufficient potential clients for the firm's services within a reasonable distance?**
4. **Who do we see as our primary and secondary customers?**
5. **How do we do what we do?**
6. **What quality of service do we endeavor to supply?**
7. **Is anyone else offering the services in the way our firm does?**
8. **Why should/would customers buy from our firm rather than from one of our competitors?**
9. **What are the trends in the profession, and how will these trends affect the firm's potential business?**

FIGURE 21-1. Questions to help a firm answer the question, "What business are we in?" These questions will be helpful in developing a marketing plan, a mission statement, and a strategic plan.

A SWOT analysis looks at the skills, abilities, and interests of employees. This review can uncover interests or skills of employees that have been underutilized and that can help the firm create new service offerings. The operational processes of the firm should also be reviewed for ways to increase productivity and, again, possibly to determine underutilized skills that can be used to market the firm.

The firm must also look outside itself in market analysis. Many small firms do not even recognize other designers within their local association chapter as potential competitors. Yet they may well be. Understanding one's competitor's design style and method of business, regardless of size of the firm, will be an asset to a design firm that is interested in expanding its own market. Of course, when the economy is good, few small firms worry about this issue.

The economic situation in the design firm's marketplace and the legal and political issues relevant to a particular community can also have a dramatic impact on the design firm. The changes in building codes, licensing of interior designers, and changes in political control of a geographic area can positively or negatively impact any size interior design firm or design department. Keeping abreast of what is happening in these areas can lead the designer to new clients or, if neglected, a loss of business.

Marketing analysis should assist the design firm in determining marketing goals and budgets. It provides a body of knowledge about the firm's practice and staff, the kind and amount of clients available, general economic and legal trends or restrictions prevalent in the area, and the competition. The design firm can then use this knowledge to prepare a definite plan in order to achieve results that are specifically related to the firm's overall marketing or strategic plan.

Marketing analysis must not be a one-time endeavor. It should be considered a critical part of strategic planning and of the annual business plan.

The Marketing Plan

Marketing plans should be developed in connection with a strategic or annual plan. Marketing plans help create goals that set down what the firm wishes to accomplish, as well as how the firm intends to accomplish the goals through various strategies and tactics. For the most part, a marketing plan looks at the future year's activity. Yet goals, strategies, and tactics also should be developed for the long term—those that are expected to take from three to five years or more to accomplish. The establishment of long-term goals are important so that the design firm can keep thinking ahead and anticipating the changing needs of its basic or desired market.

Marketing plans are prepared to help the firm determine what it intends to do to meet its goals in terms of marketing. Goals might be to increase awareness of the firm in its present market or to target a specific group of new clients. Perhaps the goal is to introduce the design firm to a totally new market or type of client. Maybe the goal is to gain greater recognition as an expert in a certain area of design.

Whatever the goals, the process of creating a marketing plan and actually writing it down helps the owner and employees see the goals before them and, by design, makes them consider how they can best accomplish those goals. By developing a plan, the design firm considers which promotional tools (discussed in the next chapters) are most appropriate to help achieve its goals. This decision then help the firm, in turn, produce budgets that will ensure that the resources are available or need to be obtained to develop the appropriate tools and strategies.

Just as there is no perfect business plan, there is no one outline for a marketing plan for all interior design firms. Some firms will want to have a very formal plan with a table of contents, references, and budgeting information. If the plan is to be used internally so that the owners, managers, and staff know what is going on, a more informal format can be used.

Figure 21-2 shows a portion of a sample marketing plan. Some of the items that the formal plan should cover include the following:

1. *An introduction*. Statements based on the information that was used to prepare the plan and statements about the use and purpose of the plan.
2. *Goals statement(s)*. A revised statement of general business goals based on the information gathered in the analysis.
3. *Capabilities*. A discussion of the firm's abilities, related to the kinds of clients who previously hired the firm.
4. *Services*. A listing of the services the firm can and is going to offer. Subsequent sections should discuss who will be responsible for these services and how they will be done.
5. *Clientele*. Quantitative information as to potential numbers, market share, and possible growth in each client category. Both existing and new client objectives should be stated.

II. Client Base
  A. Current Year
    1. Our current client base is primarily from the Midland area. Current clients within the city limits represent 80 percent of total sales. The remaining 20 percent is made up of clients outside the city limits but within a 30-mile radius.
    2. The majority of current work is residential. Eighty-five percent of clients purchase merchandise and services for homes. Fifteen percent of clients purchase merchandise and services for offices or other commercial facilities.
    3. *Services versus Merchandise*
       Of residential sales, 70 percent of all revenues are merchandise sales.
       Twenty percent are from design fees, and 10 percent represent other services, such as repairs, which do not require the purchasing of additional merchandise.
       Of commercial sales, 90 percent of all revenues are merchandise sales.
       Design fees only represent 10 percent of revenues from commercial projects.
    4. *Type of Purchaser*
       Sixty-five percent of residential customers purchase goods or services for their existing home.
         1. Sixty percent of purchases are for only a few replacement items in one or two rooms.
         2. Thirty percent of purchases are for new floor coverings, window coverings, and/or wall coverings.
         3. Ten percent of purchases are for many items in two or more rooms.
       Twenty percent of residential customers purchase goods or services for a new house.
         1. Forty-five percent of purchases are for new floor coverings, window coverings, and/or wall coverings.
         2. Thirty-five percent of purchases are for only a few replacement items in one or two rooms.
         3. Twenty percent of purchases are for many items in two or more rooms.
       Fifteen percent of residential customers purchase goods or services for a second (vacation or rental) house.
         1. Fifty-five percent of purchases are for only a few replacement items in one or two rooms.

FIGURE 21-2. A page from a sample marketing plan.

6. *Policy decisions*. A discussion of such things as how the firm will charge services to clients, how the firm will charge for consultants, whether or not the firm will bill reimbursable expenses, whether or not the firm will sell merchandise, and what policies there will be related to purchasing of products for resale.
7. *Marketing organization*. A statement of who will be responsible for ongoing marketing analysis.
8. *Marketing effort*. Answers to such questions as, "In what ways will the firm accomplish its goals?" "How will it use advertising and public relations?" How will results be monitored to see whether or not they are successful?" "How much financially will be committed to marketing?"
9. *Evaluation*. A discussion of how the goals will be measured so as to indicate the success of the marketing plan.
10. *Forecasts*. Amount of sales, profit, number of new clients, and additions to personnel. These should be stated as both quantitative and qualitative measures.

It is wise to involve the entire staff in the analysis and the planning for the yearly marketing plan. Final decisions, of course, should be made by management. It is almost always true that when plans are passed down by management without staff input, the staff feel resentful. If the staff do not believe in the plan, it will not be very successful.

As with any plan, it is important for a process of monitoring the progress and success of the plan to be instituted. It does no good and is, frankly, a waste of time and resources for the firm to go through the process of developing and writing a marketing plan if it is not committed to its execution. Monitoring the plan's progress helps, though it cannot guarantee the success of the plan.

Summary

Responding to, or depending upon, referrals is a common marketing technique that is used by interior design firms of any size. Referrals, however, are oftentimes not a sufficient method to provide a steady number of clients.

Whether the owner of the interior design practice depends on referrals or uses other marketing techniques to attract clients, thinking through the entire marketing process is a valuable endeavor. Good professional business practices require the analysis of possibilities and a focusing on those aspects of the market that are reasonable for the firm, considering the resources that are available.

This chapter discussed the technique of target marketing, has explained the four common factors of product, place, promotion, and price that are considered in the developing of marketing strategies. It also discussed the analysis process that is necessary for developing a formal marketing plan. The next chapter will look at the concept of promotion and many of the promotional tools that can be used to aid in the marketing effort.

REFERENCES

Bachner, John Phillip, and Naresh Kumar Khosla. 1977. *Marketing and Promotion for Design Professionals.* New York: Van Nostrand Reinhold.

Bangs, David H., Jr. 1998. *The Market Planning Guide*, 5th ed. Chicago, IL: Upstart Publishing.

Bennett, Peter D., ed. 1995. *Dictionary of Marketing Terms*, 2nd ed. Chicago, IL: American Marketing Association.

Berry, Leonard L., and A. Parasuraman. 1991. *Marketing Services.* New York: Free Press.

Bly, Robert W. 1991. *Selling Your Services.* New York: Henry Holt.

Collier's Encyclopedia. 1975. Vol. 15, s.v. "Marketing." New York: Macmillan Educational Corporation.

Connor, Dick, and Jeff Davidson. 1993. *Getting New Clients*, 2nd ed. New York: John Wiley.

Cook, Kenneth J. 1995. *AMA Complete Guide to Small Business Marketing*. Lincolnwood, IL: NTC Business Books.

Coxe, Weld. 1971. *Marketing Architectural and Engineering Services.* New York: Van Nostrand Reinhold.

Crandall, Rick. 1998. *1001 Ways to Market Your Services*. Lincolnwood, IL: Contemporary Books.

———. 1996. *Marketing Your Services.* Lincolnwood, IL: Contemporary Books.

Czinkota, Michael R., Masaaki Kotabe, and David Mercer. 1997. *Marketing Management Text and Cases.* Cambridge, MA: Blackwell Publishing.

Davidson, Jeff. 1994. *Marketing on a Shoestring*, 2nd ed. New York: John Wiley.

Davidson, Jeffrey P. 1990. *Marketing for the Home-Based Business*. Holbrook, MA: Bob Adams.

Drucker, Peter F. 1973. *Management: Tasks, Responsibilities, Practices.* New York: Harper & Row.

Edwards, Paul, and Sarah Edwards (with Laura Clampitt Douglas). 1991. *Getting Business to Come to You*. New York: Tarcher/Putnam.

Forsyth, Patrick. 1999. *Marketing Professional Services*, 2nd ed. London: Kogan/Page.

Frost, Susan E. 1995. *Blueprint for Marketing*, 2nd ed. Portland, OR: SEF Publications.

Gordon, Ian H. 1998. *Relationship Marketing*. New York: John Wiley.

Hayes, Rick Stephan, and Gregory Brooks Elmore. 1985. *Marketing for Your Growing Business.* New York: Ronald Press.

Jones, Gerre L. 1983. *How to Market Professional Design Services*, 2nd ed. New York: McGraw-Hill.

Kotler, Michael. 2000. *Marketing Management*. Millennium ed. Upper Saddle River, NJ: Prentice Hall.

Lovelock, Christopher H. 1996. *Services Marketing*, 3rd ed. Upper Saddle River, NJ: Prentice-Hall.

Martin, Jane D., and Nancy Knoohuizen. 1995. *Marketing Basics for Designers.* New York: John Wiley.

McCarthy, E. Jerome. 1981. *Basic Marketing*, 7th ed. Homewood, IL: Richard D. Irwin.

McCarthy, E. Jerome, and William D. Perreault, Jr. 1993. *Basic Marketing*, 11th ed. Homewood, IL: Richard D. Irwin.

Morgan, Jim. 1984. *Marketing for the Small Design Firm.* New York: Watson-Guptill.

Pickar, Roger L. 1991. *Marketing for Design Firms in the 1990s*. Washington, DC: American Institute of Architects.

Pinson, Linda, and Jerry Jinnett. 1993. *Target Marketing for the Small Business*, 2nd ed. Dover, NH: Upstart Publishing.

Putman, Anthony O. 1990. *Marketing Your Services*. New York: John Wiley.

Weitz, Barton A., and Robin Wensley. 1984. *Strategic Marketing.* Boston, MA: Kent Publishing.

Zeithami, Valarie A., and Mary Jo Bitner. 1996. *Services Marketing*. New York: McGraw-Hill.

Chapter 22

Promoting the Interior Design Practice

Competition in the design industry at the end of the twentieth century grew by leaps and bounds in all communities. It is possible that dozens of new firms with numerous new designers were started in the reader's hometown over the last decade. Existing firms, as well as new businesses, must cultivate new clients and new projects to keep employees actively involved in generating revenue. No firm, regardless of its size, specialty, or reputation can afford to let its message be lost among the competition. How is this done? Through various promotional strategies and tools that are deemed appropriate to the design firm's mission, goals, and budget.

Promotion is the method used to get the designer's message—even existence—before the client. In practical sense, promotion "includes all the activities the company undertakes to communicate and promote its products [and services] to the target market" (Kotler, 2000, p. 87). Many people use the term promotion to mean public relations, but promotion is much more than public relations. Promotion also includes publicity, publishing, advertising, personal selling, and other strategies or techniques that help get a business's message to potential clients and its market in general. Promotional activities are important for the healthy growth of all interior design businesses.

Competition forces design firms to consider many promotional activities. Is it time to publish a brochure or maybe develop a Web page and promote the firm on-line? How beneficial would it be to enter a project in a competition in order to gain publicity? Is it proper for the firm to advertise in local magazines? Should the firm attempt to get a project published in one of the trade magazines? Can a new graphic image or logo help to change the client's perception of the design firm? These questions and many more are being asked in design firms every day as a part of the continual search for new clients, new markets, and greater recognition. In this chapter, we will explore many of the ways in which the interior designer can get his or her message across to prospective clients.

The chapter begins by clarifying the strategy of public relations and publicity activities. It continues with a brief discussion of several basic promotional techniques, including the company's graphic image, brochures, press releases, referrals, and networking. These are considered basic tools, since they are the kinds of things all design firms can use effectively to promote the design practice. Additional promotional tools and strategies are discussed in the next chapter.

Public Relations

Public relations refers to all the efforts of the firm to create an image in order to affect the public's opinion of the firm. In a sense, it is an umbrella for all the activities, tools, and efforts used to communicate information about a firm to the public and especially to potential clients. Public relations (or PR) is about creating an image. Perhaps it starts with the design of the company logo and stationery, the design of the studio, and even how the designer dresses. It is about communicating information concerning the design firm through a Web page, producing a brochure or newsletter, and placing news releases in local newspapers or national trade publications. Public relations can consist of educating potential clients by writing and submitting articles on design-related topics to local publications or trade magazines; conducting an in-office product seminar for the public or other professionals; or even writing a book on a design topic. It can also consist of making contributions to professional organization fund raisers, becoming involved in legislative efforts, and participating in special events in the community. Public relations refers to all of these and much more.

This kind of work can be done internally and is often the responsibility of the owner or a few key senior staff members. Many firms hire a public relations or marketing professional to help them decide what activities and tools will best serve their marketing goals and resources. The public relations professional can then produce the tools himself or herself, or hire subconsultants to produce the desired materials or activities.

Through the firm's research about itself and the public, and the marketing plan that was discussed in the previous chapter, a picture of the activities needed within public relations, publicity, and general promotional activities will emerge. The public relations professional makes suggestions as to which activities are going to lead to success, that is, more client contacts and potential sales. He or she may suggest that a new company image be started by redesigning the company logo and graphics or by developing a brochure or a Web site. Maybe it is time for the firm to convert its marketing presentations to Power Point®. Whatever the strategy is, the result is to gain positive recognition for the design firm in the public's mind. And this recognition will eventually lead to future business and greater revenues.

Publicity

A direct form of promotion is publicity. "Publicity is what you use to get attention without paying for it. Publicity is the key to letting people know what you do" (Fletcher and Rockler, 2000, p. 1). The aim of *publicity* is to attract attention or awareness without having to pay any media charges. This is the kind of promotional communication that design firms strive to achieve as much as possible. Traditionally, this has been the accepted form of promoting professional services.

Publicity takes many forms. It can be planned (good publicity) or accidental. Unfortunately, most accidental publicity is bad publicity. Bad publicity, such as being named in the papers following a personal injury suit, is not something that a design firm desires. Design firms seek to create planned publicity that will help potential clients view the firm in a good light and seek them out for design contracts.

Good publicity could be the publication of a press release sent out by the firm about its winning a design award. Maybe a designer provides a tour of a home that he or she designed on a local morning news show. Good publicity can be obtained by providing a free lecture about a design topic on accessibility guidelines to a professional business group, such as accountants. These examples are activities that the design firm may pay to develop, but the firm does not pay to place promotional information in some type of media.

Other examples of activities resulting in good publicity are charitable and community service work related to interior design, for example, helping the community theater with props and set designs; volunteering services on restoration projects; and getting members of professional organizations involved in designing rooms in model houses or a display house for the benefit of a charitable group.

Basic Promotional Tools

Promotional tools are the mechanisms and devices that are used by the interior design firm to get itself before the public. Most of these tools are created and used for relatively nonspecific general audiences. These could be considered the basic tools that a designer might use to promote the company and include such things as the firm's graphic image, a photo portfolio, brochures, and press releases. Some promotional materials, such as a brochure, are sometimes referred to as collateral materials. Which promotional tools to use, what goes into them, and how they are delivered to prospective clients all play a role in furthering the image desired by the firm. However, for the most part, these basic tools are the most common and essential tools that the interior design firm uses to project information about itself to a wide audience or, for that matter, to any audience. The basic tools are items that even the sole practitioner needs to consider during start-up of the practice or as the company grows.

Two additional methods that are used to promote the design practice are referrals and networking. These methods are intensely personal. In different ways, referrals and networking are one-on-one salesmanship efforts to obtain new client contacts. These may be the primary way in which a sole practitioner obtains new clients.

Competitions are also included in this chapter. Even though entering a competition can be somewhat time-consuming and even expensive (because professional photography is needed), any size or type of design firm can enter design competitions and ultimately gain publicity from the entry.

The Graphic Image and Basic Stationery

By *graphic image*, we are referring to the package of materials that the interior design firm uses to identify itself. This includes the company logo, business cards, letterhead and other stationery, business forms, and drawing paper identification. The firm's graphic image can be incorporated into many of the tools that are discussed in this chapter and the next. There are many design options for stationery. This graphic image is the first impression potential clients have, which is so important for establishing a relationship with clients (see Figure 22-1). The color used for paper stock and ink, the type size, the typeface, and the size of the finished format are just some of the factors that the design firm must consider when it is developing the firm's graphic image and stationery. Some typefaces are overly decorative and may look great on some items but may be difficult to read on others. It is a good idea to consider hiring a graphic designer to create any logo and stationery designs. Even though the interior designer may feel that he or she is capable of doing so, a graphic designer is more familiar with products and processes that can be used to create the graphic image.

A *logo*, or mark, is a symbolic image of the company (see Figure 22-2). It can be a strong identification symbol for the firm, which will eventually help make the firm easily identifiable. It can be used for all of the firm's written communication as well as on many other items that are related to the firm's business.

The design and color of the logo should be the same on all materials related to the firm. This will help clients identify the logo with the firm and help bring

FIGURE 22-1. Sample of a design firm's stationery and logo. (Reproduced with permission, Debra May Himes Interior Design & Associates. Mesa, AZ; photo, Dawson Henderson)

FIGURE 22-2. A sample design firm's logo, used on the firm's stationery and related materials. (Reproduced with permission, James Tigges, Pinnacle Design, Inc. Phoenix, AZ)

about client awareness and identification. Logos are displayed in many of the figures found throughout this chapter. The rest of the design of the business card, stationery, and so forth must be compatible with the logo.

The business card is a very interesting marketing tool in itself. This small piece of stiffened paper, generally 3.5 inches × 2 inches, serves to help us remember people whom we have met or who have met us. They are sometimes thought of as tiny billboards by which a company can leave an impression of sophistication, whimsy or seriousness. It can be black and white, have a colored background, be white with type in many ink colors or just about anything else the design firm, graphic designer, or printer can come up with (see Figure 22-3). A business card can be single-faced, double-sided, folded, square, embossed, or it can have cutouts. Today, it is becoming more and more difficult to include all the information that a design firm may want on its business card by using only one side of the business card. Positioning the firm's logo, name, address, phone number, fax number, E-mail and web addresses, cell or pager number, and, finally, the person's name, affiliation, and license number makes for really tiny print! Many design firms have started using both sides of the card or a folded card. Other design firms are deleting some of these items and choosing to include only key contact points, such as the phone, fax, and E-mail numbers.

However, there is another choice today for business cards—tiny CD-ROMs. There are companies that produce a multimedia business card on a CD-ROM. These hi-tech cards can store video, text, graphics, audio, and even links to web pages. Just think of the presentation that your company can make with a CD-ROM business card! Of course, they are expensive and will remain so until they catch on.

Interior designers, being creative individuals, like to design their own logos, graphic image, and basic stationery. It is always a good idea to talk to a graphic designer about the graphic image in order to ensure that the design is going to "work," that is, that it can be reproduced effectively and project the image desired by the designer. There are many subtleties to the designing of graphic image and stationery, which are too numerous to discuss here. A graphic designer as well as a high-quality, professional printer can provide advice about paper color, weight of the paper stock, typefaces, color on the stationery, and many other things.

FIGURE 22-3. Examples of logos used on business cards. Clockwise from top right: Scamp Sound Masking Systems by K. R. Moeller Associates, Ltd., Ontario, Canada; Gail Adams Interiors, Phoenix, AZ; Bast/Wright Interiors, San Diego, CA; Vining Design Associates, Inc., Houston, TX; Sandy Friend, Ashland, OR; Jain Malkin, Inc., La Jolla, CA; Exclaim Design, Scottsdale, AZ. (Photo: Dawson Henderson)

There are many other items that the design firm can use to display its logo or otherwise to help make itself visible to prospective clients.

Photo Portfolio If there is one other promotional tool that the start-up interior design firm is going to need, it is the *photo portfolio*. A selection of project photos taken by a professional architectural photographer, the photo portfolio is very important to help the start-up interior design firm show what it can do in meetings with prospective clients. It is an important tool for the existing firm as well. A photo portfolio in today's design world is really a generic term for the establishing of a library of project photos that can be used as part of many kinds of promotional tools.

Today, many designers use digital cameras to take their own photographs of job sites. This works very well for designers who do not need the high-quality print images produced on regular film. An advantage to a digital photograph is that the image can be checked immediately, and, if there is something wrong, such as underlighting or overlighting, adjustments can be made and a new image can be taken. Digital photographs also can be manipulated on the computer with software like Photoshop®. Subtle changes—even dramatic ones—can be made on the computer in order to improve the photo or to incorporate other elements.

Photographs that are shot in a transparency or negative format generally produce the sharper, high-quality photographs required of magazines and book publishers, and for quality prints that hang on a wall in the office. Enlargements made from negatives or transparencies are generally sharper than from digital photos. Transparencies can be used for audiovisual presentations and look better as part of Power Point presentations. A book filled with photographs of installations can be shown to the client during the marketing stage of a design project. They will also translate a bit better when they are used to create color copies on copying machines for proposals.

It is important to get the permission of the client and to have anyone appearing in the photo sign a release, especially if the photo will be published. This protects the designer from being sued for invasion of privacy. There should always be a clause in the design contract that gives the design firm permission to photograph and submit for publication all work, whether the firm expects to do this or not. The photographer has the release forms, in case there are people in any of the photos.

Brochures

A brochure can be a helpful promotional tool. It can provide information to interest clients, grab their attention, and allow the design firm to showcase its design style and expertise. It is most useful to a design firm when clients do not know about the design firm and it still needs to build credibility in the marketplace. Brochures are least useful to interior design firms that have frequent repeat customers or that rely on referrals to generate new business, that is, if the designer expects the client to refer others to the design firm and give them a brochure.

The brochure gives the interior design firm the opportunity to show selections of its best work and to tell clients something about itself (see Figure 22-4). Although a four-color brochure on standard letter-sized paper can be expensive, small brochures can be produced at a reasonable cost. The image on the brochure should mirror the firm's image. The cover should be attention getting and interesting, and the copy should be written with the client's point of view in mind. It should be well done and should have the highest quality photography that the design firm can afford. A few excellent photographs of very good installations is far superior to many inferior shots and wordy copy. The graphic identification should relate to the other graphics.

Copy must be well written and brief, since clients do not have a lot of time to read a lengthy history or philosophy that a designer may wish to include. The copy and photos of a brochure are meant to provide just a "taste" of what the design firm is about and to "invite" the potential client to call the designer so that a face-to-face presentation can be scheduled. The copy should tell potential clients about the firm, the services it offers, and perhaps should list

PHOENIX CITY HALL

Size:	550,000 s.f.
Estimated Cost:	$55.3 M
Construction Cost:	$53.8 M
Completion Date:	1993
Location:	Phoenix, Arizona
Client/Contact:	City of Phoenix Sheryl Sculley Assistant City Manager 602.262.7915

Project Features

- Careful programming consolidated 20 city departments into a centralized, citizen-friendly facility which has become an icon in the downtown Phoenix landscape. The project has received numerous awards including AIA Award of Merit, APS Energy Award and Valley Forward Crescordia Award.

- City staff were relocated to a highly flexible and efficient 80% open office and 20% closed in the new building from approximately 80% closed offices and 20% open.New workstation standards were developed, enabling the City to more efficiently utilize space.

- Security is accomplished inconspicuously with carefully planned access to sensitive areas, and bullet-resistant panels in millwork, providing protection for staff and officials, and a level of comfort for visitors.

LANGDON WILSON ARCHITECTURE PLANNING INTERIORS

FIGURE 22-4. One-page inserts used by many firms in place of formal brochures. (Reproduced with permission, Langdon Wilson Architecture Planning Interiors, Phoenix, AZ)

former clients. Today, many graphic designers and PR professionals recommend that the copy be written using the second person (you/your) rather than the first person (we/us). It needs to be attractive and written in a language that the potential client can understand. Do not fill it with industry jargon and buzzwords that a client will not understand. The copy should set the stage for further discussions.

Care must be taken that the photographs chosen do not date the brochure. Featuring photos of the design staff is a compliment to each designer, but when one of them leaves the design firm, his or her photograph in the brochure can date or even negate the brochure. Always remember that a brochure is not, by itself, going to win new clients. It is a promotional and sales tool to help in the long-term process of attracting new clients to the interior design firm.

Creating a high-quality brochure takes expertise in graphics, composition, photography, and copywriting. Although the firm may wish to prepare the conceptual content of the brochure, it is recommended that the actual production be left to public relations professionals or professional graphic designers.

Press Releases

When the design firm has some important news, the primary way to get that news out to the public is through a press release. A *press release* is a method of providing information about the design firm that might be of interest to the news media. It is an effective, inexpensive way for any size design firm to achieve increased public awareness. Almost any kind of news or announcement can be prepared as a press release. However, newspapers and magazines, having limited space, usually only use those items that they feel are about significant, newsworthy events. If the firm has recently been named the primary design firm for a large or unusual project, a press release is in order. Perhaps the firm is sponsoring a seminar or a workshop of interest to a wide variety of businesses or consumers. A press release is also in order if the interior design firm has won a design award—especially a prestigious national award. Even the opening of a new interior design firm or the relocation of an existing interior design firm can be announced with a press release (see Figure 22-5). Due to space constraints, in most cities, announcements about promotions and new hires are relegated to a minimal statement in a business briefs column of the newspaper.

PR professionals have experience in preparing press releases; they also have many contacts with local and national print, radio, and television media. These contacts can be utilized to obtain the best coverage for press releases. If an in-house individual uses good journalistic techniques, however, then he or she can prepare a press release. Since preparing a press release is a relatively easy assignment and is an inexpensive way to obtain some publicity for any size firm, it will be covered in some depth.

Editors do not have a lot of time to read all the unsolicited materials they receive each day. Giving them the information in a form that the publication essentially uses in terms of standard style and format helps get the design firm's press release read and published. In general, the text should be prepared in concise journalistic style, using the classic five "Ws" and "H": who, what, when, where, why, and how. The most significant information should be presented in the first paragraph, and additional details can be presented in subsequent paragraphs. Text should be typed double-spaced, with wide side margins for editorial comments. One- or two-page press releases have the best chance of reaching the media. When the editor or news director reads a press release, he or she may have additional questions. The contact information—name, address, telephone number, fax, and even the E-mail address of the contact person—should be placed at the top of the first page.

Interior Associates, LLC
Contract Interior Designers
1776 E. Commerce Street
Atlanta, Georgia

For Immediate Release

For further information,
Contact: John Adams
404-555-3506
Interior Associates, LLC Awarded ________ Golden Achievement Award

Atlanta, January 10—Interior Associates, LLC will be the recipient of the twenty-third annual ________ Golden Achievement Award presented at the ________ awards banquet on February 20, Patrick Smith President, announced.

The award is granted to an interior design firm within the metropolitan Atlanta area that has achieved an outstanding record of community service during the year.

______ notes the achievements of Interior Associates with the Northside Hospice, MacAlister Center for Battered Women, and the Home Start Youth Center as representative of the outstanding interior design work contributed by the firm. Jillian Connell, administrator for the MacAlister Center for Battered Women said, "The sensitive design of our resident areas by Interior Associates has provided an atmosphere desperately needed in this facility."

Interior Associates, LLC has been specializing in healthcare facilities as well as facilities for the aged for 20 years. The firm has completed projects throughout Georgia, as well as Florida, North Carolina, Tennessee, and Alabama.

End

FIGURE 22-5. A sample press release.

Often, press releases are prepared for immediate release. The words *Immediate Release* indicates that all the information in the text is timely and ready for publication. If this is the case, it should be indicated at the top of the press release, as shown in Figure 22-5. Otherwise, the date of preferred release should be clearly indicated.

Supplementary materials, such as line drawings or photographs, provide information that the text cannot easily explain. They also may make an otherwise routine story more interesting. Magazines prefer color transparencies rather than color photographic prints. If a black-and-white photograph is sent, it should be a glossy print. Newspapers readily use black-and-white glossy prints but are less likely to use color photographic prints. When line drawings, such as floor plans, are submitted, be prepared to send PMTs or high-quality mylar reductions. PMT is a name for a diffusion transfer process (sometimes called a "stat") that results in a positive reproduction of line copy or artwork.

If people are in the photographs, their names and titles, and signed model releases should be provided. Not providing a model release with the photograph could prevent the photograph from being published. Be sure that the client or organization has been informed about your press release and model releases, and has provided written clearance for the information to be released.

It should be pointed out that even providing the best written, concise, informative press release about a truly significant event does not guarantee that print media will use it. Being selective, especially at a local level, about who receives the press release may help get it noticed and published or even broadcasted. All areas of the media like to "scoop" their colleagues. Knowing that the design firm has attempted to provide that "scoop" just may help to get the press release noticed.

Many editors do not like to receive press releases from unknown sources via E-mail. Like everyone else, editors receive lots of E-mail every day, and some find it annoying to get a press release in this way. Check out the policy of the publication before you send an E-mail. It is also a good idea to save and send your E-mail messages in plain ASCII text so that they can be read by any word-processing software that the publication uses. Do not E-mail graphics or other attachments with an unsolicited press release! They take up a lot of space and will take a long time to download—if they download at all. Mention that graphics are available and briefly describe them. The editor will let you know if you should send the graphics by a messenger or mail.

When you send a press release, do not forget to follow up with a phone call to the editor. This is something that public relations professionals do as part of their services. It ensures that your message has been received. Even if the editor is not going to use your press release, it gives you the chance to talk to him or her briefly in order to better understand what they look for, so that you will be prepared when future newsworthy items occur at your firm.

Referrals

Word-of-mouth or referral marketing is an effective way to market interior design. A *referral* occurs when one client tells another person who may be looking for interior design services about a particular design firm—hopefully your firm. For years, many design firms have depended on this method of promotion for finding new clients. It costs nothing, since no promotional materials are needed for a client to recommend the design firm to someone.

Referrals do not just happen, however. Even the most satisfied clients may not think about mentioning your firm to a friend or a business associate. On the other hand, they will if the work was done incorrectly or poorly, or if there were problems, since it is far more likely that clients will tell numerous people—even total strangers—about poor service than mention positive service. What this means is that the designer must "manage" referral marketing.

One way to do this is to develop strategies that will encourage the client to refer the design firm to potential clients. This starts with doing everything for each existing customer as perfectly and as positively as possible and not allowing errors or problems to occur. If a problem does occur, it should be taken care of with a smile and as quickly as possible. "Studies have shown that each time customers had a positive experience with you or your place of business, they will tell 4 other people. On the other hand, any time they have a negative experience, they'll tell 11 people" (Burg, 1999, p. 114).

The designer should also ask for referrals. Many customers do not understand that designers market in this way and that referrals are important. Even if they do understand the importance of referrals, as many in business will, most clients will not give referrals unless the designer encourages them to do so. Designers can encourage clients to give referrals by helping the client understand ways to go about doing so. One of the easiest strategies is to include a sentence in a follow-up letter or thank you card at the end of the project. A sentence that says something like, "My business depends on referrals. Please consider mentioning my company to people whom you feel may benefit from my services." When a client provides a referral that results in a viable client, it is acceptable not only to thank him or her but also to give the client a thank you gift, such as a gift certificate to a restaurant. In fact, some firms make it a practice to offer incentives to obtain referrals. Perhaps the incentive is a gift certificate, a special discount, or something else that might have value or meaning to a former satisfied client.

Related to referrals are testimonials or letters of reference from clients. *Testimonials* are statements that the client has made in a letter that he or she sends or gives verbally to the designer concerning their satisfaction with the design firm's work. A letter of reference states positive attributes about the design firm to either a specific client or in general. When design firms respond to requests for proposals from clients, letters of reference are often required or submitted along with the other documents. Testimonials and letters of reference lend credibility, because someone else is making the positive comments or lending evidence to claims made by the design firm. These letters can also be used in brochures, direct mail items, on the firm's web site, and in many other marketing materials.

A word of caution about referral marketing and asking clients for referrals is in order. Never make it look like the firm is begging for work. The firm must focus on satisfaction and how it can help acquaintances of the client rather than on the design firm's need for business. If the designer somehow makes it sound like the firm is desperate or in real need of business, the client will wonder if something is suddenly wrong with the firm.

Here are some tips to improve success with referrals:

- Always provide a positive experience with existing clients. Do not let problems sour a relationship. Make sure that your reputation keeps improving.
- Make it a policy to always deliver more than you promise and never promise what you cannot deliver. When a client gets something positive that he or she did not expect, the client will generally be more interested in referring your company to others.
- Develop an in-depth mailing list of existing and past clients. Send them something each month, such as article reprints, newsletters, or announcements about seminars that you may be giving. This will keep your firm in their minds.
- Identify the clients who are most likely to provide referrals and focus your efforts on them.
- Position yourself as an expert. Being very good at your niche in interior design means you will be thought of first when a client hears of someone who needs your expertise. If your firm provides excellent service and is an expert in an area, clients will feel very comfortable in recommending your firm to others.

Networking

Networking is another word-of-mouth marketing technique. In this case, the designer is the one who is doing the talking, not the client. According to the *American Heritage Dictionary of the English Language*, (2000, p. 1181), a network is "an extended group of people with similar interests or concerns who interact and remain in informal contact for mutual assistance or support." *Networking* is the cultivating of mutually beneficial relationships; it is getting to know people you can help and who can help you. *Mutually beneficial relationships* are the key words here.

Many interior designers think about networking as an opportunity to get together with colleagues at professional association meetings. Certainly, this is true, and it is always enjoyable to meet and mingle with designer friends whom you have not seen for weeks, months, or even years. However, the purpose of networking is to use it to meet people outside the design industry who might help in other ways. It is a very good way of meeting potential new clients. This kind of networking goes on at social and community clubs, seminars, church groups, schools, and the like. Because many of the reasons that a client will work with an interior designer are based on relationships, it is important to build contacts at organization meetings and groups with which potential clients may affiliate.

Whether your purpose in including networking as a marketing tool is to meet colleagues in your area or to uncover possible clients, remember that networking is a two-way street. Do not expect the other person to help you more than once if you are unwilling to help them. Becoming involved with your church's building committee just to meet clients and not really contributing to the committee will leave a very sour taste in the mouth's of the rest of the group. Asking colleagues at an association chapter meeting about suggestions for vendors without at some time giving them similar or other information will turn your colleagues away from you.

Determine what your purposes are for networking and who you want in your network. Will they be strictly designers and maybe vendors who can help you with sources? Are you looking for new clients? What other sources of help are you looking for? Go through your Rolodex files or list the names of people whom you think can help. Be sure to ask yourself, "Why these people?" and "What kind of help am I hoping they can give me?" Invite them to coffee or lunch to talk about mutually beneficial topics. If the purpose of your networking is to obtain a reference or a recommendation, you are, in effect, saying to them that you respect their opinions. And when you are asked, it means that other people respect yours. It is extremely flattering to be asked your opinion. Be willing to share information, and others will think of you as well.

Networking, like any other kind of marketing, works better if you have a plan. If you are looking to meet people at various kinds of meetings or groups, you need to learn to "work the room." Get to the meeting early so that you can scope out the meeting place and participate in the social part of the business or organization meeting. Ask the greeters if the people whom you are hoping to meet are expected. Perhaps they can even introduce you. When you attend a CEU class, get to the class early so that you can introduce yourself to other participants and the speaker.

Always have some small talk or conversation openers prepared: "Do you come to the meetings every month?" "This is a beautiful facility. Have you been here before?" Open-ended questions like these can get the other person to start talking, and before you know it, you will find yourself in a conversation. Do not simply find people you know and stay with them all through the event. You already know them. Say hello, be friendly, and move on to meet others. Make sure that you have enough business cards, and ask for cards from people who really interest you. Get back to those individuals whose cards you have obtained. If you want something from them, do not wait for them to get in touch with you. Consider staying to the end of the meeting. Some of the best contacts can be made at the end of the evening or meeting. The leaders of the organization almost always are among the last to leave.

Using networking to expand your group of acquaintances and to meet potential clients is a very effective and inexpensive marketing technique. Realize that gaining a positive relationship with someone—even a business colleague—does not happen overnight. Take the time to build your network with positive sharing, and before you know it, you will be called upon to share your knowledge in ways that you never expected. Pushing yourself on someone whom you have not met before can backfire, because they may find you aggressive or manipulative. Wanting to tell your story or ask your questions without giving something back is also impolite. Figure 22-6 provides some additional tips on how to "work a room" in order to meet new people and expand your network.

Networking has become quite a hot topic in recent years. There are many books that can help you network, regardless of your purpose for using this technique. Two of the better book are Susan Roane's *The Secrets of Savvy Networking* (1993) and Bob Burg's *Endless Referrals* (1999). The complete information for these two books can be found in the References at the end of the chapter.

Competitions

A promotional activity that can bring a designer or a design firm a great deal of publicity is design competitions. Interior designers may produce incredi-

- Place your name tag on your right side. As you shake hands, the other person's eye will be directed to your name tag. Of course, some people believe that putting the name tag on their lower jacket pocket or belt is more interesting. If it suits your personality and the occasion, go for it!
- Have a ten-second introduction prepared. When asked the common question, "What do you do?" have something to say besides, "Oh, I'm an interior designer." Perhaps you might say, "I help make people's dreams come true." This will get a conversation going!
- If you want to give your business card to someone, ask the person for his or hers first. If the person does not offer you a card, then it is okay to ask for one.
- Take care of eating at a meeting first, if possible, since it is difficult to balance a drink, a plate of food, and get at your business cards. Freshen up and then progress to meeting people and exchanging cards.
- Know why you are attending the meeting. If you want to meet people, plan to introduce yourself. Do not complain later that the meeting was a waste of time if you end up spending the evening with an old friend or sitting like a wallflower.
- Do not drink too much alcohol. Sometimes it is a good idea not to drink at all during a meeting if you are trying to meet business contacts. At the very least, know your limit.
- Always have a sufficient number of business cards for the occasion. Nobody is impressed when you say, "I just gave out my last one." Use a card holder or put a few in your jacket pocket.
- As soon as possible after you get a card from someone (but not in front of the person, unless it seems appropriate), write a brief note as to where and when you met the person and something that will clue you in later about why you have their card.
- Make others feel comfortable at meetings. If you have been to the meeting before and you see someone new, go up and talk to the person. Introduce the person to others. In a way, appoint yourself a hostess. At the very least, you will get to meet one or two new people and will gain experience at extending yourself.
- Be sure and follow up in an appropriate manner. If you have promised to call or to send something to someone whom you have met, do so promptly. Be sure to get in touch with the chair, if you volunteered to help out at the next meeting. And do not forget a thank you card, if one is needed.

FIGURE 22-6. Tips on how to "work a room" when you are networking.

ble design work, but sometimes only a few people get to see how creative this work is. Competitions provide a great deal of publicity. Since the competitions are judged by design peers, peer recognition for outstanding work is recognized.

Design competitions are sponsored by many venues. Many local association chapters sponsor annual competitions. With the client's permission, the designer can enter recent work. These competitions are juried by other interior designers or those in the interior design industry. The award itself is always something that can be displayed in the office and serves to announce to potential clients that the designer has a reputation for doing exceptional work. In addition, the competition organization generally submits information about the award winners to the local media. Local awards are sometimes announced in national trade publications.

Competitions occur on the national level, sponsored by professional associations or manufacturers. Awards are announced at national conferences, and information about the awards is often published in trade magazines. The information is commonly submitted to the local media in the award winners' hometowns. Many competitions have categories for student entries. The *Publicity Directory of the Design, Engineering and Building Industries* is a catalog of award programs. It can generally be found in most large libraries. You can find out about competitions through associations' announcements on their web site, announcements in trade magazines, some of which are mailed directly to designers.

The numerous opportunities for entering competitions throughout the year means that a design firm must target which competitions to enter. Competitions are somewhat expensive, because professional photographs are needed and also time is needed to prepare the materials in the required format. Most have some sort of entry fee. A particular competition may not require that photographs be taken by a professional, but few interior designers win competitions, especially at the national level, with nonprofessional photographs. Photographing a project can cost several thousands of dollars. Like any other promotional tool, however, the photos and time invested in preparing an entry for competition must be weighed against the possible benefits.

The professional recognition that comes with winning or placing in a competition is very worthwhile. Recognition from peers is especially nice to receive, and recognition from peers in one's professional association is even sweeter to some designers. However, look at competitions in other ways, too. The photographs taken for a competition can be used in many ways—for the firm's photo portfolio, as well as in brochures, newsletters, case studies, and direct mail programs. They might be needed for proposal pamphlets, and they also can be integrated into the firm's web site.

It is advisable to prepare entry materials very carefully and professionally. Jurors are likely to respond to a dramatic presentation as much as to the creativity shown in the project. The design firm must prepare its entry to meet the requirements of the competition. Deviating in any way can eliminate an otherwise excellent project from consideration. Do not forget to get the client's approval before submitting drawings and photographs. In fact, many competitions include a required release form as part of the competition package. If your firm is new to the awards competition scenario, start on the local level or with smaller competitions. Get your feet wet and then move up to the more prestigious ones. Remember, the larger the pool of competitors is, as in a large, national or international competition, the more difficult it will be for you to win. Good luck!

Summary

Depending on the firm's position in the life cycle of a business (discussed in Chapter 9), marketing and promotional strategies and tactics are very important. If the firm is new or trying to enter a new market, it will likely need a variety of promotional strategies to make itself known to potential clients. Existing firms depend more on referrals than on active marketing. However, no firm can succeed without using some of the marketing tools discussed in this chapter. Potential clients will want to know something about the firm, so having a brochure or marketing letter available to give them, or even prepared resumes of staff for inclusion in a proposal are needed.

The promotional concepts discussed in this chapter suggest that there are many tools that the firm can utilize to promote itself to potential clients. Used independently or in combination, all sizes of design firms must promote themselves to a target market. Whether this is accomplished by using press releases, entering competitions, distributing a brochure, or using any of the other tools discussed in this chapter and the next, keeping the design firm's name in the client's mind is very important. The next chapter discusses several additional, more complex—and expensive—promotional tools.

REFERENCES

American Heritage Dictionary of the English Language. 2000. 4th ed. Boston, MA: Houghton-Mifflin.

Austin, Richard L. 1984. *Report Graphics*. New York: Van Nostrand Reinhold.

Bachner, John Philip, and Naresh Kumar Khosla. 1977. *Marketing and Promotion for Design Professionals*. New York: Van Nostrand Reinhold.

Bangs, David H., Jr. 1998. *The Market Planning Guide*, 5th ed. Chicago, IL: Upstart Publishing.

Barr, Vilma. 1995. *Promotion Strategies for Design and Construction Firms*. New York: Van Nostrand Reinhold.

Berkowitz, Eric N., Roger A. Kerin, Steven W. Hartley, and William Rudelius. 1994. *Marketing*, 4th ed. Burr Ridge, IL: Richard D. Irwin.

Bly, Robert W. 1991. *Selling Your Services*. New York: Henry Holt.

Burg, Bob. 1999. *Endless Referrals*, rev. ed. New York: McGraw-Hill.

Cook, Kenneth J. 1995. *AMA Complete Guide to Small Business Marketing*. Chicago, IL: American Marketing Association.

Coxe, Weld. 1971. *Marketing Architectural and Engineering Services*. New York: Van Nostrand Reinhold.

Crandall, Rick. 1998. *1001 Ways to Market Your Services*. Lincolnwood, IL: Contemporary Books.

———. 1996. *Marketing Your Services*. Lincolnwood, IL: Contemporary Books.

Davidson, Jeff. 1994. *Marketing on a Shoestring*, 2nd ed. New York: John Wiley.

Davidson, Jeffrey P. 1990. *Marketing for the Home-Based Business*. Holbrook, MA: Bob Adams.

Edwards, Paul, Sarah Edwards (with Laura Clampitt Douglas). 1991. *Getting Business to Come to You*. New York. Tarcher/Putnam.

Fletcher, Tana, and Julia Rocklin. 2000. *Getting Publicity*. North Vancouver, B.C., Canada: Self-Counsel Press.

Frost, Susan E. 1995. *Blueprint for Marketing*, 2nd ed. Portland, OR: SEF Publications.

Harding, Ford. 1998. *Creating Rainmakers*. Holbrook, MA: Adams Media.

Haviland, David. 1994. *The Architect's Handbook of Professional Practice, Student Edition*. Washington DC: AIA Press.

Hays, Rick Stephan, and Gregory Brooks Elmore. 1985. *Marketing for Your Growing Business.* New York: Ronald Press.

Hiebing, Roman G., Jr., and Scott W. Cooper. 1999. *The One-Day Marketing Plan*, 2nd ed. Lincolnwood, IL: NTC Business Books.

Jones, Gerre L. 1983. *How to Market Professional Design Services*, 2nd ed. New York: McGraw-Hill.

———. 1980. *Public Relations for the Design Professional.* New York: McGraw-Hill.

Karasik, Paul. 1992. *How to Make It Big in the Seminar Business.* New York: McGraw-Hill.

Kliment, Stephen A. 1998. *Writing for Design Professionals.* New York: W. W. Norton.

———. 1977. *Creative Communications for a Successful Design Practice.* New York: Watson-Guptill.

Kotler, Philip. 2000. *Marketing Management*. Millennium ed. Upper Saddle River, NJ: Prentice Hall.

Kotler, Philip, and Gary Armstrong. 1999. *Principles of Marketing*, 8th ed. Upper Saddle River, NJ: Prentice-Hall.

Krannich, Ronald L., and Caryl Rae Krannich. 1989. *Network Your Way to Job and Career Success.* Manassas, VA: Impact Publications.

Kremer, John, and J. Daniel McComas. 1997. *High-Impact Marketing on a Low-Impact Budget.* Rocklin, CA: Rima Publishing.

Levinson, Jay Conrad. 1993. *Guerrilla Marketing*, rev. ed. Boston, MA: Houghton Mifflin.

Marconi, Joe. 1999. *The Complete Guide to Publicity*. Lincolnwood, IL: NTC Business Books.

Martin, Jane D., and Nancy Knoohuizen. "Create a 'Bang' with Easy-to-Use Marketing Techniques." *ASID Professional Designer.* July/August 1997, 14–15.

———. 1995. *Marketing Basics for Designers*. New York: John Wiley.

McCarthy, E. Jerome. 1981. *Basic Marketing*, 7th ed. Homewood, IL: Richard D. Irwin.

McCaslin, Barbara S., and Patricia P. McNamara. 1980. *Be Your Own Boss*. Englewood Cliffs, NJ: Prentice-Hall.

Morgan, Jim. 1984. *Marketing for the Small Design Firm.* New York: Watson-Guptill.

Popyk, Bob. 2000. *Here's My Card.* Los Angeles, CA: Renaissance Books.

Putman, Anthony O. 1990. *Marketing Your Services.* New York: John Wiley.

Roane, Susan. 1993. *The Secrets of Savvy Networking*. New York: Time Warner Books.

———. 1988. *How to Work a Room.* New York: Time Warner Books.

Row, Heath. "These Cards Mean Business." *Fast Company.* August 1998, 62.

Stanley, Thomas J. 1993. *Networking with the Affluent*. New York: McGraw-Hill.

Windham, Laurie (with Ken Orton). 2000. *The Soul of the New Consumer.* New York: Allworth Press.

Zeithami, Valarie A. and Mary Jo Bitner. 1996. *Services Marketing.* New York: McGraw-Hill.

Chapter 23

Advanced Promotional Tools

The previous chapter discussed several basic methods or tools for promoting an interior design practice. The tools discussed in this chapter are those that any size or kind of interior design firm can use but are more commonly used by the larger firm, because it has greater financial resources. Of course, a design firm does not need to use all these promotional methods. The sole practitioner should be able to afford to implement one or two of them.

Promotional tools discussed in this chapter include various kinds of publication opportunities, direct marketing, seminars, and Internet marketing. For commercial interior designers, the preparation of a proposal in response to a request for proposal (RFP) from a client is a very important marketing tool. The chapter concludes with a discussion on advertising and how this promotional activity can be used by interior design firms.

Publication

There are many possible ways for the interior designer to utilize print media to gain publicity for the firm beyond the press release. For the most part, the publication of photographs and text (or editorial copy) is a relatively inexpensive way for the design firm or designer to obtain publicity since the interior designer does not pay for it. However, preparing materials to submit for publication takes time. Excellent quality photographs are very important. In some cases, the publication will pay for the photography and even prepare the editorial material (the text), though this is not common. This section will discuss four ways of using publication as a promotional tool: (1) project submissions, (2) newsletters and case studies, (3) general design articles, and (4) books.

Project Submissions

A most sought after kind of publicity is publication of projects in trade and shelter (or consumer) magazines. Trade magazines or journals are those that focus on a particular profession, business, or industry. These publications are sold by subscription primarily to those within the publication's target market. However, some are found on newsstands. Examples of trade magazines in interior design include *Interior Design*, *Contract*, *Interiors*, and *Interiors and Sources*. There are several others. Shelter or consumer magazines are sold by subscription or on newsstands for the general public. Examples of consumer magazines in interior design include *American Homestyle and Gardening*, *Southern Accents*, *Architectural Digest*, and *House Beautiful*. There are dozens of others. A few trade magazines cross over to the consumer market. Large bookstores or magazine stands often carry *Interior Design*.

Because of the different types and proliferation of magazines and other print media, when a firm decides to submit materials to a magazine or other print publication, it must decide who the audience should be and the purpose for submitting the material. As mentioned, each magazine or other type of print media has a different audience. Some are very specific, and the designer needs to understand who makes up the readership of the magazine before he or she submits the project (or article). ASID has prepared a pamphlet called *Professional Exposure: how to get design work published*. This pamphlet lists general guidelines for preparing publication material for many of the trade and shelter magazines. The pamphlet also provides information concerning the type of projects and kinds of materials each of the magazines might be interested in publishing. Designers can also contact a magazine's editorial offices to receive information about submission requirements. This type of research is commonly part of a public relations professional's responsibilities.

Publication of a project in a interior design or built environment trade publication generally means that there will be a limited audience for it, consisting of primarily professional peers. Residential designers may want to have projects published in local or national shelter magazines or possibly the home section of the local newspaper. Many cities have local magazines that are used for promoting the good qualities of the city or state. These magazines often include articles on residences or commercial properties, giving designers an outlet to consumers. Some of these magazines even have special issues that focus on the local design community. In addition, many of these publications welcome articles or even have ongoing columns written by local designers. These articles help educate the reader on various topics in the interior design firm.

Commercial designers may seek to publish their projects in the trade magazines that are read by the target clients. For example, if the purpose of the publication of a project is to have clients gain more awareness of the interior design firm, the firm can obtain reprints and mail or give them to prospective and former clients. Such magazines as *Hospitality Design*, *Law Practice Management*, *Modern Physician*, and *Corporate Design* run articles on outstanding interior design projects. To locate a publication that focuses on a particular design specialty, refer to *Ayer's Directory of Publications*, published by Ayer's Press. This directory lists information on all the magazines published annually in the United States and is available at most public libraries.

Newsletters and Case Studies

Newsletters have long been popular with architects and larger interior design firms. With the software that is available today, even the smaller design firms can produce a newsletter for promotional use. There are two basic kinds of *newsletters*. One is the simple in-house newsletter that tells everyone whose birthday it is and other tidbits of interest to employees. The other is the promotional newsletter that is used to inform clients about projects or otherwise provide information that clients might find valuable (see Figure 23-1).

When a firm makes a commitment to publish a newsletter, the first thing to remember is that it has made a commitment. Once the firm begins to publish a newsletter, it must follow through. The firm should keep publishing the newsletter to show this commitment to its clients. This being said, one of the first decisions that the firm will need to make is to determine what will be the purpose of the newsletter and the budget for producing it. Part of this decision is determing how often it will be published. With a large in-house staff, a

Perkins&Will

Chicago, New York, Washington
Architects, Engineers, Planners, Interior & Graphic Designers

PROGRESS

Facilities Management: Controlling Physical Assets

Reduction in demand for basic and consumer goods and services, slow receivables, lay-offs, and changing capital markets are phenomena almost all sectors of the economy have faced to some degree during the early 80's. The result has been commitment to tighter management of an organization's assets. Asset management includes people, equipment, and facilities. It is no surprise, then, that a full service architecture, engineering and interior design firm like Perkins & Will has experienced increased interest from its clientele in a specialized section of this process—Facilities Management.

In its most comprehensive sense, facilities management is the process of inventorying and evaluating the location, condition, function, and economic value of an organization's physical assets. In other times we called this systematic effort Master Planning. While the terminology has changed, the intent has not. Whatever it is called, the objective is to make the best economic use of the real estate owned and/or occupied by an institution. The required activities fall into two categories.

- Identification in an organized and retrievable manner of all pertinent data related to real estate and property assets.
- Analysis of this data to determine the most appropriate means of using and managing the asset.

These analyses take on many different forms depending on an organization's specific objectives. They can deal with land, buildings, improvements, interior space, or furnishings. They can address immediate needs for space or cash, or they can position the company to respond intelligently to future conditions.

Furnishings

Beginning with the most tangible facilities, companies are looking at their furnishings, carpeting and other moveable equipment to determine whether they are functional, for how long, and what they are worth. When one real estate investment trust recently acquired two neighboring, but dissimilar office buildings, it decided to market the buildings as one unit. To achieve this, the public had to view the two buildings as related even though the architecture, bay

continued on page 2

HARTFORD PLAZA
Chicago, Illinois

Two downtown Chicago high-rises were the focus of efforts to unify the buildings visually through new signage programs and renovation of main floors and public areas. Tenant standards were developed for various interior design elements; the overall conceptual scheme was designed to allow for phased implementation so the buildings could remain open while renovation proceeded.

April 1983 1

FIGURE 23-1. A sample of a newsletter that provides information about projects with which this design firm recently has been involved. (Reprinted with permission, Perkins & Will, Chicago, IL: Photo: Eugene Balzer)

design firm might be able to produce enough project announcements or other information to issue a newsletter on a quarterly basis. A small firm might plan on publishing a semiannual newsletter. Of course, a monthly newsletter is best, but any regular publication is better than none. It will be necessary also for the firm to determine how many pages will be produced, how often, and what type (if any) graphics will be included. Of course, the basics, like type style, format (two or three columns?), and use of color also must be determined.

Then the firm will need to decide on the overall content of the newsletter. Perhaps it will be primarily announcements about project contracts and completed projects. Maybe the firm intends to provide useful information, such as changes in code requirements, that clients should know about. Finally, a determination must be made as to who will have the responsibility of producing the newsletter. Someone in-house may be able to take on the responsibility, but this means that the hours spent on this task are not billable. A freelance writer or consultant can be hired, which saves time for the staff but will raise the expense of producing the newsletter. None of these decisions can be taken lightly.

Of course, a newsletter can also be integrated into the design firm's web page. In fact, many firm's have given up producing a printed promotional newsletter and have put all this information on their website. More will be discussed about the web later in this chapter.

A case study of a particularly interesting or challenging project can be produced as a separate publication. A *case study* tells what the design program was and some unique features of the project, and may include before and after photographs. A case study can also discuss the solution and ideally contains some quotes from the client regarding the quality of the project. Many commercial design firms develop a variety of simple case studies to include in materials needed for proposal submissions (see Figure 23-2). A case study can be as short so as to fit on one page, with space for a photograph. Complex projects, obviously, will require a longer case study, in order to include several photographs. They also can be inserted into a brochure to show the firm's special expertise. Some firms also include case studies as part of their web page. The same kinds of considerations mentioned for a newsletter need to be taken into account when the firm is determining whether or not to utilize case studies as a promotional tool.

Neither the newsletter nor the case study needs to be printed in color but should be well done. Today, high-quality, color laser printers and color photocopiers make it much easier for smaller design firms to incorporate color into their newsletters and case studies.

General Design Articles

The twenty-first century has certainly become the information age. Everyone wants to learn more about a wide variety of topics. And there are certainly a wide variety of topics covering the interior design and built environment industry. Designers who are comfortable with gathering information and writing find that proposing general design articles is an effective way of marketing themselves and their businesses. "Publications provide one proof of who is real and who isn't . . . published work tells [a potential client] that the author must have substantial experience, and that she has reflected more deeply on her businesses than some" (Harding, 1994, p. 24). Clients many times view designers who have articles published in print media as experts or at least as having more expertise than others. And clients like to hire experts. When a potential client sees an article by a designer in a magazine or a newspaper, this indicates to the client that the designer must have some expertise that his or her peers do not. The fact that a magazine has printed an article by a designer might also inspire a trade association to ask the designer to speak at a meeting.

Material submitted to a magazine is reviewed and considered by an editor who is looking for good information that will be appropriate for the publica-

AvMed Health Plan

This $800 million, non-profit HMO has been growing so fast and reconfiguring furniture so frequently, employees tease that the company's name is Latin for "change." Which is why, at their Gainesville, Florida, headquarters campus, AvMed built a workplace where everything is changeable. Now they can make changes faster, cheaper, and with far less disruption than ever before.

Organizational Goals

Skyrocketing membership. That's how AvMed expects to maintain its position as Florida's largest and oldest HMO. New services, new-member drives, and acquisitions of smaller healthcare providers are among the ways AvMed plans to nearly double its membership from 400,000 today to 700,000 next year.

More members means more incoming phone calls and more claims. To accommodate this internal growth and alleviate overcrowding in existing facilities at their headquarters campus, the HMO needed another building. And because AvMed's corporate mission is to improve the health of members and employees while keeping rates low, the new workplace needed to help reduce day-to-day costs while providing a healthy, attractive environment for their employees.

"We believe the physical environment plays a large role in how satisfied and effective people are in their work."

Bob Hudson, chief operating officer

This claims support group work area used to be scattered among different floors. Now that they're together and have instant visual access to one another, they're getting more work done in a day.

Workplace Objectives

Employees were crammed into AvMed's two existing facilities. To accommodate the rapid growth of the workforce, workspaces in the open plan had shrunk below corporate standards and departments were scattered among floors.

The company's technological needs had grown just as rapidly. Additional equipment on each desktop had increased the number of power and communication cables beyond AvMed's expectations. Also, the company's "home run" method of laying cables from the communications closet all the way to the desktops proved too slow and costly for this dynamic organization. Reconfiguring a typical workspace required help from three vendors, took more than a week, cost $940, and disrupted adjoining workspaces.

To meet AvMed's needs, the new facility would have to:

- accommodate technological growth
- reduce life-cycle costs
- support worker effectiveness
- promote employee health, safety, and comfort
- re-use existing Avenir® workstations

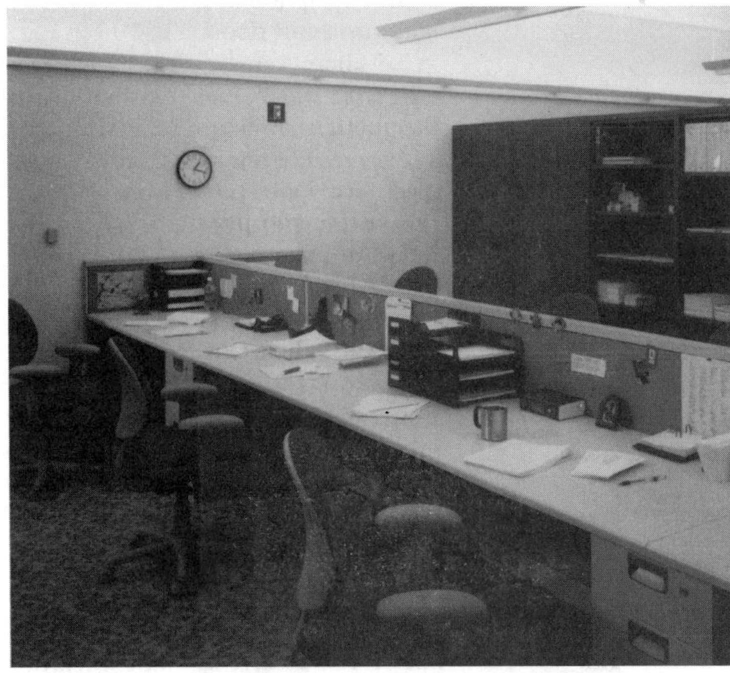

FIGURE 23-2. A sample project case study used for marketing purposes. (Reproduced with permission, Steelcase, Inc. Grand Rapids, MI.)

tion. The writer must have some credentials, along with an ability to write, in order to be considered a columnist or even a contributing writer to a publication. The editor also is looking for good writing and a sense that the person who is writing the article knows what he or she is talking about. Designers who submit articles generally must submit a brief resume that explains the designer's expertise in the topic.

Once an article has been published, the author can request reprints. These reprints can then be used as part of the design firm's total marketing plan and strategies. Reprints can be included in packets that are given to clients during marketing presentations or in packets that are mailed to prospective clients. Designers can also send along a reprint when they are writing to a former client.

In order to achieve publication, the designer must do some homework. First of all, the designer should investigate the publications in the firm's geographic area. Determine what kinds of articles are commonly found in those publications. Major cities have local resident and tourism magazines that cover issues of interest to local residents but also are used to attract out-of-town tourists. This type of magazine occasionally has a few issues that contain articles on interesting interior design and architecture. Magazines such as *Phoenix Magazine, Los Angeles,* and *Chicago* are of this type.

When you find a magazine that you think targets your potential clients, check a few issues to see what style of writing and types of editorial material the magazine publishes. If what you want to submit does not fit the editorial content of the magazine, you will be wasting your time and that of the publication's editorial staff. Most magazines review unsolicited manuscripts, but usually they do not return them if they are not used. Because of this (and other reasons), writers should send query letters first, to save time. A query letter explains the concept of the article and even gives a little "taste" of it by including the first paragraph. If the editor is interested, the editor will contact the designer. Then arrangements can be made concerning length, whether or not graphics or photographs are needed, deadlines, and even whether the magazine will pay for the piece.

When you suggest an article, make sure that the article is something the magazine normally publishes. Come up with an idea that is interesting to the magazine's readers. Make sure it is something you know something about and can easily research for additional background, if necessary. Provide a good focus to the article—most magazines limit the length of articles submitted from nonstaff writers to 500–1500 words.

If the editor is interested, he or she will send you information about the magazine's style guidelines, which include information about margins, word count, requirements for camera-ready photographs or drawings, and basic grammatical style that is appropriate for the publication.

Although an article will not result in the phone ringing off the hook from new clients' inquiries, it does provide one more promotional tool that the interior design firm can use. Articles provide awareness; they get the design firm's name or designer's name in front of more clients than can be reached by the efforts of the designer alone. And writing can be fun!

Books

Writing a book is another way of demonstrating expertise and authority and can be a very effective promotional tool for the interior designer. Of course, books take longer to write and require greater commitment than writing an article. However, it is a way of showing more expertise and credibility, especially if the topic is related to the designer's specialty.

Perhaps a designer's expertise is in retail store design and he or she writes a book on that topic. A book about the many considerations that go into designing an effective sales background for a retail store can be a very useful promotional tool for that designer. The book will give prestige to the interior designer, and the designer can add this to his or her resume.

A few words of caution about writing books, however. They take time—sometimes a great deal of time—to research, write, rewrite, obtain photographs or other graphics, and go through the editing process. Do not contemplate writing a book as a promotional tool if you are disorganized and your business does not allow your being away while you write the book. Publishers only give the writer a certain length of time to complete the manuscript. They expect to receive it on time—or nearly so.

You can find complete instructions on how to submit a manuscript proposal from many book publishers. There are also numerous reference books at bookstores on this topic.

Direct Mail

Another type of promotional activity is the process of mailing solicited and unsolicited materials to potential clients. *Direct mail* can mean just about anything—from mailing letters to any number of the items already listed. Since printing and postage are ongoing expenses, the key is to get the mailed items to the right people. To do this, the firm must have a good mailing list. The mailing list for most designers starts with past and existing customers. Additions to the list might come from researching chamber of commerce membership lists, appropriate professional association membership lists, or even the phone book.

We all receive a huge amount of unsolicited "junk" mail. A promotional mailing from a design firm will be considered junk mail by many receivers. Most junk mail ends up in the wastebasket. Often, junk mail that is sent to businesses ends up the same way. Even the best prepared mailings from business to business receive a small return rate when they are mailed to unknown people (Bly, 1994, p. 42). Therefore, it is important to consider carefully what is being mailed, why it is being sent, and to whom it is being sent.

Mailings must have some impact and should be designed to catch the eye of the receiver. They need to be well designed and creatively thought out. A good graphics designer or marketing specialist might be the answer for designing the mailing. Direct mailings that are used by interior designers are usually cover letters accompanied by a brochure or a newsletter. But direct mailings might also be announcements of sales, holiday promotions, and seminars. They give the firm a chance to see how the receiver reacts to the mailing and to make an appointment to further discuss its contents or answer any questions that the receiver may have. It is best if the mailing list includes only former clients and contacts, although some direct mail programs are meant to announce the firm to potentially new clients.

Direct mail can be sent to residential clients as well as to businesses. The items sent should be prepared for, and focused on, that particular audience—a letter or brochure for a commercial client, obviously, will not be received well at a residence, and vice versa. The items sent should provide information and should be sufficiently interesting to entice the receiver to call or write for more information. But nothing will happen automatically. For the greatest possible number of leads from direct mailings, the designer should follow up with a personal call.

An example of a twenty-first-century version of direct mail is sending an unsolicited fax or E-mail announcement. Many who receive these unsolicited faxes and E-mails are annoyed by them. Having been the recipient of unsolicited faxes at 2:30 in the morning at my home office, this author cautions against using these technologies for marketing purposes. It is also no fun, indeed, to wade through unsolicited E-mails if one regularly receives dozens of business E-mails in any one day.

There are a great number of techniques and strategies in direct mail that the designer can use as a promotional tool to develop client leads. The professional who wants to consider using direct mail is urged to check the references at this end of the chapter. For direct mail programs to businesses, the best book that the author has found is Robert W. Bly's (1994) *Business to Business Direct Marketing*.

Speaking at Seminars and Meetings

Another way to demonstrate expertise and to generate client leads is by presenting seminars. Whether the designer is in residential or some area of commercial interior design, speaking at seminars can be a very rewarding process and tool. Residential clients are interested in all kinds of topics related to the design of homes, and interior designers who make themselves available to speak to civic and club groups may find a ready group of listeners, as well as potential customers. Local business trade associations are always looking for experts who can provide them with information at their monthly meetings. The designer may even be asked to speak at regional or national conventions of professional groups of potential clients. Many interior designers have found this to be a successful way to market themselves or their design firm.

As with articles and books, the designer should choose a topic of interest to the potential audience and something that can help project expertise. For example, a author was asked to speak to a local accounting group shortly after the Americans with Disabilities Act went into effect. This professional group was concerned about how the law would impact their offices. A presentation was made on the law, in general, and how design issues could resolve the impact of this law on their offices.

Obtain conference proceedings or convention brochures from last year's convention to help determine what an appropriate topic might be for the next convention. Send your proposal in early. The next year's convention is planned shortly after this year's convention ends. If you want to start speaking at the local level, contact association or club program chairs. They often set schedules a year in advance as well.

At the presentation, bring along plenty of business cards, your brochure, or other handouts that the audience can take with them to keep your name in front of them. This is completely proper, unless the organization has a policy against it.

If you are afraid of making a presentation—and this is feared by a great number of people—work up to giving a presentation by speaking to smaller groups. Volunteer to give a presentation or critique at interior design program classes. Chair an association committee so that you have to speak before groups. Take a public speaking class—a good idea for students and also for professionals. The class can help you polish your presentation techniques and build confidence.

If you do not want to actually give the seminar, host one. Playing the host will force you to speak before a group. This will, again, help you gain confidence so that someday you will be ready to take the podium yourself! There are many books on how to prepare presentations. Check the references at the end of this chapter and Chapter 25 for suggestions.

Premiums

Interior designers are used to receiving premiums from vendors and suppliers. A *premium* is a product that has a logo, slogan, or other words or graphics printed on an object. It is something the firm usually gives away, for example, a coffee mug or a pen with the firm's name and logo. A premium can also be something that the company sells, such as the classic logo T-shirt. Giving a premium is an easy way for the firm to get its name recognized by a reasonably wide audience. Just think of how much recognition Mouseketeer ears have brought Walt Disney Corporation!

Premiums can be quite costly or reasonably priced. They come in all types, colors, and price ranges. Even the small firm can offer a premium by having its logo and name printed on something small and useful, such as memo pads or pencils. Remember that the premium itself says a lot about the firm, just as the message you have printed does. If you want your firm to be known for quality, do not send out cheap pens that break after a few uses or a scale that is not in scale!

Multimedia Presentations

Interior designers today have many forms of media from which they can choose for possible promotional assistance. Gone are the days in which a designer was confined to using glossy photographic prints in a portfolio or a slide presentation. These media, of course, are the basis of many multimedia presentations. Photographs of jobs can be turned into reliable slides, scanned on CD-ROMs, and integrated with animation on film or a CD-ROM. Digital photographs can be incorporated into multimedia presentations in many different variations. Film also can be taken relatively inexpensively with affordable videotape cameras. Computer-based presentations, using software such as PowerPoint, are relatively easy to put together. Photos, drawings, text, and animation can be blended together to create a dynamic presentation. Many larger design firms have moved away from distributing printed brochures and use some sort of multimedia presentation instead. Figure 22-3 shows one example of what a CD-ROM card can look like. There is almost no end to the ways in which a multimedia presentation can be produced to suit the budget and needs of any size interior design firm.

A multimedia presentation takes some thought and time to produce. Someone needs to be in charge of the production. It can be an in-house project, but this takes time away from billable hours. A consultant might be necessary to help with development and production, especially if the presentation will take the place of a printed brochure. It is necessary to determine what should be included and to prepare an outline so that a script or a story board (sketches of each frame or page) can be created. Then the actual integration and production will take place. A narrator may be needed as well.

Obviously, a multimedia presentation is not an inexpensive promotional tool, unless the firm is using a tailored slide presentation or prepares a computer-based presentation in-house. As with any other promotional tool, the firm must consider it in light of the budget and the goals of the firm before it commits to anything. References on how to prepare some types of multimedia presentations are listed at the end of this chapter.

Internet Marketing

By the time this book has been published, the question of whether an interior design firm needs an Internet presence or not may be a moot issue. Since 1995, the use of the Internet and the World Wide Web have exploded. The meaning of the two concepts—the Internet and World Wide Web—sometimes causes confusion. The Internet is a large, worldwide network by which all computers around the world can be connected to one another. The World Wide Web (also called the Web and even tri-dub) is a subset of the Internet, made up of servers—large computers—that store the information that Internet users can access. The visual that most readers are familiar with is the web page (see Figure 23-3). The web page is a document that is written using a special programming language, referred to as HTML (Hypertext Markup Language). With the use of secondary software, commonly called plug-ins, the HTML basic document can use text, graphics, animation, audio, and video to create a finished web page.

At first, the Internet and the World Wide Web was just a great place for people to find information. It opened up libraries around the world to researchers, educators, and students. In addition, it provided a place for writers to submit material on an almost limitless assortment of topics. The Internet quickly grew from being a vehicle for government agencies and the military to exchange information to being a wide open highway of information, commerce, and marketing venues.

According to *Fast Company* magazine, the number of domain names (addresses on the web) was only 26,000 in 1993. It grew to over 5 million in 1999, and who knows how many there will be when you read this text (Rosenfeld, 2000, p. 210). The article further reported that, in 1995, on-line retail sales did not hit $1 billion dollars but, by 2002, business-to-business (referred simply as B2B) sales will reach $1.3 trillion (Rosenfeld, 2000, p. 213)! Sales to consumers will naturally increase as well, but many end users have remained somewhat reluctant to do all but a limited amount of web purchasing.

There are, of course, all kinds of uses for an Internet connection. Besides searching for information, using E-mail is one of the most common. Electronic mail is fast, reliable (for the most part) and certainly cheap. Business communications of every kind can be sent by E-mail as attachments. Many design firms in 1997 were already using E-mail to communicate with clients around the country and the world. Some were beginning to use E-mail in those early years to transmit orders for goods from suppliers. Others found the speed of transmitting drawings electronically an amazing advantage.

Because not everyone uses the same operating system for their computers, a person must be careful when sending attachments via E-mail. In many cases, the use of ASCII text must be used. When graphics such as floor plans are attached, even more problems can occur. Utility programs that can translate the encoded graphics may be needed.*

E-commerce and E-tailing (electronic retailing) are becoming quite common. Ordering via the Internet using E-mail or direct placement systems is

* Since systems and software change very fast, the reader should contact a hardware/software consultant to determine the right products for his or her situation.

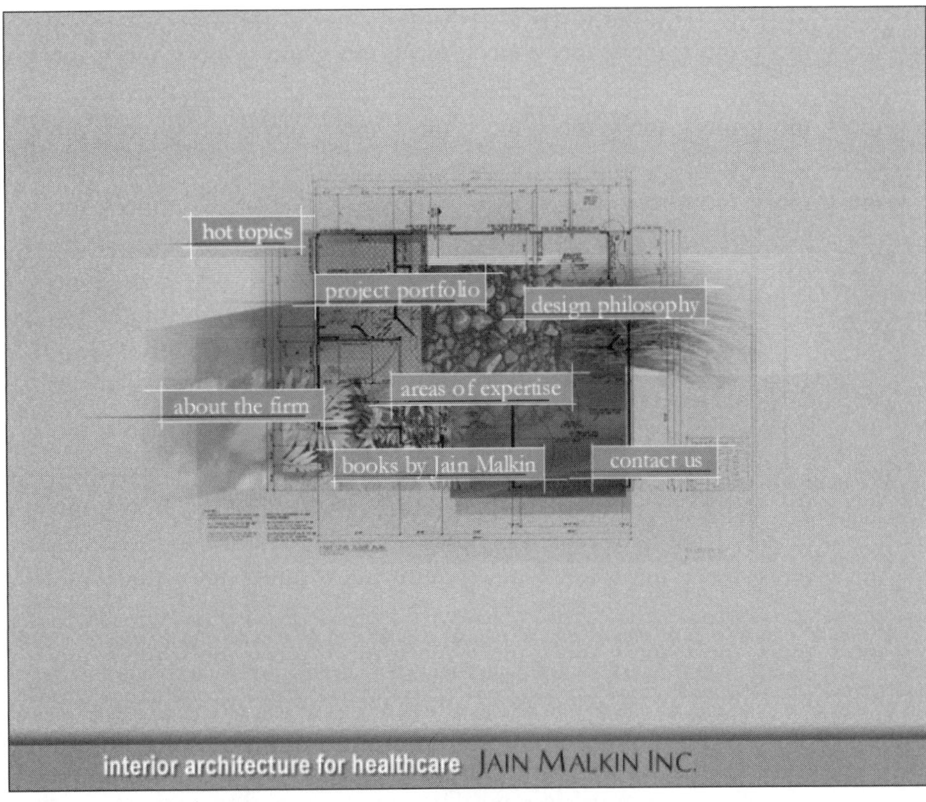

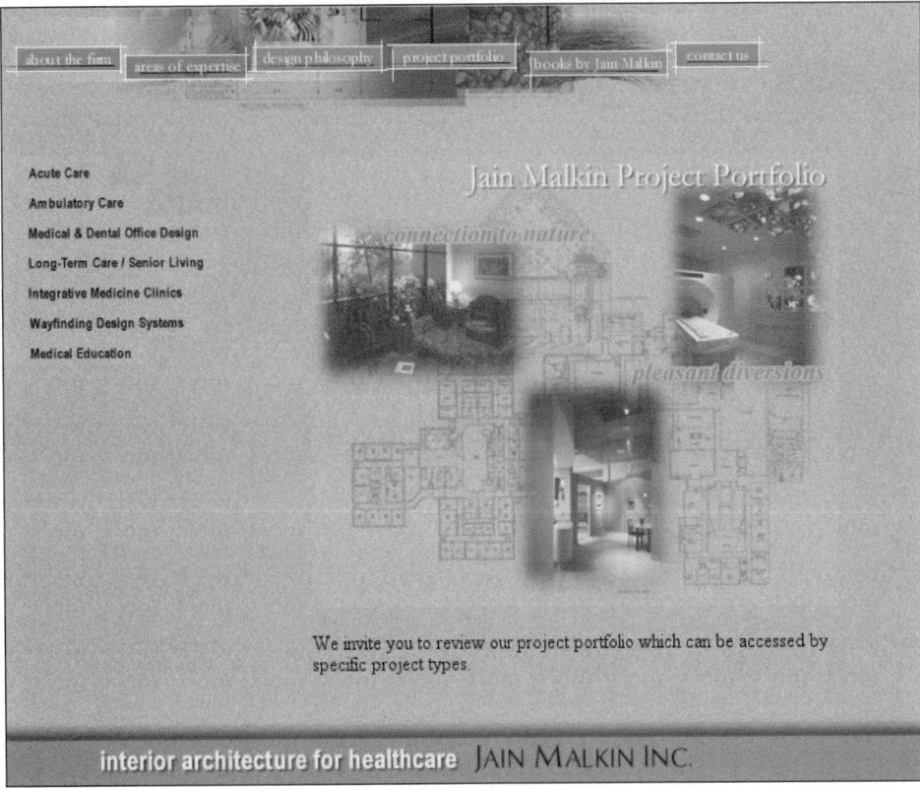

FIGURE 23-3. The home page (a) and internal web page (b) from the web site of Jain Malkin Inc. (Reproduced courtesy Jain Malkin Inc. La Jolla, CA)

commonplace for businesses. Consumers have been slower to accept the Internet for purchasing goods because of privacy and security issues.

For the interior designer, an extremely useful tool on the Internet is design libraries. These are web sites that provide information, graphics, even purchasing capabilities for the products that the interior designer specifies and sells to clients. This resource makes many products that were not available before to the designer very accessible and frees up office space, because the need for keeping a library of catalogs is lessened. In addition to design libraries are the web sites of manufacturers. Designers can get information on a wide variety of products directly from manufacturers by going to their web sites. Depending on many factors, it also may be possible for the designer to order directly from the manufacturer. This use of the web is discussed in Chapter 28 (see Figure 28-4).

Let's look at the use of a web site as a marketing tool. Interior designers had a web presence fairly early. Large firms, in particular, were the first to embrace web marketing, since they were already very familiar with the use of CAD in the 1980s. The opportunity to have a worldwide marketing presence was understood immediately by these firms. Smaller firms have found the possibilities of the web more slowly, but their use of the web increases every day.

A firm should first decide why it might be necessary to have a web site. Does the firm seek a web site because it seeks clients in its immediate area or around the world? Is it prepared to work with clients on the other side of the globe, or is it content to stay in its area? If the design firm thinks having a web site will immediately bring dozens of new clients, it is wrong. A web site does provide exposure—no question, but, like advertising, it rarely provides clients instantly.

What should be on the web page is another decision that the firm needs to make. The firm can display photos of recent jobs, award-winning projects, text that can describe the firm's design philosophy, and service offerings and client list (see Figure 23-4). The firm can integrate graphics, animation, and video to make the pages look interesting. Since there is so much that can be put into a web page, the firm must decide what information about the company will intrigue someone who finds its website.

What does the firm want the viewer to do after he or she surfs through the web site? Certainly, the firm wants the viewer to communicate with the firm, so contact information is necessary. The simplest way to do this is by E-mail. Thus, the web site should include a link to the E-mail address of the owner or other staff. It is also possible to have a space where the viewer can leave contact information. Perhaps the firm wants the viewer to request information, make personal phone call for an interview, or maybe purchase something offered for sale on the web site. Many web sites have a link to "FAQ," an acronym for "frequently asked questions," where the viewer will find a list of things that he or she can ask about the site. To save both the viewer and the firm time, the viewer can go to this page for many inquiries. However, a danger is that, if the firm provides too much information in this way, the prospective client may not bother to contact the firm for an interview.

Another decision concerns selling merchandise over the Internet. A great deal of thought must go into this issue. It involves deciding what will be sold, pricing, purchasing arrangements, security for purchasing, display of product photos, and much more.

The answers to these basic questions form the foundation for the computer code that must be written to prepare the web site pages. It is something any interior designer can do if he or she has the time. However, the interior

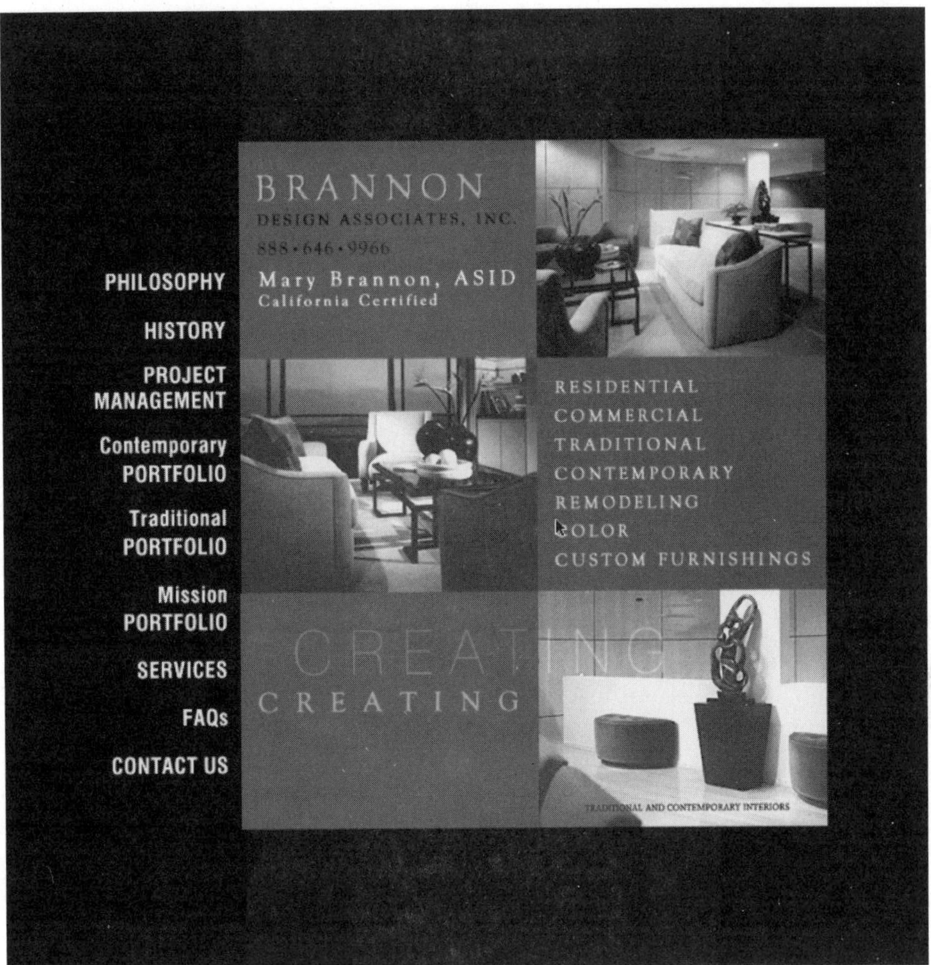

FIGURE 23-4. The home page from the web site of Brannon Design Associates, Inc. (Reproduced with permission, Brannon Design Associates, Del Mar, CA)

designer probably would be better off hiring a web site designer to produce the site and spend his or her own time working with interior design clients.

When the design firm chooses to market itself on the Internet, the relationship between client and design firm is harder to achieve. Because of the lack of a physical connection, the relationship starts with the image projected on the web site. Image definitely comes across on a web site. The quality of the photos, the style of language in the text, the colors used for backgrounds all play a part, similar to a printed brochure or hard-media promotional pieces. The ease (or lack of it) in moving from page to page and link to link within the web site will also impact that relationship.

Finding ways to get the viewer to stay at the web site is very important. If the design firm has a lot of graphics, and/or animation on the web site, or has a very large site, it will take time for it to load on the viewer's computer. Some people have a short attention span and may not wait for it to load, if the information is very complex. The viewer certainly will not come back if the information is time-consuming to load and does not really provide enough information. There are little things that can be done to get the viewer to come back. One is to include a changing page of "tips" or "hint of the week," where the designer can provide design ideas or information to target consumers. A commercial designer could include code information, while the residential designer might supply hints on holiday decorating. This should be something that the design firm can commit to upgrading, or the viewers will not come back.

Investigate several web sites of other interior designers. Maybe there are colleagues in your area who have web sites already. You can probably get their addresses from association directories or just key in *interior design company* with a search engine and start looking. Watch your spelling and try more than one search engine. Make notes on what you like and bookmark sites that you like. You also may want to read books or attend seminars on Internet marketing.

Now, re-examine why you want to be on the Internet and start creating specific notes for your web site designer. If you don't have a mission statement, write one. You might not include your mission statement, but the philosophy of why you are in the business of interior design will be important in the creation of your web site. Then gather your information and get the web site designed!

Unfortunately, there is not enough space in this text to include a discussion on web site design and other general issues about the Internet and web marketing. There are so many different opinions about how and what information should be placed on a web site, that it is impossible to do justice in the space permitted. In addition, so much is changing relative to hardware, delivery, and software, that it would be impossible to speak with sufficient depth in this text. Some assistance is available through professional associations at the local and national offices. Readers may wish to refer to the many references in this chapter, as well as to books and magazines on the net and in bookstores that they may find. An incredibly interesting and complete book on this topic is *Communication and Design with the Internet* by Jonathan Cohen (2000). It focuses on the architectural profession, but the concepts Cohen presents are applicable to all design areas. Figure 23-5 provides some additional tips and considerations on the use of web sites for marketing.

Proposals

As competition has increased, clients have had their pick of design firms. Although the proposal process has been around for many years, it has taken on greater significance for interior design firms that are marketing themselves during the last five to ten years. The term "proposal" has been used for many years to mean a contract proposal or an overview of how the designer intends to proceed with a project. In this context, however, the *proposal* is a response to a request for a proposal (RFP) issued by a client. It is not a contract.

The proposal has become an efficient way for clients to obtain information and, to some extent, ideas on how to solve their project issues for the last five to ten years. A client issues an RFP to design firms whom it might like to consider to have execute a project. An RFP can also be issued to search the design market for a design firm that has the qualifications the client feels are important for the project. Proposals have thus become an important, even critical, marketing tool for many interior design firms. The formal proposal that we are focusing on in this section is most commonly produced by commercial interior design firms; residential designers must engage in this activity to a far lesser extent.

From the client's point of view, the RFP involves gathering a lot of information on perhaps dozens of design firms. The proposal prequalifies the firms, because the information required is very specific, and if a firm cannot meet the requirements and supply the information requested, it will not generally even

Why do you want a web site?

- Increase awareness
- Sell products
- Develop leads for design consulting
- Provide information about the firm
- Market worldwide
- Develop a mailing list through the "hits"

What information will you include?

- Job photos
- Owner and staff photos
- Owner and staff resumes
- Client list
- Design philosophy
- Services list
- Photos and descriptions of products to sell
- On-line place information distribution

Tips for creating a successful site are the following.

- Make sure you know why you want a site.
- Keep it simple.
- Provide a reason for the viewer to come back to the web site.
- Target the audience through design techniques.
- Respond quickly to inquiries.
- Keep it updated on a regular basis.
- Promote your web site.
- Provide an easy way for potential clients to contact you.
- Keep your links to other sites at a minimum so that you don't lose the reader.

FIGURE 23-5. Tips for using a web site for marketing an interior design business.

bother to reply. Since developing a proposal takes so much time, it also results in proposals being returned only by firms that are seriously interested in the project. The proposals are reviewed by the client, and he or she can eliminate any other firms that do not meet the qualifications spelled out in the RFP. This actually saves the client time and money, since the client (1) gets responses from firms that he or she might never have thought of for the project; (2) reviews proposals at his or her convenience; (3) does not invest a large amount of time interviewing a large number of design firms, some of which may be unqualified; and (4) may find a group of highly qualified firms (theoretically).

From the interior designer's point of view, an RFP gives firms sufficient information about the project so that they can decide if they wish to take on the project. Since the client prepares the RFP, the design firm finds out about some projects that the firm might never have known about. In carefully reviewing the RFP, the design firm also can forecast the possibility of obtaining an interview with the client; that is to say, if the design firm has an insufficient amount of experience in executing certain sizes of retail spaces, it is unlikely that it will be granted an interview. In such cases, it would not be reasonable for the design firm to spend the time putting the proposal materials together.

Clients do not make a decision about a design firm purely on the basis of the proposal. After the proposals are reviewed, a list of design firms that the client most wants to interview emerges. This list is usually called a *short list*, because the number of firms is commonly limited to three to six (depending on the size and complexity of the project). Interviews are then set up with each firm on the short list. The decision as to which firms the client will interview rests on the material provided in the proposal. This makes the proposal a very important document.

The client controls the content and format of the proposal. This is spelled out in the RFP. This control is used by the client so that all proposals will be treated equally. The design firm has an obligation to provide all the information requested and to present it in the order required. Leaving out sections or making the proposal presentation different from what was requested can lead to disqualification.

A typical proposal contains the information outlined in Figure 23-6. If a design firm decides to respond to an RFP, it will have to include information pertinent to each of these issues. The instructions in the RFP will inform the design firms as to how much latitude they have in what is to be stated and what additional information can be included. Each part is critical and must be written in response to the specific project, client, and instructions. Although many proposals allow room for what amounts to "boiler plate information,"

- Cover letter
- Title page
- Table of contents
- Executive summary: Overview of contents
- Problem analysis: Design firm's opportunity to explain its understanding of the client's needs
- Scope of services: What will be done
- Project experience: Information about projects similar in nature to the proposed project
- Project approach: Information about how the firm will provide services and will manage the project
- Staffing: Who will be responsible for the project (resumes commonly included)
- Schedule
- List of deliverables: Documents the firm expects to prepare for the project
- Budget
- Financial information on the design firm
- References
- Miscellaneous information:
  Additional project case studies
  Article reprints
  Other information the firm wishes to provide

FIGURE 23-6. A typical outline of a proposal in response to an RFP. Note that the actual content of the proposal is governed by the information requested by the client.

that is, standardized sections that can apply to more than one project, the proposal must still read as if it were written only for the client. Other parts are written specifically for the project. For example, information on past similar projects may very well be reusable "boiler plate information," while comments about a firm's experience with green environmental issues may be very specific to the project's needs. Proposals for commercial projects can easily run about 25 pages for a small project and more than 50 pages for complex projects. So this activity should not be taken lightly.

Design firms that have been successful with the proposal process are exceptionally good at identifying hot button issues within the RFP. A *hot button issue* is one of critical concern to the client. For a school district, the hot button issue might be quality design at an economical price. Other frequent hot button issues include a very tight schedule, a concern for value engineering, a desire for innovative design ideas, and a concern for cultural design influences. Other clients do not describe needs as succinctly or as obviously, and the design firm would then have to attempt to identify the issues. This, obviously, is more difficult and challenging for the design firm.

Proposals are not design contracts. A proposal is a marketing tool by which a design firm gets to tell its story as to why it is best qualified to do a project. Generally, the proposal does not include the same information that a contract must have. However, RFPs from clients may ask design firms for their desired fee for the project. This is usually provided under a separate cover letter in a sealed envelope.

Good writing is a must. It should be clear and factual, using language that will be easily understood by the client, not interior design jargon. And, of course, it must have perfect spelling and grammar. The proposal is a verbal selling tool that must convey the personality of the design firm and at the same time must be a professional business communication. The interior design firm will not have the opportunity to have a one-on-one meeting with the client unless it makes the short list, so it must speak completely to the issues that the client has stated as well as what the firm wants to convey to the client.

With the availability of digital photography, relatively inexpensive photoshop software, and color photocopying, the proposal can be a very interesting visual presentation (see Figure 23-7). Even if the firm cannot afford to manipulate the color graphics in-house, this type of work can be done by copy stores and, of course, by graphic designers. Proposals read better if they are presented in two or three columns rather than one column. It is interesting to integrate color in bullets or headlines as well. All in all, it should look very professional and finished but not overly expensive, unless that is called for. If the client is looking for budget conscious ideas, an expensive looking proposal may very well give the wrong impression. As a final note, the firm should consider using loose-leaf pages rather than binding the pages. This makes it easier to insert additional items and move things around. Many of the references at the end of the chapter can provide additional help and ideas on preparing a proposal. Chapter 25 provides information concerning the presentation phase of the proposal process.

Advertising

Advertising is defined as any kind of paid communication in media, such as newspapers, magazines, television, or radio. If a design firm pays the newspaper to run an announcement of some kind about the firm, it is considered

FIGURE 23-7. Proposal materials in response to an RFP (Reproduced with permission, Fred Messner, Phoenix Design One, Phoenix, AZ; Photo by Dawson Henderson)

advertising. If the newspaper runs an announcement or article about the firm and the firm does not pay for it, it is considered publicity (see Figure 23-8).

Advertising as a means for professionals to promote their services has been controversial until about the 1980s. Professional associations at that time loosened up their stand against members' advertising. For example, in 1981, the Institute of Business Designers (now IIDA) (1980, p. 3) stated in its code of ethics that "members may purchase dignified advertisements and listings in newspapers, periodicals, directories, or other publications. . . ." Today, even professional associations themselves regularly use advertising in print and

FIGURE 23-8. Magazine advertisement. (Reproduced with permission, Langdon Wilson Architecture Planning Interiors, Phoenix, AZ)

television media. Perhaps you have seen the AIA's advertisement on television or ASID's advertisements in major business magazines, like *Fast Company* and *Fortune.*

Nevertheless, there has always been a reluctance on the part of the professions to engage in advertising of services. There is no standard as to the use of paid advertising by interior design firms. For some firms, advertising plays an important part in the firm's overall promotional plan. Others never even consider using a paid advertisement for any reason. Most firms fall somewhere in between these two extremes.

Firms that are designer/specifiers rarely advertise. However, they may occasionally do so in special editions of trade magazines in their local market. Designers who produce revenue from selling products advertise more often. It may be a general awareness advertisement in which a photograph of a client installation is featured. Or it may be an advertisement announcing a sale on inventory or special purchases. Of course, retail stores in this industry regularly advertise in local magazines and newspapers. In general, the more the firm depends on product sales and showcases products in a retail store or a studio, the more the firm will use advertising.

Part of the decision to advertise or not is also affected by the firm's clients. If the design firm's clients are exclusively or primary commercial, the advertising used consists of print ads placed in trade magazines or newsletters targeted to commercial specialties. In business-to-business (B-2-B) advertising, the design firm needs to target where the business's clients are, and the local newspaper may or may not be a satisfactory location for a B-2-B ad. Residential designers locate print advertising in local home magazines or national home magazines like *House Beautiful*.

If a design firm primarily deals in services and tries to advertise to bring in new projects, it will be disappointed. Advertising for service businesses rarely brings an immediate response. Instead, it is a way for the design firm to create awareness when it places an advertisement in publications that reach its target audience. A viable client might not contact the design firm until months after the advertisement has been published.

A common form of direct advertising that all designers use is a yellow-page advertisement in the phone book. Many rely on ads in which the firm's name, address, and telephone number are printed in very small type. These ads are placed to announce the firm's presence in the local area. Firms that sell furniture out of retail showrooms or small studios often take out larger-size yellow-page ads.

Manufacturers of many kinds of products use photographs of their products in installations in paid advertising. Designers should seek to negotiate for the project designer's and the firm's name to be incorporated into the ad. These manufacturers' ads can go into trade or shelter magazines, in the company's brochures and catalogs, on their web page—almost anywhere that the manufacturer chooses to advertise. This type of advertising is commonly called *co-op advertising*. This means that the manufacturer and designer generally share in the cost of the advertising, or the manufacturer provides an incentive to the designer to sell a particular product. This was discussed in Chapter 19. While this type of promotion is not truly public relations, it does serve to market the firm to new clients.

Advertising is expensive. One ad can use a small design firm's total marketing budget for the year. For example, a quarter-page black-and-white advertisement in many local magazines starts at $1000 for a one-time use. National magazines will charge far more. Of course, ads in the newspaper announcing a sale on a particular product can bring in results quickly. It is, therefore, important for the design firm to understand what the goals are for placing and paying for an ad.

Advertisements placed in newspapers are cheaper than those placed in magazines. They can reach a broader audience, but they also reach a generally untargeted audience. An ad in the newspaper may get response from callers who really are not prepared to work with the interior designer or to pay the designer's fees. Yet the designer will have taken the time to talk to the prospective client on the phone or during an interview. As with any other promotional tool or strategy, care must be taken in considering the why, when, how, and where of advertising. These are the kinds of issues discussed in Chapter 21 that are related to target marketing and marketing plans.

Summary

Deciding how to go about promoting the interior design practice is never an easy one. The small firm has a limited amount of resources in both dollars and time to devote to finding new clients. Yet, in some ways, it has the greatest need to market itself. Larger firms can often depend upon its reputation and referrals. Nevertheless, it must budget for many kinds of promotional tools when collateral items are needed for presentations, proposals, and prospective client requests.

Chapters 22 and 23 have presented a great deal of information and ideas on the kinds of promotional tools that are available to interior design firms. Which items are right for any one firm can best be determined by a review of Chapter 21 and the marketing plan. The next two chapters essentially discuss what a design firm should do once a prospective client shows interests in the firm. Chapters 24 and 25 focus on the selling and presentation processes.

REFERENCES

Bachner, John Philip, and Naresh Kumar Khosla. 1977. *Marketing and Promotion for Design Professionals.* New York: Van Nostrand Reinhold.

Barr, Vilma. 1995. *Promotion Strategies for Design and Construction Firms.* New York: Van Nostrand Reinhold.

Berkowitz, Eric N., Roger A. Kerin, Steven W. Hartley, and William Rudelius. 1994. *Marketing,* 4th ed. Burr Ridge, IL: Richard D. Irwin.

Bly, Robert W. 1998. *The Lead Generation Handbook.* New York: American Management Association.

———. 1998. *The Six Figure Consultant.* Chicago, IL: Upstart Publishing.

———. 1994. *Business to Business Direct Marketing.* Lincolnwood, IL: NTC Business Books.

Cohen, Jonathan. 2000. *Communication and Design with the Internet.* New York: W. W. Norton.

Collin, Simon. 1997. *Doing Business on the Internet.* London: Kogan/Page.

Conlon, Ginger. "Cashing In." *Sales and Marketing Management.* June 2000, 95–102.

Coxe, Weld. 1971. *Marketing Architectural and Engineering Services.* New York: Van Nostrand Reinhold.

Crandall, Rick. 1998. *1001 Ways to Market Your Services.* Lincolnwood, IL: Contemporary Books.

———. 1996. *Marketing Your Services.* Lincolnwood, IL: Contemporary Books.

Edwards, Paul, and Sarah Edwards (with Laura Clampitt Douglas). 1991. *Getting Business to Come to You.* New York. Tarcher/Putnam.

Edwards, Paul, and Sarah Edwards (with Linda Rohrbough). 1998. *Making Money in Cyber Space*. New York: Tarcher/Putnam.

Elias, Stephen, and Patricia Gima. 2000. *Domain Names: How to Choose and Protect a Great Name for Your Website*. Berkeley, CA: Nolo Press.

Emery, Vince. 1996. *How to Grow Your Business on the Internet*. Scottsdale, AZ: Coriolis Group.

Feather, Frank. 2000. *future consumer.com*. Toronto, Canada: Warwick.

Gaulden, Joan. 2000. "The Business Value of the Internet." (Seminar handout).

Gerbert, Philipp, Dirk Schneider, and Alex Birch. 2000. *The Age of E-tail*. Oxford, UK: Capstone Publishers.

Goldsborough, Reid. "Changing the Future of Doing Business." *Interiors & Sources*. June 1999, 40–41.

Harding, Ford. 1998. *Creating Rainmakers*. Holbrook, MA: Adams Media.

———. 1994. *Rain Making*. Holbrook, MA: Adams Media.

Haviland, David. 1994. *The Architect's Handbook of Professional Practice, Student Edition*. Washington DC: AIA Press.

Haylock, Christina Ford, and Len Muscarella. 1999. *Net Success*. Holbrook, MA: Adams Media.

Hays, Rick Stephan, and Gregory Brooks Elmore. 1985. *Marketing for Your Growing Business*. New York: Ronald Press.

Holtz, Herman. 1998. *The Consultant's Guide to Getting Business on the Internet*. New York: John Wiley.

———. 1998. *Proven Proposal Strategies to Win More Business*. Chicago, IL: Upstart Publishing.

———. 1990. *The Consultant's Guide to Proposal Writing*, 2nd ed. New York: John Wiley.

———. 1987. *Expanding Your Consulting Practice with Seminars*. New York: John Wiley.

Institute of Business Designers. 1980. *Code of Ethics*. Chicago: Institute of Business Designers. (Pamphlet P105).

Kliment, Stephen A. 1998. *Writing for Design Professionals*. New York: W. W. Norton.

———. 1977. *Creative Communications for a Successful Design Practice*. New York: Watson–Guptill.

Kotler, Philip, and Gary Armstrong. 1999. *Principles of Marketing*, 8th ed. Upper Saddle River, NJ: Prentice-Hall.

Ligos, Melinda. "Clicks and Misses." *Sales and Marketing Management*. June 2000, 69–76.

Martin, Jane D., and Nancy Knoohuizen. 1995. *Marketing Basics for Designers*. New York: John Wiley.

McCarthy, E. Jerome. 1981. *Basic Marketing*, 7th ed. Homewood, IL: Richard D. Irwin.

Merle, Jan S. "The Internet: Hype or Harbinger of Business, 90s Style?" *ASID Report*. November/December 1995, 16–18.

Muoio, Anna. "Should I Go .com?" *Fast Company*. July 2000, 164–172.

Parker, Roger C. 2000. *Relationship Marketing on the Internet*. Holbrook, MA: Adams Media.

Patti, Charles H., and Sandra E. Moriarty. 1990. *The Making of Effective Advertising*. Englewood Cliffs, NJ: Prentice-Hall.

Pickar, Roger L. 1991. *Marketing for Design Firms in the 1990s*. Washington DC: AIA Press.

Putman, Anthony O. 1990. *Marketing Your Services*. New York: John Wiley.

Ries, Al, and Jack Trout. 1993. *The 22 Immutable Laws of Marketing*. New York: Harper Business.

———. 1986. *Positioning*. New York: Time Warner Books.

Rosenfeld, Jill. "Information as if Understanding Mattered." *Fast Company*. March 2000, 203–219.

Schonfeld, Erick. "Corporations of the World, Unite! You Have Nothing to Lose but Your Supply Chains!" *eCompany*. June 2000, 123–132.

Smith, Rob, Mark Speaker, and Mark Thompson. 2000. *The Complete Idiot's Guide to e-Commerce*. New York: QUE/Macmillan.

Stern, Linda. "The Perfect Proposal." *Home Office Computing*. February 1995, 81–86.

Stone, Janet, and Jane Bachner. 1994. *Speaking Up*, rev. ed. New York: Carroll & Graf Publishers.

Talarico, Wendy. "Listening to Computer Experts." *Architectural Record*. August 1999, 74–78.

Walters, Dottie, and Lilly Walters. 1997. *Speak and Grow Rich*, rev. ed. Paramus, NJ: Prentice-Hall.

Chapter 24

Selling Your Services

The best design idea will become a reality only if the designer and design firm can convince the client to buy it. In addition, the client will not buy a great design idea if it is the wrong idea. Designers sell services or products, but it is their clients who buy them. Certainly, in some situations, a client may walk into a studio, see a terrific product, pay for it immediately, and take it home. There is not much selling skill involved in this situation. But, most of the time, a relationship between the client and the designer must be built, and the designer must work very hard to finally obtain agreement from the client. Most of the time, the designer needs a lot of skill in selling to achieve an agreement.

Interior designers are involved in many different selling situations. First, they must sell themselves to get the opportunity to talk to the client. After that, designers must sell the design contract (or any other method by which they wish to be compensated) in order to begin the project. Designers must also sell their design concepts as the project progresses. Designers also sell products—literally and figuratively.

Some designers find it extremely easy to sell concepts or products. Others feel frustrated by a lack of success in this area. We hear about the proverbial "born salesperson." But designers who can successfully sell ideas and products are not just "born." It is a skill that becomes easier with practice and experience. Learning techniques about how to sell more effectively also helps make the selling situation more successful.

This chapter discusses several selling techniques that are used by designers. The focus of this chapter is on selling interior design services; however, much of what is discussed applies also to the selling of products. We begin by discussing the differences in selling services versus products. This section is followed by comments on relationship selling. The chapter continues with an overview of the selling process and concludes with a few techniques that can help bring the sales encounter to a successful conclusion. Chapter 25 will focus on design presentations and discuss the parts of the selling process that relate to making a successful presentation.

What Is Selling?

Selling, like marketing, involves finding out what the client wants and providing it. But, unlike marketing, *selling* consists of personal, often one-on-one, communication. According to the *World Book Encyclopedia*, selling "involves two-way communication between a salesperson and a customer. It enables the buyer to ask questions about a product [or service] and receive additional information about it immediately" (*World Book Encyclopedia*, 2000, p. 62). Some people do not like selling or salespeople, because they believe that selling involves manipulating people to get them to buy what they do not want. Unfortunately, this kind of selling is practiced by many so-called salespeople, but this is not the kind of selling we wish to talk about.

Interior design professionals, in their interaction with clients, do their utmost to find out what their clients really want in the way of design services and products, and then try to provide those services and products. Satisfying clients and making a sale makes both parties winners. It is not necessary for the designer to try to sell clients what they do not want. In fact, it is bad for business.

Interior designers, whether they wish to admit it or not, are involved in many selling situations. They must learn techniques that help them navigate through these encounters as effortlessly and successfully as possible. Many times clients pose objections to concepts, floor plans, colors, and products that the designer has worked so hard to research and prepare. The designer must find ways to handle these objections, explain why certain things have been specified, and bring the presentation to a successful conclusion. Sometimes this means making changes in the design as it is being presented. This back and forth communication forms the heart of the sales association with the client. And, as many interior designers will tell the uninitiated, none of this is easy to do.

Selling Services versus Products

In many respects, what makes selling interior design services so difficult is that the service and the proposal are intangible; it is, after all, a concept that the designer is selling the client. At first, it exists only in the mind of the designer. The designer must translate that concept into words and graphics so that the client understands it and "sees" it as the designer sees it. It only becomes real when the project has been completed. However, the designer must convince the client to trust him or her in order for it to be completed.

Selling a service is selling an action that is yet to be performed. For the client, it is difficult to know what he or she is going to get until it is done. In addition, the client does not keep the service; the client keeps the result of the service—in this case, a beautiful interior. Perhaps this is why so many people have difficulty understanding what goes into doing an interiors project. The client often does not "see" all the work that is done to complete the concept of a project before he or she is presented with floor plans, boards, and specifications.

A lot of what constitutes interior design service is the creation of a concept and getting the client to buy that concept. How the living room will really look or how the restaurant will look is difficult for many clients to understand. Most have a difficult time visualizing the colors and fabrics on the pieces being recommended. Many clients also are not used to reading floor plans, which makes it difficult for them to visualize the interior space plans. The designer must use all of his or her technical training and verbal selling skills to explain how the space will look—before it has been completed.

It is generally a lot easier to sell a product, because it is tangible. Clients can see it, feel it, and use it. They like it or they don't like it. They either agree with the designer that the piece would be perfect in the living room or office, or they don't agree.

"Whereas most goods are produced first, then sold and consumed, most services are sold first and then produced and consumed simultaneously" (Zeithaml and Bitner, 1996, p. 20). The designer must sell the client on his or her ability to solve the client's problem, execute the requirements of the project within a budget, and actually make it all happen. The client has to have a great deal of trust in the designer's ability to actually follow through with the plans. This is why experience in a design niche, reputation, knowledge of the design process, and knowledge about products are so important for the interior designer to develop and for the client to accept.

Finally, a service is said to be "perishable." What this means is that, since a service only takes place *as* it is taking place, it cannot be inventoried or resold. Goods, of course, can be inventoried and sold or subsequently returned, and the product can then be resold to someone else. Once a designer has committed to work for a client, he or she cannot spend that *same* time working for another client. Of course, designers may work on more than one project at a time, but not literally. He or she cannot draft a floor plan for one client and literally draft a different floor plan for another client at the same time. If something happens that causes the client to not be satisfied with the results, the designer might not get the compensation that he or she was expecting. In addition, if the designer is committed to one project, he or she probably cannot take on another project that perhaps might be more interesting.

Successfully selling the design concept is the culmination of the design-selling responsibilities of the interior design professional. Understanding the differences between selling services and selling products points out how important it is for the interior designer to understand the selling process and learn how to be successful in navigating that process. Neglecting to learn these differences will impact the designer's ability to sell services and produce sufficient revenue to maintain the business.

Building Client Relationships

Marketing and sales experts continually discuss the importance of building client relationships in this highly competitive world. In building client relationships, the focus is on helping the design firm and the client become partners—ideally working toward long-term commitments. It pays for the designer to build an ongoing relationship with the client, since the cost of prospecting for new clients is greater than that of maintaining existing client relationships. Clients prefer to work with someone whom they already know rather than to find a new interior designer. If you go to a particular restaurant on a regular basis, do you ask for the same waitress? Do you have a favorite sales clerk at your preferred clothing store? The same concept can be applied to the interior design profession. Relationships should be built so that clients think of the same designer and firm whenever they need interior design services.

Certainly, it is not easy for designers to develop this type of partnership with many clients. For some clients, interior design services are something that they purchase once, maybe twice in a lifetime. These encounters may happen many years apart. Because these encounters happen with many intervening years, a relationship with an interior designer is not easy to sustain. Furthermore, for some clients, the relationship does not last, because they had a bad experience.

Clients sometimes hire a designer to design an office and then their home, or the other way around. Later, the designer may be retained to design another home or commercial facility. Designers and clients may become friends, not only working with each other, but also socializing.

The interior design of a residence is an intensely personal experience for clients. It is their home. It is where they will raise the children, share family accomplishments and perhaps tragedies, and entertain friends and business associates. Bringing a stranger into the home can be difficult for the family. The designer must show concern, thoughtfulness, and empathy for the clients' interiors problems. Being totally businesslike certainly has its place, but so does having a sense of humor and knowing when it is all right to relax and be casual.

The interior design of a commercial space is less personal, but the relationship that must be built between the parties is no less important. The client may trust the designer to specify hundreds of thousands of dollars worth of construction and products, using the client's financial resources. The client certainly must trust the designer to create an interior that solves whatever the goals and needs of the client may be. This trust is a very important part of the relationship. Since many commercial projects take several months or even years to complete, a personal relationship may also develop between the client and interior designer.

Developing a sustainable relationship with clients is not an easy task. Despite the difficulty, doing so will very likely result in repeat business, referrals, and success for the design firm. The trust that must be built between the designer and the client takes time; it is easy to lose and difficult to gain but worth every effort to achieve.

The Selling Process

In all selling, a flow of activities and communications takes place in order for the selling process to be successful. The reader already understands the design process; now we will discuss the selling process. It is generally accepted that there are seven steps in the selling process. These are shown in Figure 24-1. The first three—prospecting, qualifying, preparing—are covered in this chapter, whereas the last four are discussed in the next chapter.

Prospecting

It would be nice if clients purchased services from interior designers on a regular basis—once a happy customer, always a happy customer! Unfortunately, interior design services are not a commodity that can be repeatedly obtained by the client in a sustained manner. Some types of service firms have this continuation of service—attorneys and accountants, for example. Of course, clients do sometimes come back to the same designer. However, finding new

1. Prospecting:	Locate viable prospective clients
2. Qualifying:	Clarify if these prospects can work with you
3. Preparation:	Do homework and prepare everything needed for the presentation
4. Presentation:	Make appropriate presentation to the client
5. Overcome Objections:	Resolve client questions or concerns
6. Close:	Ask for the sale or job
7. Follow up:	Provide documentation or actions promised during the presentation

FIGURE 24-1. The steps in the selling process.

clients is really an important activity for all types and sizes of interior design practices.

Prospecting is the process of locating new clients and obtaining appointments with them in order to discuss how the design firm may assist the client. *Prospects* are potential clients in the firm's business area or target market who may require design services. They include clients who have worked with competitors, though not clients who already are under contract with competitors. Target market research and the marketing plan are used to identify potential clients in the firm's business area (see Chapter 21). Potential clients or prospects can also be found in other places. They may be members of social or civic groups to which the designer belongs. They can result from any one of the promotional activities discussed in Chapters 22 and 23. Potential clients can be located through direct mailing of letters or literature to a mailing list that the designer develops of the firm's target clients. There are many sources of potential clients.

Another method of finding prospects that designers sometimes use is cold calling. The technique of *cold calling* means that the designer is contacting potential clients whom the designer has not met before. Telephone solicitations and unannounced visits are forms of cold calling.* Designers do not particularly enjoy cold calling; many feel that it is unprofessional. However, competition sometimes forces designers to make use of cold-calling techniques in order to obtain an initial in-depth meeting with potential clients. Still, cold-calling techniques such as telephone solicitations and drop-in visits are not the most effective means of marketing one's services.

When a prospect begins to show interest in a firm, he or she might be referred to as a *lead*. Clients who call after seeing an article about the design firm in the newspaper or a trade magazine can be considered leads. Those who respond positively to the idea of a face-to-face meeting to discuss possible design services are leads. By generating leads, the design firm identifies the best prospects for selling the interior design firm's services. When leads are identified, the designer begins the crossover into the next phase of selling—qualifying prospects.

It is not uncommon for the designer to make a brief prospecting presentation before the client allows the designer to make a full presentation. It is difficult to know exactly where this falls in the selling process. Is it part of prospecting or qualifying? Or is it really a type of presentation? Most designers would agree that it doesn't matter; it just needs to occur!

A prospecting presentation requires that the designer gather enough information to explain to the client who the designer is and why the designer is contacting him or her. Since such contacts are usually quite brief—perhaps occurring over the telephone—the designer must get to the point quickly. For example, the following might be the kind of opening a designer could use to make a cold call on a potential client: "Hello, Mr. Stevens. My name is Rhonda Tower, and I am the design director at Robbins and Porter Commercial Interiors. I saw in the Dodge Reports that your firm is planning to add office space at your Dallas facility. It would be our pleasure to make a presentation to you on how Robbins and Porter Commercial Interiors might be of service to your company." Depending on the client's response, Tower either has a solid lead or should go on to the next lead on her list.

* The author is not advocating using the approaches of door-to-door salespersons or today's telemarketers for locating clients. However, some individuals who work in commercial design make drop-in visits to potential clients.

The goal of prospecting presentations is to obtain an appointment with the client so that the designer may then make a marketing presentation. In order to make a prospecting presentation, the designer must prepare carefully, just as he or she would for any kind of presentation. The designer should script what it is he or she wants to say beforehand. This allows the designer to anticipate questions and objections. It is important for the designer to emphasize the benefits for the client of the potential meeting, not simply how great the designer or firm is. The details of the firm's services can be given at the marketing presentation. Through the script, the designer must tell the client that he or she is interested in being of service to the client.

It is important for the designer to take notes as he or she talks to the potential client. The script may have room for notes below each question. Some designers develop contact sheets or cards to record calls. It is also important for the designer to keep track of names, titles, and key words that might give the designer a hint about the potential of the contact. The call should not be tape recorded. Recording a telephone conversation or a face-to-face meeting without the other person's permission can be illegal.

Qualifying

Identifying potential prospects is only part of the process. The designer must also qualify prospects. *Qualifying* a prospect means that the designer is determining whether or not there is sufficient reason to pursue a prospect. A qualified prospect is one who has been determined to be reasonably likely to contract with the interior designer.

To be most effective, the designer should devote time to those potential clients who have the greatest likelihood of retaining the designer. This is a key point about qualifying clients. Those clients who have the greatest likelihood of retaining the designer are those target clients identified in the marketing plan. Qualified prospects must have a need for interior design services. Of course, not all potential clients in the firm's business area are really viable prospects. For the design firm that specializes in restaurant design, for example, facilities that have been open for only a year or so will not need design services for some time. Restaurants that have been open for several years, however, may be looking for some kind of assistance.

Qualified prospects must also be able to pay the fees expected by the interior designer. As we have seen from previous chapters, there are all kinds of ways to charge for services, and the experience level of a designer impacts his or her level of fees. Can the potential client afford the level of fees the designer requires? Credit ratings of commercial clients can be checked, and diplomatic discussions and questioning can be used to check whether the residential client has the income level to afford hiring the designer. Of course, credit checks can also be conducted on residential clients.

Another qualifying criterion most associated with commercial design is whether the prospect has the authority to make a purchasing decision. Not everyone associated with an office or restaurant, for example, actually has the authority to set up an appointment, even if the person really thinks the office or restaurant needs a fresh look. The designer must get to the person who is in charge, or he or she could be wasting time. Sometimes it is not easy to get to a decision maker. Assistants to upper-level management personnel are very good at keeping unsolicited callers from getting to those executives.

Once the prospect has become a fully qualified lead and an appointment has been made, the designer moves to the next step—the preparation of a marketing presentation.

Preparation

Whatever the purpose of the presentation, a certain amount of preparation is wise. The more important the presentation is, the more preparation should be undertaken. The author has heard of many designers who like to "wing" a presentation—they simply go to the meeting and discuss things as they come up. This technique might work for a project presentation to clients with whom the designer has a good relationship but is very unwise for the designer to use when he or she is trying to win a contract with a new client or make the final presentation.

Marketing presentations require a great deal of preparation. Whoever has made the initial contact with the client already has obtained some valuable information about the direction and content of the presentation. The following are just a few of the questions that the designer must answer in order to prepare the best possible marketing presentation.

1. What are the prospective project requirements?
2. To whom will the presentation be made?
3. How many people will attend the presentation?
4. Where will the presentation take place?
5. Who from the design firm should be involved in the presentation?
6. What is it about the design firm that the client will want to know?
7. What kind of graphics will be used to evidence the design firm's design expertise?
8. What materials and documents will be given to the client to keep?

The answers to all of these questions and perhaps others will have an influence on the content and format of the presentation itself.

The designer must set the objectives of the presentation yet must keep in mind the concerns of the client. The designer needs to ensure that the presentation addresses the prospective client's questions and concerns or, frankly, the designer will be wasting his or her time. Obviously, the design firm's objective is to obtain the go-ahead to prepare a design contract. But there can be other goals as well. Making sure the prospective client learns about the design firm's design philosophy, methodology in project management, and expertise is very important. With these goals in mind, the designer needs to make decisions about the questions posed above.

An important step is to clarify the identity of the decision makers, that is, who the person is who has the authority to hire the designer. This seems obvious (whoever the designer has contacted to arrange for the presentation); however, this is not always the case. In commercial design, for example, it is not uncommon for the design firm to make the initial contact with a purchasing agent, not the owner or the principal of the company. In such cases, the designer may make an initial presentation to the purchasing agent and a more formal presentation to the owner at a later time. Presentations for many commercial projects often are made to a group of clients. For example, a medical office building may be owned by a group of doctors. In residential design, the designer rarely consults in this early stage with anyone but the owner of the home and the family, but who is the decision maker in the family—the husband or wife?

Who will be involved during the project at the interior design firm must also be determined. This seems obvious; however, in large firms, the owner or design director must establish who will be expected to execute the project at about the same time that the firm is still trying to secure the project. Some designers may need to be involved in the presentation, since the client likes to know who he or she will be working with during the project. Be careful not to have so many representatives from the firm at the meeting that the client is overwhelmed. Commercial design firms commonly intimidate clients by bringing great numbers of people to the presentation, thinking—mistakenly—that the client wants to see the entire team. Remember that anyone from the design firm who attends the presentation must participate in the presentation, or he or she should not be there.

Deciding and preparing what to show the client are also very important. For example, clients do not really care to see slides showing how many doctors' offices a design firm has designed if the project involves a retail store. A variety of materials and strategies can be used for the content of a marketing presentation. For a few people, a photo portfolio of previous projects would work quite well, but for a larger group, it would be more effective to use slides, a video presentation, or, more commonly today, a computer-based presentation.

Equipment should be checked to make sure that everything works as it is supposed to. Backup equipment, such as a projector bulb or an extension cord, might be necessary if the presentation is at the client's home or facility. Slides have an uncanny habit of going into the tray upside down. Boards or drawings need to be clean and neat. The middle of the marketing presentation is no time to discover that something is broken or missing.

Preparation includes determining where the presentation will take place as well as who will represent the design firm. Designers generally like to make presentations in the firm's office or studio, if at all practicable. This allows the designer to control the environment, keeping distractions to a minimum while the designer is putting his or her best foot forward. More will be said about the presentation environment later in the next chapter.

The designer will probably have about one hour, maybe two, to make the presentation. It is very important to stick to the time limit, unless the client allows the presentation to continue. An outline is always a good idea to have. Notes, key words in slides, or a computer-based presentation help the designer to cover all the important topics and help ensure that nothing is forgotten. Memorizing the presentation is generally not a good idea, no matter how critical the presentation is. A memorized presentation usually sounds just like that—canned and not personalized for the client.

In organizing the outline of the presentation, the designer should follow the basic form for outlining and organizing material for any report or presentation:

1. Tell them what you are going to tell them.
2. Tell them.
3. Tell them what you have just told them.
4. Ask for the sale.

The first step, *tell them what you are going to tell them,* is quite simply to present an overview of what will be discussed at the meeting. This first step should include reviewing the agenda, introducing other members of the design firm, and briefly describing what each person will discuss. Part of the purpose of the first step is to stimulate the potential client's attention and interest. Even though the client has agreed to meet with the designer (which automatically suggests interest), the client still needs to be given a reason to listen to the presentation. The designer must provide that reason during the *tell them what you are going to tell them* step. The designer uses this opportunity to provide that reason.

The second step, *tell them,* consists of giving the body or the presentation itself. It is important for all the presenters to be enthusiastic, alert to the client's body language, and responsive to the client's questions. The designer should involve the client by asking questions of him or her. The content of this portion of the presentation focuses on a discussion of everything that the firm wants the client to know about it, as well as how the firm will approach the client's potential project. Answers to specific questions that the client has asked in any early conversations should also be given. If the discussion digresses from the outline, the designer should go back to any item that he or she feels still needs to be covered.

Step three, *tell them what you have just told them*, consists of giving a summary of the points that you have made during the presentation. Do not forget to remind the client of the important points that he or she has heard. Remember to highlight the features and benefits of your services as they relate to the needs that the client has expressed (see Chapter 24).

The last step, *ask for the sale*, amounts to requesting that the client give the go-ahead for the firm to prepare a design contract, sign the already prepared contract, or in some other way provide a positive conclusion to the presentation. In other words, this is the "close" of the marketing presentation. More about closing will be discussed in the next chapter.

The last part of the preparation involves making an impression. There is an old saying that you only have one chance to make a first impression. Even though the designer may already have met the prospective client, he or she should not let this mean that appearances can be taken lightly. Everyone should dress professionally and appropriately to meet the client's expectations.

The biggest mistake that the designer can make during the marketing presentation is to ignore the client's goals and questions during this very early phase of a potential project. Too many designers get carried away with telling their story and forget to tell the client what he or she wants to know. The designer who has been careful to cover what the design firm wishes to tell about itself as well as to answer the client's questions will conclude the presentation on a positive note.

The remaining parts of the selling process are discussed in the next chapter. We continue with a brief discussion of some verbal techniques that can be used throughout the presentation, regardless of the type of presentation undertaken.

Selling Techniques

It is not possible to turn the reader into a expert salesperson in these few brief pages. The topics of probing, features, and benefits as techniques that help a designer sell have been used by successful designers and salespeople for many years. Perhaps these, as well as those discussed on giving presentations and the ones that will be discussed later, will assist the reader in taking steps to improve their selling and presentation skills.

The designer's discovering techniques that will help the designer sell his or her services and products is a very personal business. What works for one designer can lead to frustration and failure for another. Although interior designers use many techniques to help them sell, two important characteristics have always been present in the presentation methods used by successful designers. Those characteristics are enthusiasm for what they are doing and interest in the needs of the client. Successful professionals must have a genuine interest in their clients and the needs of their clients. When the designer realizes this, it is a lot easier to bring the encounter with the client to a successful conclusion.

Clients come to interior designers for help in solving their problems in making their home or business attractive and functional. Clients also come to designers to help them make decisions, because many have a difficult time making decisions or are reluctant to do so. Showing a sincere interest in trying to help the client will achieve positive results for the designer. However, because clients are afraid that they will be blamed by a boss, coworker, or spouse if the decisions they make are wrong, interior designers must help them understand the process and make a decision to buy the designer's services and products. Sometimes certain techniques can be used to help that decision become reality.

Probing

Probing is a technique for asking different kinds of questions in order to uncover the needs of the client. Some questions that the designer may ask will elicit what is referred to as a *closed probe*, which generally results in a closed response—"yes" or "no." Other questions that the designer may ask will hopefully force the client to provide a response so that the client is encouraged to talk. This second kind of probing question is called an *open probe.*

Closed probe questions are geared toward eliciting specific information. They are also used when the client is not particularly responsive to other kinds of questions. For example, a designer might ask this short series of questions:

DESIGNER: "Do you have a preferred color scheme?"

CLIENT: "Not really."

DESIGNER: "Do you prefer warmer colors, like oranges, rusts, and yellows?"

CLIENT: "No."

DESIGNER: "Do you prefer cool colors, like blue and green?"

CLIENT: "Yes."

DESIGNER: "Would a color scheme combining blues and greens together be satisfactory to you?"

CLIENT: "I think I would like that."

Open probe questions, on the other hand, attempt to get the client talking freely about some topic. They are also used to try to get the client to expand on previously mentioned information or to talk about broader concepts. An example could be, the interior designer is interviewing a doctor who plans to open a new family practice medical suite with other doctors. The designer might say, "Tell me about any ideas you have on how to accommodate small children, their parents, and adult patients in the waiting room." Hopefully, such a question will get the doctors to provide ideas on this important topic.

By means of a careful combination of open and closed probes, the designer can obtain the information required to discover the actual needs of the client. Discovering the needs of the client allows the designer to find out what the client's goals and needs are for the project and help the designer determine what should go into the design contract. These kinds of questions also can be used successfully when the designer is handling objections that the client has raised during the actual progress of the design project.

Features and Benefits

Another important selling technique that is useful in any kind of selling situation is one of describing features and benefits. *Features* are specific aspects or characteristics of a product or service; for example, a plastic laminate top on a desk is a feature of many desks. *Benefits* are features of a product or service that directly relate to a client's need for that product or service; for example, a benefit of the plastic laminate desktop might relate to the ease of maintenance (it will not mar as easily as a wooden desk top).

When the designer is discussing services, it is far more important to discuss the benefits of the service than any features, because it is more difficult to explain and understand features of services. A feature of the design firm's services could be error-free working drawings. However, the client expects this to happen. What, then, might be a benefit of the firm's service of preparing working drawings? One benefit is that the designer provides a one-stop, single-source for documents needed for the client's project. When the designer is trying to think of benefits of services, he or she should think of outcomes that provide value to the client. What are some benefits of interior design services for a couple who is planning to build a custom home or for an organization that is planning to build a convention center?

Once the designer knows the needs of the client, it is relatively easy for him or her to point out the various features and benefits of the services or products as they relate to those needs. If the services and products meet the needs of the client, obtaining confirmation and closing the sale is much easier and quicker.

Using probing, features, and benefits can assist the designer in the selling situation. Other techniques related to the selling process are learning how to overcome objections, to negotiate, and to close. These are discussed in the next chapter. A few other ideas on how to have a successful selling outcome are offered in Figure 24-2.

- Listen carefully to the client.
- Ask questions that are thoughtful and that show you are listening.
- Be sure to let the client talk; don't monopolize the conversation.
- Have a positive attitude and be enthusiastic.
- Never interrupt.
- Never, ever argue!
- Be polite and respectful toward the client.
- Do not sound like you are begging for work.
- Do not sound insincere.
- Always work toward a win-win outcome.
- Dress and sound like a professional.
- Use third-party testimonials as evidence of the firm's expertise.
- Remember that it takes time to build a relationship. Do not feel bad if you have to come back three or four times to close the sale.
- Always say thank you and follow up promptly on any promises.

FIGURE 24-2. Tips on how to have a successful selling outcome.

Summary

Throughout this book, we have seen that there is more to interior design than being able to put colors, fabrics, and furniture together into a workable floor plan. One of the most important nondesign activities of the interior designer is selling. Without being able to quickly determine what the client needs and then having the ability to convince the client that the design ideas and products that the designer has established are what is needed, the designer cannot stay in business.

In this chapter, we have reviewed concepts that explain why selling design services can be difficult. We have discussed the first three phases in the selling process, which help the designer do a better job of making a sale or a presentation end more satisfactorily for the designer. Some of the many techniques that are used by designers to sell their services and products also have been briefly explained. All these processes and techniques, and those that will be covered in the next chapter, will help the designer conclude the sales presentation for services or products.

REFERENCES

Beckwith, Harry. 2000. *The Invisible Touch.* New York. Time Warner Books.

———. 1997. *Selling the Invisible.* New York: Time Warner Books.

Blades, William H. 1994. *Selling: The Mother of All Enterprise.* Phoenix, AZ: Marketing Methods Press.

Bly, Robert W. 1998. *The Lead Generation Handbook.* New York: American Management Association.

———. 1991. *Selling Your Services*. New York: Henry Holt.

Carlson, Richard K. 1993. *Personal Selling Strategies for Consultants and Professionals.* New York: John Wiley.

Crandall, Rick. 1998. *1001 Ways to Market Your Services.* Lincolnwood, IL: Contemporary Books.

Crandall, Rick, ed. 1998. *Celebrate Selling the Consultative-Relationship Way.* Corte Madera, CA: Select Press.

Dawson, Roger. 1992. *Secrets of Power Persuasion.* Engelwood Cliffs, NJ: Prentice-Hall.

Faria, A. J., and H. Webster Johnson. 1993. *Creative Selling*, 5th ed. Cincinnati, OH: Southwestern Publishing.

Fisher, Roger, and William Ury. 1981. *Getting to Yes.* New York: Penguin Books.

Frank, Milo O. 1986. *How to Get Your Point Across in 30 Seconds or Less.* New York: Simon & Schuster.

Gitomer, Jeffrey H. 1994. *The Sales Bible.* New York: William Morrow.

Goodman, Dr. Gary S. 1984. *Selling Skills for the Non-Salesperson.* Englewood Cliffs, NJ: Prentice-Hall.

Gordon, Ian. 1998. *Relationship Marketing*. New York: John Wiley.

Hammonds, Keith H. "How We Sell." *Fast Company*. November 1999, 294–306.

Harding, Ford. 1994. *Rain Making*. Holbrook, MA: Adams Media.

Holtz, Herman. 2000. *Getting Started in Sales Consulting*. New York: John Wiley.

Hopkins, Tom. 1982. *How to Master the Art of Selling.* New York: Time Warner Books.

Hyatt, Carole. 1998. *The Woman's New Selling Game*. New York: McGraw-Hill.

Johnson, Spencer, and Larry Wilson. 1984. *The One-Minute Sales Person.* New York: William Morrow.

Kendall, Dick. 1995. *Nobody Told Me I'd Have to Sell.* New York: Birch Lane Press.

Nirenbert, Jesse S. 1984. *How to Sell Your Ideas.* New York: McGraw-Hill.

Parker, Roger C. 2000. *Relationship Marketing on the Internet*. Holbrook, MA: Adams Media.

Putman, Anthony O. 1990. *Marketing Your Services*. New York: John Wiley.

Stanley, Thomas J. 1991. *Selling to the Affluent*. New York: McGraw-Hill.

Tingley, Judith C., and Lee E. Robert. 1999. *Gender Sell*. New York: Simon & Schuster.

Underhill, Paco. 1999. *Why We Buy*. New York: Simon & Schuster.

World Book Encyclopedia. 2000. Vol. 17. Chicago, IL. World Book.

Zeithaml, Valarie A., and Mary Jo Bitner. 1996. *Services Marketing*. New York: McGraw-Hill.

Ziglar, Zig. 1991. *Ziglar on Selling*. Nashville, TN: Thomas Nelson.

Chapter 25

Design Presentations

In the previous chapter, we reviewed the first three stages of the selling process: prospecting, qualifying, and preparation. The focus of this chapter is on design presentations. This emphasis is given to presentations because it is so very important to the overall activities of the designer. The presentation made after the potential client has shown an initial interest in the design firm is arguably the most important of these activities. If the encounter does not go well and the relationship between the designer and the potential client is not built, there will be no project to execute.

Of course, there are many other types of presentations that occur during the phases of a design project. A presentation is made in order to obtain a design contract and to get the contract signed. Designers make mini-presentations each time they meet with the client during the course of the project. And, of course, the designer often makes a final presentation near the end of the project design process.

Making any kind of presentation can be very difficult for many students and professionals. Public speaking is one of the most feared activities. Although giving a design presentation of any kind is not the same as public speaking, it still requires the designers to stand up (figuratively or literally) in front of one or more people and be in the spotlight.

Selling design involves listening as well as questioning and talking. If you do not listen, you do not catch all the words the client is saying. If you are not listening—paying attention—you also will miss the body language that may tell you whether the client is happy or puzzled. And if you do all the talking, this does not give the client a chance to tell you anything useful.

This chapter will provide some basic guidelines for making three common types of design presentations: (1) the marketing presentation to obtain consent to begin a project, (2) the proposal presentation, whose end result is the same, and (3) the project progress presentation. It also discusses the other stages of the sales process that bring the process to a conclusion: overcoming objections, closing, and follow up. This chapter includes negotiation strategies and concludes with numerous general guidelines for making any kind of design presentation.

Marketing Presentations

A marketing presentation occurs when the designer finds himself or herself discussing why a prospective client should hire the interior designer for a project. The marketing presentation can take many forms—from a somewhat informal, one-on-one presentation to a very structured, formal, and serious meeting with numerous clients and designers participating. The purpose of a marketing presentation is for the designer to explain how he or she plans to do a project and why the client should select the designer to do the project. Of course, only the larger design firms really think of this first in-depth meeting with the client as a marketing presentation. Many designers simply think of this presentation as the initial interview and do not even think of it as a presentation. Whatever it is called, it is important because it introduces the designer to the potential client, and so it should always be handled thoughtfully and professionally.

The designer is trying to achieve several specific goals in a marketing presentation. One of the most important is the attempt to establish a relationship with the client that will be conducive to doing business with that client. This relationship, as we saw in the previous chapter, is necessary so that the client will have confidence in the designer's ability to handle the project. The designer also wants to clarify the extent of the firm's experiences, ability, and interest in undertaking the potential project. It is very important for the designer to establish how he or she can and will solve the client's concerns and meet the client's goals. These three issues generally make up the bulk of the marketing presentation. Some may argue—rightly so—that the true goal of a marketing presentation is to finish the presentation with a request by the client for the designer to prepare a design contract or otherwise go forward with the project. The marketing presentation is not a time for the designer to drone on and on about how wonderful the designer thinks he or she is.

The client will have concerns that he or she also wishes the designer to address. Project management has become a key consideration of both residential and commercial clients in recent years (ASID, 1998, p. 5). Interior design projects have become more complex, and the designer's ability to manage the myriad details is very important to clients. Potential clients also want assurance that the designer has the experience and ability to handle the project. They do not want to find out sometime during the project that the designer does not have the expertise to satisfactorily complete the project. In some situations, clients are looking for preliminary design solutions at the time of the marketing presentation. Most often this is truer of smaller projects than of more complex projects, for which extensive design planning and specifications are required. However, providing specific design ideas during the marketing presentation or initial meeting is generally not advisable, regardless of the size of project. Clients are very concerned about the project costs and how long the project will take. It is generally better to not be specific about design fees at such an early juncture. It is best to speak in generalities and return with a contract for design services a few days later. Except for small projects, designers should also refrain from specifically quoting project costs for products and/or construction at this time. If the client requires estimates for products and construction, *feasibility studies*, which are in-depth estimates of the cost of planning and providing specifications, can be accomplished within a few days or weeks. The remainder of this section provides many tips on conducting a marketing presentation.

Preparation

The kind of preparation that we discussed in the previous chapter is generally required of a marketing presentation. The information will not be repeated here. Refer to Chapter 24 for ideas on how to go about preparing a marketing presentation.

The Presentation

An agenda or outline for the presentation should be prepared, and the role of each participating member of the firm should be determined. The outline helps make sure that everything that is necessary to be said will be said. This agenda can be distributed to the client for the most formal of presentations. It can be done verbally for other situations.

A conference room at the design studio or office is preferable as the location for the presentation. Ideally, the client should be positioned directly across from the designer or at a right angle to the designer (see Figures 25-1 a and b). This allows the designer to easily see and evaluate the client's body language.

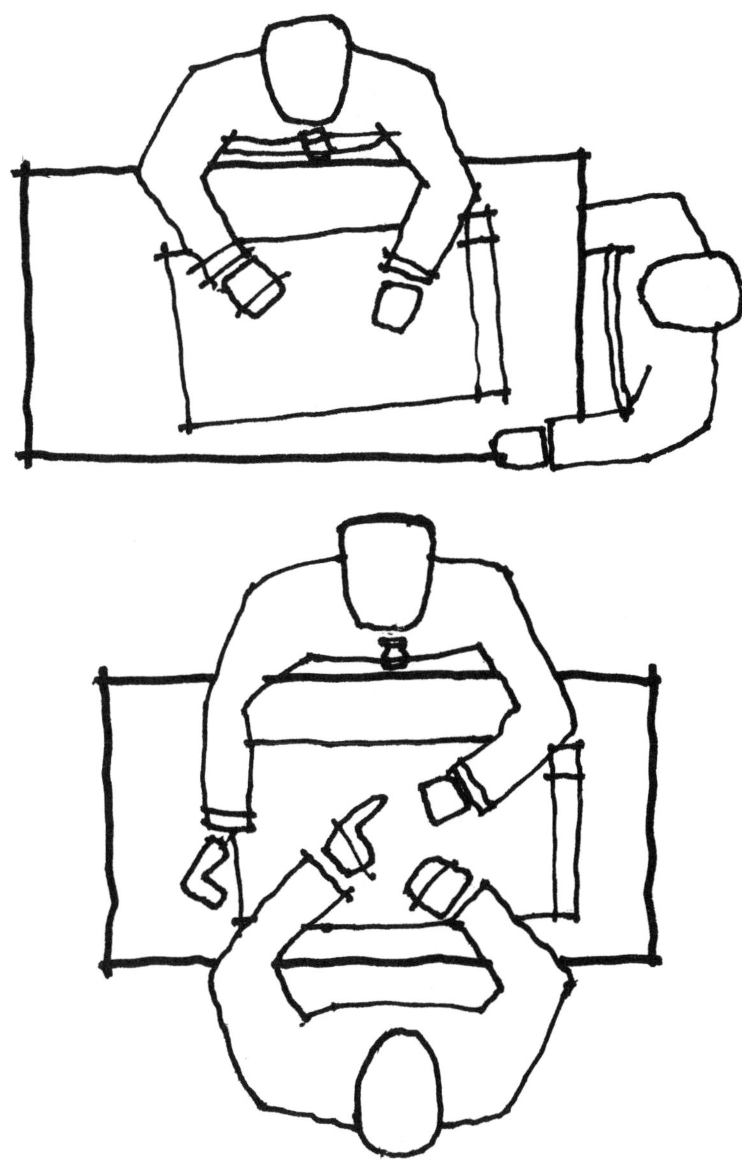

FIGURE 25-1. Sketch "A" shows the presentation arrangement in which the client and designer sit at right angles to one another at the conference table. Sketch "B" shows the presentation arrangement in which the client and designer sit across the conference table from one another. (Drawing: Charles B. Cooper, ASID)

Observing the client's body language can help the designer evaluate whether the presentation is going well or whether the client has lost interest.

If the presentation must be held at the client's office or facility, ask for the use of a conference room. It is impossible to show slides or computer-based presentations in an office. Besides, a conference room—even though it is at the client's place of business—is somewhat neutral territory. A presentation held in the client's office is not only awkward but also allows the client to be distracted by phones, people dropping in, and other interruptions.

If the presentation is held in the client's home, if at all possible, the presentation should be made in the dining room rather than the living room. For most families, the living room is the formal room, where they can easily say "no." The dining room allows the designer to sit directly across or at a right angle to the client, which is considered a more satisfactory informal situation.

During the presentation, the designer should be aware of his or her own body language and that of the client. Body language is a very powerful communication device. Nonverbal communication is said to be 75–90 percent of effective communication (Twitty-Villani, 1992, p. 2). Experts such as Julius Fast (1970) believe that body language is a more accurate indication of a person's true feelings than the words that are said. More information on body language can be found in the next chapter, and some books on this topic are listed in the References at the end of the chapter.

Many perceive eye contact as an indication of honesty and trustworthiness and the lack of eye contact as either a lack of confidence or disinterest. Good eye contact does not mean staring down the client to make him or her uncomfortable, it does mean looking the client in the eye from time to time. Maintaining eye contact with an individual for about five seconds, looking away for awhile, and then returning to eye contact so that eye contact is maintained about 50 percent of the time is a beneficial technique.

How you say what you say is also important when you are communicating a favorable message. Beware of using fillers like *er, well, okay, you see*, and *umm*. These words are indicators of powerless language. To the astute client, these fillers also show lack of preparation and lack of confidence in what the presenter is trying to say and sell. Do not say things that will dilute the feeling of confidence in you that the client needs to have. Hedges, fillers, and other meaningless words that are combined with slumped posture will make a client think twice about your ability to execute the project.

Many designers and consultants believe that handouts—and especially the contract, if one already has been prepared—should not be distributed until the verbal portion of the presentation is nearly completed. When handouts are given to the client while the presentation is being made, it is almost a certainty that he or she will look through the handouts rather than listen to the presentation. When this happens, the client often misses important points and asks questions about what was said. This can result in the designer's not being able to present everything that he or she wants to present because information must be repeated. Enough time should be allowed at the end of the presentation for distributing and going over any handouts that have been prepared for the client.

It is also commonly recommended that presentations not begin with slides, videos, or similar materials. Interest in these visuals should be built upon the verbal presentations. It is better to first get the client excited and interested in what he or she will be seeing in the visuals. When the visuals are presented, be careful not to show so many that the client falls asleep. Present a sufficient number of visuals to make a strong impression without boring the client.

After the summary and the "ask for the sale" portion of the presentation are concluded, thank the client for your taking up his or her time. Do not forget to shake hands and use the last few minutes for small talk about continued interest in the project. Be friendly and continue to show confidence in obtaining and completing the project.

Proposal Presentations

When a design firm sends a proposal in response to a RFP, the hope is that it will be received in a more than satisfactory manner so as to make the short list and be allowed to make a presentation. The proposal is the key to having the opportunity to make the presentation, whereas the marketing presentation is requested after the designer has made a few prospecting and qualifying phone calls.

Unlike the basic marketing presentation, the presentation made after a proposal submission may be the first time the designer has actually met and talked with the client. A key issue, therefore, besides being able to tell the firm's story, is to develop rapport with the client. This is difficult for many designers, since the presentation is likely to be given to a group. Many find it more difficult to speak before a group than to one or two people. These client groups, referred to as the selection committee, however, want the designers to succeed in the presentation. Having to make a presentation to a group should guide the designer in preparing the materials and selecting the type of materials that will be used.

Remember from our discussion in Chapter 23 that the RFP is often used by larger companies that want to investigate a number of design firms for a project without having to talk to each and every one of the firms. A firm that makes the short list is therefore already considered capable of doing the project. The presentation must help the designer establish the relationship that is so important when executing an interior design project.

It is essential that the presentation address the goals and needs of the client, as stated in the RFP, and address the key issues that are on the client's mind. It is critical for the designer to understand that the presentation must convince the client that the designer is the only one who truly understands the issues the client has and that the designer is there to meet those challenges. It is not the time to brag about how great the firm is. This was done in the proposal.

These presentations are commonly given at the client's place of business. It is necessary to find out about the room, what audiovisual equipment can be supplied, what the presenter must bring, and the seating configuration of the space. Some designers prefer to use a conference table; others like a U-shaped table for a group. Since the designer is using the client's facility, he or she will need to ask what is available and whether arrangements can be made to accommodate the presentation style.

All the strategies and techniques discussed in the marketing presentation section apply to this presentation as well. The decision as to who will participate in the presentation is very important. Most of the time, a principal of the firm will lead the presentation. The project manager or lead designer must also be introduced and participate. If the project is large enough for some sort of partnering with another firm, than a representative from that firm must be included. Each person plays a part, explaining some important points about the project concepts and/or methods that will be employed to execute the project.

Which presentation tools to use is also important and can be keyed to the expected group.

Appearances are important. Appropriate business apparel, clean and neat presentation materials and handouts, and working audiovisual equipment are a must. The designer may be asking the client to trust him or her with millions of the client's dollars. The interior design team must look like it can meet that challenge in a businesslike manner. A projector that does not function or a room that cannot be darkened enough so that important graphics can be seen can mean the difference in winning or losing the project.

The designer should try to find out who will be on the selection committee. There is nothing unethical in asking about the committee members and then finding out something about each one. This is not always easy to do, but phone calls to colleagues who have dealt with the client before can be helpful. Are the members budget conscious or do they prefer high style? What are their concerns about the project? This not only clues the firm into what to say but also how to strategize the presentation. A budget conscious group may not appreciate a computer-based presentation (too slick) but may think the use of flip-charts is just great.

It is very important for the firm to stick to the time limit established by the client. Most likely, all the other firms will be waiting to make their presentations that same day (if a small number of firms constitutes the short list). Stealing time from someone else is very unprofessional. Practicing the presentation ensures that it will stay within the designated limits. Leaving something out because of poor time management or forgetting to bring along a particularly important graphic can infer that the firm is not up to the challenge of the project.

Involve the client in the presentation. Encourage questions and include questions to ask members of the committee. This is important in any type of presentation but especially in this case. Listening to the comments and questions that the client makes, as well as watching body language, are important. All these strategies help gauge client interest and confirmation of the ideas the firm is offering.

Find out when you are going to present. If it is late in the day, bring along some refreshments to wake up the selection committee. Even if you are first, it is a good idea to bring the refreshments. Do not count on the client to supply you with coffee or soda! Some firms like to go first; they feel they can make a good impression that way. Many other firms like to be last—giving the last ideas and concepts that the client hears for the day. Bringing along a small, fun "gift," like the small toy construction vehicles a firm brought to a presentation. However, some clients are not allowed to take even this small gratuity.

Now it is actually time to make the presentation. Everything has been rehearsed, checked, and rechecked. Everyone knows his or her part and what to wear. Plan to arrive a little early so that you can set up your materials while the committee members are breaking between presentations. Arrange the space (if that was cleared ahead of time), and then take a deep breath and relax!

Even if this is a project that your firm really wants to get, it should not feel like the end of the world if your firm does not win. So relax, be at ease with the committee members, exhibit warmth, enthusiasm, and interest. Do not try to show off or hard sell. In all likelihood, this will turn off the committee members. Only a few designers can get away with this kind of behavior and still get plenty of work.

When it is over, say thank you, gather your materials, and leave without trying to hang around. It will probably take the committee a few days or weeks (depending on how many design firms are making presentations) to get back to you with the results. If you have had a lot of questions or the group is particularly lively when you have finished, you can assume that the presentation is successful. If they are subdued, well, you tried!

Always go back to the office and critique the presentation: What seemed to go well? What went wrong? Learning from mistakes makes the firm better at making a presentation the next time. It is also appropriate to send the selection committee chair a thank-you letter within a few days. This is not only a polite bit of business etiquette, but also it gives the firm one more chance to say a few words about how interested it is in executing the project.

Project Presentations

Project presentations may be conducted numerous times during the course of the contract. There are basically two kinds of project presentations—preliminary presentations and the final project presentations. Preliminary presentations are conducted periodically to ensure that the designer is on track with his or her design decisions. The final presentation is conducted when the designer has completed all of the planning, design, and specifications for the project that are required in the contract.

The goal of the designer during preliminary presentations is to obtain client approvals of whatever is being discussed. Obviously, approvals will not be obtained for everything at each presentation. Designers, especially entry-level designers, should not be discouraged when clients object to plans or specifications at this stage. Some objections are very common. It is necessary for the designer to learn that not all suggestions made by the designer at this stage will be automatically approved by the client. Some designers even make certain types of suggestions so as to guarantee that one of them will be vetoed in order to direct the client toward the solutions that the designer wishes to pursue. In many cases, educating the client is a big part of the preliminary presentations. Clients sometimes want the darndest things in an interior, and part of the designer's responsibility is to explain why they might not be appropriate for the client's situation and needs.

During preliminary presentations, designers often work informally. They often use rough sketches and show drawings that were made freehand. In this way, the client or designer can sketch on the rough floor plans or make notes on the sketches without being concerned about the time it took to produce the drawing. Changes at this stage do not waste a lot of the designer's time, since materials for the presentation itself are informally prepared. Many designers review floor plans and elevations on tracing paper or bring tracing paper along on which they can make sketches. Product selections can be informal as well; the designer can use the pages from catalogs and loose fabric and finish samples. This informality, as long as it is not done in a sloppy and unprofessional manner, creates a comfortable atmosphere so that the client will be involved in the project. Psychologically, it also makes the client feel like the designer is not forcing decisions on him or her, since the plans and selections are still in the preliminary stage.

It is important for clients to sign off on approved products and floor plan proposals. A form such as the one in Figure 25-2 can be used to detail preliminary and final product specifications. Note that the form provides a place for the client to initial or sign it. Signed approvals allow the designer to move on through the project with confidence. A client signature or even initials on the marked-up copy of the floor plan or specification, which signifies agreement

Product Control Sheet

Job Name: ______________________ **Job #:** ________

Room/Area: ______________________ **Control Number:** ________

Item Specification			
Manufacturer:			
Catalog Number:			
Case/ Frame Finish:			
Hardware Finish:			
Size W:	D:	Ht:	Sh:
Other:			
Special Installation Instructions:			
Fabric:			
Grade:	Yards Required/Unit:		
Repeat:	Stain Repellent:	Fire Retardent:	
COM Supplier:			

Sketch/Photograph	**Fabric**

Delivery Time: ____________ Shipping Location: ______________________

Unit Price (net): ____________	Quantity: ____________
Upholstery: ____________	
Special Handling: ____________	Freight: ____________
Total Item Net ____________	Delivery: ____________

Client Signature: ______________________

FIGURE 25-2. A typical control sheet that can be used for client sign-off on each item on which agreement has been reached.

to what has been shown, also provides a mechanism for the designer to charge clients for work that has to be redone if the client changes his or her mind *after* the initial approval.

Whether the preliminary and final presentations are held at the client's location or at the designer's office is really dependent on the designer's style, the size of the project, and the demands of the client. The client wants to feel in control of the project, so when the designer comes to the client, the client feels in control. The larger or more complex the project, the more likely the preliminary presentations will be held at the designer's office. Making the preliminary presentations at the designer's office also provides access to additional resources, such as product materials and print machines, if it should be necessary to make copies or additional prints.

Many of the design professionals that the author has spoken to prefer to conduct preliminary presentations at the client's location, unless the project is quite large and complex. "We have found that going to the job site or office is good psychologically for clients. They are paying us to develop design ideas, but they want to be serviced. Going to them in the early stages is one of the ways we service the client," related one design director. Residential designers often find that it is helpful to make the preliminary presentation at the client's home. Many interior designers who specialize in residential design report that making the presentation to the client in the environment in which the project will be completed works very well.

The key to making successful preliminary presentations is never forgetting three things. First, always give the client some choices during the presentation. Designers often use a strategy of presenting three options. One option works but is a fairly obvious poor choice (though the designer should not admit this); the second option is an acceptable alternative—something the designer can "live" with; the third option is the one the designer is most interested in using. Making it look as though the client has no say in the project often leads to the client feeling left out and can produce disagreements, even though the client may like the design concepts presented.

Second, always involve the client in the presentation. Ask the client questions, especially questions that bring acceptance of the concepts under discussion. As each item is agreed to, it will be much more difficult for the client to be opposed to the entire project at the end of the presentation. Techniques discussed in the previous chapter and later in this one can help. Getting the client involved makes it easier for the client to feel comfortable about the design concepts. Feeling comfortable about design concepts leads to a greater chance of final approval at the end of the formal presentation.

Third, keep the preliminary presentations relaxed and somewhat informal. By following this tip, you will keep the presentation "preliminary." Discussion and disagreement need to occur during the preliminary presentation. Formality might result in tension, while informality allows for the necessary give-and-take that must occur in the early stages of the project. Of course, the preliminary presentation must still be presented using appropriate businesslike behavior. There is a time for jokes and there is a time for business.

Final project presentations are done to review the design decisions one last time. The goal of the final project presentation is to obtain the go-ahead to order products or to begin the bidding process. Ideally, the designer is hoping for approval of all the design concepts and product selections. It is common that a few changes will still be necessary, however.

For very large projects, a substantial amount of time may have elapsed since the last preliminary presentation. Final presentations pull all the earlier decisions together into one package. They also are used to show the client specialized graphics, such as detailed, rendered floor plans, perspectives, sample boards, models, and perhaps computer simulations. All the last-minute hesitations by the client must be resolved at this time so that the project can move forward.

Of course, the final presentation is when other issues will be resolved. Presenting the final cost estimates (for bid situations) or actual final cost of the project is also done at this time. The designer must be ready not only to defend design decisions but also to answer any questions about costs of the project. It is advised that the designer once again obtain signed approvals on product selections and plans. The signed documents become part of the project files, just like those obtained during the preliminary presentation.

In contrast to the preliminary presentations, most designers prefer that the final project presentation be made at the designer's office. Knowing where the final presentation will occur is important so that the designer can know how to put the documentation together. In reality, presenting a relatively simple project to one or two clients can be done successfully over a conference table, the client's desk, or even a dining room table. When the project is complex and several representatives of the client need to be present, a different set of presentation graphics may need to be prepared, just as with the marketing presentation. Controlling the environment of the presentation is very useful in bringing this phase to a satisfactory conclusion.

Reviewing project materials with the client is an important professional activity. Designers need to have thought as much about how to show the drawings and other documents as what is to be said. Involving the client in the presentation, using professional language without getting hung up on jargon or highly technical descriptions, exuding confidence, and creating excitement and enthusiasm in the design solutions are all important parts of conducting successful preliminary and final presentations.

As with the other types of presentations, it is a good idea for the designer to spend a few minutes back at the office, after the presentation has been made, reviewing what went right and wrong during the presentation. Obviously, this is more important if the client had lots of questions and problems with the final presentation documents. Generally, however, this presentation requires only that minor changes to the plans, specifications, and other documents be made so that the project bid documents or purchase orders can be prepared. These next steps are discussed in Part VI.

Overcoming Objections

In any selling situation, the client will have some objections to what is being discussed or proposed. To become successful at selling services or products, one must understand how to overcome these objections. Many of the top salespeople feel that, unless the client makes some kind of objection, it is quite possible that the designer is not even making any headway.

Objections can occur because the client does not understand what the designer is talking about but is embarrassed to say so. Sometimes objections are raised because the client really cannot afford what is being discussed but will not admit it. And other objections are raised because the client is afraid of making a mistake and would rather not buy than make a mistake. Some of the most common types of objections are listed in Figure 25-3.

Although there are potentially as many different objections as there are clients, we will discuss a few of the most common objections in this section.

- Your price is too high.
- Your service was not very good the last time the client worked with your firm.
- There is a question about the designer's experience for this type of project.
- The client does not like what has been proposed.
- The competition is cheaper.
- The client cannot afford the service or product after all.
- The client does not believe your firm is big enough to handle the project.
- A competitor is willing to do the design work on spec (for free).
- The designer has not met the needs of the client.
- The client must get approval from someone else.
- The client likes the ideas but will purchase from a friend or relative in the business out of state.
- Your low price as compared to the competition makes the client suspicious.
- The client is not convinced that you can meet the client's schedule.
- The client's priorities have changed, and the client needs to spend the funds on something else.

FIGURE 25-3. Common objections raised by clients during presentations and selling encounters.

One of the most common objections has to do with price. It is rare for price not to be an issue. "Your competition charges less per hour," "I can get free design services from another studio," or "The sofa is too expensive," are typical comments heard by interior designers. Perhaps the designer can overcome such objections by restating quality characteristics of the product or by discussing how his or her services are different from the competition. How much money any design firm is ready to leave on the table in order to obtain a project or sell furniture is up to the firm's owner and/or managers, and the designer.

A second common objection is, "I need to talk this over with my spouse" (e.g., partner, boss, etc.). This objection often comes up for two reasons: first, the client is afraid of making a mistake and will not make a decision unless someone else agrees; second, the designer has not been careful in setting up an appointment with the decision makers in the first place. In the first situation, there is not much the designer can do, unless he or she can review information about the service or product to help alleviate the client's concerns. This may lead to the client making the decision without consulting with the other party. Be careful about becoming a pushy salesperson, which could result in losing the sale altogether. In the second situation, the designer must be sure that he or she understands who is making the decision as the designer gathers information during the initial presentation. The presentation should be arranged so that all the decision makers are at the meeting. In this way, the designer only makes one presentation.

An obvious part of overcoming objections is actually listening to the objection. This sounds simplistic, but it is brought up because too many designers do not listen to the client and miss the cues or even the words of the objections. It is imperative that the designer listen carefully to everything that the client is saying so that the designer will not be in the following sample situation. Sally Jones, a designer, was on a call with Bill Preoccupied, one of the project's designers. They both were at the office of Anthony Smith. Smith was responding to a question by Jones concerning color and style preferences for the remodeling of the office, and in the middle of that discourse, Smith said that he really did not like a lot of browns and tans. Preoccupied looked up from his notebook and said, "I really think that browns would be great in your new office." Both Jones and Smith looked at Preoccupied and then looked at each other. Although the names have been changed to protect the guilty, it is a true story and shows that even the most experienced designers may not pay attention and potentially can lose a client.

When objections occur, keep your sense of humor and perspective. The client is not going to like everything. Repeat the objection back and then ask questions to clarify what the problem might be. Then review the information you have already gathered about the needs of the client and summarize your point of view in terms of the client's needs and objection. It is not necessary to assume that the client is right concerning the objection. However, be respectful, since the client may not be familiar with industry concepts and terms. Never tell the client that he or she is wrong—this will only put the client on the defensive.

Whatever the objection is, the designer must listen to the objection and be ready to deal with it in a professional manner. Successful designers do not become successful by giving in to these objections without trying to understand the nature of the objection and to sway the client. However, *never* argue with the client. Getting him or her angry not only means that the problem will remain unresolved but also that the designer may lose the client.

Closing Techniques

Closing is the art of knowing when to ask for the sale. If you are lucky and the client says, "I'll hire you," or "I'll take it," without your having to ask first, you probably do not even need to read this chapter at all. If you have developed a positive relationship with the client, most likely you will not have to utilize any of the techniques discussed in this section. When a good relationship exists, the designer has a better feeling about how to answer the questions the client asks or doesn't ask, for example, what the client's face and body language may be saying to the designer about agreement or disagreement. Getting a signature or approval in order to move on with the project will then be easy.

When this positive relationship does not exist, the designer may need to use other techniques to bring the presentation or sales encounter to a conclusion. Not asking for the sale is the most common reason that the client does not buy the designer's services and/or products. Interior designers are very comfortable in designing elaborate, complex residences or commercial spaces—in the office, away from the client. Some of these same designers, however, become very uncomfortable when the time comes to present and sell those concepts. Why are designers afraid to ask for the sale? Fear, plain and simple—fear of the rejection that comes when the client says "no."

Closing techniques involve words and actions that the designer uses to ask for the sale. The sooner the designer asks, the sooner the client may sign the agreement, and the sooner the designer can move on to another project. In a very real sense, asking for the sale assumes that agreement has been reached on the issues being discussed. However, many people neglect to ask the questions that slowly confirm agreement. When the designer then tries to close, he or she is often met by one more objection. Remember, however, objections do not necessarily stop the presentation in its tracks. They are just obstacles to be overcome.

There are many techniques that are recommended by numerous how-to-sell books. Some of those books are listed in the References at the end of this chapter. The following will recount some of the techniques that other professionals use with great success. They are easily applied to selling services and products in the interior design industry.

In the previous chapter, we discussed using features and benefits to help sell services and products. Try this closing method in combination with features and benefits. When you can meet at least two needs of the client based on your features, or benefits (or those of a product), use a trial close. A trial close is simply asking for the sale; that is, you are trying to close. Supporting the client's needs with features and benefits shows the client that you are really trying to solve the client's needs and provide him or her with only what is needed, not what you want to sell the client. Remember, trying to close the sale means that you have reached an agreement on needs. Consider the following situation.

Designer: "You said that you are looking for a comfortable sofa bed for the guest room, which will have a fabric that will be easy to maintain. Is that correct, Ms. Smith?"

Smith: "Yes, it is."

Designer: "I have already shown you that this sofa bed, made by company X, has been rated by an independent testing company as having the most comfortable mattress on the market. This nylon basket weave fabric, which you liked, will be easy to maintain. Why don't I work up the final price with this fabric and see when we can deliver it to your home?"

Assuming that the price is not an issue, if the client says this will be fine, you can finish with the sale and only need to write up the paperwork. However, if the client says no, you must assume that something needs still to be resolved. You must ask more questions, support needs by discussing other features and benefits, and then try again to close.

Another frequently used closing technique is to close when the client agrees to a secondary issue concerning the sale. In the preceding example, when the designer obtained agreement about the fabric choice, he or she would then follow with questions related to the color of the fabric. When these two issues were resolved, then the designer would be ready to close.

Many designers use *third-party testimonials* (or references) or stories to help with the close. "A testimonial is a statement from a satisfied client praising you and your services" (Bly, 1991, p. 30). Recalling how a previous client was satisfied by the firm's service or products often helps to alleviate fears of the decision-making process. "Grey Fox Restaurant felt our project management techniques were outstanding and was a major reason why their fast-track restaurant project opened on time," is an example. Third-party testimonials or stories are very powerful. They do not represent the designer's opinions but a neutral third party. It is reasonable to ask clients who were particularly satisfied with your work for a testimonial. Do this by asking for comments and criticisms to improve your service in the future. You will likely gain a sentence that can then be used as part of your closing techniques or in other promotional situations. Always ask for permission to quote the client, however.

A closing technique that many designers use, though perhaps reluctantly, relates to a forthcoming event. For example, a client who might be hesitant to close the sale today, might be encouraged if he or she knew that the price on the goods were going up in a few weeks. "I can only guarantee this price for the next ten days, since we have already been informed of a price increase on January 1," the designer would say. This technique is perfectly legitimate *if it is* true. It should, however, only be used in complete honesty. Telling a client that the price of the goods is going to go up when, in fact, it will not or telling the client that the plant will close for two weeks when it will not is not professional.

Another useful, though unpopular technique, is performing some kind of physical action that will encourage the client to close the sale, for example beginning to write up the sales order for the client to sign. Another action might be placing a pen in a position so the client will pick it up and use it immediately, on top of the design contract or confirmation. If the client does not object to the activity or pull back, the designer knows that the sale is about to be closed.

These closing techniques and others are discussed in many sales books as methods that can help the designer obtain the client's signature on a design contract, perhaps achieve agreement to design concepts when reviewing plans, and sell products. Whether you use them or not is up to you. They are provided as a conclusion to the discussion on the overall sales process.

Follow-up

The designer should follow up on the marketing or proposal presentation with a letter and/or a phone call. The follow-up should cover such things as thanking the client for his or her time, restating important points of the presentation, and emphasizing continued interest in working with the client. This courtesy may be all the client needs to make a decision to use the design firm. Any documentation, site visits, third-party testimonials, or other actions that were promised during the presentation must be taken care of at this point as promptly as possible. Delays in sending these additional documents could hurt the designer's chances of closing the sale.

Losing a sale can be a great lesson, that is, if the designer takes the time to evaluate why he or she did not get the job. Whether the designer is experienced or new to the professional presentation process, his or her understanding of why he or she lost the job may be more important to future success than closing one sale. It is not pleasant to lose a sale, but it is important for the designer to try to find out why he or she did.

Records should also be kept on the results of marketing presentations and at the completion of a project. This activity was discussed in part in this chapter, at the end of the discussion on proposal presentations. The postproject evaluation is discussed in Chapter 31.

Negotiating

The reader undoubtedly has already been involved in many negotiation situations, even if he or she has not yet worked in the interior design field. Perhaps it was to stay out late on a date in high school or to get some time off from a part-time job while working during college. It could even have been to get a few extra days from a professor to complete a project or a paper. Of course, the professional designer is negotiating all the time—for better pricing from a vendor or a more favorable installation date from the wallpaper hanger, or even the hourly fee charged by the designer's accountant. In many respects, a negotiation is another form of a presentation.

Negotiating is an activity wherein two parties are trying to reach agreement about some point of discussion. Negotiating should create a "win-win" situation so that both parties are satisfied. If a negotiation reaches a "I win, you lose" situation, then it is not a successful negotiation, since only one party is happy. The "I win, you lose" situation is not a negotiation but, rather, manipulation. And manipulation has no place in the bag of skills of a successful interior designer.

Successful negotiation requires the use of strategies that are similar to those used in any other type of presentation. To be successful, you have to know what it is you want in order to understand your goals and objectives for entering into the negotiation. It is also necessary for you to have the facts about what you are asking for and what the client or other party may be looking for (or object to); this simply means that you should be prepared. In a negotiation, you are more likely to need to take a position or stand. Perhaps you are requesting $10,000 in fees to execute a design project. That is your position. Are you really willing to go below that and, if so, how far below? And why are you willing to lower your fee?

Knowing when and where to negotiate is also important. If it is possible, carry on the negotiation for a raise somewhere other than your boss's office. Take your boss to lunch and discuss this topic in a neutral place. Control of the environment is why designers prefer to make marketing presentations in their office or studio rather than at the client's location. If the client greets you at the entry with a scowl and tells you about the terrible time she just had with the maid, it is no time to negotiate or make a presentation with the expectation of obtaining a positive outcome. Reschedule if possible when the client is no longer frantic and perhaps angry. Figure 25-4 lists some tips that might help in negotiations.

Success in negotiation is not a gift that comes naturally to most professional designers, but it can be learned. Each successful negotiation affects how you conduct future negotiations. And how you go about a negotiation session will also affect the future relationship between the individuals involved.

- *Start with a plan.* When you are about to negotiate an important design contract or a salary increase, do not fool yourself into thinking that you can pull it off without planning what you are going to say.
- *Only negotiate for what you are prepared to do or are able to do.* Do not put anything on the table that you have no intention of doing or cannot accomplish.
- *Always be truthful.* A successful negotiation depends on trust between the two parties. If the parties to a negotiation do not trust each other, they will never be able to successfully negotiate anything.
- *Have patience.* The best negotiators know that it takes patience to work toward a win-win conclusion. Nobody likes being browbeaten or intimidated into making a decision. You gain an advantage when you take your time rather than rush.
- *Use your "power."* Power is based on perception. If you think you have it, you do. Using your power means having confidence in yourself and your point of view.

FIGURE 25-4. Ideas that can be used when the designer is in a situation that requires negotiation.

Other Guidelines for Making Presentations

In this chapter, we have discussed many tips for making specific types of design presentations. Frequently, these tips overlap and are a useful part of any kind of presentation. In fact, many of the items discussed can be applied to job interviews, asking for a raise or promotion, and even dealing with personal relationships out of the office. In this last section, several additional presentation guidelines that students and designers alike might find useful in their professional practice will be discussed. Some of these items will be discussed in more detail in the next chapter.

- You only have one chance to make a first impression. Remember that the first 30–60 seconds create the strongest impression. Do your best to make this initial contact as professional and confidence-building as possible.
- Dress appropriately. Business clients expect designers to look as though they understand business. Residential clients generally are more comfortable with trendy attire than with conservative business clothing. Keep the client in mind, though. Wearing an expensive designer suit to a meeting with budget conscious clients will make them feel they cannot afford your services. On the other hand, wearing budget-priced and unkempt clothing to meet with a high-end client may very well have them thinking that you are not very successful, and they will be unwilling to hire your firm.
- Use professional language. Part of being a professional is sounding like a professional. Use proper language and speak distinctly. It is okay to use technical words, but be prepared to explain any technical language that you incorporate into your presentation.
- Use good posture. Stand and sit straight, shoulders back—just like Mother always said!
- Listen. "Listening is a selfless act. You must suspend your own ego and interests and focus on the other person."* Listening also involves focusing your mind on what the person is saying rather than on what you are trying to say. Most people can tell when someone is truly listening or pretending. Do not pretend. Listen, learn, succeed.
- Anticipate the other person's responses and questions. Trying to determine the other person's concerns will make you more thorough and professional.
- Be enthusiastic. Clients cannot get excited about a project if you are not enthusiastic yourself.
- Stick to your time limit. Be sure you understand how long you have for the presentation and never exceed the time limit, unless the client gives you permission to do so.
- If you make a mistake, do not make a big deal out of it. Calling attention to the problem only will make you feel worse and may totally throw you off balance. Say something like, "Let me clarify that last point," and move on.
- Never be late for the presentation or begin the presentation late. In fact, plan on arriving a little early. In that way, you will always have time to repair a board that has been damaged in transit, freshen up, and relax before you must begin.

* Excerpted with permission of Chandler House Press, from *Knockout Presentations* by Diane DiResta. Copyright © 1998 by Diane DiResta www.chandlerhousepress.com.

- Final presentations must not be taken lightly. Designers need to be thinking about how they are completing the necessary presentation documents. Exactly how the final presentation will be made can be decided as the project is being completed. The method of presentation will impact what graphics are needed and how much time must be allotted to prepare them.
- If you develop standardized presentations, be sure to tailor them for each individual client; for example, lawyers want to know about how you have handled law offices, not homes.
- Think of the little things. Are you going to drag armloads of catalogs and samples under both arms, or carry them in a nice satchel or bag? Be respectful of the client's time by not spending a lot of time in small talk, then having to rush through the presentation or taking up too much of the client's time. Little things like this (and many more) can mean a lot in building rapport and a positive working relationship with the client.
- Plan breaks, if necessary. Especially long presentations, such as many major, final project presentations, may take two hours or more. Plan breaks into your presentation and use the time to set up additional visuals. Since it is your presentation, arrange for providing refreshments as well.
- Prior to making a presentation, do not consume milk products, salty foods, or alcohol. These items dehydrate most people, and most designers do not need to get "cotton mouth" in the middle of a presentation. If you are susceptible to dry mouth, be sure you have a glass of water handy.
- Talk to the client, not to the board or the screen. Too many designers and students direct what they are saying to the board or screen rather than to the audience. The client does not want to admire your back. He or she wants to see your face as you are talking.
- Do not criticize your competition. If the client asks you what you think of a competitor, say something simple like, "I understand that he is a competent designer." Bad-mouthing the competition is unprofessional and will only come back to haunt you later.
- Facial expressions should be relaxed and friendly. Do not scowl or look so tense that you appear as if you are about to have a root canal. If you know what you are going to say and have confidence in your ability to pull off the presentation, it will be easy to look as though you are having a good time. You should not have to fake a smile either. Clients can read right through that. Be enthusiastic about your project solution, your company, your own abilities, and you will be rewarded.
- Do not smoke during your presentation, even if your client does. The cigarette will get in your way and will distract the client from what you are saying.
- If a piece of equipment does not work properly or if there is a problem with a sample board, for example, quickly determine if you can proceed without the item. If it is critical to your presentation, have one of the other members from the design firm fix the item while you continue presenting other information. If this is not possible, suggest taking a short break so that you can fix the item without the client watching. Of course, this would not have happened if you had checked everything before you began the presentation.
- If the potential project is out of the country or with a foreign company, bone up on body language and customs of the other country. This kind

of homework is absolutely necessary if your firm seeks to work with international clients.

- Use an outline or script. Designers who lack in presentation experience or are uncomfortable with making presentations need to write out what they want to say. However, it is unwise to read the script back to the client. It will sound very unnatural.
- Always define your goals. If you do not know what you want to say or accomplish in your meeting, you will almost always be dissatisfied at the end of the meeting.
- Use gestures carefully. Gestures are helpful to emphasize important points. Hands that are constantly in motion are distracting.
- Practice, practice, practice! The more often you run through a presentation, especially with a colleague who can critique it, and the more often you make presentations, the easier and more effective they will become.

Summary

Making a presentation is a part of the overall selling process. Some interior designers might argue that it is the only part of the selling process that really applies to interior design practice. However, Chapters 24 and 25 have shown that all the parts of the process play a part in the professional practice of interior design.

It makes little difference if the presentation is to gather additional information after an initial meeting, actually make a marketing presentation of some kind, or defend design plans and specifications during the course of a project. Designers are constantly making presentations. Although we did not discuss how to make seminar presentations, many of the basic concepts of preparing, making, and following up on a marketing presentation, a proposal, or project presentation can be applied to the seminar presentation. Successfully navigating through the presentation will help the designer build confidence and increase his or her professional competence.

Educational programs strongly emphasize giving critiques of design work. Although this is a great way to understand the good and bad points of a project, it does not focus attention on the type of presentations that designers have to make in the professional world. Students should consider taking a speech or acting class in order to gain confidence in speaking in front of a group. Professional designers often join networking clubs, where they must make a brief presentation from time to time. Of course, a professional who is uncomfortable in front of a group can also gain from taking a speech or acting class.

In this chapter, we have discussed many techniques and have provided numerous guidelines on structuring and performing design presentations. Utilizing these concepts when faced with making a presentation should help students and professionals become more effective. The next chapter is new to this text. It will explore additional concepts that can positively affect the professional success of students and professionals alike.

REFERENCES

American Society of Interior Designers. June 1998. *Strategic Mapping Research. Phase III.* Washington DC: American Society of Interior Designers.

Axtell, Roger E. 1991. Gestures. New York: John Wiley.

Barr, Vilma. 1995. *Promotion Strategies for Design and Construction Firms*. New York: Van Nostrand Reinhold.

Blades, William H. 1994. *Selling: The Mother of all Enterprise*. Phoenix, AZ: Marketing Methods Press.

Bly, Robert W. 1991. *Selling Your Services*. New York: Henry Holt.

Breighner, Bart. 1995. *Face to Face Selling*. Indianapolis, IN: Park Avenue.

Dawson, Roger. 1999. *Power Negotiating*, 2nd ed. Englewood Cliffs, NJ: Prentice-Hall.

———. 1992. *Secrets of Power Persuasion*. Englewood Cliffs, NJ: Prentice-Hall.

Delmar, Ken. 1984. *Winning Moves—The Body Language of Selling*. New York: Time Warner Books.

DiResta, Diane. 1998. *Knockout Presentations*. Worcester, MA: Chandler House Press.

Elsea, Janet G. 1984. *The Four-Minute Sell*. New York: Simon & Schuster.

Faria, A. J., and H. Webster Johnson. 1993. *Creative Selling*, 5th ed. Cincinnati, OH: Southwestern Publishing.

Fast, Julius. 1970. *Body Language*. New York: Simon & Schuster.

Girard, Joe, with Robert L. Shook. 1989. *How to Close Every Sale*. New York: Time Warner Books.

Hoff, Ron. 1988. *I Can See You Naked. A Fearless Guide to Making Great Presentations*. Kansas City, MO: Andrews and McMeel Books.

Holtz, Herman. 1998. *Proven Proposal Strategies to Win More Business*. Chicago, IL: Upstart Publishing.

Hopkins, Tom. 1982. *How to Master the Art of Selling*. New York: Time Warner Books.

Hyatt, Carole. 1998. *The Woman's New Selling Game*. New York: McGraw-Hill.

Jones, Gerre. 1983. *How to Market Professional Design Services*, 2nd ed. New York: McGraw-Hill.

Kendall, Dick. 1995. *Nobody Told Me I'd Have to Sell*. New York: Carol Publishing.

King, David, and Karen Levine. 1979. *The Best Way in the World for a Woman to Make Money*. New York: Time Warner Books.

Kliment, Stephen A. 1998. *Writing for Design Professionals*. New York: W. W. Norton.

LaBella, Arleen, and Dolores Leach. 1983. *Personal Power*. Boulder, CO: New View Press.

McCracken, Laurin, and Ann Carper. "Designers on Stage." *Contract*. November 1992, 66–67.

Murray, Katherine. 1997. *Power Point 97*, 3rd ed. San Francisco, CA: Sybex.

Nirenberg, Jesse S. 1984. *How to Sell Your Ideas*. New York: McGraw-Hill.

Nierenberg, Gerard I., and Henry H. Calero. 1971. *How to Read a Person Like a Book*. New York: Pocket Books.

Nierenberg, Juliet, and Irene S. Ross. 1985. *Women and the Art of Negotiating*. New York: Fireside.

Peoples, David A. 1988. *Presentations Plus*. New York: John Wiley.

Rabb, Margaret Y. 1993. *The Presentation Design Book*, 2nd ed. Chapel Hill, NC: Ventana Press.

Reck, Ross R., and Brian G. Long. 1987. *The Win-Win Negotiator*. Kalamazoo, MI: Spartan Publications.

Reilly, Brian. 1997. *Create Power Point Presentations in a Weekend*. Rocklin, CA: Prima Publishing.

Roth, Charles B. (with Roy Alexander). 1995. *Secrets of Closing Sales*, 6th ed. Paramus, NJ: Prentice-Hall.

Smith, Terry C. 1984. *Making Successful Presentations*. New York: John Wiley.

Stanley, Thomas J. 1991. *Selling to the Affluent*. New York: McGraw-Hill.

Stasiowski, Frank. 1985. *Negotiating Higher Design Fees*. New York: Watson-Guptill.

Thompson, Jacqueline, ed. 1981. *Image Impact*. New York: A & W Publishers.

Twitty-Villani, Teri. 1992. *Appearances Speak Louder Than Words*. Portland, OR: Voyager Press.

Ziglar, Zig. 1991. *Ziglar on Selling*. Nashville, TN: Oliver Nelson.

———. 1982. *Zig Ziglar's Secrets of Closing the Sale*. New York: Berkley Books.

Chapter 26

Personal Power*

Personal power involves making a positive first impression. Some people say you have only ten seconds to do so. Others say you have as much as four minutes. Does it really matter? The point is, research shows that you have a very short time to make a positive impression on your client, boss-to-be, new friend, or whomever you meet for the first time. In only a few seconds or minutes, people make judgments that can affect your career, daily business responsibilities, and personal relationships. Of course, you are making similar judgments about them.

Whether the client signs the design contract or you get your first job in interior design can depend on how you present yourself to the world. If you look like a professional, you will be treated like one; if you look like a student, you will be treated like one. If you look unkempt and disorganized, others may very well not trust you. "Not fair!" you might think, but it is true nevertheless. The impression you make does make a difference in people's perceptions about your ability, personality, and trustworthiness to do the job.

This chapter has been added so that the reader can become aware of many nonverbal communication elements that can impact their professional effectiveness in dealing with clients, an employer, or their peers. Both students and professionals alike will find the information useful. Chapter 26 discusses issues related to image, appropriate business dress, and business etiquette.

Image—Nonverbal Cues

Seventy to 90 percent of effective communication is nonverbal (Twitty-Villani, 1992, p. 2). This means that how you dress and your body language and posture, gestures, and facial expressions send powerful messages about you at a particular time. Remember the scene in the movie *Pretty Woman* when Julia Roberts goes shopping for clothing on Rodeo Drive in Beverly Hills? If you are unconvinced, try this experiment. Dress very casually and visit a high-end clothing or jewelry store. Walk around and observe how you are looked at. If a clerk approaches you, what does he or she say? About a week later, put on a nice business suit, and go back to the same store. Now, how are you treated? Even in today's more casual world, appearances do make a difference.

* This is also the title of a book by LaBella and Leach (1983).

What creates the impression others have of you is based on the image you project—how you dress; a sincere smile; a firm handshake, eye contact, posture, and what you say—even how you say those first words. All of these play a part in how a client or a potential employer will react to you. Gender, physical appearance, skin color, and age also influence decisions and impressions.

Students sometimes have a difficult time making the transition from wearing casual clothing to wearing attire that is more appropriate to a business setting. Clothing does make the man and the woman in a business environment. What you wear is a reflection of you, your company, and even your perception of your professionalism and worth as an interior designer. Mom was right when she kept telling you to sit up straight and not slouch when you walk. Posture can be a powerful indicator of confidence or the lack of it.

Improving your self-image is a matter of learning ways to overcome the factors that hold you back from achieving greater success in your career. It involves making changes in the areas of personal image and presence that detract from your potential for success. I hired a young woman straight out of school several years ago. She was a very competent designer and was very pleasant, but she was finding it difficult to be taken seriously by many clients. She appeared one day with a shorter hair style (it had been below her shoulders). "Why did you cut your hair?" I asked. She replied, "I am tired of not being taken seriously just because I am young."

The self-image you portray begins with many subtle things. A smile, a handshake, and the tone of your voice give those to whom you come in contact an inkling of what you are like. Several of these subtle elements will be discussed in this next section. Other ingredients that influence your self-image are your apparel and your body language. These two items will be treated separately.

Give a Gift

When you meet a new person, do you give that person a gift? I do not mean a bouquet of flowers or a box of candy. I mean something of yourself—a smile, a warm handshake, eye contact, listening to him or her, and enthusiasm. These are gifts that are welcomed by most people and that influence your self-image and how others think of you. What happened the last time you smiled at the harried cashier at the grocery store? Didn't she sort of let out a breath and smile back? Wasn't it interesting to reflect on how rapt the client was when you spoke to her with genuine enthusiasm about the plans she had for remodeling her kitchen?

When you give this type of gift, people will want to work with you. Confidence will radiate from you as you make presentations to clients, talk to an overworked tradesperson, solve the problem of an irate client, or perhaps convince your boss to give you a raise.

It is said that smiling can disarm someone who is angry with you. How can the person be angry at someone who is smiling? Smiling also can help when you don't really feel very confident. Sure, lots of people can plaster on a fake smile, but I'm not talking about this type of smiling. Creating interiors is a fun way of making a living, so why aren't you smiling? Every day you get to spend other people's money wisely, and you didn't have to take a finance class to do so. Why aren't you smiling? "A smile does not say, 'I am a person with no problems and everything is perfect' " (Twitty-Villani, 1992, p. 8). A smile says you think the other person deserves respect, even if you are having a bad day.

Touching is very powerful, and the traditional handshake in North America has become an important nonverbal communication business tool. The handshake has its roots in ancient times, when men would show their palms to indicate they were unarmed. Hundreds of years later, during the Industrial Revolution, men would confirm a deal with a handshake (Zunin, 1972, p. 104).

Decades ago, women generally did not shake hands, except with other women, and only if they both wore gloves. Today, however, it is almost expected for a woman in a business situation to shake hands with a man or another woman.

A handshake should be firm, not bone shattering. A weak handshake is often interpreted as meaning that the person is timid or lacking in confidence. The dainty fingertip handshake used by some is said to show weakness and submissiveness. When someone grasps your hand firmly and then places his or her other hand over the two hands, this sends a very powerful signal that is sometimes called the "politician's" handshake. Between friends it can be taken as a warm gesture; between strangers, it is usually considered rather ingratiating or phony. A "wet" handshake from someone with sweaty palms is also interpreted as a sign of weakness. If you get nervous and your hands sweat, be ready to discreetly dry your hand just before you shake hands.

When you talk to someone, do you look the person in the eye, letting him or her know that you acknowledge the person's presence? Knowing how to use eye contact is another gift. It is a gift of honesty, as far as the other person is concerned, and it is a sign of self-confidence. Of course, it is not impossible for someone to look you in the eye and lie. It has probably happened to you. But it is not easy to do. Your eyes can tell someone if you are happy, bored, excited, sad, or lonely. Perhaps you are unsure about the solution to a floor plan because you did not take enough time to work out alternative solutions. It is going to be difficult to convince the client that the floor plan is the right solution if you cannot look the client in the eye and say so.

How you say what you say also conveys a lot of meaning, and language experts say that the tone of your voice is often a true reflection of what is really inside your head. Are you having a bad day? The "hello" you give as you greet a client on the phone is not going to be very welcoming. If you are enthusiastic about what you are showing to clients, it is infectious. They will like what you are talking about. If the tone of your voice is even slightly off, they will have a difficult time being convinced, even if they really like what you are showing them. Some clients will be comfortable with a formal tone; others will think you are a snob.

Language and the way you talk can be powerful or powerless. When you talk rapidly, the listener's heartbeat will accelerate; if you talk calmly, the listener will relax. If you use a lot of industry jargon, the client is likely to look at you like you have just arrived from a foreign country. If you talk down to them, they will just as likely turn you off. Powerful language is assertive, conversational, and inclusive. Powerless language is strewn with fillers (words that mean nothing), for example, "Like, you'll like, love this chair." Powerless language is also full of phrases and words that reduce the listener's confidence in what you are saying: "I'm not sure, but I think a code of some kind applies to this situation." The nuances of language are so important that you are urged to read more about this skill.

According to research studies, we spend 40 percent of our time listening and 35 percent of our time talking; the remainder we spend reading or writing (Burley-Allen, 1995, p. 2). Some listen better than others and the individuals who are better listeners tend to be more successful. When you give the gift of listening, you learn a lot more about what the client (or your boss) wants than when you are talking. The gift of listening does not mean that you are sitting there thinking of what you want to say next while the other person is talking. This is not listening. Listening means that you are paying attention to the person who is talking, using eye contact so the person knows you are really listening, and not interrupting in the middle of sentences. "There are two major reasons why people don't listen well: because most of us aren't trained to listen well, and because it requires putting the other person first. Most of us don't want to suspend our own egos long enough to truly listen (DiResta, 1998, p. 89). Isn't it nice when you know that someone is really listening to you? Give that gift back and watch your positive results with clients increase.

Well Suited

What we wear makes a difference in how people perceive us. Put on any well-tailored garment and you will probably find yourself standing up a little taller. In business, clothing does speak volumes to those with whom you interact. Whether you are designing a home or an office for the chief executive officer of SONY or the managing partner of a local law firm (or whoever the client may be), what you wear to the interview and subsequent meetings will influence whether or not you get the project. Of course, how you dress for an employment interview is also important. This is discussed in Chapter 33.

We all play roles in our interactions with clients, vendors, peers, coworkers, friends, and associates. What is appropriate dress for one role is not necessarily appropriate for a different role or the same role at a different time. You may hear people talk about dressing for a particular situation. A designer with whom I consulted at one time was spending the day in the office dressed somewhat casually—slacks and a short-sleeved shirt. The next day, when he went to visit several clients, he wore a beautifully tailored suit. He dressed the part—appropriate for the situation.

One nice thing about being in a creative career such as interior design is that you can wear clothing other than a conservative navy blue, black, or charcoal gray suit. In fact, some clients probably expect an interior designer to wear trendy attire. Others are looking for that conservative suit. Nonetheless, there are some conventions or standards that apply to appropriate business attire in the interior design profession. Most of the rules, however, are made by each individual designer or a business' dress code. The business' owner sets the tone for what is appropriate at a particular time.

Designers who work in commercial design firms tend to wear more traditional, conservative apparel. The well-tailored suit is always appropriate for meetings and giving presentations to clients. Pant suits in the office may be permissible for women depending on the firm and the designer's position in the firm. When you are expected to be in the office, "dressing down" means that women can wear a pants suit and men can wear a sport shirt (not a team T-shirt) or dress shirt without a tie. Casual days may be pretty casual in some commercial companies if no client appointments are scheduled. But "business casual" does not ever mean that attire should be sloppy.

In residential design, women have more flexibility than the men in terms of what they can wear. Women residential designers often wear dresses with more flair and color. Others like to wear lighter-colored business suits, especially during the summer. Pants suits or pants outfits in the office and perhaps to see a client are also appropriate. Men generally still need to wear a suit for most business situations. Slacks, a dress shirt, and tie, or sport shirt and maybe a sweater are appropriate for more casual days and situations.

According to John Molloy (1988, p. 41), the suit remains the most important garment. "It is the central power garment—the garment that establishes our position as inferior, equal or superior in any in-person business situation." Since suits are usually worn by people who help us make important decisions about our lives, such as doctors and attorneys, we are more willing to accept the wearer as an authority figure and important. People who wear suits are usually given more respect than those who do not wear a suit. The jacket is as important for a woman as a suit is for a man. A woman who wears a jacket is thought of as a serious person who wields authority and power. It is not necessary for a woman to wear a suit to project this image. She can wear a jacket with a dress, trousers, or a nonmatching or matching skirt; these all are generally appropriate and project authority.

A suit is not always the best thing for you to wear. It is important for you to dress for the situation. Take into consideration the type of design firm you are working for and the type of clients (traditional, conservative, professional, trendy, or budget conscious) with whom you will interact. When you meet clients for the first time, your appearance should impress on them that you are a serious business person. Your portfolio and what you say should convince them of your talent. For subsequent meetings, you can dress more on the "business casual" side, leaving the navy blue suit at home and wearing something less traditional. Of course, this still depends on who the client is.

When you visit job sites, it is not necessary for you to dress up, but it is not good to dress too casually either. Remember, you lose authority when you dress down. Foremen and tradespeople must still recognize you as an authority. Consider also the issues of safety and of getting dirty. Do not wear high heels at a construction site (even if the construction is the remodeling of a home); change into a pair of flats. This would be an appropriate time for women to wear a pants outfit and for men to leave their suit jacket in the car and wear a dress shirt and tie.

Accessories act as the final touch to complete a garment and the wearer's look. Since trends in accessories change each season, only a few comments will be made here about accessories in general. The purpose of accessories in apparel is the same as in interior design—they help to finish the look, not overwhelm it. Women should limit wearing jewelry to only a few items. If you are dressing conservatively, then you can wear simple earrings along with perhaps a bracelet and a necklace. Save the trendier earrings, bangle bracelets, or other showy accessories for more casual times. Apply perfume lightly—do not leave a trail behind. Perfumes, by the way, came into existence to hide the body odor of royalty back in ancient times, when bathing was not common. For men, accessories should be simple—a good-quality watch, a handkerchief, and possibly other small items. The gold pen was the ubiquitous power symbol in the 1970s. A fine-quality fountain pen could be the power symbol today. (Never use a throwaway pen when you are meeting with an affluent client, by the way.)

Today, many of you have to juggle a cell phone, an electronic organizer, documents, samples, drawings, and maybe a laptop computer when they are on a call to a client. You may need an attaché case or a large satchel to carry papers, samples, a tape measure, and the other items needed by any interior designer when he or she is on a call to a client. A woman's handbag is for the pens, wallet, keys, and other small items that she needs to have with her.

A few tips on shopping for business garments is in order:

- Before you go shopping, review what you already have in your closets so that you can pinpoint your needs. This may take some of the fun out of shopping, but if you are on a limited budget, it will help you get what you really need in order to project the image you want to project.
- When you shop for business apparel, wear a similar type of garment. For example, if you are looking for a suit, wear a suit. You will have a more accurate idea of what you will look like in that suit than if you go shopping in shorts and a top. This includes wearing the kind of shoes you are most likely to wear with the new clothing.

- If you are looking for a higher-quality suit, shop where you can get in-store tailoring or alterations done. In this way, you can get assistance from a sales clerk who knows how to fit you properly.
- Fit is very important. Buy what fits, not what you think you will get into if you go on a diet. A poor-fitting, expensive garment will look worse on you than a good-fitting, moderately priced garment.
- For women who are on a limited budget, buy separates rather than dresses—but still of the best quality you can afford. Separates allows you to mix and match, which provides more versatility to a limited wardrobe.
- A high-quality garment will have its patterns match at the seams. Seams should all lie flat and be straight. A jacket and the openings around collars should be lined and lie or drape smoothly when they are open. When you buy a ready-to-wear suit, the better-quality suit jacket will have the pockets tacked closed. These must be opened carefully so that you don't damage the material.
- Wool is still preferred for suits, although polyester/wool blends wrinkle less. Even in the summer time, a fine-quality wool suit looks good, does not loose its shape, and wrinkles less. Cotton and linen are more comfortable in the summer, but they wrinkle and hold their wrinkles until they have been cleaned and pressed.
- Women carry *handbags*, not purses. A purse, according to my friends who teach fashion merchandising, is used to carry coins. A handbag is what women use to carry everything else that they need to carry. However, a "power" handbag should not be as big as an attaché case. It should be on the small side, such as rectangular clutch or a shoulder bag.
- Sales clerks pay more attention to and more quickly help those customers who are "dressed up" than those who are wearing shorts, T-shirts, and hiking boots—even on a Saturday.
- Put color psychology to work when you are selecting garments. Blues, gray, and tans are preferable for men. The darker the color, the more authoritative the person will be perceived. Black is very formal and is associated with funerals in the United States and in many other cultures. But black has become popular for business apparel. However, it can make the wrong statement if you are trying to be approachable. Grays, tans, and lighter blues, can help you appear approachable.

As was said earlier in this section, interior designers play many roles. You will be called upon to market to corporate executives or to affluent residential clients; to provide instructions to tradespeople and craftspeople at their shop or on the job site; to input CAD drawings or hand-drafted plans to your computer; to be on the job and spend time as the authority, psychologist, and "friend" to clients during the project. Perhaps your role is the owner of the firm or maybe the person who cleans the sample library from time to time. Each role requires different skills and behaviors, and each role means something a little different in terms of the clothing you wear for that situation.

Body Language

The study of body language comes from the scientific study of the meaning of body positions and gestures, called *kinesics* (Fast, 1980, p. 1). Body language is very powerful nonverbal communication. Studies have shown that the clues we give through body positions and gestures often more accurately reflect what we are thinking than the words we use. If you know how to read these signals, you will be able to interpret whether your client (or anyone else) is, for example, really interested in what you are saying or bored; upset at what is being discussed, even though he or she hasn't said anything; or wanting you to back off and leave the client alone. You, of course, also are giving cues to what you are thinking. The signals you send tells clients (and others) such things as whether you are confident about your suggestions, interested in doing the project, interested in working for the firm, and many other things.

There are many different gestures and body positions that have been studied, which are related to body language. We can discuss only a few of them here.

One of the most important elements of body language is eye contact. We have already discussed this, but I do want to make one more comment about it. Not making eye contact can be interpreted as meaning that you do not really think the other person is important. When you fail to use eye contact, you are also sending a message that can be interpreted as arrogance: "I'm better than you." Both of these messages are bad to send to your client or to anyone else, for that matter. Let me give you an example of how powerful eye contact can be. I have twice had the opportunity to shake hands with President Bill Clinton. He has an uncanny ability to look into your eyes, smile, and make you feel like you are the only person in the room when, in fact, there are hundreds, if not thousands, around you. Whether you like President Clinton or not, his ability to give everyone with whom he shakes hands his undivided attention is very powerful. Just think of what this skill can do for your ability to work positively with a client!

Another aspect of body language involves what we do with our hands. We shake hands, we put our hands in our pants pockets, behind the back, or sometimes over our mouth slightly while talking, or we put our fingertips together to make a triangle. What do these gestures mean? Putting your hands in your pockets is not the use of good body language. Often it is interpreted as meaning that you are secretive or unsure of yourself. Placing your hands behind your back can be a power stance, many police do this when they walk a beat. It also makes you look stiff and uncomfortable, especially if your posture is somewhat rigid. Remember that, in ancient days, men showed the palms of their hands to foes in order to show that they were unarmed. If you are standing, let your hands fall naturally to your side or perhaps fold them softly (so it does not look like you are madly gripping your hands) at your waist. If you are seated, fold them softly in your lap or rest them comfortably on the arm of the chair. Don't drum your fingers! Keep your fingers and hands relaxed. If you are the presenter, don't fidget with a paper clip or drum your fingers. This means you are nervous, losing interest, or getting impatient. Any kind of fidgeting is a signal that you are inattentive or nervous. Do not do this yourself and watch if your client does so!

Do you know someone who generally puts his or her fingers over his or her mouth while talking? This is commonly interpreted as meaning that the person is not very confident about what he or she is saying. It can also mean that the person is not being completely truthful. Eliminate this gesture from your body language.

Placing your fingertips together to create a triangle with the hands is referred to as steepling, since the shape resembles a church steeple. People who use this gesture usually feel they are in a powerful position. They may be considered smug or egotistical. It may be used when one is sitting or standing but is more commonly used when sitting. The higher the steeple is, the more confident the person feels. However, those who know about body language sometimes use steepling when they feel they are in a weak position and are pretending that they are in a position of power. Watch out for someone who uses this body language!

When you stand to give a presentation, be relaxed but maintain good posture. Face the client or group as much as you can rather than place your back to them. Keep your hand movements slow and small; don't flail around with your hands or arms. Stand with an easy stance, without slouching. Walk with your head up but not with your nose in the air!

When you are sitting, you can lean forward to show interest in what you are saying and what the client says in response to your statements. If the client leans or pushes away from the table, then possibly he or she is losing interest in what is being said. If you are standing and lean over the conference table or desk toward the other party (or this is done to you), it is generally considered to be an aggressive posture. Most people will then lean away from the person who is leaning toward them.

If the client folds his or her arms across the chest, it might mean that the client does not like what is being said. Depending on how tightly the client is clenching his or her fists or arms, the client may be getting angry. The more frowns, tightly laced fingers, crossed arms, pushing away from the table, and tightly crossed legs you see, the more resistant the client is becoming. At this point, it is best to stop and ask some questions. The client has heard something that he or she doesn't like. You may have insulted the client without being aware of it.

There are many other gestures and body positions that can help you better understand what your client, boss, coworkers, or others are actually saying when speaking. Figure 26-1 highlights a few more, but you are urged to read one of the books on body language in the References or in others you might find.

Business Etiquette

Interior designers are hired because of their design expertise by executives, professionals, and those at the upper end of the residential market who are in

- Impatience
  - Pushes away from table or desk
  - Taps fingers or a pen or pencil on the table
  - Shifts from one foot to another while standing
  - Clenches hands tightly
- Boredom
  - Turns body toward exit
  - Rests head in the hand
  - Doodles
  - Stares blankly
- Secretiveness and suspicion
  - Turns body slightly away from you
  - Looks everywhere but at you
  - Covers mouth with fingers while speaking
  - Smiles superficially or glances sideways

FIGURE 26-1. A few hints on how to interpret the body language of others. (*Source*: Nierenberg and Calero, 1993; Delmar, 1984; Fast, 1970)

positions of power and influence. Working with the elite is unfamiliar territory for many designers if they have not been raised in that environment themselves. However, appropriate business etiquette, or manners, is part of being the consummate professional, whether one's client is Bill Gates of Microsoft, a senator, the owner of a mansion in a city, or the owner of a small family business. According to Letitia Baldrige, former chief of staff for Jacqueline Kennedy, "An atmosphere in which people treat each other with consideration is obviously one in which a customer enjoys doing business. . . . A company with a well-mannered, high-class reputation attracts—and keeps—good people" (Baldridge, 1985, p. 3)

In this section, we will not try to teach basic manners. It is a given that students who enter interior design generally know what constitutes basic politeness and manners. However, entry-level designers—and designers at every level of the professional chain—may find themselves in situations in which they are unfamiliar with what is appropriate business etiquette. This section will focus on business entertaining and travel. We begin with a few common courtesies related to business.

Common Courtesies

There are some common courtesies that everyone should know but that seem to have been forgotten in today's fast-paced society. However, if you are dealing with clients who are used to receiving preferential treatment, such as older clients, executives, and the affluent, you will be expected to show certain courtesies to those with whom you will be working.

NAMES

Always use the client's surname when you address him or her until the client gives you permission to use the client's first name. This means using "Mr. Cruise," "Mrs. Bush," and "Ms. Roberts," not "Tom," "Barbara," or "Julia." If you encounter someone you met a while ago and find you have forgotten the person's name, reintroduce yourself so that (hopefully) the other person will do the same.

SMOKING

If you are a smoker, do not smoke if you are speaking to a group and there are nonsmokers in the group, even if you are the host. Do not ask if its okay; just do not smoke. If you are a nonsmoker and the host asks about smoking, say something like, "I would prefer it if you did not smoke."

GREETINGS

If you are seated and someone approaches to shake your hand, always stand up, whether the person is a man or woman. If its impossible for you to stand, for example, if you are in a restaurant booth, do a slight 'bob,' in which you rise slightly but do not fully stand. Men don't have to wait for a woman to extend her hand to shake hands anymore. Never stay behind the desk in your office when a client or other person who is introduced to you arrives. Stand and move around your desk to greet the person.

INTRODUCTIONS

Always introduce the person with the highest "status" to the people with lower status; that is, introduce the client to your boss, your boss to a coworker or a friend.

Business Entertaining

A significant amount of business is conducted across a table in a restaurant. Interior designers often meet with clients at a restaurant after a presentation or to discuss a topic that does not require reviewing of plans and samples. Manufacturers' representatives often invite designers to lunch. An employee may go to lunch with a supervisor or the owner of the firm. The designer meets colleagues at professional associations, and they often meet to chat and network.

Table manners can play a part in a job interview as well. Some companies have daylong interview sessions. It is quite possible that the interviewer is carefully evaluating the job seeker's etiquette during the lunch or, for that matter, all day. The firm does not want to hire someone who does not know basic etiquette. It is quite obvious that there are all sorts of situations in which an interior designer will need to use appropriate table etiquette.

The main purpose for a business meal is to continue to develop rapport between the designer and the client. Business *is* discussed, but it is usually done after some small talk has occurred. As was pointed out in other chapters, getting to know the client is very important in a service industry. Thus, it is not only acceptable to ask the client about his or her hobbies and interests or other general topics that might be appropriate but also helpful in developing a business relationship with the client. However, unless you know the person very well, stay away from talking about politics and religion!

If you have invited the client to the meal and you both will be arriving at the restaurant separately, be sure to arrive at the restaurant a little early. In this way, you can greet the client rather than have the client stand around waiting for you. If you don't know the client very well, wait for him or her in the lobby rather than at the table. Your client should not have to come find you. If you do go to the table first, proper etiquette says that you should not order beverages (or start eating the bread) until the other party has arrived.

If you are meeting a client whom you do not know at a restaurant for the first time, it is especially important for you to wait in the lobby. It is never easy to match the person with a description given over the telephone, so give the client a hint by telling him or her what you will be wearing. Do not go to the table. If you do, you could end up like the designer who relayed the following story. The designer did not see anyone who seemed to match the description of the person whom she was to meet in the lobby. She decided to have the hostess seat her. After sitting there for 15 minutes, she spied another woman who was sitting alone across the room. Finally, she went over and asked her name, and sure enough, it was the client! This is an embarrassing situation, to say the least.

If you are the host, the guest should be waiting for you to be seated first or for you to indicate where you think you both should be seated. If you are dining with only one other person or if you are the host, the person should sit at your right. Sitting across from someone in many restaurants makes it difficult to conduct a conversation. It is up to the host to signal the waiter when service is needed and to control the pace and purpose of the meeting.

Perhaps you have gone to dinner with a group. Do you have difficulty determining which bread dish is yours or which water glass to use? The rule is this—liquids to the right, solids to the left—which means that your water and other beverages will be on your right, whereas your bread plate will be on your left. If the person next to you picks up your glass or uses your bread plate, don't make a big fuss. If the person is a friend or colleague, you might want to politely thank the person for the roll and start eating it. The person will get the message! If the person is your client, you can forgo the bread or ask for another service set from the waiter. Make sure you do not embarrass the client.

When you are faced with numerous utensils, work from the outside in. An exception is if you order a salad as an entree. Then you would use the dinner fork, not the salad fork. Pass food or the condiments to the right, counterclockwise. Offer items like sugar or cream to the guest first and then

- If you invite someone to lunch, the guest will assume that you will be paying for it.
- If you invite someone to a business meal, it is your responsibility to call and make the reservations. It is also your responsibility to cancel the reservations if the meeting has to be canceled or postponed.
- Never order the most expensive item on the menu, even if you are the host.
- Do not pull out business papers during the meal. Discuss business, if you must, after you have finished eating.
- If food you do not like is served, allow it to be served, but it is okay for you not to eat it. Do not make a big fuss over the fact that you have been served food you do not want to eat.
- When you are finished eating, fold your napkin and place it on the right of the place setting.
- Be aware of time restraints. Check with the client regarding the amount of time he or she has and stick to that time limit. If necessary, instruct your waiter and tip extra for faster service in a slow restaurant.
- Do no personal grooming at the table. This includes applying fresh lipstick. Excuse yourself and go to the restroom.

FIGURE 26-2. A selection of tips related to business meal etiquette.

take what you need. In the American style of dining, when you want to "rest" between bites, place the knife at the top of the plate, with the serrated edge facing you, and place the fork, tines up, with the handle in the lower right side of the plate (or lower left, if you are left-handed). When you are finished eating, place both the knife and the fork in the center of the plate, with the handles on the right. The fork tines should be facing down.

Most companies do not allow the drinking of alcohol during business hours. Refrain from drinking hard liquor or wine during lunch, especially if you will be discussing business. Having a drink during dinner is frequently left up to the discretion of the employee. However, be sure you use care in how much you drink. If the client does not drink or is not drinking, refrain from ordering a drink for yourself. If you don't know and you are the host, you can always say something like, "I was wondering about some wine with dinner." Gauge your response from what he or she says.

Wait for everyone to be served before you start eating. This is especially important for the guest, as he or she should wait until the host takes the first bite.* It becomes awkward if you are finished eating before the client, or vice versa. Try to order entrees that will allow you to eat at a similar pace with the client. If you order a huge salad entree, you will probably not finish it or may still be eating it while the client is sitting with a cleaned plate and hands folded. Keep pace by asking questions so that the client is forced to pause to talk while you eat, and vice versa.

The host also sets the protocol for ending the lunch or dinner. Coffee is ordered after the main meal, not during, so after the plates have been cleared, if you choose to have dessert, wait until the plates have been cleared to drink your coffee. When you arrived early, you should have told the maitre d' that the bill should be presented to you or that you would take care of it on the way out. This may sound silly, but sometimes women designers have to fight male customers for the bill, even in this new century! Figure 26-2 provides some additional tips related to business meal etiquette.

Business Travel

Having the opportunity to travel on business does not mean that you should leave good manners at home. In fact, they may be even more important when you are traveling. You never know if the person sitting next to you on the

* Most of us think that it is the other way around; it is not!

airplane might turn out to be a potential client. Being friendly and courteous on an airplane will be appreciated by those around you, even if you are never going to see them again.* Sometimes you will travel with a colleague, client, or your boss. If you need to discuss business, be sure arrangements are made so that this can happen. It's not much fun sitting in the middle seat in coach for a long trip, but it might be necessary if you are traveling with colleagues.

When you fly during the work week, it is best to wear business clothing, even if you are traveling alone. Then you will be prepared for conducting business once you get off the plane. If you are traveling in the evening, wearing business casual attire is okay, and on the weekends, casual is fine, unless you are being greeted by the client! Be sure you have any documents, computer disks, or other items that you will need to conduct business in your attaché case or carry-on bag. If you are traveling in order to make a presentation, be sure to have the necessary materials in your carry-on bag. If at all possible, do not schedule your arrival or departure so tightly that you must leave early or that a flight delay would result in your missing your connection or presentation.

If you are sharing a cab, the person of junior rank should be prepared to take care of the fare if the boss does not. The designer should always take care of the fare when in a cab with a client. The same rules would apply to limousine service.

Remember, on any kind of business trip, your boss or your accountant will want receipts for tax purposes. Cab drivers will give a receipt, but usually it is blank. Write down the correct amount as soon as possible. Restaurant receipts often are from a charge card. If you are eating with a group of colleagues and you all need receipts, ask about requesting separate checks. Some restaurants will do this. If the restaurant will not, then ask for duplicate copies of the receipt so that everyone will have what they need for reimbursement or tax purposes.

Just because you are out of town does not mean that your manners and good sense should be forgotten. There is nothing funny about seeing a colleague get drunk at a conference and embarrass the design firm. Use the same business etiquette that you would use at home. This means dressing appropriately for business. It is fairly common for designers who are attending a conference that will last several days or a week to wear business attire on weekdays and business casual on the weekends.

If you have traveled to visit a client, your time is really the client's time. Most likely, you are getting paid for the time you travel and meet with them. Although you may think evenings are your own, you will probably have dinner with the client. A lot of very good relationship building can happen over dinner.

Conference expenses may be paid for by your employer or by you. If the expenses are being paid for by your employer, you have an obligation to attend meetings or seminars and perhaps pick up materials to bring back to the office. Many firms that send designers to Neocon expect them to give a report to the rest of the design team when they return. Even if you are paying the expenses rather than your boss, you have an obligation to conduct yourself in a businesslike and appropriate manner.

Telephones, Cell Phones, and E-mail

Interior designers spend quite a bit of time on the phone and using E-mail to communicate with clients, coworkers, vendors, and others. There are common courtesies regarding telephone communication that have been used for many years. Cell phone courtesy has become a hot topic, since it seems almost

* Of course, you would hope that those around you would extend the same courtesy.

everyone, from children to the highest level executive, has a cell phone. E-mail courtesy is also becoming a concern, because the misuse of E-mail annoys many people.

TELEPHONE Your telephone greeting says a lot about you and your design firm. If you have an overly casual manner when you answer the phone, this can affect a potential client's impression of you and your firm. If you are an employee, the owner has probably instructed you on how to answer the phone. If you are a sole proprietor, be sure you have a phone system at your home office that allows you to keep your personal phone line and your business line separate. If you are calling long distance, say so. While we are speaking of long distance, remember that there are time zones. People who work on the East Coast sometimes forget about the three-hour time difference to the West Coast and Western states, and vice versa! This sometimes makes it very difficult to get in touch with people.

When you call someone, give your name and the name of the person with whom you wish to speak in a pleasant manner, for example, "Hello, this is Susan James. I would like to talk to Mel Adams, please." Or, "Hello, this is Susan James. Is Mel Adams available, please?" If the person is not there, it is a good idea to ask when the person might be available. Do not ask that the person call you back if the person does not know you at all (cold calling) or if the person may not remember your name. The usual rule is that the one who has something to gain from the conversation should call back.

Voice-messaging systems are very prevalent today. If you have to leave a message, speak distinctly, especially when you are giving your phone number. Make the message short as well. Busy people find it annoying to listen to messages that drone on if the important information, such as the phone number of the caller, comes at the very end of the message. Sometimes these long messages are cut off before the pertinent information has been left!

Return all your messages promptly—no later than the next day, if this is at all possible. Because of the prevalence of fax machines, cell phones, and other time-saving equipment in our fast-paced society, clients expect responses right away. Not getting back to someone quickly can be very annoying to the other person. And this might mean that you have lost business. Never be the one who is difficult to reach. If you are playing phone tag with a client or someone else to whom you really need to talk, be sure to give the person solid information as to when to reach you, or ask the person to leave a message as to when you can get that person.

CELL PHONE Courtesy and cell phones sometimes do not seem to go together. The ubiquitous ringing phone and people who seem to be talking to themselves can be annoying. For some reason, people seem to talk louder when they are using a cell phone than when they are using a regular phone. If you must use your cell phone around others, be conscious of how loud you are talking. Not everyone is interested in hearing your conversation.

Cell phones ringing in restaurants is becoming a major problem. Many restaurants (as well as other businesses) are posting signs that say that the use of cell phones in their facilities is forbidden. Since most cell phone plans allow for voice messaging, turn your phone off while you are dining in a restaurant or other quiet place. Only you are impressed by your own self-importance when you feel you must respond to a call on your cell phone in such environments. If you are expecting a very important phone call and it comes while you are meeting with someone, excuse yourself. Go outside or to a quiet place in order to carry on your conversation.

If you must use a cell phone in your car, take advantage of the hands-free devices. No call is so important that you should risk having an accident while you are driving, which could result in injury to you or an innocent person. I was told of a case in which a buyer was riding in a car with a salesperson. The cell phone of the driver rang, and she proceeded to talk while driving about 50 miles per hour through city traffic. Then she started making notes on a note pad! Incredibly, nothing happened, but how inconsiderate this salesperson was of her client!

E-MAIL Using E-mail is definitely a great way to communicate with clients, vendors, and friends. However, there are some courtesies that should also be mentioned with regard to using E-mail. DO NOT USE ALL CAPITAL LETTERS when you are writing an E-mail. It may be easier to read, but it is considered shouting and is not necessary. Be careful what you write. Once you click the Send button, there is no way to take back what you have sent. It goes to the recipient, and he or she can mull over meanings and interpret words in his or her own way. Also realize that E-mail can be printed out at the other end and thus becomes a legal document in many ways. Be careful when you are sending large attachments or E-mails with graphics. These take a long time for the recipient to load and even have been known to crash someone's system. Always check your spelling. It is easy to make typing errors in E-mails, and this will not look good if you are sending it to a client or someone else whom you need to impress. One last item. Be careful when you "Reply to All" or "Forward" an E-mail. The original document goes with these, and something may have been said that someone else should not read. Perhaps the vendor has E-mailed you an estimate, which you would not want the client to see, as well as some specification information that you want to get to a client.

International Etiquette

Interior design is practiced around the world—so much so that ASID, IIDA, IDEC, FIDER, NCIDQ, IFMA, and other professional associations embrace members from around the world. Trade markets take on an international flavor, because designers from many countries travel to the United States to see what new products are being offered. Manufacturers have offices, showrooms, as well as factories around the world. The Internet makes locating interior design businesses and conducting business internationally easy.

Those readers who wish to conduct business outside North America must, therefore, be sensitive to cultural differences and etiquette issues in the countries to which they may travel. Books exist on this topic; thus, it is left to those other authors to provide an in-depth discussion of international etiquette. If you are traveling on international business or have been contacted by a client outside the country, make it a point to read up on the country's differences in etiquette, which literally can mean the difference between having a positive encounter or causing an international incident.

A smile is universal, but a handshake is not. A handshake is a Western gesture of greeting and is not done in numerous other countries. A gesture of greeting might be a slight bow, a hug, the shaking of hands and a bow, or numerous other greetings that are specific to a particular culture or country.

Most foreign businesspeople can speak English. They may, however, choose to conduct business at some point in their own language. You would be expected to do so as well or to bring along an interpreter. It is imperative that you really listen to your international clients. Their English may be very good, but sometimes their accent might make it difficult for you to decipher certain words. Never talk down to your international clients. Respect their culture and customs, and they will respect you.

Punctuality is a very interesting issue in international business relations. It is very highly regarded in some countries, appreciated in others, and somewhat relaxed in others. According to Roger Axtell (1997), the concern for promptness varies greatly in different parts of the world.* Make sure you understand this issue if you are working with international clients so that you do not get angry when they are late and they do not get angry when you get angry if they are late!

As you can see from these descriptions, the first rule in international business etiquette is to respect the cultural differences of the country in which you are traveling. Do not expect the client to conduct himself or herself as you would in North America. In addition to the differences in language and communication, what is right and proper in another country can be a dramatic awakening for many North Americans.

Summary

It is hoped that the reader will understand that the information provided in this chapter is only a small slice of what can affect your personal power and professional image. The list of references at the end of this chapter comprise only a few books that deal with these topics in detail. The author has tried to distill a great deal of information into brief discussions about various topics that are related to the interior design industry. However, as with every other topic in this text, what is said here is general; your particular experience in a particular design firm in a particular part of the country or world might be different. It is a fact of this business that there are no absolutes in how you should project your professionalism any more than there are absolutes related to what is good interior design.

As a professional, you should be interested in putting your best foot forward. How you conduct yourself in a business encounter certainly does affect your success with your clients. Perhaps you may feel that how you look, what you wear, what pen you use, or even how you speak should not matter—only your talent should be of concern. However, this is just not so. Clients have expectations of who you are—that is, the image you project—perhaps in relation to what you can do. It is a fact of life in the twenty-first century. You can meet these expectations or choose not too. But if you do not, your success in the industry will likely be diminished.

In Chapter 26, we have presented some concepts that can help you understand the issues that can add to your personal power as you see yourself in the image of the professional interior designer. The discussion on body language and business etiquette can also help you interpret your client's reactions, which will help you become more effective in discussions and presentations.

This concludes our discussion of the many issues, strategies, and activities involved in marketing interior design services and products. Part VI discusses management and business topics that are related to project management.

* Roger Axtell's books are both thorough and interesting discussions of international etiquette.

REFERENCES

Axtell, Roger E. 1997. *Do's and Taboos Around the World for Women in Business.* New York: John Wiley.

———. 1991. *Gestures*. New York: John Wiley.

Baldrige, Letitia. 1993. *Letitia Baldrige's New Complete Guide to Executive Manners.* New York: Rawson Associates.

———. 1985. *Letitia Baldrige's Complete Guide to Executive Manners*. New York: Rawson Associates.

Bender, Peer Urs. 1995. *Secrets of Power Presentations.* Willodale, Ontario, Canada: Firefly Books.

Benton, D. A. 1992. *Lions Don't Need to Roar*. New York: Time Warner Books.

Bixler, Susan. 1991. *Professional Presence*. New York: Perigee.

Bixler, Susan, and Nancy Nix-Rice. 1997. *The New Professional Image.* Holbrook, MA: Adams Media.

Burley-Allen, Madelyn. 1995. *Listening: The Forgotten Skill.* New York: John Wiley.

Casperson, Dana May. 1999. *Power Etiquette.* New York: American Management Association.

Dale, Paulette. 1999. *"Did You Say Something, Susan?" How Any Woman Can Gain Confidence with Assertive Communication.* Secaucus, NJ: Birch Lane Press.

Dawson, Roger. 1994. *The 13 Secrets of Power Performance.* Englewood Cliffs, NJ: Prentice-Hall.

Delmar, Ken. 1984. *Winning Moves—The Body Language of Selling.* New York: Time Warner Books.

DiResta, Diane. 1998. *Knockout Presentations.* Worcester, MA: Chandler House Press.

Elsea, Janet G. 1984. *The Four-Minute Sell.* New York: Simon & Schuster.

Fast, Julius. 1994. *Body Language in the Workplace.* New York: Penguin Books.

———. 1970. *Body Language.* New York: Pocket Books.

LaBella, Arleen, and Dolores Leach. 1983. *Personal Power*. Boulder, CO: Newview Press.

Lavington, Camilee (with Stephanie Losee). 1997. *You've Only Got Three Seconds.* New York: Doubleday.

Littauer, Florence. 1992. *Personality Plus: How to Understand Others by Understanding Yourself.* Grand Rapids, MI: Fleming H. Revell.

Mandell, Terri. 1993. *Power Shmoozing*. Los Angeles, CA: First House Press.

Molloy, John T. 1996. *The New Woman's Dress for Success Book.* New York: Time Warner Books.

———. 1988. *New Dress for Success.* New York: Time Warner Books.

———. 1981. *Molloy's Live for Success.* New York: Perigord Press—William Morrow.

Morrison, Terri, Wayne A. Conway, and George A. Borden. 1994. *Kiss, Bow, or Shake Hands.* Holbrook, MA: Adams Media.

Murphy, Tom. 2000. *Web Rules*. Chicago: Dearborn Financial Publishing.

National Institute of Business Management. 1989. *Mastering Business Style*. New York: Berkley Books.

Nierenberg, Gerard I., and Henry H. Calero. 1993. *How to Read a Person Like a Book*. New York: Barnes & Noble.

Pachter, Barbara, and Marjorie Brody (with Betsy Andrson). 1995. *Complete Business Etiquette Handbook*. Englewood Cliffs, NJ: Prentice-Hall.

Post, Peggy, and Peter Post. 1999. *The Etiquette Advantage in Business.* New York: Harper & Row.

Sabath, Anne Marie. 2000. *Beyond Business Casual*. Franklin Lakes, NJ: Career Press.

Siress, Ruth Herrman (with Carolyn Riddle and Deborah Shouse). 1994. *Working Woman's Communications Survival Guide.* Englewood Cliffs, NJ: Prentice-Hall.

Stone, Janet, and Jane Bachner. 1994. *Speaking Up: A Book for Every Woman Who Talks*. New York: Carroll & Graf.

Thompson, Jacqueline. 1981. *Image Impact.* New York: A & W Publishers.

Twitty-Villani, Teri. 1992. *Appearances Speak Louder Than Words.* Portland, OR: Voyager Press.

Williams, Terrie (with Joe Cooney). 1994. *The Personal Touch*. New York: Time Warner Books.

Zunin, Leonard (with Natalie Zunin). 1972. *Contact: The First Four Minutes*. New York: Ballantine Books.

Susan Coleman, FIIDA, FIDEC, CID has 35 years of experience as an interior design practitioner and 25 years of experience as an educator at Orange Coast College and California State University, Long Beach. Among her numerous leadership positions, Coleman is currently the Vice President to International Regions for the International Interior Design Association and represents the North American design community on the International Federation of Interior Design board.

In order to prepare students to compete in the global workplace, we must focus on teaching students how to learn. The most valuable skill that we can teach our students is how to access, analyze, and apply information to the "real world" of design practice. Teachers must become the facilitators of learning. As we move from the industrial age to the age of technology, we must equip students with the skills to become lifelong learners.

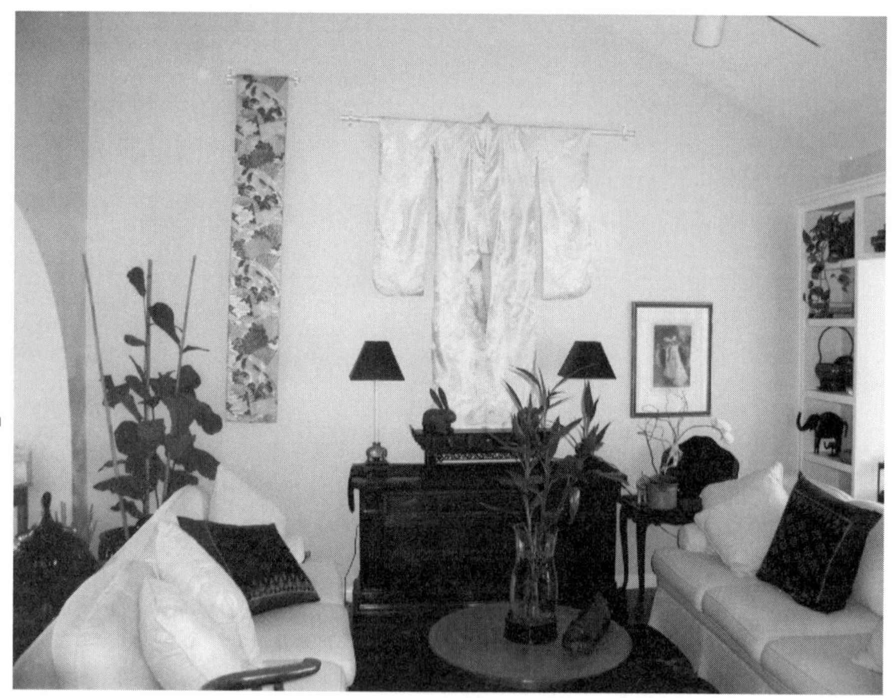

Part VI

Project Management

27. Project Management Techniques
What is Project Management? *Phases of an Interior Design Project* *Working Relationships* *Project Schedules* *Project Budgeting* *Time Records* *Time Management* *Project Files or Job Books* *Value Engineering*

28. Working with Trade Sources
Manufacturers *Sales Representatives (or Reps)* *Market Centers, Marts, and Showrooms* *Local Showrooms* *Retail Specialty Shops* *Manufacturer's Dealers* *Tradespeople and Craftspeople* *Construction Contractors* *Selecting Trade Sources* *Technology and Trade Sources*

29. Contract Documents and Specifications
Contract Documents *Specifications* *Competitive Bidding* *Modifications* *Submittals*

30. Contract Administration
Construction and Procurement Administration *Order Processing* *Shipping and Freight* *Expediting*

31. Contract Administration: Delivery and Project Closeout
Delivery and Installation *Project Closeout* *Postoccupancy and Follow-up*

Chapter 27

Project Management Techniques

Interior design is a process by which the designer obtains and assimilates information in order to convert that information into design concepts, floor plans, specifications, and construction drawings. Sketches or renderings may be needed, and color schemes are coordinated. These graphic and written forms of design documents are used to explain the design concepts to the client and show the client how goals will be accomplished. Yet, once all this has been done, only about 50 percent of the project has been completed.

In principle, it does not matter if the project is a huge, new Las Vegas hotel or the remodeling of a second home. The design process, the project phases, and the project management are the same. All projects must be managed so that the required work is done quickly, correctly, and with as few problems as possible. This is not an easy task. As one senior project designer related, "My dream is to have a project go from start to finish with no problems, no extra worries, no delays. After 14 years of commercial work, it still hasn't happened." For this edition, I went back and asked that same designer if his dream had occurred yet. He said, "No."

This chapter offers a very complete, though brief, discussion of the project management process. It begins by providing a brief overview of what project management is and the role of the project manager. A section in which the phases of a complete design project are discussed is followed by an overview of the working relationships that are part of the overall project. The chapter continues by explaining scheduling methods that help the designer and design manager keep track of activities for each project. Other controls or project management techniques included are project budgeting, time record keeping, time management, and project files or job books. The chapter concludes with a brief discussion on value engineering—a process borrowed from architecture that has found its way into interior design.

What Is Project Management?

Interior design projects are increasingly complex, whether they are commercial or residential. The size of the projects is larger, the amount of product specification is greater, and the overall scope of services has grown. Added to this is the speed with which decisions must be made and information transmitted. Clients complain if the interior designer does not get back to them within a few hours, if not a few minutes. Every client feels that his or her problem or question has priority. "It is getting difficult to project manage today because there is so much to manage!" could be said by many interior designers today.

Project management is the process of organizing and controlling an interior design project from beginning to end to satisfactorily solve the client's problems and provide a reasonable profit to the design firm. A project solution that does not solve the client's problems or does not provide a reasonable profit for the design firm should not be considered a successfully managed project. In order to be a successfully managed project, the *project manager*, who most often is the interior designer in charge of the project, must use both the creative and analytical sides of the brain. The client is looking for a creative solution, yet in many cases, the client is looking for a solution that solves his or her problem, whether or not it is a creative solution. The client is also looking to the interior designer to manage all the details and installation of the project.

As for the interior designer, he or she certainly wishes to provide a creative solution, for that is why most designers go into the interior design business in the first place. But as a businessperson, the interior designer must also execute his or her responsibilities so that the firm can earn a reasonable profit. Engaging in work that will not generate a reasonable profit should be left to those times the interior designer engages in community service work—not for clients.

All of these goals are not in opposition to each other. They require planning, management, communication, and business skills that all function together. Perhaps these are all orchestrated by a sole practitioner who is working with minimal assistance from an office manager or a student intern, or by a senior project manager who has numerous years of experience and is fortunate enough to have a team of designers and office staff as backup. The basic responsibilities are the same. The intensity of the tasks is the same as well. The point is this: few designers can be successful without carefully managing their projects.

Successful project management requires many things. Key issues are listed in Figure 27-1. The skills used to perform these and dozens of other tasks are acquired by the designer as he or she works alongside experienced interior designers until the responsibility is thrust upon the designer. The designer learns about scheduling, for example, by first learning how long it takes for common tasks to be achieved and then by being responsible for scheduling. Learning the various management skills plays a critical part in the designer's success so that he or she can control the project instead of letting the project control the designer. This chapter and others in Part VI discuss these skills and tasks.

Phases of an Interior Design Project

Interior design projects have several distinct phases. The tasks of a design project are broken down into five phases: (1) programming, (2) schematic design, (3) design development, (4) preparation of contract documents, and (5) contract administration. Obviously, not all work done by all interior designers always involves the many activities that fall into each of these project phases. Some of the typical activities that relate to each phase will be discussed in this section. Other information concerning the activities in each phase are presented in Figure 18-8, related to the development of the scope of services in a design contract. Understanding what goes on in each phase as it relates to the business

- Prepare the proposal and contract.
- Establish and oversee the project schedule.
- Select a project team.
- Serve as primary client contact.
- Supervise the design team.
- Establish and oversee the budget.
- Coordinate with consultants.
- Oversee the project files.
- Supervise quality control.
- Provide design input.
- Utilize good communication skills.
- Prepare and distribute project status reports.

FIGURE 27-1. Key tasks of a project manager.

management of the firm is very important to professionals and students alike and of most concern in this text. This section will not attempt to describe fully how these phases or how a project should be done. There are many other books the reader might use for this purpose.

In small firms, managing these phases is the responsibility of the project designer. In other firms, a project manager who is also, in all practicality, the project designer, is the one who is assigned this responsibility. The activities involved in prospecting for a client and in preparing a design contract or other designer/owner agreements that are needed to begin a project are discussed in many of the earlier chapters of this book and will not be discussed in this chapter.

Before we begin, however, there are two terms that are associated with the preprogramming phase but are continually a part of the entire project. They are the work plan and deliverables. The *work plan* is "a document defining all the tasks that are needed to take a project from inception to completion" (Piotrowski and Rogers, 1999, p. 312). It helps the designer clarify everything that has to be done and in the correct order so that the project schedule can be more easily determined. As part of the work plan and considered in the preparation of the design contract are the *deliverables*. Documents and presentation materials that must be prepared to explain the design concepts and eventually allow the project to be built and installed are deliverables. Examples are floor plans, sample boards, models, construction documents, and bid documents. They are called deliverables because they must be "delivered" (or provided) to the client.

Programming Phase

The *programming phase* is often thought of as the information-gathering portion of an interior design project. The designer seeks from the client and other individuals involved as much information as possible on such things as client expectations, functional needs, aesthetics, and factors concerning the interior space itself. Client interviews are conducted to determine the client's goals and objectives, visits are made to the job site, or floor plans are obtained from the client or architect in order to understand any physical limitations of the project spaces. An inventory and an analysis of existing furnishings and equipment are conducted to help in later determination of product specification. In addition, interviews with employees might be conducted. If architectural drawings do not exist, designers may be required to field measure the site. A review of applicable codes is also necessary to be sure that any legal restraints are taken into consideration. Much time must be spent and careful notes must be taken in order for the interior designer to successfully design and prepare the documents required for completing the project. These comments describe only some of the activities in this very important first phase of the design project.

Designers are helped through this process by utilizing a variety of specialized forms. Client interview forms developed by many firms help define the client's needs that are related to space requirements and furnishings and equipment requirements. For large commercial office projects, designers might find that using employee questionnaires is a more efficient use of time. Office systems manufacturers, such as Steelcase, Herman Miller, and Haworth, provide detailed workstation and employee interaction questionnaires for use by designers. When the client feels that he or she needs to use existing equipment, the designer can use a special form to analyze and inventory the furniture and equipment that the client already owns. These are just a few examples of the special forms that designers create to help obtain the information they will need about the client's requirements and the interior space to be designed.

Schematic Design Phase

The *schematic design phase* involves the execution of preliminary design decisions through the development of written design concepts, bubble diagrams, preliminary floor plans, design sketches, as well as the initial selection of furniture, materials, finishes, and equipment. From a project management point of view, the designer is working with estimating forms for the architectural finishes, furniture specifications, construction estimates from contractors, and budgets. Estimating forms such as the one shown in Figure 27-2 help designers in this phase of the project.

With the review and approval of the selections and graphic documents, the designer is ready to move on to the next phase of the project. It is very important for the designer to obtain client signatures or at least the initialing of plans, drawings, and specification sheets prior to moving to the next phase. Obtaining client sign-off during the schematic phase provides the designer with assurance of proper reimbursement for any changes that the client makes while the designer is preparing finalized drawings and documents.

Design Development Phase

The *design development phase* of a project involves the preparation of all final furniture plans; presentation graphics, such as perspectives or axonometric drawings, sample boards, if they are to be used; and specifications for all the FF&E. Depending on the designer's contract, he or she may also prepare construction specifications, at least at the preliminary level. Along with these graphic documents, the designer prepares a more complete project budget, which is necessary at this stage. Figure 27-3 shows an example of a form that the designer can use to develop a budget for a project that will not be put out for competitive bidding. Depending on the project and the actual design responsibilities, the client will receive either the actual pricing and equipment lists for furniture, finishes, and equipment or an estimate with broader specifications pending formal bidding. This is the point at which the final presentation discussed in Chapter 25 takes place. At the conclusion of the presentation, the designer should have obtained written client approvals of all drawings and specifications before moving the project on to the contract documents stage.

G. S. Hinsen Company
2133 Bandywood Drive
Nashville, Tennessee 37215
Phone: (615) 383-6440
Fax: (615) 269-5130

QUOTE REQUEST
WINDOW TREATMENTS

Workroom:__________

DATE:__________ CLIENT:__________ ROOM:__________

DATE QUOTE REQUESTED:__________ NUMBER OF WINDOWS:__________ SIZE OF WINDOWS:__________

FABRIC(S) to be used:	TYPE/CONTENT	WIDTH	REPEATS
(1)__________	__________	__________	__________
(2)__________	__________	__________	__________
(3)__________	__________	__________	__________
(4)__________	__________	__________	__________

SPECIFICATIONS:

LINING:__________

BLACKOUT LINING:__________

INNER LINING:__________

PLEAT STYLE:__________

HANDSEWN (circle): yes no

TRIM TYPE:__________

TRIM APPLICATION:__________

HARDWARE: SUPPLIED BY:__________

	DIMENSIONS	QUANTITY	FINISH
RODS:__________	__________	__________	__________
BRACKETS:__________	__________	__________	__________
FINIALS:__________	__________	__________	__________
RINGS:__________	__________	__________	__________

NOTES:

____

____

____

*PLEASE QUOTE YARDAGE/MATERIALS NEEDED SEPARATE FOR EACH PIECE WINDOW.

FIGURE 27-2. An estimating form that helps the designer establish the window treatments needed for a project. (Reproduced with permission, Grei Hinsen, G. S. Hinsen Company, Nashville, TN)

The Design Collective Group, Inc.
2129 South U.S. Highway 1
Jupiter, Florida 33477

Estimate P3029

Bill To: Ship To:

SALESPERSON		PROJECT	SHIP VIA	SHIP DATE	TERMS		DATE	PG.
Michael A. Thomas		Alum. Tables 3029			C.O.D.		4/27/00	1
Quantity	**Item**	**Description**		**Price**	**Unit**	**Mark**	**Extended**	**Taxed**
1	Ironwork	Material and labor to fabricate aluminum table base for circular table on East Patio of Beach House. Finish work not included. Includes 42" diameter x 1/2" glass to with ogee edge.		$1,370.00		(25%)	$1,712.50	X
4	Ironwork	Material and labor to fabricate aluminum triangular occasional tables for Patio of Beach House. Finish of aluminum base is not included. Includes 1/2" glass top.		$497.00		(25%)	$2,485.00	X
1	Ironwork	Material and labor to fabricate aluminum cocktail table base as per drawing. Quote does not include finish of aluminum. Quote does include finished wood top.		$3,325.00		(25%)	$4,156.25	X

Deposit Required $ 4,400.00. Please sign and return with deposit to above address.	SALE	$8,353.75
	FREIGHT	$0.00
	SALES TAX	$501.23
	TOTAL	$8,854.98
	PAID TODAY	$0.00
	BALANCE	$8,854.98

■ **FIGURE 27-3. A sample partial project budget estimate, which is part of the company's standard paperwork system. (Reproduced with permission. Michael Thomas, The Design Collective Group, Inc., Jupiter, FL)**

Contract Documents Phase

The *contract documents phase* of the design projects involves the final preparation of all construction or working drawings (sometimes referred to as CDs), schedules, and specifications that are required to build and install the design project. These plans, drawings, and other documents are described in Chapter 29. They are technical construction drawings, not furniture floor plans or other presentation drawings like perspectives. Care in the preparation of these drawings is very important, since serious liability issues are at stake if errors are made in the construction drawings.

For projects that will be procured through the competitive bid process, detailed specifications concerning the furnishings, finishes, and equipment are prepared along with the construction specifications. The designer who is responsible for also managing the competitive bid assembles several other documents that are necessary for the competitive bid process to occur in an orderly, fair, and appropriate manner. The competitive bid process will be discussed in Chapter 29.

Many residential projects and small commercial projects do not require a competitive bid. In these cases, project management at this stage includes preparing lists of recommended vendors or contractors in the name of the client or that are recommended to the client.

Contract Administration Phase

The *contract administration phase* is the portion of the project that involves the competitive bid process or the placing of orders for all the furniture and equipment, as well as the actual construction and installation work. The project management responsibility for the interior designer at this stage centers on the finalizing of bid documents and assisting or supervising the bid process with regard to all the work that is the responsibility of the interior designer. In addition, the interior designer's project management responsibilities might also involve the supervision of construction or installation of the FF&E. Over the last several years, all postinstallation or postoccupancy activities have been acknowledged as being a part of the contract administration phase rather than a separate phase. This includes site inspections, called a walk-through, where the designer, with the client, determines if there are any omissions or damages. Notations are made on a form, commonly called a punch list. Final payment to the designer is often withheld until all items on the punch list are taken care of. Larger design firms often prepare postoccupancy evaluations a short time after the client has moved in. Forms commonly associated with the ordering and delivery of merchandise are discussed in Chapter 30. The walk-through, punch list, and postoccupancy evaluation are discussed in Chapter 31.

Work supervision, along with the ordering of merchandise or letting construction contracts, occurs during this phase. Coordination and cooperation with the architect, general contractor, and subcontractors is necessary to insure that the handling of the overall project is accomplished smoothly. Interior designers are traditionally responsible for the installation supervision of the architectural finishes and furnishings that they have specified for the project. Today, interior designers in many jurisdictions must hold the proper license to legally perform installation supervision or must be willing to relinquish this responsibility to a licensed contractor. This issue was discussed in Chapter 7, and the reader is advised to learn what the law requires in his or her jurisdiction.

One form that is used by design firms throughout the phases of the project is the transmittal letter (see Figure 27-4). The *transmittal letter* is a form letter that can be used for many purposes. It can be used to send information to the client, consulting architects and/or engineers, subcontractors, leasing agents, manufacturers, or anyone who is involved with the project.

JAIN MALKIN INC.
7855 Fay Avenue
La Jolla, CA 92037
858/454-3377
858/454-9996 Fax
www.jainmalkin.com
e-mail: info@jainmalkin.com

LETTER OF TRANSMITTAL

To: | Date:
Re:
Job No:
Sent Via: ☐ Mail ☐ Messenger

Purpose of Transmittal: ☐ For Review and Comment ☐ For Approval ☐ As Requested
☐ Correct and Resubmit ☐ For Your Use ☐

Date	No. of Copies	Shop Drawings	Plans/Blueprints	Tracings	Specs	Other	Description

Comments:

By: | Copies:

■ **FIGURE 27-4. A typical transmittal letter. (Reproduced with permission, courtesy Jain Malkin Inc., La Jolla, CA)**

The transmittal letter is designed to eliminate the need to write a separate letter or memo in order to transmit or ask for information. The fill-in-the-blank format makes it easy to use for a variety of purposes and is most commonly sent with materials or drawings of any kind. As can be seen by the example, it provides space to tell the receiver what is being sent and for what purpose, and it also gives instructions to the receiver for resubmittal or any action that the sender requires. It is an invaluable aid to speedy correspondence. Usually it is a two-part form, the original goes with the material being sent, and the copy is placed in the job file.

Working Relationships

A project may seem to be an adventure that is embarked upon only by the client and the interior designer. But they happen to be only the main players on the team. An interior design project may have many other individuals or groups involved in it, depending, of course, on how large the project is and how complex the design is.

Anyone who is involved in the project and somehow has an interest in the project is commonly referred to as a stakeholder. The project manager (or project designer) is responsible for ensuring that the members of this sometimes widely diverse group know what each member of the team is supposed to do and when and how they are supposed to do their tasks, and, for the most part, checks to be sure that they have accomplished their tasks. As any interior designer, from the sole practitioner to the senior project designer at the largest interior design firm, would agree, this is hardly ever an easy task.

For the sake of this discussion, let us assume that the design firm is one that employs several designers of varying responsibilities as well as a support staff. Let us also assume that the project is fairly complex, requiring a full range of design services, from programming through contract administration. However, almost all interior design projects involve most of the relationships that we will describe.

One set of working relationships involves the design staff. In our hypothetical project, the lead designer, called the project manager, has need of one or more other designers who will help gather information, produce all the design documents, and keep the project manager informed about the progress of the project. To make this relationship work, proper communication between the project manager and the design team and adequate delegation of responsibilities are necessary. The team members must know what must be done, how and when it must be done, and so on, to meet the expectations of the designer and the client. The designer must trust the team members if they are to carry through with their responsibilities; that is, the project manager must properly delegate work to the team members.

Another working relationship very often occurs between the design team and the technical consultants. The project manager first must determine which technical consultants, such as architects, engineers, or specialty designers like a lighting designer are required. He or she may hire these individuals as part of the design firm's contract or may recommend certain ones to the client.

As the design team begins to specify products for the job, another working relationship grows between the designer and various trade sources. Suppliers provide product information and pricing, possibly obtain samples for the designer, and give other assistance that might be needed. This working relationship is complex, since the designer might require information from dozens of suppliers and craftspeople.

If we assume that demolition or construction work occurs as part of the project, another working relationship occurs between the designer and the general contractor and subcontractors. In this situation, clear communication between the designer and the general contractor and subcontractors is necessary. Scheduling is also very important to ensure that the scheduling of the tradespeople does not negatively affect the progress of the project.

Because the relationship between the project manager and the client is mentioned last does not mean that it is the least important. On the contrary; it is the most important. It is placed last in our discussion, though, because the designer must manage all the other relationships effectively in order to keep this most critical one in order. Clients expect the designer will keep them informed of the progress of the project. In some cases, the client will be satisfied with an occasional phone call telling him or her that all is well and on schedule. Other clients request and require monthly, even weekly, meetings—sometimes because they want to feel "in control" of the project, and having the designer constantly report to them makes them feel in control. Others need the information to ensure that they will be prepared for the eventual move into the new facility. A residential client may be selling one home to move into another; a business that is moving from one location to another has a burdensome task. A move, as the reader no doubt understands, is a time-consuming, stressful period for some clients.

Clients also want to know how the activities of the project will be undertaken. It is the responsibility of the project manager at the earliest meetings with the client to explain how the project will proceed through its phases and what will happen during each phase. Although it is quite likely that the project manager for the design firm will be the contact for the client, the designer must know very early who the contact will be for the client. In a commercial project, it is required that the design firm designate the project manager or some other individual as the single source of contact. A *single source of contact* is one particular individual who has the authority to make decisions regarding the project and to whom all communication is to be directed. When the final negotiations are taking place, the design firm wants to know who the client's single source of contact is. For large projects, it is not uncommon for the single source of contact for the client also to have the title of project manager.

Remember to caution the client about directly instructing workers on the job site. Construction workers, in particular, are not required to be diplomatic and to respond to the instructions of clients. Be sure the client understands that he or she should direct questions and changes to the proper foreman or to the designer. For example, on one residential construction project, the owner, being retired, spent most of every day on the site. He kept questioning and interrupting the workers until one day the framer said, "I was hired to do this job according to the plans. If you want to do the work, here's a hammer. I'll go home."

It certainly helps when all of these working relationships run smoothly. It is "hats off" to the project manager who can keep these relationships running smoothly on a consistent basis.

Additional information about the people with whom the designer coordinates all of the tasks on an interior design project will be discussed in the next chapter.

Project Schedules

Throughout these project phases, a very important project management responsibility is scheduling. Project schedules are prepared during programming as part of the revised work plan, are refined during schematics, and are updated throughout the project. The project manager/designer carefully monitors the schedule, informing the client of any changes that can impact the due dates of upcoming activities and the completion of the overall project. Project schedules help the designer maintain control of the project. Breaking down a large task into manageable units helps the designer get the task done on time.

Project schedules can take many forms, depending on who is using the information. For the project designer, the schedule may be day-by-day or, at least, week-by-week descriptions of what must be done to reach the target completion date. For the project manager or design director, a week-by-week or monthly schedule is needed to aid in accepting, estimating, and assigning new work.

Computer software is available to assist with project scheduling, from very sophisticated systems used by large design firms that are responsible for complex projects to simpler programs for firms involved in projects that are complex but require budget-priced software. Depending on the complexity of the software, the program can produce numerous reports once data about time lines, activities, and due dates have been entered. The three most common methods used for visualizing the project schedule are the milestone, the bar chart (also called a Gantt chart), and the critical path method.

Milestone charts may be the easiest method of scheduling a project. In this method, the designer outlines the activities required for the project and establishes a target date for their completion (see Figure 27-5). Space can be included to indicate who has responsibility for each activity. The actual date of completion should be noted, as this will aid in future estimating. The biggest advantage in using the milestone chart for scheduling is that it is so easy to use. It is a very good method for controlling the schedule of small projects that are not very complex. No specialized software is required, since it can be set up using common word-processing software; however, it may also be an option on specialized project management software.

A more graphic method of showing the scheduling of a project is by use of a bar chart. Figure 27-6 provides an example. *Bar charts* consist of a description of tasks required in the left-hand side and horizontal bars on the right-hand side, showing the time in days, weeks, or months that is required to complete

Project: Weldone Residence
Designer: Maryanne

Task Name	Days	Earliest Start	Earliest Finish	Latest Start	Latest Finish	Actual Finish
Interview Client	3	9/23/0X	9/26/0X	10/3/0X	10/8/0X	9/23/0X
Obtain Floor Plan	1	9/24/0X	9/25/0X	10/7/0X	10/8/0X	9/24/0X
Inventory Existing Furniture	1	9/25/0X	9/25/0X	10/7/0X	10/8/0X	10/5/0X
Sketch Preliminary Plan	7	9/26/0X	10/7/0X	10/8/0X	10/17/0X	10/6/0X
Make Preliminary Selections	5	9/26/0X	10/3/0X	10/10/0X	10/17/0X	10/7/0X
Prepare Preliminary Budget	2	10/6/0X	10/7/0X	10/15/0X	10/20/0X	10/8/0X
Meet with Client	1	10/7/0X	10/8/0X	10/17/0X	10/20/0X	10/8/0X
Revise Preliminary Plan	5	10/8/0X	10/15/0X	10/20/0X	10/27/0X	10/14/0X
Revise Selections	3	10/7/0X	10/20/0X	10/27/0X	10/30/0X	10/17/0X
Prepare Final Budget	1	10/20/0X	10/20/0X	10/29/0X	11/3/0X	10/23/0X
Make Final Presentation to Client	2	10/20/0X	10/22/0X	10/30/0X	11/3/0X	10/24/0X

FIGURE 27-5. A sample milestone chart. The chart indicates the activities to be performed, the estimated days for completion, and the target dates for starting and stopping each activity.

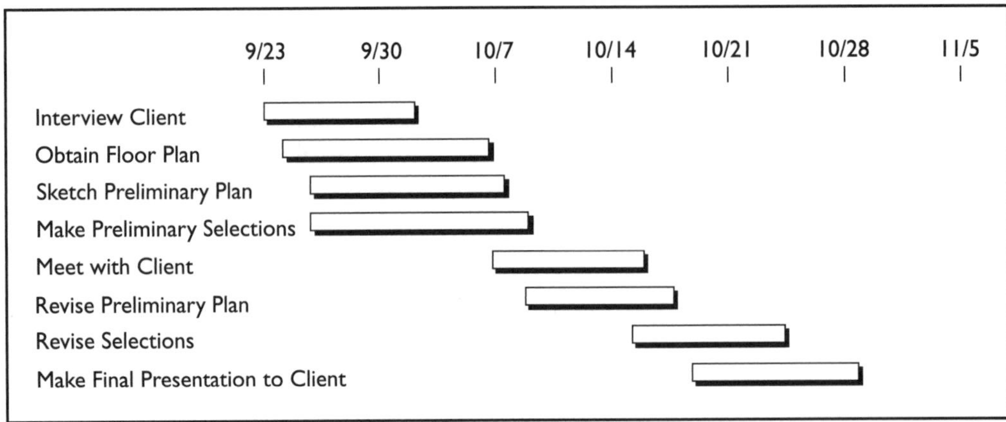

FIGURE 27-6. A bar chart that graphically shows the time span required to complete designated project activities.

the task. As a management tool, designers can use this chart on a daily or weekly basis to show their responsibility if they are working on more than one project. To assist with overall project management, the project manager can prepare a monthly chart for each designer to help the design manager determine whether they are available for additional work.

A disadvantage of using the bar chart is that it does not necessarily show how one activity affects another activity or which is the most important activity needed to complete the project on time. Analysis of the most important activities can be developed with more careful project analysis and a more complex color-coded bar chart. It works well for most small to somewhat complex projects, although it is not particularly appropriate for large or very complex projects. It can be done manually; some firms put bar charts up on a wall to show the project's or firm's progress on the work being done in-house. Computer software is also available for creating bar charts.

If the design project is quite complex so that the interrelationships of the required tasks are critical, the third method of scheduling may be called for, the *critical path method (CPM)*. This scheduling method is dependent upon the interrelationships of activities and the detailed tasks of each activity. Any one activity in a sequence cannot be completed unless the previous tasks and related activities have been completed. Generally, only the larger interior design firms find CPM appropriate for project scheduling when they are involved in large projects. CPM is commonly used by architects and the construction industry to maintain control of the interrelated construction process, however. This method would be very difficult to manage manually, so the project manager should obtain some type of computer project management software.

Briefly, CPM scheduling starts by identifying the interrelationships of the tasks to be performed. This analysis shows the project manager which tasks must be done before the next or other tasks can be performed, thus establishing the critical path (see Figure 27-7). A simple critical path in an interior design project occurs when the designer obtains the client's needs, prepares floor plans, obtains the client's approval, orders products, and installs and/or delivers products. It is clear that it is impossible, as well as unwise, to try to do any one of these tasks prior to completing the one directly preceding it. As the interrelationships are entered into the computer, along with due dates and the duration of each task, the computer automatically makes the calculations to adjust for changes in the schedule. Then new charts are produced, which can

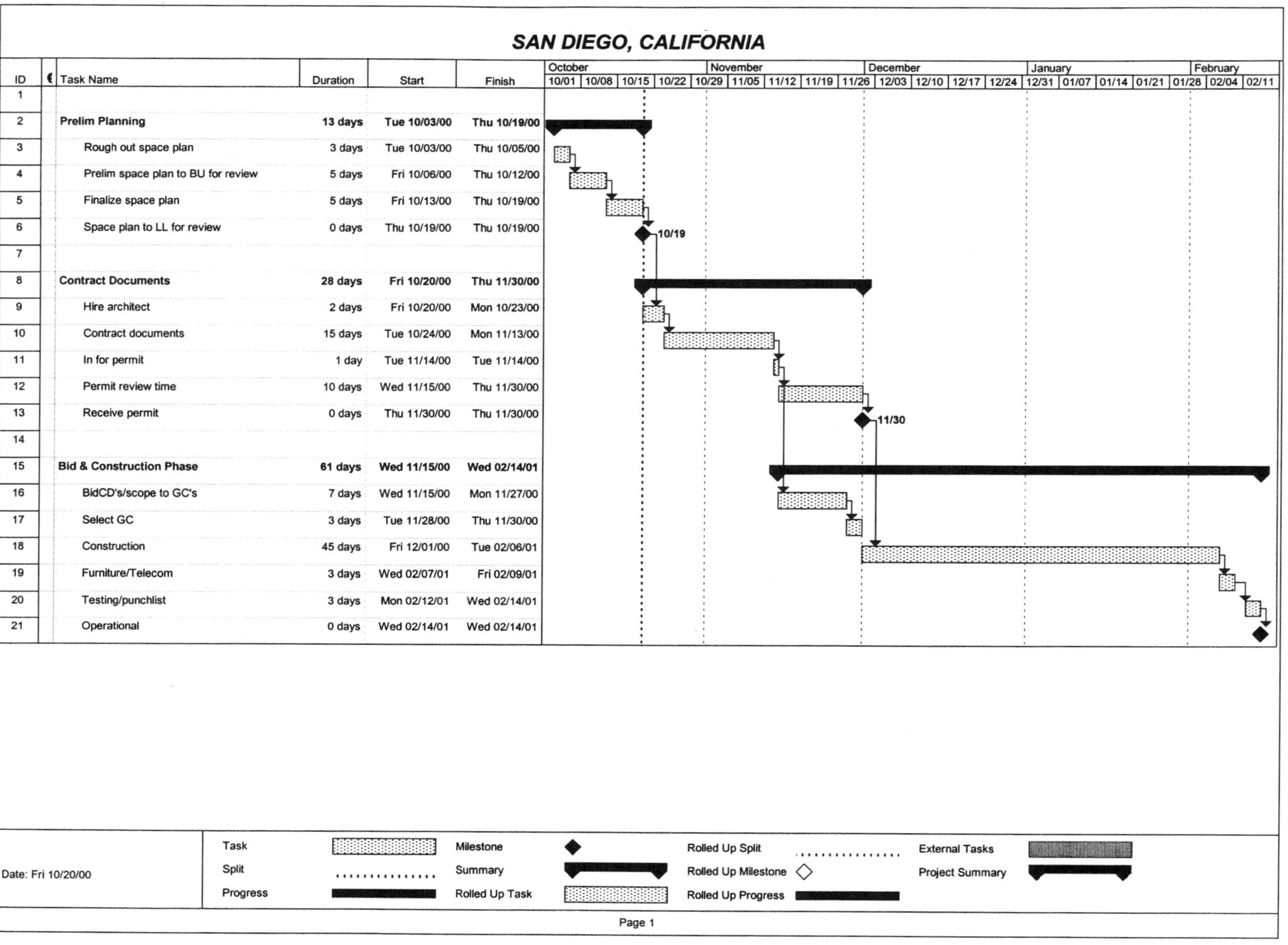

FIGURE 27-7. Critical path method chart. (Reprinted with permission, Allyson Grenier, Allied Member ASID, Phoenix, AZ)

be given in different formats to the interior design team members, the client, and other stakeholders.

Project Budgeting

Budgeting is a very important function of the interior designer and a significant responsibility. Specifying a project that comes in significantly over the client's budget can lead to a potential lawsuit and ethics charges. These reasons alone make accurate project budgeting a concern for all interior designers. Clients do not give designers free reign with an unlimited budget to do any kind of project. In fact, the budget that the client has in mind is almost always smaller than can reasonably be accomplished. Many clients do not tell the designer what the budget is. Perhaps these clients think that, by revealing the budget, the designer will spend that much and not less; by keeping it a secret, they think that perhaps the project will come in below what he or she wanted to spend.

Many interior designers are hired after other budget decisions already have been made. At this point, the client, architect, and contractors already have made design decisions that affect what can be done and how much is left that can be spent on the interior design and finishing of the project. It then becomes more of a challenge for the interior designer to effect the same creative and exciting ideas that he or she would want if he or she had been involved in the project at an earlier stage. It is never an easy task to convince the client to upgrade finishes, modify structural elements, or purchase higher-quality furnishings after these kinds of decisions have been made.

Project budgeting for the interiors will involve estimating the costs of furniture, architectural finishes, accessories, and perhaps nonload-bearing construction of such things as partitions, lighting, cabinets, or other built-ins, and the like. For example, depending on its size, a new kitchen with all new cabinets, counters, wall and floor finishes, ceilings, and lighting can start at $10,000 for something modest and can reach $25,000 and more quite easily, before appliances are included. The furniture alone for an office of around 175 square feet can start at about $15,000 (retail). How does the less experienced designer go about determining a budget?

One method that can be used concerns developing quality ranges. Design firms can develop three or four quality ranges from among the manufacturers with which they commonly do business. In a way, it would be like using the grade ranges of fabric for upholstered goods. The lowest grade or group of manufacturers would be those with budget lines. A second group would be those that provided medium-quality goods—goods that would be serviceable and would provide several years of satisfactory use. A third group would be many of the high-end manufacturers, whose products are known for their high quality. The last group would be those manufacturers that could supply custom goods or that are known to carry the very best quality items. Some design firms find it useful to develop a checklist that describes these ranges. These checklists can be shown to the client as a means of clarifying the differences in the product groups. The furniture representatives or the manufacturers' literature can be helpful sources of information to develop these quality ranges.

A second budgeting technique is the use of "typicals." Commercial interior designers who have a significant amount of experience with certain kinds of spaces develop layouts of typical spaces, for example, offices or a doctor's exam room, or even a hotel guest room. At its simplest, this technique starts with an average or typical furniture arrangement. There can even be more than one typical arrangement for a similar space—something that is commonly done for hotel guest rooms. Adding a quality level to the typical space provides a budget idea that the designer can discuss with the client. Residential designers also find this method useful as a starting point when they are helping a client understand the potential overall cost of furnishing a portion of the home.

It is also possible to do product budgeting based on a square foot factor. In this case, the designer utilizes historical data that he or she has collected on a variety of project types and conditions. As preliminary discussions of project feasibility and budget are conducted, the designer can use these factors to clarify potential costs to the client. For example, a residential design firm can use this information to give a "ballpark" budget of all furniture and finishes for a high-end house based on the livable square footage of the house. A commercial designer may use historical square foot factors to provide information to a client who is considering furnishing a law partner's office. The designer can even show the client that a contemporary style office might cost X dollars per square foot, while a traditional style will cost some other factor per square foot.

Of course, the designer can also estimate each item by using standard materials cost and labor charges for individual items such as window treatments, carpeting, tile, and so on. Materials estimates can also be obtained by the designer's use of reference books.

There are, of course, a few built-in problems in using any of these techniques for budgeting. Clients may make decisions based on price rather than on the quality required. This may back the designer into a corner, and he or she may be forced to use products or design concepts that do not provide for the best finished project. Another problem is that the client may assume that the budget is the designer's final price and may go elsewhere in order to find a less expensive solution. This is why most designers commonly quote budget ranges rather than single numbers. Ranges give the designer flexibility in the specification of products without appearing to be always over the budget when the actual prices are determined.

Time Records

In my talks with interior designers, they have often asked me whether they were charging enough for a certain project. My first question has always been, "Are you keeping track of your time?" The common response is, "I'm too busy to keep track of my time!" If an interior designer is too busy to keep track of his or her time, how can he or she know if the fixed fee or markup method or whatever fee method a designer uses is fairly compensating him or her for the time that the designer puts into the project?

It is crucial that the designer keep accurate time records for all professional services, even if the designer does not actually charge the client by the hour. Keeping time records is not a difficult task. It does, however, take discipline to record the different activities and times involved, as accurately as possible on projects and/or other company business. Here are several good reasons to make time record keeping a habit:

1. Accurate time records are necessary for billing if the design firm is charging by the hour for professional services. Some clients wish to see time records before paying the bill.
2. Time records help the designer or firm owner check on the progress of current jobs. This is necessary in order to determine if too much time is being used. If the project is running over the estimated time,

the reasons need to be analyzed. Does the client change his or her mind often? Is the designer nonproductive? Was there an error in the requirements or plans? Has enough time been budgeted?

3. Keeping accurate time records helps a designer or a design firm determine what kinds of projects are actually profit making. When a firm is working with many clients who require a lot of hand-holding or the firm's time for activities like specification writing and drafting, certain fee methods provide more potential revenue (and profit margin) than others. This cannot be determined accurately if time records are not kept.
4. A record of time worked on previous projects helps the design firm determine budget and fees for new projects. For example, if the firm knows that a 3000 square foot model home can be completely designed in X hours, that information saves the firm time and errors in writing new contracts.
5. Historical time records can also help a firm decide if it even wants to take on certain kinds of projects, since they may be very time-consuming while returning a very small profit margin.
6. Time records can be of assistance to managers when they are arranging performance reviews of employees. Interior designers in many firms are looking for the majority of the designer's time to be billable. Time records help the firm determine if designers are productive for the firm. Depending on how important this is to the design firm, those designers who are billing closest to their goals are more likely to receive salary increases or to be rewarded in other ways.*
7. Time records and historical utilization records† assist the firm's owner in making overall budget and planning decisions that are necessary for the continued future health and growth of the design firm.
8. A wide variety of management control reports can be generated from time sheets. Some of these reports were discussed in Chapter 16.

Time records are only as accurate as the design firm owner and employees keep them. How exact the records need to be is a function of management control. For most companies, it is practical to keep track of time to the quarter-hour; that is, the designer reports work on any project or house time that is related to 15-minute intervals. (Keeping track to the exact minute is micro-managing and will only annoy most designers.) Designers record the activities of a normal work day plus any overtime (See Figure 27-8).

It is easy for most people to keep track of a day's activities on one sheet of paper and then transfer the time related to individual projects and nonbillable time to the appropriate sheet for that project. Many designers use some type of computer-based daily planner to keep track of appointments, so recording of time becomes quicker and less of a hassle. The records can be kept on a daily basis and, depending on the needs of the firm, can be compiled on a weekly or a monthly basis. Figure 27-9 shows a page from a computer-based contact system. Each record includes the client's name or the project's name, the designer's name, a description of the work performed, and the hours of work per description. The computer system allows for a great deal of additional

* *Billable hours* is an important issue for commercial design firms, since billing is more commonly based on an hourly rate. It is a less important issue in many residential design firms that are less likely to bill at an hourly rate.

† Utilization was discussed in Chapter 16.

Time Record

Designer: ______________________________ Week of: ____________________

Page: ________ of ________

		Task	Billing		
Date	Project Code	Description/Notes	Time	Fee Rate	Bill Amount
		Totals			

FIGURE 27-8. A sample time record-keeping form used to keep track of all billable hours worked by the design staff.

Thu Oct 26, 2000

To-Do's

think about artafactual furniture	2-18-00
call barry for lunch	10-16-00
Proposals due on TSG Call C	10-26-00
verify FFE deliv sched on Credit union	10-26-00

7	
8	8:00a - 9:00a meet w K French re:PCC
9	
10	10:00a - 2:00p OSW Des Dev
11	
12	
1	
2	2:00p - 3:00p Az Biz conf call
3	
4	4:00p - 5:00p ASSCU weekly jobsite meeting
5	
6	
7	

Printed 8:43a 10/20/00 1

FIGURE 27-9. A computer based-time record system. (Reprinted with permission, Fred Messner, Phoenix Design One, Inc., Phoenix, AZ)

information to be included in the database. The computer system also can be interactive so that each staff member can check on the appointments of other designers, if necessary.

Time Management

We have just discussed some reasons why time record keeping is important. Yet a big part of consistently and accurately recording time is having reasonable time management skills. Workloads continue to increase. The client continually demands that turnaround time on information be faster. We receive and transmit large amounts of information in the blink of an eye. We barely have time for our personal lives amid all our other responsibilities. There never seems to be enough time to get everything done. The Internet has brought us 24/7/365; this means that a business (essentially) can be contacted over the Internet 24 hours a day, 7 days a week, 365 days a year. Effective time management is not an option in the 2000s—it is a necessity.

To an interior designer, one of the absolute truths is that time equals money. Whether the designer is paid by the hour or receives compensation in some other way, the efficient, productive use of time has a direct bearing on the designer's yearly income. It is, therefore, very important for the interior designer to make the best use of his or her time while on the job.

Time management and organization problems have probably existed for many, many years. The first book this author found on the subject was *How to Get Control of Your Time and Your Life* by Alan Lakin, published in 1972. Time management theories were not developed to make a person a slave to his or her job but, rather, to help the person organize his or her time to be as productive as possible on the job. Its purpose is not to control time but to control the *use* of time. Today, books discussing time management techniques abound. There are even books especially for women or creative people. However, the basic premise is based on similar concepts of creating to-do lists, prioritizing those lists, handling papers once, and keeping a calendar and a reminder notebook handy.

Time management has to do with planning, decision making, and control. A designer plans the day (or week or month) by making decisions about what will be done and will not be done, hopefully, during any one time period. These plans and decisions then help the designer better control what he or she does with time. Time management does not mean that a person controls his or her time so rigidly that there is no room for flexibility to meet emergencies. In interior design, it sometimes seems that every day is filled with emergencies. Nor does the person control it so loosely that he or she is prohibited from getting anything of value done. Figure 27-10 suggests ten common time wasters.

Alan Lakin and other time management experts discuss the 80/20 rule. As it relates to time management, the *80/20 rule* maintains that, when activities are arranged in order of importance, 80 percent of a person's time will be spent performing 20 percent of the activities. What this means is that, in a list of ten items, if a person accomplishes the two most important items, he or she has achieved 80 percent of the total value of time spent. Most companies can look at sales records and see that approximately 80 percent of the sales was generated by 20 percent of the sales staff. The main thrust of the 80/20 rule is that one should concentrate one's efforts on the few items on the list with the highest priority to generate the greatest value or return.

Effective time management starts with a to-do list. This list must be prioritized to have even a remote chance of achieving the success of the 80/20

- Inadequate planning
- Telephone interruptions
- Procrastination
- Personal disorganization
- Unrealistic time estimates
- Attempting too much
- Inability to say no
- Crisis management
- Socializing
- Making mistakes

FIGURE 27-10. Typical reasons people waste time on the job.

principle. Many designers have such busy schedules that they plan their entire week on Sunday night or Monday morning. Whether you plan your week or only one day at a time, take a few quiet minutes early in the morning or very near the end of the day and prepare a list of what has to be done that day or the following day, or that week. Items on this list come from previous lists, calendars, schedules, memos, and so on. Once the list has been determined, decisions can be made with regard to what needs to be done for the day—or at least attempted. This can include "Complete the floor plan revisions for Jones's house" or "Select the carpet for the Andrews' living room" or even "Pick up cleaning on the way home."

Items on the list should also include the expected time it will take to complete the task (see Figure 27-11). How long will it take to complete the floor plan revisions, and so on? If expected time allowances are not planned for, a person tends to get frustrated with a never-ending list that never seems to get done. Because interruptions and emergencies occur, it is wise to plan for one less hour of work per day. For example, plan for a seven-hour work day rather than a full eight-hour day. The one hour of padding allows for phone calls, drop-in visitors, emergencies, and so forth. If you are planning for the week ahead, allow a few hours extra padding by Thursday and Friday for emergencies and unexpected opportunities that are bound to arise. Of course, if you plan a week at a time, you will need daily lists also. Each day unfolds in its own way and will affect those perfectly planned other days.

The next step is to prioritize the list. The classic way of doing this is by categorizing each item as A or B. A items are the more important tasks that need to be done that day. Depending on the item, noncompletion of an A task could damage the designer's reputation or the reputation of the company. The completion of B tasks is less pressing; B tasks can be finished the next day or some other day. Once all items have been listed as A or B, they should be prioritized further by number. After this numbering has been done, the 20 percent of tasks that will give the 80 percent of value will appear.

Work on accomplishing A1 first, then move on to A2, and so on. If A2 cannot be done (e.g., A2 was to call a client, but the client was not in), move on to A3 and plan to go back to A2 a little later in the day. Record that the call was made but that the client could not be reached. (Record also if a message was left for the client.)

Crossing items off the list as they are completed shows accomplishment and allows for a feeling of satisfaction. Those tasks not completed are trans-

ITEM	ABC	DAILY TASK LIST	TIME EST.
		Check and respond to emails	:30
		Call Sally James: carpet pricing for Smith	:15
		Call Ned for Lunch ?? Thursday	
		Verify RFP pickup for Hospice Center	:15
		Discuss Hospice center proposal with Jim	:45
		Review Allegro plans with Tom	
		12:00 Lunch with Barbara W at Green Gables	1:30
		Finish Allegro plans review	1:00
		Check and respond to emails	:30
		4:00 Conference call with DKD	:45
		Time sheets	
		Specs for MicroAge 3rd Floor	

FIGURE 27-11. A prioritized to-do list showing activities and time estimates for the completion of each task.

ferred to the next day's list. If an item continually shows up on the list but never gets done, the task may need to be labeled an A1 someday! It also may point to a problem (e.g., a habit of procrastinating too much on certain kinds of activities) or a need to reassess an effective use of time during the day.

A key to the to-do list is to break down big projects into small segments. Any large-sized task should be broken down into manageable segments and be assigned target dates. This method will help ensure that the designer will complete the project on time.

It is important to keep the to-do list handy, along with a daily appointment calendar. Designers use several sizes of notebook organizers in configurations of calendars, note pads, phone numbers, and so forth to meet personal needs. Others use handheld electronic organizers that can be downloaded back and forth to their computer. Still others use organizer software or contact software on their computer and print out daily and weekly calendars to carry in their attaché case. Regardless of the system used, it is best to have a monthly calendar, a day-to-day calendar divided by hours, pages for a to-do list, memo paper, and address pages. These should constitute the absolute minimum.

Of course, there is a lot more to time management than these simple strategies concerning to-do lists and prioritizing tasks. Time management also involves confident decision making, becoming more organized, and learning how to deal with procrastination. It also involves learning how to handle interruptions, how to delegate effectively, and even how to say NO, which sometimes can be very difficult. Time management also requires that you learn to reward yourself when you meet goals and, on the other hand, not beat yourself up when you are not making the progress that you would like.

Time management works, but it takes a certain amount of discipline to get into the habit of creating to-do lists and prioritizing them every day, and learning all the other techniques that will help you become a more effective employee or owner. Even though new habits are difficult to establish, it is necessary to keep at it in order to become a designer who rapidly earns promotions and responsibility.

Project Files or Job Books

Keeping all the records and documents concerning a particular project so that the project designer—or anyone else in the office—can quickly track the answers to questions is a very important task for the project manager. Creating a *project file* or project job book is the mechanism used for this type of control. The project file usually consists of file folders or notebooks in which the designer keeps all the pertinent data and paperwork related to the work in progress. It might be supplemented with boxes or other binders containing swatches and samples of materials. The project file serves as a complete record of all the designer's efforts to organize a project and can be used to create the installation manual.

Keeping a project file up to date and organized requires discipline, just as time management does. But it is immensely useful to the designer, to the design firm, and to the client. All the information the designer needs about the project is in one place. As questions arise or changes are made, the designer has a complete reference to use when talking to a client, vendors, or personnel in the design firm. The well-organized project file makes an impressive statement to the client about how the designer and the design firm keep control of projects.

Having all the information in one place saves valuable time when questions arise. There should be no need to scour the office for information or to answer questions.

If the designer in charge of the project is absent for any reason, the project file allows other members of the firm to seek out answers to clients' and vendors' questions. Even if the lead designer leaves the firm, another designer should be able to pick up the project file and complete the project successfully.

The project file also is invaluable as a future reference tool. If the client wants to replace items or is in need of repairs of items specified, it is easy to check the project file for exact product information. If legal problems arise during or after the project, the project file will serve as a thorough reference tool for the firm.

Although projects are all different, many have similar qualities. Project files help the firm with projects that are similar in many ways. For example, project files can help determine

1. Why the design time estimate was or was not accurate
2. Whether or not products performed as specified and if vendors were a problem
3. If taking additional work from the same client would be inadvisable, perhaps because an inordinate number of changes were made by the client

A project file is helpful as a sales tool in marketing efforts. Clients may wish to see how the firm expects to control their project, so displaying a well-organized project file, with all its various parts, may be the answer.

The project file should have the following categories of information: meeting notes, correspondence, samples, and floor plans.

Note Taking

An important habit for designers to develop is the taking of notes while attending meetings. Of course, most people do take notes, but some choose to trust their memories rather than put notes in writing. Perhaps they feel that, by taking notes, they are not giving their undivided attention to their client. However, memory is not always perfect, so being able to show notes taken over a period of time can become important in court if any type of legal challenge has been raised. These notes should contain the date and time of the meeting and the names of those in attendance. In fact, it is a useful habit for students to date all notes and drawings—even rough sketches—to help them get into the habit and to see a progression of their design solutions. These notes are the original notes taken during the various meetings that the designer may have attended with the client, contractors, manufacturers, subcontractors, or architect. Telephone notes to any of these parties should also be kept in this section.

Meeting notes should include the notes taken during the initial interview, which are used to develop the design contract, and all subsequent interview notes or forms obtained concerning client needs. Many designers send transcribed copies of meeting notes back to the client or other interested parties to be sure that there are no misunderstandings as a result of the meeting. Preprinted forms that are specially designed for recording the meeting notes can be used. Some designers use electronic organizers for quick notes, but these still seem impractical when interviewing clients. Other designers use a laptop computer for taking notes, since this negates the necessity of transcribing the notes later. Most designers simply take notes. Always take notes. Take a lot of notes. Do not trust your memory.

Correspondence

There are all kinds of correspondence that must be kept in a project file. These items generally fall into two broad categories: general and project documents. General correspondence includes correspondence to and from clients; to and from factories and representatives; and construction correspondence. Copies of all correspondence sent to, or received from, the client should be kept in the project file. First among this group is a copy of the signed design contract. Many firms find it best to retain the original, signed design contract in a separate file, held by the design director or the owner of the design firm. Project designers use a copy that can be marked up and file the original to protect it from loss or damage. Insert any other letters or memos sent to, or received from, the client as well. This includes any E-mail messages. A hard copy should be printed out of your E-mail messages to a client and any responses from the client. Correspondence to and from factories and representatives include letters concerning pricing, special treatments or fabrics, custom work, availability for shipping, freight charges, and so on. When the design project involves construction activities, the file includes correspondence to and from the general contractor or subcontractors. Again, all E-mails concerning the project should also be printed and placed in the project file.

A large number of original or, in some cases, photocopies of project documents should be in this section of the project file. Figure 27-12 lists some of these documents. In-depth discussions of many of these forms are contained in Chapters 29 through 31.

Everything that goes into the file should be accurately dated. Do not throw away any of the preliminary work sheets, even when finalized sheets have replaced them. Murphy's law often clicks into effect just after something has been thrown away. In addition, a client signature, pricing information, or brief comments might be on preliminary sheets that did not get into the final documentation but that are needed to clarify or defend some action or decision. Leave cleaning out the files until after the project has been installed and all moneys have been collected. A backup copy of the computer-based correspondence and notes produced by the design firm should be stored in a fireproof file.

Samples

Fabric samples for all items being specified should be included in the project file. Samples should not be stuffed into a box or a folder with no identification. These must be accompanied by a full description, including the manufacturer, the product name and/or number, the color name or number, and a code for determining what furniture item (for upholstery) or room name/number (for window treatments, wall treatments, and floor finishes) goes with which sample.

Samples may be organized piece by piece or room by room, with all samples for one room going on one sheet. Using a form such as the one shown in Figure 25-2 or perhaps a smaller form printed on card stock can help the firm keep track of all the materials that are specified for a project. The control sheet, or some variation of it, is ideal for setting up an installation manual so that the installation of furniture items will go more smoothly.

Designers use different storage systems for filing their samples, depending on the type of project. Residential designers find it necessary to maintain samples in boxes rather than in notebooks or files. Designers use sturdy, solid-faced magazine storage boxes, clear plastic boxes (that can hold shoes), or even medium-sized storage tubs to hold samples and the necessary records for their projects. These storage solutions have become necessary as projects become larger and more complex. They are also used because fabric samples, in particular, must be obtained in larger memo samples to appropriately show patterns to the client. Commercial designers generally use a notebook or expandable,

- **Correspondence**
  - Signed design contract
  - Memos and transmittals from vendors and suppliers
  - Meeting minutes and subsequent replies from client and vendors
  - Other correspondence related to the project
- **Project-Programming Documents**
  - Client interview questionnaires
  - Job site analysis
  - Space-programming questionnaires
  - Employee work area summaries
  - Existing furniture inventories
- **Project Specifications and Budgets**
  - Furniture specification sheets
  - Estimates for architectural finishes and window treatments
  - Other budgeting forms
  - Samples and approved cuttings
- **Drawings**
  - Preliminary plans drawn from site measures
  - Preliminary sketches, especially those approved by the client
  - Contract documents
  - Shop drawings
  - As-built documents
- **Bidding and Procurement**
  - Bid specifications
  - Purchase orders
  - Acknowledgments
  - Invoices
  - Shipping documents
  - Change orders
  - Punch lists
  - Site inspection reports
- **Miscellaneous**
  - Warranties
  - Maintenance documentation
  - Postoccupancy evaluations
  - Internal postproject documentation
  - Anything else pertinent to the project for future reference

FIGURE 27-12. Typical documents included in a project file.

closed file folders to store samples. However, for some projects, they would also use other storage systems.

Floor Plans

At the very least, the project file should have a copy of the final floor plan. This may be both the entire project plan or room-by-room plans for very complex projects. If the project is very large, it might be convenient to have the large floor plans reduced on smaller sheets. The copy of the signed, approved floor plans should also be included in the project file. Of course, backup copies of the CAD file should be maintained in a fireproof file.

Preliminary plans also should be maintained until all moneys have been collected and the project has been fully installed and approved. Disputes at the time of installation often can be mitigated by referring back to approved preliminary drawings and plans. In addition, maintaining these earlier plans and sketches allows the designer more leverage when charging clients for changes at the very end of the project.

The design firm should develop a system of coding the plans to the control sheets, as previously discussed, and to the written specifications. This makes it easy to identify specific items on the floor plan and is a key in the development of installation manuals. An example of this is shown in Figure 29-1.

Other Items

Some projects have additional items that should be placed in the project file. Depending on the organization and the size of the design firm, copies of many forms that normally would be in the bookkeeping area, in the warehouse, or in the hands of the managers might be included in the project file. These items might include a copy of the formal bid specifications, equipment lists, invoices from manufacturers, time records, and freight information. Follow-up notes, if done by management, concerning profitability, marketing information, problems, or successes may also be kept in the file.

Value Engineering

Value engineering is a method of analyzing and specifying products and design solutions based on cost-effectiveness. It is discussed in this chapter because it is easily associated with many phases of a design project and thus is part of the overall project management process. Value engineering can be applied in order to find acceptable substitutions to higher-cost design concepts in order to provide quality outcomes at lower cost. This concept started with engineering and architectural firms. It is best applied at the early stages of a project, before many design decisions have been made. Actually, it has more to do with the specification of products or materials. When this method is utilized at the beginning of a project, it saves the designer time in analyzing various options against the known budget.

At times designers have referred to value engineering as "making a silk purse out of a sow's ear." Of course, many designers feel that this is just not possible. A more positive approach to value engineering is that it involves doing the very best design job possible at the lowest cost to the client. Sometimes this can be relatively simple, such as substituting a rayon blend fabric for silk for an upholstered item or using a textured vinyl wall covering rather than natural grass cloth.

Clients, however, may use the method as a pure cost-cutting mechanism, especially at the end of a project. This can create a wide range of difficulties for the interior designer. The best way to prevent cost cutting at the end of the project is to have frank and complete budget discussions with clients at the beginning of the project. Residential and commercial clients appreciate interior designers who show them up-front estimates for design projects. Residential clients, who may lose track of how expensive it is to design or remodel a home, appreciate budget estimates.

Value engineering can be another useful tool for interior designers to use when they are showing clients how they offer value and knowledge in design. In addition, applying value engineering in appropriate ways can be useful when the designer is trying to show how he or she may be different from competitors.

Summary

Project management is a very important part of a satisfactory design experience. With so many firms vying for design dollars, customer service via good project management means the difference between a healthy firm and one that may go out of business.

It is vital for the interior designer to be able to manage his or her time and the time of the firm's employees. It is also important for the designer to keep the projects under control. This means that the designer must develop the discipline and skills of time management and the firm must develop a satisfactory means of project management and of scheduling the various projects that come into the office. Project files are used to control the project itself.

In this chapter, we have looked at the basic concepts of project management, work relationships, different scheduling methods, budgeting, time records, time management, and the value of the project file. All of these help the designer and the firm manage projects.

REFERENCES

American Society of Interior Designers. "The Road Map to Growth." *ASID ICON*. November 1999. (Reprint.)

———. *Strategic Mapping Research. Phase III*. June 1998. Washington, DC: ASID.

———. 1997. "Clients Are Impressed by Project Management." *ASID Professional Designer*. March/April, 17.

Birnberg, Howard G. 1999. *Project Management for Building Designers and Owners*. Boca Ratan, FL: CRC Press.

Blanchard, Ken, Donald Carew, and Eunice Parisi-Carew. 2000. *The One-Minute Manager Builds High-Performing Teams*. New York: William Morrow.

Bliss, Edwin C. 1984. *Doing It Now*. New York: Bantam Books.

Brandt, Roslyn. "Can You Manage?" *Contract Design*. April 1995, 76–77.

Burstein, David, and Frank Stasiowski. 1982. *Project Management for the Design Professional*. New York: Watson-Guptill.

Cook, Marshall. 1999. *Time Management*. Holbrook, MA: Adams Media.

Farren, Carol E. 1999. *Planning and Managing Interior Projects*, 2nd ed. Kingston, MA: R. S. Means.

Friday, Stormy, and David G. Cotts. 1995. *Quality Facility Management*. New York: John Wiley.

Hale Associates, Inc. 1998. *Analysis of the Interior Design Profession*. Washington, DC: National Council for Interior Design Qualification.

Haviland, David, ed. 1994. *The Architect's Handbook of Professional Practice, Student Edition*. Washington, DC: AIA Press.

Karlen, Mark. 1993. *Space Planning Basics*. New York: Van Nostrand Reinhold.

Katzenbach, Jon R. 1998. *Teams at the Top*. Boston, MA: Harvard Business School Press.

Kliment, Stephen A. 1998. *Writing for Design Professionals*. New York: W. W. Norton.

Lakin, Alan. 1973. *How to Get Control of Your Time and Your Life*. New York: Signet, New American Library.

LeBoeuf, Michael. 1983. *The Productivity Challenge*. New York: McGraw-Hill.

———. 1979. *Working Smart*. New York: Time Warner Books.

Levy, Sidney M. 1987. *Project Management in Construction*. New York: McGraw-Hill.

Lewis, James P. 1995. *Project Planning, Scheduling and Control*, rev. ed. Chicago, IL: Richard D. Irwin.

Lientz, Bennet P., and Kathryn P. Rea. 1995. *Project Management for the 21st Century*. San Diego, CA: Academic Press.

Loebelson, Andrew. 1983. *How to Profit in Contract Design.* New York: Interior Design Books.

Lundy, James L. 1994. *Teams.* Chicago, IL: Dartnell Press.

MacKenzie, Alec. 1997. *The Time Trap*, 3rd ed. New York: American Management Association.

Means, R. S. 2000. *Means Interior Cost Data 2001*. Kingston, MA: R. S. Means.

Pinto, Jeffrey K., and O. P. Kharbanda. 1995. *Successful Project Managers.* New York: Van Nostrand Reinhold.

Piotrowski, Christine M., and Elizabeth Rogers. 1999. *Designing Commercial Interiors.* New York: John Wiley.

Sampson, Carol A. 1991. *Techniques for Estimating Materials Costs and Time for Interior Designers.* New York: Watson-Guptill.

Siegel, Harry (with Alan M. Siegel). 1982. *A Guide to Business Principles and Practices for Interior Designers*, rev. ed. New York: Watson-Guptill.

Silber, Lee. 1998. *Time Management for the Creative Person.* New York: Three Rivers Press.

Snead, G. Lynne, and Joyce Wycoff. 1997. *To Do, Doing, Done!* New York: Fireside Books.

Stasiowski, Frank A., and David Burstein. 1994. *Total Quality Project Management for the Design Firm.* New York: John Wiley.

Stitt, Fred A., ed. 1986. *Design Office Management Handbook.* Santa Monica, CA: Arts and Architecture Press.

Thompson, Jo Anne Asher, ed. 1992. *ASID Professional Practice Manual.* New York: Watson-Guptill.

Williams, David J. 1996. *Preparing for Project Management.* New York: American Society of Civil Engineers.

Chapter 28

Working with Trade Sources

The booming economy of the late 1990s into the twenty-first century has certainly helped make interior design an exciting profession. One of the things that makes it so exciting is the wide variety of furniture, materials, architectural finishes, fixtures, accessories, and all the other goods that are available for projects. Sometimes there are too many choices and not enough time to investigate them all. Sometimes there are not enough choices—or so it would seem! If you consider all the variations on products, colors of textiles, and the other permutations of products, the number of choices most designers have for specifying their interiors projects is almost incalculable.

For the student, understanding who all the trade sources are and what they offer is a big task. This chapter tries to help the reader sort out the different places designers can go to obtain products and services. The various trade sources not only represent the manufacturers and/or suppliers of the goods and services but also provide information to help the designer make choices and even to help the designer's clients make choices.

Trade sources are the groups of manufacturers, suppliers, and tradespeople who provide the various goods and services a designer uses to complete a project. Designers work with many kinds of trade sources. The majority of them comprise the manufacturers of different furniture and furnishings products. Others are the suppliers and tradespeople who supply a custom product or install a product. The designer finds these trade sources in many locations.

Vendor, a term used often in this chapter and subsequent chapters, encompasses all the listed sources and even the interior designer. A *vendor* is someone who sells products or services either to the end user or to some other person, like the designer. Commercial clients are used to working with vendors, whom they classify as anyone from whom they purchase any product or service. Residential clients, on the other hand, are used to working with salespeople or designers and may not be familiar with the term vendor.

It is essential for the designer to find the trade sources that complement his or her business ideals. In this chapter, we will look at the different kinds of trade sources utilized by interior designers.

Manufacturers

In the 2000 *Interior Design Magazine* "Buyers Guide," there were 37 pages that listed (in small print) manufacturers of various kinds of furniture. There were 238 companies listed as manufacturing seating alone, 75 manufacturers of carpet, 102 manufacturers of lighting fixtures, and 83 manufacturers of wallpapers. They did not list any other categories. Perhaps you get the picture—the manufacturing of furniture and furnishings products is big business in the twenty-first century.

Most of the goods that a designer specifies and/or sells to clients come directly from the manufacturers. In addition to making and selling the products that the interior designer specifies and sells, the manufacturers provide specification information, manufacturing criteria, and maintenance information on their goods. Designers obtain product catalogs, fabric samples, price books, tear sheets, and even sample products from manufacturers. In addition, manufacturers help the interior designer obtain special products or semi-custom-designed products when the standards in the catalogs are insufficient.

Most of this information comes from the manufacturers' sales representatives (discussed below), though some factories deal directly with the designer. Unless a designer is dealing with a small manufacturer, discounts and special pricing decisions also filter to the designer through the sales representative.

The designer needs to be sure that he or she understands the terms and conditions of ordering and selling for each manufacturer with which he or she deals. Terms will vary, and finding out, for example, that a company charges a 25 percent restocking charge for a canceled order after it has been canceled is bad for business. The catalog provides a lot of general information on how to order. And, of course, the representative can explain all the conditions. A design firm needs to establish credit with each manufacturer with which it wishes to deal, or it will be faced with having to pay for the goods at the time of ordering. The smaller firm has the hardest time establishing credit and must be prepared to make substantial prepayments when ordering from many manufacturers for the first time. Other information about working with trade sources and getting orders placed correctly will be covered in Chapter 30.

Sales Representatives (or Reps)

Representatives, or *reps*, are terms used to refer to the men and women who either work for the manufacturer or represent the manufacturer to the architecture and design (A&D) community. There are two kind of reps: independent representatives and factory representatives. *Independent reps* basically work for themselves or a sales-representing group. Many handle several manufacturers' products. These products may be related (e.g., all are from lighting manufacturers) or, as is more often the case, may be a combination of furniture and other products. *Factory reps* work for one particular manufacturer as employees of the company. They only represent that manufacturer's products or possibly only a segment of the manufacturer's product line. Both kinds of representatives are extremely helpful to the interior designer, and most small firms would not survive without their valuable assistance.

Reps provide information that the interior designer uses to make specification and pricing decisions. Representatives quote prices, give product information, make special product presentations, arrange for samples to be sent to the designer, provide the designer with information needed to write specifications, and distribute catalogs to the designer and, in some cases, to the end user. Some reps bring information and even samples of new merchandise to the attention of designers by having a trunk show. A *trunk show* occurs when a manufacturer's rep invites one or more interior designers to view a small selection of new merchandise. The trunk show could take place at the designer's studio, or the rep may invite more than one designer to a hotel conference area. The trunk show refers to the use of a trunk to transport the selection of goods that the salesman wishes to show retailers at the retailer's store. Today, a trunk show may be conducted by use of a laptop computer and CD-ROM disks or other computerized presentation hardware. The term is also associated with the garment industry and retail, in general.

Manufacturers' sales representatives also have a role in generating sales independently of a designer or a dealer. For products generally used in commercial design, reps make calls on potential clients. Leads are generally turned over to dealers or are referred to designers. Sometimes, of course, the representatives sell directly to the client, bypassing the designer or vendor.

Market Centers, Marts, and Showrooms

Market centers are concentrations of trade sources in one area of a city. *Market* is a term that many interior designers use to mean that they are going to visit one of the annual shows held at marts or convention centers. A *mart* is a building in which many firms have separate showrooms or share showroom space. A showroom is the leased or owned space that a manufacturer uses at a market center or other location to display merchandise to the trade. This allows the designer the opportunity to see firsthand samples of the products that he or she is specifying. Designers often bring clients to the mart so that the client can see the items that are being specified.

The largest marts are located in the major urban areas of cities such as Chicago, New York, Toronto, and Los Angeles. The Merchandise Mart in Chicago is still the largest single mart in the United States and holds the largest national contract market. Regional marts are located in many other cities. *Interior Design* magazine, in its January 1994 "Buyers Guide," lists 72 regional marts. Fifty-five regional marts are listed in the January 2000 issue of *Interior Design* magazine's "Buyers Guide" in just the United States. It is interesting to note that, in the first edition of this book, *Contract* magazine (December 1985) listed only 45 regional marts in the United States. *Contract* magazine, in its 1999–2000 "Source Guide," listed 49 trade buildings.

Traditionally, marts and trade showrooms have building access policies, and, in many cases, admittance to the building and its many showrooms is to the trade only. Market centers that are open only to the trade require special passes for gaining admittance. These passes are obtainable by trade members from the mart's leasing agent or other mart officials. Showrooms generally admit individuals without passes if they have proper credentials that identify them as members of the trade. Proper credentials might include a business license, a tax license, business checking account information, an association membership card, or other documentation beyond a business card that establishes the individual as a representative of a design business. Student members of ASID and IIDA or other professional organizations are able to get into most of the showrooms by showing their student membership card. Showrooms, however, have their own policies, and some do not admit anyone unless he or she has an official building pass. It should be noted that admittance to a showroom does not automatically allow the individual to purchase products from the manufacturer. Some manufacturers have retail stores or showrooms away from mart showrooms. These stores are, of course, open to the general public. Designers may be given credit and discount privileges at these stores.

As we enter the twenty-first century, manufacturers' products are also available for viewing on the Internet. Manufacturers know the value of putting information about their company and products on the World Wide Web for potential end users to review. This will be discussed further later in this chapter.

Merchandise, if it is priced in the showroom, is often tagged with a suggested retail price or a price code. This is done to protect the designer's profit policies as he or she shows clients the products specified for the project. Occasionally, showrooms have sales, in which discontinued items or slightly damaged floor samples are sold to the trade at very good prices.

The larger marts have shows in which manufacturers introduce their new products. Probably the largest furniture show in the United States is held at the Neocon Market in Chicago's Merchandise Mart. Frequently, more than 50,000 interior designers, architects, facility planners, and related professionals travel to Chicago in June to see the new products. Although contract furniture is highlighted, many residential products, as well as floor coverings, wall coverings, lighting, and accessories, are shown. These shows often include seminars, workshops, and continuing education classes. The combination of educational programs and the opportunity to inspect a great number of products is an important updating tool for designers. Recall from Chapter 1 that furniture shows began in the nineteenth century!

Other large furniture shows are held in other parts of the country. The market in New York City is now called Neocon New York and is held in late October or early November. Rather than touring individual showrooms, designers walk the aisles of a large convention center, viewing displays of new products. Designers may also visit regular showrooms in Manhattan and the surrounding area. The International Home Furnishings Market is held in April in High Point, North Carolina, and other trade shows are held in Los Angeles. Specialty shows are also held at these same marts either just prior to the major market shows or at other times of the year. Other specialty shows where products can be viewed are held in various cities during the year. Actual dates and locations of furniture and specialty shows, as well as of the many conferences for interior designers are published in the trade magazines. The January "Buyers Guide" issue of *Interior Design* magazine has an extensive calendar of industry events. Most of the smaller regional marts also have shows. These generally attract the local design community.

Market shows like Neocon Chicago or New York are exciting, energizing events, especially for students who are attending them for the first time. Even professionals approach markets as an endurance contest, hoping their feet will hold up to all the walking! There is so much going on that it is difficult for designers to decide what to do each day. There is a tendency for first timers to overload themselves with brochures and catalogs. Instead of taking home more catalogs than can fit in your luggage, it is wise for designers to bring an abundance of business cards and request materials so that manufacturers can mail their catalogs to the designer. Owners of small design firms who have had problems with getting mailings may want to bring their business license or resale license as well. Students should be cautioned to not grab for every sample, catalog, brochure, or gift lying around. It is true that some reps do not like to talk to students, but students who act and dress professionally, ask intelligent questions, and request that information be sent to them often earn respect and gather much information from representatives. The major shows generally include presentations and events planned for students.

When students enter a trade showroom, they should be respectful of the employees who work there and should be courteous enough to listen to the sales presentations. They can ask the rep questions but should pay attention to their answers. Designers and students who attend markets with serious intent find new product lines and helpful reps who can add immeasurably to their future business.

Local Showrooms

Many manufacturers locate regional showrooms or showroom/sales offices in other markets. Some of these are for major furniture manufacturers, like Herman Miller, and Knoll International, or various suppliers of fabrics, wall coverings, carpet, and floor materials. These showrooms generally are restricted to the trade and have similar policies for admittance, pricing, and purchasing as showrooms in the marts.

Designers can often place orders directly from small, local showrooms. The usual establishment of credit, prepayment, and other terms of sale exist when working with small, local showrooms as with buying directly from manufacturers.

Retail Specialty Shops

Many designers who work with smaller firms, especially sole practitioners, often frequent retail specialty shops to purchase items that they need in a hurry. Retail stores that sell lighting fixtures, accessories, art objects, or even furniture pieces can be a convenient source for the interior designer. They are generally not owned or franchised by any of the manufacturers whose products are displayed.

Some manufacturers have retail outlets. Until fairly recently, these retail outlets have been primarily for specialty items, like paint and floor coverings. Ethan Allen has had retail stores for its furniture products for many years, and other residential-type furniture manufacturers are now getting into the retail business.

Retail specialty shops often give trade discounts to interior designers. These trade discounts are reduced prices given to trade members so that designers can then resell them to their clients. The reader may wish to refer back to Chapter 19 for more information on trade discounts.

Manufacturer's Dealers

Manufacturer's dealers are usually retail furniture stores, as opposed to specialty shops, that have made special arrangements with one or more manufacturers of furniture. In this case, they are generally not owned or franchised back to the manufacturer but are privately owned businesses. *Manufacturer's dealers* (or just dealers) feature selected products in their showrooms and frequently stock inventory of considerable size. However, they sell a wide variety of products—not just ones from one or two manufacturers.

A full-service dealership offers design, selling, and installation services. It may also provide in-house installation of flooring and wall coverings. In other words, it can help a client through the entire design process, from programming to completion. This sometimes is referred to as turnkey design.* Of course,

* In architecture, *turnkey projects* commonly include financing assistance, perhaps even property acquisition.

these full-service dealers also have interior designers available to assist clients. Smaller dealerships may function a bit more like a retail store and also provide bidding on projects specified by other dealers or outside interior design and architectural firms.

The term manufacturer's dealer is most associated with office furnishings dealers. However, there are many residential furniture retail stores that actually serve as dealers. Dealerships often offer a trade discount to independent designers, since some of their products are only available through dealers.

Tradespeople and Craftspeople

Tradespeople and craftspeople provide goods and services to the design community and the general public. Cabinetmakers, painters, carpet and floor-covering installers, and wallpaper installers are a few examples. Drapery workrooms primarily manufacture for designers and retail specialty stores, and do not generally market directly to the end user. There are also craftspeople who make custom products of various kinds, especially furniture items, and who work with interior designers and may somehow market to end users.

It is important for designers to work with quality craftspeople. New craftspeople and tradespeople should be investigated by the designer. This investigation should include obtaining references from their clients and inspecting their work by visiting previous job sites.

It is also important, when the designer is hiring tradespeople, such as painters and carpet installers, to determine whether these individuals are licensed contractors. Individuals who are involved in structural work or installation of architectural finishes are often required to be licensed by their state. Remember, from our earlier discussion, that hiring unlicensed contractors in states that require licensing can leave the designer open to lawsuits.

When beginning to work with new tradespeople, the designer should be sure that he or she understands how the tradespeople work, not just what they make and the quality of their work. Will the cabinetmaker prepare working drawings of the custom furniture from just a plan and elevation, or is the designer expected to prepare all of the working drawings? If materials must be sent to the tradespeople, for example, fabric to an antique refinisher, how will freight charges be handled? Will the installer accept delivery of goods (such as carpet) in the designer's name, or will the designer have to receive the goods and have the installer pick up the carpet from the designer? These are just a few questions that the designer must ask of potential tradespeople.

Construction Contractors

Design projects that involve structural work necessitate the use of one or more construction contractors. *General contractors* (often called the GC) are contractors that hold a license that allows them to contract and supervise all phases of a construction project. Commercial designers regularly work with general contractors or construction management companies that oversee the entire project. A *construction manager* is an individual who oversees the construction project as an agent for either the general contractor or the owner. These general contractors often hire *subcontractors* (also called subs) to do the specialized work. There are specialized subcontractors who do concrete work; plumbing; electrical work; framing; sheet metal; heating, ventilation, air conditioning (HVAC); painting; roofing; carpet installation; ceramic tile; landscaping; and many other specialized trades and crafts involved in the construction and finishing of commercial and residential buildings. There can even be *secondary subcontractors* who are hired because the project may require special skills or equipment that the subcontractor does not have. For example, in construction, when a cinder block stem wall is required, it is usually filled with a special cement mixture to strengthen the wall. The masonry subcontractor may hire a secondary subcontractor to take care of this job, since it requires a special piece of equipment.

There is a type of etiquette that is required of designers when they are working with contractors and subcontractors. The men and women who work in the trades professionally do the work as it is drawn, specified, and contracted, that is, not how it is supposed to be or how someone tells them it is supposed to be, but how it was drawn, specified, and contracted. This is why working drawings have to be done correctly, or the work might be stopped if corrections are required. Of course, a contractor or a subcontractor who sees errors in the drawings and specifications that could be dangerous or that violate codes will call this to the attention of the designer. Making changes in a job after the contract is let (awarded) requires a change order.* Change orders usually result in higher prices for the project, because something extra had to be done that was not called for in the original drawings and specifications.

It is important for the client to understand that he or she should not try to give directions or in any way supervise the subcontractors, unless, of course, the client is his or her own general contractor. Fights have been known to break out when subs refuse to make a change that is requested—or demanded—by the client. If the client or the designer has a question or wants to make a change, the change order needs to be issued by the general contractor, who will check with the architect or interior designer and then direct the work to the subcontractor after a change order has been prepared.

Designers must also be careful about giving instructions to subs on the job. Designers should always request changes through the supervisor of the tradespeople involved or through the general contractor. Again, subs might just ignore any request made by the designer. In some states, designers must hold either a contractor's license or a specialty license to give instructions and supervisory information to installers—even carpet and wallpaper installers. The designer should know the law in his or her jurisdiction.

It is the responsibility of the interior designer to instruct the client, who may never have had a custom home constructed, experienced a remodeling or renovation project on a home or a commercial space, on the process that will take place. The designer should clarify the chain of command and how the various decisions and communications will take place right from the beginning of the project to its completion.

Selecting Trade Sources

Working with trade sources is a two-way street. Vendors and suppliers are there to assist the interior designer by providing the goods and services that the interior designer wishes to sell or specify. The trade sources are in business to make money. In highly competitive or economically recessive times,

* Change orders are forms describing any modification in construction projects after the contract has been awarded. The concept is also applied to interiors furnishings projects. Change orders are also discussed in Chapter 29.

the street is not always smooth or a two-way street. Reps and suppliers complain about designers who demand specification fees (an activity that is considered unethical by the professional associations). And designers have complained about reps and suppliers who are stingy with information or who "buy" jobs.* Both camps need each other and need to cooperate with each other.

Designers receive mailings, phone calls, and drop-in visits from reps and suppliers constantly. An interior designer's library can easily become clogged with sample books, catalogs, flyers, and price lists. "I still think they are like rabbits. You turn your back on your library, and it doubles," complained a small design studio owner. Managing a firm's resources and selecting resources are important tasks in an interior design practice. Of course, today, many product catalogs are virtual catalogs—available on CD-ROM disks or able to be viewed on the Internet. This helps, yet the designer still requires information on the products and how to get the information that he or she needs about these items. Some items need to be real, tangible, and on shelves or in drawers at the designer's studio. Fabric samples for upholstery, drapery, and the like; carpet and many other types of floorings; wood for furniture; many wall treatments; stone for counters or table tops; plastic laminates; and other materials are better evaluated from actual samples and need to be stored.

The firm's business plan and annual plans give management guidelines on what to keep as resources. If the firm is not doing residential design, there is little need for residential grade carpet. Design firms that are lucky enough to work with high-end clients have little use for budget furniture catalogs. But then, these comments only state the obvious. How does a design firm really find and maintain the best sources? Some suggestions follow.

1. *Clarify the business plan*. The design firm should prepare a business plan if no plan exists. This will show the firm who its client groups are, the kinds of design services the firm is prepared to offer. It will help direct the firm to the kinds of trade sources that are needed.
2. *Review current resource materials*. Gradually, the design firm should clean out its current library and resource materials. Catalogs with five-year-old price lists may need to be discarded, especially if no one in the office can remember buying from the source recently. Besides, that old price list could get the firm in trouble if discontinued goods are specified. The firm should request new tear sheets or even entire catalogs from manufacturers that they use frequently. They should call the representative so that he or she can update the firm's catalogs and samples. It is, after all, part of the service that the rep provides. The firm should obtain CD-ROM catalogs for products that it uses frequently. It can set up bookmarks on the Internet for the most frequently used web-based catalogs.

   If existing employees do not have time to do the library work, the firm can hire an interior design student who, with direction, can pull out old items and purge sample books. The student will benefit from the opportunity to learn about products, and the firm will get an updated library. It is also a good idea for the firm to review its project files and purchase order files in order to determine which major vendors have been the most successful for the design firm. It

* *Buying a job* refers to the practice of pricing the goods or fees at an unusually low level in order to make the sale.

should consider eliminating suppliers that have given the firm poor service, regardless of the products the suppliers offer.

3. *Carefully review new sources*. The design firm should keep only those new items that fit the design firm's product and jobs profile. It should return or discard those items that do not add to the firm's library. The firm should get to know the representatives or the craftspeople from the resources the firm maintains. It can make an appointment to talk to the rep and get answers to questions on pricing, delivery schedules, exclusivity, customs, warranties, quality, and manufacturing. The owner, design director, and lead designers should understand all the terms and conditions of sale from new sources.
4. *Try to work with sources on the firm's terms*. Small design firms need to find sources that will take lower prepayments with orders. Smaller firms might also have to work with firms that are closer to the design firm geographically, because the design firm may have to drop ship goods directly to the client. This method also reduces the cost of the project, because freight charges are somewhat reduced. Unless designers enjoy constant interruptions, they should require reps to make appointments to show new items. Long ago, larger design firms began requiring reps to meet with the design staff during lunch hours, and the reps provided the meal. This works well, and reps do not complain about the cost, unless very few of the design staff show up. Firms that demand this of representatives, must be sure that all of the staff is available for these lunch meetings.
5. *Designers must do their job*. Designers sometimes try to pass the buck when they make a mistake or create a problem, and try to pass it on to the trade source. Of course, it can be argued that designers have learned this from trade sources who pass the responsibility back to the interior designer. However, this is not the point. A professional, responsible, and ethical interior designer who does his or her job does not to have to worry about passing the buck because of liability issues.

By now, the reader has an understanding of the vast amount of responsibility that an interior designer has in the execution of a design project. Many things can go wrong, including providing incorrect information to vendors, making mistakes on drawings, forgetting to tell tradespeople about site conditions or perhaps peculiarities of the client. It is important that the designer only take on projects for which the designer is qualified. He or she must do the necessary research to understand the proper specification of any product that goes into the project. It is the designer's responsibility to be sure the client knows about any special maintenance of products installed in the project. The designer must carefully prepare the documents needed for the job. He or she should develop good project management procedures and provide adequate communication with the client and all the other stakeholders. Above all, the interior designer should take care of problems that arise as quickly and professionally as possible.

Technology and Trade Sources

In several places in this chapter, we have mentioned the use of the Internet and other computer applications for activities related to finding trade sources.

Every day several new sources go on-line or offer CD-ROM substitutes for printed catalogs. It is nearly impossible for the interior designer to ignore the computer in the everyday operation of an interior design practice.

Faxing orders and receiving faxed acknowledgments is quite common today. Some companies now E-mail orders and acknowledgments. It is becoming very difficult to function without these business aids. Certainly, they are sometimes curses as well. For the sole practitioner who works from home, receiving a fax at 2 A.M. is not a very pleasant experience. Receiving junk faxes from every conceivable business is annoying. Spamming—sending unsolicited E-mails—is so annoying that there is legislation to try to curb it.

For all its possible problems, computer technology opens the world to the designer. Hundreds, if not thousands, of manufacturers, suppliers, and professional associations of importance to the interior designer are on the World Wide Web or will be soon. More are added every day. Recall the estimates of B2B Internet sales, mentioned in Chapter 23.

Catalog libraries have been created on the Internet so that designers now have access to the catalogs of numerous vendors and manufacturers without having to leave their office or to have the catalog on their shelf. Once an item is found, the picture and information can be downloaded and printed for later reference. If the designer has a color printer, a product picture in color can be added to a sample board without cutting up an existing in-store catalog. Some of these on-line libraries are for reference only, meaning that the designer cannot order the merchandise. The designer would have to order merchandise through a local rep. Others do provide some purchasing capabilities.

On-line libraries are to the trade only. A designer has to subscribe to the library in order to receive a password that will give the designer access to the information (Figure 28-1). This serves the same purpose as a closed showroom; it gives the interior designer access to product information and pricing that are not available to the general public. The information in these on-line libraries gives the small practitioner access to products from hundreds of manufacturers around the world. These resources add more suppliers to their libraries every day and have product listings for both commercial and residential needs. Some companies may also have chat rooms to exchange information, provide planning tips and assistance, provide industry news, and other features.

On-line libraries usually bring the smaller and specialty suppliers into the virtual catalog. Large manufacturers like Herman Miller, Baker Furniture, Collins & Aikman Floorcoverings, Nevermar (laminates), and Thomasville Furniture, to name just a few, have their own web sites where designers may obtain information.

Other kinds of information can be obtained from the World Wide Web as well. The Sweets catalogs for construction, architecture, and interiors products are also available on-line. The professional associations have web sites for members and some web pages for nonmembers. A designer can also search for information on business operations, marketing, or financing. The types of information that can be obtained from on-line sources is unlimited.

In addition, there are many auction sites and possibly thousands of very small tradespeople and craftspeople who sell specialty items via their own web sites. The World Wide Web has certainly brought a new dimension to searching for products and the ability to make an interior even more special.

Web addresses for many companies are listed in the buyer's guides and source guides of the many trade magazines. As a product resource, company web pages and on-line libraries have revolutionized product source research for the interior designer.

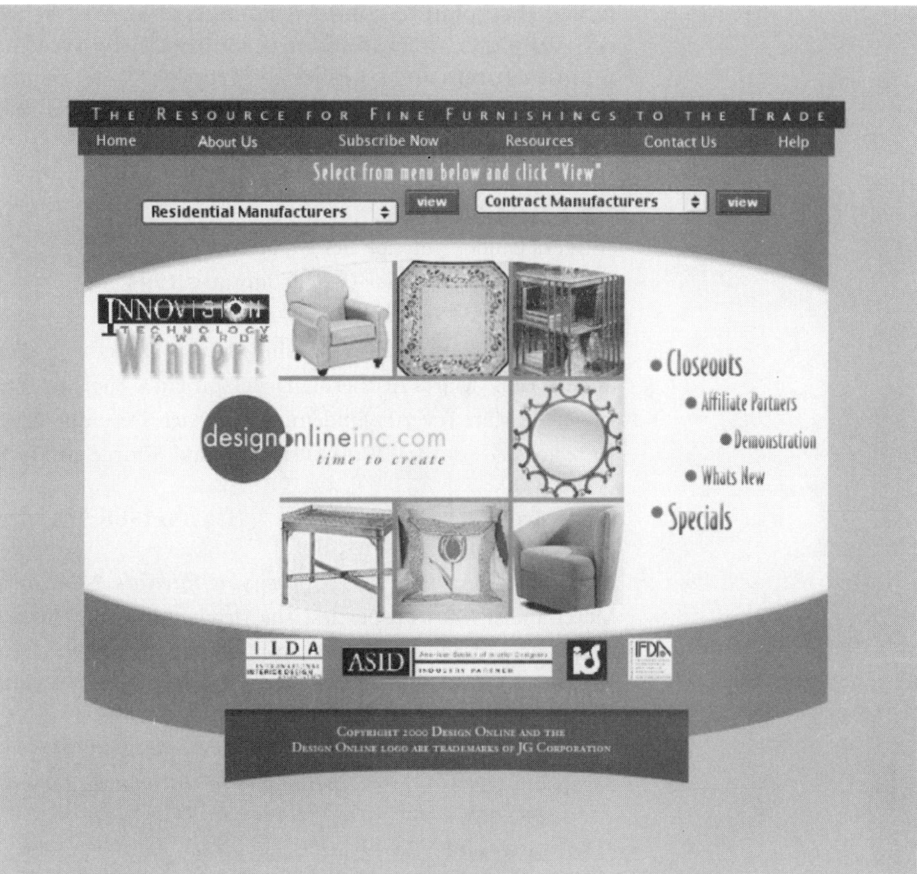

FIGURE 28-1. Home page for designonlineinc.com web site, one of the first design libraries on the World Wide Web. (Reproduced with permission, designonlineinc.com, Greenville, SC)

Summary

The sources that the design firm uses or maintains information about are many and varied. Those chosen regularly by the design firm should compliment the firm's work. Trips to market shows give designers a very good opportunity to review sources and to talk to sales representatives or factory salespeople. Because of the wealth of products available to designers, it is important for designers to carefully select the products, representatives, and other trade sources that fit into the firm's type of business.

The Internet has brought a new dimension to finding just the right product for a client. On-line libraries, web sites of major manufacturers, and even web sites of specialty craftspeople help make themselves known to potential clients. Although there are, at the time of the writing of this revision, questions about privacy and security when people purchase via the Internet, its future is strong by many accounts.

The discussion of trade sources in this chapter that are utilized by the interior designer provides some information about where designers can find the products and services that they will use for their clients. Professionals can easily become familiar with the sources available in the geographic areas in which they plan to conduct business that may be available from manufacturers, suppliers, or craftsmen throughout the world. Students can learn about manufacturers and suppliers by reading trade magazines, going on the Internet and searching out products, visiting local trade showrooms, visiting one of the market shows, or visiting local design offices.

REFERENCES

"Buyers Guide." *Interior Design.* January 1993.

"Buyers Guide." *Interior Design.* January 1994.

"Buyers Guide." *Interior Design.* January 2000.

"Contract Furniture and Furnishings Mart Directory." *Contract.* December 1985.

Corlin, Len. "Marts Accelerate Development." *Contract.* December 1986.

———. "Mart Fever Is Epidemic." *Contract.* December 1985.

"Interiors & Sources 2000 Directory and Source Guide." *Interiors & Sources.* January 2000.

Knackstedt, Mary V. (with Laura J. Haney). 1988. *The Interior Design Business Handbook.* New York: Watson-Guptill.

McGowan, Maryrose. 1996. *Specifying Interiors.* New York: John Wiley.

Merchandise Mart Properties. *The Merchandise Mart Buyers Guide*. June 2000.

"Open vs. Closed: The Results Are In." *Interior Design*. June 1992.

Poage, Waller S. 1987. *Plans, Specs and Contracts for Building Professionals*. Kingston, MA: R. S. Means.

Reznikoff, S. C. 1989. *Specifications for Commercial Interiors*. New York: Watson-Guptill.

Sampson, Carol A. 1991. *Techniques for Estimating Materials Costs and Time for Interior Designers.* New York: Watson-Guptill.

"The Source Guide 1999–2000." *Contract.* January 2000.

Veitch, Ronald M., Dianne R. Jackman, and Mary K. Dixon. 1990. *Professional Practice.* Winnipeg, Canada: Peguis Publishers.

Wakita, Osamu A., and Richard M. Linde. 1984. *The Professional Practice of Architectural Working Drawings.* New York: John Wiley.

Chapter 29

Contract Documents and Specifications

If the interior designer is responsible for preparing space plans and necessary drawings for the construction of partitions and other non-load-bearing features, specific documents must be prepared. These contract documents and formal specifications are used when it is necessary for the client to obtain competitive bids, or prices, for the completion of an interiors project.

Contract and construction documents and drawings are needed whenever partitions and other non-load-bearing structural design is part of the designer's responsibilities. Projects that have minimal or no construction work involved are often referred to as *FF&E* projects. That acronym stands for furniture, furnishings, and equipment.

When an interior designer is contracted by a client or teams up with an architectural firm to design large projects, competitive bidding is generally required. This is especially true for projects involving large-sized private entities, such as a hotel, a corporate office center, or a department store. Public projects for any level of government agency also generally require competitive bids. Utility companies are often thought of as quasi-public and also are normally required to use competitive bidding for interiors and construction projects. Depending on whether a project is FF&E, construction and FF&E, public, quasi-public, or private, certain processes in the preparation of construction documents and specifications will be different. This chapter primarily discusses the documents that are associated with projects that must be competitively bid and the bid process, with emphasis placed on formal bid specifications and bid documents.

Contract Documents

The fourth phase of a project is referred to as the contract documents phase. It is in this phase of a project that all the documents needed to build and bid (or purchase) the project are completed. *Contract documents* are all the drawings and specifications that together describe what is required for a project, along with contracts or agreements between the project owner and the designer and other interested stakeholders (Haviland, 1994, p. 706). A complete set of contract documents (also called CDs) include architectural drawings, schedules, specifications, modifications, and contracts related to the actual build-out of the project. *Construction documents* are "a set of legal contract documents of drawings and specifications that graphically and verbally describe what is required for a specific construction project" (Wakita and Linde, 1984, p. 549). A set of construction documents includes all of the contract documents, along with the bid documents.

Construction documents are very important, because they insure that the project will be executed according to the design concepts and wishes of the interior designer and the client. They insure that the project will be done as designed, since they are legal documents—a contract. Technically, to vary from the construction documents without approval constitutes breach of contract. These documents must be prepared carefully and accurately. Errors in the drawings or other documents will result in liability issues for the interior designer, which can mean loss of revenues as well as reputation and even penalties imposed by a court.

This section of the chapter will briefly discuss construction drawings and schedules. The less familiar documents—specifications, documents for the competitive bidding process, and modifications—will be covered separately.

Construction Drawings

The *construction drawings* portion of contract documents typically consists of all plans, elevations, and details required for building the structure or the interior. For an interiors project, a set of CDs would include dimensioned partition drawings, section drawings, mechanical drawings, including electrical and telephone location plans, reflected ceiling plans, plumbing plans, HVAC plans, other mechanical plans (such as for sprinklers in a commercial building), interior construction elevations, and construction details. Additional specialized drawings, such as plans from lighting designers, commercial kitchen and foodservice designers, healthcare systems designers, and others, might also be included. Preparation of additional drawings would be done by the person who designed the exterior structure.

Many interior and architectural firms also include equipment plans or furniture plans in the working drawings. Equipment plans show the location of, and identify by code, the movable equipment in the project. By movable equipment, we mean furniture and other equipment, such as refrigerators, that can be easily moved and are not part of the structure. Movable equipment is rarely bid with the construction of the walls. In most projects, furniture and equipment drawings are provided to the general contractor for information only. They are, however, necessary for the furniture bid.

This section describes how the equipment or furniture plan should be prepared as part of the construction documents and how this plan relates to written specifications. The equipment plan for bidding purposes must be very clear and understandable. When projects are to be bid, it is common for interior designers to prepare a separate equipment or furniture floor plan for information and use in installation. Some designers use codes that correspond to information in the written specifications to clarify each furniture item in the bid. Codes may be simple numbers or letters, accompanied by a furniture schedule describing these items of furniture (see Figure 29-1) or more complicated multinumber codes. Codes are used to indicate generic types of furniture and furnishings, not specific product information, just as generic information is often used in notations on construction drawings. These codes then need to be further explained in the specifications.

The exact format and coordination between plans and specifications must be clear enough for the vendor to know what he or she is bidding on. They

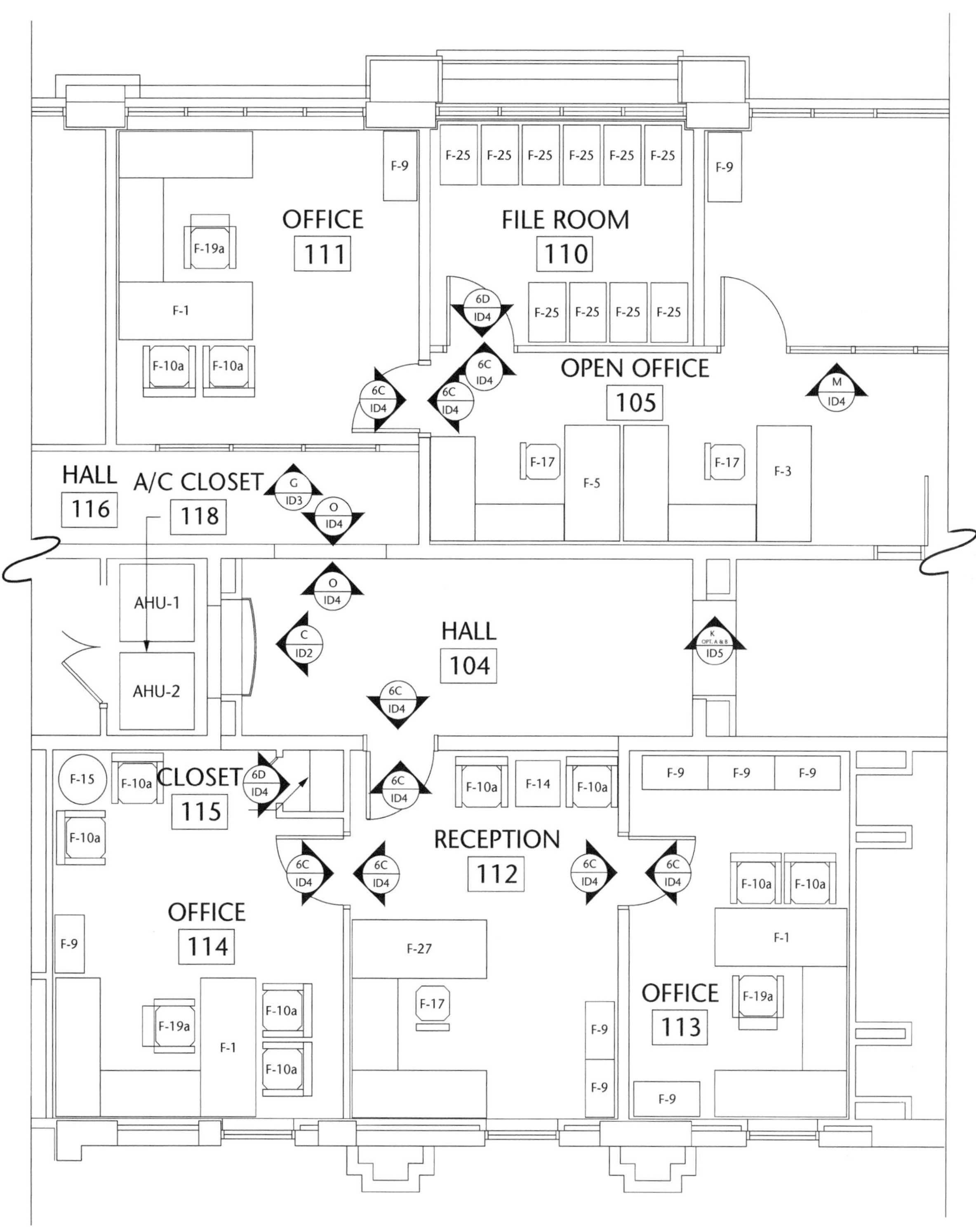

■ **FIGURE 29-1. Coded furniture schedule—partial floor plan. (Reproduced with permission, Sally Thompson, Personal Interiors by Sally Thompson, Inc., Gainesville, FL)**

must also be easy enough for the design firm to produce and also to make any required changes to the plans. However, the design firm should individualize the formats since they are, in part, a marketing tool.

Trade names and product numbers should not be used on the equipment plans, since errors can occur. It is easy to transpose numbers, and if the designer must write product names and numbers many times, it would be easy to make this kind of error, resulting in an incorrect bid. If it becomes necessary to change or substitute a different product, forgetting to make the changes in product numbers on the plans can cause incorrect bidding or the wrong product being ordered. Trade names and product numbers, if used, should be limited to the written specifications. All information in schedules or code keys should be generic descriptions.

Although it is better to use generic names for furniture, furnishings, and room names, generic descriptions can lead to misinterpretations if the terms used are not clarified. For example, *chair* can mean guest chair, arm chair, posture chair, club chair, dining chair, stool, occasional chair, or executive chair. *Table* can mean dining table, coffee table, end table, cocktail table, occasional table, conference table, table desk, or Parsons table. And *rest room* can mean ladies' room, men's room, powder room, lavatory, bathroom, or lounge.

Many other examples of generic furniture, furnishings, and room terminology exist. Although it is important for designers to use generic terms, it is equally important for terms to be consistent, clear, and defined within the specifications. To aid in defining all generic terms, a key needs to be placed either in the specifications or on one of the sheets of equipment plans.

Schedules

In this situation, a *schedule* is usually a tabular chart or graphic used to clarify project items that cannot easily and completely be distinguished from representations on floor plans and other construction drawings. Schedules are commonly prepared for doors, windows, and interior room finishes. Interior room finish schedules include information for walls, floor treatments, and ceiling heights and treatments. Schedules for other specific items, such as lighting fixtures and furniture, are also used by designers. Finish schedules are commonly prepared in tabular form, while door and window schedules are commonly prepared in graphic form. The format of these schedules varies greatly from office to office. Tabular schedules can be computerized by using word-processing or spreadsheet programs.

For the same reasons given for equipment plans, the information provided in the schedules should be generic. Trade or manufacturer's names are to be supplied in the written specifications. For interiors projects that are not very large or complicated, some designers include a materials key with the finish schedule. The materials key is similar in format to the finish schedule. This materials key does name manufacturers. If it is used, it should be used in the specifications. It would not be appropriate to use a materials key if a performance or descriptive specification were used.

Specifications

The *specifications* portion of the contract documents is the written instructions to the general contractors and vendors. Specifications (simply referred to as "specs" by many in the industry) are prepared in a technical fashion and provide information about descriptions of the materials or products required, qualities and workmanship, installation requirements, responsibilities of bidders, and the like. They are needed for structural materials and designs as well as for the FF&E required for the interior. This section discusses the types of specifications used for the FF&E. If the reader is in need of information on the preparation of specifications for structural work, he or she should refer to the References at the end of the chapter for suggestions.

Small interior design firms that work directly with the client for specification and subsequent purchase of the products will likely use a simple, though detailed, specification list to clarify what is to be provided for the project. Of course, it is necessary for the designer to clarify the quantities, description, and perhaps pricing on these simple specifications. Figure 19-1 showed a example of this type of simple equipment list. If a custom item or an attachment is part of the project, the interior designer may prepare notes concerning the quality and installation procedures required for those items as part of the equipment list or separately. Many of the documents discussed later in this chapter are not utilized in this case, because the terms and conditions concerning ordering the merchandise previously have been agreed to by the designer and the client.

When a project is specified and the whole or part of the construction and/or procurement of the goods is to be procured by competitive bid, a different type of specification is required. Written specifications for a project can be quite complex. There are many opportunities for mistakes if the firm preparing the specifications is careless. Sometimes discrepancies occur between what is shown on the drawings and what is stated in the written instructions. Since it is easier for people to interpret the written word than drawings when there are discrepancies between the two, the courts often base judgments on the specifications. It is, therefore, important for the designer to prepare the specifications clearly, without any ambiguity, errors, or omissions.

The specifications should complement the drawings, not duplicate them. Specifications should describe what is needed, along with quality standards. In addition, the drawings should show dimensional and location information. Drawings can also indicate quantities, sizes, generic identification of materials, and interrelationships of space, materials, and equipment. Some designers also provide quantities of the goods required in the written specifications. Although this is very helpful to the vendors who are bidding, vendors commonly are required to be responsible for the quantities.

When a specification is written for a product such that no other product can be substituted for it, it is commonly called a *closed specification*. Closed specifications require that only an exact match of the specification be provided by the vendor. Substitutions are not allowed.

An *open specification* is one in which the owner is willing to consider substitutions to what was originally specified. This type of specification usually has the words *or equal* incorporated into the specifications. The *or equal* term means that products that are the same as, or very closely similar to, what has been specified will be considered.

There are four customary kinds of formal specifications. These four types of specifications identify the goods and/or materials needed in different ways. This is done so that the designer and the client can have better control over what is actually bid by vendors. Concern for control of the bidding process is desired by both the interior designer and the client. The four types of specifications are: (1) proprietary, (2) descriptive, (3) performance, and (4) reference.

Proprietary Specification

A *proprietary specification* names the products and materials by manufacturer's name, model number, or part number. With a proprietary specification, there is no doubt about what the designer and client wish to have bid (see Figure 29-2). The basic proprietary specification is a closed specification, since it does not allow for any substitutions. If the specifications allow for no substitutions or do not have an "or equal" clause (which would allow for a substitution), then the proprietary bid might be called a base bid. "The term *base bid* means that all people who wish to provide materials for the project must base their bid on the product named in the specification" (Reznikoff, 1979, p. 231). The proprietary specification that allows for substitutions is considered an open bid, because it allows for many products to be substituted for the item being specified. If it is a base bid, it is considered a closed bid.

The advantages of the proprietary specification are as follows:

1. It is the easiest specification to write. In many cases, the designer only needs to provide the basic descriptive information of manufacturer, product number, and finishes/fabrics to complete the specifications. When more detail is needed, manufacturers often provide information to the designer that can be reproduced in the specifications.
2. It is easier to use for preparing drawings. With known product sizes, drawings are more accurate. The designer does not have to allow in the drawings for possible larger or smaller sizes of a product that might be bid.
3. The designer has maximum product control over the project. The carefully worked out design concept can be realized, since the products used to develop the design concept will be the ones purchased.
4. The time element from invitation announcement to order entry is faster, since alternate products do not have to be evaluated by the client. Since everyone is bidding on exactly the same products, the competitive bid concept is more fully realized.

There is an important disadvantage to using proprietary specifications. This type of specification can limit competition in some markets. Most private businesses and public agencies go through a bid process to obtain more than one price for a project. Sometimes there are not sufficient numbers of bidders in a given market area that can provide the products. When this is the case, it is often necessary to have an "or equal" clause in the specifications.

When the specifications must include an "or equal" clause, extra time is required for the designer and/or client to evaluate the bids and the substitutions. Design control can be lost, since the client may choose a product that is similar in appearance but lower in price than the original specification. What is equal in this situation is open to subjective judgment on the part of the client, the designer, and the bidders.

Reception Area

ITEM	QUANTITY	DESCRIPTION	UNIT	TOTAL
LC-5	4	Knoll 250LS Barcelona Chair Leather: Black		
T-3	1	Knoll 56T-MIN Mercer Coffee Table 44 1/2" x 44 1/2" Finish: Nero-black Marble		

FIGURE 29-2. Sample of a very simple proprietary specification.

Another problem with a proprietary specification is that government agencies generally require that more than one product be specified. This allows for competition for government contracts. A proprietary specification can work in this case only if an "or equal" clause is allowed. If more than one product is specified, it is no longer a proprietary specification—at least not technically.

To protect all the parties concerned when they have to deal with an "or equal" clause, definitions of what procedures will be followed concerning the submittal of alternates must be included in the specifications. A common practice recommended by the Construction Specifications Institute (CSI) is to submit requests related to substitutions prior to the close of the bid. These requests might include detailed descriptions of the substituted product. In some cases, clients ask that a sample product be submitted prior to the close of the bid for evaluation. Some firms require that vendors pay for the time the interior designer must spend in evaluation of substitutions, especially if substitutions are *not* allowed.

Descriptive Specification

A *descriptive specification* does not use a manufacturer's name or trade name for the goods being specified. Rather, it describes, often in elaborate detail, the materials, workmanship, fabrication methods, and installation of the required goods. The descriptive specification is considered an open bid.

There are two advantages to the descriptive specification. First, it allows the designer to prescribe exactly what he or she wishes to specify for the project. When there are many similar products that have subtle differences, such as happens with floor coverings, a descriptive specification helps to ensure that what is bid is actually equal to what is being specified, even if the goods come from different manufacturers. There are also situations in which the client wants a certain product for the project but may have a difficult time obtaining sufficient numbers of competitive bids on that product if he or she is using a proprietary specification. A descriptive specification helps to narrow the "or equal" alternates so that the client can get what he or she wants.

Second, the descriptive specification allows for some performance criteria to be used in the situations for which a complete performance specification is not appropriate. With floor coverings, many manufacturers have carpets that can meet the simple descriptive specification of such things as fiber, pitch, stitches per inch, and pile height. This may not be enough to be sure that the carpet or carpet quality required of the project is bid. Performance criteria related to such factors as static electricity, delamination, and crocking can be included in the specification for these kinds of goods. Other goods, such as furniture, which may not have such stringent requirements, can be written as descriptive specifications (see Figure 29-3).

There are a number of disadvantages to using descriptive specifications. First, it requires time to produce them, and also they can be quite lengthy. Second, it also requires more precise descriptions of the products. The descriptive specification of an open office system work surface would have to read something like this: "A cantilevered hanging work surface, 64 inches wide by 30 inches deep by 1 inch thick. The finished top surface shall be a light ash, wood grain laminate, and the edge shall match. Support finishes shall be black." The same description in a proprietary specification would read as follows: "Herman Miller, A2310.3064LALABU."

Third, the volume of information needed to prepare a descriptive specification can lead to errors and loopholes, which allows for products being bid that were not intended. In the previous example, if the designer did not write in "a light ash, wood grain plastic laminate" but only wrote "plastic laminate,"

12.7 Work Surface

A. General
1. Work surfaces shall suspend from architectural walls or freestanding panels. Components attached to the work surface shall be removable by hand or with the use of a minimum of tools.
2. Vertical support elements (VSE 1–12) shall support hanging components on one-inch intervals and shall easily allow for vertical height adjustment of the work surface.

B. Component
1. Work surfaces shall be made of warp resistant materials and have squared corners and edges.
2. Work surfaces shall be finished using high-pressure plastic laminates that are scratch and heat resistant (up to 250°) available in a variety of colors. Edges shall be finished with a matching vinyl material.
3. All work surfaces must be provided with cantilever-type support brackets that allow for easy installation and removal from panels and wall-hanger strips with a minimum of tools.
4. Work surface tops shall be capable of having various undercounter drawers, storage units, or other accessories suspended below, installed with a minimal use of tools.
5. Cantilevered work surfaces shall be able to support up to 200 pounds when weight is located at the front edge of work surface. (Test data must be provided.)
6. Work surfaces shall be available in the following nominal sizes:
   WST-1: 24" deep by 30" wide
   WST-2: 24" deep by 36" wide
   WST-3: 24" deep by 42" wide
   WST-4: 24" deep by 48" wide
   WST-5: 24" deep by 54" wide
   WST-6: 24" deep by 60" wide
   WST-7: 24" deep by 66" wide
   WST-8: 24" deep by 72" wide
   WST-9: 30" deep by 30" wide
   WST-10: 30" deep by 36" wide
   WST-11: 30" deep by 42" wide
   WST-12: 30" deep by 48" wide
   WST-13: 30" deep by 60" wide
   WST-14: 30" deep by 66" wide
   WST-15: 30" deep by 72" wide

FIGURE 29-3. Sample descriptive specification for open-office systems work surfaces.

the client would not get what he or she desired—the light ash wood finish—but would probably get a plain or neutral finish.

Finally, the descriptive specification, unless it is written very carefully, can result in the designer losing control of the product and design concept. As the example shows, an omission in the specification can result in the wrong finish being specified for the job. It would be within the rights of the bidder to ask for additional moneys to change the product finish to the intended light ash. The omission and resulting cost to the client could also lead to the client's being able to sue the designer.

Performance Specification

Another specification, the *performance specification,* is written without trade names. The performance specification establishes the product requirements based on exact performance criteria. Any product that meets the performance criteria can be used. The performance of the goods is based on the end product of the goods, and thus performance criteria are based on the accomplishment of that end. The performance specification is considered an open bid. For example, a performance criteria for carpeting is shown in Figure 29-4.

Performance specifications are based on qualitative or measurable statements. It is common for specifications to require that certain tests and methods of testing be done and for bidders to submit test data with their bids. This information is available from the manufacturers for the designer's use in writing the specifications. Manufacturers can also submit testing information through the bidders.

When data from the manufacturer is not available or appears inconclusive, it may be necessary for the bidder to supply a sample of the product for testing, as is often the case with various textiles. For example, if the designer wished to use a carpet material on the wall, it would be necessary for the designer to specify some kind of performance criteria for that textile and for the manufacturer to either supply data for its use or to supply a sample that could be tested.

Some designers prefer this type of specification, because it allows for flexibility in what can be bid. Other designers feel that this is a major problem with a performance specification. Advantages are the same as for the descriptive specification: full control when it is not appropriate to use proprietary specifications. Disadvantages are also the same: extra preparation and evaluation time, possible errors, possible loss of design concept, and loss of product control.

SPECIFICATIONS

PILE FIBER CONTENTS	100% Advanced Generation Nylon
CONSTRUCTION	Dense Cut Pile Graphic
GAUGE	1/10
PILE HEIGHT	.250
PILE WEIGHT	30 Oz.
PRIMARY BACK	Polypropylene
SECONDARY BACK	ActionBac
YARN SIZE	
PLY	2 Ply Heat Set
DYE METHOD	Beck Dyed
TOTAL WEIGHT	60 Oz.
STITCHES PER INCH	8.3
PATTERN REPEAT	

TESTING

RADIANT PANEL (ASTM E-648)	Class I
SMOKE DENSITY NBS (ASTM E-662)	Less than 450
FHA-HUD	
DOC FF-1-70	Passes
STATIC PROPENSITY	Built-in Antistatic Control

NOTES

Specifications listed above are subject to normal manufacturing tolerances.

Chair pads are necessary under office chairs, with roller casters to prevent premature or accelerated wear and to preserve appearance.

Color may vary from dye lot to dye lot.

FIGURE 29-4. Performance specification for carpeting. (Reproduced with permission, Wade Carter, Interior Surfaces Guild, Scottsdale, AZ)

Reference Specification

A *reference specification* utilizes an established standard, such as the standards of the American Society for Testing and Materials (ASTM) and the American National Standards Institute (ANSI), rather than written, detailed descriptions or performance criteria for required products. These established standards generally provide minimal acceptable standards of performance for various kinds of products. Because of this, the reference specification is considered an open bid.

The designer must check these standards to be sure that these minimums are satisfactory for the needs of the project. If the standard is too low, the reference specification cannot be used. It is also necessary for the designer to be fully familiar with the standards, because the standards sometimes provide options for materials or workmanship. The designer must be sure that he or she specifies the standard or level of standard required for the project. If this is not done, the bidder then has the option of using a lower standard than the one the designer may have intended to use. Reference specifications are more widely used in construction. They may be utilized by the interior designer for such things as wall and floor products and installation.

One advantage to using a reference specification is that it saves time, because only the standard must be stated; there is no need to write a long, descriptive specification or performance specification. Another advantage is that a reference specification also can be used to help explain a complex performance specification or descriptive specification for specialized products or installations.

The disadvantage is that, if the designer is not fully aware of the complete, up-to-date standard, the designer may allow for products and workmanship that do not meet the desired requirements.

Specification Organization

Because of the complexity and potential depth of the project, it is necessary to organize the specification in such a manner that it is easy to prepare and to locate information in an orderly fashion. As legal documents, specifications should not be written in obscure language or with information omitted. Even with the use of computer applications in the preparation of specifications, this document requires a great deal of time, thought, and accuracy.

Following a standardized organization allows for greater speed and accuracy by the vendors who will be providing bids. The furniture vendor is only interested in what furniture and furnishing items are required. The framer, electrician, plumber, and all the other trades are likewise only interested in what they are being asked to provide.

The organizational format most frequently used in the design and construction professions was developed by the Construction Specifications Institute (CSI). The CSI is a nonprofit organization whose purpose is to improve professional documentation, especially specifications. With its membership spanning the full range of the construction professions, CSI has been able to develop a common language of construction and a standardized format for the preparation of specifications. The address for CSI is listed in the Appendix.

Masterformat™, published by CSI, is the most widely accepted method of organizing specifications. Figure 29-5 shows a portion of the CSI system. The detailed numbering system, organized by materials, trades, functions, and space relationships, reduces the chances of omitting important information. It also makes it much easier for the designer to make changes while the specs are being written.

With a word processor, the design firm can establish its own version of standardized specification language. All the popular word-processing software products provide sufficient flexibility for the designer to develop template sections that are needed in a furniture and finishes specification.

MasterFormat™

LEVEL TWO NUMBERS AND TITLES

- INTRODUCTORY INFORMATION
- BIDDING REQUIREMENTS
- CONTRACTING REQUIREMENTS
- FACILITIES AND SPACES
- SYSTEMS AND ASSEMBLIES
- CONSTRUCTION PRODUCTS AND ACTIVITIES
  - DIVISION 1 GENERAL REQUIREMENTS
    - 01100 SUMMARY
    - 01200 PRICE AND PAYMENT PROCEDURES
    - 01300 ADMINISTRATIVE REQUIREMENTS
    - 01400 QUALITY REQUIREMENTS
    - 01500 TEMPORARY FACILITIES AND CONTROLS
    - 01600 PRODUCT REQUIREMENTS
    - 01700 EXECUTION REQUIREMENTS
    - 01800 FACILITY OPERATION
    - 01900 FACILITY DECOMMISSIONING
  - DIVISION 2 SITE CONSTRUCTION
  - DIVISION 3 CONCRETE
  - DIVISION 4 MASONRY
  - DIVISION 5 METALS
  - DIVISION 6 WOOD AND PLASTICS
  - DIVISION 7 THERMAL AND MOISTURE PROTECTION
  - DIVISION 8 DOORS AND WINDOWS
  - DIVISION 9 FINISHES
    - 09050 BASIC FINISH MATERIALS AND METHODS
    - 09100 METAL SUPPORT ASSEMBLIES
    - 09200 PLASTER AND GYPSUM BOARD
    - 09300 TILE
    - 09400 TERRAZZO
    - 09500 CEILINGS
    - 09600 FLOORINGS
    - 09700 WALL FINISHES
    - 09800 ACOUSTICAL TREATMENT
    - 09900 PAINTS AND COATINGS
  - DIVISION 10 SPECIALTIES
  - DIVISION 11 EQUIPMENT
  - DIVISION 12 FURNISHINGS
    - 12050 FABRICS
    - 12100 ART
    - 12300 MANUFACTURED CASEWORK
    - 12400 FURNISHINGS AND ACCESSORIES
    - 12500 FURNITURE
    - 12600 MULTIPLE SEATING
    - 12700 SYSTEMS FURNITURE
    - 12800 INTERIOR PLANTS AND PLANTERS
    - 12900 FURNISHINGS RESTORATION AND REPAIR
  - DIVISION 13 SPECIAL CONSTRUCTION
  - DIVISION 14 CONVEYING SYSTEMS
  - DIVISION 15 MECHANICAL
  - DIVISION 16 ELECTRICAL

FIGURE 29-5. A partial listing of the Construction Specifications Institute (CSI) MasterFormat™Level Two Numbers and Titles, 1994 edition. (Reprinted with permission from the Construction Specifications Institute (CSI), and Construction Specifications Canada (CSC), 2001. For more information, call 800-689-2900 or CSINet URL: http://www. csinet.org.)

Larger design firms may be interested in obtaining one of the standard text systems. Standard text systems on computer disks are available from trade associations, manufacturers, and some of the professional organizations. These standard text systems have a fill-in-the-blank format. However, these standard text systems require that the user have a thorough understanding of the construction process in order to know what to leave in and what to take out of the specification.

Another standardized specification is the ARCOM AIA Masterspec™ Interior Design. It has 75 short-form master specifications, which follow the CSI format. This specification program has specification information for interior construction, finish, and equipment items for several types of commercial facilities. It also has reference materials and provides background information on the various materials. This system is the first set of specification standards for interior materials and products. It simplifies interior product specifications, since it is a user-friendly system that is used to complete intricate interior specifications. Figure 29-6 shows a sample page for wood flooring. The materials are available from the publisher, ARCOM Master Systems, which is listed in the Appendix.

Whatever format the firm chooses to use, it should remember to keep the language of the specifications clear and direct. In the field of interior design, sentence structure traditionally uses the indicative mood. For example, "The vendor shall remove all cartoning and packaging materials." Another alternative recommended by specification writing professionals is the use of the imperative mood. In this case, instructions do not use the phrase "the vendor shall" or the "contractor will." Words such as "shall" and "will" are omitted, creating an imperative mood. In the preceding example, in the imperative mood, the sentence would read, "Remove all cartoning and packaging materials."

A few other examples showing the need to use language carefully are given below. They show that words can have a double meaning (Reznikoff, 1989, p. 251).

Shall and Will	Often used incorrectly. "Shall" is used to designate a command; "Will" implies a choice.
All	"The Contractor shall assume the responsibility for all unacceptable work." This sentence leaves no doubt about the contractor's responsibility.

Writing technical specifications and preparing the remaining documents needed for a bid are time-consuming activities. In truth, neither is an activity that many designers enjoy. Small firms that infrequently produce formal contract documents and bid specifications may wish to hire specification-writing consultants. Independent practitioners provide consulting services to design professionals who do not feel qualified or who do not have the time to prepare construction and/or detailed interiors specification for bids. Larger firms may assign a staff member to be responsible for the preparation of all specifications issued by the firm. These specialists need to be experienced in interior design and/or architecture, and should have an eye for and interest in detail and a thorough knowledge of such things as materials, products, construction methods, and building codes. CSI has developed a certification process for qualified specifiers, who are entitled to refer to themselves as certified construction specifiers (CCS).

Competitive Bidding

Competitive bidding is a process whereby the client has the opportunity to obtain comparative prices from a number of contractors and/or vendors for

The Hardwood Plywood and Veneer Association (HPVA) publishes ANSI/HPVA LF, *Laminated Wood Flooring*. This standard establishes requirements for grade of plies, moisture content, machining, bond line (delamination resistance), construction (ply assembly), formaldehyde emissions for products made with ureaformaldehyde or melamine-formaldehyde adhesives or surface coatings, and finish of engineered-wood flooring. Veneers for the face ply can be of one or more species. Common species used include pecan, hard maple, red oak, white oak, birch, ash, beech, black walnut, southern pine, and black cherry. Face Grades established by the standard are Prime (practically clear with minor imperfections) and Character (sound wood variations and a greater allowable level of imperfections than Prime). Veneers are rotary cut, sliced, or sawed from a log, bolt, or flitch. Sawed veneers are the most durable and look the most like traditional solid-wood flooring products.

APPLICATION CONSIDERATIONS

Controlling the moisture content of wood is critical both before and after installation. Wood is hygroscopic, meaning it changes dimensionally with the absorption or release of moisture. Swelling and shrinking varies with the wood species, cut, and type of flooring. Because engineered products' cross-ply construction adds dimensional stability, moisture control for engineered-wood flooring is less critical than for solid-wood flooring.

Manufacturers kiln-dry wood flooring so it will behave predictably. During transit, delivery, and storage, it must be protected from moisture. Before installation, wood flooring must stabilize at (acclimatize to) the temperature and relative humidity of space in which it will be installed. After installation, and even after finishing, fluctuations in environmental conditions cause shrinking and swelling.

Wood flooring installations must accommodate movement. An expansion space is required at the perimeter of the installation. For larger installations, more expansion provisions may be required.

Concrete slab substrates must be dry and protected from subsurface moisture by appropriate grading and drainage, a capillary water barrier of porous drainage materials, and a membrane vapor barrier. Temperature, relative humidity, and ventilation affect concrete drying time. A slab allowed to dry from only one side generally takes 30 days for every 1 inch (25.4 mm) of thickness to dry adequately.

For adhesive attachment to concrete, slabs must be clean and free of curing compounds, sealers, hardeners, and other materials that may interfere with an adhesive bond.

Spaces below wood flooring must be dry and well ventilated. Cross-ventilate crawl spaces and cover the ground with a polyethylene vapor retarder. If solid-wood flooring is installed over wood sleepers on a concrete slab, NOFMA recommends covering the sleepers with a polyethylene vapor retarder and making provisions for ventilating the airspaces between sleepers.

TROPICAL WOODS

Tropical moist forests, including rainforests and seasonal or monsoon forests, provide the hardwoods generally called *tropical woods*. The destruction of rainforests is an important environmental issue. More than half the plant and animal species on Earth are found in tropical rainforests concentrated mainly in the South American Amazon Basin, Africa's Congo Basin, and Southeast Asia.

Land-use changes, not the timber industry, are the major cause of rainforest destruction according to most reports. Some organizations assert that boycotting the use of tropical woods may accelerate the destruction of rainforests because it devalues the timber as a resource and encourages changes in land use to those uses that immediately profit the local human population. Organizations concerned with preserving rainforests generally also have social agendas. They encourage responsible, sustainable forestry-management practices and timber production as a means of providing for a region's human population. If desired, verify that

FIGURE 29-6. Sample specification page from Masterspec Section 09640—Wood Flooring Evaluations. (Used by permission of ARCOM Master Systems, publishers of Masterspec for The American Institute of Architects)

the construction or supply of the project. It takes place after all the construction drawings, specifications, and schedules have been completed. Competitive bids almost always are required by law for projects involving federal, state, and local agencies, as well as for public businesses, like utilities. Most private businesses also require competitive bids on construction projects and large furniture or equipment orders. A residential project will likely use competitive bidding for the construction of the house but rarely for the interior FF&E.

Of course, many clients do not use the competitive bid process. Depending on the size of the project and the client's policies concerning project procurement, the client can purchase goods directly from a vendor of the purchasing department's choosing. In most cases, this happens only for a project that has a small dollar value. Most private companies and government agencies have policies that state that any project over a certain dollar amount must be put out to bid. That dollar amount might be as small as $500 or much larger. In other cases, the client may directly negotiate with a particular vendor because of some unique quality of the product, project, or circumstance. For example, if the client has a large inventory of Haworth office systems, the client may be able to negotiate directly for additional purchases, regardless of the size of the purchase.

The idea of the bid process is that it allows the client to purchase the products and services required for the project at a price that is as low as possible while maintaining the quality and intentions of the original design concept. This assumption is valid as long as the goods or services being bid on are either the same or can objectively be compared as equal. This, however, is not always possible. When substitutions are allowed, it becomes difficult for the interior designer and client to evaluate the differences in the various products being bid on objectively. Questions then arise about possible compromises in order to maintain the quality and/or design intentions of the specifications. When there are sufficient bidders of a like product, then competitive bids based on the original idea are possible. When a project is designed and/or specified in such a way that few bidders can supply the same product at a fair price, then the bid process is suspect.

Clients who are ready to purchase large quantities of a product and are required to use the bid process often are under pressure to accept the lowest bid. For the designer, this can mean the loss of the original design concept for the project, since a different product that does not have the same aesthetic appearance as the original one might be purchased. For example, picture if you will the specification of Knoll Barcelona chairs for a reception area. A bidder may offer a knockoff* of the Knoll Brno chair instead. The appearance and quality are far different from what has been specified. For the client, it can mean that he or she will now own a product that does not meet the performance criteria of the original design. In this example, it is unlikely that the knockoff Brno Tubular chair will hold up as well as the Knoll Barcelona chair.

Competitive bidding may also be more expensive than it would for other purchasing methods. There is a greater amount of preparation time of complicated contract documents and specifications for the goods and services. Also, additional documentation related to the bid procedure, general conditions for performance of the bid contract, and other conditions related to the bid and subsequent work must be prepared. When similar but unequal products are bid or products are bid based on performance, the client and designer will be involved in time-consuming evaluations either before the bid submittal or

* *Knockoff* means an imitation.

before the awarding of contracts. Additionally, there is a potential for claims and lawsuits related to the bid award if one or more bidders feel that the award was improper.

The bid process will continue to exist for most major commercial and governmental projects. The interior designer must include the services for monitoring and coordinating the bid phase in his or her contract. This will help the designer keep control of the design concepts and aesthetic intent of the project. Architects have done this for years. Interior designers, regardless of the size of their practice, must do the same.

In addition to the contract documents, four bid documents must be produced in order to complete a bid. They are: (1) the general conditions, (2) the invitation to bid, (3) instructions to bidders, and (4) the bid form.

General Conditions

Bid documents for projects involving any kind of construction include a section of general conditions. These *general conditions* set forth the legal responsibilities, procedures, rights, and duties of each party to the contract. A standardized set of general conditions used by many designers and private business owners is the AIA form, AIA Document A201. It is commonly used because it has stood the test of time; however, the standardized form is quite long and cumbersome. Many designers and clients modify the conditions of the document for their particular situation.

Items covered in the general conditions include definitions of the contract document, the names of the designer and owner, ownership of documents, the responsibilities of the designer and the owner, definitions and responsibilities of the contractors and subcontractors, clauses concerning payments, the time period of project, claims, insurance, change orders, dispute resolution considerations, and other definitions or statements related to the contractual relationship of the parties.

For bids that concern only furniture, AIA document A271, "General Conditions of the Contract for Furniture, Furnishings, and Equipment," can be used. The general conditions in this document are similar in scope to the ones in Document A201 but are related to interior furniture and furnishings rather than construction.

Since both of these forms are lengthy, generalized legal forms, it is necessary for the designer to prepare supplemental conditions for the projects. The supplemental conditions spell out any conditions that are related to the specific project. A supplemental condition that must be stated if the designer uses either of these forms is that the words *designer* or *interior designer* should be substituted wherever the word *architect* is used. The AIA also has Document A571, "Guide for Interiors Supplementary Conditions," available to help the designer prepare the supplemental conditions for Document A271.

Documents similar to the AIA standardized documents are available from ASID and IIDA. Copyright law should be respected, since these documents belong to the AIA, ASID, and IIDA. It is necessary for the designer to obtain permission from the association in order to make copies or to modify the documents in any way. Should the designer/specifier wish to prepare his or her own set of general conditions, these should be reviewed by the design firm's attorney before being submitted to the client. Copies of these forms can be ordered from local AIA chapter offices or by contacting the AIA national office (see the Appendix). Sample documents from ASID and IIDA must be ordered from the association national offices.

The Invitation to Bid

The first step in the bid process is to prepare and conduct an invitation to bidders (also called an advertisement for bids). The *invitation to bid* notifies potential bidders of the existence of a project. Government and public agencies most likely will advertise a bid in newspapers. This process is called *open competitive selection*. In this case, anyone interested in the project who meets the qualifications that are spelled out in the invitation to bid may submit a bid. Private businesses rarely advertise a bid, though they may do so for a very large project. Some private organizations, through careful legal preparation, may have an acceptable "bid list" of potential designers and vendors who would receive the notifications. This selection process is called *closed competitive selection*. In this situation, the client will contact several designers/vendors to make them aware of the project. Only those invited to bid in this manner are allowed to bid on the project.

The advantage of a bid list is that bidders are prequalified by the client so that those bidders who have experience with the particular kind of project for which the bid list has been prepared, proven personnel, capital to procure the goods, and so on, are the only designers and vendors with whom the client will deal. This also allows the client to maintain a reasonable number of bids, rather than a very large number of bids that would will require additional evaluation to eliminate unqualified bidders.

One disadvantage of closed competitive selection is that too few bidders may be used, resulting in possibly a higher price for the project. There is also the probability that less experienced, yet qualified, designers and vendors will be prohibited from entering the bid process. Yet, if it is possible to get a sufficient (by the client's estimation) number of qualified bidders through a prequalification bid list system, it is a satisfactory and legal method of obtaining competitive bids.

The invitation to bid provides a summary of the project, the bid process, and other brief pertinent procedures for the project. It informs potential bidders of the project, its scope, and ways in which they can obtain further information. The invitation also states whether a security bond is required, how much it will be, and how long it will be held. The size or length of time for which the bond will be held may discourage some designers and vendors from bidding. The information shown in Figure 29-7 is common to an invitation to bid.

Instructions to Bidders

The *instructions to bidders* document informs bidders how to prepare bids for submittal so that all submittals are in the same form. This helps make the

- Identification of the client
- Identification of the architect and interior designer
- Project location
- Description of the scope of work of the project
- When and where bid documents can be obtained
- Prequalification standards, if any
- Description of any bonds or deposits that are required
- Place, day, and time where bids are to be received
- Statements concerning the client's right to reject any and all bids
- Description of any laws or regulations affecting the bid
- Identification of the company or organization responsible for issuing the bid

FIGURE 29-7. Items commonly included in an invitation to bid.

various bids easily comparable. It is common for some bidders not to bid on portions of the project. When this occurs, the items not bid on are called *exclusions*. Thus, it is not always easy to start with absolutely comparable bids.

Information in the instructions should only tell how to prepare and submit the bids. The following represents what is commonly found in the instructions: it will inform the bidders what form and format to use; information on how, where, and when bids are due; statements related to site visitations and familiarization responsibilities; statements related to resolution of interpretation of any discrepancies in the documents; information on how bids can be withdrawn; the procedure for awarding the bid; conditions for rejecting bids; and any other pertinent instructions that may be required by the client (see Figure 29-8). Much of the same information that is in the invitation to bid are also repeated in the instructions to bid.

Important parts of the instructions are the portions of the bid documents that are usually referred to as the "drawings and specifications." These consist of working drawings and/or equipment plans and the written specifications related to products, materials, and construction methods. The instructions to bidders should only mention where and how these documents can be obtained, how they are to be used by the bidder, and if substitutions or exclusions are allowed (and how they are to be submitted). The actual drawings and specifications do not appear in this portion of the documents.

The Bid Form

The *bid form* (also sometimes called a tender form) is a document prepared by the designer or the client and provided to the bidders. The bid form is the document that the vendor uses to inform the client of the bid price. The format generally is set up as a form letter from the bidder to the client. The bid form has blank space in appropriate places to be filled in by the bidder. Figure 29-9 shows a sample bid form. If no substitutions or exclusions are allowed in the instructions, a statement reinforcing disqualification of a bidder who submits a substitution or exclusion should be provided here.

Bond Forms

Bond forms are legal documents used to bind the designer or vendor to the contract as assurance that the designer or vendor will perform the requirements of the contract as agreed upon. There are three bond forms commonly used in the bidding process: (1) the bid bond, (2) the performance bond, and (3) the labor and materials payment bond.

The *bid bond* is required to assure that the designer or vendor awarded the contract will sign the contract and execute the project. Most firms that submit a bid expect to go through with the contract. However, some firms submit bids only to find out how the competition is pricing services or products. In addition, if a firm has made an error in its bid, it may want to withdraw even after the bid has been awarded. The bid bond thus acts as insurance that all who bid are actually interested in going through with the contract. The bid bond may be a lump sum or a percentage amount of the bid. This security amount may be given by using a bond, cash, a certified check, or another method approved by the project owner.* The bid bond of the successful bidder is usually held by the client for some time after the contract has been signed and other bid securities have been obtained. For unsuccessful bidders, the bid bond is returned promptly.

* During construction, the "project owner" can be either the client who will occupy the space, or the contractor who has responsibility to build-out the project. In the later case, the contractor relinquishes ownership to the client.

AIA Document A771

Instructions to Interiors Bidders

1990 EDITION

TABLE OF ARTICLES

FIGURE 29-8. "Instructions to Bidders" (AIA Document A771). (Reproduced with permission, American Institute of Architects)

INSTRUCTIONS TO INTERIORS BIDDERS

ARTICLE 1
DEFINITIONS

1.1 Bidding Documents include the Bidding Requirements and the proposed Contract Documents. The Bidding Requirements consist of the Advertisement or Invitation to Bid, Instructions to Bidders, Supplementary Instructions to Bidders, the bid form, and other sample bidding and contract forms. The proposed Contract Documents consist of the form of Agreement between the Owner and Contractor, Conditions of the Contract (General, Supplementary and other Conditions), Drawings, Specifications, and all Addenda issued prior to execution of the Contract.

1.2 Definitions set forth in the General Conditions of the Contract for Furniture, Furnishings and Equipment, AIA Document A271, or in other Contract Documents are applicable to the Bidding Documents.

1.3 Addenda are written or graphic instruments issued by the Architect prior to the execution of the Contract which modify or interpret the Bidding Documents by additions, deletions, clarifications or corrections.

1.4 A Bid is a complete and properly signed proposal to do the Work for the sums stipulated therein, submitted in accordance with the Bidding Documents.

1.5 The Base Bid is the sum stated in the Bid for which the Bidder offers to perform the Work described in the Bidding Documents as the base, to which Work may be added or from which Work may be deleted for sums stated in Alternate Bids.

1.6 An Alternate Bid (or Alternate) is an amount stated in the Bid to be added to or deducted from the amount of the Base Bid if the corresponding change in the Work, as described in the Bidding Documents, is accepted.

1.7 A Unit Price is an amount stated in the Bid as a price per unit for materials, furniture, furnishings, equipment or services or a portion of the Work as described in the Bidding Documents.

1.8 A Bidder is a person or entity who submits a Bid.

1.9 A Sub-bidder is a person or entity who submits a Bid to a Bidder for labor, materials, furniture, furnishings or equipment for a portion of the Work.

ARTICLE 2
BIDDER'S REPRESENTATIONS

2.1 The Bidder by making a Bid represents that:

2.1.1 The Bidder has read and understands the Bidding Documents and the Bid is made in accordance therewith.

2.1.2 The Bidder has read the bidding documents, contract documents or record drawings for other portions of the Project, if any, being bid concurrently or presently under contract and understands the extent that such documentation relates to the Work for which the Bid is submitted.

2.1.3 The Bidder has visited the Project premises, or, if not yet constructed, has reviewed the documents pertaining thereto, has become familiar with local conditions under which the Work is to be performed and has correlated the Bidder's personal observations with the requirements of the proposed Contract Documents.

2.1.4 The Bid is based upon the materials, furniture, furnishings, equipment and services required by the Bidding Documents without exception.

ARTICLE 3
BIDDING DOCUMENTS

3.1 COPIES

3.1.1 Bidders may obtain complete sets of the Bidding Documents from the issuing office designated in the Advertisement or Invitation to Bid in the number and for the deposit sum, if any, stated therein. The deposit will be refunded to Bidders who submit a bona fide Bid and return the Bidding Documents in good condition within ten days after receipt of Bids. The cost of replacement of missing or damaged documents will be deducted from the deposit. A Bidder receiving a Contract award may retain the Bidding Documents and the Bidder's deposit will be refunded.

3.1.2 Bidding Documents will not be issued directly to Sub-bidders or others unless specifically offered in the Advertisement or Invitation to Bid, or in supplementary instructions to bidders.

3.1.3 Bidders shall use complete sets of Bidding Documents in preparing Bids; neither the Owner nor Architect assumes responsibility for errors or misinterpretations resulting from the use of incomplete sets of Bidding Documents.

3.1.4 In making copies of the Bidding Documents available on the above terms, the Owner and the Architect do so only for the purpose of obtaining Bids on the Work and do not confer a license or grant permission for any other use of the Bidding Documents.

3.2 INTERPRETATION OR CORRECTION OF BIDDING DOCUMENTS

3.2.1 The Bidder shall carefully study and compare the Bidding Documents with each other, and with other work being bid concurrently or presently under contract to the extent that it relates to the Work for which the Bid is submitted, shall examine the Project premises and local conditions, and shall at once report to the Architect errors, inconsistencies or ambiguities discovered.

3.2.2 Bidders and Sub-bidders requiring clarification or interpretation of the Bidding Documents shall make a written request which shall reach the Architect at least seven days prior to the date for receipt of Bids.

FIGURE 29-8. Continued

3.2.3 Interpretations, corrections and changes of the Bidding Documents will be made by Addendum. Interpretations, corrections and changes of the Bidding Documents made in any other manner will not be binding, and Bidders shall not rely upon them.

3.3 SUBSTITUTIONS

3.3.1 The materials, products and equipment described in the Bidding Documents establish a standard of required function, dimension, appearance and quality to be met by any proposed substitution.

3.3.2 No substitution will be considered prior to receipt of Bids unless written request for approval has been received by the Architect at least ten days prior to the date for receipt of Bids. Such requests shall include the name of the material or equipment for which it is to be substituted and a complete description of the proposed substitution including drawings, product data, performance and test data, and other information necessary for an evaluation. A statement setting forth changes in other materials, equipment or other portions of the Work including changes in the work of other contracts that incorporation of the proposed substitution would require shall be included. The burden of proof of the merit of the proposed substitution is upon the proposer. The Architect's decision of approval or disapproval of a proposed substitution shall be final.

3.3.3 If the Architect approves a proposed substitution prior to receipt of Bids, such approval will be set forth in an Addendum. Bidders shall not rely upon approvals made in any other manner.

3.3.4 No substitutions will be considered after the Contract award unless specifically provided in the Contract Documents.

3.4 ADDENDA

3.4.1 Addenda will be mailed or delivered to all who are known by the issuing office to have received a complete set of Bidding Documents.

3.4.2 Copies of Addenda will be made available for inspection wherever Bidding Documents are on file for that purpose.

3.4.3 No Addenda will be issued later than four days prior to the date for receipt of Bids except an Addendum withdrawing the request for Bids or one which includes postponement of the date for receipt of Bids.

3.4.4 Each Bidder shall ascertain prior to submitting a Bid that the Bidder has received all Addenda issued, and the Bidder shall acknowledge their receipt in the Bid.

ARTICLE 4
BIDDING PROCEDURES

4.1 FORM AND STYLE OF BIDS

4.1.1 Bids shall be submitted on forms identical to the form included with the Bidding Documents.

4.1.2 All blanks on the bid form shall be filled in by typewriter or manually in ink.

4.1.3 Where so indicated by the makeup of the bid form, sums shall be expressed in both words and figures, and in case of discrepancy between the two, the amount written in words shall govern.

4.1.4 Interlineations, alterations and erasures must be initialed by the signer of the Bid.

4.1.5 All requested Alternates shall be bid. If no change in the Base Bid is required, enter "No Change."

4.1.6 Where two or more Bids for designated portions of the Work have been requested, the Bidder may, without forfeiture of the bid security, state the Bidder's refusal to accept award of less than the combination of Bids stipulated by the Bidder. The Bidder shall make no additional stipulations on the bid form nor qualify the Bid in any other manner.

4.1.7 Each copy of the Bid shall include the legal name of the Bidder and a statement that the Bidder is a sole proprietor, partnership, corporation or other legal entity. Each copy shall be signed by the person or persons legally authorized to bind the Bidder to a contract. A Bid by a corporation shall further give the state of incorporation and have the corporate seal affixed. A Bid submitted by an agent shall have a current power of attorney attached certifying the agent's authority to bind the Bidder.

4.2 BID SECURITY

4.2.1 If so stipulated in the Advertisement or Invitation to Bid, or supplementary instructions to bidders, each Bid shall be accompanied by a bid security in the form and amount required, pledging that the Bidder will enter into a Contract with the Owner on the terms stated in the Bid and will, if required, furnish bonds covering the faithful performance of the Contract and payment of all obligations arising thereunder. Should the Bidder refuse to enter into such Contract or fail to furnish such bonds if required, the amount of the bid security shall be forfeited to the Owner as liquidated damages, not as a penalty. The amount of the bid security shall not be forfeited to the Owner in the event the Owner fails to comply with Subparagraph 6.2.1.

4.2.2 If a surety bond is required, it shall be written on AIA Document A310, Bid Bond, unless otherwise provided in the Bidding Documents, and the attorney-in-fact who executes the bond on behalf of the surety shall affix to the bond a certified and current copy of the power of attorney.

4.2.3 The Owner will have the right to retain the bid security of Bidders to whom an award is being considered until either (a) the Contract has been executed and bonds, if required, have been furnished, or (b) the specified time has elapsed so that Bids may be withdrawn, or (c) all Bids have been rejected.

4.3 SUBMISSION OF BIDS

4.3.1 All copies of the Bid, the bid security, if any, and other documents required to be submitted with the Bid shall be enclosed in a sealed opaque envelope. The envelope shall be addressed to the party receiving the Bids and shall be identified with the Project name, the Bidder's name and address and, if applicable, the designated portion of the Work for which the Bid is submitted. If the Bid is sent by mail, the sealed envelope shall be enclosed in a separate mailing envelope with the notation "SEALED BID ENCLOSED" on the face thereof.

4.3.2 Bids shall be deposited at the designated location prior to the time and date for receipt of Bids. Bids received after the time and date for receipt of Bids will be returned unopened.

4.3.3 The Bidder shall assume full responsibility for timely delivery at the location designated for receipt of Bids.

FIGURE 29-8. Continued

4.3.4 Oral, telephonic or telegraphic Bids are invalid and will not receive consideration.

4.4 MODIFICATION OR WITHDRAWAL OF BID

4.4.1 A Bid may not be modified, withdrawn or canceled by the Bidder during the stipulated time period following the time and date designated for the receipt of Bids, and each Bidder so agrees in submitting a Bid.

4.4.2 Prior to the time and date designated for receipt of Bids, a Bid submitted may be modified or withdrawn by notice to the party receiving Bids at the place designated for receipt of Bids. Such notice shall be in writing over the signature of the Bidder or by telegram; if by telegram, written confirmation over the signature of the Bidder shall be mailed and postmarked on or before the date and time set for receipt of Bids. A change shall be so worded as not to reveal the amount of the original Bid.

4.4.3 Withdrawn Bids may be resubmitted up to the date and time designated for the receipt of Bids provided that they are then fully in conformance with these Instructions to Interiors Bidders.

4.4.4 Bid security, if required, shall be in an amount sufficient for the Bid as modified or resubmitted.

ARTICLE 5
CONSIDERATION OF BIDS

5.1 OPENING OF BIDS

5.1.1 Unless stated otherwise in the Advertisement or Invitation to Bid, the properly identified Bids received on time will be opened publicly and will be read aloud. An abstract of the Bids will be made available to Bidders. When it has been stated that Bids will be opened privately, an abstract of the same information may, at the discretion of the Owner, be made available to the Bidders within a reasonable time.

5.2 REJECTION OF BIDS

5.2.1 The Owner shall have the right to reject any or all Bids, reject a Bid not accompanied by a required bid security or by other data required by the Bidding Documents, or reject a Bid which is in any way incomplete or irregular.

5.3 ACCEPTANCE OF BID (AWARD)

5.3.1 It is the intent of the Owner to award a Contract to the lowest responsible Bidder provided the Bid has been submitted in accordance with the requirements of the Bidding Documents and does not exceed the funds available. The Owner shall have the right to waive informalities or irregularities in a Bid received and to accept the Bid which, in the Owner's judgment, is in the Owner's own best interests.

5.3.2 The Owner shall have the right to accept Alternates in any order or combination, unless otherwise specifically provided in the Bidding Documents, and to determine the low Bidder on the basis of the sum of the Base Bid and Alternates accepted.

ARTICLE 6
POST-BID INFORMATION

6.1 CONTRACTOR'S QUALIFICATION STATEMENT

6.1.1 Bidders to whom award of a Contract is under consideration shall submit to the Architect, upon request, a properly executed AIA Document A305, Contractor's Qualification Statement, unless such a statement has been previously required and submitted as a prerequisite to the issuance of Bidding Documents.

6.2 OWNER'S FINANCIAL CAPABILITY

6.2.1 The Owner shall, at the request of the Bidder to whom award of a Contract is under consideration and no later than seven days prior to the expiration of the time for withdrawal of Bids, furnish to the Bidder reasonable evidence that financial arrangements have been made to fulfill the Owner's obligations under the Contract. Unless such reasonable evidence is furnished, the Bidder will not be required to execute the Agreement between the Owner and Contractor.

6.3 SUBMITTALS

6.3.1 The Bidder shall, as soon as practicable after notification of selection for the award of a Contract, furnish to the Owner through the Architect in writing:

.1 a designation of the Work to be performed with the Bidder's own forces;

.2 names of the manufacturers of furniture, furnishings, equipment and materials proposed for the Work; and

.3 names of persons or entities (including those who are to furnish materials or equipment fabricated to a special design and those performing installation or assembly on the premises) proposed for the principal portions of the Work.

6.3.2 The Bidder will be required to establish to the satisfaction of the Owner and Architect the reliability and responsibility of the persons or entities proposed to furnish and perform the Work described in the Bidding Documents.

6.3.3 Prior to the award of the Contract, the Architect will notify the Bidder in writing if either the Owner or Architect, after due investigation, has reasonable objection to a person or entity proposed by the Bidder. If the Owner or Architect has reasonable objection to a proposed person or entity, the Bidder may, at the Bidder's option, (1) withdraw the Bid, or (2) submit an acceptable substitute person or entity with an adjustment in the Base Bid or Alternate Bid to cover the difference in cost occasioned by such substitution. The Owner may accept the adjusted bid price or disqualify the Bidder. In the event of either withdrawal or disqualification, bid security will not forfeited.

6.3.4 Persons and entities proposed by the Bidder and to whom the Owner and Architect have made no reasonable objection must be used on the Work for which they were proposed and shall not be changed except with the written consent of the Owner and Architect.

ARTICLE 7
PERFORMANCE BOND AND PAYMENT BOND

7.1 BOND REQUIREMENTS

7.1.1 If stipulated in the Bidding Documents, the Bidder shall furnish bonds covering the faithful performance of the Contract and payment of all obligations arising thereunder. Bonds may be secured through the Bidder's usual sources.

7.1.2 If the furnishing of such bonds is stipulated in the Bidding Documents, the cost shall be included in the Bid. If the furnishing of such bonds is required after receipt of bids and before execution of the Contract, the cost of such bonds shall

FIGURE 29-8. Continued

be added to the Bid in determining the Contract Sum.

7.1.3 If the Owner requires that bonds be secured from other than the Bidder's usual sources, changes in cost will be adjusted as provided in the Contract Documents.

7.2 TIME OF DELIVERY AND FORM OF BONDS

7.2.1 The Bidder shall deliver the required bonds to the Owner not later than three days following the date of execution of the Contract. If the Work is to be commenced prior thereto in response to a letter of intent, the Bidder shall, prior to commencement of the Work, submit evidence satisfactory to the Owner that such bonds will be furnished and delivered in accordance with this Subparagraph 7.2.1.

7.2.2 Unless otherwise provided, the bonds shall be written on AIA Document A312, Performance Bond and Payment Bond. Both bonds shall be written in the amount of the Contract Sum.

7.2.3 The bonds shall be dated on or after the date of the Contract.

7.2.4 The Bidder shall require the attorney-in-fact who executes the required bonds on behalf of the surety to affix thereto a certified and current copy of the power of attorney.

ARTICLE 8
FORM OF AGREEMENT BETWEEN OWNER AND CONTRACTOR

8.1 FORM TO BE USED

8.1.1 Unless otherwise required in the Bidding Documents, the Agreement for the Work will be written on AIA Document A171, Standard Form of Agreement Between Owner and Contractor for Furniture, Furnishings and Equipment Where the Basis of Payment is a Stipulated Sum.

FIGURE 29-8. Continued

BID FORM FOR FURNISHINGS CONTRACT

CONTRACT NUMBER: ______________________________

PROJECT: ______________________________

BID OF: ______________________________

(name of bidder)

- a Corporation organized under the laws of the State of ______________
- a Partnership, with the following individuals as partners:

____

- a Limited Liability Company with the following member as General Manager:

____

- a Sole proprietor.

Present Bid To:

____

At: Hunter / Noble Inc.
3114 N. 38th St.
Phoenix, AZ

The Undersigned acknowledges receipt and review of the Project Documents, consisting of ________ pages of drawings and ________ pages of written specifications, and addenda No. ________ through ________, and hereby proposes to furnish all materials, labor, and miscellany necessary to provide and install the furniture and furnishings as specified in the aforementioned documents.

The Undersigned further agrees to hold his/her Bid open for thirty (30) days after the receipt of bids. Should the bidder be awarded the contract, he/she shall furnish a Performance Bond and a Labor and Materials Payment Bond in accordance the General Conditions of the Bid, to the owner within ten days after award of bid.

No substitutions or exclusions to what was specified shall be allowed. Any bidder not bidding on all items as specified shall be disqualified.

The undersigned agrees to supply and perform, in accordance with the specifications, all of the materials, labor, and miscellany as specified for:

______________________________Dollars ($______________).

The Bid Bond and all other required documentation is attached by the undersigned bidder.

It is understood that the owner reserves the right to reject any or all bids, to withhold the award of bid for any reason, and reserves the right to hold all bids for thirty (30) days after the date of opening.

Date of Bid: ______________________

Name of Bidder: ______________________________

Address of Bidder: ______________________________

Authorized Officer: ______________________________

FIGURE 29-9. Sample bid form.

The *performance bond* is required of the winning bidder as a guarantee that the designer or vendor will complete the work as specified. It also protects the client from any loss up to the amount of the bond as a result of the failure of the designer or vendor to perform according to the contract. It is customary for the performance bond to be an amount equal to 100 percent of the value of the bid contract. The designer or vendor, however, pays a surety company a smaller percentage for the bond insurance. This actual amount varies, based on the actual project conditions and the surety company. The performance bond is returned after completion of the project.

A *labor and materials payment bond* is required of the winning bidder to guarantee that the designer or vendor will be responsible for paying for all the materials and labor that have been contracted for in the event that the designer or vendor defaults on the project. This is to prevent the client from being held responsible to subcontractors for goods not delivered. This bond is also customarily an amount equal to 100 percent of the contract price. It also is returned after completion of the project.

A legal recourse that is related to the labor and materials payment bond is the *mechanic's lien*. This lien is an action filed by the contractor, subcontractor, or possibly the designer with the county clerk to prevent the owner of the property from giving or conveying title or a deed of trust to the named property until the mechanic who has filed the lien has been paid. In this situation, a mechanic is one who is an employee, subcontractor, or vendor who has been hired to do work by the client or a general contractor.

More simply stated, contractors, subcontractors, their vendors, and, in some states, architects and interior designers may find it necessary to file a lien against the property in order to insure that the owner of the property will pay the contractor any moneys due. A properly filed lien prevents the owner of the property from selling or conveying title of the property until the lien has been settled. Not all states have provisions that fully allow for a mechanic's lien. The designer should check with the attorney general or registrar of contractors of his or her state to clarify how liens might affect the workings of the designer.

Bid Opening

Almost always a bid proposal is required to be sent to the client or designer in a sealed envelope. The exact labeling of the envelope, where it is to be delivered, to whom, and by what day and time are stated in the instructions to bidders. If a bid is delivered after the day and time specified in the instructions, it will be left unopened and rejected. Any bid received that does not conform to the instructions can be rejected. It is also customary that bids not be withdrawn after the closing date and time for the receipt of bids, even if the bid opening has not yet taken place. However, the instructions may stipulate the conditions under which a bid can be withdrawn, especially if there are errors in it that would create a hardship for the bidder. In almost all situations, bidders should not be allowed to modify or alter a bid once it has been received and opened.

Bids for governmental agencies or public companies, such as utilities, are required to have the *bid opening* at an open public meeting. The place and time is noted in the invitation to bidders. At that meeting, the client or person charged with administering the bid announces each bidder and his or her bid price. The client usually does not award the bid at that time. The invitation to bid should have informed bidders about the length of time that the client will take to evaluate the bids and to make the decision as to who will be awarded the contract. Although most public agencies most likely take the lowest bid, they are not bound to do so if there are legitimate reasons for rejecting the lowest bid. Care must be taken by the client, therefore, not to announce that firm X is the lowest bidder at the bid opening, since this announcement could later bind the agency, even if it wanted to reject the bid.

For private companies, the bid opening is not required by law to be open to the public. This means that each bidder might not have the opportunity to know what the competition has bid, if his or her own bid is low in comparison to all the others, or if the bidder made an error in reporting his or her prices. According to Justin Sweet (1985, p. 469), the courts expect the client who uses a closed bid opening to act in good faith with the bidders if a bid comes in substantially lower than all other bids and not penalize the bidder who makes a legitimate mistake.

Depending on the provisions in the contract between the interior designer and the client, the designer will assist the client in evaluating the bids. This service can help a client interpret appropriateness of substitutions or any conditions that bidders may have included in their bid document. After a reasonable length of time, the contractor or client will award the bid based on the bid values, negotiate further (assuming there are small changes that need to be made) with the winning bidder, or reject all bids and consider rebidding the project.

Bid Award Notification

After the bids have been evaluated and a decision has been made as to who the successful bidder is, each bidder must be notified of the result. A simple form letter is usually sent to each one of the unsuccessful bidders, thanking each one. It is not legally necessary to inform them as to who the successful bidder is or the amount of the bid. It is often a good idea to include a comment that the bids of the unsuccessful bidders will be held for a certain length of time, as stated in the invitation to bid, in the event that the successful bidder does withdraw. This means that the bids of unsuccessful bidders remain valid offers until the end of the holding period.

Should the owner wish to speed up the actual ordering and/or construction process, a *letter of intent* is sent to the winning bidder. This letter is a signal to the supplier or contractors to begin work (see Figure 29-10) on the project. Other documents that are used concerning the winning bidder and the continuation of the project are discussed in Chapter 30.

Modifications

Modifications are changes in the construction documents. If the changes are made before the contract has been awarded, they would be made by an addendum. Changes made after the contract has been awarded is made by the use of a change order.

Addenda

Addenda are additions or changes made to the contract documents once they are in the hands of contractors and vendors and they determine their prices for the project. A change in the project may result because the client wants to alter some part of the project, even at this late time. Clarifications also may be needed because of a question from one or more of the bidders or because of errors or technical requirements regarding the documents that are discovered during the bid process. Addenda are used to clarify these changes in relationship to the previously prepared contract and/or construction documents. Addenda become part of the contract documents.

Each addendum must be written and sent to all bidders. Corrections or clarifications should not be made or accepted orally. All addenda should be

LETTER OF INTENT

1999 EDITION
FORM IIDA03L

Consultation with legal counsel is recommended regarding the completion or modification of this document.

AUTHORIZATION

made as of the ____________ *day of* ____________ *in the year of* ____________
[in words, indicate day, month and year]

TO *the Client*

COMPANY ____________

ADDRESS ____________

PHONE/FAX/E-MAIL ____________

REGARDING

PROJECT NAME ____________

PROJECT NUMBER ____________

Dear (Client) ____________,

This letter will act as authorization for (Interior Designer) ____________ *to proceed with professional services in accordance with our proposed Agreement dated* ____________, *pending its execution.*

Please indicate your approval for (Interior Designer) ____________ *to proceed by signing both copies of this letter and returning one to me.*

Sincerely,

(Interior Designer)

Approved as a duly authorized signatory and representative of (Client) ____________

NAME ____________ TITLE ____________

SIGNATURE ____________ DATE ____________

I|I D|A

FIGURE 29-10. A letter of intent—Form IIDA3L. (Reproduced with permission, International Interior Design Association)

prepared as quickly and as clearly as possible. They should come from the person who is responsible for creating the documents. If an allied professional or other design team member finds a questionable item, it should be called to the attention of the specification writer, and that person should prepare and send the addendum. When addenda are mailed to bidders, there must be sufficient time for bidders to react to the addenda prior to the close of bid. Recall that notification begins upon receipt of the notification, not at the time of mailing. Addenda supersede and supplement the appropriate part or parts of the construction documents or bidding documents.

According to Harold J. Rosen (1981, p. 177), addenda are used to provide any of the following kinds of information to bidders:

1. Correct errors and omissions.
2. Clarify ambiguities.
3. Add to or reduce the scope of the work.
4. Provide additional information that can affect the bid prices.
5. Change the time and place for receipt of bids.
6. Change the quality of the work.
7. Issue additional names of qualified "or equal" products.

Of course, other conditions or situations may occur that would require a change in the documents prior to awarding of the contract.

Note that an addendum can also be used to issue instructions after the awarding of the contract has occurred. However, when this term for a change is used at this time, it is only with regard to a change order to the winning bidder or contractor.

Change Orders

Changes or modifications made after the contract is awarded is generally and most commonly referred to as change orders. *Change orders* are written permissions or instructions concerning any aspect of the project that modify design concepts, construction designs, or product specifications. Change orders happen for reasons that are similar to those for addenda. Changes may occur during the course of the project. Perhaps the client wants a window moved to a new location. Maybe the paint color for the doctor's suite must be different. A lighting fixture specified in the restaurant dining room might not be available by the time the project is underway. Any of these examples and many more can occur during the actual construction, ordering, and installation of the project. The use of change orders is also discussed in Chapter 30, and an example is shown in Figure 30-1.

It is good professional practice for designers not to allow any change to occur without a written change order being issued to all necessary parties. Unfortunately, many designers and contractors allow changes to occur without giving written authorization or notification to the various parties. Clients have been known to tell the contractor to make a change and then forget to inform the interior designer. A seemingly simple change can, in fact, be quite a big deal. If the change is major, such as moving a window, it can affect other trades, schedules, space layouts, product specifications, to name the most obvious. A good working relationship between the designer and the client and other stakeholders, as well as professional project management by the interior designer, can prevent changes being made without proper authorization and notification.

Changes made after the contract has been awarded also can result in additional charges. Just as the interior designer wants to be compensated to replan a space once the client has given approval, a contractor or vendor will want to be compensated for making changes after the contract is in process. Changes made at this point usually cost the client much more than if the issue had been addressed and changes had been made prior to the issuing of contracts. For example, if the client approved a certain flooring material as part of the bid and then, for some reason (not the fault of the vendor or designer), decided to change the material, the new product could be significantly higher in price, even if essentially the same grade of material as the original is used.

Submittals

Sometimes at the beginning of the contract administration or perhaps during the course of this phase, materials, drawings, or documents may need to be provided by the vendor for approval. As a group, these are referred to as *submittals*. For example, the vendor may have to submit items such as finish samples for furniture, literature from manufacturers, or test results or certificates related to life safety code requirements. Submittals of shop drawings for custom pieces or special installations also may be required of the vendor.

In addition, the vendor may have to provide other submittals. One would be updates to the designer and owner about construction or delivery schedules. In some cases, the bid documents and instructions to bidders may require that mock-ups be provided by the vendor. A *mock-up* might be a full-scale wall painted or otherwise finished to specifications so that the client and designer can check the colors, texture, pattern, and so on; setups of systems furniture so that the client can see the actual arrangement of the furniture; even the construction of a full-scale room, such as a patient room in a hospital, with all furniture, finishes, and equipment shown.

At some point, in a project that involves bid documents, as described in this chapter, it will be necessary to order the furniture, furnishings, and equipment. The process and documents associated with ordering products is discussed in Chapter 30. Of course, this process is very similar for projects that are not bid. Project finalization and postordering issues and forms are covered in Chapter 31.

Summary

It is important for interior designers whose practices involve any structural design work or formal bid specifications to be familiar with contract documents and the bidding process. Commercial designers normally are familiar with them, but residential designers must also understand how to prepare contract documents if they become involved in remodeling projects or custom manufacturing of products. There is a substantial amount of terminology associated with contract documents, and the student and professional should be familiar with this terminology.

Floor plans and other working drawings, equipment plans keyed to equipment lists or formal specifications, and various schedules are all part of the contract documents. Most familiar to designers are the formal specifications needed when the client requires competitive bids. Four different kinds of bids are discussed in this chapter: proprietary, descriptive, performance, and reference. For designers who are not commonly associated with the bid process, this chapter also discusses how this important method operates.

Once the bids have been received and the contract for the products and construction has been awarded, the project moves into the contract administration phase. This is the phase when the actual construction, ordering of products, and eventual installation of the FF&E occur. Information related to these activities will be covered in the next two chapters.

REFERENCES

Clough, Richard H. 1986. *Construction Contracting*, 5th ed. New York: John Wiley.

Cushman, Robert F., James C. Dobbs, eds. 1991. *Design Professional's Handbook of Business and Law.* New York: John Wiley.

Haviland, David, ed. 1994. *The Architect's Handbook of Professional Practice, Student Edition.* Washington, DC: AIA Press.

International Interior Design Association. 1999. *Forms and Documents Manual.* Chicago, IL: International Interior Design Association.

Lohmann, William T. 1992. *Construction Specifications. Managing the Review Process.* Boston, MA: Butterworth Architecture.

Meier, Hans W. 1978. *Construction Specifications Handbook*, 2nd ed. New York: Prentice-Hall.

O'Leary, Arthur F. 1992. *Construction Administration in Architectural Practice.* New York: McGraw-Hill.

Poage, Waller S. 1987. *Plans, Specs and Contracts for Building Professionals.* Kingston, MA: R. S. Means.

Reznikoff, S. C. 1989. *Specifications for Commercial Interiors*, rev. ed. New York: Watson-Guptill.

———. 1979. *Specifications for Commercial Interiors.* New York: Watson-Guptill.

Rosen, Harold J. 1981. *Construction Specifications Writing*, 2nd ed. New York: John Wiley.

Simmons, H. Leslie. 1985. *The Specifications Writer's Handbook.* New York: John Wiley.

Stasiowski, Frank. 1985. *Negotiating Higher Design Fees.* New York: Watson-Guptill.

Sweet, Justin. 1985. *Legal Aspects of Architecture, Engineering and the Construction Process*, 3rd ed. St. Paul, MN: West Publishing.

Thompson, Jo Anne Asher, ed. 1992. *ASID Professional Practice Manual.* New York: Watson-Guptill.

Wakita, Osamu A., and Richard M. Linde. 1999. *The Professional Practice of Architectural Detailing*, 3rd ed. New York: John Wiley.

———. 1984. *The Professional Practice of Architectural Working Drawings.* New York: John Wiley.

Chapter 30

Contract Administration

It is difficult to define when one phase of the project ends and the next begins. Yet, it is generally agreed that once the bids have been received and the contracts have been awarded for the primary work, the last phase of the project begins. In contract administration, activity centers on the actual construction, placing of orders, and completion of the project. At this critical point in the project, all the other work that has been performed by the interior designer and others come together to make design concepts become reality. All of the activities and responsibilities discussed in this chapter and the next require that the designer take utmost care in the execution of tasks, responsibilities, and paperwork and their supervision, all of which are part of project management.

Exactly what role the interior designer plays during contract administration depends on the laws and regulations within the jurisdiction of the project and the scope of services specified in the contract. The interior designer's role can be as uncomplicated as the ordering of merchandise and the checking to be sure that it has been delivered and placed properly. It can be very complex and involve activities such as obtaining permits, coordinating the procurement and supervising the installation of the FF&E, supervising the installation or construction work of subcontractors, conducting site inspections, and issuing documents related to the conclusion of the project work. Or it can be anything in between.

Most of the time, the interior designer is indirectly involved in the construction of the building or interior. As the reader knows, the interior designer is very limited in what he or she can do concerning load-bearing construction. But this does not mean that the interior designer should be ignorant of the tasks and the paperwork that are necessary during this phase of the project.

This chapter begins with a brief discussion of the paperwork associated with contract administration that might be part of the designer's responsibilities. Because so many interior designers sell merchandise, the chapter provides a more detailed explanation of the paperwork involved in procuring merchandise for the client.

Construction and Procurement Administration

With the exception of the installation of architectural finishes and the delivery of furniture, most construction or remodeling that is done on either residential or commercial sites requires a *building permit*. A building permit is an authorization from the city (or other jurisdiction) so that the plans and specifications submitted for construction meet local codes and regulations. It allows the construction work to proceed.

In order to obtain a building permit, sets of construction documents along with a permit application are submitted to the building department within the jurisdiction of the project. The building department reviews the plans (or performs a *plan check*) to ensure that the documents meet local building, fire safety, accessibility, and other codes that may apply to the particular project.* In some cases, the plans may be reviewed by the local fire marshall, the public works department, and the state (or provincial) health department. Plan checkers may find problems with the drawings and will red line the plans. Red lining refers to the fact that plan checkers use a red pencil to make notations and comments on the plans, indicating problem areas. A meeting is held with the building officials and the client, or the client's agent (such as the interior designer or architect) to go over the plans. Depending on the quality of the drawings at this stage, a permit may be issued or the plans may have to be redone and reviewed again before a permit can be issued.

The interior designer may have been retained to work with the client in selecting contractors and initiating the construction contracts. Throughout the construction process, building inspectors will inspect the work. They will check to see that the project is built according to the plans, specifications, and appropriate methods. The interior designer (or general contractor) also will inspect the project. If an interior designer is not allowed to give direct supervisory instructions to subcontractors, he or she will provide memos to either the client or the general contractor on discrepancies or changes that are needed.

When the project is ready to begin, it is very important that the client understand the potential for disruption in the family or work environment. Remodeling a home cannot be done without some mess and inconvenience to the family. Major remodeling or additions might make it necessary for the family to move to other quarters for several months during the project. For commercial remodeling projects, few businesses can survive if they must totally shut down, even if the project involves only installing new carpet. If the client is moving into a new facility, the interior designer may include move-management in his or her scope of services. *Move-management* can include a wide range of services to help the client schedule packing and moving furniture and belongings into the new home or commercial site. For example, when a move is involved, additional scheduling must be planned so that employees can pack up their belongings that are in desks and file cabinets or inventory and mark items that need to be moved to the new location. Obviously, this would be true of a family as well.

Commercial projects often must be scheduled outside normal business hours, with pricing that includes overtime for installers and delivery persons. Special permits for the construction and even delivery and/or installation of furniture may be required. Many times these types of moves are made on the weekends; the move begins at the end of business on Friday, and the employees move back in on Monday morning. It can be a Herculean effort to schedule all that must be done, but it is an effort that is part of the interior designer's responsibilities.

* Remember, the plans must meet the codes that apply in the jurisdiction of the actual project site, not that of the interior designer's office location.

Even if the interior designer is not directly responsible for making inspections during construction, the designer retains a responsibility to the client during this time. Clients become very nervous during a project. They see the changes taking place, but the changes always seem to happen too slowly. It is very important for the designer to spend time explaining how the project will proceed, prior to initiating orders and starting the construction process. The designer needs to go over the schedule with the client at the very beginning of the project, so that the client has a chance to question the designer and understand why the ceramic tile will not be installed until after the walls have been painted or why it is not a good idea to install the carpet until the painting and several other trade activities have been completed.

It is very important that the client understand the scheduling of a project. The designer should spend a lot of time showing the client how each part of the construction and finishing of the project will be done and approximately when each phase will occur. There are reasons that projects often only have one or two tradespeople working on the job site at one time. The designer and tradespeople understand the problems that can occur when multiple tradespeople are on the job site at the same time. However, clients generally do not understand that problems can occur in this situation. For example, rough plumbing and rough wiring are done when the building is in the same condition, but it is not a good idea for the designer to schedule both tradespeople to do their work on the same day. The plumbers will need to be where the electricians are, and vice versa. General contractors and job foremen have had to break up fights when electricians have unintentionally dropped wiring on the head of plumbers. An entire project has been known to shut down because nonunion furniture installers was on a job site while union workers were also on the job site finishing their work on the project.

The designer needs to schedule regular meetings with the contractor as well as make regular visits to the construction site. In this way, the designer will know what is going on and can easily keep the client informed of the progress of the project in relation to the interior designer's contract responsibilities. Designers issue *progress reports* to the client so that the client knows what is going on. This is especially helpful in those cases in which the client wishes to be very involved in the project. For out-of-town projects, the designer must include the expenses of traveling to the project site in the contract and have these visits approved by the client prior to the visit. Design decisions regarding any necessary changes in the plans or the orders that are being placed for goods are far more effectively made with this kind of coordination.

Clients can become quite frustrated and stressed over the myriad decisions that they must make during the course of the project or during construction. The designer needs constantly to assure the client that everything is under control and to clarify where the project is on or off schedule. This, of course, means that the designer must be fully informed of the progress of the project. Holding weekly meetings with the client is not always necessary, but having periodic meetings with the client to discuss the schedule and what will be happening next are important to keeping the client comfortable with the progress of the project. Many large design firms have found that assigning an installation supervisor, in addition to a design project manager, is a very good investment for efficient project administration.

If problems occur that affect the timely completion of the project, it is important that the designer inform the client immediately. The concept of taking care of things and thinking that "what the client doesn't know won't hurt him or her" might sound good, but clients do need to know when things are going awry. As long as the designer or the firm is working on a solution to the problem, the client most likely will not become unduly nervous when the designer calls to inform him or her that all the furniture for the client's project was damaged in a shipping accident. Obviously, the client will be nervous about hearing something like this, but if the designer has a solution prior to calling the client, the client will feel that the designer has already taken care of things.

Changes or corrections made because of errors and omissions that have occurred during the construction need to be brought to the attention of the designer. Changes can easily impact the aesthetic and functional goals of the project. Too often, the designer gets cut out of many of these decisions as the contractors and the client rush to complete the project. Changes should only be done when a change order has been issued (see Figure 30-1). This form was discussed in Chapter 29.

It should be noted that contractors often bid projects very low. Changes during the course of construction can be charged at far higher prices than the original bid. The designer must caution the client about making arbitrary changes on the project. "It sure would be nice to have a window on that wall of the bedroom," says the client to the contractor. "Yes, I suppose it would. But that window will now cost you about $700, since the wall already has been framed. It would have cost only about $200 if you had thought of it sooner."

If the designer has a minor role in the construction process, his or her energies will shift to the administration of the ordering of the goods. At an appropriate time, the FF&E for the project will be ordered. The ordering of architectural finishes is often included in the general construction contract rather than in the interiors contract, although this varies. The reader will recall from Chapter 19, anything that has to do with the actual building of the structure or that becomes physically attached to the structure is considered real property. In construction, this is often referred to as *capital construction* or *capital improvements*. The furniture, fixtures, and any equipment that is movable is generally not purchased as part of the capital construction. These various furniture items are considered *movable equipment*, in construction terms.

When it is time for the designer to order movable equipment, the designer will either do so directly or will coordinate with vendors who will do so. Now let us look at the paperwork and process involved in the ordering of goods for a client.

Order Processing

Order processing can be a responsibility of the designer, who also has developed the concepts for the project, or it can be the responsibility of the supplier. As has already been mentioned, many residential designers and small interior design studios, regardless of their design specialty, also sell merchandise to clients. The interior design firm or vendor responsible for purchasing and delivering merchandise is required to order, track, and deliver perhaps several hundred—even thousands—of pieces of furniture, fixtures, and equipment.

Many things can and often do go wrong when interior designers order merchandise. Product numbers can be transposed, the manufacturer may put the wrong item in the box, or the merchandise may be damaged in transit. Sometimes the ship date is weeks after the move-in date, the client may not pay his or her bill, the client may claim that the merchandise delivered is not the merchandise specified, and many other problems can easily and commonly happen to designers who sell merchandise. It is, therefore, important for the design firm to develop clear policies about how to go about ordering merchandise and handling the paperwork involved in ordering merchandise. This is no

Change Order

Project Name____________________ Change Order #: ____________
Project #: ____________________
Date Prepared ____________________ Phone: ____________
Project Designer/Manager: ______________

Change Requested by:

Description of Change to Project or Contract:

Cost Estimate for Change (Attach Additional Paperwork if Necessary)

This is an Authorization to proceed with the change as detailed in **Change Order** ________.

Authorized Agent (Client)	*Date*	*Authorized Agent (Design Firm)*	*Date*

Only valid if signed by *both* Agents

These changes will impact Final Completion Due Date until: ___________. (No Change)

FIGURE 30-1. A sample change order form.

time for sloppy handwriting, oral agreements, procrastination in reviewing paperwork, or even the lack of careful consideration of a client's credit worthiness. Profit margins on merchandise are too small and competition is too keen for any firm, large or small, to allow itself to be careless in conducting order processing.

The ideal situation is to have an expediter—an individual who is familiar with the company's paperwork system and the requirements of the many manufacturers—be responsible for this order processing and subsequent tracking function. However, in most firms, this function is the responsibility of the designer who has been put in charge of the project, an office manager, or an assistant office manager. In retail stores, some of this detail is taken care of by others. Whatever the case, the designer should have a working knowledge of the paperwork system and terminology related to paperwork in the interior design office. This chapter covers the kinds of forms that are generally used, including the purchase order, acknowledgment, and invoice. It also provides additional information about shipping concerns and contract administration.

Credit Application

Interior designers specify and sell thousands of dollars worth of products to their residential and/or commercial clients. Unfortunately, some of these clients turn out to be bad credit risks. Therefore, interior designers need to have policies about investigating the credit worthiness of clients before they special-order merchandise or begin extensive design services. Firms that display items on a showroom floor or in inventory may find it impractical to require a credit check for all purchases, since many sales may be "cash and carry." Management may decide, with the advice of the firm's accountant, that special-order purchases or design fees over some specific dollar amount require that a credit application be completed by the prospective client.

A credit application form should be easy for the client to fill out. After it has been completed, the form should be turned over to a financial institution or a credit agency for review and recommendation. Although the firm should take the opinion of the financial institution or credit agency very seriously, the final decision as to whether or not to extend credit to the potential client should be that of the owner or the appropriate manager.

A credit application never provides 100 percent assurance as to the credit worthiness or good intentions of a client. However, the procedure gives the design firm a greater opportunity to work with clients who will honor their financial obligations.

Confirmation of Purchase, Purchase Agreement, or Proposal

Many firms proceed with ordering merchandise on the basis of a verbal agreement given by the client. As the reader will recall from Chapter 19, a verbal contract for the sale of goods whose value is over $500 is not legally binding on the client. For this reason, many firms require that a *confirmation of purchase*—also called a sales agreement, a purchase agreement, or a contract proposal—be completed and signed by the client. This form legally requires the client to fulfill his or her financial responsibility to the designer. Company policy should be clear that no furniture or furnishings should be ordered or begun until a signed purchase agreement has been obtained from the client.

The design firm should use a two-page (or longer) form so that the design firm and the client will have a record of the sale (see Figure 30-2). When it is signed by the client, the confirmation becomes a legal contract for selling the described merchandise. The designer must sell the described merchandise at the prices quoted, and the client must pay for that same merchandise. To be legally binding, the form must contain quantities, descriptions, and prices. It

112699

CUNNINGHAMS INTERIORS

BETTY J. UPTON, OWNER

2221 EAST SEVENTH AVENUE • FLAGSTAFF, ARIZONA 86004 • 520-526-0633

SALES AGREEMENT

Date of Order____________________19____

Purchaser______________________________Phone______________

Address____

Street City State Zip

Install at: Name______________________________Phone______________

Address____

Street City State Zip

SPECIAL INSTRUCTIONS:____________________________________

MATERIALS AND SPECIFICATIONS	Price Each	TOTAL

Additional charges may be incurred for undisclosed defects or conditions that was not identified as part of the estimate.

- ☐ Subject to final billing for floor preparation
- ☐ Subject to final measurements
- ☐ The buyer has provided own measurements and is therefore responsible for all amounts herein
- ☐ The buyer is responsible for protection of his articles when floor or wall preparations are done.

TOTAL MATERIALS $________

Labor ________

Sub Total ________

Tax ________

Total ________

Read the back of this page before signing. The provisions on the back side of this page are part of this agreement.

Deposit Due________ Deposit Paid ________

Sales Representative________________ CK# ________ Balance Due $________

Purchaser____________________

FIGURE 30-2. A sales agreement (or confirmation of purchase), used as the contract for the sale of merchandise. (Reproduced with permission, Betty Upton, Cunninghams Interiors, Flagstaff, AZ)

is impractical for a firm to use a series of these forms for a large volume of items. In such cases, a statement such as, "The undersigned agrees to purchase the items described per the attached list" will suffice.

The terms and conditions of the sale must be stated on the proposal agreement, and the client must be made aware of the terms (see Figure 30-3). Terms and conditions might relate to partial deliveries, changes in the job site, warehousing when the client is not ready to accept delivery, and warranties. These terms and conditions should be prepared with the advice of the firm's attorney.

Do not forget to have the client sign the confirmation. The client's signature is important for creating a legally enforceable contract for the sale of goods. Ordering merchandise without obtaining the client's signature is risky, because, without a signed confirmation document, the firm has no concrete evidence that the client has agreed to purchase the goods.

Many small design firms, especially sole practitioners, use the purchase order (discussed in the next section) as a confirmation of purchase. The argument is that the residential client, in particular, does not like to sign a lot of documents during the design process. Making this judgment call is up to the owner. It is more difficult for the designer and owner of the firm to control proprietary information, such as pricing, which the designer may wish to include on the purchase order, if the purchase order also serves as the confirmation of purchase. It is better business practice today, since clients are more willing to balk or threaten to file all sorts of liability lawsuits, to use a confirmation that has been signed or at least initialed by the client before ordering goods.

It should be noted that a designer who is engaged in commercial design will also receive purchase orders from clients. In some ways, these can be considered a confirmation of purchase, although since they come from the client, they are really a purchase order that signifies the buying relationship. Businesses are used to issuing a purchase order to proceed with a furniture order. It may also be faxed or E-mailed. As clients become more and more comfortable with purchasing goods over the Internet or by fax, even the smaller design firm must become familiar with these methods of confirming and ordering merchandise for interior design projects.

Purchase Orders

One of the most important forms of paperwork is the *purchase order*, often referred to as a PO. The interior designer uses the purchase order to initiate orders for merchandise and services from manufacturers, tradespeople and craftspeople, and other vendors. Additionally, many interior designers use purchase orders to initiate orders for supplies or other items that are used by the design firm.

The purchase order must be designed so that all the information that the vendor or supplier needs to complete the order quickly and correctly can be easily found. Considering the scope of projects and the number of different clients that a design firm may be dealing with at any one time, it becomes apparent that the format must be standardized and must complement the recording methods of the remaining paperwork and accounting systems used by the firm.

All firms, regardless of their size, should have a policy prohibiting telephone orders. It is even scarier to think of designers placing orders over their cell phones while they are in their car! In any case, many manufacturers do not honor telephone orders until the written order has been received. Telephone orders for any kind of product or service can lead to making mistakes in interpreting verbal instructions or in a duplication of orders and can leave the

FACILITEC
INTERIORS FOR
BUSINESS

4501 EAST MCDOWELL RD.

PHOENIX, AZ 85008

PHONE 602/275-0101

FAX 602/275-0202

TERMS AND CONDITIONS

Applicant (hereafter referred to as **Customer**) agrees that the extension of credit by **Facilitec, Inc.** (hereafter referred to as **Facilitec**) shall be subject to and in consideration of the following Terms and Conditions:

1. Payment is due net 30 days from the invoice date. The **Customer** warrants and affirms that it is financially able to meet the commitments made to **Facilitec** and will pay promptly when due any invoice rendered by **Facilitec** on or before the due date set forth on each invoice. Any deposits required by the manufacturers will be billed to **Customer** and are due upon receipt.

2. The **Customer** should understand that **Facilitec** invoices for product as it is received at the **Facilitec** warehouse or at the job site. **Facilitec** cannot control the schedules of the manufacturers, therefore, multiple invoices can occur on a proposal. It is the **Customer's** responsibility to match the invoices to the corresponding **Facilitec** proposal. If the **Customer** requires a deviation from **Facilitec's** normal billing procedures, additional charges may be applicable.

3. **Customer** agrees to pay a finance charge of 1.5% per month (annual percentage rate of 18%) on all past due balances. Balances are past due after thirty (30) days from the invoice date.

4. At any time, any invoice is delinquent, the **Customer** understands that **Facilitec** may, at it's sole option, suspend credit terms to the **Customer**. If any legal action is required to collect monies due to **Facilitec**, the **Customer** promises to pay, in addition to finance charge, all costs of collection, including attorney's fees.

5. Partial shipments: **Facilitec** agrees to make every effort to deliver and install all products as quickly as possible. However, due to manufacturers shipping schedules and methods, **Facilitec** may only be able to deliver and install portions of the job at a time. **Customer** agrees to pay 90% of invoice amounts and may withhold 10% until completion of the job.

6. Storage: If **Customer** is unable or unwilling to accept installation or delivery of the products according to the specified schedule, the product may be stored at the **Customer's** request in the **Facilitec** warehouse, solely as a convenience to the **Customer. Customer** shall pay 90% of the invoice amount within thirty (30) days of the invoice date. In addition, **Customer** shall pay a warehouse charge of 1% per month of the invoice amount of such products so warehoused, payable monthly.

7. If **Customer** cancels an order with **Facilitec,** cancellation fees may be applicable.

Company Name	Authorized Signature
Company Address	Print Authorized Signature
Date	Phone Number

FIGURE 30-3. Typical terms and conditions on the back side of a confirmation of purchase. (Reproduced with permission, Facilitec Interiors, Inc., Phoenix, AZ)

design firm responsible for paying for unwanted products. Designers should use the telephone to find out about product availability or to request that yardages of fabrics be held, pending a confirming purchase order, but should not let the telephone substitute for proper paperwork.

Another very good procedure used by many smaller firms is to request a cutting for approval (CFA) from fabric suppliers before the order actually has been placed. This notation can go on the purchase order if time is of the essence, or a separate form can be faxed to the fabric supplier so that the sample will be received in a timely fashion. When the sample has been received and approved, a notice can go to the supplier to proceed with the order. Of course, this same CFA procedure can be applied to wall coverings, floorings, and specialty finishes of many kinds. What this procedure does is help to ensure that the color of current stock will work with all the other materials that will be used.

Many firms now order from vendors electronically. Purchase orders are prepared and faxed to appropriate vendors. When the designer faxes a purchase order, it is a good idea for the designer to have the fax machine set so that a transmission report will be printed for each order and page (see Figure 30-4). This provides a record that the fax was actually sent to the correct party. Vendors often fax back an acknowledgment, showing the receipt and confirming the order.

Many suppliers are able to accommodate E-mail order entry. In this case, the designer can send a purchase order either directly from his or her order system as an attachment to an E-mail. Due to possible system incompatibility, the attachment should be sent in ASCII type or as a text file so that the vendor is assured of being able to read the attachment. Although, at this time, only larger design firms use this procedure, it is something that all interior designers who wish to purchase goods for clients must eventually master.

Larger office furnishings dealers and retail showrooms utilize direct ordering to some vendors via E-mail. In the most sophisticated arrangement, once the client has signed an order confirmation and has provided a purchase order, the design firm can E-mail the order directly to the manufacturer. Copies of these E-mail orders should be printed so that the design firm will have a hard-copy backup to the electronic message. While ordering by fax is becoming commonplace, in a few more years, E-mail ordering will be a normal process for most design firms, regardless of their size.

Whether the order is placed by mail, fax, or E-mail, purchase orders play an important role for the design firm that sells merchandise to their clients. The first role, of course, is that it serves as the means of obtaining the needed goods and services in the client's interests. A second important role of the purchase order is that it acts as a record of all outstanding orders. This role plays a part in the financial accounting of the firm for income tax and loan application purposes. A third role of the purchase order is that it acts as a control mechanism for billing clients. Many small firms with a very simple paperwork system use the purchase order as a delivery ticket as well. What is shown as delivered on the form keys the bookkeeper to send the necessary billing to clients. A fourth role is that it can be used for checking the correct pricing of various suppliers. If the supplier acknowledges a price that is different from the one shown on the purchase order, the designer should immediately find out what has caused the discrepancy.

What the exact content and format of the purchase order will be should be established by the needs of the individual firm and its accounting practices. Figure 30-5 shows an example of a typical purchase order. The following information should be a part of the purchase order, either as preprinted information or left as blank spaces:

```
                    **********************
                    ***   TX REPORT    ***
                    **********************

TRANSMISSION OK

TX/RX NO                0833
CONNECTION TEL
CONNECTION ID
ST. TIME                09/18 13:10
USAGE T                 00'34
PGS. SENT                 1
RESULT                  OK
```

PURCHASE ORDER

№ 13374

G. S. HINSEN COMPANY

Grace's Plaza, 2133 Bandywood Drive, Nashville, TN 37215
(615) 383-6440 FAX (615) 269-5130

CONTACT Rhett Black	TELEPHONE	FAX	DATE 9/18/00		
TO Murals / Pacific Showroom West			SHIP TO G S Hinsen		
ADDRESS			ADDRESS		
CITY	STATE	ZIP	CITY	STATE	ZIP

CLIENT	REFERENCE NO.	DATE REQUIRED	HOW SHIP	TERMS

	QUANTITY ORDERED	PLEASE SUPPLY ITEMS LISTED BELOW	UNIT PRICE	TOTAL PRICE
1	1	#LMP-4-6152 Art Lamp		
2		Murals C+M in brass		
3		finish		
4		29 3/4"w x 9"d x 2 1/2"h		
5				
6		12 week lead time		
7				
8				
9				
10				
11				
12				

FIGURE 30-4. Example of a "TX" fax transmission reply, showing that the fax was sent. (Reproduced with permission, Grei Hinsen, G. S. Hinsen Company, Nashville, TN)

The
DESIGN
Collective Group, Inc.
2129 South U.S. Highway One
Jupiter, Florida 33477
IB# 0864

Voice: (561) 745-4146
Fax: (561) 745-0361

Purchase Order

•IMPORTANT NOTICE : Within 5 Days of Receipt, Vendor Must Provide Our Firm With An Acknowledgement, Confirm Costs And Provide Firm Delivery Schedule. We Reserve All Rights To Cancel If Vendor Fails To Provide This Information.

Our Reference # ____ - ____ - ____

Today's Date ____________

Vendor ____________
Address ____________
City, ST, Zip ____________

Sidemark ____________
Must Complete By ____________
Ship Via ____________

Ship To ____________
____
Address ____________
City, ST, Zip ____________

Terms ____________
- This Order may be canceled without penalty if Vendor is not able to ship by date specified or fails to notify of any delay.
- No changes nor any substitutions without prior approval.
- Acknowledgements, Shipments & Invoices must be clearly marked with Our Reference Number and Complete Sidemark.
- Any Additional Costs Must be Approved Prior to Proceeding.
- Vendor agrees that acceptance of this order and the terms outlined supercede any other terms and conditions set forth.

Quantity	Specification	Cover, Color, Finish	Each	Total

Special Info?

Subtotal	
Other Charges?	
Freight	
TOTAL	

Authorization To Proceed With This Order Subject To Terms Above :
By ____________ Date ____________

White - Vendor Yellow - Client Binder Pink - Billing Gold - Receiving

FIGURE 30-5. An example of a purchase order. (Reproduced with permission, Michael Thomas, The Design Collective Group, Jupiter, FL)

1. *Preprinted sequenced numbers*. Using numerically sequenced purchase orders allows the firm to keep track of each purchase order, whether it is used or thrown out.
2. *The firm's name and billing address, telephone number, fax number, and E-mail address of an appropriate party*. Preprinted forms look more professional, negate mailing or shipping errors resulting from illegible handwriting, and save time.
3. *Space for the supplier's/vendor's name and address*.
4. *Space for the "ship to" location*. This is very important if the design firm does not have the merchandise shipped to the design firm's office location. On occasion, designers *drop ship* orders. This means that the order is to be delivered to some location other than the designer's office. It usually means that the shipment will be made to the client's address or job site.
5. *Preprinted boxes or space for additional shipping instructions*. These instructions relate to expected ship date, the preferred freight company, and collected or prepaid charges.
6. *Space for the "tag for" information*. The *tag for information* (or "special info?" box in the figure) can be placed at the bottom or the top of the purchase order. The client's name or a project number* is usually written in this space as a further means of identifying the client who ordered the merchandise or service. Some firms also put other brief instructions on the purchase order that will help the receiving party clearly identify where the items are to be located at the job site.

The body of the purchase order should have space for the following information:

1. *Quantity*. This is not only needed by the supplier, but also it is required by the UCC to create a sales contract.
2. *Catalog number*. This should exactly reflect the sequence of numbers and/or letters that the supplier uses to call out the products from his or her catalog. Reversing one number can lead to the wrong product being shipped.
3. *Description*. The method that the supplier uses in the catalog should be followed. This helps prevent having the wrong item shipped. However, it should be remembered that many suppliers process orders by the catalog number on the purchase order, not the description. The description acts as a check against the catalog number. There is no guarantee that the supplier's order input person will read the description.
4. *Net price*. Putting the expected net price on the purchase order works as a good pricing check. Net pricing on the purchase order can also help the firm attempt to utilize a cost accounting method for managerial control. Note that the net price should not be included on the purchase order if a copy of the form will be given to the client.
5. *Line item number*. Many firms use *line item numbers* as another method of controlling an order. Each item† on the sale order is given a line item number. This number is cross-referenced in the appropriate column

* Some design firms use project numbers rather than the client's name on all paperwork that travels out of the office. This is done for the purpose of maintaining client confidentiality.

† Multiples of the same item for the same order are considered one line item.

on the purchase order. Problems and questions about orders can more easily be tracked with this number. Goods also can be tagged with the line item number.

The bottom of the form should provide space for the authorizing signature. This signature will be either that of the firm's owner or of an authorized manager. Additional information that the design firm wishes the supplier to be aware of can be added in appropriate places. An example of this is instructions asking the supplier to acknowledge receipt of the purchase order and to provide an expected shipping date.

Each supplier involved in a project receives a separate purchase order. Multiple items to the same supplier for the same client can, of course, be sent on the same purchase order. If the designer is placing orders for multiple items to the same supplier but for two or more *different* clients, a different purchase order should be prepared for each client. Even though some firms place two or more customer orders to the same manufacturer on the same purchase order, better control is maintained by initiating separate purchase orders for each customer.

If two suppliers are involved in the completion of one finished product, such as a *customer's own material (COM)** sofa, the designer must prepare two different purchase orders. One purchase order is written to the sofa supplier, referencing (according to the supplier's requirements printed in the supplier's catalog) the COM fabric. A second purchase order is written to the fabric supplier, referencing the information required by the sofa supplier. This information is often written as an expanded "tag for" block of information in the body of the purchase order, rather than in the normal "tag for" space. Most furniture manufacturers require that the fabric be shipped prepaid to the factory. The designer must be sure that the fabric supplier does this, and the designer must remember to add the estimated shipping charge to the cost of the sofa. It is, after all, part of the cost of completing the sofa.

For a small design firm, two to three copies of the purchase order are required. To help the firm visually track the various copies, it is best if each sheet is a different color. The first sheet is always white. The other copies may be any color. They are used as follows.

- The white, or original copy, is the copy that is mailed or faxed to the supplier.
- The second copy should go in the "open purchase order file." If the order is being faxed, the original copy can go in the "open purchase order file" after an acknowledgment has been received from the supplier.
- The third copy should go in the client's active file and be used for reference.

The open purchase order file consists of all numerically sequenced purchase orders that have been mailed or faxed but against which merchandise or services have not yet been received. In a small design firm, the design assistant or the bookkeeper may keep track of this file. When acknowledgments are received, they should be checked for accuracy against the information on the purchase order. Discrepancies should be dealt with immediately. When merchandise has been received and delivered, the bookkeeper can bill the client. The designer or other responsible staff member can track orders not yet received

* *COM* indicates that the designer is not using a fabric available from the chair or sofa manufacturer. The desired fabric has to be ordered from a different supplier and sent to the chair or sofa manufacturer.

by checking the expected ship date on the order against the current date. If an order appears to be late, the designer who was responsible for placing the order should contact the supplier to establish the reason for the delay.

One or more additional copies of the purchase order might also be used. Commonly, an additional copy is sent to a warehouse or warehouse service. This helps the warehouse effectively service the design firm, because the warehouse will know in advance the quantity and expected arrival dates of all the merchandise that the firm has ordered. If, on occasion, the merchandise is shipped to the client's location rather than to the warehouse, the warehouse has the responsibility to unload and inspect the merchandise as it comes off the truck.

Some firms use a copy of the purchase order as a delivery ticket. In this case, pricing is blocked out of the copy that is given to the client. The client would sign or initial the items that have been delivered. Any back orders* or needed repairs also can be noted on the delivery ticket copy of the purchase order.

Acknowledgments

Acknowledgments, or confirmations (sometimes called order updates) are the forms that the supplier sends back to the designer to indicate what the supplier interprets the designer's order to be (see Figure 30-6). Depending on the supplier and whether the purchase order has been mailed, faxed, or E-mailed, the designer receives an acknowledgment anywhere from a few hours to up to ten days later.

Although acknowledgments vary in format to suit the needs of specific suppliers, it is likely that the following kinds of information will be provided on them:

1. An order number assigned by the supplier.
2. The design firm's purchase order number.
3. The date on which the acknowledgment was prepared.
4. A scheduled shipping date. The order will be shipped some time during that week, not necessarily on that day.
5. What the expected shipping situation will be (e.g., "Collect—Roadway" means that the design firm will have to pay the shipping charges and that the merchandise will come from the Roadway shipping company).
6. Notations as to who ordered the merchandise, the billing address, and the shipping address.
7. What the "tag for" instructions are.
8. A restatement of quantity, catalog number, description, and pricing information. Many manufacturers put the net price on the acknowledgment. However, others still quote retail prices. If the retail price has been quoted, the acknowledgment will often also quote the discount that the designer will receive for that order.
9. Other information related to billing and shipping.

Faxed or E-mailed acknowledgments should also contain similar information. E-mailed acknowledgments need to be downloaded into the designer' order system, or hard copies should be printed so that the designer will have a record of the transaction.

* *Back orders* are items that the vendor cannot ship with other merchandise or are otherwise not available for some period of time.

THIS IS NOT AN INVOICE
CONFIRMATION

Knoll International, Inc.
P.O. BOX 157, EAST GREENVILLE, PA 18041

FURNITURE
TEXTILES

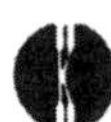

KNOLL ORDER NUMBER	CUSTOMER P.O. NUMBER	CONFIRMATION DATE	SCHEDULED SHIPPING WEEK
7070001	502147	11/11/87	12/23/88

PAGE 1

BILL TO — CUSTOMER NO.
SAME AS SOLD TO

SHIP TO — CUSTOMER NO.
SAME AS BILL TO

SOLD TO — CUSTOMER NO. 673911
CREATIVE INTERIOR DESIGNS
4156 N CRANE DR
FLAGSTAFF AZ 86001

PAR DEALER — CUSTOMER NO.

SHIP VIA: FOB EG D W POOL
NBD:
ORDER MARK FOR: MARTHA KWAS

SHOWROOM CODES			PS.	DISC.	ACCOUNT NUMBER
SOLD	SPEC. BY	SHIP	CODE	CODE	
107	107	107	000	35	

ITEM NO.	QUANTITY	PATTERN NO.	BCD	DESCRIPTION	UNIT PRICE	EXTENDED AMOUNT
1.0	1.000	1053F	03 G	SOFA,LEATHER/FEATHER AVAIL FOR SHIPMENT 12/23/88	1770.72	1770.72
1.1	318.000	K6A	G	KNOLL SUEDE SAGE 5001000 *****	N/C	
2.0	2.000	245	01	CHAIR,BRNO FABRIC AVAIL FOR SHIPMENT 12/23/88	1388.40	2776.80
2.1	3.400	K78426		KNOLL VELVET/CAMEL 200300 5080	N/C	
3.0	1.000	252		TABLE AVAIL FOR SHIPMENT 12/23/88	2264.08	2264.08
				MERCHANDISE TOTAL		6811.60
				TOTAL TAXES		840.58
				TOTAL AMOUNT OF ORDER		7652.18

SHIP SCHEDULE -A- ONE LOAD DURING THE SHIP WEEK NOTED ABOVE.

THANK YOU FOR PLACING YOUR ORDER WITH KNOLL.

K2012 R 7/87

CUSTOMER COPY

FIGURE 30-6. An acknowledgment telling the designer what the manufacturer believes to be the merchandise or service order. (Reproduced with permission, Knoll International, New York, NY)

Depending on the size of the firm and its organizational structure, someone from the firm must be responsible for checking the acknowledgment information against the purchase order. In smaller design firms, this person is the designer, an assistant, or the bookkeeper. Checking acknowledgments is usually the responsibility of the expediter in larger design firms. The expediting function will be discussed later in this chapter. Comparing the acknowledgment information against the purchase order should be done immediately so that any discrepancies between the two forms can be found. Any discrepancies, but especially those in quantity, catalog number, description, and price, should be discussed with the manufacturer immediately. Delays in calling attention to errors often result in the design firm's receiving the wrong merchandise. Such delays can lead to angry clients and/or reduced profit margins. Discrepancies regarding the expected shipping date or other shipping information also should be checked to see how they may affect the project's completion.

Speedy review of the acknowledgment against the purchase order is also necessary, since there is generally very little time for the designer or the client to make changes in the order. Major suppliers often give only ten days and certainly no more than three weeks "from receipt of order" to make any changes in the order. Time, therefore, is of the essence.

The supplier may send the design firm an original copy, a fax, or possibly an E-mail version of the acknowledgment. Again, depending on the firm's size and paperwork structure, the copy that comes from the supplier should be attached to the corresponding purchase order in the open purchase order file. A copy may be added to the active project file, for reference purposes.

Someone in the design firm also must be responsible for checking all outstanding orders. Many firms use a "tickler file," keyed to the days of the month. This file is checked daily (in very large firms) or weekly in smaller firms to make sure that goods have been received within the expected ship dates. Checking can be done immediately on orders that are about to be shipped or that have not yet been received, although the ship date has passed. Again, computer programs are useful tool in such situations.

Invoices

An *invoice* is simply a bill. The interior design firm sends out invoices to clients for services performed and/or goods purchased in the client's name. Suppliers send invoices to the designer for the goods or services that the interior design firm has ordered. Figure 30-7 shows a sample invoice from a supplier to a designer. Figure 30-8 shows a sample invoice from a designer to a client.

Invoices from suppliers are commonly sent at the same time that the merchandise is shipped. The invoice generally arrives at the office a few days before the merchandise. Many suppliers have invoices that look very similar to their acknowledgments; the only difference may be that there is a label. Again, someone in the design firm must be responsible for checking the invoice to be sure that it corresponds to what was ordered. Since the invoice often arrives a few days before the merchandise, it also should be checked against what is received.

It is important for the designer to check the invoice to determine if the manufacturer has extended any special pricing, especially any discount related to prompt payment. The reader can refer back to our discussion on cash discounts in Chapter 19. These discounts can amount to substantial savings for a design firm that can afford to pay the invoice within the specified time period. Not all suppliers offer this special discount to all designers.

Invoices to clients should be sent as quickly as possible. Goods should be billed within ten days after the goods have been delivered and accepted by the client. Services should be billed once services have been completed for

invoice

customer | date | invoice number

sold to

ship to

It is the orderer's responsibility to check this document for accuracy, correct fabric selections, etc. Report claims immediately. This order is subject to the terms and conditions on the face and reverse side. Federal employer I.D. 38-0837640.

order date	your purchase order number	terms	deposit	salesperson	territory	type	order number	ship date
contract number	ship to purchase order number	ship from	ship via					bill of lading number

	item number	quantity this invoice	quantity remaining	quantity ordered	quantity previously invoiced	product number	product description	unit price	extended price

FIGURE 30-7. A sample invoice from a manufacturer to a designer. (Provided courtesy of Herman Miller, Inc., Zeeland, MI)

INTERIORS FOR BUSINESS

PHONE: (602) 275-0101
FAX: (602) 275-0202

SEND PAYMENT TO: P.O. BOX 60006, PHOENIX, ARIZONA 85082-0006

"INVOICE"

SOLD TO:

INVOICE #: 62678

DATE PRINTED 09/15/00
PROPOSAL U32002
PROJECT 50-133
CUST P/O #

INSTALL AT:

PAYMENT TERMS: NET30

CUSTOMER #: 001755   SALESPERSON: HOUSE ACCOUNT

ITEM #	QTY.	PRODUCT #	DESCRIPTION	UNIT PRICE	TOTAL AMOUNT
			MERRIT MENEFEE - QPM# 166-00250 CHAIR & STOOL SPA: G951079 LEADTIME: 4 WEEKS PLUS TRANSIT TIME TAG: 50/U32002/MERRITT		
1	1.00	K700-8001 (2) ,TR- 0CM	STOOL,28" HGT,BACKLESS,ARMLESSNO GLIDES TRIM SURFACE 1 SURFACE 1 BUMPY HYDRANT	80.33	80.33
			HAWORTH FREIGHT INCLUDED		
			PRODUCT.........:		80.33
			SALES TAX.......:		6.03
			FINAL TOTAL.....:		86.36
			PAY THIS AMOUNT......:		86.36

PAGE 1 OF 1

Authorized Signature   Date

Past due invoices are subject to finance charges of 1½% per month (18% annually) on the balance due.

FIGURE 30-8. A sample invoice prepared by a design firm and sent to a client. (Reproduced with permission, Facilitec, Inc., Phoenix, AZ)

short-duration projects, on a monthly basis for larger projects, or on whatever billing basis for services was agreed to in the contract. Delays in billing goods and services can cause an increased amount of receivables and poor cash management. This is something that small and large design firms alike cannot afford to do. Delays in billing can also lead to a few unscrupulous clients not paying for goods or services at all.

To help the design firm have at least some legal basis for preventing late payment or no payment, the original contract for services or goods should contain such language as "billing upon delivery" or "payment due ten days after receipt of invoice." Some firms try to use item-by-item billing on large projects. This, of course, means that, if the project has 20 items that are to be delivered and only two arrive, the firm delivers the two items and bills only for those two items. The next time one or more items arrive, those are also delivered and billed. Although this may help the firm's cash flow, it can cause many costs and headaches to the firm. There is a cost attached each time the delivery truck delivers goods to the client. There is also a cost associated with the preparation and mailing of invoices. It is suggested that, whenever possible, deliveries be done in lots or only when the job has been completed. This will reduce delivery and bookkeeping costs for multiple deliveries.

Shipping and Freight

Chapter 19 contains a discussion of how freight and delivery charges affect the price of the goods. Chapter 20 reviewed freight concepts as regulated by the UCC. In this chapter, we will look at the forms that are related to freight services.

There are various freight matters that result in additional paperwork management for the designer. The first is the bill of lading. The *bill of lading* is the form that the supplier provides to the truck driver (see Figure 30-9) to show what is being shipped and who has title to the goods. The driver carries this form with him or her in the truck; the contents of the truck must match what is on the form. Many times the bill of lading is not a detailed list but, rather, a total quantity of items. The designer or the warehouse must check the number of items that are delivered to the firm against the number on the bill of lading. Discrepancies in quantity should be noted on the bill, as well as any notations regarding damages to merchandise.

Another form that accompanies the delivery is a packing list. The *packing list* is commonly in a plastic envelope attached to the outside of one of the items being delivered. The packing list details by quantity and description what is being shipped from a manufacturer or supplier to the warehouse at a specific time. The designer should check the packing list against all items taken from the truck and against the number on the bill of lading. Again, discrepancies should be noted on the bill of lading.

The actual *freight bill* is another use of the term "invoice." It is usually sent a few days after the shipment leaves the manufacturer. The freight bill comes from the shipping company, not the manufacturer, and is the bill for the shipping service.

It is important for the designer or a representative of the design firm (the warehousing service) to inspect all the items as they arrive at the designer's warehouse or job site. Many one-person design firms allow merchandise to be delivered to the client without the designer being available at the time of delivery to inspect the goods. This can be very costly if merchandise has

UNIFORM STRAIGHT BILL OF LADING — Short Form — Original — Not Negotiable — Domestic

On Collect on Delivery shipments, the letters "COD" must appear before consignee's name or as otherwise provided in item 430, Sec. 1.

*If the shipment moves between two ports by a carrier by water, the law requires that the bill of lading shall state whether it is "carrier's or shipper's weight." NOTE—Where the rate is dependent on value, shippers are required to state specifically in writing the agreed or declared value of the property.

RECEIVED, subject to the classifications and tariffs in effect on the date of the issue of this Bill of Lading,

SHIPPER NO. | DATE

FROM
STREET AND NO. ZIP
CITY AND STATE

CONSIGNED TO
STREET AND NO. ZIP
CITY AND STATE

ROUTING

C. O. D. $

C. O. D. FEE TO BE PAID BY CONSIGNEE ☐ SHIPPER ☐

ADVANCE	C.O.D. FEE	T.L. REV.	C.L. REV.

the property described below, in apparent good order, except as noted (contents and condition of contents of packages unknown) marked, consigned, and destined as indicated below, which said carrier (the word carrier being understood throughout this contract as meaning any person or corporation in possession of the property under the contract) agrees to carry to its usual place of delivery at said destination, if on its route, otherwise to deliver to another carrier on the route to said destination. It is mutually agreed, as to each carrier of all or any of said property over all or any portion of said route to destination, and as to each party at any time interested in all or any of said property, that every service to be performed hereunder shall be subject to all the terms and conditions of the Uniform Domestic Straight Bill of Lading set forth (1) in Uniform Freight Classification in effect on the date hereof, if this is a rail or a rail-water shipment, or (2) in the applicable motor carrier classification or tariff if this is a motor carrier shipment.

Shipper hereby certifies that he is familiar with all the terms and conditions of the said bill of lading, including those on the back thereof, set forth in the classification or tariff which governs the transportation of this shipment, and the said terms and conditions are hereby agreed to by the shipper and accepted for himself and his assigns.

NO. PKG.	HM	DESCRIPTION OF ARTICLES, SPECIAL MARKS, AND EXCEPTIONS	*WEIGHT (Sub. to Cor.)	Class or Rate	Check Column

Subject to Section 7 of conditions of applicable bill of lading, if this shipment is to be delivered to the consignee without recourse on the consignor, the consignor shall sign the following statement:
The carrier shall not make delivery of this shipment without payment of freight and all other lawful charges.

(Signature of Consignor)

If charges are to be prepaid, write or stamp here, "To be Prepaid."

Received $____ to apply in prepayment of the charges on the property described hereon.

Agent or Cashier

Per____
(The signature here acknowledges only the amount prepaid.)

This is to certify that the above-named materials are properly classified, described, packaged, marked and labeled and are in proper condition for transportation according to the applicable regulations of the Dept. of Transportation.

THE AGREED OR DECLARED VALUE OF THE PROPERTY IS HEREBY SPECIFICALLY STATED BY THE SHIPPER TO BE NOT EXCEEDING ____ PER ____

1

IT IS HEREBY AGREED THAT THE DECLARED VALUATION ON HOUSEHOLD GOODS OR PERSONAL EFFECTS IS NOT EXCEEDING 10¢ PER POUND PER ARTICLE LOST OR DAMAGED UNLESS A HIGHER VALUE IS DECLARED.

____ SHIPPER

PER ____

____ Agent, Per ____
(This Bill of Lading is to be signed by the shipper and agent of the carrier issuing same.)

FORM 212-4 (11-77)
(TREAS-146)
ISSUED 9/82

FIGURE 30-9. The bill of lading provides information about the shipper, the receiver, and the merchandise being shipped. (Reproduced with permission, Transcon Lines)

been damaged. Damaged cartons should be immediately opened and inspected. Whenever practical, all items should be unwrapped or uncartoned to inspect for *concealed damage*—damage that may exist even though the carton or wrapping appears intact. Concealed damage must be reported to the carrier as soon as possible. As the time from acceptance of shipment or the discovery of damages lengthens, successful claims become less probable.

Any damage to cartons, packing, and merchandise should be shown to the driver. Notations about damaged merchandise must be made on the bill of lading in order for the design firm to make successful claims. Many designers also take pictures of damaged merchandise. This can greatly help the firm in the filing of claims.

Since the filing of freight claims and disposition of the claims are very time-consuming, many larger firms forgo filing claims on minor damage and make repairs themselves. These charges are costed as overhead expenses. Merchandise that has sustained substantial damage in transit should be refused. However, a freight claim must still be filed, and records such as photographs, showing the extent of the damage, must be kept.

Certain documentation is generally required when the firm is filing a freight claim.

1. The bill of lading
2. The paid freight bill

3. The manufacturer's invoice for the item
4. The inspection report prepared by the freight carrier
5. Documentation of repair costs
6. Documentation of additional freight costs (if any) resulting from the damage
7. Other written or photographic documentation that attests to the damage occurring before delivery to the job site or to the designer's warehouse

Most manufacturers will not accept merchandise for return once the design firm has accepted it. Therefore, the firm must get written permission to return damaged (or incorrectly shipped) merchandise. The firm should not simply send the merchandise back to the manufacturer. Each manufacturer has its own policy concerning returns, and these policies must be adhered to in order for the firm to receive proper credit.

When the design firm contacts the freight carrier concerning a shipping question, it should have the bill of lading number, the supplier's name and location, the date of shipment, the description and number of items shipped, and the delivery location. If the information needed is not on the manufacturer's invoice, this information, along with other needed information, can be obtained from the manufacturer.

Expediting

An *expediter* is an individual who is familiar with the design firm's paperwork system and the various ordering and shipping requirements of manufacturers. In firms that are large enough to have a person responsible for this specific job function, the expediter is a person who constantly monitors all orders *after* the purchase orders have been sent and the acknowledgments have been received. He or she is responsible for the speedy processing of orders.

The first activity of the expediter is to check the acknowledgment from the manufacturer against the purchase order. This is a vital step to ensure that all the information matches the two forms and confirms that the correct products and/or services are being supplied. Discrepancies must be taken care of immediately.

Once all the product information has been checked, the expediter will look closely at the expected ship date. He or she must check to be sure that the products are going to ship within the time specified on the purchase order and that they will arrive when they were promised. If the ship date is not what is expected, the expediter should inform the designer so that the proper action can be taken. Merchandise shipped earlier than desired may have to be warehoused until the job site is ready. If this is the case, the designer must negotiate with the client as to who will be responsible for the charges and where the merchandise should be shipped. At the time of order, it is relatively easy for the design firm to request that the merchandise not be shipped until a date beyond the normal shipping date. There may be an extra charge if the manufacturer must warehouse the finished goods when the designer requests that the shipment be delayed.

It is not uncommon for the ship date to be later than expected. The designer must contact the client to let him or her know about the delay. Short-term delays may be inconvenient but are seldom critical. Delays of three or more weeks may necessitate canceling the original order and finding alternate products.

The expediter is also responsible for tracking shipments once they have left the manufacturer. He or she should alert the delivery people of the impending shipment and where it is to be delivered by the trucking company. If merchandise is to be drop shipped to a job site, someone representing the design firm must be at the site to unload, inspect, and deliver the goods to the client. Truck drivers generally are not responsible for unloading the merchandise from the truck, unpacking it, and delivering it to the client. In some firms, the expediter may also be responsible for filing return permissions as well as freight claims. However, a warehouse service may be able to provide these last two services for the design firm.

Once shipments leave the manufacturer, the designer tracks them by the bill of lading number, not the purchase order number. The firm receives from the freight company information as to what this number is. This number, along with the name and address of the design firm, the name and address of the delivery site, the name of the shipping company, the name and address of the original shipping location, a description and the number of pieces in the order, and the weight of the order must be available for tracking delayed shipments.

Summary

In this chapter, we have looked at the various kinds of paperwork that are involved once the project reaches the contract administration phase. A brief discussion concerning the permits and other paperwork that are a part of the structural work that occurs in most interior design projects begins the chapter. Emphasis has been placed on the paperwork connected to ordering merchandise or invoicing of services. Design firms that function as designer/specifiers and do not sell merchandise to the end user save themselves a considerable amount of paperwork. Those that wish to sell merchandise as well as perform the design service must be prepared to understand and handle the multitude of forms and paperwork involved. We also looked at the paperwork involved in freight or shipping of merchandise to the delivery location and the delivery responsibility.

The differences between the paperwork management for residential and commercial projects is very subtle. The forms themselves are the same. Designers who are unable to manage the paperwork should hire someone who is skilled in this area. Not doing so can result in the firm's having serious or even disastrous cash flow and public relations problems that can lead to the dissolution of the firm.

The next chapter covers the tasks of the final portions of the contract administration phase—the delivery of merchandise and the project's closeout.

REFERENCES

Alderman, Robert L. 1997. *How to Prosper as an Interior Designer.* New York: John Wiley.

Birnberg, Howard, ed. 1992. *New Directions in Architectural and Engineering Practice.* New York: McGraw-Hill.

Emery, Vince. 1996. *How to Grow Your Business on the Internet.* Scottsdale, AZ: Coriolis Group.

Entrepreneur Media, Inc. 1999. *Small Business Advisor,* 2nd ed. New York: John Wiley.

Fast Company. "The Internet: What Does It Look Like?" *Fast Company.* March 2000.

Getz, Lowell. 1986. *Business Management in the Smaller Design Firm.* Newton, MA: Practice Management Associates.

Haviland, David. 1994. *The Architect's Handbook of Professional Practice, Student Edition*. Washington, DC: AIA Press.

Jentz, Gaylord A., Kenneth W. Clarkson, and Roger LeRoy Miller. 1987. *West's Business Law—Alternate UCC Comprehensive Edition*, 3rd ed. St. Paul, MN: West Publishing.

Knackstedt, Mary. 1992. *The Interior Design Business Handbook*, 2nd ed. New York: Van Nostrand Reinhold.

Leonard, Woody. "The New Internet Security Threats." *SmartBusiness Magazine*. July 2000.

Loebelson, Andrew. 1983. *How to Profit in Contract Design*. New York: Interior Design Books.

McGowan, Maryrose. 1996. *Specifying Interiors*. New York: John Wiley.

O'Leary, Arthur F. 1992. *Construction Administration in Architectural Practice*. New York: McGraw-Hill.

Poage, Waller S. 1987. *Plans, Specs and Contracts for Building Professionals*. Kingston, MA: R. S. Means.

Siegel, Harry (with Alan M. Siegel). 1982. *A Guide to Business Principles and Practices for Interior Designers*, rev. ed. New York: Watson-Guptill.

Smith, Rob, Mark Speaker, and Mark Thompson. 2000. *The Complete Idiot's Guide to e-Commerce*. Indianapolis, IN: Que/Macmillan.

Thompson, Jo Ann Asher, ed. 1992. *ASID Professional Practice Manual*. New York: Watson-Guptill.

Chapter 31

Contract Administration: Delivery and Project Closeout

The previous chapter dealt with the different kinds of paperwork related to contract administration up to the time that products are shipped to the job site. Of course, the project is not complete until all the merchandise has been delivered and accepted by the client. In this chapter, we will look at the final activities that occur in contract administration once the orders have been processed and are ready to be delivered to the client. These activities include delivery and installation, project closeout, and postoccupancy reviews.

In small design firms, these activities are customarily administered by the designer, with assistance from others only at the delivery stage. In larger design firms, many of these activities are handled by other employees whose specialized job responsibility revolves around completing the project.

Whether these activities are done by the designer himself or herself or are the responsibility of others, the project designer always retains ultimate responsibility for the completion of the project. It is an important part of being a professional interior designer.

Delivery and Installation

Just prior to the installation of the furnishings, the designer must schedule a detailed meeting with the client concerning the final work on the project. This time is spent going over the floor plans to be sure that the client has not changed his or her mind about the placement of any of the items. If items are to be moved, revised plans need to be prepared so that the delivery and installation workers are not forced to place the items more than once. Large, commercial projects require that parking lots or even parts of streets be closed to allow delivery trucks easy access to the building. If it is necessary to close a street, the client, designer, or contractor must arrange with the city police to obtain the proper permits for the closure. For projects in buildings with elevators, the client, designer, or contractor will also have to arrange for perhaps continual access to freight elevators or one of the regular service elevators. Even the installation of furniture at a new home can mean that neighbors may get upset about the number of delivery trucks or tradespeople's trucks that are constantly seen in the neighborhood.

When the purchase order is prepared, instructions are given as to where to ship the goods. As discussed in the previous chapter, most designers have goods shipped to a warehouse before they are ultimately delivered to the job site. Delivery includes the activities concerned with moving furniture, furnishings, and equipment from the warehouse or showroom to the job site and placing them in their correct locations. Delivery involves no special activities of assembly, construction, or physical attachment of the products to the building. Installation involves assembly, construction, or physical attachment of products to the building. Let us look at delivery services first.

Delivering merchandise to the client's home or commercial facility can be an opportunity for the designer to continue to demonstrate that he or she can provide first-class customer service and even marketing. Larger design firms have the advantage of having their own trucks and warehouse. Oftentimes these delivery trucks can be "moving billboards," providing a marketing opportunity along with controlled delivery services (see Figure 31-1). It is not difficult for the firm to train the delivery staff employees in the "white gloves" procedures that lead to satisfied customers. Clean uniforms, clean hands, politeness, and respect for the client's property are just some of the factors that help a firm continue the high-level of customer service that the designer established at the beginning of a project.

The smaller design firm most commonly depends on independent delivery services within the local area. Smaller firms must monitor the performance of the delivery service to insure that the company can represent the quality of service the designer wishes for his or her clients. Whether goods are delivered by in-house staff or a warehouse service, leaving cartons at the job site, allowing fabrics to become soiled due to dirty hands, and being brusque or offensive to clients at a time when they are probably stressed is no way for a design firm to cement long-term relationships with clients.

The delivery process itself can be very stressful for clients (as well as exciting) as they finally see the design concepts and ideas that they have waited for unfold before their eyes. It is also stressful for the designer, because many important project management activities are occurring at the same time. It is important that the interior designer carefully plan delivery supervision time into the design fee, whether the goods are sold by the designer or are supplied by other vendors.

From a practical point of view, it is important for the client to sign documentation that indicates what he or she has received during the delivery portion of the project. As we discussed in Chapter 20, this signifies acceptance and transfer of title, and thereby requires that the client pay for what was delivered. If a copy of the purchase order was sent to the warehouse service or to the designer's warehouse, the client can sign off on this form. Some firms have a separate delivery ticket that accompanies the merchandise. This ticket (see Figure 31-2) is at least a three-part form. The parts are used as follows:

1. The top or original copy goes to the client.
2. A second copy is sent to the billing office.
3. The third copy is retained by the warehouse whenever a back order, which is a partial shipment, occurs.

Any notations regarding damages or discrepancies between what was delivered and what was ordered should be noted on the delivery paperwork. This helps clarify which damages are the responsibility of the design firm and which damages are the responsibility of the client.

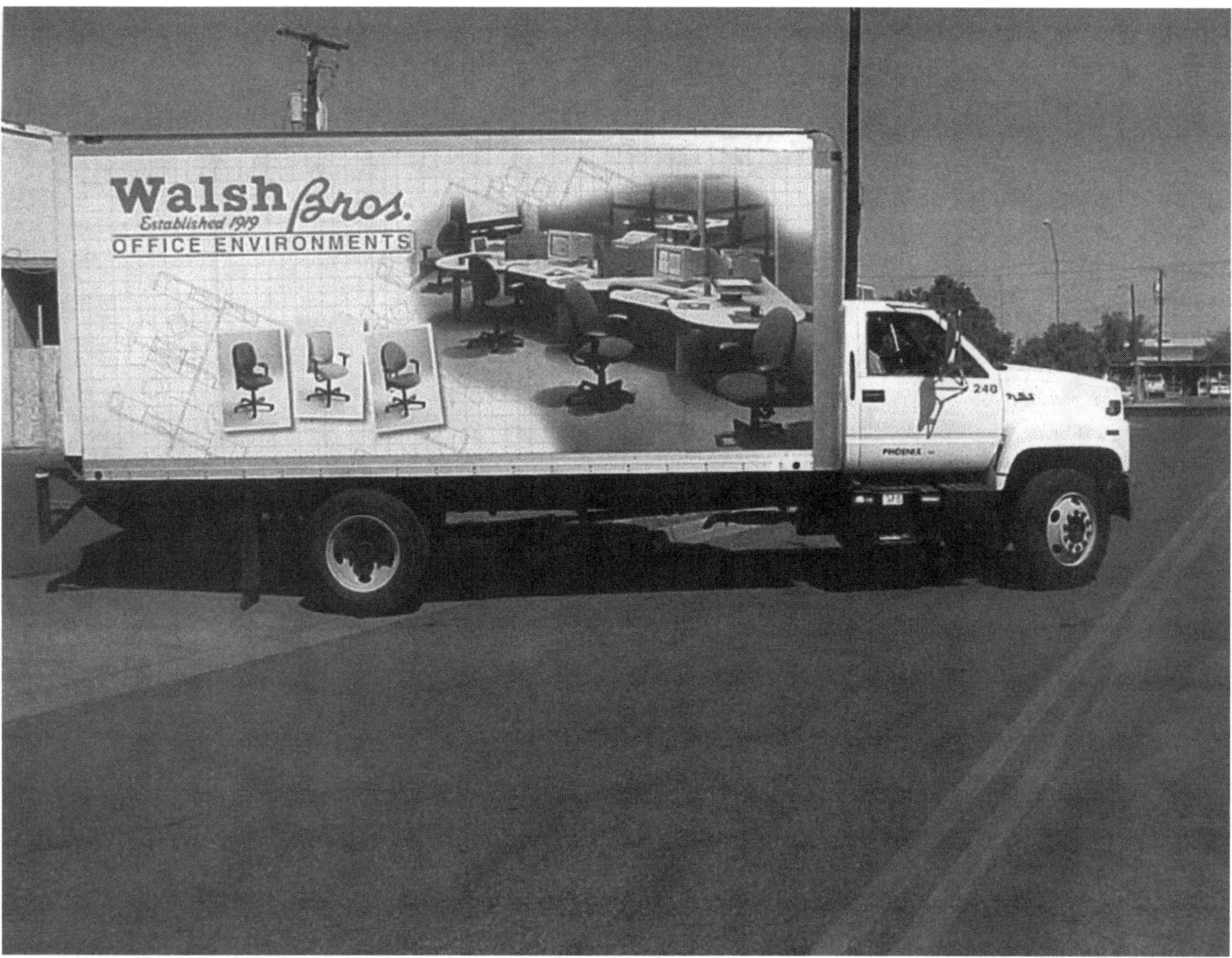

FIGURE 31-1. Delivery trucks can serve as a marketing tool as well as being a functional necessity. (Photograph courtesy of Walsh Bros. Office Environments, Phoenix, AZ)

The designer should prepare a delivery plan, showing locations for all the furniture and other items for the job, to let the delivery people know exactly where each piece should be located. This is essential for the smooth completion of the project. A floor plan keyed to the purchase order number and line item number is one way to do this if the project is small and does not involve many items. For larger projects, and especially in commercial design, other methods are used. Furniture items on the floor plan are keyed to the purchase order to facilitate delivery (see Figure 29-1).

Delivery service should include dusting and vacuuming of the merchandise, as well as carefully inspecting it for any scratches or other damage. It may also be the delivery team's responsibility to show the client how to operate certain items, such as adjustable office chairs. However, this is often the responsibility of the designer or the salesperson.

A common responsibility of the delivery team is the removal of all cartons and packaging materials. No matter how small the job is, the empty cartons and packing materials should not be left to be disposed of by the client.

Clients often expect the designer to be present at all times during the delivery and installation of merchandise. This may seem to be an impractical use of the designer's time, but it can be key for maintaining good public

MTA INTERIOR ENVIRONMENTS

Miles Treaster & Associates
3480 Industrial Boulevard
Suite 100
West Sacramento, CA 95691
916.373.1800
916.325.4877 Fax

Commercial Furnishings
Interior Design
Space Planning

DELIVERY/INSTALLATION

D/I FORM # № 6635
TODAY'S DATE __/__/__
SALESPERSON ______
PRODUCT CT # ______
INSTALL CT# ______
MTA P.O.#'s ______

☐ Installation ☐ Pickup
☐ Reconfigure ☐ Punch List (see attached)
☐ Delivery ☐ Other ______
Original D/I form # ______
Client Name ______ Proj. # ______
Site Address ______

Client Contact ______ Phone # ______
Warehouse to call client to schedule **Yes** ☐ **No** ☐
Estimated week of Installation ______

☐ Deliver/Install all P.O.'s at once
☐ Deliver/Install as arrives
☐ Keyed Alike

Detailed Instruction(s) of Service(s) to be Performed: ______

Status of Installation:
☐ Installation Complete. No follow up required ☐ Freight damage (see attached)
☐ Installation Incomplete. (see attached) ☐ Additional items needed (see attached)

For Office Use Only			
Charges: ☐ Hourly $ ______ /man hour ☐ Fixed Fee to Client $ ______ ☐ Inter dept to Project ☐ No Charge	TRAVEL TIME: (per man hour) ______ ON SITE TIME: (per man hour) ______	Installer Names: ______ ______ ______ ______ ______ ______	Distribution **W** — Warehouse **B** — Operations **G** — Originator **C** — Acct **P** — Client **Gold** — Originator

The products and services described above have been received/performed in a satisfactory manner except as noted.

Signed: ______ **Date:** ______ **Title:** ______

FIGURE 31-2. A form that is used to accompany merchandise for delivery and/or installation. (Reproduced with permission, Miles Treaster & Associates, West Sacramento, CA)

relations. The designer should allow for spending a reasonable amount of time on the job site during delivery and installation. This time should be estimated at the beginning of the project and included in the fees for the project. If the designer is at the job site during this crucial time, he or she can reassure an anxious client who may not be sure about finishes and products as they are being installed and/or delivered.

The designer who is present during the delivery and installation of merchandise can speed up the inspection process, reassure the client, and, when questions arise, help answer them. How much time the designer spends at the job site during this time will depend on the client, the contract, the particular complexity of the job, and the designer's availability.

Installation is also the part of the delivery process that involves assembly or construction of merchandise, or installing physical attachments to the building. Installation includes attaching wall-hung bookcases or other storage units, mirrors, and assembling open-office furniture. Note that the installation of wall coverings, window treatments, and carpeting and other flooring in commercial projects is often part of the construction contract and the responsibility of the general contractor. In residential projects, installation of these architectural finishes can be part of the construction contract or part of the interior designer's responsibility. The installation of such items is usually done by someone other than the supplier of the goods, but not always. Installation service often depends on some other part of the project construction and delivery process being already completed, which requires careful scheduling of the construction, delivery, and installation.

If many items of furniture are to be assembled, specialized sets of drawings are necessary. With open-office systems, for example, commercial firms prepare one or more sheets of drawings that aid in the assembly. Plans may be drawn that show panel configurations and finishes, electrical and telephone service, and either plans or elevations for the location of hanging components.

Routine architectural finish schedules, as part of the construction documents, provide the information needed for designers to specify the locations of these finishes. Graphic schedules or interior elevations inform the contractor of the locations of such items as mirrors, complex wall treatments, and various wall-hung units.

Although it does take time to prepare delivery and installation drawings, it is the easiest and simplest way for the designer to guarantee that all the specified goods will be delivered and installed in their proper location. Preparation of these documents provides the designer the assurance that he or she will not be needed on the job site at all times. Showing the client that these kinds of documents have helped on projects in the past will also indicate to the client that the firm can deliver and install the products without the designer being there at all times.

It is also important for the installation crew to take care of dusting, vacuuming, and removal of trash. Since some companies do not perform such tasks as a routine part of their service, the design firm should be sure that these tasks are included in its contract with the installer. If they are not included, the designer or client will be charged for the extra work.

Project Closeout

As the last of the products are being delivered and/or installed, the project reaches what is referred to as *project closeout*. This term, which is borrowed from architecture and the construction industry, means that the interior design project has reached the time for final inspections, providing any necessary documents such as warranties to the client, and approval of payments to subcontractors and/or vendors. The first task that the designer must perform to close out a project is make a final inspection, referred to as a walk-through.

Walk-Through

When all the furniture and furnishings have been delivered and installed, it is customary for the designer and client to have a *walk-through*. This is a final inspection of the job site to be sure that everything that has been ordered is present and that any omissions or as yet unrepaired damages are noted. As the designer, client, and perhaps contractors walk-through the job site, a list of these omissions and damages are made. This is most commonly called a *punch list* and details everything that must still be taken care of in order for the project installation to be completed. Some firms call the punch list the *site inspection report*.

A punch list should be carefully prepared by room or area so that it will be easier for the delivery and repair people to find and complete the omissions or repairs. A copy of the punch list should be given to the client. Another copy can be used by the design firm to prepare work orders, repair tickets, and memos in order to expedite missing goods. For firms that charge design fees on a phased basis, the billing of the final part of the fee cannot be made until after the walk-through is done. Many clients will not make final payments until all the items on the punch list are taken care of. It is to the designer's benefit to take care of these items as quickly as possible.

The walk-through is also a good time for the designer to fine-tune the project. Although this can involve some "free" design service, it also can result in some additional specification or sale of merchandise. Commercial clients especially have a difficult time budgeting for accessories at the beginning of the project. But when the installation is winding down, they often see the need for wall hangings, desk accessories, plants, and other items that can complete the project. Residential clients as well may be interested in buying merchandise that was originally specified but was deleted for budgetary purposes once the furniture was delivered.

Complaints and Repairs

Complaints, repairs, omissions, and replacement of damaged items should be taken care of as soon as possible. Regrettably, this is the stage at which many designers lose interest in the project. It is always more difficult for the designer to take care of nagging problems with an ongoing project than to be designing a new project. But unresolved problems cause bad feelings and can result in poor recommendations from clients. Uncollected receivables, because of these small problems, can cause serious problems with the firm's cash flow. The design firm should have highly qualified furniture repair people, who are experienced with all kinds of wood and metal furniture, available to do repair work.

As much as possible, the firm's aim should be to handle complaints and repairs before the client is even aware of them. A competent warehouse service that inspects and repairs furniture can eliminate minor damages before furniture has been delivered to the client. Delivery personnel that handle the merchandise as if it were their own also avoid potential problems. The firm should hire only competent, experienced installers. The delivery and installation people must be required to clean up the job site. And delivering all the goods at one time helps to solve a lot of complaints.

Final Documentation

As the project nears completion, several additional documents or permits are provided to the client. One of these is warranties and maintenance information on all equipment and products that are delivered as part of the project. These documents are provided by the appropriate vendors who have supplied and installed the merchandise. In addition to the documents, instructions may be required on how to operate equipment. These instructions also are provided by the vendors. If the interior designer has sold the goods to the client, then he or she should be prepared to transfer the warranties, instructions, and provide appropriate training to the client.

Commercial clients frequently request that the designer prepare maintenance schedules. In general, maintenance schedules inform the physical plant workers how to clean, wax, vacuum, remove stains from, and otherwise maintain the furniture, fabrics, and architectural finishes. Such a schedule can be made up from the information provided by the manufacturers. The preparation of a formal maintenance schedule is often a separate design service, though it is sometimes included and charged for in the design contract.

The designer or architect issues another form after the final inspection and punch list have been completed. The *certificate of substantial completion*[*] clarifies everything that has been done and indicates if something is missing. As part of issuing this certificate or notice, the designer also should make sure that any extra material, such as extra carpeting, ceramic tile, and wall coverings, are left at the job site and that suppliers have cleaned the areas for which they are responsible. If doing so is applicable to the designer's responsibility, the interior designer may also obtain a *certificate of occupancy (CO)*.[†] The certificate of occupancy is issued by the local building department and certifies that the building or space has been inspected and approved for occupancy. This certificate applies to the structure, not to the interior movable furniture products.

For a construction project, the contractor is required to maintain a set of drawings at the job site. If any changes are made, they must be added to these *record drawings* so that a complete record of the construction work exists. These drawings are often referred to as *as-built drawings*, since they reflect how the interior or building was actually built rather than what was shown in the original construction drawings. Of course, a copy of the specifications and of all the addenda and change orders are also kept with these plans. When the project has been completed, the record drawings are turned over to the interior designer or the architect. A print or copy of the as-built drawings, the specifications, and addenda are then given to the client.

Depending on the responsibility of the interior designer, contractors will invoice the interior designer or architect for work that has been completed. If the designer feels that the work has been done satisfactorily, he or she will issue a *certificate for payment*. This form tells the client that the supplier or contractor has completed parts of or most of the work and has sent an invoice for that work, and that the interior designer recommends that the client pay the supplier for that work. The term *retainage* is associated with the certificate for payment (this can also be referred to as a hold back). Depending on the contract, the client may retain a certain amount—commonly 5 to 10 percent—to ensure that all the work, omissions, and problems are taken care of.

When everything has been completed or otherwise is in accordance with the interior designer's contract, the final payment to the interior designer should be made.

* The certificate of substantial completion is associated more with construction projects.

† This is more commonly issued to the owner directly from the city.

Postoccupancy and Follow-up

The project is complete. The furniture, accessories, and all the other items in the specifications or bids have finally been delivered. Every item on the punch list has been taken care of, repaired, delivered, or replaced. The client has even paid the design firm for all outstanding invoices. This is a happy time for interior designers! "We don't have to think about the Ross project anymore," the project designer announces. Perhaps this should not be the case, however.

Simply because everything that was supposed to get done has been done should not signal to the designer that he or she can forget about the project. Does the client love his or her home? Are the workstations really adequate for employees now that they are fully up and running? Are more files needed in the medical records area of the doctor's office suite? Was this truly a successful project for your design firm? These are the kinds of questions that can only be answered a few weeks or months after the client has fully moved in to his or her new spaces and has had a chance to "break it in."

The best way to review the success of a project is to make a postoccupancy evaluation. A *postoccupancy evaluation*, or *POE*, is thorough review of the project and site visit that is conducted from both the designer's and the client's point of view. The goal of the POE is to determine the success of the project solution and project management process and whether or not the client is satisfied. The purpose is twofold: (1) to understand client satisfaction or, more importantly, dissatisfaction with the project solutions if problems exist before they become critical issues that might hurt the design firm and (2) to improve the project processes used by the interior design firm so that even better results can occur on all future projects.

Formal postoccupancy evaluations that involve questionnaires or on-site surveys, resulting in reports, can be included in the design contract or sold to the client as a separate service. Commercial designers most frequently use the formal POE, though many of them do not. An informal postoccupancy evaluation, in which the interior designer interviews the client to determine his or her satisfaction with the project, can be done by any firm for free or can be included for a nominal fee in the design contract's scope of services. Frankly, many firms do not get involved in postoccupancy evaluations of a project, because the designer is afraid of hearing criticism or because they have already moved on to the next project.

It is shortsighted for the design firm or the designer not to seek comments on client dissatisfaction. If problems exist, the designer needs to find out and take care of them before they fester and become crises. For example, an employee who is dissatisfied with a new office may not truly be dissatisfied with the office design, aesthetics, or furniture but really only needs someone to tell him or her how to adjust the desk chair, or that employee may simply need another file cabinet. If these kinds of problems go undiscovered, then criticisms made by employees can give the client the impression that the project was unsuccessful. The designer who would rather move on forgets that repeat business or referrals can come from satisfied clients. If the designer forgets his or her clients, the chance for subsequent work is likely to vanish.

A postoccupancy evaluation can best be conducted by means of some sort of questionnaire. Figure 31-3 shows a rather formal questionnaire that can be used if the client is paying for this additional service. The design firm can make up its own questionnaire, consisting of a few simple questions, when it is conducting an informal evaluation. In either situation, the questionnaire should be structured to gather information on user satisfaction concerning the

OCCUPANT SURVEY

USABLE TOOLS

We wish to conduct a post-occupancy evaluation of your building. The purpose of this evaluation is to assess how well the building perfoms for those who occupy it in terms of health, safety, security, functionality, and psychological comfort. The benefits of a post-occupancy evaluation include: identification of good and bad performance aspects of the building, better building utilization, and feedback on how to improve future, similar buildings.

Please respond only to those questions of the following survey that are applicable to you. Indicate your answers by marking the appropriate blanks with an "X".

1. In an average work week, how many hours do you spend in the following types of spaces (specify):

Space A ______________________
Space B ______________________
Space C ______________________
Space D ______________________
Space E ______________________

HOURS	A	B	C	D	E
0 - 5	( )	( )	( )	( )	( )
6 - 10	( )	( )	( )	( )	( )
11 - 15	( )	( )	( )	( )	( )
16 - 20	( )	( )	( )	( )	( )
21 - 25	( )	( )	( )	( )	( )
26 - 30	( )	( )	( )	( )	( )
31 - 35	( )	( )	( )	( )	( )
35 - 40	( )	( )	( )	( )	( )
40 + ...	( )	( )	( )	( )	( )

KEY FOR THE FOLLOWING QUALITY RATINGS:

EX = Excellent quality
G = Good quality
F = Fair quality
P = Poor quality

2. Please rate the overall quality of the following areas in the building:

	EX	G	F	P
a) Space Category A................	( )	( )	( )	( )
b) Space Category B................	( )	( )	( )	( )
c) Space Category C................	( )	( )	( )	( )
d) Space Category D................	( )	( )	( )	( )
e) Space Category E................	( )	( )	( )	( )
f) Restroom(s)........................	( )	( )	( )	( )
g) Storage...............................	( )	( )	( )	( )
h) Elevator(s)..........................	( )	( )	( )	( )
i) Stairs/Corridors....................	( )	( )	( )	( )
j) Parking...............................	( )	( )	( )	( )
k) Other, specify_______........	( )	( )	( )	( )
______________________..	( )	( )	( )	( )

3. Please rate the overall quality of Space Category A in terms of the following:

	EX	G	F	P
a) Adequacy of Space............	( )	( )	( )	( )
b) Lighting..............................	( )	( )	( )	( )
c) Acoustics............................	( )	( )	( )	( )
d) Temperature........................	( )	( )	( )	( )
e) Odor....................................	( )	( )	( )	( )
f) Esthetic Appeal..................	( )	( )	( )	( )
g) Security.............................	( )	( )	( )	( )
h) Flexibility of Use.................	( )	( )	( )	( )
i) Other, specify_______........	( )	( )	( )	( )
______________________..	( )	( )	( )	( )

FIGURE 31-3. One of many different formats used for a postoccupancy evaluation. (Reproduced with permission, from *Post-Occupancy Evaluation,* 1998, Van Nostrand Reinhold, Inc.)

OCCUPANT SURVEY

USABLE TOOLS

8. Please rate the overall quality of design in this building:

	EX	G	F	P
a) Esthetic quality of exterior........	( )	( )	( )	( )
b) Esthetic quality of interior.........	( )	( )	( )	( )
c) Amount of space.......................	( )	( )	( )	( )
d) Environmental quality (lighting, acoustics, temperature, etc.)......	( )	( )	( )	( )
e) Proximity to views......................	( )	( )	( )	( )
f) Adaptability to changing uses.....	( )	( )	( )	( )
g) Security..................................	( )	( )	( )	( )
h) Maintenance............................	( )	( )	( )	( )
i) Relationship of spaces/layout.....	( )	( )	( )	( )
j) Quality of building materials........				
(1) Floors..............................	( )	( )	( )	( )
(2) Walls...............................	( )	( )	( )	( )
(3) Ceilings...........................	( )	( )	( )	( )
k) Other, specify...______________	( )	( )	( )	( )
______________________________	( )	( )	( )	( )

9. Please select and rank in order of importance facilities which are currently lacking in your building:

10. Please make any other suggestion you wish for physical or managerial improvements in your building:

11. Demographic Information:

a) Your Room #/Building area ____________________

b) Your Position: ______________________________

c) Your Age: ________

d) Your Sex: ________

e) # of years with the present organization: _______

FIGURE 31-3. Continued

4. Please rate the overall quality of Space Category B in terms of the following:

	EX	G	F	P
a) Adequacy of Space	( )	( )	( )	( )
b) Lighting	( )	( )	( )	( )
c) Acoustics	( )	( )	( )	( )
d) Temperature	( )	( )	( )	( )
e) Odor	( )	( )	( )	( )
f) Esthetic Appeal	( )	( )	( )	( )
g) Security	( )	( )	( )	( )
h) Flexibility of Use	( )	( )	( )	( )
i) Other, specify________	( )	( )	( )	( )
________________________	( )	( )	( )	( )

5. Please rate the overall quality of Space Category C in terms of the following:

	EX	G	F	P
a) Adequacy of Space	( )	( )	( )	( )
b) Lighting	( )	( )	( )	( )
c) Acoustics	( )	( )	( )	( )
d) Temperature	( )	( )	( )	( )
e) Odor	( )	( )	( )	( )
f) Esthetic Appeal	( )	( )	( )	( )
g) Security	( )	( )	( )	( )
h) Flexibility of Use	( )	( )	( )	( )
i) Other, specify________	( )	( )	( )	( )
________________________	( )	( )	( )	( )

6. Please rate the overall quality of Space Category D in terms of the following:

	EX	G	F	P
a) Adequacy of Space	( )	( )	( )	( )
b) Lighting	( )	( )	( )	( )
c) Acoustics	( )	( )	( )	( )
d) Temperature	( )	( )	( )	( )
e) Odor	( )	( )	( )	( )
f) Esthetic Appeal	( )	( )	( )	( )
g) Security	( )	( )	( )	( )
h) Flexibility of Use	( )	( )	( )	( )
i) Other, specify________	( )	( )	( )	( )
________________________	( )	( )	( )	( )

7. Please rate the overall quality of Space Category E in terms of the following:

	EX	G	F	P
a) Adequacy of Space	( )	( )	( )	( )
b) Lighting	( )	( )	( )	( )
c) Acoustics	( )	( )	( )	( )
d) Temperature	( )	( )	( )	( )
e) Odor	( )	( )	( )	( )
f) Esthetic Appeal	( )	( )	( )	( )
g) Security	( )	( )	( )	( )
h) Flexibility of Use	( )	( )	( )	( )
i) Other, specify________	( )	( )	( )	( )
________________________	( )	( )	( )	( )

FIGURE 31-3. Continued

installation, aesthetics, and functional planning, or any other information that the individual designer and client may seek to obtain.

In addition to conducting the postoccupancy evaluation related to client issues, it is a good practice for the designer and the design team to do an in-house evaluation of the project soon after the project has been completed. This evaluation should cover a time analysis to see if the project was completed within the time estimate. It should identify any problems related to the project, the client, the manufacturers and suppliers, the delivery process, and so forth. The design director may also do a profitability analysis to evaluate whether or not the project itself was profitable. This evaluation will help the design firm determine whether it should seek this kind of project in the future.

Of course, the interior design firm or project manager should send a thank-you letter or postcard to the client at the conclusion of the project. Many designers drop off a small gift as part of the thank you. A sincere thank-you note is most effective when it is a hand-written note, even if it is really a "form letter." It shows an added measure of concern for the client and appreciation of his or her business (see Figure 31-4).

If a postoccupancy evaluation or meeting is not conducted, the design firm should solicit comments on the handling of the project from the client. Designers who are committed to providing their clients with excellent customer service carefully evaluate their clients' comments. They use the in-house evaluation and their clients' comments, obtained from follow-up mailings, to improve any phase of the service of the project that have been determined to be substandard. Poor customer service is unacceptable in a professional interior design practice.

Please accept my thanks for your recent purchase from Cunninghams Interiors.

You may count on me to do everything possible to justify your confidence in Cunninghams Interiors. If you have any questions regarding your purchase—or if you have further decorating needs—please feel free to contact me.

Enclosed are two of my cards. Please share them with your friends and neighbors who may have decorating needs. Again, thanks, and I hope you enjoy your purchase.

FIGURE 31-4. Sample of the greeting inside a follow-up thank-you note from a designer. (Reproduced with permission, Betty Upton, Cunninghams Interiors, Flagstaff, AZ)

Summary

In this chapter, we have looked at many of the final tasks of the contract administration phase. Many designers do not enjoy taking care of the paperwork or following up on the orders for the merchandise that they specify. Still, this is a very important part of project management.

This chapter concludes the overall discussion of project management. The professional designer is constantly dealing with administrative activities and paperwork. These activities, along with the creative processes of the actual design projects, are the heart of the interior design profession.

In the last two chapters, we will be looking at other issues of the interior design profession—issues of interest to both the professional and the student of interior design.

REFERENCES

Berger, C. Jaye. 1994. *Interior Design Law and Business Practices*. New York: John Wiley.

Farren, Carol E. 1999. *Planning and Managing Interiors Projects*, 2nd ed. Kingston, MA.: R. S. Means.

Haviland, David. 1994. *The Architect's Handbook of Professional Practice, Student Edition*. Washington, DC: AIA Press.

Jenks, Larry. 1995. *Architectural Office Standards and Practices*. New York: McGraw-Hill.

Kaiser, Harvey H., PhD 1989. *The Facilities Manager's Reference*. Kingston, MA.: R. S. Means.

Levy, Sidney M. 1994. *Project Management in Construction*, 2nd ed. New York: McGraw-Hill.

O'Leary, Arthur F. 1992. *Construction Administration in Architectural Practice*. New York: McGraw-Hill.

Poage, Waller S. 1987. *Plans, Specs and Contracts for Building Professionals*. Kingston, MA: R. S. Means.

Preiser, Wolfgang F. E., Harvey Z. Rabinowitz, and Edward T. White. 1988. *Post-Occupancy Evaluation*. New York: Van Nostrand Reinhold.

Charles D. Gandy, FASID, FIIDA is President of Gandy/Peace, Inc., an award-winning Atlanta design firm, which specializes in both residential and commercial interiors. An accomplished lecturer, Gandy has also written countless articles on the business of design. He has held numerous national and international academic positions, and recently collaborated with the Smithsonian Institution on a series of seminars about interior design.

When the time came for me to open my own business, I knew that in order to succeed, it would be best for me to "focus." I deal with very determined couples and individuals who respect my skills and allow me to guide them into making the best decisions for their particular situation. I have budgets and projects that allow my creativity to be exploited in ways that I didn't realize were possible. I feel honored and privileged to be a "residential" designer.

Part VII

Careers

Chapter 32

Career Options

There are so many different ways to work in the interior design field and so many ways in which an individual can find the right path that will match his or her talents and interests. Traditionally, people have assumed that a career in the interior design profession means designing (or more likely decorating) homes. To this traditionally minded person, the interior designer is one who prepares floor plans of rooms and then selects and arranges furniture, fabrics, and other materials and accessories until the residential space is a beautiful, maybe even stunning, interior. Yet, we know that the interior design field encompasses substantially more than this.

Commercial interior design has taken on increasing importance over the last 40 or 50 years. The design of public buildings, such as hotels, restaurants, medical offices, and offices of every kind, has become recognized as another career path in this profession. For the commercial interior designer, space planning, developing furniture plans, and specifying and selecting furniture products and materials always have been very important. Although all of these "traditional" activities are very definitely an important part of the interior design profession, the interior designer does much more. And the variety of career options that are open to an interior designer goes far beyond designing residential or commercial interiors.

Many students wonder, "What can someone who majors in interior design do after graduation?" Although most graduating students enter the profession as either a residential or a commercial interior designer, there are other options for the graduate. This chapter will look first at some basic concepts about making a career choice in interior design and then will follow with a discussion of the two main options in the profession—that of being a residential interior designer or a commercial interior designer. Then the chapter will also explain other career options that are available to the student or the experienced professional. A new section that explores preparing for career specialization has been added at the end of the chapter.

Career Decisions

You might think it enough to decide to work either in residential or commercial interior design. When you are looking for a position, however, that decision is just one of many that you will have to make as an entry-level professional.

It is important for the entry-level designer to understand that a lot of "chore" work occurs at the beginning of employment. Regardless of the new employee's training and talent, the interior design firm will want to train and observe the employee for some period of time before giving him or her a lot of responsibility. This is called "paying one's dues," and although no one likes it, paying one's dues is part of making the transition from student to professional.

At first the entry-level designer will be doing a lot of simple chores, like maintaining the library, filing new tear sheets and price lists from suppliers, as well as gathering materials for presentations, putting sample boards together, calling for pricing, possibly meeting with sales representatives, and many other basic chores. He or she might also attend meetings with clients to learn to take careful notes and how presentations are made by designers. This is in addition to preparing simple floor plans or sketches. As the design director or owner and staff become comfortable with, and confident about, the ability of the new designer, he or she will be given more responsibility.

Working in a small firm, the new employee has the opportunity to work on a variety of projects and have a variety of experiences fairly quickly. Small firms need people to contribute, so the expectations will be high for a new employee to dive in and assist the more experienced designers in many ways. In some cases, the entry-level designer in a smaller company will be given project responsibility more quickly. This, of course, depends on the talents and attitudes of the employee.

In a larger firm, it is not unusual for the entry-level designer to progress a bit more slowly through responsibility levels. The old joke of entry-level architects drafting bathroom partitions for a year is matched by the old joke of entry-level interior designers taking care of the library for a year. Fortunately, this has changed—somewhat. However, doing similar work, such as inputting the sketches of more senior designers day after day in a large office, is not uncommon. Larger firms give an entry-level designer the opportunity to see how a variety of bigger projects are handled and also the big picture.

Another decision that the entry-level designer has to make concerns salary options. Sometimes working for a firm at a lower salary is a good idea because of the experiences that the new designer can have with that firm. Maybe one firm has better benefits than another or benefits that appeal to the designer. Location is another issue. Wanting to live in a major city like New York City has many advantages, but the cost of living is quite high. The new designer will need to be sure that the salary and benefits pay the rent and other living expenses.

Even though it most likely will take an entry-level designer up to two years to move up in a design firm to the next job level, this varies from firm to firm. And it is another issue for the new designer to consider when he or she is thinking about options. Ambition is usually a good thing, but sometimes the expectations and ambitions of entry-level designers exceeds their competence levels and the actual standard career path that is offered at a particular design firm.

Interests in specific kinds of design work obviously influence career options. Outside interests or experiences from a previous career can move you toward a particular specialty. Understanding who you are and what your interests are will help you make the decision as to which area to go into in interior design. There is a book titled *Do What You Love, the Money Will Follow* about choosing a career. When you do what you love or what you think you will enjoy, your progression in the profession will be rewarding. And, although changing jobs frequently to find the right one is not really recommended, few people stay with the same company for decades, as our grandparents did. It is likely that you will have more than a few different careers or certainly different jobs before you actually retire.

These considerations and many more are part and parcel of deciding which way to go in this profession. It might seem overwhelming, but it really is not. Dive in. The career is just fine!

Residential Interior Design

Residential interior design primarily deals with private living spaces, and most frequently, of course, the freestanding, single-family home. Residential designers also often design variations of private living spaces such as townhouses, condominiums, and apartments. Although hotels, motels, and dormitories also may be considered private living spaces, they are actually part of commercial or nonresidential interior design. Figure 32-1 provides a list of specialties within residential interior design.

Private living spaces challenge the designer in exciting ways. Some describe the job of the residential designer as helping the home owner turn his or her dreams into reality so that the home will express beauty, culture, and style—the personality and lifestyle of the family—as well as create a functional environment that will be comfortable and efficient. Home owners want to treat their private living spaces in a very special way, and residential designers are responsible for interpreting their feelings and translating them into an environment that the client will be comfortable with and will enjoy.

An important characteristic of residential interior design is the personal relationship that usually develops between the client and the designer. Those who engage in residential interior design must have the ability to get along with people, be interested in their personal needs, and feel comfortable in becoming the client's "friend." This is due, in a large part, to the fact that residential clients are much more particular about what they buy and how their home reflects their image than those clients who purchase interior concepts and products for their businesses.

Lifestyle and client interests and desires play a significant part in the execution of a successful residential project. Thus, the residential designer must develop a sensitivity for questioning the client in such a way so as to be able to determine what the client really wants. The designer must also develop an empathy with the client so that expressed desires can be translated into a design concept with which the client can live. And the designer must develop tact and diplomacy in order to show the client the realities of good and bad design ideas.

In today's world, detailed floor plans, working drawings, shop drawings, sketches, and other graphic presentations are day-to-day realities for the res-

Single-family homes	Apartments in assisted-living facilities
Townhouses	Kitchen and/or bathroom design
Condominiums	Home offices
Patio homes	Home theater design
Apartments	Manufactured housing units
Vacation homes	Residential restoration
Model homes and apartments	Color consultation

FIGURE 32-1. A partial list of residential interior design specialties.

idential designer. Freehand sketches often are useful to explain design ideas. Experienced designers frequently are involved in projects that require technical drawings and construction documents. The amount of time that a designer must spend "on the boards," preparing technical drawings, has significantly increased in residential design in recent years. The professional residential interior designer is frequently hired not only to consult with the client but also to assist the client in communicating changes and needs to the architect. Understanding the construction process, therefore, is very important.

Product knowledge is essential. Today's families are on the go constantly, and most home owners are looking to the designer to help them select products and materials that are easy to maintain. This is not to say that a beautiful silk brocade will not be specified—it will be specified only for the right client. But this consideration—another lifestyle issue—affects what will be specified for the project. In addition, many residential clients are unfamiliar with the time it takes to acquire certain products or have specialty work done for a home. The designer who can quickly put his or her hands on just the right products will enjoy great success with clients.

Those entry-level interior designers who focus on residential spaces are frequently hired to assist an experienced designer at a retail store or an interior design studio. They may do more project work on portions of a home at first. If entry-level designers are given an opportunity to work independently with clients, they often start with projects involving single rooms within the residence or even consultations regarding individual items within a room. Once they have gained experience, they are frequently asked to design an entire home.

Commercial Interior Design

Commercial interior design involves the design and specification of public spaces, such as offices, hotels, hospitals, restaurants, and so on. Figure 32–2 gives a partial list of these specialties. In this book, we have labeled anyone who works with these public spaces as a commercial interior designer. In some books, this branch of the profession may be referred to as nonresidential or contract interior design. The word *nonresidential* is self-explanatory. The term *contract design* comes from the fact that commercial projects more frequently are executed based on contracts for services. Today, of course, both residential and interior design of public spaces utilizes contracts for services.

It is unusual for any one designer to work in all areas of commercial design. The list in Figure 32–2 indicates how difficult that would be. Commercial designers specialize in designing one or two types of public spaces. A design firm may offer expertise in multiple specialties, served by interior designers and others who have specialized knowledge in a particular type of facility.

The successful commercial interior designer must understand the business of his or her clients. It is not enough that the designer be creative. It is also important for the designer to have knowledge and appreciation of the client's business in order to be effective. By specializing, the designer gains this knowledge. It then helps the designer ask better questions about the needs and goals for the design and plan of the commercial spaces. The experienced commercial designer also understands that, even though there may be a lot of similarities between two similar businesses, they will also be different. Sometimes extensive programming is necessary for the designer to totally understand the business processes of the current client, since the client may have different processes from those of a previous client.

General Offices

Facility Planning

Corporate Executive Offices

Professional Offices

Law
Advertising/public relations
Accounting
Stockbrokers and investment brokers
Real estate and real estate development
Financial institutions: banks, credit unions, and trading centers
Architecture, engineering, and interior design
Consultants of various kinds

Healthcare

Hospitals and health maintenance groups facilities
Nursing homes and assisted-living facilities
Medical and dental office suites
Out-patient laboratories
Psychiatric facilities
Rehabilitation facilities
Medical laboratories
Veterinary clinics

Hospitality and Recreation

Hotel, motels, and resorts
Restaurants, coffee shops, etc.
Recreational facilities
Health clubs and spas
Country clubs
National and state park facilities
Sports complexes
Auditoriums and theaters
Museums and restoration of historic sites
Set design: movies and television

Retail Facilities/Merchandising

Malls and shopping centers
Department stores
Specialized retail stores
Gift shops in hotels, airports, and other facilities
Visual merchandising and displays for trade shows
Showrooms
Galleries
Boutiques

Educational and Institutional

Government offices and facilities (federal, state, and local)
Colleges, universities, and community colleges
Secondary and elementary schools
Day-care centers and nursery schools
Private schools

Prisons
Churches and other religious facilities

Industrial facilities

Corporate offices
Manufacturing facilities
Training facilities
Employee service areas, such as lunchrooms and fitness centers

Transportation

Airports, bus terminals, train depots, etc.
Tour ship design
Custom and commercial airplane interiors
Recreational vehicles

FIGURE 32-2. A partial list of commercial interior design specialties.

Space planning, space allowances, furniture specification, materials, and everything else that goes into a commercial space varies with the use of the space. Space requirements for an office in a privately owned company may be quite a bit smaller than those for government offices. A perfect fabric in a hotel lobby may be totally inappropriate for a doctor's office lobby or assisted-living facility. Great carpeting in a restaurant can look awful in a nursing home. The style of a chair in a business hotel may be inappropriate in a theme resort hotel. Therefore, the designer needs to understand the business of the business in order to make appropriate design decisions. Since much of what the commercial designer specifies in projects is specially ordered from catalogs or is custom designed, the designer must have broad knowledge of products and must be confident of visualizing product size and scale. The designer often does not have products available in stock at his or her firm's warehouse. Thus, it is important for the designer to have up-to-date information concerning availability and delivery times on a wide range of products.

Commercial interior designers commonly work in teams and must know how to contribute and work in a team environment. Individuals who have a hard time collaborating or do not feel comfortable with work assignments that seem "trivial" will have a difficult time adjusting to today's commercial design firm.

Although residential design deals primarily with satisfying home owners, commercial designers must also consider how individuals other than the owners react to their design. Although they may not be asked for their input, the employees of a commercial client must feel that the interior design of their spaces is a pleasing place in which to work. The interior must also appeal in some way to the public or to the clientele of the business. A restaurant interior that pleases the owner but does not attract the public may be a beautifully designed interior but may cause the business to fail.

Commercial interior designers must also be well versed in the legal consequences of their designs. Building codes (some of which, of course, also impact the residential designer) are extremely important in commercial design. Accessibility and fire safety codes are also critical to creating a safe commercial environment. With the exception of specific local regulations, accessibility and fire safety codes have a far less impact on the design of residential spaces.

Entry-level commercial interior designers today must have experience with computer-aided drafting and design (CAD). CAD is a prerequisite skill for any designer who wishes a career in any but the smallest commercial design firms. Experience in other types of computer software that are used for presentations, scheduling, database record keeping, and project management are often recommended, if not required.

Common Employment Options

In this section, we will look at the places where interior designers commonly obtain employment and what their working environments might be like. It is important for the designer to understand that the following descriptions are very general in nature. One person's job duties in a firm might be rather different from someone else's in another, similar firm.

Residential Retail Furniture Store

Entry-level designers often begin their careers in a residential retail furniture store as an assistant to one of the senior designers. These assistants learn the business as they help with preliminary product specifications, drafting floor plans, creating sample boards, and preparing specifications, along with many other activities. As the designer gains experience, he or she is promoted to a regular design position, which gives the designer an opportunity to work more directly with clients.

In most residential retail furniture stores, the designer works with the client in either the store or the client's home. The working relationship involves the use of both design skills in planning and creating specifications and sales skills. Depending on the size of the store and the organizational setup, projects might involve designing one or two items or might involve designing and specifying items for an entire home. The designer is encouraged to sell what the store inventories but is rarely limited to selling just those items. Most often, the design service is free to the client. For the retail store, the expense of the designer's service is covered through the sale of goods at retail (or a high markup), not the service itself. Designers most often are paid on a commission basis and draw against that commission as a weekly salary. Entry-level individuals are more often paid a salary and receive a small commission. Depending on the philosophy of the store's management, it might take an entry-level person from two to four years to move up to a full-time designer position.

Department Store

Many large department stores have large interior design departments. Working for a department store is very similar to working for a retail furniture store. A designer might sell one item or a range of products. Often, however, the designer is sometimes limited to selling what the department store carries.

Other department stores have an interior design studio that offers only a limited range of services. In this case, the interior design studio is commonly housed in the drapery department, and the designer usually sells window treatments, floor coverings, and wall treatments. It is less common for the designer to sell furniture, since this is often handled by furniture salespeople.

The design service is often offered free to the client. The designer is generally paid only a commission on sales.

Retail Specialty Store

A retail specialty store is one in which only a particular product other than furniture is sold (e.g., lighting fixtures, paint and wallpaper, or floor covering). These stores are open to the general public; their goods are almost always sold at retail. Many such stores offer trade discounts to designers and other members of the interiors and construction trades. Design services are offered at no charge. These kinds of businesses represent excellent opportunities for the entry-level designer to gain sales experience and product knowledge. Designers are commonly paid a small salary plus a commission.

Occasionally, interior designers who have a strong interest in art history also find employment in art galleries or antique stores. Whether it is obtained through training or is acquired, specialized knowledge beyond a degree in interior design is often required in this type of career. Most often, compensation is a commission.

Office Furnishings Dealer

In many ways, an office furnishings dealer is similar to a residential retail showroom. There is a division of work between outside salespeople and the design department. The company has a showroom space and an inventory of furniture to back up what is displayed. And the company commonly has its own warehouse and delivery crews. The main difference is that an office furnishings dealer rarely sells products at suggested retail. More commonly, it sells products at a discount from suggested retail or adds a markup onto the cost to the client.

As for the design employee, he or she may be part of an in-house design department or may work in a subsidiary design company that is owned by the dealership. In recent years, many dealerships have positioned their design departments to support the dealership sales staff so as not to compete with the design community. The designer works with the client either in the store or at the client's facility. Office furnishings dealers primarily design various office complexes. However, some also design other kinds of public spaces, such as hospitals and hotels. Designers who work in these organizations are often required to have substantial space-planning skills and to be experienced with CAD.

Depending on the exact nature of the firm, the client might be found by the design department or by a salesperson. Salespeople are usually not required to be designers, although many were at one time, and are often asked not to do any interior design. They are the ones who sell the goods to the client, whereas the interior designers are the ones who plan spaces and specify the project. Products are often sold to the client through the firm, whether the project originated with the designer or the salesperson.

Many office furnishings dealers have certain exclusive products that they expect designers to specify most often. Depending on the dealership, the designer can specify almost anything that the client's project requires, whether or not it is carried by the firm.

Entry-level designers do a wide variety of work for more experienced designers. It often takes at least two years to advance to a position of project responsibility, although this estimate may be less in smaller firms or in firms that have more qualified entry-level designers. The pay is usually a salary for the designers and a commission for the salespeople. Designers might be eligible for commission on certain items or for bonuses.

Architectural Office

Another option for interior designers is to work as an interior designer for an architectural office. Many architectural offices have interior design groups. These designers work primarily on projects in partnership with the architects. However, it is also common in the larger offices for the interior designers to obtain projects which do not involve the architectural side of the firm. The work might involve residential or commercial projects, or both, depending on the nature of the architectural practice.

It is common for a designer to work as part of a team, with other designers and the architects and others in the firm. This opportunity requires that the designer have very good space-planning and technical skills, as well as design creativity. Interior designers in architectural firms frequently work with construction drawings and formal bid specifications. As with office furnishings dealers, most architectural firms require that designers be experienced in the use of CAD and possibly other types of software.

Architectural firms are predominately compensated by the client by means of design fees. Thus, the compensation method by which designers most commonly are paid is a salary. Some also find it advantageous to sell products to the client, though not to the extent that he or she would in an office furnishings dealership.

Independent Design Firm

An independent design firm is one that has no affiliation with a particular product and may not have any products displayed for sale in its office or studio. Because such a firm is independent, it may specify any product for its clients that is available in the marketplace. The firm may specialize in residential or commercial work but usually does a combination of both. It may be a small, one-person design studio or a large firm that has dozens of employees. Many independent design firms design and specify but do not sell products to their clients. However, the independent design firm recognizes the added revenue potential of selling products, so many are also offering this service.

Unless the firm also sells products, income is generated through design fees. Design employee's salaries, especially in the smaller firms, generally will be lower than in other types of design situations. Firms that do not sell products pay design employees a salary, whereas those that do sell products may have a commission structure for designers.

Specialized Independent Firm

A specialized independent firm is an interior design firm that primarily designs a certain kind of commercial interior, e.g., restaurants, hotels, healthcare facilities, or any others that are listed in Figure 32-2. It is, of course, possible for a residential interior designer to specialize as well. One of the most common specialties associated with a residential interior design practice is designing kitchens and bathrooms. The projects obtained by specialized independent design firms frequently requires that the designer travel extensively, since the firm's work comes from all over the country, if not the world. The specialized firm must either market itself very successfully or else engage in other types of work to keep from being adversely affected by economic conditions that could limit its practice.

Specialized independent design firms generate revenue primarily from design fees. However, many also sell products. As with independent firms, designers are paid a salary plus a possible commission (for product sales).

Manufacturer

An individual may work for a manufacturer in several ways. A designer might work in a manufacturer's showrooms. All the major manufacturers have showrooms in one or more cities. Designers might work with the interior designers and other allied professionals who come to the showroom. Usually, the designer is in a sales position and is paid a small salary and/or a commission.

Many manufacturers also hire interior designers who have a minimum of three years' experience in the business to be sales representatives. Sales reps are almost always paid a commission rather than a salary. See the discussion of sales representatives later in this chapter and in Chapter 28 for more information about sales representatives.

When a designer is working for a manufacturer, there is often the opportunity to travel throughout the United States and to work outside the country. Many of the major manufacturers have showrooms in foreign countries. Those designers who do design layout work as an employee of a manufacturer also have an opportunity to travel within the United States.

Another way in which a designer can work for the manufacturer is as a product designer. Depending on the product, the company may require that the designer have an industrial design background rather than an interior design background. A few manufacturers, notably those that produce open-office furniture may have staff designers to aid designers and architects in planning and specifying the company's products. These last job opportunities are generally at a factory location rather than at a showroom location.

Compensation depends on the actual job. Showroom sales positions are commission based; design layout work generally is salary based; and product designer positions are salary or commission based. Sales reps are most commonly paid by commission.

Industrial and Corporate Interior Designers

Many large corporations have in-house interior designers or facility planners. These individuals either are in charge of the direct planning and design of all the corporation's spaces or work with outside designers in the design of corporate facilities. Responsibility might involve designing the chief executive officer's office as well as any group of offices or spaces within the facility. It might also involve collaboration with an architect on a new facility.

Included in this career option are corporate designers who are responsible for specialized types of designs. Hotel chains, for example, have in-house designers who work with architects and franchise owners in the design or remodeling of their facility. In some situations, the designers might travel to various company locations. Designers who work in a corporate environment are paid a salary or possibly an hourly wage.

Facility Planners

Many corporations realize the economic benefit of having their own planning and design departments as part of their facility management team. Generally speaking, facility planners are responsible for space planning for a corporation. This work is most frequently done for corporations that extensively use open-office systems products, though a facility planner can work for any type of business. Facility planners are required to have experience with CAD hardware and software. Specialized degrees in facility planning are available from a few universities, but most facility planners are interior designers or architects.

If they are designing solely for a corporation, facility planners often find traveling among the various plants and office buildings a necessity. These individuals are paid a salary.

The job of facility manager, sometimes in the same department as a facility planner, is a more specialized career and requires additional training in psychology, physical plant management, and engineering.

Of course, there are many independent designers whose firms specialize in facility planning. Somewhat similar to corporate facility planners, they are primarily responsible for programming and planning, and are not generally retained to make all color and materials selections.

Federal Government

The federal government's General Services Administration (GSA) is responsible for employing interior designers. These designers prepare space plans and systems plans, design office facilities, and participate in other kinds of government agency interior design work. The designer is commonly limited to designing with the products currently on the GSA purchasing schedule, although some projects allow additional flexibility in product specification. The GSA designer designs spaces in a certain geographic area of the country. He or she will be working on projects throughout that area, which may require some traveling away from the main office. The salary, which is based on the individual's "GS" rating, is sometimes a bit higher than an entry-level salary in the private sector, and the government, of course, offers excellent benefits.

State and City Governments

Some state and city governments have salaried interior designers and architects. These professionals function in much the same way as designers who work for the federal government. Some state agencies, like the university system, have architectural or design personnel who either design or coordinate contracted work. Few state and city governments have designers preparing layouts and specifications for the state or city, since many states have laws forbidding state agencies from performing work that competes with work from the private sector. Compensation is salary based. States and cities also have very good benefits packages.

Universities and Colleges

Many medium- and large-sized universities and colleges have a facilities planning office. This office works with architects, interior designers, and the university staff to develop new building designs and to remodel existing structures. As mentioned earlier, if the institution is part of the state system, the designer only works to coordinate what is needed by the institution with private-sector designers. Compensation is by salary.

Universities and colleges also hire faculty members who have experience in the interior design field. The minimal educational requirement for a full-time faculty position at a university or a college is a master's degree in addition to some professional experience. Most universities and colleges expect that faculty members will continue their education beyond a master's degree and/or remain active in the design profession. Universities and colleges also hire practicing interior designers as adjunct or visiting instructors to teach part-time during a semester. Teaching positions are also available at many community colleges and professional schools.

Alternative Career Options

The foregoing discussion shows many of the primary ways that interior designers can practice their profession. These typify the kinds of job opportunities that most students and the general public recognize as career options in the interior design profession. However, there are many other ways in which an interior designer who has certain specialized skills or experiences can work in the field.

CAD Specialist

Although CAD has become a necessary skill for interior designers, some design firms might utilize a CAD specialist who may or may not hold a degree in interior design. In this case, these CAD specialists are called CAD technicians. CAD technicians rarely are responsible for design decisions. They input into the computer sketches from designers and architects, and produce the drawings that are required to finish a job. CAD specialists most likely are salaried employees.

In recent years, some designers who seek to own their own business have become freelance CAD specialists. These experienced designers offer CAD services (including three-dimensional rendering) to the small interior design practice that does not have in-house CAD capability.

Other Computer Specialists

Interior design firms also use the computer in other ways. One is for specification writing. The computer can speed up the production of complicated, formal specification bid packages, as well as of detailed equipment lists for open-office systems projects. Computers are also used for project scheduling, word processing, order entry, and bookkeeping. The use of the computer has become a required skill in the everyday responsibilities of the interior designer, regardless of the size of the design firm.

Professional Renderers

The professional renderer is very skilled in perspective and various rendering media. He or she may be employed by a large interior design or architectural firm, or may be self-employed as a freelance renderer. If the individual works for a firm, he or she rarely is expected to perform other interior design functions. The renderer is compensated by a salary. Today, many of these individuals utilize computer programs and perhaps virtual-reality programs to create multiple views very quickly.

Those individuals who are self-employed work for many firms in the trade. They charge their clients based on the rendering. The size and media used for the project are important criteria for determining the fee.

Model Builders

Allied to the professional renderer are model builders. These individuals may also be professional renderers, or they may only produce architectural and interior models. A few large architectural firms have model builders on staff, but this is not particularly common. In such a situation, the employee is compensated by a salary. In larger cities, there are firms that specialize in model building. Employees in such firms are also compensated by salary. For the self-employed model builder, compensation is based on the fee that the architect or designer charges.

Model building requires that the individual have an excellent sense of scale, knowledge of the kinds of material that can be used to produce a scale model, a concern for detail, and patience to do the work required in model building.

ADA and Accessibility Compliance Consultants

The passage of the Americans with Disabilities Act (ADA) in 1992 and the expansion of accessibility standards in other countries have created a new career option for many designers. Although compliance with accessibility standards is widespread for new construction, many owners of public buildings that were built prior to local adoption of accessibility standards are unsure of what must be done to comply with the standards.

Those designers who are experienced in or are interested in healthcare or the design needs of the disabled have become consultants to interior designers, the architectural community, or business owners. Extensive knowledge and understanding of the accessibility requirements allow these consultants to review plans for new or remodeled facilities to be sure that the plans will meet the law prior to submittal for building permits. These consultants can also assist business owners when they file claims or prior to the beginning of design planning to review potential costs of meeting the accessibility requirements.

Sales Representatives

Sales representatives (reps) can work in residential retail stores, office furnishings dealers, and specialized retail stores. Sales representatives can also work for manufacturers outside the showroom.

The independent rep works for himself or herself, representing many products from a variety of manufacturers. The rep visits with all the interior design and architectural firms that might specify products. The rep is compensated with a commission whenever a product has been sold in his or her territory, whether or not the rep has had anything directly to do with that sale.

A factory rep works for one manufacturer as an employee. He or she handles all or part of the product line of that manufacturer in a specified territory of the country. Much like the independent rep, the factory representative works with designers and architects who might specify his or her product line. Some factory reps also have specific obligations to dealers in their territory. A dealer might have an exclusive right to sell a product in a specific city or area of the country.

The factory representative is paid a commission on all goods sold in his or her territory, whether or not the rep has had anything to do with that sale. Both kinds of reps may have large territories and must travel extensively. In most cases, individuals must have proven sales experience to obtain a position as a manufacturer's representative.

Sales reps in retail stores might be referred to as sales associates. In some cases, a sales associate is not an interior designer but someone who is skilled in sales techniques. Many retail stores also hire interior designers to be sales associates. This is especially true of office furnishings dealers. Interior designers in large residential furniture stores primarily are responsible for doing interior design, but they are also expected to sell furniture. Sales associates in retail stores are most commonly paid a straight commission or a small salary plus a commission.

Architectural Photographers

An architectural photographer can be an interior designer who has taken several photography classes in college. However, most are photographers by trade. These individuals specialize in the photography of exteriors and interiors, and are hired by the interior designer, the architect, or the owner of the building. It is rare that an architectural photographer is working on staff of an architectural or interiors firm. Those who work for an architectural photographer are paid a salary. Those who own their own business compensate themselves as any business owner would.

Product Designers

The independent product designer creates designs for furniture and interior products and then sells those designs to a manufacturer. Today, most product designers are industrial designers by training rather than interior designers. Compensation results from royalties paid by the firm that buys the design.

Specification Writers

Larger firms have individuals on staff who specialize in preparing formal specification bid packages. These staff positions can be filled by trained interior designers or architects, but they are filled also by individuals who have a general educational background and who enjoy the detail of specification writing.

Installation Supervisors or Contract Administrators

Some firms, especially office furnishings dealers, release project managers from on-site supervision and have others perform a distinct job called an installation supervisor. The installation supervisor (or contract administrator, in architectural and construction firms) is responsible for the on-site and in-office supervision of the installation and/or construction of a project. Depending on the actual responsibility of the design firm, this individual travels to the job site in order to make sure that the building and interior construction are not deviating from what exists on the original plans. When the furniture and furnishings are ready for installation, the installation supervisor is on the job site, ensuring that everything goes where it is supposed to go and takes care of inspecting the job site for damages, omissions, and repairs.

This vital function releases the designer so that he or she can generate more design projects. The position is not always filled by a trained interior designer. The individual with this responsibility must know how to read blueprints, understand the construction process, be familiar with the ordering process, and understand the installation process of a variety of products. Installation supervisors are most often salaried employees of the design firm, warehouse service, or installation service firm.

Interior Design Management

A position in interior design management requires extensive experience in the field or experience in general management. Most design directors are former designers who have worked their way up through the ranks. It is important for the design director to have a knowledge of interior design and a good general business knowledge or experience related to the management of personnel, marketing, and general business principles. A position in design management might involve being the director of the design department, in which the individual has almost sole responsibility for marketing the firm, or any combination of these areas. Refer to Chapter 11 for additional information on the job of the design manager.

Design management personnel most often are paid a salary, with some bonus or commission structure supplementing the salary.

Marketing Specialists

Large interior design firms frequently utilize a marketing specialist to prospect and market for new clients. This person may be an interior designer who has a special ability to market or who is a business major with an emphasis in marketing. The marketing specialist is expected to locate new clients and to respond to inquiries from potential clients. He or she assists the firm's PR consultant in the development of any promotional materials, such as brochures, web site materials, and other collateral materials. The marketing specialist is involved in marketing presentations and helps determine the outline and materials needed for these presentations. He or she may also arrange training sessions for the purpose of helping the interior design professional staff become better at selling design solutions.

As with other design management staff, the marketing specialist is paid a salary.

Construction Industry

Interior designers sometimes find interesting positions with construction companies. One of the most common is the designer working for a residential developer. The designer assists new home buyers with finish selections. Although the home builder has a group of standard materials that are calculated into the purchase price, the buyer may upgrade to more expensive materials. These designers earn a commission when the buyer upgrades any of the materials.

Other designers might be hired as construction project managers or as marketing specialists. There are also positions available for designers who help create the basic floor plans of a new development, prepare renderings of the various models, and perhaps design the model homes. However, it should be noted that model home design is a specialty of many independent interior designers.

Museum Work

Interior designers with experience or additional training in museum, restoration, or curatorial areas can work for one of the many historic site museums that exist. This can be very rewarding work for those individuals who have a keen interest in history and restoration. Most of these job opportunities require advanced degree work in such areas as art history, history, and archaeology.

Journalism

A journalism career is possible for interior designers who are very good writers or who have had training in journalism. The positions might be with a large city newspaper or a trade or shelter magazine. Some designers who find their way into full-time journalism positions might also serve as design critics.

Designers who write well but who do not wish to work full time in this specialty can submit articles to various trade, shelter, and general print media. As discussed in a Chapter 23, this can be used as an excellent marketing tool.

Merchandising and Exhibit Design

Many of the skills that an interior designer learns can be applied to visual merchandising, display, and exhibit presentation. Department stores, retail specialty shops, mall management corporations, galleries, and trade show coordinators require merchandise displays. Large department stores have in-house visual merchandising departments to constantly change merchandise displays. Others may work for exhibit companies that specialize in the coordination and setup of trade show and convention displays. Still others freelance display work to retail specialty shops and boutiques. This can be very interesting and challenging work for an interior designer.

Graphics and Wayfinding

Many interior design projects involve at least some graphic design work. This may be a graphic for the walls in a child's bedroom or in an employee cafeteria. It could also be a new logo for a commercial client. Many commercial interior design firms offer graphic design services as an additional service. Some have affiliated graphics companies that seek out any type of graphic design or desktop publishing work.

Signage design and specification is very important in commercial projects. The larger the facility and campus are, the greater the need for wayfinding signage. Wayfinding involves creating graphics and signs that will help individuals locate themselves within a large facility, such as a hospital, and easily find their direction around the building.

Additional training in graphic design and desktop computer graphics is especially useful in this specialty. Compensation is generally by salary.

With so many potential career options available—and others that are in some way related to the interior design and built-environment industry—the reader may be unsure which direction to go in in the exciting and varied profession of interior design. If the reader has read this chapter first, the author urges you to go back to the beginning of this book in order to gain an overview of the interior design profession. Chapter 1 will give the reader a sense of the requirements of the profession in terms of educational preparation and professional recognition status. Chapter 3, which discusses personal and professional goal setting, may help the reader who is confused about which of these many career options he or she may be interested in pursuing.

Preparing for Specialization in a Career

Many career specializations require some sort of additional educational training or job experience. Students or, for that matter, designers who are seeking a change in their career, need to keep this in mind when they are considering career interests. But how can one find out what experience or education is required of any specific career option in interior design?

One important way to prepare for career specialization is to interview designers who already work in that segment of the design field. Interior designers are like most people—they love to talk about what they do and are flattered to find out that others are interested in their work. Appointments can be set up with experienced designers so that the prospective designer can ask a short series of well-considered questions about their work in the specialty. It is suggested that the individual ask for no more than 30 minutes of the designer's time; this shows respect for their professional responsibilities.

If an individual is interested in a specialty area of interior design, it is also very helpful for that individual to seek additional course work that would provide general background information about that specialization. For example, someone who wishes to specialize in hospitality design should take some introductory classes in the hospitality industry. Those who wish to work in retail design in some manner would be wise to take merchandising and visual merchandising classes. Residential designers could take classes on salesmanship or human behavior. This type of introduction to a specialty will provide valuable help to the student as he or she seeks to understand the unique functional problems of the specialty.

Researching the specialty is another way of understanding the business of that specialty. The reader could subscribe to trade publications that are related to the specialty. Reading design trade magazines, textbooks, and design books on the specialty is another easy way to learn about the business of that specialty. Personal experience is another way to learn. Some students become interested in healthcare design because of a family member's health problems. Those who work in retail stores in order to work their way through college often become interested in visual merchandising or retail design.

Students should also recognize that many specialized interior design firms may not hire an entry-level designer. The author has heard from numerous specialized firm principals over the years that they simply do not hire entry-level designers. In general, the reason is that their lack of actual work experience prevents them from working at the pace and intensity that are needed in their firms. "We need designers who can hit the ground running," commented one such principal. "Entry-level designers, regardless of the quality of their talent, cannot do this," the principal continued. Their advice is for students to get good-quality actual work experience and learn what it is really like to work in design before they apply for a job in a highly specialized design firm. Of course, there is no reason a student could not apply anyway. Being in the right place at the right time has gotten many designers their first job!

Summary

One of the fascinating aspects of the interior design profession is the variety of ways in which an individual can work in the field. This chapter has reviewed many areas of interior design that an individual might find exciting and rewarding. Although some areas do require training or experience beyond the undergraduate level or the normal interior design degree, many offer positions that the trained interior designer can achieve with work experience in the field. This section shows that it is not absolutely necessary for everyone to be highly creative, a great salesperson, a great artist, or a space planner in order to find a niche in interior design.

In the final chapter, we will look at how the designer should prepare for obtaining that first or next job by reviewing portfolios, resumes, the job search, and the job interview.

REFERENCES

American Society of Interior Designers (various authors). "Design Specialties." *ASID Professional Designer*. July/August 1998.

Ball, Victoria. 1982. *Opportunities in Interior Design*. Skokie, IL: VGM Career Horizons.

Bolles, Richard Nelson. 2000. *The 2000 What Color Is Your Parachute?* Berkeley, CA: Ten-Speed Press.

Kilmer, Rosemary, and W. Otie Kilmer. 1992. *Designing Interiors*. Fort Worth, TX: Holt, Rinehart & Winston.

Knackstedt, Mary. 1992. The *Interior Design Business Handbook*. New York: Van Nostrand Reinhold.

———. 1985. *Profitable Career Options for Interior Designers*. Kobro Publishers.

Lloyd, Joan. 1992. *The Career Decisions Planner*. New York: John Wiley.

Loebelson, Andrew. 1983. *How to Profit in Contract Design*. New York: Interior Design Books.

McLain-Kark, Joan H., and Ruey-Er Tang. "Computer Usage and Attitudes Toward Computers in the Interior Design Field." *Journal of Interior Design Education and Research*. (Fall 1986) 12: 25–32.

Rubin, Harriet. 1999. *Soloing: Realizing Your Life's Ambition*. New York: HarperCollins Business.

Sher, Barbara (with Annie Gottlieb). 1979. *Wishcraft: How to Get What You Really Want*. New York: Ballantine.

Siegel, Harry (with Alan Siegel). 1982. *A Guide to Business Principles and Practices for Interior Designers*, rev. ed. New York: Watson-Guptill.

Sinetar, Marsha. 1987. *Do What You Love, the Money Will Follow*. New York: Dell.

Thompson, Jo Anne Asher, ed. 1992. *ASID Professional Practice Manual*. New York: Watson-Guptill.

Veitch, Ronald M., Dianne R. Jackman, and Mary K. Dixon. 1990. *Professional Practice*. Winnipeg, Canada: Peguis Publishers.

Chapter 33

Getting the Next—or First—Job

The ease with which you may find the next—or first—job fluctuates wildly in direct relationship to the economy. Students and professionals alike in the 1980s were frustrated by a lack of available positions. Graduates and professionals in the late 1990s had numerous opportunities as design firms all over the country and the world were in search of interior design staff at all levels. This trend is expected to grow, at least for the immediate future. The roller-coaster ride of finding an interior design position can change at any time. Because the interior design profession does ebb and flow with the economy, students and design professionals must be thorough in their approach to their career efforts. When they are ready to make a move or to start the job search process, they must do so with careful thought and planning.

The job search can be a time-consuming and stress-producing period. The number of books on how to write a resume or a cover letter, how to have a successful interview, and so on, grows every month. However, going to a bookstore to look for a guide to aid in the job search for a specific career in interior design can be frustrating.

This chapter will provide the professional and the student alike with some tips related to finding a job in interior design. All the examples are specifically based on the needs of the professional or new interior designer as he or she seeks a professional design position. This chapter will discuss the portfolio, the resume and cover letter, the job search, and the interview, and it includes a discussion concerning the use of electronic means to widen the job search process. The chapter concludes with new sections that discuss the transition from student to professional and some comments about job changing for professionals who are looking to make a major career change.

Portfolios

Whether you are a student seeking an entry into the interior design industry or a seasoned professional looking to make a job change, a portfolio will be needed. A *portfolio* is a visual presentation of what you can do as an interior designer. It must show your best work, but not just anything. It should contain design work that relates to the design position that you are seeking and the needs of the prospective employer. Keep these two thoughts in mind as we discuss the interior design portfolio.

Let us begin by saying that your portfolio is never "finished." It must be constantly updated and refined to meet current or expected needs in the job search process. For the experienced professional, the portfolio must show a range of work, with emphasis on the present. For the student who is seeking that all-important first job, the portfolio must exhibit the very best work that the student can do and also must present the breadth of the student's abilities so as not to limit the prospective employee from any reasonable, possible opportunity.

Whether the portfolio is for the professional or the student, the portfolio must be suited to the kind of job for which the individual is interviewing. A portfolio that shows multiple examples of sample boards but does not show drafting skills wastes both the employer's and the job seeker's time. It also shows the prospective employer that the job seeker has not done any homework about the design firm or its needs.

In addition, portfolios should be self-explanatory. Many times it is necessary for the designer to send his or her portfolio to a prospective employer for a review before an interview will be granted. When the designer is not there to explain his or her involvement, the parameters of the project, and how the designer arrived at the solution, the prospective employer expects the portfolio to be able to answer these questions. If it does not, then all that the prospective employer can review is the individual's technical competence in the preparation of drawings and boards.

A portfolio should also be well organized so that it clearly tells your story. A logical order is needed to help when you present the portfolio. You will be nervous, so having items in disarray will only make you more nervous. If you have done your homework and know something about the firm and its present needs, you will know how to organize the portfolio so that each piece that you include demonstrates how you can help the prospective employer. Of course, this means that you will want to make some slight adjustments to the contents of your portfolio for each job interview. Just as you would not send a resume that emphasizes a commercial design career objective to a residential design firm, you would not show a lot of residential design work to a commercial employer, unless there was a very good reason. We will talk more about this later in the chapter.

Ideas on format, general contents, and processes to produce the portfolio can be quite similar for the professional and the student. A professional's portfolio will be more extensive than a student's and will likely only show drawings or photographs of completed projects. A professional's portfolio will not contain many items from school, unless the job change is happening within only a year or two of graduation or the professional has recently gone to graduate school. Thus, the remaining discussion of a portfolio will be a generalized discussion on what to include, the format, the media, and will include some ideas about making a portfolio presentation using electronic materials, and the written materials.

What to Include

It is important that the portfolio include examples of all the skills of which you are capable. As much as is possible, the items selected should relate to the type of design work the design firm does. For example, if you are seeking a position in a residential design firm, the majority of items should show your skills in designing and executing residential projects. Of course, it is perfectly acceptable to include other kinds of work. A big part of this strategy is to show the employer that you have some understanding of the issues involved in designing the types of interiors that the firm undertakes. Obviously, a student's portfolio will not necessarily have an extensive selection of either residential or commercial projects, so a student must show a variety of items that will help demonstrate his or her skills in the techniques and processes of interior design. The professional may find it easier to emphasize certain types of work, but he or she may also have to show the breadth of his or her experiences in designing projects when making a job change.

Obviously, the portfolio should show only your best work. It is generally acceptable for students to rework (if possible) earlier project solutions once they have been graded. Since many programs emphasize residential spaces in the early part of the curriculum, these projects are often not the best examples of the student's abilities after graduation. When a student is looking for a position in a residential design studio, it might be necessary for the student to rework these early projects in order to show how his or her technical mastery, as well as concept development, have improved.

It has been suggested by many professionals that the portfolio should start out with your very best work—perhaps the one that earned you first place in a student competition. If you are a professional, you may want to start by showing a recent award-winning project. It should end with another quality piece to serve as a "last impression" of what you can do. The other items can be arranged in between the two. However, do not include poor-quality work or work you feel you have to apologize for, even if it is the only piece that shows a certain kind of skill or type of interior. If it is not very good, either rework it or leave it out.

Since you may only have 30–60 minutes for the entire interview, you need to limit the number of items in your portfolio. Twenty-five to 30 items or pages should be sufficient, especially if they directly demonstrate the skills needed for the position. You probably will not want to have more than about 45 items in the portfolio, or it will either bore the reviewer or decrease the time available for the interviewer to ask you questions. Besides, having too much to show or taking too much of the reviewer's time at some point becomes disrespectful of his or her busy schedule.

In order to present a high-quality portfolio, you should photograph them as soon as possible after having completed them. You need to store projects, drawings, models, and so on, carefully so that they do not become damaged. A former student of mine lost all her original work when her apartment roof leaked. She had no photos of any kind of her work. If you take photographs, take more than one image or have multiple copies made, so that you will have backup copies. Standard film and good-quality digital photography, even though it may be of amateur quality, can be useful. Since those of you who are professionals generally are not allowed to take drawings and documents that you have made while employed at a design firm, you may have to spend the time and money to photograph finished projects. However, be sure you obtain the client's permission to photograph the interiors. The rights clause in a design contract that relates to photographs does not cover a designer's personal use of photos.

The portfolio should include as many of the items listed in Figure 33-1 as possible. Students (and even professionals who have just a few years' of work experience) should also retain at least some preliminary work. Employers like to see the thought process behind design solutions, and sketches do this. Although most of the examples are commonly parts of projects, it is important to show at least one complete project presentation. This complete project should include the verbal explanation of the design problem, floor plans, color boards, renderings, and any other written or graphic documents that were a part of the project's requirements. A copy of your resume should be included in the portfolio. Having a neat copy of the resume in the portfolio guarantees that you

- Sketches that show the decision-making process
- Furniture floor plans
- CAD drawings
- Color boards
- Working drawings
- Freehand sketches
- Perspectives, elevations, and/or isometric drawings
- Examples of lettering skills
- Technical renderings in any media in which the designer is competent
- For professionals, slides, photographs, or publication reprints showing completed projects for which the designer was primarily responsible
- For students, at least one completed project

FIGURE 33-1. Items commonly included in a portfolio.

will be able to present an unfolded copy to the prospective employer. Be sure you know the details about everything that you have put in your portfolio. What were the project goals, and so on? You will be asked questions about many of the items, and you should be able to give reasonable responses.

Format of the Portfolio

A key decision that you will make as you create the portfolio relates to the format. You will be carrying your portfolio in taxi cabs, automobiles, trains, buses, and airplanes. They will be laid out on conference tables and desks, and possibly even be mailed across the country. Although a common format size for boards and drawings is 20 inches by 30 inches, portfolios are actually becoming smaller in size. The 20 inch by 30 inch format works well for the preparation of drawings and presentation boards, but it makes for a very cumbersome package to carry. Format sizes that are easier to present and to transport are 8 inches by 10 inches, 11 inches by 14 inches, and 14 inches by 17 inches. Thus, early on, you must make a decision about the final size of your portfolio. The larger-size formats make it easy to present original work, yet the smaller-size formats are easier to handle. Frankly, some employers still like to see 1/4-inch scale drawings and full-sized sample boards. You might have both large- and small-sized format items available. When you are finalizing the schedule for an interview, you can inquire about any preferences that the prospective employer may have.

Whatever format you decide upon, it is important as much as possible for you to present all the examples consistently in either a vertical or a horizontal manner. This will aid you during the interview because you will not have to keep flipping the items in the portfolio around. If you have used both horizontal and vertical presentation formats, you will have to give more thought as to how the portfolio will be organized and presented, and if items need to be redone (if possible), or possibly eliminated from the portfolio. An option is to group horizontal items separately from vertical format items.

Let us look at some ideas for a small-sized format presentation, since it has become so popular with students and professionals. There are different methods of binding pages, so choose one that will allow you flexibility if you know you are going to be interviewing with a variety of different employers. The pages of the portfolio will need to take a certain amount of abuse. Many items, such as sketches, renderings, and plans, can be mounted on paper that matches mat board or black photographic paper and can be inserted into plastic notebook sleeves. You have to be careful about reducing a large original. CAD drawings are generally not a problem, but hand-drafted items may be difficult to read and details may be difficult to discern. Larger sheets can be neatly folded. Remember that each side of the plastic sleeve is a "page." Use this to your advantage as you organize drawings and written statements. For written items, try to stick to one type font. Multiple type fonts can accidentally make the portfolio look messy.

The large-sized format will be more difficult for you to handle during a presentation. Remember the problem you had of transporting your projects to and from classes. That aside, when you are using a format that will accommodate up to 20 inch by 30 inch mat or foam core board, remember that these items become heavy. It will not be easy to carry 25 pieces of large mat board very far on a subway in New York City or on the Metro in San Francisco. Try to remount materials on lighter weight boards or sheets, if possible. Good organization, clean and neat materials, "pages" that include all of the written information that should go with the design elements are all important.

The physical binder itself should be of good quality and look very professional. Drawings rolled up in a tube may be convenient for carrying, but they do not communicate the right level of professionalism, nor do the cardboard portfolios that many students use during college. It is not, however, necessary to spend a lot of money on leather-bound books.

Media

If you decide to take advantage of a smaller-sized format, many items will need to be redone into other media. There are several different kinds of media that can be used to present your portfolio items.

Color-slide transparencies (35 mm) are a popular portfolio medium used by many designers. Slides are easy to transport and are relatively inexpensive to produce. A disadvantage of using slides is that you need to carry along a slide viewer. You should not assume that the prospective employer will have a slide projector available to show slide-formatted work. Carrying and setting up a slide projector is also an extra headache that the prospective employee may not want to add to the interview situation. A handheld viewer would be better than a projector, but it should be easy to operate and should be reliable. Whatever you do, try not to get stuck in a situation in which the prospective employer must hold up sheets of slides and look at them by means of the light of a ceiling fixture.

Amateur photographers can take slides of flat work themselves using a small amount of equipment. All that is needed is a 35-mm camera, a tripod, and, if daylight film is used, an area where good, consistent natural light is available. If natural light is not available, the proper combination of film and photo floodlights must be used. Using the camera's flash unit can produce glare, hot spots, and inconsistent results.

Photographic prints are easier to present but are more expensive than slides to produce. Photographic prints, whether they are color or black and white, should be at least 5 inches by 7 inches. Prints 8 inches by 10 inches are even better, yet each 8 by 10 print can cost several dollars to have made. The best quality print will come from a slide negative rather than from print film.

Many firms use the services of a professional architectural photographer to take photos of high quality or of unusual projects. Designers involved in these projects should obtain duplicates of the slides or prints from the design firm or client through the photographer to use in their personal portfolio.

A common medium used by designers is the photo mechanical transfer (PMT). A PMT is a high-contrast positive print. This is an exceptionally good medium to use when you want to reduce working drawings and floor plans that have not been originally drawn using CAD. Design items that you want produced as PMTs must be crisp, black-and-white technical work. Color work cannot be made into PMTs.

Of course, today there are many electronic media that can be used for the portfolio as well. A relatively easy and reasonably economical way of using electronic media is by transferring portfolio items to the computer. Digital photographs can be taken of work or items that can be scanned into the computer. These can be manipulated to your format and even, in some cases, to repair small errors. The images can then be printed on a high-resolution laser printer for multiple copies.

A more sophisticated use of electronic media is by transferring work to CD-ROM disks or even the web. It is easy to transfer almost all portfolio items to a writable CD-ROM disk.* CAD files can be copied directly to the disk. Other drawings can be scanned with a flatbed scanner. Digital photographs can be taken of sample boards, models, and other three-dimensional items. Digital photos of actual installations can also be transferred to the CD-ROM disk.

What is the advantage of going to the extra expense of transferring work to a CD-ROM? Flexibility with layout, ease of transport, and excellent quality of images. Using a CD-ROM also shows the prospective employer that you are on the cutting edge of the industry. Of course, you have almost instantaneous communication over the web.

With a CD-ROM, you have a preprogrammed presentation, by which the viewer experiences your portfolio as you want him or her to, without interruption. You are then getting the viewer's undivided attention during the presentation. You can integrate animation, voice-overs, and music to make it even more personalized. In addition, you control the timing, sequence, and pace of the information in your presentation.

A CD-ROM also can be created to be more interactive with the viewer; that is, the viewer can follow the sequence from beginning to end as in a preprogrammed presentation, or the viewer will have options (links) that allow him or her to move from one section to another of the material. When the presentation is controlled by the viewer, he or she can focus upon areas of interest and skip others. For example, if the company is looking for someone for its hospitality department, the design director can skip work related to other types of facilities and concentrate on the quality of solutions and technical work in hospitality.

These presentations can also be programmed into a personal web site. You may be able to link your web site onto one of the job search sites or bring your laptop along and let the interviewer look at your web site during the interview. The one caution with web site portfolios is that you must be careful about image file size and the number of images you include. As the reader probably well knows, the more graphics you include on a web site, the longer it takes for them to load. Employers may become impatient waiting for a complex portfolio to download. If the portfolio is sent as an E-mail, large attachments with a lot of graphics can crash the receiver's system. A portfolio on a web site will need to be revised and updated. The designer must either be able to program with HTML or pay someone to frequently update the site.

Students may be able to receive assistance in setting up an electronic portfolio from departmental or university computer centers. There are also many software programs that can help the professional do the work themselves. Professionals can also get help from commercial copy centers, or they can hire a graphic designer or a web site designer.

* Of course, a writable CD-ROM drive and appropriate software are needed.

Written Materials

Each section of the portfolio should be labeled. Pieces that are not self-explanatory should have brief, written descriptions of the problem or the piece. Since hand lettering is considered an important skill by many design firms, written materials could be hand lettered. However, word-processed documents are certainly acceptable. Avoid using a large variety of fonts. Different font sizes will call attention to important identification items or statements, but too many can make the material confusing and may give an impression of disorganization.

Remember that a portfolio tells a visual story about you. If it is neat and well organized and contains design documents that show a range of skills for which the prospective employer is looking, the interviewer will have a favorable impression of you. If it is sloppy and appears to have been thrown together haphazardly, it will likely lead to a short interview and a response of "Don't call us; we'll call you."

Make sure an extra copy of your resume is included so that the prospective employer has a copy for his or her files. If you are mailing the portfolio, you will need to include contact information, perhaps a career objective or design philosophy statement (if one is not included in your resume), and a cover letter. To have a complete visual package, coordinate the paper color to the overall theme you have used in the portfolio. When you ship the portfolio, also arrange to pay for the shipping costs when the prospective employer sends it back to you so that the employer will not have to pay these charges.

Resumes

A *resume* is a summary of a person's qualifications. It is a tool that plays a significant part in whether an applicant will obtain an interview for a first or a new job. In some companies, a resume is also important in reviews for promotions. The resume must instantly communicate vital information related to your work experience, education, personal information, special skills related to the desired position, and career objectives. The length of a resume for a student rarely should exceed one page. The professional who has several years' experience will have a hard time condensing all of the pertinent information to one page, so additional pages may be needed. However, few professionals need a resume that is longer than about three pages. A resume is always accompanied by a cover letter, if it is mailed or faxed. If the resume is E-mailed, it is more courteous to send a short note along with the resume. More on electronic job search issues will be discussed later in the chapter.

Content

Certain kinds of information are expected in all resumes. This includes personal contact information, a career summary or perhaps a career objective, educational accomplishments, and work experiences. It is important to include information on professional memberships and involvement with the associations, professional licensing, and NCIDQ qualification. Including information on community service and outside interests is optional and should be deleted if doing so makes the resume too long or if doing so does not add to your overall qualifications for the position.* There are different formats to use for a resume. Each will be discussed later in this section. Let us look at the common items that are included in resumes first.

* Unfortunately, certain community activities that you may have participated in can unwittingly cause a prospective employer to discriminate against you. There would be nothing you could do, since you volunteered the information.

CONTACT INFORMATION Contact information generally heads up a resume. This is simply your name, address, telephone number, E-mail address, and perhaps a fax number. Students should consider including both a permanent address and an address at school. Do not use a fax or E-mail address at work as part of your contact information!

CAREER SUMMARY The career summary, in a few brief sentences, provides a significant statement concerning your ability to handle the job for which you are applying. For example, "Ten years' sales experience for office furnishings dealers, specializing in Herman Miller and Steelcase open office systems. Exceeded sales goals 11 out of 15 years," might be a career summary for an individual who is seeking a position as a representative with a manufacturer. A career summary for an interior designer might read, "Senior project manager with 11 years' experience in hospitality design with one of the top design firms in the country. Experienced in all aspects of the design process and recipient of numerous awards for creative work."

CAREER OBJECTIVE For the student who is beginning a career or a professional who is making a major job shift, a career objective may need to be included on the resume. A career objective talks about what you want to do rather than what you have already accomplished; for example, "Energetic recent graduate seeking employment with a creative residential design firm that also includes opportunities to design assisted living facilities." When you are using a career objective, it is important that it not be so narrow as to limit other possibilities—assuming you are open to other possibilities—or so broad that it seems that you have no direction or objective. Consider this objective: "A position as an interior designer." It is too vague and indicates to the employer that you have not given much thought to your future.

EDUCATION Educational information is another category that is necessary to include in a resume. For students, this section follows the career objective, since it is the primary "experience" a student has had up to this point. A professional commonly includes educational experience farther down on the resume, since work experience is more important. Begin first with the highest degree you have earned. Included should be the name of the institution and its location; the kind of degree earned and the year granted; major, minor, and any academic or career-related activities. Students should only list their grade point average if it was exceptionally high. About a year after graduation, you should drop the grade point average from the resume. For professionals, employers are not as interested in grade point average or academic activities. Professionals should also include professional continuing education units (CEU) and any other formal educational training in this section. However, if the professional has taken a large number of CEU classes, he or she should list only the most recent and any others that show updating related to the job being sought. Students do not need to list high school education. The author suggests listing this information only if it was a prestigious school or a foreign educational institution.

WORK EXPERIENCE Depending on which format you choose for your resume, the work experience portion will be written differently. Traditionally, the work experience section lists the name and location of the company, the years worked for each, and the title of the position held. This is followed by one or more brief narrative statements about skills developed, responsibilities, and/or accomplishments in each position. For example, to describe a job with a small interior design studio, the designer could write, "Interior Design Associate. Initial assistance to all walk-in clients. Design assistant to two senior designers. Specifically helped senior designers by pulling products and samples, preparing final specifications, estimating materials, drafting floor plans, and preparing purchase orders for senior designers." Students will want to place the internship first in the work experience section, followed by summaries of part-time jobs held. Figure 33-2 provides a list of active verbs that can be used in resumes and cover letters.

Professionals need to list projects for which he or she has been responsible. The organization of this information varies with the job objective. A word of caution on project listings. It is not necessary to list every single project in which you have worked. If you have extensive experience, highlight the key projects that might be of interest to the prospective employer. For example, it would make more of an impression to note that you were the project designer for a restaurant in the Belagio Hotel than to include an unrelated list of small projects on which you worked three years ago. Be selective about your project list so that your resume does not become too long. Also, ethics are involved here, so you must be careful about how you take credit for work in which you might have been a team member but not the project designer.

PERSONAL INFORMATION What you must include on the resume is what you included in your contact information. Anything else is left up to the individual. Some applicants feel they must include marital information, names of children, service records, height, weight, and health conditions. It is not necessary to put this information on the resume. The reader should be reminded that the employer cannot legally ask for any of this information, except within the bounds discussed later in this chapter. Volunteering this information could prejudice a decision, and the applicant would not have any grounds for challenging the prejudiced decision.

REFERENCES Today, it is not necessary to list references on a resume or even to provide them without a request from the prospective employer. Most references are

Accomplished	Executed
Achieved	Formalized
Arranged	Gathered
Assisted	Improved
Collected	Initiated
Communicated	Introduced
Composed	Managed
Conceptualized	Negotiated
Conducted	Organized
Contributed	Performed
Coordinated	Prepared
Created	Presented
Demonstrated	Reviewed
Designed	Scheduled
Developed	Selected
Directed	Supervised
Established	Trained
	Wrote

FIGURE 33-2. A partial list of active verbs that can be used in resumes and cover letters.

not even checked until after the interview and before an offer has been made. Most employers assume that the work and education history are the starting point for your references. These are the people whom they will likely first want to contact.

A professional who is seeking a job while he or she is still working may not want the current employer to know that he or she is looking for a job elsewhere. If this knowledge gets back to the current employer, the professional could be instantly terminated. You can clarify why you do not want the prospective employer to contact a current employer during the job interview.

If you are concerned that a previous employer may give a bad reference, ask that the employer not be contacted. It is necessary that you provide a brief explanation of the circumstances surrounding this request to the prospective employer, however. It is interesting to note that many employers no longer give a reference—good or bad—to a former employee. This extends, in some cases, to student interns as well. Employers are concerned about the possibility of being sued by former employees if it can be shown that the bad reference is the reason the employee did not get the job. When you intend to give professors, personal acquaintances, perhaps a designer at some other firm, or a sales representative as a reference, remember that it is common courtesy to ask the individual if he or she may be used as a reference before the individual is called.

Students can also use the services of college career placement offices to maintain references. This is a convenience for those who are asked to provide personal references, since they only have to write the reference once, and then it is kept on file at the placement office. Prospective employers then request a copy of the reference from the placement office.

Format

The three most common styles of formatting resumes are called: the chronological, the functional, and the combination style. No one format works best in all cases. Which of the basic formats you should use should depend on the audience the resume is for and the purpose for the resume. The experienced designer who is attempting to make a career change from "on-the-boards designer" to salesperson will need a different format from the technician who is trying to obtain a position of total project responsibility. A student's resume will be formatted differently from that of an individual who has been out of work for some reason for a number of years.

By far, the most commonly used format is the chronological resume, which lists all experience in reverse chronological order. Functional resumes do not give specific employment history and are sometimes used by individuals who have been out of work for some time. The combination format generally combines the chronological and functional resume to help elevate the negative issues that a functional resume may raise. Information about how to structure an electronic resume is also included later in this section.

Chronological Resume

The *chronological resume* states educational and work experiences exactly when they occurred, in reverse order. This type of resume is easy to follow and clearly shows the work history of the individual. Many employers prefer to read this traditional format for resumes, since it is familiar to most people. It is not recommended, however, if the job seeker has a spotty work record, is seeking to make a significant change in his or her career, or has been out of the work force for some time.

When individuals use this format, experienced professionals should provide work history in reverse chronological order, followed by educational experience. If the experienced (and older) designer places education first, it can draw attention to age, which, unfortunately, can lead to discrimination. Work history is more important than educational experience for the professional anyway. Students should place educational experience first, since that is the most recent activity.

When you are listing your educational experience, you would commonly list the information as follows:

Education: B.S., University of Wisconsin, Madison, 1999
Major: Interior Design
Minor: Business Administration
Magna Cum Laude

Figures 33-3 and 33-4 are examples of chronological resumes and show examples of how to list work experience.

Mary Anderson

1234 Granite Avenue *Circle City, Arizona* *602-555-9782* *E-Mail: mary@xxx.com*

OBJECTIVE: Entry-level design position with a commercial interior design firm specializing in health care and hospitality. Particularly interested in a challenging position which will increase my experience and involvement in interior design.

EDUCATION: Northern Arizona University, Flagstaff, AZ. 1998.
B.S., Major: Interior Design.
Minor: Marketing.
GPA 3.8/4.0.

EXPERIENCE:

Summer, 1998 **Design One, Phoenix, AZ.**
Intern.

Commercial and residential firm specializing in hospitality.
Space planning and design documents for a bed and breakfast and two other projects.
Client meetings, interaction, and project presentations.
Meetings with manufacturer's representatives.

Summer, 1996–97 **Desert Construction Co, Mesa, AZ.**
Draftsperson.

Assisted in the preparation of working drawings for custom home builder.

COMPUTER SKILLS

- AutoCAD 13 and 14
- Microsoft Office Word and Excel for documents and spreadsheets
- Microsoft PowerPoint for presentations

HONORS/ACTIVITIES

American Society of Interior Designers
Student Chapter, 1996–1998
Chapter Treasurer, 1997
Volunteer for the Showhouse (Phoenix chapter) 1997
Phi Kappa Phi Honor Society,
Northern Arizona Chapter

FIGURE 33-3. Chronological resume prepared by a student who is seeking a first job.

Sandra A. Mathews
200 Mocking Bird Lane
Richmond, Virginia 23375
Phone (314) 555-2000
E-mail sandram@xxx.net

KEY WORD SUMMARY

Ten years' experience in health care, hospitality, and corporate office design. Project Manager, Senior Designer. AutoCAD 2000, PowerPoint, Microsoft Project. Marketing responsibility, team management, NCIDQ certified, ASID chapter leadership, BS Interior Design.

DESIGN EXPERIENCE

Carson Jefferies, Inc. Richmond, VA.

1994 to present. Project Designer
1991–1994 Senior Designer
Direct design teams of 3–8 professionals in design of hospitality and health care projects.
Space plan and design corporate offices. Familiar with Haworth and Herman Miller systems.
Responsible for obtaining contracts of over $230,000 in fees in past two years.
Hired and scheduled subcontractors and supervised installations.
Developed two presentations using PowerPoint, which have become templates for company.

Associated Interior Architects. Del Mar, CA.

1989–1991. Designer
Space plan and design executive offices, law offices and banking facilities.
Assisted senior designers with drafting, product research and specification writing.
Assisted in space planning two open-office systems projects of over 25,000 square feet each.

EDUCATION

U.C. San Diego
Part-time, 1990–1991. Classes in Marketing.
Arizona State University
1989 Bachelor of Design Science. Major: Contract Interior Design

PROFESSIONAL AFFILIATIONS

International Interior Design Association, Professional member
Chapter Publicity Committee
American Society of Interior Designers, Professional member
American Institute of Architects, Affiliate member
NCIDQ Certificate # 55555

FIGURE 33-4. Chronological resume prepared by a professional, shown in a format that is acceptable for electronic transmission or scanning.

Functional Resume

The *functional resume* presents information in order to emphasize qualifications and skills, rather than the order in which they were obtained (see Figure 33-5). The idea of emphasizing overall qualifications is to quickly interest the employer with your qualifications and possibly overlook a spotty work record. Many employers do not like the functional resume, since they are concerned with a prospective employee's work history, so this tactic often does not work. However, it is still an option for many job applicants. If an applicant presents a functional resume, it would not be uncommon for the prospective employer to ask for a chronological work history to be provided as well.

WILLIAM C. BLAKE

9700 N. 19th Street | Tallahassee, FL 32000 | (P) 850.555.9876 | blake@xxx.com

SUMMARY

Highly motivated individual seeking an entry-level position in interior design. Previous work experience provides superior work ethic and demonstrated ability to successfully work with others. Negotiated contracts in public relations areas.

MAJOR WORK EXPERIENCES

Interior Design
Part-time design assistant for a residential design firm. Select finishes and products, develop sample boards, prepare furniture floor plans under direction of design firm owner.

Technical Writer
Three years' experience in large architectural firm. Responsible for developing proposals and other marketing materials. Collaborated with the firm's PR consultant on many projects.

Event Planner
Two years working as an assistant to a major event planner in Nashville, TN. Obtained pricing information, developed schedules, supervised small party set-ups.

Public Relations
Ten years' public relations experience in private sector. Excellent print media placement record. Good writer and researcher. Skilled in organizing special events. Worked with several interior design and architecture firms. Involved in contract negotiations for events.

EDUCATION

Florida State University 200x. Bachelor of Arts: Interior Design
O'More College of Design. Intermittent. Took design classes part-time.
University of Michigan 1984 Bachelor of Science Major: Journalism/Public Relations

AFFILIATIONS

American Society of Interior Designers, Student Member
Publishers Publicity Association
Public Relations Society of America

FIGURE 33-5. Functional resume prepared by an individual who has made a career change.

Combination Resume

A *combination resume* utilizes characteristics of both the chronological and the functional resume and combines them into one. Usually, this results in a resume in which functional skills are described, as in the normal functional resume, followed by a chronological listing of educational and work experiences. A combination resume highlights skills that are related to the job being sought and deemphasizes either a limited or a spotty work history. This kind of format can work very well for students whose skills learned in school and internships will be of greater interest to a prospective employer than work history that consists of a series of part-time jobs (see Figure 33-6).

Physical Appearance

The appearance of the resume can, by itself, make a good or bad impression. It must have perfect spelling and good grammar. You should coordinate paper color, fonts, and possibly designs with the cover letter. Contact information

Jennifer Alvarado
1875 Wacker Drive
Chicago, Illinois
312-555-3000

SUMMARY

- Four years' commercial sales experience for an office furnishings dealer
- Experienced in marketing interior design services
- Design project team manager
- Seven years commercial interior design: government and corporate
- Three years residential interior design
- Computer skills: Microsoft Office, Project, and Act!

SALES AND MARKETING SKILLS

Maintained numerous commercial accounts with last employer. Developed many new accounts with government agencies and corporate. Generated over seven million dollars in sales last year (second highest total for ten sales people). Equaled or exceeded sales goals each year.
Developed successful marketing strategies for two interior design firms and two contractors.

SUPERVISION SKILLS

Hired, trained and supervised two sales assistants to help manage my accounts. First sales assistant recently began working as sales representative. Also supervised design assistants when working as a project team manager. Overall project manager for several large government agency projects.

DESIGN SKILLS

Experienced in commercial space planning and interior design. Familiar with open-office systems products, and various qualities of commercial and residential furniture and furnishings products. Some experience in residential design/sales.

WORK HISTORY

1998 to present.	Account Representative	Quality Office Furnishings, Inc.	Chicago, IL.
1996–1998	Interior Designer	Smyth Design Consultants	Evanston, IL.
1991–1996	Interior Designer	Best Interiors, Inc.	Chicago, IL.
1988–1991	Design Associate	Regal Home Furnishings	Oak Park, IL.

EDUCATION

Southern Illinois University. 1988. Bachelor of Science. Major: Interior Design.

PROFESSIONAL MEMBERSHIP

American Society of Interior Designers, Professional member since 1994.
NCIDQ certified. Certificate # 55555

FIGURE 33-6. A combination resume for a professional seeking new responsibilities in his or her career as a sales representative.

should be easy to find and easy to read. Using a different font in the contact information is acceptable, as long as it is legible. Headings should be bold so that they stand out and attract attention. Single-space the resume with double-spacing between major sections. Do not forget to leave sufficient side margins so that the prospective employer may write notes in the margins. Remember to keep your length reasonable, considering your experience.

The text should reproduce as a dark black image. Word-processed resumes are common, but use a letter-quality laser printer for the printout. When a quantity of resumes at one time is required, have them printed offset on bond paper, not photocopied. This will be less expensive than laser printing if you do not have access to your own laser printer. Do not use a current employer's equipment to prepare a resume or other job search tools!

Interior designers tend to use a creative design or a creative method of printing or folding the resume. It is rare that odd-colored paper and creative designs on resumes really help applicants get an interview. Remember that the resume will be filed in a standard letter-sized manila folder. If the resume is a strange size or shape, it might get lost or filed in the "round file." The content of the resume and cover letter are what get the interview. Stick to white, buff, or maybe a light gray paper and minimal, if any, attention-getting designs. Refer to the portion of this section on cover letters, which you will find later in the chapter, for other hints on a resume's appearance.

Finally, before you print your copies proofread your resume two or three times over a period of time or have someone else also proofread the resume. Spell checkers do not always spell words correctly. You could have a wrong word spelled correctly that seems right (manger for manager), which you might not see.

Tips for Creating an Electronic Resume

Technology affects nearly every aspect of the interior design profession. The fact that it impacts the development of a resume and the job search process should not, of course, be a surprise. According to Nemnich and Jandt (1999, p. 4), over 3 million plus resumes were posted on the Internet in 1999. By the time this book is published, the number will have dramatically increased. How many of those posted were resumes of interior designers is difficult to say. This method of searching for a job is certainly gaining favor, especially in commercial interior design, and will no doubt be widespread in our industry in a few years.

Design firms receive resumes by fax and E-mail—sometimes in greater numbers than by regular mail. Preparing a resume for fax transmission has no special needs. Posting a resume by E-mail or otherwise on the Internet calls for some special considerations.

For the most part, your electronic resume will be very similar to any printed resume. You need to include the same categories of information: contact data, a career summary or objective, education, experience, and any optional information you might like to include. The differences are more in terms of how to present the information.

SCANNING

Larger employers are scanning resumes using an OCR (optical character recognition) scanner to help speed up eliminating those that do not meet their specific needs. The computer then scans for key words so that the employer can narrow the number of resumes even further in order to meet its particular needs. Some of these key words and terms in interior design include Autocad and names of other software programs, certifications such as *NCIDQ*, a degree, job titles, professional affiliations, and terms like interior design, hospitality industry (or other specialties), and project manager. When you describe your experiences, use terminology that shows you know what the industry is about. The use of key words as well as industry jargon in resumes is important in order to have your resume "found" by a prospective employer. The employer uses a similar concept when going to a resume-posting site on the web. He or she would punch in a small string of key words that would help narrow the field, just as you do when you are searching for any information on the web.

The version to be scanned should be printed on white paper only. Do not use bullets, underlining, boldface type, boxes, other graphics, or italics to highlight items that can confuse the scanner. Many fancy fonts do not scan well into OCR programs. You should be careful to limit your fanciful fonts and stick to the basics, such as Times Roman, Courier, Optima, Futura, Helvetica, and Palatino. Fonts will scan better if the type size is 12 or 14 point. Acronyms can confuse the scanner so spell out acronyms, for example, "American Society of Interior Designers," rather than "ASID"; "National Council for Interior Design Qualification," rather than "NCIDQ"; and so on. If you think the resume will be scanned, send it flat in a large envelope rather than folded so that the folds will not cause any problems. Actually, this is a good idea even if you do not think it will be scanned.

E-MAIL You may also need another version of your resume in order to E-mail it to prospective employers. The first rule to follow when you E-mail a resume is not to use any fancy formatting as extra tabs, boldface or italics on fonts, or anything else that is nonstandard. The other important rule is to always save your text as an ASCII file. Both these issues are important, since different word processors will read (or not read) your E-mail. A third rule is to cut and paste the resume to an E-mail rather than send it as an attachment. In many cases, the person can read the E-mail message, but the attachment becomes garbled or unreadable. You know this if you have ever opened an attachment only to find gibberish, followed by a little bit of readable material, which is then followed by more gibberish.

Only E-mail a resume if you have been asked to do so. When you E-mail your resume, involve a brief cover note, reminding the prospective employer about your earlier conversation. Keep this resume to a reasonable length, though it is not necessary to keep it to one page. The page length for E-mails (and HTML) is somewhat difficult to pin down, so you can make it longer than your print version. Remember that the longer the resume is, the longer it will take to download, and a very long resume could tie up or crash the receiver's system.

WEB RESUMES (HTML VERSIONS) Many design firms have a link on their own web sites where prospective employees can get information about openings and transmit a resume. There are numerous sites where you can post your resume on the web. And, of course, you can create your own web site.

Posting your resume on the Internet can give you more flexibility with content and design than sending either an E-mail or regular printed version. You are able to use boldface, italics, colors, different font sizes, and even graphics to call attention to your information: "This on-line presence . . . demonstrates to employers your awareness of technology and may be a little extra that puts you ahead of the competition" (Nemich and Jandt, 1999, p. 75). Here are a few other hints for using a web resume: avoid photographs of yourself; do not use too many links—you may lose the employer; watch the contrast of colors of fonts against that of the background—it needs to be readable; and use simple graphics that will not take too long to download. You may want to check the References at the end of the chapter for books that can help further if you wish to prepare an electronic resume.

The Job Search

For graduates and professionals in the late 1990s, finding a job in the interior design industry was relatively easy. Many graduates had their choice of jobs.

Some design firms even offered special incentives in order to retain or attract experienced professionals. The outlook for interior design positions should remain strong in many markets, but this will not always be the case.

Whether the market for interior design jobs is good or poor, for the student, the job search begins long before graduation. The student must evaluate what part of the profession holds the most interest for him or her. Is it doing residential or commercial design? Is the student afraid to make presentations and therefore does not want to be a salesperson? Does the student find making technical working drawings boring but working with colors exciting? These kinds of questions, coupled with questions related to lifestyle choices, geographic preferences, and many others, need to be asked so that the student can determine where to seek employment and what kind of employment to seek. Sometimes using a book such as Richard Nelson Bolles's *What Color Is Your Parachute?* is a help in determining career goals more precisely.

Information about the various aspects of the interior design field and potential employers is available from many sources. College advisers and career counselors can be helpful sources of information regarding different design companies. Students can join student chapters of professional associations. If your school does not have a chapter, you should make an effort to attend the professional chapter meetings at the local level. Students are always welcome at professional association meetings.

There are other contacts that students can use to obtain information about the work of the interior designer and information about possible jobs. He or she should talk to relatives who might have worked with designers. One of the best ways to understand what the interior design field is all about is to schedule an informational interview with a professional interior designer. Who better to tell the student about what it is like to work in residential design than someone who is actively doing just that kind of work?

An *informational interview* is a way in which the student can get a better picture of what it is like to work in a certain interior design specialty or type of interior design firm. It is done by first planning several questions that you want to ask the designer. Assume that you will take only 15–30 minutes of the designer's time, so be precise about what you want to know. Choose a few designers whom you want to interview and then call and ask for that 30 minutes of their time. You could invite the designer to lunch, but more likely the designer will want to talk to you at his or her office. Be prompt, be pleasant, and do not try to turn it into a job interview. You will turn off the designer if this is your ploy. Send him or her a thank-you card within a few days after the interview.

University career placement offices have information about many corporate employers. Unfortunately, most interior design businesses are closed corporations, so information about them probably will not be listed in the resources of the placement office. It is necessary to be more creative in your research. If you are looking to move to a new city, perhaps your professors can make suggestions. Obviously, the Internet can be a great help in this situation.

Reliable standbys for gathering information on design firms include yellow pages ads, local publications, and classified ads. Yellow pages ads do not always provide the name of the owner or the manager of a design firm, but they can give some information related to the company. A small interior design practice is usually listed under the owner's name. The name of larger firms may include several names or may have been invented, like Excellent Design Inc. Firms that sell a lot of merchandise often list in their ads the product lines that the firm carries. These product lines will help the student determine if the firm is primarily a residential or a commercial interior design firm.

Local home and business magazines are filled with advertisements of many different interior designers. Perhaps once a year these magazines focus on interior design or on one of the associations so that companies will advertise in them. Also, some cities have a "promotional" magazine that covers cultural, home, business, and social events. Many design firms also advertise in these magazines.

The Sunday classified section of the newspaper is a possible place to find interior design and trade-related job notifications. These classified ads, however, often only provide the barest amount of information about a position. Sometimes the firm does not even publish its name but asks the respondents to mail resumes to a box number. The job seeker should respond to anything that sounds remotely possible and interesting. A student should not be discouraged about applying if the ad states that only applicants with X years of experience should apply.

Professionals who are looking for new positions usually hear about job openings by word of mouth. Others discreetly put out the word to allied associates, such as sales reps, that they are looking for a new position. Quite a lot of job searching and interviewing occurs during trade shows, like the various Neocon shows. This is especially true for designers and others who are interested in sales positions. However, design firms may also advertise that they will be interviewing during one of the Neocon shows.

Employed professionals who are looking for another position must be discreet. Understandably, employers do not like their employees looking for another job while they are still working. Yet, of course, not everyone can afford to quit a current job in order to look for a new job. And almost all books on searching for a job advise readers not to quit the current job before they have obtained a new job.

Here are a few hints for the professional who is seeking a new job while presently employed. Do not use company time, company telephones, or company supplies for the job search. It is acceptable to schedule appointments during the lunch hour, but it is not acceptable to fake appointments in order to go on interviews. If it is necessary for you to take an extended period of time for an interview, use vacation time; do not call in sick. Remember, the employee owes loyalty to the employer as long as the employee is on the payroll. Abusing the employer by making interview appointments or long-distance phone calls at the present employer's expense is not only unprofessional but also could be grounds for termination.

Electronic Job Search

The Internet is another place for you to search out job possibilities. According to Richard H. Beatty (2000, p. 321), by 2005, employers will be spending $13.5 billion for job postings on the Internet. The Internet has become popular for job posting because it is cheap, offers the opportunity of sending a large number of applications, and is fast.

Some design firms have links on their web sites for a candidate to obtain information about possible openings and how to apply for those positions. Professional association web sites also have links to sections where designers might find job postings.*

Executive Search Firms

It is also common for professionals to use general or specialized professional employment agencies, or other executive search firms. These professional employment agencies are sometimes called *headhunters*. It refers to those companies that search out and essentially "steal" an executive or an employee from

* This member benefit is generally not available to students.

one firm in order to place that employee in another firm. The term is commonly used today to refer to any executive search firm.

Professional designers often work with executive search companies when they seek management positions. An executive search firm works on a commission that generally is paid by the hiring employer. Because of this, the search firm is interested in helping the employer, not you. The job of the search firm is rarely to help you find a job but, rather, to fill contracts with employers. If you decide to use an executive search firm, investigate it thoroughly to be sure that it deals with the interior design and architecture industries. Names of firms that specialize in interior design and architecture positions can sometimes be found in the classified sections of trade magazines.

If you are going to use a executive search firm, know what you are looking for before you approach one. Because an executive search firm works for the employer, it may be willing to help place you only if you exactly meet the qualifications desired by the employer. If the job seeker uses an agency to obtain leads, he or she should understand all the restrictions and fees involved. This could mean that you will waste a lot of time waiting for the firm to find you something if you don't fit its profile.

Some executive recruiting companies may want you to sign an exclusive agreement with them. Employment experts suggest that you do not sign an exclusive agreement. It is not appropriate for them to want to do this. It also limits your possibilities. If you are interested in working with this type of agency, you may want to check *The Directory of Executive Recruiters* at a local library to find recruiters in your area and field.

The Cover Letter

Your cover letter is just as much a marketing tool as those discussed in Chapters 22 and 23. The cover letter will help you market yourself to a prospective employer. It is an opportunity for you to personally introduce yourself in such a way that the employer, hopefully, will have no alternative but to read your resume and call you for an interview immediately.

In the cover letter, you can point out significant skills that directly relate to the job you are seeking and express personal interest in the company. Just as the design firm targets its marketing efforts, you must target potential employers. Tailoring the cover letter to each company accomplishes this objective. Each letter must sound as if it were written only for that company, even if it contains primarily "stock" paragraphs used in practically every letter you send.

Cover letters can be created for different purposes. The first thing you must do is clarify which type of cover letter you are writing. Some are in response to an advertisement that you saw in a newspaper. Some are sent because you have had a personal contact with the employer. Others are sent based on a recommendation by a professor or an interior designer. Professional designers may also send cover letters to executive or professional search companies. Then, of course, there are the broadcast letters that you might send to maybe dozens of employers, hoping that one will interest an employer enough to call you to set up an interview.

Content

With the purpose of the cover letter in mind, as always start by doing some homework. If the letter is in response to an advertisement, look up the company in the yellow pages or check to see if it has a web site. If you are a member of one of the professional associations, you might get some information about the company by calling the local chapter office. Be sure you know how to spell the name of the person who gave you a referral, if you use the name of a personal contact. This may sound simple, but you will lose a few points if you misspell the name of the person who gave you the referral in your letter. Most likely, your professor will be able to tell you something about the company that he or she mentions to you. If you are writing to an executive search company, remember that it helps companies find employees. It does not help the employee or an applicant find a job. With a broadcast letter, do as much research on each firm as you can, as if you were responding to an ad.

The cover letter, as with most resumes, should only be *one page* in length. Longer letters, even those from experienced professionals, may not get read by busy design directors or personnel managers. It is important for the letter to get the reader's attention and to make him or her want to read your resume and then call you for an interview. This is done by using good business-writing techniques. Standard business letters include the sender's contact information in a simple format or appropriate letterhead design. Do not use the stationery of the company where you are currently working or interning! The letter must be dated, of course. The prospective employer's address should be preceded by the name of the person to whom the letter is being directed. Your research should tell you who this is by name and job title. As for the salutation, letters addressed to "To Whom It May Concern" or "Personnel Office," or that use other generic salutations usually end up in the trash. It is generally recommended by business writing consultants and employment counselors that the cover letter contain about four paragraphs, each with a particular purpose (see Figure 33-7).

The first paragraph should attract attention by stating the purpose of your letter in concise words. Write with enthusiasm and interest. You are trying to sell yourself, and this is your 30 seconds that were mentioned in Chapter 26. Let the prospective employer know that you know something about the company and why you want to work there. This is also where you begin to target your letter by stating why you are contacting this company. For example, if the letter is in response to an advertisement, this paragraph should give the name and date of the announcement. If it is a letter of inquiry, this should be clearly stated (see Figure 33-8).

The second and third paragraphs should contain specific information about the applicant's skills and interests in the position in order to keep the reader interested. Tell the prospective employer how your skills relate to the job that was advertised (or that you heard about) or otherwise meets his or her needs. Focus your attention on the prospective employer's known or probable needs, not on your need for a job. Let the prospective employer see that you have done some homework about the company. This will make a major impression. If you do not respond to the specific needs mentioned in the ad, the letter again could end up in the trash. Statements about your personal goals and interests as they relate to the particular position and company can also be placed in these paragraphs.

Although there is no set order in which this information should be presented, it is most frequently presented in terms of its importance to the position as the applicant understands it. Mention two or three skills or accomplishments that directly relate to the position. For example, if you have CAD skills, state what version software you have experience in. Professionals should describe not only skills but also other accomplishments, such as sales records and management experience (see Figure 33-9). For students, this section should deal primarily with course work. Students should point out the skills in which they are particularly proficient. Students would also want to describe responsibilities

Applicant's name
Address
Area code and phone number

Date

Name and title of employer
Name of company
Address
City, State, Zip Code

Dear Mr. (Mrs. or Ms.) Smith:

The first paragraph should state the reason for the letter. Give the employer information about the specific position for which you are applying. If you are responding to an advertisement or have gotten the contact through someone the employer will know, state that information.

The second and third paragraphs are where you can provide some specific information about yourself and why you are interested in working for the firm. Include statements that explain how previous academic training or work experience qualifies you for the position. Relate your skills and experiences to the company's needs or the job requirements.

For professionals with several years of experience, the third paragraph will probably be necessary to complete the basic information you wish to tell the employer. Whether you are a student or professional, do not simply repeat what the employer can read in the resume—expand or clarify upon what you have stated in your resume.

A final paragraph thanks the reader for his or her time and indicates your desire for a personal interview. Be concise. If you are going to be in the city at a particular time, mention that you will be calling to set up an interview at that time. If you intend to get back to the employer rather than wait for him or her to call you, indicate that. Or say something like, "I look forward to hearing from you soon." Remember to say thank you "for your consideration" or use other appropriate wording.

Add a closing greeting such as "Sincerely,"

(leave four lines for your signature)

Type your full name

Enclosure (or Enc.). This is used to indicate you are sending something with the letter, in this case, your resume.

FIGURE 33-7. A sample cover letter that shows what should go in each section of the letter.

they had during internships or other interior design or trade-related work that they did while in school.

One caution about these middle paragraphs. Do not try to use this space to repeat all the information in the resume. You are trying to get the employer interested in reading your resume by highlighting key information.

The last paragraph should tell the prospective employer what you want—most likely an interview. You want the employer to call you, but do not wait for the employer to respond. The paragraph should also state that you will be calling the employer concerning making an appointment at a convenient time. Many job seekers will plan to be in the city where the letter was sent for only a few days. If this is the case, it should be mentioned in the closing paragraph so that the prospective employer knows when the applicant will be available. However, check your calendar before you mention specific dates. Do not bother

Julie Adams
8090 S. Willamette Street
Philadelphia, Pennsylvania
215-555-1448
E-mail jadams@xxx.com

October 26, 200x

Mr. Timothy O'Niel
AAD, Inc.
1237 N. 17th Street, N.W.
Washington, D.C.
202-555-1400

Dear Mr. O'Niel:

Over an eight-year period, I have worked as a Designer and most recently a Senior Designer at a highly respected commercial design firm in Philadelphia. At this point in my career, I seek an opportunity to apply my design and supervisory skills in a management position.

During the last few years I have been personally responsible for obtaining and designing many of the largest projects ever undertaken at my company. As a Senior Designer I am responsible for supervising design teams in the execution of projects.

It is not difficult to hear flattering comments about the quality design work produced at AAD, Inc. I believe the negotiation and design skills that I have refined at Design Three will further add to the success of your firm. In addition, I grew up in Baltimore and have a strong association with the Washington, DC and Baltimore markets.

As you will see from the enclosed resume, I have broad commercial experience in health care, hospitality, corporate offices, and university facilities.

Over the past four years, I have been preparing myself for management by enrolling in courses in pursuit of a master's degree in business.

I have considerable talent, enthusiasm and interest to offer as a design manager to AAD, Inc. and would appreciate the opportunity to meet with you personally to discuss such a position. I will call you next week to confirm a convenient time for a personal interview.

Sincerely yours,

Jennifer Woods

Enc.

FIGURE 33-8. A cover letter in which an individual is inquiring about a possible position.

to call the employer on Mondays and Fridays if you can help it. Most design managers are in meetings on Mondays or otherwise are catching up after the weekend; some are lucky enough to leave early on Friday.

The last paragraph should include a reference to the enclosed resume as well as the availability of the portfolio for review. Of course, you should also thank the employer for taking the time to review the letter and resume.

Use a simple ending, such as those shown in Figures 33-8 and 33-9. Leave four spaces for your signature, with your name spelled out below. Since you

Sally Johanson
7654 W. Main St.
Boise, Idaho
208-555-1000
E-mail: sjones@xxx.com

August 18, 200x

Mr. Roger Smith, Director of Design
Myer's Interior Design
82 W. Willow Lane
Denver, CO

Dear Mr. Smith:

I found your recent advertisement on the World Wide Web too interesting to resist! I remember visiting your showroom many times with my parents when I was growing up in Boulder. The opportunity to move back to Denver and work for your excellent company is very exciting.

At university, I specialized in residential interior design—which is my passion. My training was quite complete, covering all phases of design development, production, presentation and business practices. From project evaluations, I can state that I have strong skills in space planning, color coordination, drafting, presentation skills and rendering.

My internship was completed at Beverly Miller's Interiors in Boise, where I have remained for the last six months. My responsibilities include color coordination, preparation of presentation boards, drafting, rendering and order processing. This experience has taught me about the excitement and complexity of residential interior design.

I am anxious to meet you personally so as to present my portfolio to you. My experience at Beverly Miller's Interiors has been wonderful; however, I have decided to return to the Denver area permanently. I will be calling your office on August 27 to confirm an interview appointment. I have enclosed my current resume for your review.

Thank you for your time, and I look forward to meeting you next month.

Sincerely,

Sally Jones

Enclosure

FIGURE 33-9. A cover letter that an individual has prepared in response to a listing posted on the World Wide Web.

are including a resume, the word *Enclosure* or the abbreviation *Enc.* should be placed below the signature. Figure 33-10 provides some additional tips on preparing cover letters.

Physical Appearance

The appearance of the cover letter can quite easily attract attention—positive or negative. The author remembers receiving, in response to a newspaper advertisement for an experienced interior designer, a hand-written letter on ruled paper. It certainly made an impression. Many interior designers try to make the letter as creative looking as possible, using fancy type styles, funny folds, logo style designs, and pastel colors. These techniques do attract attention, but they also often get in the way of the content and businesslike attitude for which the employer may be looking. You may use a logo, design

- Address the letter by the employer's name—never "To Whom it May Concern."
- When you can drop names, do so: "I was referred to your company by John Jones, the owner of Jones Thompson Flooring."
- Discuss accomplishments, and results. This goes for the resume as well.
- Be brief and concise. Use good grammar and correct spelling.
- It is okay to use industry jargon and buzzwords. You better know what you mean if you use any jargon you put in your letter, however.
- Do not include negative information such as "I left ABC Interiors because of a disagreement with the owner."
- Do not make your letter sound like you are begging for a job.
- Always say thank you at the end.

FIGURE 33-10. Tips for preparing a cover letter.

element, or graphic, but use discretion. Unless you are applying for a job as a graphic designer, your graphic should not be more interesting than your text (and then not even in that case).

Use quality bond paper and business size envelopes (referred to as number 10). Black ink on white, gray, or ivory paper is the most businesslike combination, though light, pastel colors are not a problem for many prospective employers. The exact job opening and the kind of design firm will dictate whether these creative techniques are a help or a hindrance to the effectiveness of the cover letter. Serif fonts (they have little "feet"), such as Times Roman and New Century Schoolbook, are easier to read than san serif fonts. Specialty fonts can be used in the letterhead and the contact information on resumes. It is very common to coordinate the paper, fonts, and general style of the cover letter and the resume.

Use letter-writing techniques that almost all personnel managers and owners will appreciate. Do your very best to make even a broadcast letter sound like it was written just for the reader. Perfect spelling is necessary, along with good grammar. Have someone else read the letter, perhaps a professor, if you are a student. A professional who still does not feel comfortable writing may want to hire a freelance writer/editor or resume writer to help with preparing the cover letter. Do not photocopy letters and then change the address. Personally address each one and laser print each letter.

How Employers Review Resumes and Cover Letters

Potential employers receive dozens of resumes by mail, fax, and E-mail every week, whether or not they have an opening. If the employer has placed an ad, he or she will scan the letters for those that match the requirements stated in the ad. Those that do not match will be put in a separate pile and may or may not ever be read again. If the company has no current openings, an employer may give the cover letter a glance and determine if they are worth retaining for future reference. Again, this review will be focused on whether an applicant has certain skills that are generally needed by the company.

Certain factors almost always will automatically eliminate a letter from consideration. Such things as poor spelling, sloppy appearance, a "To Whom It May Concern" salutation, too many pages, or an obvious lack of skills will often mean round-file filing. There are several other items that an employer either looks for or uses to evaluate a resume.

1. *Relevance to the design firm*. Employers are impressed when an applicant has done some research about the firm, for example, career objective and career summary statements that relate to the work done by the firm to which the individual is applying. If the applicant states that he or she wishes to do commercial design in a cover letter or resume that is being sent to a residential design studio, this will not make a positive impression. Employers are also looking for any statement in the cover letter that refers to the actual work done by the firm.
2. *Referring to how the applicant heard of the job opening or the firm*. "I was excited about your advertisement in the Sunday *Gazette* for a design assistant." "My senior studio professor at State University suggested I contact you about an internship." These comments show the prospective employer that you know something about the firm rather than that you have sent a broadcast mailing.
3. *Using key words or phrases to catch the reviewer's attention*. Employers are looking for certain skills, accomplishments, educational background, and other issues that are specifically related to their design specialty. When those key words or phrases are used (e.g., AutoCad 2000, increased sales, award-winning projects) they will catch the reviewer's eye, and he or she will likely slow down and pay more attention to the letter and resume. Other suggestions about using key words were made in the section on electronic resumes, discussed earlier.
4. *Clarity of employment history*. Employers want to know what the applicant did and where he or she worked prior to applying for the position. Providing every single detail in the resume is not necessary, but vagueness will get the applicant nowhere.
5. *Good communication skills*. Designers do not just communicate in their drawings. Writing skills and verbal skills are equally, if not more, important for some positions. The cover letter and resume must use proper grammar. Students, in particular, often write paragraph-long sentences. Revise your letters and resume. Have someone else make suggestions as well.
6. *"Creative writing."* Employers become suspicious of resumes filled with more active verbs or claims of accomplishment than seem reasonable for the individual's apparent level of experience. Out-and-out lying is easily discovered and should never be engaged in.
7. *Achievement*. Employers want to hire an individual with a proven level of accomplishment. They are looking for indications of successful project management, profit making, or anything else that indicates the applicant knows how to achieve goals.
8. *Broad interests*. Most employers want to hire individuals who are loyal and dedicated to the interior design profession, but they do not want one-dimensional employees. Applicants need to avoid going overboard when they are stating outside interests—he or she may sound too busy with hobbies to have time to work. Indicate involvement in professional associations, community groups, and other outside activities.

9. *Care and thought.* Interior design is a profession in which attention to detail is essential. Careful drafting, proofreading, and execution of a resume and cover letter are important. Sloppy work, poor grammar, or minimizing statements related to the employers potential needs will raise doubt as to the individual's concern for a client's project.
10. *Neatness.* This is obvious, but it is worth repeating.

Interviews

Looking for a job is serious work. You have already spent a great deal of time determining what kind of job in the interior design industry is of interest to you; preparing your resume, portfolio, cover letters; and following up with numerous phone calls in order to get an interview. Now you have one—congratulations!

This is your chance to make a good impression, to convince the employer that you are the one person in the world who can handle the job. If you are a student, this is the opportunity for which you have been working so hard for so many years. If you are a professional, this could be the start of something new: a new city, new responsibilities, more pay or whatever has brought you to decide to change your job. In just about every reference book that you might look at, you will read that the interview is where little things more often than not torpedo a good candidate. The hints and comments in this section, hopefully, will help you as you travel through the interview process to achieve success.

Preparing for an Interview

The planning and preparation for your interview is no less important than any other kind of planning and preparation discussed in this text. Once an interview has been obtained, it is necessary for you to do some preparation. You will need to check and modify your portfolio for the interview. Then you will need to prepare yourself in terms of your appearance for the interview. Recall those comments on first impressions made in Chapter 26. You also must verify details about the location of the interview. And finally, you will want to prepare yourself mentally for one of the most nerve-wracking experiences you will go through. Let us start with the easiest one—verifying details.

If the interview is in your hometown, about 24 hours before the scheduled interview, call to check on details. If the interview requires that you travel a long distance, call about 48 hours ahead, if practicable. Find out exactly with whom you will be interviewing and how to pronounce his or her name. The person who will be interviewing you will not necessarily be the person who responded to your letter. Larger design firms will have a personnel manager who is in charge of interviewing prospective employees prior to the design director interviewing them. If more than one person will conduct the interview, ask for their names and job titles. Request an agenda, so that you will know how much time you will be spending with each person.

Double-check the day and time of the interview. No matter how much time has passed from the time you set up the interview, call to confirm the time. If you have any questions about how to get to the studio or office, or you are not sure where to park, ask for directions at this time. In large cities, it is probably safer to take a cab than it is to drive, but check for suggestions about this also. If there is any reason that you cannot keep the interview, call and personally talk to the interviewer to tell him or her. Initial interviews can be as short as 30 minutes or can last 2 hours, though an hour is the average.

In either case, plan to spend about 20 minutes showing your portfolio and the rest of the time answering questions.

Now that you know what the situation is, go through your portfolio and be sure that every item is where you want it for the interview. Familiarize yourself with what you are going to show the interviewer and confirm in your mind the order in which you wish to show it. If something has become damaged, take time to repair it or try to replace it. Place an extra, unfolded copy of your resume in the portfolio. Also check to be sure that a pen and pencil are in either your portfolio, your pocket, or your handbag.

Next, work on your own appearance. The evening before the interview, check the outfit that you plan to wear. Make sure it is clean, well pressed, and that it does not have loose buttons or threads. Be sure your shoes are shined. Think about wearing something on the conservative side, since all employment experts agree that the interview is the time to dress conservatively even in a creative field like interior design. However, this does not mean that you have to wear a black or navy blue suit, unless you know that this is standard at the design firm you will be visiting.

Your mental preparation includes anticipating and thinking about the kinds of questions the interviewer may ask you and that you may want to ask the interviewer about the company. Some common questions will be included at the end of this section.

It is never permissible to be late, unless it is due to something totally beyond your control. If you are held up in traffic or miss your plane or connection, call the interviewer as soon as you can. To avoid being late, make a point of arriving at the office or studio at least 10–15 minutes early. These few extra minutes will give you a cushion in case you experience a traffic jam or difficulty in finding the office. It also gives you a chance to try to relax and collect yourself before going into the interview. Before you check in with the receptionist, go to the rest room to check your overall appearance.

When you check in with the receptionist, be sure to smile and tell the receptionist who you are, with whom you have an appointment, and what time the appointment is for. Most likely you will be told to have a seat. Try to use this time to compose yourself. Read a magazine, and try to relax. Do not fiddle with your portfolio, briefcase, or handbag.

What to Wear to an Interview

Let's take a few moments to discuss the visual presentation of yourself in a bit more detail. What you wear to the job interview is a part of the overall impression that you will leave with the interviewer. It will not get you the job, but it might lose it for you. Many interior design professionals find it acceptable to be more trendy and flamboyant in their everyday business apparel. However, most interviewers expect more conservative apparel for the interview. If you have researched the company as well as you can, you will have some idea of what normal business attire is like at that design firm. This will be your guide as to how trendy or how conservative you must appear.

Wear apparel that is comfortable. Do not use the job interview to break in a new pair of shoes. Business suits with ties for men is standard. Conservative fabrics in solid colors are commonly accepted. Women should also choose conservative suits and dresses with jackets. Sundresses, sleeveless dresses, or low-cut dresses do not project the kind of impression that businesspeople like to see.

Women also should be careful about what kind of accessories they add to their outfit. Refrain from wearing brightly colored or boldly patterned scarves, dangling, noisy bracelets, or oversized earrings—anything that attracts more attention to the accessories than to yourself. Refer back to Chapter 26 about other suggestions for general business dressing.

The Interview

Your interviewer has now arrived at the reception desk. When he or she greets you, be prepared to shake hands. It is not necessary to use a bone-crushing handshake. Just make it sincere. Prepare for this by having your portfolio, handbag, or attache case positioned so that you can pick them up with your left hand, leaving the right hand free to shake hands. Smile! Say hello, introduce yourself. You want this job, don't you?

When you arrive at the conference room or office where the interview will be held, wait for some indication from the interviewer as to where to sit. If he or she does not make any indication as to where to sit, choose a chair that is either directly across from the interviewer or at a 90-degree angle. These two positions make it easier to show your portfolio and to maintain eye contact.

Remember that the purpose of the interview is for the employer to get to know you personally, ask you questions, and try to evaluate whether or not you would be a good addition to the firm. The interview is also a time for you to evaluate whether this particular firm is really the kind of firm for which you wish to work. Just because a firm has a good reputation does not mean that you will want to work for it.

As you are sitting through the interview, try not to use distracting mannerisms. Don't play with a paper clip or pen, fuss with your hair or accessories, and so on. Let your body language and visual presentation communicate that you are an interested professional. Be sure to listen to the questions the interviewer asks. Do not think of what you want to say so that you will not hear what is being asked. Think before you speak, and do not interrupt the interviewer. Use eye contact, but do not try to stare the interviewer down. Use body language that is open and receptive to what is being discussed, not defensive. Smile, show interest. If you do not show interest in your work or if you sound bored or defensive as you describe it, you will not be making a favorable impression and you can be guaranteed of not getting an offer.

There are many different styles of interviewing. In some cases, the employer will purposely ask you questions that will put you under even more stress than you are already experiencing. The idea, as far as the employer is concerned is to find out how you might react under the worst conditions. This probably does not happen in interviews with interior design firms very often, but stress-inducing questions could come up. Stay calm, recognize what the interviewer is doing—its not a personal attack—and do not become sarcastic or attack. If the interview is conducted in a particularly stressful manner, maybe you would not want to work there anyway.

Another style of interviewing is the situational interview. In this case, the interviewer will ask a lot of questions, like "What would you do if the client vetoed every single design idea you presented at the final presentation?" The interviewer is trying to see how you think on your feet. These kinds of questions are most likely to be asked if you are applying for a management position or perhaps a project manager position rather than a position as a designer. In any case, think about your answers and take these questions seriously.

Some firms use team interviews. This means that you might be questioned by more than one person during the interview or you will be passed from staff member to staff member during the interview. This happens frequently in larger design firms, where an ability to fit into the team and existing company's culture is important. Understand that everyone probably has a preplanned part to play in the interview. One interviewer may be casual, another may be formal, and another may appear not to be interviewing you at all but observing your behavior. Be respectful of everyone and be prepared for a long interview process.

Most interviews in interior design are not designed to induce stress. In fact, many owners and managers of design firms with whom this author has talked insist that they try to make the candidate as comfortable and at ease as possible. They remember what it was like! Stress your qualifications in terms of what you can do for the company. Graduating students need to indicate a willingness to learn. Be enthusiastic in your answers and stress your positive characteristics. But do not exaggerate your experience or your abilities. It will not take much time for the employer to find out that you are not an expert with CAD, if you said you were but are not. And do not try to pass off someone else's work for yours in your portfolio. That, too, will be found out very quickly, and will always lead to dismissal.

During your interview, never bring up personal problems, argue, blame others, or beg for the job. Even if you have left your previous job under difficult circumstances, do not blame anyone at the other company for your problems. It tags you as a difficult person and will probably influence the interviewer to pass you over. If you are asked if you were ever fired, you do have to be honest. But it is not necessary to go into a long, detailed discussion of what happened. Make some brief comments about what happened and hope the interviewer moves on.

If, during the interview, you determine you are not interested in working for the company, complete the interview but inform the firm promptly that you are not interested in pursuing the position further. Those of you who are students should not accept an interview if you really have no interest in working for the company. Some students like to go on interviews to "practice" for the job they want. This is poor business etiquette that can come back to haunt you later.

Unless the interviewer brings it up, do not ask about salary and benefits until the latter part of the interview. It is considered very bad form if the first question you have is about salary and benefits. You first need to ask questions that will help you understand if you want to work at the company. Questions you might ask include the following:

- How many people work in the company?
- What are the company's plans for growth or expansion?
- What are the job responsibilities of this position?
- Will I be working with only one designer or several (for an entry-level position)?

When you have asked your questions, you might also want to ask, "Are many other people being interviewed?" "When will you be making a decision?" You need to know what will happen next.

If you get an offer, that is when you will begin to discuss details about salary, benefits, and responsibilities. Be prepared to give a salary range that you must have. Employers, of course, want to hire you at as low a salary as is reasonable for the position. But do not sell yourself short. If the salary offer is way below what you need to live on or is way below what you understand the competition is paying, say so. Remember that benefits such as health insurance, reimbursement of professional association dues, and employee discounts are important parts of the compensation package. One company with an excellent health insurance program, a profit-sharing program, and a generous discount for personal purchases but that offers a low salary might offer a better opportunity than another company offering a higher salary but weaker benefits (all other things being equal). Compensation in interior design is notoriously low in comparison to other professions. Salaries have increased during the economic boom of the late 1990s, but designers generally agree that they do not go into interior design to become rich. If you haven't read it, go back to Chapter 11 and read the section on different compensation methods.

For the most part, if you are offered a position, be prepared either to accept or to reject it at that time. If you are offered a position that is different than the one you expected or you are being offered a lower salary than you were expecting, it is acceptable to ask for time to consider the offer. If you really want the position, say so. If you have another interview that day, do not keep one employer dangling to see if someone else might have a better offer. Many designers now request that offers be put in writing. This does not have to be a formal employment contract, as described in Chapter 12, but key points concerning salary, benefits, and responsibilities might be included in it. A written offer of this kind is not generally necessary for students who are interviewing for their first job but is more common for experienced designers, especially those who are shifting into management or quasi-management positions. If you are not made an offer but there is no indication that you have been rejected, ask the interviewer when he or she will be ready with a decision. Do not leave without knowing what the salary range is if you have been given an offer.

One very good clue that the employer is interested in you is if he or she suggests showing you around the studio or office. This is usually only done if the candidate interests the employer and he or she wants to introduce you to staff members. However, if you have not actually been offered the position, don't assume anything. Every once in a while, an employer just tries to be nice and shows off his studio but doesn't offer you a job.

The time of the offer or nonoffer is the best clue that the interview is over. Watch for other clues, such as that the interviewer is stacking the job application, your resume, and his or her notes together, or the interviewer is pushing his or her chair back in preparation for getting up. This is the time to summarize your interest in the position and why you are the best candidate. State this in a few sentences so that you do not overstay your welcome at the end. When the interview is over, get up and leave promptly. If an offer has been made and you have accepted it, be sure that you understand what day you are to start, the time, and anything else that needs to be taken care of by you, either prior to your first day or on your first day on the job. In the excitement, it is not uncommon for the applicant to forget to ask about these issues!

Typical Interview Questions

There are many kinds of questions that commonly are asked in interviews. Interviewers will ask questions in order to find out about your personality and demeanor. They want to determine whether or not you will fit in to the existing group. They will ask questions to determine your overall interest in interior design and the specialty area that you are interested in pursuing. If you are a recent graduate, the interviewer probably will ask you about your educational background and the classes you took. Questions are likely to come up to find out about your ambitions in the field and, to some degree, your future plans with regard to your career. They may even ask questions to find out if you have any "skeletons" in the closet, to discover whether you left a prior job under bad circumstances. It is important that you prepare yourself for these questions in advance. The questions shown in Figure 33-11 are typical of ones asked in an interior design interview. You may want to think of some others as well.

Illegal Questions

There are many questions that can no longer be asked in a job interview and can no longer appear on a job application. These questions relate to age, sex,

Common Interview Questions

General Questions for Any Candidate

Why do you wish to work for us?
What do you know about our company?
How did you hear about our company?
Have you applied to any other companies?
Tell me about the qualifications you have for this position.
Are you willing to do the traveling out of town that is necessary for this position?
Tell me about yourself.
How long have you lived in this city?
How much compensation are you expecting?
What will you add to our company?
Describe what you consider to be your weaknesses.
How do you plan to overcome those weaknesses?
Could you name a co-worker that we could contact that could tell us something about you?
Do you have any objections to taking our entry psychological tests?

For Entry-Level Positions

Why did you select the college or school you attended?
Why did you select a major in interior design?
Did you have any leadership experience in college?
How do you think your colleagues in your major would describe you?
How do you view this job in relationship to your long-term goals?
Describe your reactions when your work was criticized.
What are your ambitions for the future?
How long would you expect to stay with our company?
Did you find it comfortable to work in the classroom studio?
How long do you think it will take you to make a meaningful contribution to our firm?

For Candidates with Prior Professional Experience

Tell me about your previous experience and how those positions relate to this position.
How do you think you can best contribute to this firm?
Why are you looking for another position?
Are you a leader?
What are your ambitions for the future?
You appear to be overqualified for this position. Why are you applying for this position?
If you are offered a position with this company, tell me what you would do during the first month on the job.
How much are you worth?
How would you describe your supervisory (management) style?
How have you increased sales or profits at your present employer?
How do you think your present boss would describe you?
May we contact your present employer?
Please tell me how many days of work you missed last year.

FIGURE 33-11. Common interview questions.

religion, and ethnic origin. For example, the employer cannot directly ask you how old you are, your date of birth, your religion, or your native tongue. Keep in mind that many questions that do not seem to be sexually discriminatory actually are. Questions directed at women, asking whether they are single or married, what their husband does for a living, whether or not they plan to have children are all considered illegal. These discriminatory kinds of questions must not influence the employer's decision as to whether or not to offer a job to an individual.

There are ways in which certain discriminatory questions can be asked so as to make them legal. This is especially true if the question has a direct bearing on the ability of the individual to perform the job. Although it is illegal to ask you, "How old are you," it is legal to ask, "Are you between the ages of 25 and 45?" You may wish to review appropriate sections from the books of Lewin G. Joel III, Fred S. Steingold, and Steven Mitchell Sack listed in the References for specific ways in which questions can and cannot be asked during interviews or on job applications.

When you are asked a question that you believe to be illegal or about which you feel uncomfortable answering, you must be prepared to say something. Many of the job-hunting books suggest that you answer the question, forget about it, or say something like, "I do not understand what that has to do with the requirements of the job or my qualifications to do the job." Some interviewers may not have hired anyone for some time and may not be aware that some questions cannot be legally asked anymore. Making a big issue of such questions, if you honestly feel the person is asking the question innocently, could result in your not getting the job. If the interviewer asks too many of these kinds of questions or ignores your hesitancy in answering them, you always have the right to terminate the interview and to obtain a job somewhere else.

It is sad to say, but discrimination in hiring decisions will occur. However, if you feel you have been denied a job based on discrimination, you have a recourse should you choose to pursue it. "You may have a cause of action if you can prove that you were discriminated against in the job application process. . . . If you feel you have a legitimate gripe, the first step is to file a complaint with your state human rights commission or the EEOC" (Lewin, 1996, p. 46). Of course, you can hire a private attorney and file a civil suite if you wish. Only you can decide whether or not you want to work for a firm that appears to discriminate.

Follow-Up

The job search can be a quick process, or it can seem to take forever. You must manage this process right from the beginning. Keep a record of all correspondence. Make a copy of each letter and resume that you have sent to each employer. Add a sheet of notes concerning responses to your phone calls, asking for an interview, what was said, and anything else that will help you make future encounters positive. Look at each negative response as an opportunity to learn how to make future inquiries positive.

As soon after the interview as is practical, make notes to yourself about what transpired. This is true whether you have accepted an offer, rejected an offer, or not even received an offer. Notes related to salary, benefits, expected performance levels, and your general impressions of the firm can be important if you have not made a decision about the company or the company has not made a decision about you. If an offer was not made or you were rejected, these notes will help you understand what may have gone wrong so that you can correct the errors during future interviews. This same information will be important in the future, so that you will know what your agreed upon responsibilities are on which you will later be evaluated.

Good business etiquette also calls for you to send a thank-you letter to the interviewer immediately after the interview (see Figure 33-12). Thank the interviewer for giving you his or her time, restate your interest in the position, if you are still interested, and follow through on any promised information you agreed to supply.

If you have been offered a position but have asked for time to consider the offer, it is best if you call the interviewer promptly and follow up with a refusal or an acceptance letter. In most situations, the employer is hoping for an immediate response. Depending on the situation, you can ask for 24–48 hours. Waiting longer can be a problem and can indicate to the prospective employer that you are not interested. It also can start you out in the job

Marilyn Norton
2571 N. Paradise Lane
Sacramento, California
(916) 555-2410

February 18, 200x

Mr. Sandford Hopkins
Hopkins, Dodge, and Russell, Inc.
1849 Grass Valley Avenue
Reno, Nevada

Dear Mr. Hopkins:

Thank you for giving me the opportunity to meet with you yesterday and discussing my joining your firm as a Project Designer.

While you interview the other individuals you are considering, I hope you will take the time to examine my resume and will decide in my favor. I feel confident in my ability to be a productive contributor to the on-going success of Hopkins, Dodge, and Russell.

I would like to review three important facts that show I am the most qualified candidate for the position of Project Designer. First, I have seven years' experience with a full-service commercial design firm, where my responsibilities involved all areas of a design project from programming through contract administration. Second, my experience and knowledge of AutoCAD 14, 2000, and PowerPoint allow me to contribute immediately to your firm. Third, since I am already NCIDQ certified, you will be hiring a designer who will easily be licensed in Nevada.

Should you need any further information, I will be happy to provide it. I look forward to your positive response to my application at the end of the week, when you conclude your remaining interviews. Thank you again for your time and consideration.

Sincerely,

Marilyn Norton

FIGURE 33-12. A sample follow-up thank-you letter that would be sent after a job interview.

relationship on a sour note, if you decide to accept the offer. By responding within a reasonable time frame, the company knows whether or not you are interested in the position and, in the case of your refusal, has a letter for the company's records.

If you are interested in a position with the firm but you know that the firm is still interviewing others, it is necessary to keep the design firm interested in you. Be sure to add a short paragraph summarizing your qualifications and stating how you can contribute to the company.

Following up is a way of continuing the good impression of yourself that you have left with the prospective employer. A short note, which should be typed using good business letter form, will indicate to the prospective employer that you are a professional. Even if the firm does not have an opening for you, you will be remembered later.

The First Job

The last semester of school can be a nerve-wracking time for students. It is when their classes in their major seem to be the most difficult at the same time that they are busily putting together their portfolios and resumes for jobs or internships. As graduation looms, they realize that friendships nurtured over the past few years will change or fade as they and their friends go in different directions and possibly end up on opposite sides of the country. The transition from student to professional is not easy for most individuals.

Almost all interior design curriculums today require or at least recommend that students include an internship as part of their major. These internships, which last six weeks or longer, in a design office or studio, help students see how all the course work that they have taken relate to the work done "in the real world." In addition, internships provide students some work experience that they can include on their resume. Of course, the internship experience is different for everyone. However, the point is to get the most from the internship. You should have had something to do with arranging it, and you should discuss your responsibilities with the employer. The focus should not be on whether you are being paid or not; the focus should be on what you will learn. You must remember that you will only get out of the experience what you are willing to put into it. So, if you sit back and wait for someone to teach you something during your internship, you will probably be very disappointed with your experience. You may even have earned a poor recommendation from the employer.

Your first job is important, because it becomes the groundwork for your career. This is not to say that your first job represents what you will always do in interior design. If you ask any professional who has been working for 15 years or more about his or her career path, you will find that a career in interior design is never a straight path. It zigs and zags and even may throw you a few curves. I once had a student who always finished her commercial projects very quickly in comparison to everyone else in the class. I asked her about it one day, and she said, "I hate doing commercial projects so much, I just want to get it over with." Naturally, her first job was with a residential design firm. About a year later, she was visiting the school, and we got to talking. "Say, do you know of any commercial design firms that are hiring?" she asked. "I hate residential design!"

Your first job is also important for other reasons, for it is where you will learn to work in interior design. You will learn methods of pulling together design projects that you never heard of in school, not because your professors didn't know them, but because each designer and each design firm has different ways of working. You will begin to make business and industry contacts as you socialize with professionals in your area. Attending and participating in professional associations will help, since you will be able to network with designers of all levels of experience. You also will learn how to dress, how to "talk," and how to act like an interior design professional. And, hopefully, that first job will help you build your confidence as a designer.

Because it is your first job, do not be cavalier about the experience. Most of you will learn very quickly that you must park your egos at the door, because you will be directed, reprimanded, and pushed to learn from bosses, other designers, and even clients. Just because you graduated from a wonderful, FIDER-accredited school (or anywhere else, for that matter) does not mean that you know more than your boss. I have often told students, much to their chagrin, that now that they are graduating, they will begin to learn about work and how to do interior design.

Don't be afraid to ask questions. The only dumb question is the one you don't ask. You are not expected to know everything. Keep your eyes and ears open, ask to be involved, ask questions, and your colleagues will start giving you more responsibility. Figure 33-13 lists a few suggestions about how you can prepare yourself for the transition between student and professional. I am sure your professors will have others.

A few years ago when I was on a sabbatical, I spoke to many interior designers about their expectations of the entry-level employee. A few of the

- Talk to professionals who are doing the work you want to do. People love to talk about what they do and their work. Make appointments and come prepared with about 15 good questions to ask that will help you find out what it is like to work at a particular kind of company or in a particular type of design specialty.
- Examine your motives and establish goals. Set goals that interest you. Think about what you want to do two, five, or ten years from now.
- Get involved with a professional association. Visit chapter meetings of the different organizations in your area. Students are always welcome. When you are sure about which one(s) you want to join, get involved. Volunteer for committees. It is a great way to get to know people in the business.
- Begin to be a professional. One or two days a week—maybe for studio classes—dress professionally, as if you were going to the office. Get used to being dressed up. You will also likely feel more confident on those days.
- Begin to work like a professional. Use a time management system of some kind. Treat the school day as a work day; that is, start the day at 8 and work until 5.
- On your internship:

  Don't play the critic. You are there to learn, not to criticize the company.

  Don't be lazy or blase. If you want a good recommendation from this company, cheerfully complete all assigned tasks. Look for things to do or to help out as well.

  Ask questions. They expect you to ask questions.

  If you want to work for this company, show that you want to be there by doing all that is asked and then some.

  When you have nothing to do, don't just read magazines (though that is a good way to learn). Straighten catalogs or review samples and catalogs. There is a lot to learn about current products by cleaning up the library from time to time.

FIGURE 33-13. Suggestions to assist students as they make the transition from student to professional.

comments they made—in no particular order—were as follows: be punctual, reliable, accurate, detail oriented, able to communicate verbally, a team player, well organized, disciplined, and motivated. I also asked these same professionals to describe the ideal employee. Probably the best answer was, "Someone who wants my job." Think like the owner. Consider his or her problems as a designer and a businessperson. Aspire to learn all you can about the business, and there will likely be no end to your success.

Making a Career Change

At some point, many interior design professionals start thinking about making a career change. This author has spoken to numerous senior designers in recent years who have considered leaving a full-time practice in order to enter the teaching field. Other designers seek the possibilities of additional income by obtaining positions as sales reps with manufacturers and vendors. And, frankly, some leave the profession to do something else.

Interior design, as has been pointed out many times in this text, can be a fun way to make a living. It is also, to many, a stressful type of work. In today's economy—and this likely will continue to occur into the twenty-first-century—many clients want interior designers to work "cheaper, better, faster." What this means is that there will be increasing pressure on design firms to provide a more comprehensive scope of services at a lower fee. There is a great deal of competition today in the interior design industry in most cities, and clients sometimes give no extra consideration to one design firm over another. The attitude in many cases has become, "If you can't do it for less, I will go to someone who will."

At the same time, clients want the work to be done for less money, they also expect it to be perfect—no errors, no omissions, no problems, no excuses. This is probably one of the big reasons that CAD is used so prevalently—as long as the designer has entered certain data correctly, the drawings and documents will always be correct. If something goes wrong, clients today are more willing to threaten lawsuits, file ethics complaints, or simply not pay for the work.

Finally, interior design work has to be done faster, in many cases. Once clients get their funding, they do not want to lose the interest rate on their mortgage, whether it is for a house or a commercial development. "I sent you an E-mail this morning. Why didn't you get back to me right away!" scream clients. Deep down inside, they may realize that you have other clients, but many of them really do not care. They feel that they are the only important clients. With the ability for communication to be instantaneous, clients now have come to believe that interior design solutions and specifications can be done more quickly as well. Many simply do not seem to understand that the creative problem-solving process that is required for the design of their home, office, hotel, or whatever, still takes time.

What does all this mean in terms of making career changes? Many senior interior designers "burn out" from working 12-hour days, 6 days a week to just keep up. It takes its toll, and many start looking for other jobs or possibilities, as mentioned earlier.

One day you may find that your current job does not suit your needs anymore. "You can come up with a million (untrue) reasons why you can't leave a situation you dislike. But when you deny reality (or the depth of your unhappiness), it has a way of catching up with you" (Hirsch, 1996, p. 149). If you are unhappy, you may need to go all the way back to books like Bolles' *What Color is Your Parachute?* to discover some new direction. Answer the questions in Figure 33-14. Just be sure that you know why you are dissatisfied before you "cut the cord" and move on to something else. Talk to someone who knows you well and who will keep your confidence as you contemplate making a career change. If it is going to be something dramatic, such as moving from a design/planning position to one in sales, talk to people who already are working in that position, especially those who have been designers before. They can help you understand what it is like to make a transition and problems with making a career change.

When you are sure about your new career path, check to make sure that you can afford to make the change. For example, senior designers who want to go into full-time teaching careers are often shocked to learn about the salary differentials. They also may not have the academic credentials necessary for seeking a full-time teaching position. Do not burn your bridges. Walking in and quitting one day without giving notice, with projects unfinished will cause a lot of problems for the company and yourself, since the company may not be very willing to give you a recommendation, assuming you may need it.

Remember that finding a new job, especially in a different field, will take time. Figuring out for sure what it is you want to do and where you want to do it is just the start. How might this impact your family? When are you going to find time to obtain credentials, such as a master's degree, if you want to teach? When are you going to be able to interview without the boss finding out?

Once you know what you are going to do, give ample notice, say thank you for the experience of working there, and say good-bye gracefully. And remember, for most of you, Thomas Wolfe was right—*You Can't Go Home Again*.

Summary

Each of us grows in our own way as we seek fulfillment in our careers. As the professional gains experience in the field, he or she seeks greater levels of

- What is scariest about changing careers?
- List three to five reasons why you want to leave your present job.
- List three to five reasons why you should stay in your present job.
- What was the reason—the last straw—that helped you decide to leave?
- Did you regret leaving a previous job?
- Do you wish that you had left that other job (or this one) sooner?
- Is there a particular circumstance that would convince you to stay?
- If you leave, how will you support yourself during a transition, should you be fired during the job search?
- If you leave, are you really acting in your own best interests?
- Why do you think it is time to make a total career change?
- What will you be looking for in a new career that the current one does not provide?
- Are you prepared for a major difference in income if you embark on a totally new career?
- Do you have a plan for your future related to making a career change?

FIGURE 33-14. Questions that a professional should consider when he or she is contemplating making a job or career change.

responsibility and challenges in the workplace. Often, it is necessary to seek new responsibility in another firm, even in another city. For the student, the first job is an important first step in establishing a successful and satisfying career in the interior design profession. Obtaining a position does not come easily to most of us.

At one time or another, preparing portfolios and resumes, and embarking on the job search and the stressful interview process will affect all who read this book. It is hoped that the information in this chapter will help each one of you make achieving that "right" position possible.

REFERENCES

Allen, Jeffrey G. 1997. *The Complete Q & A Job Interview Book*, 2nd ed. New York: John Wiley.

American Society of Interior Designers. "Preparing Your Portfolio." *Report.* April 1981.

Angel, Dr. Juvenal L. 1980. *The Complete Resume Book and Job-Getter's Guide.* New York: Pocket Books.

Beatty, Richard H. 2000. *The Resume Kit*, 4th ed. New York: John Wiley.

Besson, Taunee S. 1999. *National Employment Weekly. Cover Letters*, 3rd ed. New York: John Wiley.

Bolles, Richard Nelson. 2000. *The 2000 What Color Is Your Parachute?* Berkeley, CA: Ten-Speed Press.

Buschy, Jennifer Thiele. "Wanted: Architects and Designers for Hire." *Contract.* September 2000, 96.

Catalyst Publications. 1980. *Marketing Yourself.* New York: Bantam Books.

Cochran, Chuck, and Donna Peerce. 1999. *Heart and Soul Internet Job Search.* Palo Alto, CA: Davies-Block Publishing.

Dahle, Cheryl. "Fast Start—Your First 60 Days." *Fast Company.* June/July 1998.

Gardella, Robert S. 2000. *The Harvard Business School Guide to Finding Your Next Job.* Boston, MA: Harvard Business Reference.

Goodale, James G. 1992. *One to One.* Englewood Cliffs, NJ: Prentice Hall.

Grensing, Lin. 1991. *Employee Selection*, 2nd ed. North Vancouver, British Columbia: Self-Counsel Press.

Haldane, Bernarad. 2000. *Haldane's Best Cover Letters for Professionals.* Manassas Park, VA: Impact.

Heim, Pat, and Susan K. Golant. 1995. *Smashing the Glass Ceiling.* New York: Fireside Books.

Hirsch, Arlene S. 1996. *Love Your Work and Success Will Follow.* New York: John Wiley.

Joel III, Lewin G. 1996. *Every Employer's Guide to the Law.* 2nd ed. New York: Random House.

Jones, Nancy L. with Phil Philcox. 2000. *The Women's Guide to Legal Issues.* Los Angeles, CA: Renaissance Books.

Josefowitz, Natasha. 1980. *Paths to Power.* Reading, MA: Addison-Wesley.

Kendall, Pat. 2000. *Jumpstart Your Online Job Search.* Rocklin, CA: Prima Publishers.

Kennedy, Joyce Lain. 1995. *Hook up, Get Hired! The Internet Job Search Revolution.* New York: John Wiley.

Krannich, Ronald L., and Caryl Rae Krannich. 1994. *Dynamite Salary Negotiations*, 2nd ed. Manassas Park, VA: Impact Publications.

Linton, Harold. 2000. *Portfolio Design*, 2nd ed. New York: W. W. Norton.

MacMillan, Pat. 1992. *Hiring Excellence.* Colorado Springs, CO: NavPress Publishing Group.

Marquand, Ed. 1981. *How to Prepare Your Portfolio*, rev. ed. New York: Art Direction.

McKinney, Anne. 1996. *Resumes and Cover Letters That Have Worked.* Fayetteville, NC: PREP Publishing.

McLaughlin, John E., and Stephen K. Merman. 1980. *Writing a Job-Winning Resume.* Englewood Cliffs, NJ: Prentice-Hall.

Medley, H. Anthony. 1984. *Sweaty Palms: The Neglected Art of Being Interviewed.* Berkeley, CA: Ten-Speed Press.

Milshtein, Amy. "First Timers." *Contract Design.* November, 1994, 84.

Nemnich, Mary B., and Fred E. Jandt. 1999. *Cyber Space Resume Kit.* Indianapolis, IN: JIST Publications.

Roberson, Cliff. 1992. *Hire Right, Fire Right*. New York: McGraw-Hill.

Sack, Steven Mitchell. 1998. *The Working Woman's Legal Survival Guide*. Paramus, NJ: Prentice-Hall.

———. 1990. *The Employee Rights Handbook*. New York: Facts on File.

Schlesinger, Eric, and Susan Musich. 2000. *E-Job Hunting*. Indianapolis, IN: Sams/ Macmillan.

Steingold, Fred S. 1999. *The Employer's Legal Handbook.* 3rd ed. Berkeley, CA: Nolo Press.

Wilson, Robert F., and Adele Lewis. 2000. *Barron's Better Resumes for Executives and Professionals*, 4th ed. Hauppauge, NY: Barron's.

Yate, Martin. 1990. *Hiring the Best*, 3rd ed. Holbrook, MA: Bob Adams.

Glossary

Acceptance. In contract law, one person agrees exactly to the conditions in the contract set by the other party.

Accounts. Financial entries with different names for clarification to show additions (increases) and subtractions (decreases) to the account.

Accounts payable. Claims from suppliers for goods or services ordered (and possibly delivered) but not yet paid for.

Accounts receivable. What others owe to the firm as a result of the sale of, or billing for, goods and services.

Accrual accounting. An accounting method in which revenues and expenses are recognized at the time they are earned (in the case of revenues) or incurred (in the case of expenses), whether the revenue has actually been collected or the expenses actually have been paid.

Accrued expenses. Expenses owed to others for a given time period but not yet paid; salary owed during an accounting period but not yet paid is an example.

Acknowledgments. The paperwork forms that a supplier sends to a designer to indicate what the supplier interprets the designer's order to be; sometimes called confirmations.

Addenda or order updates. Corrections or changes made to contract documents by the issuance of addenda (addendum is the singular form) and written by the person or firm responsible for the original set of contract documents.

Advertising. Any kind of paid communication in media, such as newspapers, magazines, television, or radio.

Advertising allowance. A special discount or other incentive given when a designer uses a manufacturer's product in promotions and advertising.

Agency relationship. The common-law relationship that exists when one person or entity agrees to represent or do business for another person or entity. Today's employer-employee relationship is a reflection of the agency relationship.

Amortize. Results from the concept that the value of intangible assets, such as copyrights, patents, and trademarks, are reduced; similar to depreciation.

Arbitration. When a disinterested third party evaluates the arguments of two parties to a contract.

As-built drawings. Working drawings prepared after a project has been completed that indicate exactly what has been built rather than what may have been shown in the original construction drawings.

Assets. Any kind of resource—tangible or intangible—that a firm owns or controls and that can be measured in monetary terms.

Assignment. When rights in a contract are transferred to a party that was not originally part of the contract.

Back orders. Items that a vendor cannot ship with other merchandise or are otherwise not available for some period of time.

Balance sheet. An accounting form that shows the financial position of a firm at a particular moment in time, including a statement of its assets and liabilities; sometimes called a statement of financial position.

Bar charts. A scheduling method consisting of a description of tasks required on the left-hand side and horizontal bars on the right-hand side showing the time in days, weeks, or months that is required to complete each task.

Barrier-free. Codes created and enforced to make public buildings more accessible to the handicapped.

Base bid. Refers to a proprietary specification that contains an "or equal" substitution allowance. All bidders must base their bids on the goods specified by product name.

Basis of the bargain. Information provided by a salesperson that is the primary influence on the buyer's decision to buy a product.

Benefits. Features of a product or a service that relate to the needs of the client.

Bid. An offer for the amount a person will pay to provide the specified goods and/or services required.

Bid bond. Required of all bidders to ensure that the designer or vendor who has been awarded a contract will sign the contract.

Bid form. Document prepared by the designer or the client and provided to the bidders. The vendor (bidders) submit their prices for the goods or services on this form. Sometimes also called a tender form.

Bid opening. The time that the owner of a project reveals who has bid on the project. In most situations, the bid opening is private, and only the owner and the designer who is responsible for creating the contract documents are present. Governmental agencies and many public utilities are required to have bid openings open to the public. In this case, anyone may attend the bid opening and find out what others have bid for the project.

Billable hours. The number of hours that a designer works on projects under a contract for design fees. The fees can be charged by any method, if the client is actually being charged for the hours that the designer works.

Billing rate. A dollar amount, combining salary, benefits, overhead, and profit, that is used as the basis for charging clients for services; usually expressed as an hourly rate.

Bill of lading. The form that the supplier provides to the truck driver to show what is being shipped and who has title to the goods.

Bond forms. Legal documents used to oblige the designer or vendor to the contract as assurance that the designer or vendor will perform the requirements of the contract as agreed upon. Three common bond forms are the bid bond, the performance bond, and the labor and materials payment bond.

Bonus plan. Method of paying extra compensation based on the employee's producing more than a specified personal quota.

Box burns. Furniture damage caused when a shipping carton rubs against fabric or frame materials.

Breach of contract. Breach simply means "to break." A breach occurs when one of the parties of a contract does not perform his or her duties as spelled out in the terms of the contract.

Break-even point. The point at which revenues equal expenses. At this point, the firm is neither making nor losing money.

Budgeting. Involves annual managerial goals expressed in specific quantitative terms, usually monetary terms. Budgeting encourages the manager to plan for the various events affecting the firm rather than to react to them.

Building codes. Regulations that primarily concern structural and mechanical features of buildings.

Build-out. An industry term for the construction process.

Building permit. A permit granted by local governmental agencies that allows for the construction of a new building or major interior remodeling.

Building standard workletter. This document outlines what quantity and quality of work will be undertaken by the developer in the construction of a tenant's office or other commercial space.

Buyer. A person who contracts to purchase or who does purchase some good.

Buying a job. A practice in which a firm prices goods or services at an unusually low rate in order to make the sale.

Capital construction. The cost for actually building the structural components; also referred to as capital improvements.

Career objective. A statement that explains what kind of work the job applicant seeks. It generally is used in the resume and/or cover letter.

Career summary. In a resume, a significant summary statement of experiences and skills concerning the applicant's ability to handle the job for which the applicant is applying.

Case study. A marketing tool that tells what the design program was for a particular client, and discusses some unique features of the project.

Cash. The cash on hand in the firm's bank accounts, checking accounts, and cash registers, or petty cash boxes; considered a current asset.

Cash accounting. The accounting method whereby revenue and expense items are recognized in the time period in which the firm actually receives the cash or actually pays the bills.

Cash discount. An accounting term referring to an extra discount given when a designer or design firm pays an invoice promptly. A notation that commonly looks like "2/10 net 30" appears on the invoice to notify the designer or design firm of the cash discount.

Certificate of occupancy (CO). A certificate provided by the local building department after the construction of a building has been completed, which means that the owner may now legally occupy the building.

Certificate for payment. A form that tells the client that the supplier has completed parts of, or most of, the work and that the supplier has sent an invoice for that work. This certificate recommends that the client pay the supplier for the invoice.

Certificate of substantial completion. A form that reports what has been done and indicates if something is missing concerning the construction of the structural elements.

Chain of command. The formal reporting links that exist between one level of employee and another; this helps everyone in the organization understand what the formal communication patterns are.

Change order. Written permission or instructions concerning any aspect of a project that modify design concepts, construction designs, or product specifications.

Chart of accounts. A list of all the accounts that a firm is using.

Chronological resume. States educational and work experiences exactly when they occurred, in reverse chronological order.

Close corporation. A corporation whose shares of stock are commonly held by only a few individuals. The stock is not traded on any of the public stock markets; also called family corporation or closely held corporation.

Closed competitive selection. Occurs when an acceptable list of potential bidders receive notifications of impending bids and are allowed to bid on a project.

Closed probe. A sales technique in which the designer asks the client a question that generally results in a closed response from the client such as "yes" or "no."

Closed specification. A bid specification that is written for a product such that another product cannot be substituted for what is being specified.

Closing. The art of knowing when to ask for the sale.

Codes. Systematic bodies of law created by federal, state, and local jurisdictions to ensure the safety of the public.

Cold calling. When a designer contacts potential clients whom he or she has never met before.

Combination resume. Utilizes qualities of both the chronological and the functional resume, and combines them in one resume.

Commercial interior design. The branch of interior design concerned with the planning and specifying of interior materials and products used in public spaces, such as offices, hotels, airports, hospitals, and so on; sometimes called contract interior design because it involves a contract for services.

Commission. A method by which an agent acting on behalf of the employer is paid; usually a percentage amount paid to the agent (interior designer), calculated on the agent's sale of goods and/or services.

Compensation. The method of paying an employee for work performed.

Compensatory time. Time off given salaried employees during the normal work week to make up for the overtime hours they have worked.

Competitive bidding. A process whereby the client has an opportunity to obtain comparative prices from a number of contractors and/or vendors for the construction or supply of the project.

Concealed damage. Damage to goods that is not obvious because the original packaging is not damaged. Most often occurs when items are shipped in cartons.

Conditions, covenants, and restrictions (CCRs). Specific regulations for condominiums, townhouses, and some other types of residences in planned communities. If a community has CCRs, it might not allow a home-based business to operate in the community.

Confirmation of purchase. The business form that spells out what goods the designer has agreed to order or sell to the client; also called a sales agreement, purchase agreement, or contract proposal.

Conflict of interest. Occurs when a person puts his or her self-interests before his or her public or fiduciary responsibilities.

Conforming goods. The delivered goods as described in the sales agreement.

Consideration. The "price" one pays to another party for fulfilling a contract.

Contract administration phase. The fifth phase of a design project, in which the project is actually constructed and orders for goods are issued and installed.

Contract documents. All the drawings and specifications that together describe what is required for a project, along with contracts or agreements between the project owner and the designer and other stakeholders.

Construction documents. Legal documents consisting of working drawings, schedules, specifications, and bid documents, describing what is required for the completion of an architectural and/or interiors project.

Construction drawings. The typical plans, elevations, and details required for building a structure or an interior.

Construction manager. An individual who oversees the construction project as an agent for either the general contractor or the owner.

Contract. A promise or agreement made between two or more parties for the performing or not performing of some act. The performance or lack of performance of this act can be enforced by the courts.

Contract administration phase. The portion of a project that involves actual construction work as well as the placing of orders for all the items required; also called the construction and installation phase.

Contract documents phase. The fourth phase of the design project; it involves the final preparation of all construction or working drawings (sometimes referred to as CDs), schedules, and specifications that are required to build and install the design project.

Contractual capacity. Each party to a contract must have the legal capacity to enter into a contract.

Control function. A management function that requires that a manager monitor the activities of the firm and take any necessary steps to ensure that the plans, policies, and decisions of the manager and the firm are being carried out.

Conversion. When the rightful property of one person is taken by another, a tort has been committed; can also be a crime of theft.

Co-op advertising. A manufacturer and designer generally share in the cost of the advertising, or the manufacturer provides an incentive to the designer to sell the particular product being advertised.

Copyright. The method of legally protecting, for a specified period of time, written materials and graphic designs.

Copyright notification. In order to begin the legal protection of written materials and graphic designs, the following must appear in a conspicuous place on the work: (1) "Copyright," "COPR," or ©, (2) year of publication, and (3) the name of the copyright claimant.

Corporation. An association of individuals created by statutory requirements, which is a legal entity. The corporation has existence independent of its originators or any other member or stockholder. It can sue and be sued by others, enter into contracts, commit crimes, and be punished. A corporation has powers and duties distinct from any of its members and survives even after the death of any or all of its stockholders.

Cost-of-living adjustment. An across-the-board compensation increase meant to offset inflation; also referred to as COLA.

Cost of sales. Refers to the costs paid in the direct generation of revenues. Called cost of goods sold in retail sales businesses; in this case, it refers to changes in inventory.

Cost plus percentage markup. A design fee method that allows the design firm to add a specific percentage to the net cost of the merchandise being purchased by a client.

Cost price. The price that the designer must pay for the goods.

Counter offer. An agreement to the offer in which the terms of the offer have been changed.

Credit. In accounting, this term means the right-hand side of an account.

Crime. When a person (or a business, in the case of a corporation) commits a wrong against society that is regulated by statute.

Critical path method (CPM). A scheduling method that begins by identifying the interrelationships of the tasks to be performed. This analysis shows the designer which tasks must be done before the next or other tasks can be performed, thus establishing the critical path.

Current assets. Resources that the firm would normally convert to cash in less than one year.

Customer's Own Material (COM). When a designer uses a fabric on a specially ordered, upholstered furniture item that is different from one of the fabrics available from the furniture manufacturer.

Debit. In accounting, this term means the left-hand side of an account.

Debt capital. Business loans that come from creditors, such as commercial banks.

Decision making. The act of making reasonable choices between available alternatives; an important part of the management function.

Deep discounting. An extremely large discount from the suggested retail price that is given to a designer or a design firm when placing very large orders.

Defamation. The wrongful harming of a person's good reputation. If the defamation is in writing, it is called *libel*; if it is oral, it is called *slander.*

Deferred revenues. Revenues received for services that have not yet been rendered or the sale of goods that have not yet been delivered.

Delegation. When one person gives his or her responsibilities to another.

Deliverables. Documents and presentation materials that must be prepared to explain design concepts that are given to the client.

Delivery. Includes the activities concerned with moving tangible items from the showroom or warehouse to the job site and placing them in their correct locations.

Deposit. Money that is part of the purchase price, prepaid by the buyer as security in contracts for the sale of goods or real estate.

Depreciation. Results from the concept that capital equipment has a limited, useful life. It is intended to express the usage of a fixed asset in the firm's pursuit of revenue.

Descriptive specification. Describes, often in elaborate detail, the materials, workmanship, fabrication methods, and installation of the required goods.

Design development phase. Involves final design decisions for plans, specifications, and preparation of final presentation documents.

Destination contract. A manufacturer retains title of goods until they are delivered to the buyer's delivery address; also referred to as FOB destination.

Direct labor. The time employees spend directly involved in the generation of the revenues of the firm.

Direct personnel expense (DPE). A number that includes not only the salary of employees but also any cost of benefits, such as unemployment taxes, medical insurance, and paid holidays.

Discounting. A reduction, usually stated as a percentage, from the suggested retail price. A full or normal discount from suggested retail is 50 percent.

Doing Business As (DBA). A filing required when the name of the business is other than the names of the owners.

Domestic corporation. A corporation formed in one state and doing business only in that state. Domestic corporations are also corporations formed within the United States.

Door-to-door. The client is charged from the time the designer or the delivery truck leaves the designer's studio or warehouse loading dock to the time it leaves the client's location.

Down payment. A portion of the total selling price paid at the time goods are ordered.

Drawings. In accounting, the withdrawals from the profits of a business by owners in proprietorships and partnerships.

Drop ship. When the designer requests that a manufacturer ship goods to an address other than the designer's business location or warehouse.

80/20 Rule. A business rule used in many situations. From a list of ten items arranged in the order of importance, if one accomplishes only the two most important items, one achieves 80 percent of the total value of time spent.

Employee handbook. A concise reference of company policies for all employees.

Employment at will. The doctrine that an employee, who is not bound by a written contract and who has no written terms of his or her employment spelled out, has the right to quit his or her job without notice but can also be fired by the employer at any time, with no explanation.

Empowerment. Giving employees the opportunity and authority to carry out the activities of the company without prior approval of a supervisor or a manager.

End user. The ultimate consumer of goods or services; can also mean consumer.

Entrepreneur. Someone who starts and manages his or her own business.

Equities. Claims on a balance sheet by outsiders and/or owners against the total assets of the firm.

Equity capital. Business funding that comes from investors, such as stockholders.

Errors and omissions coverage (E & O). Insurance that covers an interior designer in the event that he or she is responsible for errors or omissions for work performed or advice given to a client.

Ethical standards. What is right and wrong in relation to the professional behavior of the members and even the practice of a profession.

Exclusions. Portions of a competitive bid on which a vendor does not bid.

Expediter. An individual who is familiar with the design firm's paperwork system and the various ordering and shipping requirements of manufacturers. The expediter is responsible for the speedy processing of orders.

Expenses. The amount of outflows of resources of a firm as a consequence of the efforts made by the firm to earn revenues.

Express warranties. Promises, claims, descriptions, or affirmations made about a product's performance, quality, or condition that form the "basis of the bargain."

FF&E (Furniture, Furnishings, and Equipment). Acronym for projects that have minimal or no construction work involved.

Factory reps. Manufacturer's representatives that work only for one particular manufacturer as employees of the company.

Feasibility studies. In-depth estimates of planning and providing specifications for a project.

Features. Descriptions of specific aspects or characteristics of a service or a product; used during selling.

Fiduciary duties. An individual acts in a position of trust or confidence for someone else.

Financial accounting. Concerned with day-to-day and periodic measurement and reporting of accounting information for use by individuals outside or inside the firm.

Financial management. Act of planning and analyzing all the financial aspects of a firm in order to help owners manage and control the performance of the firm; often called managerial accounting.

Fire safety or life safety codes. Regulations that provide a reasonable measure of safety in a building from fire, explosions, or other comparable emergencies.

Firm offer. When a merchant makes an offer for the sale of goods in writing, whether or not any consideration has been given by a buyer.

Fixed assets. Resources that are also called property, plant, and equipment, which are the long-lived items used by the firm.

Fixed fee method. Some dollar value determined by a designer for the performing of all the services required of a project. The client is then charged that amount, whether the project takes a shorter or longer time than the estimate; also called the flat fee method or lump sum method.

Fixture. In tax terms, a product that could be considered personal property that has become affixed to a building, such as a mirror.

FOB, Destination. When the manufacturer retains ownership of the goods, pays all shipping expense, and assumes all risks until the goods reach the destination.

FOB, Factory. When the buyer assumes ownership or title of the goods when they are loaded on the truck at the factory. The buyer assumes the transportation expenses and all risks.

FOB, factory—freight prepaid. The interior designer has ownership and responsibility for damages during transit, but the manufacturer pays the transportation charges to the destination.

Foreign corporation. A corporation formed in one state but doing business in another state is referred to by the other state as a foreign corporation.

Four Ps of Marketing. The four basic variables (product, place, promotion, and price), that create a firm's marketing mix.

Fraud. When someone intentionally misrepresents facts to deceive another party for personal gain.

Free on Board (FOB). When the shipper must assume the expense of loading the goods onto the truck as well as the expense and risk for shipping the goods to the FOB destination; also referred to as freight on board.

Freight bill. The bill from the shipping company for moving goods from the supplier to the designer or the receiving location; it is a type of an invoice.

Fringe benefits. Direct or indirect additional payments made to the employee for work performed. Benefits may include paid vacations, profit-sharing plans, and group health insurance.

Functional resume. Presents information in order to emphasize qualifications and skills of the applicant, rather than the order in which they were obtained.

General conditions. Documents that set forth the legal responsibilities, procedures, rights, and duties of each party to a construction project; part of the bid documents.

General contractor. Individual or company that holds a license to contract and supervise all phases of a construction project; often called the GC.

General partnership. When two or more people join together for the purpose of forming a business; they alone share in the profits and risks of the business.

Goals. Broad statements, without regard to any time limit, about what a firm wishes to achieve.

Goods. Tangible items that have physical existence and can be moved.

Graphic image. The package of materials that the interior design firm uses to identify itself. This includes the company logo, business cards, letter head and other stationery, business forms, and drawing paper identification.

Gross margin. The difference between revenues and cost of sales. Represents the amount of revenue available to cover overhead (selling and administrative) expenses.

Gross profit. Another term for gross margin. Does not represent profit.

Gross revenue. All the revenue, prior to any deductions, generated by the firm for a given accounting period.

Gross salary. The amount of employee compensation before any deductions are taken.

Headhunters. A term associated with professional executive search and employment agencies that will search out and essentially "steal" an employee from one firm in order to place the employee in another firm.

Hot button. An issue that has critical importance to the client.

Hourly fee. The most commonly charged fee; based on the firm's direct personnel expense. For each hour or portion of an hour that a designer works on a project, the client is charged some dollar amount.

Hourly wage. A compensation method in which a employee is paid some dollar amount per hour for every hour worked.

HTML. Stands for Hypertext Markup Language. It is the computer language source code used to develop World Wide Web sites.

Implied contract. A contract formed by the actions of the parties rather than by an expressed written agreement.

Incentive compensation. Compensation over and above regular compensation.

Income statement. An accounting report that formally reports all the revenues and expenses of a firm for a stated period of time. The result shows the net income (or loss) for the firm during the period; also called a profit-and-loss statement.

Incorporate. To create a corporation.

Incorporation. The act or process of forming a corporation.

Independent contractor. Someone who works for himself or herself and is not subject to the control of an employer.

Independent reps. Manufacturer's representatives who work for themselves or a sales-representing group; they usually handle several manufacturers' products.

Inferior performance. Work that varies quite considerably from what is required in a contract.

Informational interview. An informal interview that allows a student to find out something about the work in a particular profession.

Infringement. Any unauthorized use of copyrighted materials.

Installation. The specialized part of the delivery process that involves assembly, construction, or physical attachments of products to the building.

Instructions to bidders. A document that informs bidders how to prepare bids for submittal so that all submittals will be in the same form.

Invasion of privacy. A legal harm against a person's right to freedom from others' prying eyes.

Inventory. Goods purchased and held by the business for resale to clients.

Invitation to bid. Summary of the project, the bid process, and other brief pertinent procedures for the project. It informs potential bidders of the project, its scope, and where to obtain further information; also called an advertisement for bids.

Invoice. A bill that is sent from the manufacturer or supplier to the designer, indicating how much the designer must pay. The designer also uses an invoice to bill the client for goods and/or services provided.

In lots. Products for one order are transported from the manufacturer to the designer in partial shipments.

Job description. Communicates the qualifications, skills, and responsibilities of each job classification within a design firm.

Joint venture. A temporary contractual association of two or more persons or firms in which they agree to share in the responsibilities, losses, and profits of a particular project or business venture.

Journal. In accounting, a chronological record of all accounting transactions for a firm.

Kinesics. The scientific study of the meaning of body positions and gestures.

Labor and materials payment bond. Required of the winning bidder to guarantee that, should the designer or vendor default on the project, the designer or vendor would be responsible for paying for all of the materials and labor that have been contracted for.

Ledger. In accounting, the ledger is a group of accounts; often called a general ledger.

Letter of agreement. A simplified form of contract.

Letter of intent. A letter sent to the winning bidder allowing them to begin work on a project.

Liabilities. In accounting, amounts that the firm owes to others due to past transactions or events. Liabilities always have first claim on the firm's assets.

Libel. A wrongful harming of a person's good name through a written communication.

Lien. When someone other than the person who has ownership or possession of goods has a security interest in the goods.

Limited liability company. A type of business formation that is a hybrid of the general partnership and the corporation, and which grants limited liability to its members.

Limited partnership. A business formation created according to statutory requirements. A limited partnership is formed with at least one general partner and one or more partners who are designated as limited partners.

Line item number. On a sales order, items are identified in numerical order. This number helps the firm cross-reference merchandise to purchase orders and other documents.

Line of credit. Short-term business loans that last for one year or less.

List price. Generally accepted as being the same as suggested retail price—a price to the consumer.

Logo. A symbolic image of a company or an organization; also called a mark.

Management. The effective direction of staff members and financial resources under a manager's control toward goals and objectives that the owners of the firm have established.

Manufacturer's dealers. Retailers that feature selected products from a particular manufacturer in a showroom that is open to the public.

Markdown. A term used in retail to represent discounts taken from the normal selling price.

Market. In reference to designer resources, a term that many interior designers use to mean they are going to visit one of the annual shows held at the marts.

Market centers. Concentrations of trade sources in one area of a city.

Marketing. Includes all the activities of moving goods and services from producers to consumers.

Marketing analysis. Involves gathering and analyzing data concerning such things as the abilities and interests of the staff, potential clients, the economy, and the competition in order that the owner and managers can make better plans and decisions about the direction of the firm's business efforts.

Marketing mix. Operational elements that the design firm can control in the process of marketing and selling goods and services.

Market segment. A group of customers that has a common characteristic.

Markup. A term used in retail to represent percentage amounts (converted to dollars) added to the net or cost price to the designer.

Mart. A building in which many firms have separate showrooms or share showroom space.

Mechanic's lien. A legal recourse related to the labor and materials payment bond. It is an action that prevents the owner of the property from giving or selling the property to anyone until the lien has been satisfied.

Merchant. Anyone who is involved with the buying and/or selling of the kinds of goods with which he or she is dealing. A person acting in a mercantile capacity.

Merit pay. An amount added to an individual's basic annual compensation amount, often for the reward of quality work done in the past.

Milestone charts. An easy scheduling method whereby a designer outlines the activities required by the project and establishes a target date for the completion of each task.

Mirror image rule. Unequivocal acceptance of the offer in a contractual situation.

Misrepresentation. The altering of facts to deceive or the use of fraud in order to receive personal gain.

Mission statement. A philosophical statement of what the firm sees as its role in a profession. It contains broad statements of what the firm wishes to achieve during an unspecified time period.

Mock-up. A full-scale, usually nonfunctional, portion of a design project, such as a hotel guest room.

Modifications. Additions or changes made to the contract documents (*see also* Addenda and Change order).

Movable equipment. Items such as furniture, accessories, and equipment items that are not fixed to a building structure.

Move management. A process to help a client get ready to move and the actual move from one location to another.

Multiple. A billing rate based on a calculation of salary rate, expenses, and a profit margin.

Multiple discounts. A series of discounts from the suggested retail price, given by manufacturers to designers for placing very large orders.

Mutual assent. The giving of a contractual offer and acceptance of the offer must be done willingly.

Negligence. A failure by one party to use due care, resulting in injury sustained by another person or a person's property.

Negotiating. When two parties are trying to reach agreement about some point of discussion.

Net income (or loss). The amount of income or loss that results when all expenses are subtracted from revenues. If the result is positive, net income represents the dollar amount of profit the firm has made for the given time period. If the result is negative, net loss indicates that expenses have exceeded revenues for the given time period.

Net price. A price representing a 50 percent discount from suggested retail.

Networking. Cultivating mutually beneficial relationships for the purpose of marketing oneself or one's design firm.

Niche. A very specific or unique focus concerning services or products provided by a firm.

Nonconforming goods. Any goods that are not as described in a sales order or a purchase order.

Offer. In contract law, one party makes an offer to provide something or do something for another party.

Offeree. The person to whom an offer has been made in a contract negotiation.

Offeror. The person who makes the offer in a contract negotation.

Open competitive selection. When clients, such as government agencies, advertise impending bids so that anyone who is interested in the project who meets the qualifications that are spelled out in the invitation to bid may submit a bid.

Open probe. A sales technique in which the designer asks the client a question that generally results in an open response so that the client is encouraged to talk.

Open specification. A bid specification written in such a way that many products can be substituted for the item being specified.

"Or equal." A term in a specification that allows bidders to substitute what they believe to be products of equal quality to that which was specified.

Other assets. Financial assets such as patents, copyrights, and investment securities in another firm.

Overhead expenses. Those expenses that are incurred whether the firm produces any revenues or not; also called selling and administrative expenses.

Owner's equity. The section on the balance sheet showing the amount the owners have invested in the firm.

Packing list. A detailed list by quantity and description of what is being shipped to the designer from a manufacturer or a supplier. It is commonly placed in a plastic envelope attached to the outside of one of the items being shipped.

Patent. An exclusive right to make, sell, and use a product for a specific period of time.

Percentage of merchandise and product services method. A fee method that allows the designer to negotiate a percentage of profit on the cost of the goods and installation that will be involved in the project.

Percentage off retail method. A fee method in which a percentage is determined and the dollar amount is subtracted from the retail price of the merchandise.

Per diem. A dollar amount that is charged to the client to cover hotel, meals, and transportation costs when it is necessary for the designer to travel out of town in the interests of the project. It can also represent a day rate for services.

Performance. In contract law, when each party does or provides what was agreed upon in the contract, performance has occurred. There are three types of performance: (1) complete, (2) substantial, and (3) inferior.

Performance bond. Required of the winning bidder as a guarantee that the designer or vendor will complete the work as specified and will protect the client from any loss up to the amount of the bond as a result of the failure of the designer or vendor to perform according to the contract.

Performance evaluation. Systematic evaluation of the positive and negative work efforts of an employee. It is used to review past performance in relation to agreed-upon responsibilities, which then forms the basis for salary increases, promotions, and/or retention.

Performance specification. A specification establishing product requirements based on exact performance criteria. These criteria must be based on qualitative or measurable statements.

Photo portfolio. A collection of photographs, slides, or other photographic media that represent projects for which the designer was responsible; used as a promotional tool.

Plan check. The act of a jurisdiction's building department's review of construction documents before issuing a building permit.

Plan review board. A local governmental agency whose responsibility it is to review construction drawings prior to issuance of building permits.

Planning. Involves research of capabilities and resources in order to provide direction for the firm.

Portfolio. A visual presentation of what an individual can do as an interior designer.

Postoccupancy evaluation (POE). Site visit and project review that are conducted to evaluate the existence of any problems in the design and installation of a project.

Posting. The transferring of a journal entry to the correct ledger account.

Practice acts. Guidelines established by legislation concerning what a person can or cannot do in the practice of a profession in a particular state. Individuals whose profession is guided by practice acts must register with a state board and meet exacting requirements.

Premium. A product that has a logo, slogan, or other words or graphics printed on an object, such as a T-shirt or a coffee mug.

Prepaid expense. The early payment of expenses in a period prior to their being required. The prepaid expense is an asset, since the value of the prepaid expense, not yet due, still has value to the owner.

Press release. Information provided by the design firm or its representatives that might be of interest to the news media.

Prestige pricing. Certain special products can be priced unusually high due to status or special aspects, like exceptional quality or materials, associated with the product.

Price. Any kind of payment from a buyer to a seller, including money, goods, services, or real property.

Primary sources. Information that provides specifics and comes from first-hand sources, such as a questionnaire.

Private, or general, corporation. The most common type of corporation formed for private, profit-making interests.

Probing. A selling technique for asking questions in order to uncover the needs of a client.

Professional corporation. A special form of corporation created by individuals in professions such as law, architecture, and accounting.

Profit-and-loss (P&L) statement. Another name for the income statement.

Pro forma. Projected financial information, such as the pro forma income statement; it can also mean "in advance" and be associated with credit.

Programming phase. The information-gathering portion of an interior design project.

Progress reports. Correspondence or verbal reports to the client so that the client is kept informed of the progress of the project and any problems.

Project closeout. The point at which a project has reached the time for final inspection and for providing necessary documents to the client to bring the project to completion.

Project file. File folders or notebooks in which the designer keeps all the pertinent data and paperwork related to a project in progress.

Project management. A process of organizing and controlling an interior design project from beginning to end in order to satisfactorily solve a client's problems and provide a reasonable profit to the design firm.

Project manager. Individual who is responsible for making site visits and telephone calls in order to keep a project on track; also the job title for a designer who has overall responsibility for all phases of a design project.

Promotion. Providing information about services or products from the seller to the buyer; includes publicity, publishing, advertising, and direct selling.

Proposal. An overview or other response to a request for a proposal (RFP) from a client. It is not necessarily a contract. Some designers use the term proposal to mean a contract, however.

Proprietary information. Information, graphics, or other property that belongs to a particular person or firm.

Proprietary specification. This specification names products by the manufacturer's name, model number, and/or part number.

Prospecting. The process of locating new clients and obtaining appointments with them.

Prospects. Potential clients in a firm's business area.

Proximate cause. A legal term that connects unreasonable conduct of a designer (or others) to harm that is caused by that conduct.

Publication. When the creator of a copyrightable work has somehow distributed the work to others for review without restricting its use.

Publicity. A direct form of promotion that is not paid for.

Public corporation. Those formed by some government agency for the benefit of the public. The US Postal Service is an example of a public corporation.

Public relations. All the efforts of a firm that go into creating an image of the firm in order to positively affect the public's opinion of the firm.

Puffing. A salesperson's statements of opinion, not facts, about a product.

Punch list. A list that records in detail everything that must be taken care of in order for a project's installation to be completed; also called the site inspection report.

Punitive damages. Compensation in a tort case or breach of contract; given in order to punish the guilty party because the harm is grievous.

Purchase order. The business form that a designer uses to order goods and/or services for the client or to order supplies needed by the design firm.

Qualifying. A term associated with determining whether or not a potential client is really worth pursuing as a prospective client.

Quantity discount. A discount greater than the normal 50 percent discount, given because a large quantity of merchandise has been purchased at one time.

Record drawings. The set of drawings kept at the job site on which any changes made to the building are recorded. These later will be used to create the as-built drawings.

Red lining. Notes or corrections made in red pencil or other media that call attention to problems or errors on drawings that a jurisdiction checks before issuing a building permit.

Reference specification. An established standard such as the standards of the American Society for Testing and Materials (ASTM) and the American National Standards Institute (ANSI), rather than written, detailed descriptions or performance criteria for required products.

Referral. Occurs when a client (or other party) tells another person who may be looking for interior design services about a particular design firm.

Reimbursable expenses. Costs that are not part of the design contract but that are incurred in the interest of completing the project.

Representatives, or reps. The men and women who act as the informational source to the interior designer about various manufacturers' products. Independent reps work for themselves and are usually responsible for many different manufacturers' products. Factory reps work for only one manufacturer as an employee.

Request for proposal (RFP). A document used by clients to obtain specific information about a large number of design firms that may be interested in providing design services for a project.

Residential interior design. The plans and/or specifications of interior materials and products that are used in private residences.

Restocking charge. A fee charged by the designer for taking back merchandise that the client has ordered but does not want.

Restrictive covenant. In an employment contract, a provision that does not allow an employee to work for a competitor; also called a noncompete agreement.

Resume. A summary of a designer's qualifications.

Retail method. A fee method in which the design fee is derived by charging the retail or suggested retail price for goods sold to clients.

Retail price. Generally means the same thing as suggested retail price; the price quoted to the consumer.

Retainage. Money held back by the client to ensure that all the work, omissions, and problems associated with the project are taken care of.

Retained earnings. The claim on the assets arising from the cumulative, undistributed earnings of the corporation for use in the business after dividends are paid to stockholders.

Retainer. Payments to a professional to cover future service or advice by that professional. In interior design, the retainer is customarily paid at the signing of the contractual agreement.

Revenue. The amount of inflows from the sale of goods or rendering of services during an accounting period.

Right of refusal. After a contract has been signed, a buyer has 72 hours to refuse the purchase of goods or services; in many jurisdictions the right of refusal only applies to contracts signed in a residence.

S Corporation. A special form of corporation that utilizes many of the benefits of a corporation but that pays taxes as a partnership; formally called a subchapter S corporation.

Sale. Occurs when the seller transfers title or ownership of the goods to a buyer and the buyer has provided some consideration to the seller.

Schedule. A tabular chart or graphic that is used to clarify sizes, location, finishes, and other information related to certain nonconstruction parts of an interior or structure. Schedules are commonly prepared for doors, windows, and interior room finishes.

Schematic Design phase. The phase of the design project in which preliminary design decisions and documents are prepared.

Seasonal discount. A special discount given to retailers to purchase certain goods earlier than normal. The goods are generally associated with a season or a holiday.

Secondary sources. Information that generally comes from existing materials, such as a magazine or newspaper article.

Secondary subcontractor. A subcontractor hired by another subcontractor to provide a portion of the work required of the first subcontractor.

Secured loan. A loan for which collateral is required as protection against nonpayment.

Self-employment tax. A tax required of self-employed individuals on income earned.

Seller. Any person who sells or contracts to sell goods to others.

Selling. Finding out what a client wants through the use of personal communication and then providing it.

Selling price. Refers to the actual price that is quoted to the client.

Sexual harassment. Unwelcome sexual advances or requests for sexual favors from a supervisor directed at an employee in order for the employee to be hired, or promoted, or to otherwise influence the work performance of the employee.

Shipping contract. When the title to goods passes to the buyer at the time the goods are placed on the truck, which is located at the manufacturer's factory. Also referred to as FOB, Factory.

Shop right. The employer holds a nonexclusive license to any creation or invention of tangible products an employee designs that are a part of the employee's normal working duties.

Short list. A small number of interior designers or design firms that are selected from a larger group, that have been selected by a client for a presentation in order to negotiate a contract for design services.

Single source of contact. One particular individual who has the authority to make decisions regarding a project for the design firm as well as the client.

Slander. The wrongful harming of a person's good reputation through oral communication.

Sole proprietorship. The simplest and least expensive form of business. The company and individual owner are one and the same.

Specifications. The written instructions to contractors and vendors concerning the materials and methods of construction or the interior products that are to be bid on a project.

Specific performance. A type of remedy related to breach of contract that a court requires. The breaching party is ordered to perform the specific, breached terms of the contract.

Square foot method. A method of calculating fees whereby the designer determines a rate per square foot and multiplies it by the amount of square footage of the project.

Stakeholders. All the parties to a project who have a vested interest in the completion of the project, such as the client, interior designer, architect, and vendors.

Statement of cash flow. An accounting statement reporting, for a specific period, the changes in cash flows from operating, investing, and financing activities.

Statute of frauds. Statutory requirements that call for written contracts in certain circumstances. For the interior designer, these include a contract for the sale of goods that have a value over $500, any contract that will take more than one year to complete, and any sale of real estate.

Stocking dealer. A vendor that stocks a certain inventory level of goods at all times. These sellers and designers often receive larger discounts because of the volume of products they carry.

Straight salary. A fixed amount of salary paid to an employee no matter how many hours in the week he or she works.

Strategic planning. A process for creating a specific written vision for a firm and for the future of that firm.

Strategies. Specific actions that are part of a business or marketing plan for which definite time limits within the year have been set for completing them.

Strict liability. When a seller is held liable for injury to others, resulting from a product's defects, regardless of fault.

Subcontractor. An individual or company that is licensed to contract and perform specialized work on an interiors or construction project; also called a sub.

Submittals. Materials, drawings, or documents that may need to be provided by the vendor to the designer or contractor for approval.

Substantial completion. Contract performance that cannot vary greatly from what has been spelled out in the contract.

Suggested retail price. A term related to the price, to be used by the seller and suggested by the manufacturer.

SWOT. A planning analysis technique used by firms to develop many kinds of plans. SWOT stands for strengths, weaknesses, opportunities, and threats.

Tactics. Highly specific actions needed to accomplish goals and strategies. They are even more specific than strategies and are usually short term.

Tag for. Information that a designer requests that a manufacturer affix to the goods and note on the invoice in order to help the designer deliver the goods to the correct client.

Tangible personal property. Any property that is movable, can be touched, or has physical existence.

Target marketing. A marketing method that helps a design firm identify one or more groups of potential customers who are most likely to utilize the services of the firm.

Tenant improvements. Improvements to a commercial space paid for by the tenant; also called leasehold improvements.

Testimonials. Statements that the client has made in a letter that he or she sends, or gives verbally to the designer concerning their satisfaction with the design firm's work.

Third-party testimonials. When an interior designer uses a statement from a former client as a reference to help sell his or her services and/or merchandise to a new client.

Title. In sales law, title refers to the legal ownership of goods. The person who holds title to the goods owns the goods.

Title acts. Legislative measures concerned with limiting the use of certain professional titles by individuals who meet agreed-upon qualifications and who have registered with a state board.

Tort. When a person commits a wrong against another and causes injury to the harmed party. Torts are civil matters and, therefore, are not legislated by statute.

Trade credit. When a supplier allows a designer to purchase on credit, the designer is working with the supplier's money.

Trade discounts. Discounts given as a courtesy by some vendors to designers and others in the trade. These are usually a small percentage off retail.

Trademark. Legal protection for distinctive names, logos, or symbols.

Trade sources. Groups of manufacturers, suppliers, and tradespeople who provide the various goods and services that a designer uses to complete an interiors project.

Transaction privilege (sales) tax license. Allows the interior designer to pass on the state sales tax to the consumer; issued by state and municipal taxing authorities.

Transmittal letter. A form letter that a designer can use to send information to anyone involved with the project or to anyone from whom information has been requested.

Trunk show. Occurs when a manufacturer's rep invites one or more interior designers to view a small selection of new merchandise.

Turnkey project. In architecture, a project that commonly includes financing assistance, property acquisition, and all the design and specification services associated with architecture or interior design.

Unemployment taxes. Funds provided by the employer to eligible employees in the event that they are laid off from their job; paid to the employee through the state.

Uniform Commercial Code (UCC). The body of law that guides the relationships between the various levels of buyers and sellers in business transactions.

Unsecured loan. A loan that does not require collateral as a guarantee.

Use tax. A tax on goods that a business purchases from a supplier in another state for use within the state in which the purchasing business is located.

Utilization rates. A factor identifying the amount of time that a designer spends on billable hours versus nonbillable work.

Value engineering. A method of analyzing and specifying products and design solutions based on cost-effectiveness.

Value-oriented fee method. A fee method by which a design firm prices its services based on the value or quality of the services rather than on the cost of doing those services; also called value-based method.

Variance analysis. A managerial technique in which one looks at financial and numerical data in relation to the differences between planned or budgeted amounts and actual amounts.

Vendor. Someone who sells products or services either to the end user or to another merchant, like the designer.

Vignette. A display of furniture and furnishings in a store or a showroom that simulates an actual room.

Walk-through. A final inspection of a job site to be sure that everything ordered is present and that any omissions or damaged goods are noted.

Warranties. A statement or representation made by a seller concerning goods. Warranties are related to quality, fitness of purpose, or title.

Wholesale price. A special price given to a merchant from a merchant at a value lower than what the goods would cost the consumer.

Worker's compensation insurance. An insurance program paid for by the employer that provides funds to the employee to cover the expenses of work-related injuries.

Work in process. Work under way for a client that has not yet been billed.

Work plan. All the tasks that are required to complete an interior design project.

Wrongful discharge. Firing an employee without good cause.

Zone pricing. A manufacturer determines two or more shipping zones based on geographic distances from the factory. Each zone has a different price for the product.

Zoning variance. Issued by a local jurisdiction so that a business can operate in a residentially zoned area. Other zoning variances may apply, depending on the jurisdiction.

Appendix*

Interior Design Professional Associations

American Society of Interior Designers (ASID)
608 Massachusetts Avenue N.E.
Washington, DC 20002
202-546-3480
www.asid.org

Association of Registered Interior Designers of Ontario (ARIDO)
717 Church Street
Toronto, ON M4W 2M5, Canada
416-921-2127
www.arido.on.ca

Association of University Interior Designers
Miami University, Cook Place
Oxford, OH 45056
513-529-3730

Foundation for Design Integrity
1950 N. Main St., #139
Salinas, CA 93906
650-326-1867
www.ffdi.org

Foundation for Interior Design Education Research (FIDER)
60 Monroe Center N.W., #300
Grand Rapids, MI 49503
616-458-0400
www.fider.org

Interior Design Educators Council (IDEC)
9202 N Meridian St., Suite 200
Indianapolis, IN 46260
317-816-6261
www.idec.org

Interior Designers of Canada (IDC)
Ontario Design Center, 260 King St. East, #414
Toronto, Ontario Canada M5A 1K3
416-964-0906
www.interiordesignerscanada.org

Interior Design Society (IDS)
P.O. Box 2396
Highpoint, NC 27261
919-883-1650

International Facility Management Association (IFMA)
1 E. Greenway Plaza, Suite 1100
Houston, TX 77046
713-623-4362
www.ifma.org

International Interior Design Association (IIDA)
998 Merchandise Mart
Chicago, IL 60654
312-467-1950
www.iida.com

Institute of Store Planners
25 North Broadway
Tarrytown, NY 10591
914-332-1806

National Council for Interior Design Qualification (NCIDQ)
1200 18th St. N.W., Suite 1001
Washington, DC 20036
202-721-0220
www.ncidq.org

Allied Professional Organizations and Trade Associations

American Hospital Association
840 N. Lake Shore Drive
Chicago, IL 60611
312-280-6000

American Hotel and Motel Association
1201 New York Avenue N.W., Suite 600
Washington, DC 20005-3931
202-289-3100

*This information is current as of January 1, 2001.

American Institute of Architects (AIA)
1735 New York Avenue N.W.
Washington, DC 20006
202-626-7300
www.aia-online.org

American National Standards Institute (ANSI)
1819 L St. 600
Washington, DC 20036
212-642-4900
www.ansi.org

American Society of Furniture Designers (ASFD)
P.O. Box 2688
521 Hamilton Street
High Point, NC 27261
919-884-4074
www.asfd.com

American Society of Landscape Architects
636 Eye Street N.W.
Washington, DC 20001
202-686-2752
www.asla.org

American Society for Testing and Materials (ASTM)
100 Barr Harbor Drive
West Conshohocken, PA 19428
610-832-9500
www.astm.org

ARCOM Master Systems
332 East 500 South Street
Salt Lake City, UT 84111
800-424-5080
www.arcomnet.com

British Contract Furnishing Association
Business Design Center
Suite 214
52 Upper Street
London N1 OQH England
0044 207 22666
www.bcfa.org.uk

Building Owners & Managers Association (BOMA)
1201 New York Ave. NW, Suite 300
Washington, DC 20005
202-408-2662
www.boma.org

Business and Institutional Furniture Manufacturers Association (BIFMA)
2680 Horizon Drive S.E., Suite A-1
Grand Rapids, MI 49546
616-285-3963
www.bifma.com

Center for Health Design
3470 Mount Diablo Blvd., Suite A-150
Lafayette, CA 94549
925-299-3631
www.healthdesign.org

Color Marketing Group (CMG)
5904 Richmond Highway, Suite 408
Alexandria, VA 22303
703-329-8500
www.colormarketing.org

Construction Specifications Institute (CSI)
99 Canel Center Plaza, Suite 300
Alexandria, VA 22314
703-684-0300
www.csinet.org

Contract Furnishings Council
1190 Merchandise Mart
Chicago, IL 60654
312-321-0563

Contract Furniture Dealer Division,
National Office Products Association
301 N. Fairfax Street
Alexandria, VA 22314
703-549-9040

Home Furnishings International Association
110 World Trade Center
P.O. Box 420807
Dallas, TX 75342
214-741-7632
www.hfia.com

Illuminating Engineering Society of North America (IES)
120 Wall Street, 17th Floor
New York, NY 10005
212-248-5000
www.iesna.org

Industrial Designers Society of America (IDSA)
1142-E Walker Road
Great Falls, VA 22066
703-759-0100
www.idsa.org

International Association of Lighting Designers (IALD)
Merchandise Mart, Suite 11-114A
200 World Trade Center
Chicago, IL 60654
312-527-3677
www.iald.org

International Code Council
5303 Leesburg Pike, Suite 600
Falls Church, VA 22041
703-931-4533
www.intlcode.org

International Furnishings and Design Association (IFDA)
1200 19th Street NW, Suite 300
Washington, DC 20036
202-857-1897
www.ifda.com

National Fire Protection Association (NFPA)
1 Batterymarch Park
P.O. Box 9101
Quincy, MA 02269
617-770-3000

National Kitchen and Bath Association (NKBA)
687 Willow Grove Street
Hackettstown, NJ 07840
908-852-0033
www.nkba.org

National Trust for Historic Preservation
1785 Massachusetts Ave. N.W.
Washington, DC 20036
202-588-6000
www.nationaltrust.org

Neocon Trade Shows
Merchandise Mart Properties, Inc.
Suite 470, The Merchandise Mart
200 World Trade Center Chicago
Chicago, IL 60654
800-677-6278
www.merchandisemart.com

Ontario Ministry of Industry and Technology
900 Bay St. Hearst Block, 9th Floor
Queen's Park
Toronto, ON M7A 2E1 Canada
416-325-6666

Quebec Furniture Manufacturers Association
1111 St-Urbain Street, Suite 101
Montreal, Quebec H2Z1Y6
Canada
514-866-3631
www.qfma.com

Business Advisors

Allied Board of Trade, Inc.
200 Business Park Drive
Armonk, NY 10504
914-273-2333

American Demographics, Inc.
P.O. Box 68
Ithaca, NY 14851
800-828-1133
www.marketingtools.com

American Management Association
135 West 50th Street
New York, NY 10020
212-586-8100

American Women's Economic Development Corporation
The Lincoln Building
60 E. 42nd Street
New York, NY 10165
212-692-9100

Directory of Newspapers and Periodicals
426 Pennsylvania Avenue
Fort Washington, PA 19834
215-628-4920

Department of Commerce
Herbert H. Hoover Building
14th Street and Constitution Ave. NW
Washington, DC 20230
202-482-2000
www.doc.gov/edu

Department of Labor
Bureau of Labor Statistics
Washington, DC 20230
www.bls.gov

Department of Justice*
10th Street and Constitution Avenue N.W.
Washington, DC 20530
202-724-2222

Department of Justice (Form I-9)
Immigration and Naturalization Service
425 I Street N.W.
Washington, DC 20536
800-777-0777
www.ins.usdoj.gov

Dun and Bradstreet Corp.
299 Park Avenue
New York, NY 10171
212-593-6728
800-234-3867
www.dnb.com

Encyclopedia of Associations†
Gale Research Company
Book Tower
Detroit, MI 48226
800-877-GALE

Equal Employment Opportunity Commission (EEOC)
1801 L Street N.W.
Washington, DC 20507
800-669-4000
www.eeoc.gov

Minority Business Development Agency
US Department of Commerce
14th & Constitution Ave. N.W.
Washington, DC 20230
202-482-5061
www.mbda.doc.gov

National Small Business Association
NSB Building
1604 K Street N.W.
Washington, DC 20006
202-293-8830

Organization of Black Designers (OBD)
300 M St., S.W., Suite N-110
Washington, DC 20024
202-659-3918
www.core77.com/obd

Register of Copyrights
Copyright Office
Library of Congress
Washington, DC 20559
202-287-9100
www.loc.gov/copyright

Society for Marketing Professional Services
99 Canal Center Plaza, Suite 320
Alexandria, VA 22314
703-549-6117

* Americans With Disabilities Act Information
† Provides help in locating trade associations.

Standard & Poor's Register of Corporations, Directors, and Executives
Standard & Poor's Corporation
25 Broadway
New York, NY 10004
212-208-8000

US Hispanic Chamber of Commerce
2000 M Street N.W., Suite 860
Washington, DC 20036
202-862-3939

US Small Business Administration
1414 L. Street
Washington, DC 20416
800-827-5722
www.sbaonline.sba.gov

US Small Business Administration
SBA Publications
P.O. Box 30
Denver, CO 80201
202-205-6665

DEFINITION

SHORT DEFINITION The Professional Interior Designer is qualified by education, experience, and examination to enhance the function and quality of interior spaces.

For the purpose of improving the quality of life, increasing productivity, and protecting the health, safety, and welfare of the public, the Professional Interior Designer:

* analyzes the client's needs, goals, and life and safety requirements;
* integrates findings with knowledge of interior design;
* formulates preliminary design concepts that are appropriate, functional, and aesthetic;
* develops and presents final design recommendations through appropriate presentation media;
* prepares working drawings and specifications for non-load bearing interior construction, materials, finishes, space planning, furnishings, fixtures, and equipment;
* collaborates with licensed practitioners who offer professional services in the technical areas of mechanical, electrical, and load-bearing design as required for regulatory approval;
* prepares and administers bids and contract documents as the client's agent;
* reviews and evaluates design solutions during implementation and upon completion.

LONG DEFINITION (SCOPE OF SERVICES) The interior design profession provides services encompassing research, development, and implementation of plans and designs of interior environments to improve the quality of life, increase productivity, and protect the health, safety, and welfare of the public. The interior design process follows a systematic and coordinated methodology. Research, analysis, and integration of information into the creative process result in an appropriate interior environment. Practitioners may perform any or all of the following services:

Programming. Identify and analyze the client's needs and goals. Evaluate existing documentation and conditions. Assess project resources and limitations. Identify life, safety, and code requirements. Develop project schedules, work plans, and budgets. Analyze design objectives and spatial requirements. Integrate findings with their experience and knowledge of interior design. Determine the need, make recommendations, and coordinate with consultants and other specialists when required by professional practice or regulatory approval.

Conceptual Design. Formulate for client discussion and approval preliminary plans and design concepts that are appropriate and describe the character, function, and aesthetic of a project.

Design Development. Develop and present for client review and approval final design recommendations for: space planning and furnishings arrangements; wall, window, floor, and ceiling treatments; furnishings, fixtures, and millwork; color, finishes, and hardware; and lighting, electrical, and communications requirements. Develop art, accessory, and graphic/signage programs. Develop budgets. Presentation media can include drawings, sketches, perspectives, renderings, color and material boards, photographs, and models.

Contract Documents. Prepare working drawings and specifications for non-load bearing interior construction, materials, finishes, furnishings, fixtures, and equipment for client's approval. Collaborate with specialty consultants and licensed practitioners who offer professional services in the technical areas of mechanical, electrical, and load-bearing design as required by professional practice or regulatory approval. Identify qualified vendors. Prepare bid documentation. Collect and review bids. Assist clients in awarding contracts.

Contract Administration. Administer contract documents as the client's agent. Confirm required permits are obtained. Review and approve shop drawings and samples to assure they are consistent with design concepts. Conduct on-site visits and field inspections. Monitor contractors' and suppliers progress. Oversee on their clients' behalf the installation of furnishings, fixtures, and equipment. Prepare lists of deficiencies for the client's use.

Evaluation. Review and evaluate the implementation of projects while in progress and upon completion as representative of and on behalf of the client.

Index